MY SEVERAL LIVES

A 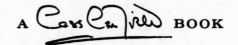 BOOK

My Several Lives

MEMOIRS OF A SOCIAL INVENTOR

BY James B. Conant

1817

HARPER & ROW, PUBLISHERS

NEW YORK, EVANSTON, AND LONDON

Grateful acknowledgment is made to the following for permission to reprint:

Harvard University Press, for excerpts from *Education in a Divided World* by James Bryant Conant. Copyright 1948 by James Bryant Conant. Excerpts from *Education and Liberty* by James Bryant Conant. Copyright 1953 by James Bryant Conant. Reprinted by permission of the publisher.

McGraw-Hill Book Company, for excerpts from *Slums and Suburbs* by James Bryant Conant. Copyright © 1961 by James Bryant Conant. Reprinted by permission of the publisher.

The Nation, for excerpts from "The Baruch Report" (September 19, 1942) by I. F. Stone, reprinted by permission of the publisher.

Oxford University Press, Inc., for excerpts from *Atomic Quest* by Arthur Holly Compton. Copyright © 1956 by Oxford University Press, Inc. Reprinted by permission of the publisher.

The Pennsylvania State University Press, for excerpts from *The New World* by Richard G. Hewlett and Oscar E. Anderson, Jr. Copyright © 1962 by the Pennsylvania State University Press. Reprinted by permission of the publisher.

Van Nostrand Reinhold Company, for excerpts from *Buna Rubber* by Frank A. Howard. Copyright 1947 by Litton Educational Publishing, Inc. Reprinted by permission of the publisher.

Walter Lippmann, for excerpts from an address made before a meeting of the Associated Harvard Clubs in Cleveland, May, 1933. Reprinted by permission of the author.

To My Understanding Wife

Contents

PART III
THE WAR YEARS

PART IV
THE POSTWAR YEARS
AT HARVARD

PART V
THE POSTWAR
INTERNATIONAL SCENE

PART VI
A LOOK AT AMERICAN SCHOOLS

Illustrations

Acknowledgments

Three people are primarily responsible for my having undertaken the task of writing an autobiography—John W. Gardner, E. Alden Dunham and Merle L. Borrowman.

Gardner, at the time he was president of the Carnegie Corporation, made the first suggestion. Dunham, who had worked with me for several years in my study of high schools, strongly seconded the idea. Borrowman, a professor of education and history at the University of Wisconsin, was in New York for a year as a member of the team I had assembled to investigate the education of teachers. He agreed with Dunham that many of the educators throughout the country who were reading my reports about public schools wanted to know what kind of person had entered their territory uninvited.

Borrowman offered to find two graduate students at the University of Wisconsin to collect material for a volume of reminiscences if Gardner would finance the project through the Carnegie Corporation. Thus it came about that in the fall of 1965, William M. Tuttle, Jr., and Charles D. Biebel started examining records and I started writing.

Tuttle was to be concerned with such nonacademic matters in my past as my interventionist activities in 1940 and my collaboration after Pearl Harbor with other university presidents in negotiations with the War Department. He completed his researches in 1967 and presented a thesis embodying his findings to the University of Wisconsin for the Ph.D. degree. The thesis is now on file in the Wisconsin library. I have drawn heavily on it in writing about the war years. Mr. Biebel prepared a series of memoranda based on his examination of the records of my own investigation of schools, starting in 1957, as well as the origin of the Educational Testing Service. I have made extensive use of this material. His rather exhaustive research in the archives of the Educational Policies Commission of the National Education Association forms a significant part of a volume I hope to publish soon, to be entitled *A Self-Appointed Investigator of the Public Schools*. This volume will more closely resemble the book John Gardner and I originally discussed than does the present volume.

I take pleasure in thanking Dr. Tuttle and Mr. Biebel for their indispensable assistance. Professor Borrowman, to whom I am much indebted, assisted me on two occasions by an examination of the presidential archives at Harvard for the period of my presidency. These archives, which are closed to public examination until the year 2003, were opened for me and my collaborators by vote of the president and fellows of Harvard in 1965. I record my gratitude to the Harvard Corporation for this action. Without it I could not have written large sections of this book.

Two chapters dealing with the formation of the Committee on the Present Danger in 1959 are largely based on the documents carefully collected and arranged by Tracy Voorhees. They are now on deposit in the library of Rutgers University. My indebtedness to Mr. Voorhees is as great as it is obvious.

It is a pleasure to express my profound gratitude to the officers of the Carnegie Corporation, which has generously financed the entire enterprise as a continuation of the subsidy of my study of American education. At the outset, the Educational Testing Service of Princeton, New Jersey, administered the grant from the Carnegie Corporation. For the assistance thus provided, I am most thankful. In the last few years I have been able to work in comfort in New York thanks to arrangements with the Teachers Insurance and Annuity Association of America. I take this opportunity to express my deep appreciation to the chairman, William C. Greenough, and his associates.

Finally, to Cass Canfield, my publisher, the late Hermine Popper and Margaret Butterfield, I am grateful for encouragement and editorial suggestions.

Preface

This book is an attempt to tell the story of several lives and ten or twelve inventions. As a chemist I patented two processes, one of which might have been important if I had been a better scientist. As a university president I invented a special kind of scholarship when scholarships were not in favor and a special type of professorship without portfolio in days before cross-fertilization of departments had begun. Borrowing ideas from others, as inventors must, I then invented a new degree for future schoolteachers (M.A.T.) which is now awarded in many institutions. The old mother "necessity" forced me to think up a new procedure for making permanent appointments at Harvard, as otherwise a faculty revolt might have forced me out of office. An unexpected bequest to improve journalism led to the invention of the Nieman Fellows in Journalism. During the war, I helped operate a revolutionary invention of Vannevar Bush—the National Defense Research Committee. After the war, as a citizen worried about the military posture of the nation, I joined with others to form a committee which I labeled the "Committee on the Present Danger." Exploring the American comprehensive high school, I discovered the need for a new concept, that of the "academically talented" and a new way of evaluating one function of secondary education by drawing up an "academic inventory." Finally, in dismay at the disarray I found in educational planning in many states, I suggested the creation of what has become "The Education Commission of the States."

The White Knight in *Through the Looking-Glass* is the model for all egotistical inventors; it was he who kept remarking that a particular gadget on his horse was his own invention. If some readers feel that I have followed too closely the knight's example, I can offer an explanation which I only recently discovered during a family luncheon party at the Harvard Club of Boston to celebrate my seventy-fifth birthday. The assembled group could not be considered young. My two sisters, Esther Conant and Marjorie Bush-Brown, aged eighty-six and eighty-one, and my brother-in-law, Harold, aged seventy-eight, almost made my wife, aged a mere seventy, feel that she should join with my son Ted and his wife Ellen to form a children's table. As the conversation became general, the younger of my two sisters began to recall the day before I was born. She remembered her excitement; the prospect of a baby, whose arrival was overdue, was almost too much for a six-year-old to bear. She went to bed with reluctance and made her aunt, who was presiding over the household, promise that if the baby was born before morning, a certain book would be left open on the table. Thus when she woke she would know whether or not she had a new baby brother or sister.

"What was the book?" I asked. "It was *Through the Looking-Glass*," said my sister. If I was, in fact, born under the sign of the great inventor—the White Knight—much of my adult behavior could be readily explained. It would require only an extension of the present trend in psychology which explains all character in terms of experience in early childhood to account for the interest in my own inventions manifested in the pages of this book.

JAMES B. CONANT

New York City
May 1, 1969

PART I

_____

HALF A LIFETIME

AS A CHEMIST

CHAPTER 1

A Yankee Childhood

I WAS BORN IN BOSTON in 1893. Yet I make no claim to being a proper Bostonian. To be sure, my maternal grandfather, Seth Bryant, had been successful in the shoe and leather trade in Boston in the 1830s. But he had come to the city from East Bridgewater in Plymouth County, Massachusetts, where his mother's family had been settled since 1623. To that portion of East Bridgewater called Joppa Village, he retired in the 1840s with his second wife, a Quakeress from Lynn. They proceeeded to raise a family of five girls and one boy.

My paternal grandfather was also of Plymouth County origin, although he was born in Pomfret, Vermont. His father had migrated to that frontier outpost from East Bridgewater with some friends and relatives right after the Revolution. The pioneer life does not seem to have appealed to all of the next generation. The pull of the "homeland" was sufficient to bring my grandfather back to Plymouth County as a young man with a wife who was a granddaughter of one of the first settlers of Pomfret.

That Bridgewater was more than a geographical entity to my Conant ancestors is clear from a letter written in 1883 by my grandfather. It is of interest because of the light it throws on the loyalties which bound together the families in New England villages almost two hundred years ago.

My father was not a soldier at the time of the battle of Bunker hill but he enlisted with several other Bridgewater boys and went to Cambridge a

3

few days after the battle which as you know took place June 17, 1775 and my father was 17 years old on the 28th of that same month. But there were no more serious battles till the next spring when Washington marched a body of troops by night around to Dorchester heights and threw up a slight breastwork from which artillery might command the shipping in Boston harbor and father was in the first detachment that broke ground on that occasion.

The British soon after left Boston and sailed for New York—while Washington moving across country to Narragansett Bay reached Long Island before them and brought on an action at Flatbush. Night put an end to the battle and Washington drew off his army under cover of the night to New York—and afterwards he retreated northward harassing the enemy on every opportunity but avoiding a general battle, at a place called White Plains. They had some pretty heavy skirmishing and it was at this place where father helped to fetch off the soldier who fell as they were retreating over a hill out of musket range. He used to tell of it in this way —on passing the brow of the hill out of sight of the enemy they came to a halt, when the captain of their company remarked that he did not want to ask any man to risk his life unwillingly to help bring off their comrade who laid in plain sight and easy range of the enemy, but he would be one of four if three others would volunteer and bring him off if possible—you know how such a proposal would be likely to affect Bridgewater boys— three step out at once, without arms, and are accepted. Father was one, they marched in open order, but were not molested. Their comrade was dead, shot through the head—he was a stranger to father. The initials S.W. were cut in the head of the wooden canteen which father always kept. Of the other two who volunteered to go with the Capt. one was Solomon Leonard and the other Joseph Pratt—both of Bridgewater. Now here is a curious coincidence—In after years when father had got him a farm and needed a wife he invited the oldest sister of Solomon Leonard,— and years after that, when she had died leaving a young family who needed a mother he invited the oldest sister of Joseph Pratt and they never said him nay.

I fancy I can envision my ancestors' life in Joppa Village at the end of the eighteenth century or even in the more recently settled Pomfret. My ability to do so depends, I believe, on the fact that my family spent the summers in a farming community of New Hampshire. One might say that I spent a portion of each year of my childhood in the horse-and-buggy age. Certainly, as far as transportation was concerned, it was the same era in which my parents and grandparents had grown up. Remove the steam train which connected the cities and the scene was the same as the eighteenth-century New England countryside.

In the winter I lived in a metropolitan area that was rapidly expanding due to the electric cars. As far back as I can remember, a trolley car was an integral part of my environment. One line from the center of Boston (Park Street) ran into old Dorchester (long since a part of the city of Boston) as far as the town of Milton, a mile beyond where I lived. At Milton one could change to another line which had only recently been completed. It headed off south to villages and towns in Plymouth County. I think my father must have bought stock in that particular electric railroad company. He seemed worried about its future. Well he might have been; by the time I was in college the company had passed from uncertainty to incipient bankruptcy. The automobile was threatening to replace the electric car except in the city itself.

My early childhood picture of the future, however, was in terms of ever-expanding electric trolley car systems. I clearly recall my belief that a trolley car line would be built one day to start at the railroad station five miles from our summer cottage in New Hampshire and come up the hill on which we lived and down to the large town five miles away in another direction. It took us nearly an hour to drive there with our horse and carriage. Before long, we would be able to make the trip in twenty minutes. Of this, I was quite certain. My father had told me about what had happened before I was born in the part of suburban Boston in which we lived; horse cars had been replaced by trolley cars. To a small boy, there seemed to be no reason why electric cars should not run in every part of the United States.

As long as transportation in and around Boston had been confined to steam trains and horsecars (running on rails) and horse-drawn carts and carriages, the towns and villages even a short distance from the city must have been very much like the Joppa Village in which my mother and father had grown up. The advent of the trolley car completely changed the scene. The suburbs as homes of daily commuters began to develop rapidly. The towns within commuting distance became parts of a metropolitan complex. Whether, like Roxbury, Dorchester and Chelsea, they were absorbed in the political structure of Boston made little difference; Cambridge, Brookline and Malden remained independent political units, yet they were all in process of losing the character of the horse-and-buggy age. The steam train had started the process. All the railroad stations within an hour's ride of the Boston station began to be centers for daily travelers to the city. The electric car completed the job, making it possible for people in the expanding towns to travel cheaply and easily either to the local railroad station or directly into the city on the electric car itself. Steam trains did not turn New England villages into commuting suburbs; the electric trolley car did.

I grew up in the new age of electricity; it was also the age of the rapidly growing low-income suburb. My father became involved in the growing process. As a newly wedded husband, he had bought a large house and stable near the Ashmont railroad station as well as some of the empty fields which must have then constituted most of the landscape of Dorchester. Although his main business was that of a photoengraver, he went into the building business as a side venture.

He had started, I was told, early in his married life by selling his horse and carriage and then tearing down the stable. (The recently opened trolley line had made the ownership of a horse a pure luxury.) A wooden two-story house accommodating two families took the place of the barn. That had happened some ten years before I was born. My father's building activities were still in full swing, however, when I started attending kindergarten. The fields were in process of being cut up into lots along paved streets soon to be lined with wooden two- and three-family houses.

I remember going with him on a walk of not more than ten minutes up a slight hill back of our house to see a new street he was just opening. He examined what the workmen had just finished. I was more interested in the street. I thought of what fine coasting there would be next winter since the adjoining street went steeply down the hill for a considerable distance. I assumed that since these streets had no trolley tracks they would be covered with many inches of packed snow in the winter. The milkman and the grocery deliveries and the coal would come on horse-drawn "pungs" (a type of commercial sled). On Saturdays and in the afternoons, the other boys and girls and I would be out with our sleds. If we were lucky, we could hook a ride on the side of one of the "pungs." Our sleds would drag alongside as the horse moved up the hill. At the top we would jump off and sled downhill on the street we had just come up.

Suburban streets in winter before the coming of the automobile were made for children's sledding, or so it seemed to me. For the rest of the year they were built for bicycles, or so my two older sisters assured me. The new streets my father and his friends were building were macadam paved and were equipped with surface sewers, making them quite unlike the New Hampshire roads I knew.

To a five-or-six-year-old, it seemed clear that before long the New Hampshire hills would be covered not only with trolley tracks but also with paved streets. Such was progress, which the grownups liked to talk about. The twentieth century, they said, would certainly bring more streets and more electric cars—possibly things called automobiles as well, though I had never seen one. No one suggested that the two- and three-family houses my father was building were, in fact, rather unattractive dwellings crowded too close together. My best friend lived in the one next door. I would have been amazed to hear anyone say a word against his home.

The house my parents had bought in 1880 must have been built before the Civil War. Dorchester was then a farming town in which a few Bostonians with money were developing estates. (The neighboring town of Milton still had such an atmosphere as late as the first decade of this century.) The house had the spaciousness of another era. It was large but not luxurious by the standards of the more modern houses of most of my friends. A front parlor and a back parlor separated by sliding curtains on a rod provided a wonderful place for charades which my sisters let me watch.

The significance of the size of the house from a small boy's point of view lay in the fact that it had enabled my father to welcome his aging father-in-law and mother-in-law as permanent guests. They occupied a pleasant room on the second floor. My Grandfather Bryant, in his late eighties, had lost his money, of which at one time he must have had a comfortable amount. His son and the other four daughters (my aunts) were not in a position to provide. My father was. The reason he wished to do so must be made clear if one is to understand my parents, which in turn requires understanding the village of Joppa before the Civil War.

As I reconstruct the story my mother told from time to time, the Bryant family lived in a large house on a prosperous farm. Her father owned a small shoe factory nearby. Across the road lived my Conant grandfather with a second wife (his first had died giving birth to my father) and his three boys. He was a shoe cutter in Grandfather Bryant's factory. The Conant family was poor; the stepmother was far from kind; my father's childhood was not pleasant. The one bright spot in it was the kindness of the grand but simple lady across the street, my grandmother, Jane Breed Bryant. She had been so good to him as a boy that there was nothing my father would not do to make his mother-in-law's old age as comfortable as he could.

Thus it happened that during the first half-dozen years of my life

I had as a constant companion my Grandmother Bryant, a sweet old lady, who would read to me by the hour. To me she embodies what my mother meant when she used the word "spiritual." In my thoughts, she is somehow quite separate from my mother, my two sisters, three or four aunts and a female cousin or two, the "regiment of women" who watched over my growing up.

I realized only years later what a sacrifice my father must have made to honor an obligation he felt so deeply. He never mentioned it, but then he was a very silent man. After my Grandfather Bryant died at the age of ninety-eight (he was born in 1800) and I was old enough to understand the ways of grown-ups, I learned that his loquaciousness as an old man had nearly driven my father to despair. I can get a hint of the differences of opinion which must have added to the difficulty by reading a thirty-two-page pamphlet my grandfather wrote at the age of ninety-four and had printed, presumably at my father's expense. Its object, the author declared in the foreword, was "to give some account of the Mitchell, Bryant, and Orr families" and "to add my efforts to those of the steadfast body of Americans who strive for the only true principle of business intercourse, free trade."

The sad fact was that in his declining years my Grandfather Bryant had become a Democrat. There had been no question of his political principles in the 1860s. Unlike another Bridgewater family into which one of his daughters had married, no one ever accused him of being a "Copperhead," a Southern sympathizer. For him sound Union principles went hand in hand with business, as Grandpa Bryant pointed out in the section of his little pamphlet headed "Shoes for the Army." As a small boy, he had heard from a sergeant who had served in Washington's special bodyguard the shocking tale of the condition of the Army's shoes; sometimes the soldiers had been forced to march in stocking feet. The story had made a deep impression. Therefore, he wrote, as soon as he heard of the outbreak of the "rebellion" (his word), he set out on April 20, 1861, for Washington. He was successful in obtaining a contract for providing shoes for the Union Army. In his Joppa factory he manufactured over 200,000 pairs of Army shoes, stamping his name on every shoe as a warranty. In recording that fact in his pamphlet, the ninety-four-year-old, retired manufacturer added with obvious pride, "Thereby the army was provided with the best shoes that any army ever had, which was a blessing greater than can be told in words."

There must have been no differences in politics when Grandfather Bryant first acquired a Joppa son-in-law. At that time for vast numbers of New Englanders the words "Republican" and "patriotic" were still synonymous. The Conant boys had served in the Union Army. I fancy it was in the first Cleveland campaign that old Seth Bryant became a free trader and then a Democrat. My father remained a staunch Republican. With age, the heresy of his father-in-law increased. In the 1890s he embraced the cause of free silver and supported Bryan. And from what I heard later, he insisted on arguing his case with anyone who would listen. I remember him distinctly, but not his conversation. It must have had its impact, however, on my embryonic political consciousness, for I recall asking my grandmother whether Lincoln had been a Democrat or a Republican—not only an illiterate question, but almost a sacrilegious one in many households. The dear old lady replied that she couldn't say, as political parties were different in those days. I believe her husband always maintained that he did not leave the Republican Party, the party had left him.

Joppa Village in the mid-nineteenth century was not, in one respect, typical of New England. The community had become a stronghold of one Protestant sect, Swedenborgianism. According to Grandfather Bryant's account, the teachings of Emanuel Swedenborg came to Bridgewater in 1818 and to East Bridgewater (Joppa Village) in 1822. By the time my two grandfathers were raising families, the Swedenborgian or New Jerusalem Church appears to have been the center of religious life. Grandfather Conant read the lesson on Sunday morning; Grandfather Bryant gave financial support to the church. My mother and my father thus shared a rather special religious faith. During the first fifteen or twenty years of their married life, they journeyed by trolley car from Dorchester each Sunday morning to attend a Swedenborgian church in Roxbury. I remember the trips and sitting through the services. I was too young, however, to attend the Sunday school and was, therefore, never exposed to Swedenborgian doctrine as were my older sisters.

About the time I entered kindergarten, my father and mother stopped these weekly journeys. I think their adherence to Swedenborgian doctrine must have been slowly losing strength. There seem to have been differences of opinion among the faithful. My mother, I remember, used to speak rather forcefully against one group whose interpretation of Swedenborg's writings she did not like at all. I was thus aware at an early age of "schisms" among churchgoers. Far more important was my mother's final and complete condemnation of

all trinitarian doctrines. She never attempted to make me a Swedenborgian, perhaps because she had become less convinced as she grew
older. She certainly succeeded, however, in making me at an early age
more than suspicious of all the standard arguments in favor of
Christianity. Of course, I might have reacted against her strong
views and joined an Episcopal High Church. As a matter of fact, I
have never had the slightest tendency in that direction.

My knowledge of Swedenborgianism comes almost entirely from
what my mother told me over a period of years, usually in answer
to my questions. The chief characteristic of the faith, she often said,
was a firm belief in immortality. Such a belief, however, had nothing
to do with rewards and punishments after death. (On the subject
of hell-fire religions, no one could be more condemnatory than my
otherwise soft-spoken mother.) Passing into the next world, as she
always called it, was entering into an existence which alone had
real significance. Here was to be found the explanation of the universe. What happened in our material world was of little moment.
The reality of the unseen world seemed to be the essence of her belief.
The prospect of seeing once again those one had known on earth
appeared not to be important. In her old age, my mother often
attended a Unitarian church. In many ways, she might have been
classified as a Unitarian, as I have usually characterized myself. The
Swedenborgian interpretation of death, however, I am inclined to
think she never lost. To this extent her religion differed from that
of many Unitarians.

My grandmother, of whom I saw so much as a very young child,
was an unquestioning Swedenborgian to the end. She calmly assumed
the distinction between the spiritual and the material (the "mere
physical," my mother would have said). One of the clearest memories of my childhood is the way I learned of my Grandfather Bryant's
death when I was five. During one of our daily talks, my grandmother
told me that my grandfather had told her he had seen a child coming
to him with a bunch of flowers. He is, of course, she said, already in
the next world—which news I accepted almost as a matter of fact;
she had spoken often of the journey to the next world my grandfather was about to take. I was not shocked. My grandmother was not
grieving. She spoke as though my grandfather had just moved into a
beautiful sunlit room. Several days later (so I have always maintained in telling the story), when I came home from kindergarten
(which was across the street), my mother said quietly, "Your grandfather is in the next world." "Yes, I know he is," I said with matter-of-

factness. "Grandmother has already told me." "But she couldn't have," my mother exclaimed, "it only happened this morning while you were at school."

My mother was gently spoken and theoretically in favor of tolerance of all points of view. But in regard to religion, as I have already indicated, the doctrine of tolerance did not mean to her equal sympathy with all creeds. And in regard to the great issue of her youth, it certainly did not mean any forgiveness of the slaveholders and those who fought under the Stars and Bars. Her strong views led occasionally to strong words of condemnation, usually uttered, to be sure, in the family circle. So, too, as regards current politics, what my mother approved and what she disapproved soon became quite clear in the course of conversation. More often than not, the clear opinion which emerged was not that of the majority of our friends and acquaintances. Mother was basically a dissenter.

The disputes in the Ashmont household between my Republican father and his Democratic father-in-law were before my day. By the time the Spanish War was over, Grandfather Bryant was dead. Public opinion divided sharply in the first year of the new century about the consequences of the American victory. Bryan was running again, this time on a plank of anti-imperialism. I heard little about the candidate but a great deal about the wickedness of the imperialists. The issue was not closed when McKinley was elected. Two of the three aunts whom I saw often were strong anti-imperialists like my mother. Dissent from Republican foreign policy thus became a continuing household attitude. Theodore Roosevelt's accession to the presidency increased the dissent to a point where I am sure it had a reverse effect on me. By the time the new President stood for election in his own right, he had become a hero in my eyes.

What Father's views were, I cannot say. He was massively silent for the most part when my mother and one of her sisters excoriated the Republicans and all their works. Two conclusions I can draw from these memories: I knew from an early age, first, that ladies could be emotionally involved as onlookers of the political scene and, second, that dissent was not only respectable but usually morally correct.

The Spanish War must have increased the normal interest of small boys in soldiers. All my early memories of playing with other boys are related to either playing with lead soldiers in the house or organizing sham battles out of doors. These activities must have pained my mother, who was anything but a militarist. Indeed, a decade later when Theodore Roosevelt was attacking President Wood-

row Wilson for his neutrality during the opening years of World War I,
I think she would have been glad to have been called a pacifist. In
1900, however, only a fiercely dogmatic pacifist would have intruded
ideology into the play world of male children. Two of my friends
had older brothers; they liked to be the officers and drill the younger
group. Air rifles were the weapons. The battles of the Civil War
served vaguely as models. The Memorial Day parades of the local
unit of the Grand Army of the Republic kept us aware of the military
past.

On this subject, my father was something of a disappointment.
He had served as a captain's boy with an East Bridgewater company
of a Massachusetts regiment, and later as a master-at-arms on a ship
of the Union Navy. In neither capacity did he take part in any
fighting. His stories about his war experiences were interesting,
particularly the one about his witnessing the naval battle between the
Merrimac and the *Monitor*. His reminiscences suffered, however,
according to my view, from a lack of any firsthand account of man-
to-man combat. Then, too, he was not a member of the Grand Army of
the Republic. He had refused to join, my mother said, because he
disapproved of the political activities of the organized veterans who
were always working for larger pensions. None of my friends' fathers
had been old enough to serve at all; so my disappointment was something I kept strictly to myself.

By the time I was nine or ten, playing soldiers in the many vacant
lots of Ashmont gave way to playing football and baseball. The older
brothers now were acting as coaches. On at least one occasion, they
arranged a football game with another group whose "home field" was
a vacant lot a mile or two away. There were no goal posts or formal
markers. It was strictly a rushing game, for which the players were
equipped with a variety of shoulder pads, rubber nosepieces and
padded football pants. Our side, of which I was the captain, won by
several touchdowns. Such was the only athletic victory in which I
had a part.

The next year, the old gang began to break up. The loyalties and
interest of some of us were transferred to the schools we had just
entered—mine to the Roxbury Latin School.

CHAPTER 2

Boyhood Explorations

ONE DAY in the late 1920s, I met the father of one of my boyhood friends. In the course of our exchange, he spoke of my recent appointment as chairman of the chemistry department at Harvard. "I remember," he said, "when you were a small boy playing with vile-smelling chemicals; you started young; you have kept at it ever since; it is an unusually consistent record." I might have replied that among chemists my case was not strikingly unusual. I could have named several of my acquaintances on both sides of the Atlantic who, like myself, had fallen in love with chemistry while still in school.

Sixty years ago, the appeal of chemical experimentation was novel. "Fun with chemistry" sets had not yet been invented; a boy had to be ingenious to accumulate the equivalent with the aid of the local drugstore. The experiments were simple but spectacular. The knowledge acquired about elements and compounds was so foreign to what was discussed in the daily papers or heard about in general conversation that it seemed a passport into a strange and secret land.

I took the first step into the new land of chemistry during my early teens, when I asked to have illuminating gas piped into the shop my father had recently constructed out of a large vestibule in the Dorchester house. There was nothing unusual about my having a shop. Many of my friends had one in the cellar or the attic, but none of them had a workbench with a stopcock to which a Bunsen burner could be attached by means of a piece of rubber tubing. A gas flame on the bench transformed a carpenter's shop into a laboratory. I was now in a position to buy a blast lamp, worked by a foot bellows, which yielded a flame hot enough to melt glass. I started to try my hand at glass blowing, an art in which I never became proficient. Without gas, the experimenter at home had to use the flame of an alcohol lamp, which is at best a feeble instrument for a would-be chemist. With a Bunsen burner, however, one could evaporate solutions to dryness, set up a still for making distilled water and even prepare oxygen gas by heating red oxide of mercury.

Earlier, my scientific interests had centered on electrical phenomena. Electricity, even in its simplest manifestation, was still something of a marvel. Few of the houses I knew had either electric current or a telephone. The electric doorbell was the one standard piece of electrical equipment. I was considered to be very clever by our next-door neighbor because I "repaired" the doorbell by renewing the zinc rod in the battery. A number of my friends could have done the same. It was not uncommon for a boy in those days to monkey with electromagnets, dry and wet batteries, electric buzzers and small motors. In a few years, interest in amateur wireless telegraphy would spread rapidly and widely.

Because I shared in this growing interest in science, my parents had selected the Roxbury Latin School for my college preparation. At that time in Greater Boston, the shift to a college preparatory school for the last six years of secondary education was almost compulsory for anyone who intended to go on to college. Of those who remained in public grammar school for the last two years and then went on to the public high school, few if any attended college. They went to work directly.

The reputation of the Roxbury Latin School was high on many counts and, in spite of the name, high in chemistry and physics. The six-year course was centered on Latin, French, and either Greek or German, with the usual college preparatory course in mathematics. But unlike many of the other preparatory schools in Greater Boston, the building was equipped with laboratories for both physics and chemistry, and all pupils were required to study both subjects in their last two years.

Soon after I entered the six-year course in 1903, a number of circumstances slowly moved the focus of my interest from electricity to chemistry. There were first the occasional visits to my father's "office," a photoengraver's establishment in Boston. Photoengraving had grown out of wood engraving during the last decades of the last century. My father had started his own wood-engraving company in a few rooms in an office building in Boston not long after the close of the Civil War. When the halftone process entered the printing business, a rapidly-growing branch of chemistry entered the commercial world. My father became an applied chemist, though he would have denied any knowledge of the science of chemistry. I am not sure that he could have carried out the complicated set of procedures involved in etching the copperplates, which his son followed so eagerly when he had a chance. He was, however, a competent photographer in the days before dry plates; preparing and developing wet plates was then a complicated chemical operation.

A second incentive was supplied by the teacher of physics and chemistry at the Roxbury Latin School. I doubt if any schoolteacher has ever had a greater influence on the intellectual development of a youth than Newton Henry Black had on mine. His lectures on elementary science to the second-year class were for those days remarkable. They stimulated the interest in science of a good fraction of the class. What appealed to me most were the final lectures on chemistry. My early fascination with the mysteries of photoengraving must have formed a receptive attitude, but at the time I was quite oblivious to any such connection. I simply thought it would be fun to do such simple things as to set up a hydrogen generator at home.

I became one of the small group of boys who brought their sandwiches to the physics laboratory at lunch hour. Almost all the others were concerned with the wireless; they were the forerunners of what became the large group of radio "hams." I had tried my hand at making an induction coil and a radio receiver with no success. So I began discussing my chemical experiments with the other boys, and from time to time with Mr. Black himself. I was not in a frame of mind, however, to desire a real chemical workbench in my home until a clerk in the corner drugstore set me on the path. It was from him that I had purchased the acid necessary for making hydrogen. He took an interest in my chemical interest, and one day suggested that I might take up qualitative analysis. He explained that one could obtain a set of directions as to how to analyze a solution to determine its chemical content. A set of simple reagents, a glass funnel and filter papers and a method of boiling water were all one needed.

During one of the lunch hours at school, I asked Mr. Black about my friend's suggestion. He thought it excellent, named the book I should buy (A. A. Noyes' *System of Qualitative Analysis*) and offered to provide me with solutions to analyze. So began what developed into a tutorial relationship. I received a little bottle every week or so and reported to Mr. Black during one of the noon periods what I had found; for example, silver and tin but no copper or lead. It was an exciting business, and I kept coming back for more unknowns. Before long I began rather systematically to follow the laboratory manual of the high school chemistry text and to study the text itself, which I had previously only looked into as my fancy chose.

A letter I wrote my sister Marjorie who was studying painting in Paris provides evidence as to a small boy's excitement on discovering chemistry. The date is March 29, 1908 (three days after my fifteenth birthday). After expressing appropriate thanks for a gift which had just arrived, I unashamedly looked forward to another present.

By the way about the book that you said you would try to find for me, if you are really going to get one I wish you would get one on *Chemistry* rather elementary, though most anyone would do, in *either German* or *French*. Mr. Black is the instructor in Physics and Chemistry as you perhaps know and is quite a friend of mine. We had him out for Super [sic!] last Sunday night and I showed him my shop etc. I am going to talk "shop" now. I hope I won't bore you.

Last Wednesday I took my weights to school to calibrate them to Mr. Black's—that is to see how much they were not correct. He showed me how to use his best balances which cost about 60 to 100 $ and then I used them it was great fun. But when I say that by one wrong twist of my wrist I could have ruined them you see you had to be pretty carefully [sic!]. They are awfully sensitive. I weighed to milligrams that is 1/1000 of a gram and as a gram is about 1/31 of an oz and as 16 oz make a lb. you see that's pretty small about 1/31,000 of an oz or 1/31,186,000 of a lb. [sic!]. [Calculations were never my strong suit.] I have been working in my shop quite a lot and I have great fun there. The new apparatus I bought [a blast lamp and bellows] enables you if you're clever enough and have practiced enough to work glass into all shapes and sizes. I have also been analyzing ores and finding what's in them. I have all the ores right except one and that didn't act as it should.

My birthday party was quite a success as mother, Esther I and the cat attended. Father was away on bussiness [sic!] that night. The cat sat up in father's chair and put his paws on the table and drank any quantity of milk out of a saucer. We had a birthday cake, your candy and bon bons.

Well I must say "so long" now but listen, if you get me a book, and I wish you would, a good one is in German, I don't [know] if they sell 'em in Paris, by Ostwald entitled "Schule der Chemie" in 2 volumes. This is just a suggestion as to what would be nice.

Your loving brother,
James B. Conant

Mr. Black must have been skeptical about how much chemistry I had really learned by my course of self-instruction. There had been no tests or examinations—only conversations about analysis and experiments. One day in the spring of my fourth year, he chose what appeared to be an accidental method of finding out how well based had been my talk. Some of the members of the graduating class were taking a trial college entrance examination in chemistry. An examination paper of a few years before was given to each member of the group, together with a bluebook. A dozen questions or so had to be answered in an hour in the blank pages of the bluebook. I happened into the laboratory as the examination started, and Mr. Black said casually: "Why don't you try and see what you can do?" With some hesitancy, I accepted the challenge and did the best I could. Mr. Black read the bluebook at once and said, with a trace of surprise I still remember: "The grade is A." I had backed into the successful study of school chemistry by starting with qualitative analysis, a subject usually reserved for college sophomores. My career was now clearly marked. I was to be a chemist.

I had learned enough to pass the written college board examination in chemistry, but I had no school record in that subject. Therefore Mr. Black arranged for me to repeat in the school laboratory some of the experiments I had done at home and others that were usual for a school course. In particular, he had to emphasize quantitative experimentation. Since I had no adequate balance at home, this fundamental aspect of chemistry had been neglected. A laboratory notebook properly certified by Mr. Black was thus ready for the examiners when I took the first set of college board examinations at the end of my fifth year, in June 1909.

The last year in school I had the use of the workbench in Mr. Black's own private room, which opened off the school's main chemical laboratory. He intended to have me anticipate the Harvard freshman chemistry course. He himself had obtained the degree of A.M. at Harvard only a few years before and therefore was known to the professors of chemistry. In October 1909, he wrote to Professor Theodore William Richards, the chairman of the department, reminding him of a conversation a few weeks earlier about a boy "named Conant anticipating chemistry"; he asked what decision had been made. Before the month was out, Professor Richards replied (I have the letter) that the department of chemistry voted yesterday "that Conant, considering his extraordinary ability, be allowed to anticipate Chemistry 1 by taking the final examination in the course next June [1910], and submitting to such other tests as the instructor in Chemistry 1 may deem necessary."

The vote was consistent with the admission procedures then in force in Harvard College. It was usual to have permission granted to take examinations in such freshman courses as trigonometry. If the candidate was successful, he was credited with a course (or half-course) toward the total of sixteen which were required for the degree of bachelor of arts. President Lowell once called the scheme, which he abolished, the cash-register system. What was quite as important to Mr. Black and me was that by anticipating Chemistry 1 I could enroll in a sophomore college course in my freshman year. Mr. Black's ambition for his pupil, however, went even higher. In expressing his appreciation to Professor Richards for the department's kindness in regard to Chemistry 1, he stated he was "very anxious that Conant shall be able to take Math 2 [calculus] and Chemistry 2, 4, and 8 next year." Chemistry 2 was a half-course in organic chemistry (the study of carbon compounds); Chemistry 8 was Professor Richards' own course in the history of chemistry; Chemistry 4 was quantitative analysis. What he was asking was that I anticipate not only freshman chemistry but qualitative analysis. Without raising the question of credits, he hoped that the department would accept his statement at the end of the high school year that he considered his pupil to have done the work of Chemistry 3 (qualitative analysis).

Once again the department was willing (though the notations on the correspondence, which eventually came into my possession, indicate the vote was not unanimous). In his second letter, Professor Richards suggested that some correspondence with the dean of Harvard College might be necessary. A freshman was not usually permitted to take so many courses not regularly open to freshmen. He added: ". . . but we shall back you up in the negotiations."

In these enlightened days, the action of Harvard College in 1910 can only be regarded as preposterous. The chemistry department, by following the recommendation of a young secondary school teacher, was aiding and abetting the early specialization of a youth whose record showed no high degree of academic talent. Not that any tests were given to discover scholastic aptitude—the phrase had not yet been invented. The total school record was available, but no one examined it. The admission requirements were in terms of passing college entrance examinations in separate subjects. Someone in authority might have required that my marks on the first set of college board examinations in June 1909 should demonstrate unusual ability. No one considered my case from such a point of view. The fact that only in physics and chemistry were my grades A, and in algebra B, was no one's concern. In the 1960s, when every college admission officer looks at the entire record, it would be questioned whether a candidate who had shown aptitude only in science would be able to survive the college course. Certainly, drastic exceptions to the rules and regulations governing the choice of collegiate studies would be doubtful for such a youth. Indeed, specialization at so young an age for a person with obviously limited scholastic ability would not be recommended.

Regarded as a "case," the admission of J. B. Conant in 1910 to special advanced standing by the department of chemistry at Harvard, largely on the basis of one schoolteacher's judgment, may well be considered a deplorable example of the consequence of the nineteenth-century educational ideas prevalent a half-century ago. Fortunately for me (if it was good fortune that I could spend half a lifetime enjoying chemistry), concern for the education of the "whole man" had not yet been manifested in Cambridge, Massachusetts. That Conant had been well prepared for college was evident from his program; he had studied Latin and French, each for five years, German for three, English literature and ancient history sufficiently to pass the college board examinations in these fields. What more would anybody ask? Some might say it was regrettable he had chosen German instead of Greek in school, but times were changing; three years of Greek were hardly sufficient anyway. No one in those days would have dreamed of inquiring whether this product of a selective six-year Latin school could speak or understand any foreign language. It would be only after two world wars, the American occupation of several foreign countries and the advent of commercial airplanes that such an obvious question would be raised, even among those who had spent their lives teaching foreign languages.

CHAPTER 3

Harvard in Transition

THE HARVARD COLLEGE I entered under such favorable circumstances in 1910 was A. Lawrence Lowell's college. Yet the spirit of Charles William Eliot's university had by no means disappeared. Eliot had resigned after forty years as President in May 1909; in his inaugural address in the fall of the same year, Mr. Lowell made it quite plain that he intended to bring about drastic changes in the education of the undergraduates. Some of these changes occurred so rapidly that I, as a member of the first class to which they applied, can speak of my undergraduate education in terms of Mr. Lowell's reforms. Nevertheless, my training as a chemist might be said to have taken place in Eliot's university.

At the time Eliot had become president of Harvard in 1869, relatively few additions had been made to the collegiate fare that was offered at Harvard and other colleges before the Civil War. Based on the classical tradition and with a heavy emphasis on developing a reading and writing knowledge of Latin and Greek, it was a closely circumscribed program. The introduction of courses in modern foreign languages, history and natural science was just starting (Eliot was himself a chemist).

By introducing what was called "the free elective system," whereby all that was necessary to obtain a degree was a passing grade in sixteen courses. Eliot laid the base for the growth of instruction in a variety of fields. The proliferation of college courses

20

started under his regime at Harvard, and was duplicated in many other colleges as the elective system grew in popularity. If one were to compare the educational opportunities offered to the Harvard College students in the late 1850s with those offered twenty years later, one would have a measure of the revolution that had occurred.

In the 1880s and 1890s, the expansion of collegiate instruction had been hailed with joy in the academic world, except for a few reactionaries. By 1900, however, in Harvard and elsewhere, the elective system was no longer a new liberalizing idea; it had fulfilled its first function and had begun to be attacked. It was easy to see some of the unfortunate consequences of giving the undergraduate complete freedom in choosing his courses. Almost all the courses might be of an elementary nature, or they might all be in one subject, or in a group of subjects so closely related as to make a narrowly bounded field.

Even before Lowell became president, a faculty committee had been at work revising the free elective system. Therefore, within a year of his inauguration, the faculty voted overwhelmingly in favor of what became known as the "system of concentration and distribution." The class of 1914, to which I belong, was the first to which these new requirements applied. No longer could a student study only chemistry, physics and mathematics, for example; no longer could one accumulate enough credits to graduate by electing only freshman and sophomore courses. A framework had been constructed by the faculty to which one's desires for knowledge must conform. Yet it was an extremely flexible framework. Six of the sixteen courses had to be in one field—this was concentration; six courses had to be distributed among three different groups of courses—this was distribution. Lowell hoped that in this way the Harvard College graduate would have studied deeply one field so that he would have some awareness of what it meant to talk about the frontiers of knowledge; he would also, because of the distribution requirement, have had some acquaintance with a variety of intellectual activities.

During the last decade of Eliot's administration, it had often been said that the able students in the college were treated much like German university students. The aim of these undergraduates was to obtain as soon as possible a professional degree in law or in medicine, or the Ph.D. granted by the faculty of arts and sciences. The course of study was often planned so that the requirements for the first degree of bachelor of arts or science could be completed in three years. The senior collegiate year then became the first year in graduate school. Moreover, the administration had developed in such a way that the instruction given to Harvard College undergraduates and that given to students in the graduate school of arts and sciences merged.

When A. Lawrence Lowell took office, he had a definite plan for reconstituting the college. Indeed, in the *Harvard Monthly* of 1887, years before he had become a professor of government, he had already published part of his plan. Entitled "The Choice of Electives," the article stated the problems of the elective system and suggested the direction of change which he was himself to urge as president twenty years later. There is no evidence to indicate whether at the time it was published the article had any influence or not. What is significant is the fact that at the age of thirty-one, on the basis of his experience as an undergraduate, a law student and an interested alumnus, he had confidently drawn a blueprint for the future of one highly important aspect of undergraduate instruction. Such foresight was characteristic.

As he told his friends from time to time in later years, President Lowell had a clear conception of what he thought a four-year undergraduate college should offer to American students. The modification of the elective system, the emphasis on honors work, the repudiation of the drift to a three-year college, the freshman dormitories, the introduction of the tutorial and general examination system, and finally the House Plan—all these were in his mind, so he said, in the first years of his administration. He did not, however, reveal even to his closest friends all the details of his plan. Indeed, he is said to have remarked toward the end of his presidency that if he had made a blueprint of his ambitions for Harvard College and given it to the world at the time of his inauguration, many people would have objected to various portions of the outline and made its realization impossible.

The story of President Lowell's twenty-four years as president was to be an extraordinary one. I doubt if there is any other example in academic history of a single individual taking over the leadership of a college or university with the intent of making so many radical changes and succeeding in the course of a little more than two decades in effecting all of them. His ideas about education were greatly influenced by his intimate knowledge of Oxford and Cambridge. The colleges in these universities were his model in many ways. Yet I do not recall his ever having suggested publicly that an American college should imitate a British institution. It was through a process of slow

evolution guided by his skillful hand that the Harvard College of today came into being.

The first step in the transformation was the reform of the elective
system. Closely connected with it was Lowell's firm determination
to eliminate the possibility of an undergraduate's obtaining an A.B.
degree in three years. The close of Eliot's administration and the
opening of Lowell's had been the occasion for the new president
to set forth in some detail his plans for remaking Harvard College.
The reverberations of the inaugural address were still strong when
a year later I entered Harvard as a freshman. The retiring president, present but silent, had been almost openly fearful of what
his successor would do. For years he had tried in vain to reduce
the undergraduate years to three; now a new president declared
forcefully his intention of making a four-year course of instruction
so significant that it could not be reduced to three.

My first indication that I had, indeed, entered a college in transition was an argument with the dean of Harvard College, a close friend
and associate of President Lowell. Looking at my proposed program,
he noted that I was planning to complete the requirements for an
A.B. degree in three years. He tried to persuade me to forgo this ambition and to rearrange my study plan so that I would use all four years
to fulfill the requirements for the first degree. Since my whole collegiate future had been planned by Mr. Black in terms of the Eliot
tradition, the credit I had already received for work in chemistry had
passed me almost halfway through a four-year course. I held to the
three-year plan.

Along with many other members of the class of 1914, I completed
the requisite sixteen courses by the end of the junior year. In my
fourth year, I enrolled in the Graduate School of Arts and Sciences;
some of my friends entered the Law School, some the Medical School.
Socially we were all seniors and roomed in the dormitories in the
College Yard, which were reserved for members of the senior class.
Before long, the rules and regulations were altered and it became
more and more difficult to finish the collegiate work in three years,
even if one attended summer school, as many of us had done. By the
time I had completed the work for the Ph.D. in 1916, four years of
undergraduate study had become the accepted pattern. It so remained
during all the subsequent years I was in Cambridge as a student, professor and administrator.

Only in the 1950s, with the introduction of the advanced placement program of the College Board, did it again become possible for

an entering freshman to anticipate certain college courses. Today, I am told, an increasing number of students at Harvard and other colleges are taking advantage of the new arrangements; by virtue of their preparatory school work they complete the requirement for an A.B. degree in three years. The similarity between this development and the dispensation I was granted in 1910 needs no underlining. I must admit to a certain chagrin when I record that it was only after I had left the university administration that the advanced placement program was accepted.

Though President Lowell's reforms for the most part lay in the future during my undergraduate days, the concentration and distribution requirements did have an influence on my curriculum. I recall that one had to elect at least one full course in either mathematics or philosophy. Since as a future chemist I had to study calculus, there was no compulsion for me to study philosophy, but I did so, largely as a consequence of my mother's urging. She as well as my two sisters, both considerably older than I, and two of my older Harvard cousins were full of apprehension about my college education. My advanced standing was viewed with misgivings. The enjoyment with which I studied chemistry and only chemistry was regarded as a bad omen. Was I going to be nothing but a narrow-minded chemist?

My cousins urged extracurricular activities; they suggested that I should become a candidate for election to the editorial board of the *Harvard Crimson*. Why not? I had been editor in chief of the school paper. Yet "going out for the *Crimson*" was a time-consuming operation. The candidates did all the reporting. Their efforts were scrutinized by the managing editor and a couple of his colleagues. From time to time the number of aspirants was reduced either by voluntary or forced withdrawal from the competition. I was eliminated after a month. A second attempt in my sophomore year was successful, though I nearly wrecked a half-year of work. What made all the effort worthwhile was the fact that success opened the doors to my election to a highly selective literary club, the Signet. Here I found my general education. In this club, around the luncheon table, conversation was kept at what we believed to be a highly sophisticated level. These discussions were probably far more significant in broadening my interests than all the lectures in the courses I took to fulfill the distribution requirements, except a course on the art and culture of Italy in the Renaissance, which I elected on the advice of an upperclassman.

Those who concentrated in chemistry at Harvard in the first two decades of this century rarely, if ever, included athletes, managers of teams or editors of undergraduate publications. The demands of the laboratory did not allow sufficient time for extracurricular activities, which, in those days, consumed far too many afternoons and evenings. Only because of my advanced standing was I able to spend so many hours on the *Crimson*. As a consequence, I had two separate groups of friends. Those on the *Crimson* and in the dormitories were my contemporaries; those concentrating in chemistry were a year or two my seniors.

The courses in chemistry, with the possible exception of the freshman course, were distinguished by a professional spirit. I found myself as a freshman talking to sophomores and juniors and even occasionally seniors in the chemistry courses in which I was enrolled. Thus in terms of formal instruction, I felt myself part of a Harvard University not unlike that which had accommodated those who were my seniors by a few years. In the advanced course in chemistry, I was on the same professional footing, so to speak, as many seniors and first-year graduate students. My circle of chemical acquaintances by the time I was in my fourth year included those who were about to receive their Ph.D. Indeed, through the Harvard chapter of a chemical fraternity, I became acquainted with one or two who had completed their graduate work before I obtained my bachelor's degree.

The point is significant only because through my many talks with those older students I came to know the way young chemists looked at their profession before World War I. Of the thirty-three men who were awarded the doctorate in chemistry at Harvard between 1907 and 1917 (I knew all but two or three), there was hardly one who did not intend to become a college professor. Ten years later—that is, between 1917 and 1927—the majority of those who received the advanced degree would enter industrial employment either at once or after a few years.

The significance of scientific research for the prosperity of an industry was just beginning to be talked about while I was an undergraduate. I recall hearing a lecture in 1912 or 1913 by Willis Whitney, the founder of the research laboratory of the General Electric Company. He told how he had persuaded a young man to leave an academic laboratory and join his group. Whitney had offered the professor an opportunity to carry on in the GE laboratory the same line of research he had been pursuing. In making the offer, Whitney told us, he had been confident that once the new recruit had a chance to look around, he would find more fascinating questions in industry than the problem he was bringing with him. In a short time, his confidence was justified. Experiments designed to provide more information about the physics and chemistry of electric light bulbs became so important that the erstwhile professor lost interest in what had once been his sole concern. The main burden of Whitney's remarks that evening was to the effect that industry abounded in problems which lent themselves to attack by a trained research man irrespective of the field in which he had gained his experience. The story made a deep impression.

CHAPTER 4

The Changing Role of the Chemist

Not only Harvard, it seemed, was in transition during my undergraduate and graduate years. The chemical profession, too, was undergoing profound changes. To explain what I have in mind, I must first retrace the chronological record and describe the Harvard chemistry department as it existed in the first fifteen years of this century.

Far and away the most eminent member was Theodore William Richards. It was he who as chairman had responded so favorably to Mr. Black's proposals about my education. Later when I learned about his own quite unusual entry into chemistry, I realized that his readiness to allow a schoolboy to anticipate college work might reflect the beginnings of his own career. He had entered Haverford College as a sophomore on the basis of what he had learned at home. After obtaining the bachelor's degree at the age of seventeen, he entered the senior year at Harvard, receiving a second bachelor's degree, followed by a doctorate at twenty. His thesis involved painstaking quantitative experimentation, and to this type of work he dedicated the remainder of his life.

While still in his twenties, Richards became the world authority on the determination of the atomic weights of the elements. His many papers, published for the most part in German scientific periodicals, attracted wide attention. A revised atomic weight of an element was news. Moreover, as one element after another was studied,

27

the chemical world realized that here was a young American experimentalist of genius who had, indeed, an infinite capacity for taking pains.

In 1901 he received a call to Goettingen. President Eliot, however, urged him to stay at Harvard, asking him what he would like to make his position more attractive. The upshot was that he remained in Cambridge under conditions more favorable than before. Harvard had agreed to a prompt promotion to a full professorship (salary $4,000); a reduction in the number of lectures; better pay for an assistant; as much relief as possible from administrative work, including service on faculty committees.

In later years, Professor Richards referred more than once to the importance of being relieved of any obligation to serve on faculty committees. Perhaps such service in 1900 was more time-consuming than it later became. One suspects, however, that the young chemist did not so much regret the hours spent away from the laboratory as he did the consumption of nervous energy in academic quarrels. The passionate investigator abhorred disagreement. He did not enjoy even the mildest form of the give-and-take of debate. He joined a social gathering gladly provided that no highly controversial subject was likely to be raised. His courtesy, charm and sensitivity made him welcome. He was not a person, however, who relished a strenuous meeting of minds.

Richards felt that a new chemical laboratory was needed, and President Eliot agreed. But a suitable building would cost a half-million dollars and at least $250,000 a year as endowment. Eliot insisted particularly on the necessity of a large endowment. In a letter to the young chemist, he remarked that benefactors and trustees were beginning to understand that a building by itself, if not endowed, could be an embarrassing gift. Eliot made no commitment, however, to seek funds to build a laboratory or even to assist in such a quest; any idea that the Harvard Corporation might out of its own free funds provide the endowment was in those days beyond imagination. (When I bargained with Mr. Eliot's successor nearly twenty-five years later, such a proposition seemed by no means out of the question. In the booming financial atmosphere of the late 1920s, a Harvard president could promise a yearly grant for research expenses for a period of five years. In the early 1900s, however, every ambitious professor was expected to find his own endowment.)

Half a dozen years after the call to Goettingen, when Richards was adding to his international reputation by his lectures in the

University of Berlin as an exchange professor, a friend of his father, Joseph Wharton of Philadelphia, volunteered to give $50,000 toward such a building. The offer, duly transmitted to President Eliot, was the start of a combined effort of a small group of well-to-do friends to raise the money to construct and endow a separate laboratory building (the Wolcott Gibbs Memorial Laboratory) for Professor Richards. The building was completed before World War I. Professor Richards and his research students (of whom I was one) were enjoying its almost luxurious facilities when he received the Nobel prize in the fall of 1915.

Richards' father, William T. Richards, had been a successful painter of marine scenes, and his pictures were highly valued by those in the Eastern cities who knew and loved the New England coast and could afford to buy them. The family was not wealthy, but family friendships extended to many who regularly supported museums and orchestras. Some might consider it a pleasant duty to help a university provide adequate facilities for the son of a famous artist who had himself just achieved international fame. Viewed in this light, the interest of Joseph Wharton in a laboratory for Theodore W. Richards is far from extraordinary.

It was not a building for the chemistry department that he had in mind, let it be noted. The plans for new chemical facilities at Harvard at that time took the form of small buildings, each primarily under the jurisdiction of one professor. Such an arrangement lent itself to the desires of individual donors to assist the work of a specific professor. After World War I the custom was abandoned. The upkeep of small separate laboratory buildings proved too costly. Two buildings to house the entire department were then envisioned; to raise the requisite money, a formal campaign was organized in the mid-1920s. An appeal went out to all alumni and to all friends of chemistry—an entirely different approach from that of the group who made possible the erection of the Wolcott Gibbs Memorial Laboratory for Professor Richards. The department now dominated the thinking. The needs of the undergraduates for adequate laboratories had equal priority with the needs of graduate research men.

This history of the way a young American academic chemist obtained support for his investigations in the opening years of this century may serve as a reminder of how closely the few leading American universities were then connected with the German world of scholarship and science. A call to Goettingen in 1901 was sufficient to establish a reputation. No one begrudged the recipient of the call a new laboratory built for his own and his students' use. Richards had stipulated that he would remain in charge of physical chemistry; this meant that no one else would be called to a full professorship in that subject. At the same time he agreed that he would continue to lecture to a considerable number of undergraduates as well as keep in close touch with the few graduate students who worked in his own laboratory.

Richards adhered faithfully to the agreement. He not only gave the lectures and organized the laboratory work in physical chemistry, but continued to give a half-course in the history of chemistry. In this way, many who were not concentrating in chemistry heard him present his interpretation of the advance of science. They left with an increased understanding of the way chemists thought and with what was perhaps more important: the knowledge that they had had the rare privilege of sitting at the feet of an American chemist of world-wide renown. All of which was in the German tradition.

Indeed, the atmosphere in Cambridge before 1914 resembled in many respects that of a typical German university town. (The same was probably true of New Haven and Princeton.) Everyone of any importance in the academic community had studied in a German university. To provide instruction for undergraduates, it had proved necessary to have more instructors of professorial rank than in Germany; yet the number of full professors remained small. And in each subject usually only one had received wide recognition as a scholar. He and his family were expected, like their German counterparts, to be dedicated to things of the mind and the spirit. Their standards were far removed from either the marketplace or the political forum. The evaluation of literature, art and music was considered an essential extension of their scholarly interests. As distinguished, learned men, they were entitled to be regarded as the social equals of anybody in the United States. (In Germany in the early 1900s, as a German professor said to me wistfully in 1925, professors were outranked only by the nobility and the generals. Yet in terms of financial compensation, the rewards were slight; a young Ph.D. usually expected to marry money.) American professors could live on their salaries in those days, but one could hardly say they were either well-to-do or high in the social scale.

Professor Richards, as a young man studying with the great professors in Germany, had become totally committed to pure research. To him, the advancement of the science of chemistry was an all-absorbing occupation. He had no time to give to problems in the area of applied science, which was beginning to assume importance in the first decade of this century. His two most brilliant pupils of the early days shared his views. They were Gregory Paul Baxter, who became a full professor of analytical chemistry at Harvard, and Gilbert Newton Lewis, the physical chemist who went to Berkeley just before World War I. Both became famous, the one for his continuation of Richards' endeavors to improve the accuracy of atomic weight determinations, the other for his original ideas in physical chemistry. Lewis served as an officer in the Chemical Warfare Service during World War I, but aside from that he manifested no interest in the rapidly expanding area of applied chemistry. I doubt if either Baxter or Lewis ever accepted a consulting position with an industrial firm.

I never heard Professor Richards say anything derogatory about those who did consulting work. He only made it clear that from his own point of view pure science was so demanding that he had no energy to give to problems which were not closely connected with the developing framework of theoretical chemistry.

His aim was high. Atomic weights, he believed (erroneously, it turned out), had fundamental theoretical significance. The physical measurements he made were related to his own theory of compressible atoms. I recall referring one day to his impressive list of papers, in which were recorded a multitude of meticulous observations. "What a record of accomplishment!" I exclaimed. "Perhaps," he replied, "but I am far from sure there is a contribution in any of them which history will record as marking the turning of a corner." His hero was Michael Faraday. Unless one aimed at a degree of fame which placed an investigator in the same class as Faraday, one would have set one's sights too low. What Professor Richards' graduate students learned by working with him was an appreciation of the grand strategy of the advance of science. Every one of his research undertakings was, in his mind, significant because of its relations to the fundamental theories of his science. The idea of making new observations just for the sake of publishing an alleged contribution to the advancement of science was anathema to him.

The tactics of research in the field of organic chemistry I learned from a man of Professor Richards' age who had joined the Harvard department while I was still an undergraduate. Elmer Peter Kohler was called from Bryn Mawr in 1912 to give the freshman course in general chemistry and the advanced course in his own field, organic chemistry. When the chemistry department turned to Kohler, they must have had in mind his reputation as a teacher; for though he had been a professor since 1900, he had no list of important papers to his credit. At Harvard he quickly proved that those who thought of him in terms of an exciting course in freshman chemistry had been correct.

Because of the advanced standing I enjoyed, I was eligible to enroll in a research course in my third year. I took advantage of the opportunity to request the permission of the new professor of organic chemistry to do a piece of research with him, though I could give only a small fraction of my time to the enterprise. I did so on the advice of some of my older friends in the graduate school who were enthusiastic organic chemists. They suggested I should find out what research in their field was like before embarking on a Ph.D. thesis under Professor Richards, as I had planned to do as far back as my days in the Roxbury Latin School.

What was intended as an exploration of a neighboring field turned out to be an introduction to my lifework as a chemist. Kohler in his first year at Harvard had few research students; therefore he gave a disproportionate amount of time to me. I was enormously impressed by him as a man and as a scientist. Under his direction, I prepared in a few months a new organic compound. The feat, which I was later to learn was a common experience in research laboratories, seemed to me an important step into the unknown. The attractions of experimentation with carbon compounds began to make me wonder whether I wanted to be a physical chemist after all.

In the middle of the same year (1912–13), Professor Kohler offered me the position as his assistant in charge of the laboratory work in his course in organic chemistry (Chemistry 5) for 1913–14. I am not sure that he, a newcomer to the Harvard scene, quite realized that though I would have been awarded my A.B. degree by June 1913, I would still be socially a member of the class of 1914 and a senior. The chances were that some of my friends who were majoring in chemistry would be taking the advanced course in organic chemistry. If so, I should have the novel experience of being responsible in part for their instruction. Actually, the prospect intrigued me and may have inclined me to accept the offer, which I did. What was far more important was the probability that if I continued with Professor Kohler, I could finish the research problems on which I was already engaged.

The course of organic reactions, like that of true love, does not run smooth. In this case, it ran quite contrary to Professor Kohler's

predictions. It happened that I stumbled upon an unorthodox explanation of the experiments which puzzled us; I was anxious to demonstrate the correctness of my hypothesis, as in fact I eventually did.
So I decided to present a double thesis for the Ph.D: The first part
would be in organic chemistry, the second in physical chemistry. If
this were to be the program, then the assistantship in Chemistry 5
for 1913–14 fitted nicely, provided it could be continued in 1914–15.
Because of the demands of the teaching, only half of the time could
be counted toward fulfilling the Ph.D. residence requirements (two
years as an assistant would be the equivalent of one year on full
time); my research as an undergraduate didn't count at all. I asked
for a place as a full-time student with Professor Richards for 1915–16
and my request was granted. With a Ph.D. awarded for a two-part
thesis, I would be theoretically prepared to undertake research in
either organic or physical chemistry. Actually, by the time commencement 1916 came around, I was a committed organic chemist. By a
series of accidents, Mr. Black's scheme of having his favorite pupil
become a physical chemist had been thwarted. I had deserted the
path of chemical science which he had laid out for me so long ago.
I think he never forgave Kohler.

I worked with Kohler so closely as a research student, a teaching
assistant and later as a junior colleague, that I am sure many of my
attitudes and opinions are a consequence of his views. As an investigator, he was a great tactician but no strategist. To be sure, it was
not easy in the organic chemistry of that period to pick problems
whose solutions would affect basic theory in a significant way. The
great work of constructing the fundamental concepts had already
been completed. Some of the German professors who regarded the
entire area of the chemistry of carbon compounds as a national preserve were turning their attention more and more to the elucidation
of the structure of alkaloids and other products of nature. The chemistry of the sugars and proteins had been put on a sound basis by the
brilliant pathbreaking work of Emil Fischer of Berlin.

Kohler was not moved to follow in any such direction. He was
interested in the mechanism of organic reactions. His students, including myself, never lost the enthusiasm for this subject which he
generated. To focus this interest on specific questions was difficult
if one used only the classic methods of following the course of chemical reactions. Until much later, when the resources opened by the
physical chemists were available, the study of the interaction of
organic compounds usually amounted to attempts to isolate the prod-

ucts of some new combination and determine their structure. To accomplish this in those days, one was almost forced to choose compounds which were crystalline solids or whose interaction would produce crystalline material. Complex mixtures of solids could be separated by fractional crystallization; mixtures of liquids could not then be resolved by any known techniques. It was a matter of great skill then (as I am told is still the case) to manipulate the solutions containing many substances so that pure crystalline compounds could be separated from each other.

Kohler was a master of such manipulations, which he performed in his own laboratory with his own hands. He continued until a few weeks before his death to carry on himself the experiments he regarded as crucial. The puzzles that such a line of investigation continually presented came to constitute for him the beginning and end of what was important. To their solution he devoted all his energies and rarely permitted himself the luxury of inquiring whether the puzzles were worth solving. The enjoyment he obtained from doing his own experimentation made him a great tactician. The same zest for the detailed, difficult tasks prevented him from taking those steps which might have given to his publications more enduring worth. To a considerable degree, the same judgment could be passed on many of his contemporaries and his students. The first three decades of this century were not a great period in the history of American organic chemistry.

The contrast between strategist and tactician was not the only difference between the two men who initiated me in research. In many ways, they were the antithesis of each other. Yet they worked together as members of the same department without the slightest friction. Richards had an international reputation. Kohler did not and was entirely indifferent to reputation; he had almost no friends among other chemists, and as far as I could ascertain had never even visited a laboratory in another university, either in the United States or Europe. He kept abreast of the chemical literature and was continually introducing new material into his lectures. He seemed to have no feeling, however, that he was a member of an international fraternity of learned men. As a bachelor, his cultural home was still his ancestral home in Egypt, Pennsylvania. His values reflected those of the German-American farm community which had existed in Lehigh Valley since pre-Revolutionary days. The solidity of his down-to-earth common-sense judgments on human problems, however, soon won him a highly respected place among not only those of his own department but those from other fields who came to know him on committees. The same qualities made him for me a highly prized adviser on all manner of things while I was cutting my teeth as a green assistant professor and for many years thereafter.

One of the strange contradictions of Kohler's character was his success as a lecturer and his lifelong diffidence as a public speaker. His delight as an artist was clear when he presented a brilliant lecture, either to freshmen or to advanced students in organic chemistry, or on very rare occasions to a "journal meeting." His anxiety before every such performance was equally real, but known to only a few. This almost pathological apprehension explained why Kohler made it a firm rule never to speak outside his lecture room. But explanations were seldom given for a policy that appeared so curious and arbitrary to many fellow chemists. He rarely if ever attended scientific meetings. All of this gained him the entirely undeserved reputation of being an academic snob. He suffered thereby the fate of more than one shy person whose aloofness is attributed to pride.

One episode in Kohler's freshman teaching deserves to be recorded for all who enjoy the hazards of experimental demonstrations before a class. The main subject of a certain lecture in general chemistry was explosives. The long lecture table was covered with samples of gunpowder: mammoth pieces used in naval ordnance, open vessels of smaller grains used in army guns, samples of powder for shotguns and rifles for sportsmen. About the middle of the hour, Professor Kohler introduced the topic of gunpowder with the following words: "There is a common misapprehension that when gunpowder is ignited it explodes, but actually if lighted in the open it burns with a quiet flame." Thereupon he poured a little black powder onto an asbestos sheet, struck a match and applied the flame. The result was a flash along the entire table, a roar and heavy clouds of smoke. An old-fashioned chain reaction had taken place; a spark had jumped from the demonstration to the nearest sample of powder and started off the entire exhibit. The students rushed for the fire escapes. Kohler, who had ducked behind the table, emerged and held up his hand to quiet the incipient panic. Through the smoke one could just see him from the back of the hall. As the milling throng quieted down, he said, "I have sent for some more gunpowder." After the laughter and cheers had subsided, he performed the experiment without mishap, and then firmly stated, "You see it does burn with a quiet flame. The class is dismissed!"

There was nothing exhibitionistic about Kohler's teaching: he used lecture-table demonstrations not for show but to demonstrate a point. He drove home with relentless logic whatever he undertook to expound; he had no patience with ill-formulated ideas or partial truths. In short, as a teacher he was at one and the same time both interesting and rigorous. His approach was entirely his own. No textbook has ever been written or ever will be that can in any way accomplish what he succeeded in achieving.

If ever the lecture system for advanced students had a justification, it was in Kohler's Chemistry 5. His success came from the combination of years of experience and great native skill in the art of speaking to small audiences. His consistent refusal to speak outside his classroom coupled with his annual destruction of his lecture notes kept this skill from being damaged by those forces that slowly erode the pedagogic talents of so many academic men. Who but a bachelor, however, whose life was centered in his subject could find the time and patience to work over every year a completely new approach to his subject?

Kohler kept turning around in his mind for a week or so before it was due the way he was going to present a certain topic "this year." He would drop a remark or two to a junior colleague that betrayed his preoccupation. And then, if one were bold enough to intrude on the actual preparation of the lecture the day before, one would find Kohler sitting at his small desk in his office making notes on pages torn from the backs of old examination bluebooks. He seemed never to write out even a fraction of the entire lecture. His notes, when one could catch a glimpse of them, appeared to consist of a series of opening sentences of paragraphs—these and some formulas of the complicated transformations so dear to the heart of the organic chemist.

Kohler shared the attitude of Richards toward industrial chemistry. He had no interest in the application of chemistry. Because of his aversion to speaking in public, he never attended meetings of the American Chemical Society. He was almost unknown to his contemporaries except for a few academic men in New England. Who was wise enough to have him called to Washington in World War I as civilian adviser to the chief of the Chemical Warfare Service, I do not know. But I do know that in the year and a half during which Kohler was in Washington he was immersed in problems of applied chemistry. As a consequence, he might have been drawn into the orbit of one or more of the companies that were expanding their research departments rapidly in the 1920s. The experience with the application of chemistry to production procedures might have altered his outlook. It did not. As soon as possible after the armistice, he returned to his own laboratory and the delights of his own personal experimentation.

The months in Washington had one result. The value of Kohler's shrewd estimates of men became known in a wider circle than before. He became one of the elder statesmen of science. Graduate students in increasing numbers came to Harvard to work with him. Thus his influence began to spread throughout the United States. The way in which he combined devotion to research with excellence in lecturing was an example to many of my generation and to the still younger men who received their doctor's degrees in the 1920s and 1930s.

At least at Harvard, before and during the First World War, lecturing was considered a fine art which should be mastered by all graduate students who expected to become professors. To this end, those who had the status of teaching assistants listened to the lectures of the full professors with critical attention. I recall that our judgments were merciless, though the evaluations were not much different from those of the undergraduates. There were good lecturers and mediocre ones. Kohler was an example of the best. We attended his lectures to try to learn his skill. There was no formal instruction in the art of lecturing whatsoever. Indeed, Kohler would have been embarrassed by any reference to his success as a lecturer. We graduate students knew, however, that in recommending a new doctor of philosophy for an academic position, the potentialities of the candidate as a lecturer would be a matter of first importance. The senior professors who listened to the short reports presented by graduate students at research meetings were able to estimate this potential; while little was said about it, everyone was well aware of the fact. Thus concern with undergraduate teaching through lecturing was almost as great as concern with the preparation of the Ph.D. thesis.

One must remember that before the growth of an American chemical industry during the war, the graduate student expected to obtain his first academic job as a professor in a small college. Teaching in such a position would be his main concern. Only if he was fortunate and could squeeze in some research, could he prove his competence as an investigator. He might slowly develop a double record on which he could be assessed, and might then be called to a large university where he would find graduate students to work with him. If so, the scene would change dramatically. Real opportunities for research would, for the first time, be open to him. Not many professors outside of the large universities were carrying on experimental studies and publishing papers. In most cases, time and energy were almost exclusively devoted to teaching. Many professors measured their success (privately, at least) by the number of promising students they could win year by year for the profession of chemistry. These young men they recommended for scholarships and teaching assistantships in a major university.

As I was to discover in the 1920s, a professor who received one of these outstanding college graduates as a research student was most fortunate. The three most brilliant of those who worked with me for a Ph.D. degree enrolled as a consequence of the recommendation of a friend on the faculty of each of three famous small New England colleges. These friends were fellow members of a small social club of New England professors of chemistry to which I had been elected soon after World War I. The annual meetings rotated from one city or town to another. In visiting the colleges, one came to know colleagues whose interests were exclusively in the undergraduates. None were themselves active investigators. There was no feeling of superiority on the part of those of us who were on the staff of a university and certainly no inferiority on the part of our friends in the small colleges.

I doubt if the equivalent of these joyously committed teachers is to be found today. From what I hear, every collegiate teacher must now be involved in a research project or suffer a diminution in prestige. The distinction in attitude between university men who were supposed to be engaged in research and collegiate professors who were not seems to have disappeared. Whether the change is permanent is open to question. I am inclined to prophesy that as the position of the two-year community college becomes stabilized, the staff of these institutions will develop a spirit of independence from the four-year colleges and universities. In time, a group of excellent professors will develop who judge themselves and ask to be judged as teachers, not as investigators. If this occurs, a group of teachers will arise who can inspire young people as did the New England college professors earlier in the century.

I have described at some length the Harvard department of chemistry in order to provide a basis for exploring the nature of the changes in the chemical profession in the United States in the years leading up to World War I. By the time I had entered Harvard, the commitment to pure research combined with a teaching career, which had been at the center of Richards' and Kohler's lives, was already giving way to the challenges of applied science; the temptations of jobs in industry were starting to appear. With the advent of war, still newer opportunities would be opening up in the government and indeed in industry itself. In the 1920s it became common practice for a professor to be a consultant to a manufacturing company. Richards and Kohler and their contemporaries had rarely had any connection with industry. (I am speaking of the professors who had academic chairs. Members of engineering faculties were different. They were expected to be in close contact with rapidly developing areas such as electrical engineering. In one or two institutions, chemical engineering had developed before 1914. In the Massachusetts Institute of Technology, in particular, the application of the principles of physical chemistry to industrial processes was making great strides.) I must emphasize that the changes to which I am referring were changes in the American scene. In Germany, the manufacture of dyes and pharmaceuticals had assumed the proportion of a major industry which was already employing scores of young Ph.D.s long before World War I started.

I had a chance to learn something about the opening opportunities for chemists in industry when, during the summer of 1915, I worked at the Midvale Steel Company in Philadelphia. Midvale had made a start on a research program as early as 1908. A few years later a Harvard instructor, George Leslie Kelley, had joined the company's research department, and Kelley in turn had brought with him one of my friends, Richard H. Patch, who had received his Harvard Ph.D. in 1914. I was offered the chance of learning about the steel industry by Patch, who knew me well, and Kelley, who knew me only as a student in his course in organic chemistry. The job was in Dr. Kelley's laboratory, developing new analytical procedures. Thus in the summer of 1915, two former Harvard instructors and one aspirant to a Harvard Ph.D. had appeared in what a few years earlier had been a control laboratory manned by a single technician.

What I learned about steelmaking I forgot in a few years. What I learned about the inner politics of a manufacturing plant has remained with me ever since. So, too, has Kelley's way of thinking about production problems. The actual laboratory work concerned the introduction of a new electrochemical method of determining the vanadium content of steel. This was a rewarding experience in itself. What was even more significant were the long talks with Kelley at his home on Sundays after a wonderful dinner served by his wife. Then Kelley would think out loud about how a more scientific outlook could be brought to bear on steelmaking.

Kelley and Patch, experienced as investigators in the realm of organic chemistry, could not claim to bring specific knowledge and techniques to help the practical steelmakers at Midvale. Their reason for being there rested on the assumption of top management that these two young doctors of philosophy had acquired in the course of their academic research work a point of view which would be helpful in a steel mill. Obviously, they themselves shared this belief. The practical men who headed the various divisions, however, were not convinced. Trained as engineers, they resented more or less openly the intrusion of any ideas these "doctors" might have about how to make steel. It was implied that Kelley and Patch had better stick to the analytical methods of the chemical laboratory—which was just what they had *not* been hired to do. In the next two decades I was to hear often of similar tensions between the practical operating men and the newcomers with research training.

Thus in the summer of 1915 I had the privilege of an intimate preview of one aspect of the young marriage of chemistry and American industry. When I returned to Harvard in the fall for my final year of work toward my Ph.D., my view of the possibilities open to a graduate chemist had been greatly enlarged.

CHAPTER 5

A Scientist in World War I

WHEN WAR BROKE OUT IN Europe in August 1914, I was a graduate student attending the Harvard summer school. By the time college opened in mid-September, all my elders had taken sides. To my amazement, the professors who had spoken so well of German research were not only pro-Ally but violently anti-German. What seemed to me a strange, sudden change in attitude was accompanied by bitterness toward the few colleagues who were pro-German. When I learned that one of the senior members of the faculty, a German by birth and a professor of Germanic studies, had been cut dead on the street by one of his neighbors, I was horrified. I recalled the words of a professor of philosophy who a year earlier had been speaking to a small group about the nationalistic furor during the Spanish-American War. At that time some zealots had been ready to have us go to war with Germany because that nation appeared to be on the Spanish side. "Just imagine," the professor had said, "our fighting Germany, with which we in the universities have so much in common." Now this same professor was on the anti-German side.

Such reversal of sentiment brought to the surface all my New England contrariness. When I heard someone denounced for an attempt to justify the invasion of Belgium, I became a pro-German apologist. Nor was I alone. Many of my friends who had either just graduated from college or who were about to graduate were reacting in the same way. We were not pro-German, but we were highly critical of the emotional anti-German remarks of our professors.

41

There was no thought of American involvement in 1914, of course. The issue was only where one's sympathies lay. The more pro-Ally the faculty became, the more skeptical became the attitude of some of us in the younger generation. (By the time I had taken my Ph.D. degree in 1916 and become an instructor in September 1917, the situation was vastly different. President Wilson's policy of keeping us out of the war had become the acute issue. A whole series of incidents, exploited by British and French propagandists, had swung the sympathy of the young as well as the old in Cambridge to the side of the Allies.)

In the first year or two of World War I, my education as a chemist was little affected by the European conflagration. Before long, however, the alteration in the American industrial scene had had its effect on departments of chemistry and the ambitions of chemists in the universities. Nineteen-fifteen was the year in which it became clear that the great European war would not be a short war. The Germans' plans for a rapid victory had been thwarted. The belligerents had settled down to the horrors of trench warfare, with no end in sight. American businessmen made up their minds that the importations from Germany of dyes and drugs and fine chemicals would not start up again within the foreseeable future. An American industry must be developed to manufacture these products. Organic chemists were in demand.

I recall a canvass of the employment situation for Ph.D.s in organic chemistry which was made by George Kelley in the course of a conversation on the porch of his home one hot evening during my summer at Midvale Steel. I was only a listener. E. K. Bolton, a friend of Kelley's from Harvard, had called to ask advice about accepting an offer with the Du Pont Company, which at that time was essentially a manufacturer of gunpowder. The company was proposing to go into the production of dyestuffs and "intermediates." Other companies had similar ambitions. As compared with working for a steel company, all such possibilities still seemed highly speculative. When the European war ended, what would happen to the new prospects? Was it research or the production of organic chemicals that these various companies had in mind? Bolton was just back from Berlin, where he had spent two years working with one of the great masters of organic chemistry. He was just the type who a few years earlier would have been considering academic openings. Not in August 1915! No university or college positions were even mentioned. The research chemist in industry was the topic of the talk. The young listener, who did not yet have his Ph.D., was all ears.

E. K. Bolton finally decided to sign up with Du Pont, where he made a brilliant record and eventually became one of the top policy-making officials. He was well on his way to success when I called on him in Wilmington, in the early summer of 1917, in the middle of my own uncertainty about what a chemist should do in wartime. Bolton was good enough to talk with me, though he did not offer me a job. This was not my last meeting with Bolton nor my last interview with Du Pont officials. In the 1920s I became a consultant for Du Pont and had many opportunities of coming to know Bolton well. By this time he was head of one of the research divisions. Indeed, it was through him that arrangements were made for the Du Pont Company to take over the rights to polymerization under extremely high pressure which Professor P. W. Bridgman and I patented just before I left the chemical laboratory for an administrative career.

As the end of my graduate studies approached, I realized that my professional training would be incomplete if I did not spend a year in Germany. With a war in progress on the continent, however, Germany did not seem the nation in which to spend a year. The United States was still officially neutral, but growing less so as regards the attitude of its citizens, at least in the Eastern cities. Some of my friends had volunteered for the American Ambulance Service and were serving on the battlefields. I played with the idea of combining a year of post-Ph.D. study at the famous Institute of Technology in Zurich with some months in the Ambulance Service—much to the horror of my former teacher, Newton Henry Black, and my parents. I soon discovered, however, that nothing less than a full year's enlistment in the Service was acceptable. I was not ready to invest that much time away from the chemical laboratory, a decision which may be a measure of any devotion I had for the Allied cause as late as 1916. Though, of course, the Ambulance Service was noncombatant and in theory neutral, joining it was often regarded as an expression of a strong desire to help the Allied cause. In fact, in some cases, it seemed far more a manifestation of a desire to come dangerously close to a dangerous adventure without running much risk of becoming a casualty oneself.

Meanwhile, two other friends, who had majored in chemistry, suggested that we go into business together to manufacture those chemicals which were selling at fabulous prices because their importation from Germany had ceased. On paper, it was easy to calculate that vast profits were in store for those engaged in such an operation. Without building a large plant one could, in theory, prepare relatively simple organic chemicals in small batches and sell them without difficulty. I emphasize the words "in theory." Practice proved to be quite another matter. The three of us—Stanley B. Pennock, Chauncey C. Loomis (both of the class of 1915) and myself—proposed to form a company, raise a little capital and proceed to manufacture one or more products then in great demand in the pharmaceutical industry. We proposed to operate only until the war was over; we supposed the imports from Germany would start up again once the fighting ended. I dreamed that I could take up an academic post with a comfortable bankroll to supplement what I knew would be a meager salary.

The undertaking ended in disaster. We rented a one-story building in the Queens section of New York City. As a result of some experimentation, we developed in a few weeks a new process of making benzoic acid from toluene. In attempting to transfer a laboratory-scale procedure to a pilot-plant operation, Loomis and I, in the small hours of a hot August morning, succeeded only in setting fire to our small building, which was rapidly and completely consumed. The insurance negotiated on our behalf by Pennock a few days earlier enabled us to rent and equip another building, this time in Newark.

As we were preparing to move, I received a startling letter from Professor Gregory P. Baxter, by then the chairman of the Harvard chemistry department, offering me the position of instructor in organic chemistry with the duty of presenting elementary organic chemistry in a half-course of lectures. Roger Adams, who had been holding the appointment, had just accepted an offer of a professorship at the University of Illinois. A decision had to be made at once. My partners were most understanding. They realized that such opportunities occurred rarely. My inclination to accept was fortified by their attitude. We proceeded to make new business arrangements and parted, they for Newark, I for Cambridge.

Within a few months, a second plant had been constructed, and then another and more terrible catastrophe occurred. The laboratory work on which the new process was based (and which yielded a patent eventually) proved to be incomplete. On a pilot-plant scale, the reaction started too soon; it quickly became an explosion, for reasons we never discovered. A fire demolished all but the concrete walls of the plant. Stanley Pennock and a plumber who was repairing the piping were killed almost at once. Loomis escaped with minor injuries. The shock of this tragedy requires no underlining. Because I had not even seen the new plant, and had not witnessed the first trial run which ended so appallingly, I could not help feeling I had deserted a post of danger. The account Loomis gave me of what had actually happened showed that the procedure had been formulated erroneously, which was no one's fault except my own.

This tragic experience with applied chemistry should have discouraged me for a lifetime. In fact it did not; within eighteen months I was to become involved again (as a chemist in military uniform) in developing a new manufacturing process for a certain chemical— this time a poison gas. Meanwhile, I was busy with my first teaching assignment.

My career as an academic chemist had started because Roger Adams had left Harvard for Illinois. To attempt to fill his shoes was a formidable undertaking, for while he had not as yet established a reputation as an investigator, he had proved himself in Cambridge to be a lively lecturer. Elementary organic chemistry can be dull; a body of complicated information must be mastered. A majority of the students who elected the half-course in the subject were either premedical students or those who were just sampling courses in different fields. Less than a dozen were future chemists. To hold the interest of such a group required vigor and imagination. Lecture-table experiments could be used to advantage by an ingenious person, and Adams used them to the full. His lectures were famous for their humor and their liveliness. He left an outline, of course, and I was given good advice by Kohler as to how to start off in a pungent and challenging way. Perhaps it was fortunate that I had less than two weeks to prepare for what lay ahead. I was forced to consider each lecture only a day or two before it was delivered, thus, by necessity, following Kohler's example. As a result, a certain degree of freshness was assured. There were no notes, which might have tempted me to stand before a class and repeat what had been said the year before.

My greenness must have been painfully apparent to all those enrolled in Chemistry 2. I could not have been less experienced. I had never spoken to any audience except the small groups who came together in graduate colloquia. What rescued me was the attitude of the undergraduate audience. The word was passed around on the first day that I was a "pinch hitter." Adams, whom they had expected to hear, had left; in his place was a friend who had never faced a class before. One or two with whom I was acquainted constituted themselves as my defenders in advance. They let it be known that I was the sort of young instructor who should be given a chance. Their point of view prevailed. I finished the half-course of lectures with the feeling that my efforts had been well received. The examination papers at midyear showed that about as many had learned how to manipulate the spider-web formulas and put together series of reactions as could reasonably be expected. If the United States had not entered the war, I would undoubtedly have been reappointed as a one-year instructor.

In the presidential election of 1916 I was pro-Wilson. I have long had a clear picture in my mind of meeting a classmate the morning after the election outside the building of the *Harvard Crimson,* on whose bulletin board the latest returns were being posted. Hughes had been leading during the night; it was the vote from California that made Wilson the victor. To our mutual surprise, my classmate and I discovered that we were both for Wilson and happy at the turn the news had taken.

From my permanent, clear image of those few minutes, I drew the conclusion that I voted for Wilson; I have often said so. Yet a close examination of my personal history now reveals that such an act would have been impossible. To have voted in Cambridge in November 1916, I would have had to establish a Cambridge residence. Actually, it was only just as college opened that I returned to Cambridge to take on the unexpected job of giving the introductory course in organic chemistry.

I have recounted this trivial error in my memory to underline the difficulty of writing an autobiography. If a person cannot recall with accuracy his participation in a crucial presidential election, how can he hope to reconstruct what he was thinking some decades back? What one remembers (or at least what I remember) is so often not an event or attitude but a later reconstruction of the event or attitude. Sometime between 1916 and the 1930s I evolved the theory that I had cast a ballot for Wilson. I write "the 1930s" because I recall having made the erroneous statement about my voting record in a discussion of Hitler's Germany. Once having decided that I had taken part in the presidential election of 1916, I never bothered to question the "fact."

For many of us, as I have indicated, the emotional tensions of 1917 were different from those of 1914. The discussion as to whether one's sympathies were with the Germans or the Allies had given place to a far more serious debate about whether the United States should or should not enter the war on the Allied side. (In terms of the violation of American rights on the high seas, there were many grounds for our declaring war on Great Britain, but no one of importance ever proposed such a course.) My alignment with the Democrats in the fall of 1916 (I am certain of my attitude, at least) was probably due less to sympathy with Wilson's policies about the war than to a negative view of what Hughes' supporters were saying. For the first time in my life (but not the last) I was witnessing a violent denunciation of the President of the United States. Objections to his domestic legislation were being coupled with attacks on his failure to take a bold stand on the side of Great Britain. In their zeal to elect Hughes by discrediting the President, it seemed to me that many writers and speakers were showing far more emotion than reason. Included among them was Theodore Roosevelt, for whom I would have voted if I had been of voting age and duly registered in 1912. I thought the critics were overstepping themselves; as a dissenting youth I adhered to the other camp.

When the submarine warfare by Germany began to move into its unrestricted phase, I was still skeptical about the United States' becoming an ally of Great Britain and France. I remember that when I heard over the news ticker at the Harvard Club in Boston the account of President Wilson's address before Congress asking for a declaration of war, I was far from happy. The chief reason for my distress, however, was not because Wilson, having been re-elected on a platform of noninvolvement, was now asking for complete involvement. It was because of the effect on my own personal plans. By what seemed to me a miracle, I had gotten my foot on the bottom rung of the Harvard academic ladder; I was anxious to hang on. I had received my Ph.D. and been made an instructor responsible for an important course the same year. If my luck continued, I might move up in a year or two.

Now such prospects were jeopardized. Teaching chemistry was no place for a young man in wartime. Even before the United States had entered the war, some students had responded to the pro-Ally sentiment by volunteering to serve in one of the fighting forces facing the Germans. Before long, I would have to decide what to do when the academic year ended. It was easy to foresee what lay ahead for me when I read President Wilson's words. It was going to be a period of painful choice. These highly personal considerations reinforced my lack of sympathy with the interventionist, pro-French, pro-British sentiment which had been building up in Cambridge. The spectacle of older men urging younger ones to fight seemed to me far from edifying.

Less than a month after we entered the war in the spring of 1917, the administration's plans for building an army were given to the public. The officer corps was to be trained through the camp at Plattsburg. All able-bodied young men were urged to apply. Many of my classmates did. It would have been easy for me to have obtained a leave of absence for the balance of the academic year in order to enter such a training camp. President Lowell had been extremely pro-Ally from the start and, like all college presidents, was anxious to cooperate with the government as soon as we entered the war.

My senior colleagues, however, thought I would be crazy even to consider the possibility of becoming a combat officer. My place as a trained chemist was not in the infantry or artillery. Perhaps it was in industry, perhaps in a government laboratory. I made trips to Wilmington, Delaware, and Washington. I was not going to stay at Harvard, of that I was certain. My friends were going to be involved directly in the war. To stand aside was out of the question. How to reconcile my determination to participate with what I was told should be my role as a chemist was the problem. There could be no question of holding my place on the academic ladder. If I wanted to do that, I could, of course, accept another year's appointment as an instructor and take my chances with the draft. In June 1917 it was not at all clear how the proposed draft would operate. But to wait until its long arm reached one would be ignominious. That alternative, at least, I would not even consider.

Finally, I accepted a position with the Bureau of Chemistry in Washington. Here I worked in the first part of the summer of 1917 on a process for manufacturing a drug which had hitherto been imported from Germany. My endeavors were only remotely related to the war. I had just about made up my mind to enlist as a noncommissioned officer in a branch of the Army organized to provide defense against poison gases (later the Chemical Warfare Service), when I ran into Professor James F. Norris of M.I.T., whom I had known quite well in Cambridge. He was in the process of organizing a research group under the direction of the Bureau of Mines. When I told him I planned to go overseas as part of an outfit concerned with gas masks, he expressed consternation, saying, in effect, that this would be a waste of my talents and training. Norris had been authorized to organize one or more research teams which would work at the American University in Washington, and he offered me on the spot the leadership of one of these groups. I accepted and thus started down a lane of endeavor which was to have considerable influence on my subsequent career.

After we had spent a few months in civilian status, the government decided to put all the research men at the American University into uniform. Thus I became a first lieutenant in the Sanitary Corps of the Army. Shortly thereafter, another shift and promotion made me a captain in the Chemical Service branch of the Army. I ended, in the summer of 1918, as a major in the Chemical Warfare Service in charge of the chemical work in a highly secret operation in Willoughby, Ohio.

I had been moved to Ohio from Washington because the group I headed had been charged with elucidating the structure of a new poison gas, which had been discovered rather by accident. It was called "lewisite" and was alleged to be most potent in its effectiveness on the skin as well as on the lungs—much like mustard gas. We were also charged with the construction of a plant to manufacture it. Before we could do more than operate a pilot plant, however, the war came to an end. Later, I learned that there had been many doubts as to whether lewisite was, in fact, effective. Whether the plant would actually have gone into production was open to question.

All of us involved in this secret undertaking were thankful when the armistice was announced. We were now through with this strange adventure in applied chemistry, which was tied to the highly un-attractive task of producing poisons to be used in combat. With a great deal of relief, we proceeded to demobilize and re-enter civilian life.

While I am writing on the subject of poison gas, I may as well answer a question that in 1968 seems to be in many people's minds, though in 1917 I heard it only rarely. The question pertains to the morality of the use of poison gas in warfare. Early in the war, the Germans had introduced the gas chlorine. Since everything German was being condemned, no one was inclined to justify its first use. By the time the United States was in the war, however, phosgene and mustard gas (actually a liquid) were being used by both sides.

To me, the development of new and more effective gases seemed no more immoral than the manufacture of explosives and guns. Tear gas for the use of police forces was a gift to the forces of law and order from the Chemical Warfare Service, so to speak. I did not see in 1917, and do not see in 1968, why tearing a man's guts out by a high-explosive shell is to be preferred to maiming him by attacking his lungs or skin. All war is immoral. Logically, the 100 percent pacifist has the only impregnable position. Once that is abandoned, as it is when a nation becomes a belligerent, one can talk sensibly only in terms of the violation of agreements about the way war is conducted, or the consequences of a certain tactic or weapon. Adherence to international rules of war or departing from them involves the same sort of moral question as obeying the laws designed to make our society function as a free society.

I would use the words "moral issue" with caution, however. When the issue was first discussed at the close of World War I, the argument against the use of gas was often as follows: Poison gas cannot be controlled with accuracy; it may damage a civilian population adjacent to a battlefield; insofar as that is true, it differs from the use of artillery and hence its use is immoral. Much the same chain of reasoning led all pro-Ally Americans to condemn unrestricted submarine warfare. To those of us who have lived in intimate contact with the development of aerial bombing in World War II, such an argument sounds old-fashioned. Civilian casualties became not only a necessary consequence of bombing, but one might almost say an objective of the fleets of bombers directed by the British, the Germans and the Russians, as well as by the Americans.

During the war months of 1917 and 1918, a group of organic chemists came to know each other intimately. The consequences of this association affected many of the activities of all of us in the postwar years. Roger Adams was clearly the leader of the group. During the months in Washington when he and I each headed research groups and both reported to Professor (then Colonel) Norris, a close friendship developed. It was to Adams that I would turn when, in 1940, Vannevar Bush asked me to organize the chemical work of the National Defense Research Committee. In 1918 we should have considered demented anyone who suggested that we would once again work together on chemical research for the armed forces. During the next fifteen years we were to consult frequently, but not in terms of war.

Adams had produced the brilliant idea of a cooperative venture involving a handful of young men. He proposed that we should publish annually a book detailing the best procedures for carrying out certain well-known chemical reactions. What was novel was that some member of the editorial board would be responsible for checking the instructions by having them carefully followed in his own laboratory. The scheme became a reality in the early 1920s in the form of the annual publication, *Organic Syntheses*. The series received a hearty reception and has been published ever since.

The chemistry department of the University of Illinois under Adams' leadership became one of the outstanding departments in the nation. His reputation as an investigator combined with his imaginative and warm approach to human problems made him in the decade after the First World War not only the first organic chemist of the land but an internationally famous scientist. After World War II he went on to win more laurels for his investigations; equally important for the nation was his success with his graduate students. He inspired and instructed as few other masters of research have ever done. Those who had completed their theses with him became his disciples and within a decade were to be found in leading positions in industry, research institutes and universities. Employers took his evaluations at face value because they had learned that while Adams was a sympathetic teacher, he was completely frank in his recommendations.

The older chemical and mechanical engineers who were involved in the Ohio adventure assumed that I would return to my former position as instructor at Harvard; they proceeded to urge me not to do so. Thinking of an academic career as it had been in the first decade of the century, they contrasted what they imagined to be the placid, sheltered life of a college professor of pure chemistry with an exciting life among aggressive men in an industrial organization. When you are involved in production, they said, you can see a product coming off the line; when you are a teacher, how do you know if you have accomplished anything? I have thought of this question many times in the last fifty years. The arguments of the summer of 1915 in the Midvale Steel Company were being repeated. I could understand them better now, but was still not convinced that I should enter industry. I shed my uniform with the intention of returning to university life as an organic chemist.

My decision to turn a deaf ear to any offer of a position in industry remained firm in the ensuing years. Yet my attitude toward activities outside of a laboratory was far different in 1918 from what it had been four years earlier when I was a senior in Harvard College. My summer at Midvale had given me a glimpse of the world of engineers and production men. My own disastrous attempt to enter the world of business had left a permanent mark. I had participated in organizing a manufacturing company. After the tragic catastrophe, the company had been liquidated and the stockholders paid off, thanks to the royalties on a patent based on my work. I had learned at first hand something about the hazards of free enterprise. As head of a team of engineers and chemists at Willoughby, I had directed the efforts of the key unit in a large undertaking. I came to know both the frustrations and the satisfactions of a leader and the excitement which goes with the making of decisions. All these experiences obtained outside the laboratory walls had altered my point of view. The ideal dedicated scientific investigator no longer stood alone on a high pedestal. I recognized that there were other fascinating ways of using one's energies. I cherished a carefully hidden ambition to try my wings someday in other fields than the scientific.

My wife has more than once reminded me of a conversation shortly after we had become engaged. Looking into the distant future, I said that I had three ambitions. The first was to become the leading organic chemist in the United States; after that I would like to be president of Harvard; and after that, a Cabinet member, perhaps Secretary of the Interior. What is interesting in this revelation of my secret thoughts in 1920 was the implied limitation on my strivings as an organic chemist. I did not aim at world-wide recognition such as that enjoyed by Professor Richards. I only hoped to be the leading American organic chemist; I did not contemplate staying with chemistry for a lifetime. Even my administrative targets were those not of a committed man but of a restless soul. I wished to lead three lives in order to sample a variety of excitements; such seemed to be the burden of what I told my future wife. As a matter of fact, I ended by settling for several careers, three of which were a reasonable fit to a young man's dreams.

When I returned to Washington and Cambridge for a visit before I was mustered out, I found that Roger Adams was returning to Illinois. My opposite number in chemical engineering, Bob Wilson, was returning to M.I.T. (though he shortly thereafter entered the industrial world). Others were weighing one offer against another. The Harvard authorities indicated that they were ready to make me an assistant professor on September 1, 1919, and I accepted just before another university made an equally attractive proposition. My seniors in Cambridge released me from any obligation flowing from my early acceptance of the assistant professorship. Indeed, Kohler hinted that I would do well to try my wings elsewhere. But I was stubborn. I had cherished for so long the ambition to carry the title of "Professor" at Harvard that I was quite unwilling to consider other opportunities.

Any higher grade than *assistant* professor was, of course, quite out of the question. Indeed, Professor Baxter, after my appointment had been settled, pointed out how meager was the public record on which the department had based its recommendations. One year of lecturing experience, a single paper of my own (concerned with a totally unimportant reaction), some papers with George Kelley, and my work for a Ph.D. with Kohler and Richards (still unpublished) were all there was. Baxter more than implied that I had been fortunate. The war had created an unreasonable demand for young organic chemists; I was the beneficiary for the time being of a new situation; I had better get busy and complete some investigations before my luck ran out. I agreed heartily and started in haste down what proved to be a blind alley. It was a year and more before I hit pay dirt as an investigator.

CHAPTER 6

Member of the Harvard Faculty

IN THE FALL OF 1920, I persuaded Grace Thayer Richards to agree to marry me. We had first met in her father's house in 1916 when, as one of the graduate students working with Professor Richards, I had been invited to Sunday dinner. During the next year when I was struggling with my first course of lectures in organic chemistry, I enjoyed the Richards' hospitality from time to time, and I met at their home a widening circle of friends. "Patty" Richards was preparing to follow in the footsteps of her grandfather, William T. Richards, the painter. She was studying at the Boston Museum of Fine Arts. On my return to Cambridge after the armistice, we renewed our friendship. In the summer of 1920, Norris F. Hall, an instructor in the chemistry department, and I visited Professor Richards and his family at Seal Harbor on the coast of Maine. Not long thereafter, I proposed and was accepted.

My wife has often said that the best of my arguments was a promise of a honeymoon in Europe. We were married in Cambridge in April 1921 and sailed for England in June. When I began these memoirs, my wife surprised me by uncovering a cache of my old letters, including several written to various members of my family in the course of our honeymoon. Since I have more faith in contemporary letters than in my own memory, I paraphrase from some of these letters and quote from others.

London was the home base from which we departed for energetic sightseeing and visits to the universities of Liverpool, Manchester and Oxford. Thanks largely to Professor Richards, we were cordially received wherever we went. I was introduced to a variety of chemists, visited their laboratories and met some delightful people who entertained us royally.

The visits to the chemistry departments of the universities were especially rewarding. I was trying to arouse interest in the publication of *Organic Syntheses* which, as I explained in the last chapter, was to be an annual publication. I was encouraged by the interest shown by several of the older professors in different universities with whom I talked. Our trip to Oxford was a delightful introduction to a scene with which I was to become familiar in later years. We did our best in two days to explore the ancient colleges and glorious gardens.

We returned to London, and immediately left for a brief junket to the continent, which is described in the following letter, dated July 3, written on our return to London. The letter was directed to my older sister and gives a report on an international meeting of chemists in Brussels on June 26 to June 30 (Conférence Internationale de l'Union de Chimie Pure et Appliquée). I had been invited to attend as one of the American representatives with the more or less explicit understanding that my name was on the list because of Professor Richards' fame and the likelihood that the publication of an international table of atomic weights would be on the agenda for discussion. The meeting had been organized by the victorious Allies. The Germans and Austrians had been excluded; all their scientists were considered to be tainted with war guilt and not fit to attend international meetings. The new nations which had been carved out of the old Austrian Empire had been given prominent positions; clearly the French were in command. The letter follows:

Yesterday morning we arrived in London after a most successful trip to Brussels. Here is a brief outline of it all—it would take a book to do justice to all the details! Saturday night (a week ago) we had a very pleasant night trip to Antwerp (via Harwich). Just as easy as going to N.Y. on the old Fall River line. Lots of sleep and no sickness! We visited Antwerp till about 5 P.M., taking in the delightful combination of Dutch (Flemish, really) and French atmosphere which makes the city interesting. It's the first really *foreign* city that either of us had ever seen—and we were both delighted by it. The view from the cathedral tower (a long ascent) was beautiful—a mass of red tiled roofs, quaint Flemish outlines, paved squares and in the distance the very places where a few years ago the Boche had done this and done that. The cathedral is also very fine with its famous Rubens paintings; there are a lot more of the same school in an old church,

St. Jacques, which we also saw. Personally, I'm not so terrifically enthusiastic about these paintings, but then. Well, I must get on with my story.

At Brussels we stayed at a very nice French pension, Mlle. Thevonet,
$1.60 a day per person, meals and room. The conference lasted till Friday.
The meetings were held in the Palais des Académies, a very delightful
spot. There were a good many social activities which Patty enjoyed a lot
as well as I. . . . Patty's excellent French and her social grace put us on the
wave at all the parties and we had a delightful time. We came in for a
good deal of "kidding" about our "voyage de noces" and about my "beau-
père." Both these points of attack and the fact that Patty was the only
Anglo-Saxon lady present at least served to keep things interesting. I wish
I could take time to tell you about the many amusing people and little
events.

The official side was also very interesting, though almost *everybody*
talked and understood *French* and with one or two exceptions *French only*.
You'd have been surprised; perhaps you don't realize that literally I never
spoke a French sentence in my life before a month ago. Patty's tutoring
on the boat helped enormously—till then I never could pronounce a word
and also thought the final -et and -ent were sounded! However, of course,
I was for the most part completely sunk, particularly during the sessions
of the conference and the various committees. However, a few kind souls
acted as interpreters, officially, occasionally, and often unofficially. In
personal conversation, I got on better—I could make myself understood
with a great deal of difficulty and understood enough to keep afloat. I improved during the week (Patty says a lot and thinks I did excellently!) (?),
and that's a lot in itself.

I managed to get my little personal business (promoting *Organic Syntheses*) slipped in at just the right moment and Patty wrote a "note" in
French about it which was read and will be printed in the report of the
conference. There were a lot of distinguished French, Dutch, Swiss and
Italian delegates present. I was very glad to see them. The Englishmen with
one exception (Sir W. Pope) and the Americans weren't anything scientific-
ally. There was one man at the conference that understood much less
French than I and spoke much less and that terribly—he was the *head* of
the U.S. delegation.

Without my dear wife I shouldn't have been anywhere at all—with her
(as always) it was very nice and fine. . . .

The next letter, also to my older sister, is once again from London
dated July 16, 1921, and describes our trip to Scotland after we had
returned from the continent to London.

Since last writing you we've been to Leeds—an awful spot where I saw
a chemist and we nearly didn't get a room in a hotel—to Ayr, Edinburgh,
Durham, York and return.

At Ayr we had a bit of a rest and made some interesting observations on people and scenery. The scenery which we saw via a motor was splendid. Wild mountainous moors, with heather and thistles—inhabited by many sheep but very few people. We also took another drive along the rugged shore of the Scottish coast and admired the view of an old feudal stronghold perched high on a rocky cliff.

Ayr is about forty miles south of Glasgow on the coast. It's full of historic interest as well as having a beautiful view of hills and islands across the Firth of Clyde. Burns was born just a few miles away and we saw his whitewashed cottage. Bruce rampaged around this part of the country, and the famous parliament-murder held by the English in a barn (do you remember it, each guest was hanged as he entered) took place right in Ayr.

Edinburgh was all that people say. . . . Unfortunately, we spent only a day and a half there—this rushing through things is certainly iniquitous and typically American! The wonderful old houses, streets, arched alleys, etc., as well as the Castle high on a rock, and the vast rocky hills close at hand make the city absolutely unique, I'm sure. Of course, it's all gray stone and rather cold and somber but when you once get used to its chilly lack of color, it is very beautiful as well as intensely interesting. The romantic figures of Scotch history, of course, are closely associated with every turn and that adds to its romantic grip on one.

We pass from one beautiful spot to another. Durham, I think, is the best yet in some ways. A wonderful Norman cathedral dominating the surrounding green country and the quaintest old medieval town possible. A chemist I met in Newcastle (thirty-one miles away) lived in Durham and showed us some of its beauty. It's a wonderful old town and very unspoiled by factories or tourists—in this latter respect quite different from Chester, for example.

We spent an afternoon, the night and a morning in Durham. Then we "hopped" a train and in good old U.S. form, "dropped off" at York for three hours, saw the cathedral, walked on the walls, etc.—jumped on another train and arrived here at 10:15 P.M. quite ready for bed. . . .

Tonight we leave for Paris by the night boat. Bag and baggage and—I forgot to add—an old brass lantern wished on us by Patty's "Uncle." All we needed to make our traveling outfit complete was a parrot in a cage; we have now got the full equivalent.

A letter to my father from Florence, dated August 20, completes the description of a young man's enthusiasm for Europe in general and Italy in particular. The reader must remember that I had as a guide a young lady who had spent some time as a serious art student and was therefore an eager and excited visitor to churches and museums.

Since leaving Paris and its intense heat, we've been having a country vacation first in Switzerland and then in the Italian lakes. Switzerland seemed to me to be the most wonderful and beautiful scenery imaginable until I saw Lake Como. But the Italian lakes aren't imaginable, that's just it. One can't imagine them, much less describe them. As a so-called scientist, I should very much like to know what particular arrangements of atoms, molecules and electrons are necessary to produce such an effect on the human soul! Such colors of water, hills and (I was about to say air!). It's a problem of colloidal chemistry (see Black and Conant)* and of the law of chance or else the final work of a perfect God—or perhaps it's both; at any rate, the effect is intoxicatingly divine.

We left Switzerland from the little town of Brig and passed through the very heart of the wall of mountains by the longest tunnel in the world— the Simplon; then we were in Italy and, behold, all the scenery, color and everything was different! After no less than five changes, including two boat trips and four passport inspections, we arrived at Lugano, which happens to be in Switzerland though geographically in Italy and on Lake Lugano. Here we stayed a day and basked in the Italian sun. It was a strange contrast to the inch or more of snow we had at Riffelalp only three days before!

The next day we went on to Italy once again (more passport inspection) and to Paradise—Villa Serbelloni, Bellagio, on Lake Como—a wonderful old villa, high on a bit of land running into the lake. The view from our room and from the terrace where we breakfasted was superb. Back of the villa was a wonderful old garden with palms, cactus, etc., and the ruin of an old castle. We stayed a day longer than we planned, making practically three days at Lake Como in all.

Now we are in Florence and are already mad about it. Fortunately, it's fine weather and cool (for Italy); in a Palm Beach suit, I am comfortable. We've seen the Cathedral, Baptistry and a bit of the streets this morning; this afternoon we drive to Fiesole for tea.

After a week here and a few days in Siena or Assisi we return to France for a week before sailing.

On our return to Cambridge in the fall of 1921, we moved into a small house, one of a group of a dozen which had been built at the time of World War I in a portion of Cambridge known as Shady Hill. Our neighbors were for the most part academic people. A ten-minute walk brought one to the Harvard Yard. We considered ourselves fortunate to have been able to rent such a convenient house in such attractive surroundings. It was a bit small, but served us well for a number of years as our family expanded. We were living there when our first son, James Richards Conant, was born in May 1923 and our second, Theodore Richards Conant, in July 1926. Fortunately, our

* A few years earlier, Mr. Black had asked me to collaborate in writing a high school chemistry text.

income expanded with the size of the family, and this fact enabled us to look for a larger house. We were again fortunate. Two new chemical laboratories had just been opened. One, the Mallinckrodt Laboratory, was on Oxford Street, the other, for organic chemistry, was just behind it. A house next to the Mallinckrodt Laboratory belonging to Harvard became vacant; we hastened to rent it. Since proximity to his laboratory is an important ingredient in the satisfaction of a chemist, I should have been completely happy with the new house, and I was. Looking back, these seem to have been the best years of my life. Only when my job changed did we desert Oxford Street for Quincy Street and the President's House.

Before that was to occur, I was to have many adventures in research. I shall make no attempt even to summarize them. Far too much technical language would have to be thrust upon the reader if I were to explain their nature. In very general terms, one might say that I was at first concerned with the use of physicochemical methods to study the transformation of compounds of carbon (organic compounds). Later, when I was able to employ research assistants, the center of my interest became the structure of the green coloring matter of plants, chlorophyll. The fact that I had presented for my Ph.D. thesis two contributions, one in organic chemistry under the direction of Professor Kohler and one in electrochemistry with Professor Richards, placed me in a rather special situation.

I was familiar with the electrochemical apparatus which had been developed fairly recently. Indeed, the summer I spent in the research laboratory of the Midvale Steel Company had been devoted to the use of such equipment in analytical chemistry along lines determined by Dr. Kelley. Yet, though equipped by my training to carry on experimentation in one branch of electrochemistry, it was as an organic chemist that I hoped to make my reputation. I was interested in the field to which Professor Kohler was directing his students, namely, the discovery of the ways in which one organic compound reacted with another. Before long, I thought of a series of possible experiments which combined organic chemistry with electrochemistry.

I decided that it should be possible to construct an electric battery in which one pole was a platinum electrode immersed in a solution of a mixture of two closely related compounds differing from each other only by a pair of hydrogen atoms. If my reasoning was correct, the voltage of such a battery would depend on the ratio of the amounts of the two substances present in the solution that surrounded one of the two poles. I constructed the type of battery I had envisioned and to my delight found that it worked just as I had anticipated. I thought I had made a great discovery. But, alas, a few days later when I was explaining my "original" discovery to an older colleague, I learned that a famous German chemist, Fritz Haber, had performed the same experiment before World War I! Those who were specialists in electrochemistry were well aware of Haber's work, I was assured, though no organic chemist had chosen to continue this line of investigation.

In spite of my disappointment, I continued my experiments (which were well along when the past caught up with me). The measurement of the potentials of electric cells containing certain pairs of organic compounds soon became one of the topics I assigned to students who wished to do research under my direction. Other chemists had been thinking along similar lines, and before long the scientific journals were full of papers on "oxidation and reduction potentials." The component of the solution surrounding one electrode of the battery which had more hydrogen atoms in its molecule was said to be the "reduced" compound, the other the "oxidized" form. The oxidized form could be transformed into the reduced form by adding one of several substances known as reducing agents. Thus the electrical battery could be so arranged that the potential varied with the amount of reducing agent added to the solution of the oxidized compound under study. Such was the arrangement I had set up before I heard of Haber's work. The same arrangement I next used in the study of the red coloring matter of the blood—hemoglobin.

My excursion into the field of biochemistry was the result of my friendship with two contemporaries who were working in the laboratories of the Harvard Medical School in Boston. They were both concerned with proteins; from time to time we discussed various aspects of their work. One was investigating a set of variables involved in the exact formulation of the conditions under which hemoglobin combines with oxygen. As I uncovered a way of following the oxidation of several types of organic compounds, we speculated on whether or not the combination of hemoglobin with oxygen could be studied in the same way. I suggested certain experiments that I could carry out in my laboratory if I had a solution of hemoglobin. My friend provided the necessary basic material—fresh horse blood—which I stored in the family ice chest, much to my wife's horror. I was instructed in the art of purifying this protein solution and soon had in hand a relatively pure solution of hemoglobin to place in my electrical apparatus.

The experiments, which I performed with my own hands, soon provided some striking information. The combination of hemoglobin with oxygen was *not* an oxidation. If hemoglobin was oxidized, another compound, methemoglobin, was formed. Methemoglobin could not combine with oxygen. It could be reduced back to hemoglobin, however, and when this was done by adding a reducing agent to the solution, the capacity to absorb oxygen was restored. A solution of hemoglobin and methemoglobin could serve as one part of an electric battery. The amount of reducing agent required to transform methemoglobin to hemoglobin was the equivalent of only a single hydrogen atom, not a pair of hydrogen atoms as in the other compounds I had been studying. I knew that the hemoglobin molecule contained a single iron atom, and I concluded that what was involved was the state of oxidation of this atom. If it was in the oxidized state in methemoglobin, only one hydrogen equivalent would be needed to reduce it to hemoglobin. These observations were new and cleared up a confusion about the relation of three molecules: hemoglobin, oxygenated hemoglobin (both containing iron in the reduced or ferrous state) and methemoglobin (iron in the oxidized or ferric state).

I had strayed into a foreign field, namely, that of biochemistry. I submitted the paper recording my experiments to the *Journal of Biological Chemistry* instead of the *Journal of the American Chemical Society*, which usually printed the communications from my laboratory. Thus the results were quickly noted by biochemists. Shortly after the publication of the paper, I met at a scientific meeting one of my contemporaries who was *the* authority on the use of electrical methods for studying the degree of acidity of solutions of significance to biologists (in technical terms, the pH values). He greeted me heartily with the exclamation: "When I read your paper in the *Journal of Biological Chemistry*, I felt like shaking your hand to congratulate you and at the same time wringing your neck with my other hand; I was just on the point of making the same experiments myself!" Remembering my chagrin when I had learned that my "original" experiment on oxidation and reduction had been anticipated a decade or more earlier by Professor Haber, I could understand his feelings.

One more set of experiments I must mention because they are not unrelated to the chemistry of synthetic rubber, which was to involve me in a considerable amount of technical activity during World War II. Making synthetic rubber is basically a process of forming giant molecules from small ones. The transformation is known as "polymerization." To explain the term to a lay reader, I can do no better than to quote from my own textbook on organic chemistry (*The Chemistry of Organic Compounds*, Conant and Blatt; the fifth edition, of 1959, was largely the product of my collaborator, Professor A. Harold Blatt of Queens College, New York. The book is now superseded and out of print). The cross heading "Polymerization" introduces a paragraph in which the behavior of the gas ethylene under high pressure is described. (Ethylene is one of the simplest hydrocarbons; its molecule contains only two carbon atoms and four hydrogen atoms.) If a little oxygen of the air is present, many ethylene molecules combine with each other; the process is called polymerization. The next paragraph in *The Chemistry of Organic Compounds* I quote in full for reasons which will be evident in a moment.

The product, polyethylene, is of great commercial importance. It is a tough solid, melting around 118°, which has valuable insulating properties and which is little affected by most chemical reagents and solvents. It is used as a protective coating and for making containers. These and a host of other uses have made polyethylene an important product whose production is expected to amount to over 500,000 tons per year in the United States by 1960.

When Professor Blatt wrote this paragraph to illustrate by the simplest example the meaning of the word "polymerization," he introduced a word, "polyethylene," which gives me a pang every time I hear it or read it. I have no doubt we joked over this fact when I first read the paragraph. For the story of how I missed discovering polyethylene is one that I have told to all who would listen since the end of World War II. It starts with the fact that in 1928 or 1929, Professor Percy W. Bridgman of Harvard, a Nobel prize winner in physics, and I had collaborated in a study of the effect of pressures of 2,000 to 12,000 atmospheres on organic compounds. Some years earlier, Professor Bridgman had invented a way in which small samples of materials could be subjected to such enormous pressures.

We found that the polymerization of the hydrocarbon molecule "isoprene," the basic unit in natural rubber, was essentially complete in fifty hours at room temperature when the pressure was 12,000 atmospheres. The product was a tough, transparent, rubber-like solid. (The older method of polymerizing the same hydrocarbon was to heat the compound in the presence of metallic sodium for several weeks.) Unfortunately, we (or rather I, since I was the chemist involved) failed to try the effect of high pressure on ethylene. Some years later, the chemists in a British company produced the first sample of polyethylene.

If I had used ethylene in one of the experiments, it would certainly have polymerized. It is pleasant to imagine that I would have recognized the valuable characteristics of the product; since at that time ethylene, unlike isoprene, had never been polymerized, the Du Pont Company, to whom we assigned the patent, would have had the monopoly on the production of a new commercial product now used on every hand. Added to Bridgman's and my satisfaction in the role of discoverers, the financial rewards might have been considerable. These increase in size almost every time I tell the story.

CHAPTER 7

Widening the Academic Horizon

A FEW YEARS AFTER my wife and I had enjoyed our first sight of Europe, we received an unexpected opportunity to gain a wider view of the American scene. Again, Roger Adams comes into the story. He had been scheduled to give the 1924 summer course in organic chemistry at the University of California in Berkeley. A sudden illness had forced him to cancel his plans. On very short notice, Gilbert N. Lewis, the head of the chemistry department, asked me to substitute for Adams. I accepted with alacrity; my wife courageously started making plans for a transcontinental journey with a one-year-old baby. We had neither of us been west of the Mississippi River. Looking out of the train window for several successive days seemed an adventure in itself.

Caring for a baby in transit in those days made traveling no care-free vacation. Commercial preparations of supplies to meet a baby's needs had not yet appeared. I can still see my wife mixing dried milk and cooking carrots over an alcohol stove in a swaying bedroom compartment of a Union Pacific express. A violent head cold I picked up at the start made me worse than useless as an assistant. When we finally disembarked at the Berkeley station, I felt as though we had been in a covered wagon, fighting off Indians day and night. However, the view of the setting sun over the Golden Gate from the cottage we rented in Strawberry Canyon, overlooking the Berkeley campus, rapidly banished thoughts of the traveling troubles we had endured.

The weeks we spent in Berkeley were our first introduction not only to the Pacific Coast but to a far wider academic world than the one we had grown up in. The summer session of the university was renowned for its international character. Famous professors of many subjects from the United States and Europe participated in the instruction for the entire six weeks. (With Chicago three days distant by the fastest trains, a visiting lecturer came to pay a real visit—not as in the 1960s to stay twenty-four hours and then fly off.)

At the outset, Professor Lewis and his associates introduced me to many of those who regularly lunched at the Faculty Club. Before long, I was on my own. With considerable trepidation, I would join a group at one of the round tables and listen to the erudite conversation which went gaily back and forth. On one occasion, I found myself sitting beside one of the older men, whom I knew by reputation as a distinguished British scholar. I was too shy to attempt a conversation. My neighbor, sensing the difficulty, proceeded to break the ice by the usual inquiry as to my subject and my university. The information that I was an assistant professor of chemistry at Harvard led to the obvious question as to my training. After I had stated that I had obtained both my Ph.D. and A.B. at Harvard and that I had been born and gone to school in Boston, we both joined in laughing at my parochialism, which contrasted so strikingly with the cosmopolitan atmosphere around us.

The chemistry department at Berkeley was a creation of Gilbert Lewis. When he had come to the university just before World War I, he had been given a free hand. He had called a few young men to professorships and, within a decade, had selected others from among the graduate students. His own ideas about the development of physical chemistry naturally were very much in the air. Yet he was far from being an academic tyrant. If a young man wished to hear the latest advances in physical chemistry discussed, he could find no more exhilarating spot than the University of California. If he wanted to see an example of one way of solving the old problem of the relation of teaching to research, he could do no better than examine the arrangements Professor Lewis had made. Every member of the department was required to participate in the instruction of the freshman course. One professor gave the lectures, but the laboratory instruction, instead of being left in the hands of graduate students, was conducted by other professors or instructors. No one was exempt. Lewis was eloquent about the advantages of his scheme and the disadvantages of the usual procedure of leaving the teaching to graduate students. I had no doubt then (or later) that Lewis was right.

I did not return to Cambridge, however, with any enthusiasm for the importation of the California scheme. It struck at the foundations of the Ph.D. program. Little was said about it, but everybody knew that the only way a professor could get on with his research was with the help of graduate students to whom he assigned problems. Almost no graduate student of chemistry could afford to study unless a large part of his expenses were paid. Hence, ever since the 1890s there had developed in the larger universities the tradition of employing graduate students as half-time teachers in elementary courses. Abolishing this practice would unquestionably improve the freshman course, but at the price of a drastic diminution in the number who were working for a Ph.D. degree. I could not imagine any group of senior professors being party to a revolution so inimical to their own interests.

Lewis was an iconoclast in other fields besides chemistry. He had little use for the state universities. He employed all his academic political skills (which were formidable) in preventing the University of California from conforming to what was becoming the traditional picture. The Morrill Act of 1862, establishing the land-grant colleges, followed by the Hatch Act of 1887, providing funds for agricultural research, had put the federal government squarely behind the growth of agricultural experiment stations as part of state universities. What might be called an indigenous American research tradition had thus been created. Taxpayers' money had started to flow to universities to support research, but only applied research.

Lewis had no sympathy with this trend. He said that it was unnecessary and unwise to attempt to persuade a state legislature to support research because of its practical results. There was no guarantee that the ills of the farms would be cured by the work of the professors; indeed, from time to time they might be made worse. The propaganda emphasizing applied research was likely to boomerang. At all events, the University of California would have none of it. Lewis and his friends on the faculty were going to demonstrate that the way to obtain generous public support was to appeal to the pride of the citizens. They would make the university so famous the world over that the voters of California would be glad to see public funds expended on pure research.

If the reader is familiar with the history of research on the Berkeley campus, he will recognize that what Lewis told me in 1924 was an amazing prophecy of the decades that lay ahead. Sometime after World War II, when I had the privilege of being the Charter Day speaker at Berkeley, I noted that the president did not fail to mention the number of Nobel prize winners on the faculty. What had been planned and pushed by a group of faculty people thirty years earlier had become a reality.

Our trip abroad in 1921, especially the political maneuvering and the exclusion of the Germans at Brussels, had given my wife and me a preview of the strains which would soon develop in the world created by the Versailles Treaty. That summer had enabled us to meet chemists from England and some European nations. Our outlook was broadened. Yet I had not come any closer to finding answers to my curiosity about German universities. What was clearly needed was several months in the country which almost all agreed had brought European civilization to the brink of ruin. Reading the daily papers was enough to indicate that there were obstacles to such an expedition. An unsettled political situation in Germany, amounting almost to civil war, had been followed by a devastating inflation. One of our friends who had close German relatives advised strongly against any effort to visit German laboratories in 1922 or 1923. Finally in 1924, it looked as if some degree of stability would soon be reached. Therefore, my wife, who shared my curiosity about postwar Germany, agreed in the late fall that by midyear of 1925 we might make the trip we had so long planned.

I applied for a half-year's leave of absence without salary (I had not served long enough to rate a sabbatical leave). It was granted; the department made the necessary arrangements, though my father-in-law was far from enthusiastic about our plans. His condemnation of the Germans in 1924 was as total as it had been in August 1914. He had made no move to re-establish communications with his former scientific friends in what he now considered to be a hopelessly barbaric land. Obviously he felt somewhat embarrassed by the fact that his son-in-law, a chemist, was now planning to make the round of German universities. He did not applaud, but he did not protest; he put the best face he could on the young people's folly. He even wrote letters to a few professors whom he had known well in former times.

We sailed from New York in February 1925. Our destination was Munich, where we hoped to find suitable quarters and someone to help look after our son, now a year and a half old. Before too long, we were settled in a pension recommended to us by a Harvard family. It had sheltered a succession of American academic people before the war and was still in operation. Through the good offices of the owners, my wife located a young lady who was glad to assist with the baby for a price our cramped budget could afford. We were the only Americans in the pension. Most of the guests seemed to be impoverished survivors who had once seen far better days. They had nothing good to say about the government of the Weimar Republic. As a matter of fact, in this regard they were like almost all the chemists I met in the ensuing eight months. (I heard only one academic man during the entire visit speak well of the Socialist Party then in control of the government.) My recollections of postwar Germany in 1925 were to prove of great value when I went back in February 1953 as High Commissioner.

We had settled in Munich for a number of reasons. I did not intend to enroll in the university, though I did ask permission of Professor Richard Willstaetter to attend his lectures on organic chemistry until they came to an end in March. I wished to avail myself of the good offices of Professor Otto Hoenigschmid, who had not only worked with Professor Richards but had made a career in Germany by importing his methods. He was cordial and extremely helpful. Indeed, without his sponsorship I should never have been received as I was in many laboratories and at three meetings of chemists. During the course of the spring, I visited Hamburg, Frankfurt, Goettingen, Marburg, Tuebingen, Erlangen, Wuerzburg, Berlin, Dresden and Leipzig. My wife stayed in Munich with the baby. Her rapid mastery of the German language, which contrasted with my continuing difficulties, enabled her to tap the store of prejudices of many of the pension guests. Thanks to her and an occasional digression into political discussions with chemists, we obtained a rather intimate view into the way the Weimar Republic looked to those who were still at heart monarchists. Their bitterness toward the victorious Allies left a deep impression.

One conversation stands out in my mind. A small group of senior academic and industrial chemists were examining the immediate past of their country in utter frankness, unmindful of my presence. Indeed, they may have thought my knowledge of German was too slight for me to understand what was being said. They were marveling at the improvement which had taken place in the past two years. The mark had been stabilized; the French had withdrawn from the Ruhr; General Hindenburg had been elected President. "That's all very well," one of the industrialists remarked, "but let us not forget the debt we owe to those men who went out, revolver in hand, and assassinated those who were leading the Fatherland astray!" To which all present enthusiastically agreed. Such sentiments made my hair stand on end. I had never heard assassination justified before. I wondered to myself how a republic could be built on such a foundation of violence. In 1933 the Nazis proved that it could not.

My travels were in search of an answer to a question: What had made German science, particularly organic chemistry, so fruitful? I suspected it was the German university system. My suspicions were confirmed by everything I heard. The striking differences between American and German universities were brought out by my talks with the younger men. (From the elder distinguished professors, I learned little except their anguish at their ostracism by chemists in other lands.) In the first place, there was only one full professor in each subject. In the second place, quite contrary to American practice, a young man was never promoted within the university where he was teaching. Third, there was an unofficial, yet permanent, hierarchy of institutions, with Berlin, Munich and Goettingen at the top and Erlangen at the bottom. This seemed at first extremely strange. Yet I slowly realized that only the existence of such a hierarchy made possible the operation of a system in which being called to another university was the equivalent of the American practice of promotion to higher rank within a university. The absence of anything like an undergraduate college I noted, of course, but I had little interest at that time in any educational patterns except those directly relevant to the training of research chemists. An exploration of the wider problems of German universities was to come forty years later.

When I slowly fitted together the information I had been assembling, a picture developed as follows: The German road to a full professorship and director of an institute was in its first stages not unlike the first steps in an academic career in the United States. The organic chemist, for example, after listening to lectures and performing laboratory experiments, enrolled as a research student under the direction of the professor of organic chemistry in any one of the German universities. The relation between the professor and his students was more formal than in the United States, but that was the only difference. The research problem was chosen by the professor, but the myth was maintained that the doctor's thesis was an "original" piece of work. Unlike the American practice, a would-be professor was not considered ready to join a faculty after receiving a Ph.D. A period of trial still lay ahead; one must complete a truly original study and present a special thesis (a *Habilitationsschrift*) to the faculty of some university. If the thesis was accepted, one obtained a "right to teach" in any university. Then, and only then, was a man eligible for appointment as a *Privatdozent* (the equivalent of an instructor) in a university. Some chemists entered industry at this point; those who did not proceeded with the research they had started when preparing their *Habilitationsschrift*. One moved from being a *Privatdozent* at a famous university to a position as an associate professor or even full professor at a less famous institution and waited there for a call to a better university. With high ability and luck, a man might receive such a call in his forties, but usually much later.

The German system might be characterized as highly competitive. The rate of progress through the various steps depended on the judgment of senior professors. These judgments conformed to high professional standards. Personal considerations were, as far as possible, excluded. The preparation of a *Habilitationsschrift* was of crucial importance. Ambitious individuals endeavored to find positions as assistants in the laboratory of one of the three or four leaders of the field. While working independently, the young man was usually expected to report before informal gatherings. The famous professor who was director of the laboratory examined carefully the investigations which were incorporated in the *Habilitationsschrift* and presided over the oral examination that completed the process of obtaining the right to teach in a university. While all who surmounted the final hurdle stood on the same basis theoretically, in practice the judgment of the director of the laboratory largely determined a person's future. I saw the system operate in Munich. Professor Willstaetter's opinion of each of two candidates was made evident by his comments at the public examination; both passed, but one was highly praised, the other not; one shortly received an appointment that opened the door to a brilliant academic career, the other entered industry.

What might be called the "screening process" continued until an individual reached a top position or was so old that he was obviously permanently stuck as a *Privatdozent* or as a professor in a second-rate university. The papers published by a recently appointed *Privatdozent* were scanned by each senior professor in all or almost all the universities. People were on the lookout for future Nobel prize winners. Meetings of chemists where scientific papers were presented provided an opportunity for the older generation to appraise the qualities of members of the younger group.

One such gathering was the annual meeting of an informal association of university teachers of chemistry in southwest Germany. I was fortunate enough to attend the 1925 session as a special guest of Professor Hoenigschmid. He explained that while I would meet all the leading professors of chemistry in the universities in the southwestern part of the country, I would not hear any of them speak. By tradition, the closed meeting was a place where only the most promising of the young men were invited to speak. The older people sat back, listened and made note of their qualities. He said frankly it was a sort of horse fair in which the full professors looked over the junior men. Both the originality of the research presented and the mode of presentation were under review. Clearly the potentialities of a young man as an investigator and as a lecturer were scrutinized. A recognition of this fact must have been an incentive for many a *Privatdozent* to work hard in improving his mastery of the art of lecturing.

I made a mental note that in the United States no meeting of chemists served the purpose Professor Hoenigschmid had so openly stated. No one would think of proclaiming as an objective the setting up, even informally and quietly, of a mechanism to differentiate between one newcomer to the faculty ranks and another. Our American meetings were social as well as professional. We listened patiently to papers which ranged from brilliant to mediocre or worse. An adverse comment might be passed privately and politely to the speaker when the session was over, but no one would be rude enough to question the results publicly. In a corresponding German meeting, a devastating question from the floor might be met by a vigorous show of approval by the audience. The intensely competitive spirit did not make for a relaxed atmosphere.

The system over the decades had certainly been most effective. The rivalry among universities as well as among individuals had resulted in a ruthless intolerance of mediocrity and showmanship. Yet the German system, to an American, seemed heartless. Not even within a single university was there any room for give-and-take among individuals of equal rank. There were no departments in the American sense of the word. There was one professor of organic chemistry, one professor of analytical chemistry, one of physical chemistry. Each had arrived at his position of eminence by a decision of the government of the state, based on the recommendation of the faculty of natural science. Each had bargained with the cultural department of the state government for the laboratory facilities and the number of assistants. A ruthless demand for excellence was the justification of what foreigners regarded as an inhuman academic world.

My trip to Germany was my first introduction to what became almost a lifelong study of the German university system. I slowly realized the origin of the tradition of devotion to the advancement of pure science, which my two teachers, Professors Richards and Kohler, had so clearly personified. One could trace it to the history of the modern university tradition. The founder was Karl Wilhelm von Humboldt. He created the model for all the institutions of advanced instruction in German-speaking lands. He and his friends regarded themselves as reformers who were freeing the advancement of learning from the encumbrance of professional training. "Solitude and freedom," they declared, were the principles that characterized the realm of pure scholarship. The law faculty in the new model university, for example, was to be concerned not with training lawyers but with the scholarly development of legal principles.

When a generation later a place had to be found for natural science, every effort was made to avoid the contamination of the study of the laws of chemistry by concern with their application. At first this was easy. One could distinguish clearly between the empirical rules of an industrial chemical art such as soapmaking and the new concepts which were portions of the growing theoretical structure of chemistry. By the end of the century, however, there came to be a considerable degree of mythology in the Germans' stubborn adherence to the belief that university professors must be engaged only in pure research. As the twentieth century advanced, a number of professors in the universities became involved in one way or another with advances in applied chemistry. In the 1870s, however, when President Daniel Gilman of Johns Hopkins imported the German university tradition into the United States, the cleavage between pure and applied research was still clear-cut; the Humboldt dogma was unchallenged. Therefore, in those American colleges which were becoming universities—including, of course, President Eliot's Harvard—it was generally assumed that the professors of chemistry had the duty to advance their science and ought to turn their backs on its application.

Leaving aside the stimulation I received from conversations with fellow chemists in Germany, the most important immediate consequence of the trip was my discovery of the role of research assistants. Until I visited the laboratories in the leading German universities, I had thought that the massive contributions flowing from these institutions were the products of students working under the direction of the full professor. I found out that such was not the case. In addition to directing candidates for the Ph.D. degree, *the* professor of organic chemistry might have as his assistants men who had already obtained a doctor's degree. These assistants might stay with the professor several years. Because of their experience, they could handle problems too difficult for students. In Munich, for example, the elaborate and tricky investigation of natural products which had brought international fame to Professor Willstaetter had been carried on entirely by research assistants, while the direction of Ph.D. candidates had been turned over to an associate professor. The more I learned about the arrangement, the more I realized that it was to a large extent responsible for the impressive output of research in organic chemistry in the pre–World War I period and the equally impressive flood of papers at the time of my visit. Why could not an American professor receive similar support? I looked for an opportunity to test the validity of the question in the context of an actual situation.

My wait was short. In 1927 Professor A. A. Noyes of the California Institute of Technology made me a most attractive offer to join the Institute. What had been the Throop Institute in Pasadena was in process of being transformed into a small, highly selective organization with emphasis on research of top quality. Noyes himself had moved from M.I.T. a few years earlier. He had been followed by the most eminent of American physicists, Professor Robert A. Millikan. Together they were guiding the transformation.

My own reason for leaving Harvard would be to increase my opportunities for research. Since I was still the junior member of the department in the field of organic chemistry, few of the better graduate students elected to prepare their doctor's thesis under my direction. In time, the situation might change, for Kohler was already quietly suggesting to more than one uncommitted student that he work with me. If I moved to Pasadena, however, I would be *the* professor of organic chemistry and all the Ph.D. candidates in that field would automatically turn to me. The idea of following that German example with regard to research assistants stimulated my interest still further.

Noyes had invited Mrs. Conant and me to spend two months in Pasadena so that we could see for ourselves the attractions of Southern California. He provided not only all the expenses of the trip but also the services of a nurse in Cambridge for our two small children. Without such provision, my wife refused to take another trip across the continent (still by train, please remember), and without her I refused to go at all. The weeks we spent in Pasadena in 1927 offered a second opportunity for us to come to know something of California. We visited Berkeley again, of course. I remember discussing Professor Noyes' offer with Professor Lewis; one point he made I added to the list of items to be discussed in Pasadena. The chief drawback of living in California, Lewis said, was the distance from the East Coast and Europe. To overcome this distance required money. Therefore an annual traveling allowance for myself and my family would be in order if I were to move to the California Institute of Technology. When I broached the subject to Noyes, he at once agreed. Indeed, such an allowance was to be only a small part of the annual budget at the research laboratory of organic chemistry which I was to head.

Noyes asked me what laboratory and other facilities I thought would be suitable for the organic chemist in the California Institute of Technology. Without committing myself to accept the proffered position, I suggested a research budget which would enable the professor to hire two or three men or women who had already received the doctor's degree. He did not like the idea at all. Quite apart from the size of the budget, he thought my proposal to carry on research with the aid of research assistants was absurd to the point of madness.

Roger Adams, with whom I discussed the offer, rejected completely my idea of importing a German practice. He had had a post-Ph.D. year in Berlin before the war. He could speak with authority about the situation in that city's university. He granted my diagnosis of the reasons why some of the German professors had been so productive, but was certain no American professor could successfully imitate the practice. Millikan was even more explicit. He spoke in terms of the best way of expending money. He had been publishing papers of great significance. The experimentation had all been done by graduate students as part of the fulfilment of the requirements for the Ph.D. They had been supported by teaching fellowships. What Millikan said, in effect, was that any given sum of money invested in teaching fellowships would yield at least twice as many helping hands as would the same amount used for hiring Ph.D.s as research assistants.

I remained unconvinced. If one planned to tackle the kind of problems in organic chemistry on which the leading German chemists were working, one needed more mature help than any student, however bright, could give.

On our return to Cambridge, we had about made up our minds to leave Harvard. But the president of Harvard was yet to be heard from. In an interview, he said, in effect, that I would be foolish to throw in my lot with what amounted to an unknown institution whose financial base was by no means secure. (My father-in-law had expressed the same opinion.) "If you go to California," said Mr. Lowell, "they will end by making you president." To which I was brash enough to reply that he could hardly himself regard such a fate as a misfortune. At which he gave me a little lecture about why he had taken on the task of being president of Harvard. Accepting the presidency of a college, he said, was like marrying—one should not take the step unless one were in love! His ancestors had done a great deal for Harvard College. He had felt certain changes were badly needed, and he had agreed to undertake to make them because he was in love with the institution. These sentiments at the time seemed to me completely irrelevant to the subject we were discussing, namely, my accepting the generous offer of the California Institute of Technology.

President Lowell and I were both anxious to avoid anything that looked like bargaining—we talked entirely in general terms. A few days later, Dean Clifford Moore was more specific. He offered an annual research budget for five years at a certain figure. I declined with regret, saying that the opportunities in California were so much superior that I should have to accept the invitation to go west. At which, without a moment's delay, Moore said, "But I understand you would stay at Harvard if the figure was $——" (adding several thousand dollars more). "Yes," I replied. "Then it is a bargain," said Moore, "and you are staying here." I agreed. Then and only then did he state that I would be made a full professor and my salary increased by a thousand dollars.

I have no memory of how and when I broke the news to Noyes. He was in the East at the time, and we must have met and talked. He and his colleagues did not seem to hold the long flirtation against me. Indeed, a few years later when the depression hit, they may have rejoiced that at least one liability they had been ready to assume in the boom years of the late 1920s was not now on their books.

When the Harvard Corporation matched the Pasadena offer in terms of the size of the research budget, I proceeded to use it by hiring some of Roger Adams' recent doctors as research assistants to work on the structure of chlorophyll. They were excellent men, well trained, and they performed as I expected.

Professor Richards in the 1890s had built his international reputation largely on experiments performed with his own hands. Similarly, Kohler's own personal research at Bryn Mawr had resulted in those papers which justified his call to Harvard. He continued to work in the laboratory himself until his death. On the other hand, by the time Richards had his own laboratory building, he had moved from experimenting with his own hands to guiding the labors of graduate students. I am inclined to think I was the first American organic chemist to take the next step and transfer the most significant inquiries to research assistants. Today this has become standard practice in many American universities.

When I negotiated with Harvard about research facilities in 1927,

I had in mind the advancement of knowledge, not its application. Steeped in the German tradition, I thought of a university laboratory as a place for pure research. I was oblivious to the significance of another research tradition—the American—which had been slowly growing in the land-grant colleges. It was this second research tradition which Lewis was really attacking when he spoke disparagingly of a state university's concern with agricultural problems. Yet by World War II the second tradition had gained a position of equality. As I have already indicated, even as early as the end of World War I some professors of chemistry were showing an interest in industrial problems. In the period between the two world wars, professors in engineering schools were changing their aloof attitude toward the academic departments of physics and chemistry and vice versa. In the agricultural faculties of the large and prosperous Midwest institutions before the depression, imaginative men trained as chemists and biologists had made highly significant discoveries. The line between pure and applied science was becoming more and more difficult to define.

Then, too, the medical schools the nation over had been transforming themselves between the wars. Research had become the key word. In three cases which came to my attention while I was still a chemist, leading medical schools looked for their professors of biochemistry not among those who had received an M.D. degree, but among those who had had no experience with medicine or biology but were promising young physical or organic chemists. What might be called the fundamental disciplines—physics, chemistry, biology— were being drawn closer and closer to such applied fields as agriculture, electrical engineering, chemical engineering and medicine.

If the depression had not hit the universities in full force in the early 1930s and been followed by World War II, I am convinced that revolutionary changes in the support of university departments of science would have occurred. What we have seen in the 1950s and '60s, I regard as a postponed logical continuation of what was just starting before the great depression, including the merger of the German and the indigenous American research traditions. With this merger has come the clear recognition of the university in America as an institution which can and should serve the public directly. No such function, outside the agricultural schools, would have been recognized when I was a young professor of chemistry.

What one might speak of as the long pause in university history started in the 1930s and only ended several years after the conclusion of World War II. I ceased to be a professional chemist just as the first phases of this long pause were setting in. How I should have reacted as a chemist to the sudden restriction of funds (which would have surely affected my own grant from the Harvard Corporation), the decreasing enrollments in the colleges, the massive unemployment including chemists and engineers, I shall never know. How I did, in fact, react as a university president is a story which starts in May 1933 and to which I now turn.

PART II

A UNIVERSITY PRESIDENT:

THE DEPRESSION YEARS

CHAPTER 8

The Laboratory Door Closes

It all started because as a professor of chemistry and chairman of the department I had not learned to keep my mouth shut. One day in the early winter of 1933, a member of the Harvard Corporation, Robert Homans, came to my house for tea. I barely knew who he was, since he had only recently become a member of one of Harvard's two governing boards. Harvard has an unusual trustee arrangement. A self-perpetuating body of seven (the Corporation), which includes the president, the treasurer and five fellows, makes all the major decisions, subject to a possible veto by an elected Board of Overseers, thirty in number.

I knew, of course, that Homans would ask me who I thought should be the next president of Harvard. In November, President Lowell had announced his forthcoming resignation. A classmate and old friend, Charles P. Curtis, who had been a member of the Corporation for many years, had already canvassed my views. I had declared without question for one of my oldest friends, Kenneth B. Murdock, professor of English literature and dean of the faculty of arts and sciences. Indeed, it had been the dean who in November had told me in strictest confidence of the forthcoming resignation.

Although no one will believe it, it never occurred to me that Homans was exploring the possibility of my becoming president. To me the visit meant an opportunity of speaking frankly to one of the six men who, with the new president, would control the future of

Harvard College. I had many faults to find, though no personal grievances. Indeed, I had had occasion for gratitude only a few years before, when the Corporation had provided me generously with a special research budget.

What I thought was wrong about the faculty of arts and sciences stemmed basically from President Lowell's persistent efforts to secure the future of those who were giving tutorial instruction. I was skeptical as to the applicability of a system of individual tutoring. The chemistry department had been almost alone in refusing to accept Mr. Lowell's offer of additional funds to hire tutors. As to the educational value of the scheme in other fields, I was not prepared to say. But I was disturbed by its effect on appointments. Looking over the fence at other departments and listening to the usual faculty gossip, I was convinced that we were filling up the younger ranks with mediocre men whose merit consisted largely in their willingness to be tutors. The older men had accepted the tutorial idea in theory, but only a few had themselves been tutors for a few years. For tutorial purposes, young men were needed. The standards for promotion were not high enough to suit me. All this and more I poured out to the unknown Homans in a way I had not done to Charlie Curtis, whom I knew too well and who, I suspected, was too close to President Lowell to be ready to listen to my strictures.

Homans was more than a sympathetic listener. He seemed to be anxious to hear negative views about the tutorial system and appointments. At one point he brushed aside my remark that I was, perhaps, being unduly critical. "Go on," he said, helping himself to another toasted muffin, which he branded as delicious. When he left after an hour or so, I felt we had hit it off in an extraordinary way. As I recorded in some notes made a year later, "The meeting left me with the peculiarly subtle feeling that Mr. Homans and I were kindred spirits and that he was interested in me as a possible candidate." Not a word had been said to indicate the latter. I was distinctly surprised to find myself in this situation. I rather doubted my intuitions and was inclined to discount them as products of an overexcited brain. My wife, recalling my youthful dream of three lives, which I had forgotten, noted the gleam in my eye when I told her of Homans' interview. She felt fate was closing in on her.

Up to this point, no one had even mentioned my name in connection with the presidency of Harvard—which had been much talked of for more than five years as the rumors of Mr. Lowell's resignation kept coming up anew. At a monthly meeting, the previous January, of a small social club to which my wife and I belonged, a long list of possible candidates had been read off by one of the members. I had the grippe and could not attend, but the list of some forty names was reported to me in part by my wife; I was *not* included. On hearing this news, I must admit to having been somewhat piqued. I couldn't help feeling that it was a bit hard to be considered beyond the pale of discussion. However, the verdict was clear, and there was little honor or pleasure in being gossiped about in that connection. Now this visit from Homans apparently put matters in a different light. He subsequently told me he had made up his mind on our first meeting that I was his candidate. So I had talked myself, if not into the job, at least into being a leading candidate for a position for which I had not apparently, been seriously considered.

Why did Homans and I so quickly come to a meeting of minds about the failure of the appointment system as it was then operating in Harvard? Because I had outlined to him in a few words the importance of what might be otherwise considered a technical administrative matter in a smooth-running university. And he had understood. A university, we both agreed, was a collection of eminent scholars. If the permanent professors were the most distinguished in the world, then the university would be the best university. The quality of those appointed to life positions was therefore fundamental. If a man was made a professor for personal reasons, as I believed was happening, or even for being a helpful member of a department or for devotion to Harvard, then Harvard was to that extent betraying its trust. Out of my own experience as a scientific investigator, I knew how few positions there were in 1932 in the United States where a professor could carry on research. To fill one of these positions with a second-rate person was to betray a trust—to be guilty of almost criminal negligence.

I don't doubt I showed considerable emotion (for a New Englander) in describing what I thought was going on at Harvard in this matter of choosing professors. Of course, I was not speaking or, indeed, thinking solely in terms of natural scientists. I knew from my friends in the humanities and social sciences what was happening in these areas, and I thought the present policy was leading Harvard downhill. The caliber of the student body was also of great importance, as I was to emphasize as soon as I became president; but that afternoon, talking to a member of the Harvard Corporation in search of President Lowell's successor, I was speaking first about appointing professors who should be outstanding scholars.

Homans might have challenged the fundamental premise I so passionately held. He didn't, as I remember it; but later, before the decision was made, the senior member of the Corporation, Thomas Nelson Perkins, did. He asked, in effect, why scholars (including scientists) were so important. My answer in the spring of 1933 was somewhat different from what it was to be a few years after I had been president, and considerably narrower than in the later years of my administration. The ideal university remained for me in those days the best of the German universities. Ever since I had started on a career as a student of chemistry, those who had advanced science were my heroes. The university was their home. My eight months in Germany in the 1920s had reinforced this belief. The idea that the university as an *institution* had special obligations to the community, the state or the nation was still almost completely absent from my thoughts.

The creative scholar as an individual, a completely independent worker like a poet or an artist, was to me the important personage. The university made his work possible. The justification of such a belief—a narrow one, I would say today—I had presented a year earlier before the graduating class of my "alma mater," the Roxbury Latin School. In an address which I am sure was over the heads of most of the audience, I had declared that arguments for scientific research based on the good effects of applied science, or against it based on the evils of mechanization, the use of poison gas and mass unemployment, canceled each other out. I quote a portion of the address:

Perhaps we might liken the growth of modern science to the building of a medieval cathedral. It is the work of many hands and has, like the cathedral, arisen slowly and to some extent irregularly. Only very few masterminds have had the privilege of planning the larger aspects of a medieval cathedral, and in the same way only a few scientists have had the joy of mapping out the larger aspects of the subject. A multitude of people have, however, contributed to the growth of the subject and it stands today incomplete but a stimulating example of what the collective human spirit can accomplish.

Civilization is, after all, the development of man and not the history of the material things which he accumulates or constructs. Two thousand years from now radios and poison gas may seem as unimportant as do Delphic oracles and Roman gladiators to us, but our art, literature, philosophy and science, if not lost, will be of significance to any real successor of our civilization. Experimental natural science is a newcomer to this list—an addition in the last 200 years. It has not yet been demonstrated that science will survive as a human force; in fact, many people wonder if a scientific material age like the present one can keep alive any civilization, even that which has come down to us. It is clearly the first task to meet this challenge and to be worthy custodians and transmitters of all the beauty and truth which the human spirit has struggled so long to create.

In spite of my inclusive bow to the humanities, the speech could easily be labeled a bit of scientific snobbery. The example of collective creative enterprise with which I concluded was drawn from the history of organic chemistry.

After I became president of Harvard and people began asking, "What is this new man like?" I sent the manuscript of the Roxbury Latin School address to an old friend, Frederick Lewis Allen, the editor in chief of *Harper's Magazine*. He sent it back with a kind but decisive rejection. He suggested that the argument needed to be expanded and worked over, and advised that I place the manuscript in a drawer for consideration at some later date. I did so and only saw it again in 1966 when I was going over old papers. I should have been more grateful for the advice than I was. If the speech had been printed in 1934, it would have hung around my neck during the next twenty years like the albatross of the Ancient Mariner.

I did not have to spell out my belief to Homans in any detail. An expression I was fond of using, namely, that professors are engaged in creating things "the world would not willingly let die," may at least have portrayed my sincerity. And I illustrated my conviction of the survival power of universities by reference to the history of Oxford and Cambridge during the Puritan rebellion in the mid-seventeenth century. The faculties had been purged by Royalists or Rebels as one side or the other obtained physical possession; yet with the restoration of the King came a return of all their rights and privileges. One phrase I used came right out of the history of the Puritan Commonwealth. I suggested that the Harvard Corporation might adopt "a self-denying ordinance," thus cutting through a question that Homans indicated was troubling them, namely, whether one of their own members might be the man to choose as the new president. Whether Homans recognized the source of what has become a hackneyed phrase, I do not know; but my knowledge of the seventeenth-century history of Oxford and Cambridge he may well have regarded as relevant.

I have often wondered whether my rather extensive study of the history of the Great Rebellion as a hobby was an asset or a liability as I stepped from the laboratory to the president's office. It certainly proved useful when I had to make speeches about Harvard's 300th anniversary, which we celebrated in the fall of 1936. But that was fortuitous. What I have in mind is the ancient question: Does one learn anything from history? I have for years been an advocate of reading history. My taste was awakened by an undergraduate course in the history of chemistry given by my future father-in-law, Professor T. W. Richards, and was later nourished by talks with Professor George Sarton, a true pioneer in this field.

The usual defense made for the study of history, particularly the history of our own country, is that we can only understand the present in terms of the past. One can make a good case for this judgment when speaking of the development of the United States as a nation. But the relation between English politics of 1640–60 and that of the twentieth century is tenuous at best. What I had derived from my reading of Burnet's *History of My Own Time* and Clarendon's *History of the Rebellion* and other contemporary documents, as well as twentieth-century interpretations, was an insight into human nature. The Puritan rebellion furnishes many examples of conduct under stress (including the conduct of scholars). My tendency to expect the worst when dealing with other people may well be traced to a prolonged self-inflicted dose of British seventeenth-century history.

One might well say that a future college president in a turbulent period required no such lesson. He would face, soon enough, the liar, the "double-crosser" and the intriguer. It might have been better if he had not already acquired a drab view of human nature by the vicarious experiences provided by studying history. He should have started out with the almost naïve optimism of one who had lived in a strife-free college—the twentieth-century equivalent of an ivory tower. As I recall my first errors as an administrator, I am not sure whether being forewarned was really being well armed.

Quite apart from this question, however, immersion in the Puritan period is rewarding to anyone. The study of the leading characters in the struggle between Parliament and King Charles (and among the Parliamentarians) brings to light an important fact not without its relevance to our own time: The words inscribed on the banners of contending armies (or political groups) are only rarely an accurate expression of what the fighting is all about. With important exceptions, they are mere rallying cries for groups who seek power for power's sake. One does not have to subscribe to the Marxist interpretation of events to see that what separated the Presbyterians and

Independents in seventeenth-century Britain was not church doctrine so much as the position of the central figures as powerful leaders of groups of loyal followers.

How many of these thoughts I shared with Homans during that first visit in 1933, I no longer remember. I do remember, however (with the assistance of the notes I kept at the time), that after his call things began to happen. Other members of the Corporation called; under the pretext of asking my opinion about potential candidates, they sized me up. Toward the end of February 1933, a few of my friends began telling me that they had heard on "good authority" that my name was being considered. My wife and I started asking each other whether we should consider the matter. Discussing the pros and cons of taking a job that no one had even hinted might be offered officially seemed a rather silly business.

Charlie Curtis called again and debated with himself in my presence whether the next president should be a faculty man or an outsider. I naturally produced strong arguments for an academic man. Then Charlie edged off to the personal question: "How would you feel about it yourself?" The query was immediately followed by strong protestations that he was speaking only for himself—this was in no sense an offer. I replied that I certainly did not want the job, but if it were offered, I would take it.

A few days later, I was interviewed in New York by still another member of the Corporation, Grenville Clark. He was even more frank than Curtis. We discussed the possibility of my being president. Again, however, it was made clear that I was not being offered the post. My position was awkward, and the situation was becoming worse. I learned that while I was out of town Professor L. J. Henderson, my wife's uncle by marriage, had paid her a formal call to gather details for the Harvard Corporation about my family and my youth. He made it plain that he was carrying out a mission which he thought slightly ridiculous. He may have been asked to perform this service by either Perkins or Curtis, as he was a close friend of both.

A few days later, Henderson came to see me himself. He reported that President Lowell had asked him to come to his office to talk about the possibility of my being the next president of Harvard. In the course of the conversation, the president had said that the choice appeared to be between Grenville Clark and myself, that he believed I wanted the job, but that I would be a fool if I took it. At any rate, would Professor Henderson have a talk with me and report back how

I looked as presidential timber? Henderson said he would if he could be quite open with me about the matter. He thereupon asked me a few questions. Obviously, he had no taste for his role.

The next development was a visit from Thomas Nelson Perkins, the senior member of the Corporation, a formidable person by reason of his long service on the Corporation as well as his reputation as a lawyer who had served the government on more than one occasion. He went right to the point, as I was to learn he always did. Did I want the job? I answered that this depended on what one meant by the word "want." I was not at all anxious to have it, but I would take it if offered, though I thought myself a great fool not to refuse to have anything to do with the proposition. Then Perkins set forth at great length his theory of the creation of a new post of vice president to be filled by an academic man; the president would be a man of affairs. I combated the theory at length and, in reply to a direct question, said that under no circumstances would I take the position of vice president. We then discussed the conflict between research and teaching, and I put forth the view that there was no problem—a man could be both a good scholar and a good teacher.

Mr. Perkins, like Charlie Curtis and Grenville Clark, made it plain that I was not being offered the job. The Corporation was having difficulty making up its collective mind. As I learned afterward, Lowell, following Harvard tradition, had absented himself from all discussions about his successor. Yet the members must have known how he felt. Indeed, he told me frankly after I was elected that he urged another name, but the Corporation did not agree. Certainly with my negative attitude toward the tutorial system (at least in science), my deep concern with my own research budget and no manifest interest in wider academic affairs, I could hardly be the candidate of his choice.

Toward the end of April, Professor Henderson came to see me in my laboratory in a state of considerable excitement. The situation had become complicated. Lowell had called Henderson in and said that two members of the Corporation had told him (the president) that they would vote for Conant if that were acceptable to Lowell; otherwise, they would vote for Clark. Lowell said he had very little belief in me as a future president, but was inclined to take a long gamble, since he regarded Clark as a poor choice for this position. He had all along stated that he thought the man should be from the faculty. He asked Henderson to see Perkins (who was, therefore, clearly not one of the two who had come to him) and urge him to vote for me rather than for Clark. Henderson agreed, but again insisted that he be free to tell me about the whole transaction. During all my talks with Henderson, he had made it clear that his candidate was and always had been Dr. Roger I. Lee, a Boston physician and a member of the Corporation; but for some reason Lee's candidacy had failed to materialize. I am inclined to believe that the two who approached Lowell were Curtis and Henry L. Shattuck, the treasurer, or perhaps Curtis and Homans; it is clear that Homans was my particularly strong supporter throughout and that Perkins was the least favorable.

On Sunday evening, April 23, Shattuck called. We spoke directly about the possibility of my election. I tried to make my position clear to the treasurer, and stated that I should require a good salary as I had no money of my own. The call was brief. I felt certain the election would take place that evening or the next day, since the members of the Corporation were in the habit of dining together Sunday evenings before the Corporation meeting, and a meeting was scheduled for Monday, April 24.

Monday was one of those unusually sultry days that come sometimes even in April. I waited—at home and in my office at the Converse Laboratory—a few hours in one spot, a few hours in the other. About three o'clock, the president's secretary telephoned the laboratory office and said Mr. Lowell was on his way over to see me. I tried to continue the calculations connected with the paper I had been pretending to write all day. President Lowell came in, sat down and said simply and rather coldly that the Corporation had that morning elected me president of Harvard. My only reply was a rather resigned "Well."

"It is a great honor," he continued, "but a very great responsibility." I made some rather feeble remark about its being equivalent to being ordered to go over the top.

President Lowell then explained the mechanism of the formal election, which would not take place for two weeks. (In a sense, no election had so far occurred—it had merely been agreed that I would be elected.) He emphasized the unanimous decision and told me that President Eliot had refrained from voting at the time of his election and that Dr. Walcott (the senior fellow), not Eliot, had brought the word to him. President Lowell spoke briefly about the finances, the balanced budget, the surplus and, without a trace of warmth, enthusiasm or friendliness, said that it was to me that he was turning over all these assets. He pledged himself not to interfere in any way with what I would do; he was quite prepared to think it would be very different from what he had done. It was painfully evident that he expected the worst.

At that moment, I most unfortunately raised the question of salary. "They said you want twenty thousand dollars," he replied, "and you shall have it." "I can't do it on that, I'm afraid," I replied. "See them about it," he said, obviously irritated that I should raise this issue at all. He made a few remarks about his having given money to the university and not bothered with salary, and departed.

I was thoroughly angry at myself for having made such a poor start, and returned at once to our house at 20 Oxford Street to try to put the blame on my wife, a usual procedure. In the midst of a somewhat hectic discussion of our personal finances, Charlie Curtis was announced. We welcomed him cordially and at once told him our troubles about the salary question. We had two little boys, and the prospect of having to maintain a large official residence was troublesome. "Don't worry," was his reply. "You don't understand at all your future relations to the Corporation. Let the figure stand, and if you need more, raise the question any time. Of course, you'll get it." This was most encouraging and reassuring. He chatted on merrily and asked us to come out to his house the next Saturday for the afternoon —he would invite some other members of the Corporation. In fact, the meeting turned out to be with only Curtis and Shattuck, but was extremely valuable.

So it was settled. That was a relief anyway. A scheduled trip to Europe in June was moved forward to May, so that my family and I could leave immediately after the official Corporation meeting. I was quite certain I must have a look at Oxford and Cambridge, which had played so large a part in President Lowell's thinking. I also needed to get away from my friends, who would be eager to give good advice. A few days later, my wife and I dined alone with Mr. Lowell at the President's House in the Harvard Yard. After dinner, the three of us talked for two or three hours. During that time, the atmosphere seemed to change miraculously—a chill beginning and a remarkably warm ending. In fact, Professor Henderson reported that when he spoke with the president the following morning, it was evident that he had changed his mind.

The change may have been due to the fact that I had spent some hours two days before with Curtis and Shattuck, who filled me in on many aspects of the university's current problems. Then, too, I imagine President Lowell was relieved not to find me belligerent about the need for change. He himself had become president because he believed Harvard College needed drastic reforms; therefore he perhaps expected me to declare war at the outset. Nothing could have been further from my mind; the fundamental issue of the effect of the tutorial system on the problem of appointments was not the kind of subject I was prepared to start debating, despite my rash remarks to Homans. It would be four years before this issue emerged with an almost revolutionary force, which nearly blew me out of office.

Either at this dinner or shortly after, President Lowell told me about his own inauguration, when he had spoken to a large audience assembled in the Harvard Yard, saying, in effect, that the way to make Harvard a vital institution was to make four years of college a rewarding experience. After the excercises were over, an old friend came up to him and said: "Well, it looks as if we are going to have a new ship." "Not at all," was the reply. "It will be the same old ship, but on a new tack." President Lowell loved this nautical analogy. He repeated it more than once in the next few years. After our first two chilly encounters, relations between us were cordial as well as correct. He said he would give me no advice unless I asked for it. He would stay out of my way—something Eliot had not done with him, he remarked rather bitterly.

This bit of Harvard history I knew quite well. The gossip in the faculty in the 1920s was that Lowell had only become a free man after Charles William Eliot had died in 1926. There seems no doubt that Eliot had appointed a number of youngish men to important positions with the hope of perpetuating his policy. I could recall at least one faculty debate in which a member of the old guard referred to the fact that some of those present had just been visiting Mr. Eliot, and strongly implied that the views of the president emeritus were in accord with those of the dissenters. I also recalled a meeting just before or after World War I, when young faculty members and alumni were addressed by President Lowell and President Emeritus Eliot. Eliot, who was then in his mid-eighties, proposed that the administration of the college needed reorganization. The position of president had become too burdensome; a vice president was needed. Lowell picked up the challenge and politely, but strongly, said his predecessor was wrong. He (Lowell) was doing very well, thank you; no vice president was needed. I remember being mildly shocked as a young profesor-to-be at this public challenge of a relatively new president by a very old one. Thinking back to that experience, I could see what President Lowell meant when he vigorously asserted that he would not interfere. He kept his word.

The official method of choosing a president of Harvard is a formal affair based on the college charter of 1650. If a vacancy in the seven-member Corporation (which includes the president) occurs, the remaining members are authorized to fill the vacancy, with the advice and consent of the Board of Overseers. The composition of the body known as the Overseers had changed from time to time over the centuries, but, as far as I knew, the words of the charter had never been violated. Whether they would be in spirit in 1933 became a matter of an amusing controversy between the president of the Board of Overseers and President Lowell.

Though I had not as yet been elected, President Lowell decided to tell the president of the Overseers, George Agassiz, what the Corporation intended. The news brought Agassiz at once into action. As president of the older, though less powerful, of the two boards, he had *in theory* a strong voice about who should succeed Lowell. And no hint of the way the discussion within the Corporation had been going had been conveyed to him either officially or unofficially. He raised at once the constitutional question that was to bedevil me for twenty years: Were the members of the Board of Overseers, and particularly the president of the board, to be treated as rubber stamps?

I learned that Agassiz, who knew my father-in-law well and was proud of his friendship with a Nobel prize winner, had been aghast at the news that I had been offered and had accepted the presidency of Harvard. His horror was made plain in our first interview. He told me I was making a great mistake; it was incomprehensible. Why should I give up a promising career as a scientist to take a job he, Agassiz, wouldn't give a rotten apple for? (One must remember that George Agassiz, though not himself a scientist, was a son of one famous investigator and the grandson of another.) Then he referred to several of my contemporaries who had *not* forsaken science for an administrative post. Next he raised the question whether there was any evidence that I could handle an administrative position. I mentioned my experience in World War I when, as a major in the Chemical Warfare Service, I had been in charge of a research and development group isolated in a small Ohio town. Agassiz suggested that my superior officer, now once again a civilian chemical engineer, might provide a reference, so to speak. On his urging, I reluctantly provided the name and address. (The response he received, I subsequently discovered, was satisfactory. At the dinner of the Harvard Club of Boston in the fall, given in my honor, Agassiz read the letter with pride, proving to his satisfaction that the Board of Overseers had made no mistake in consenting to the Corporation's decision.)

When I reported Agassiz' rather negative attitude to President Lowell, he replied: "His bark is much worse than his bite. I have no worry that he will vote against you." The real question troubling the president of the Board of Overseers, President Lowell went on to say, involved the public announcement of the election. The procedure at the coming meeting of the Overseers on May 8 was to be as follows. Following the wording of the charter and the tradition of several hundred years, the members of the Corporation would meet in a room next to the large room in University Hall where the Board of Overseers would convene. The president of the university, as an ex officio member of both boards, would be an intermediary carrying messages between the two. First he would preside at the Corporation meeting, which would vote to request the permission of the Overseers to proceed to the election of a president. Then he would place this request before the Overseers, who were expected to grant it by voice vote. (No one predicted trouble at that point, though I later discovered by reading Harvard history that in 1869 the Overseers had refused this request, knowing Charles William Eliot would be the choice; the matter was settled in favor of Eliot in subsequent negotiations and a formal meeting.)

President Lowell explained that Agassiz was concerned about what would happen when the president of the university returned from the meeting of the Corporation in the adjacent room and placed before the Board of Overseers the name of the man who had just been officially elected. The Overseers' own rules forbade any immediate action; the matter had to go over to their next meeting, which would be on Commencement Day in June. Would the press be told that I had been elected but not as yet confirmed?

At a meeting of President Lowell, President Agassiz and myself, I heard the two men argue the matter rather vigorously. Agassiz insisted that the dignity of the Board of Overseers required that my name be kept from the public on May 8. The Corporation decision should be released only after the Overseers had had a chance to veto it. Otherwise, the Overseers would be deprived in reality of their freedom of action. A *public* challenge of the Corporation's decision was unthinkable. In other words, a secret of some interest must be kept until Commencement Day, more than a month away. President Lowell said this was impossible. When asked who would betray the secret, he replied promptly: "You or one of your fellow members will, as soon as the meeting is adjourned." It was finally agreed to leave the decision to a vote of the Overseers. Apparently a majority agreed with President Lowell, for the news of my election—subject to confirmation of the Overseers—was sent out at 11 A.M. on Monday, May 8, 1933.

When I was interviewed by a committee of the Board of Overseers a few days after the announcement, I discussed cautiously some of the problems I thought faced the new administration. Although 1933 was the year of the closing of the banks, the inauguration of Franklin Delano Roosevelt and the coming to power of Hitler, none of these world-shaking events was referred to in our talk. That we were living in the midst of a financial crisis was, of course, a premise everyone accepted. Yet no member of the Corporation or of the Board of Overseers asked me about raising money. This is an incredible fact, when looked at from the viewpoint of the 1960s, a fact that underlines the kind of America we were living in in the first years of the great depression. Raising money! Out of the question, everyone would have said in May 1933. The problem in those days of catastrophe was how to hang on to what little we had and spend it wisely.

President Lowell had assumed that, in spite of Agassiz' misgivings, the announcement of my election would be made on May 8. Therefore, a few days before the fateful Monday, he sent a young man to talk with me about how the newspapers were to be informed. Word came to me that my caller was the only person in all of Harvard who was in touch with the journalists who covered Harvard news. He was obviously worried and impressed with the difficulties of introducing a new president to the press. His first question was: "Will you be on hand so you can be interviewed at once?" The answer was "No." I had a long-standing engagement to lecture in Philadelphia on Monday evening. "Most unfortunate," the young man said. He would face imperious demands for a lengthy, detailed story the moment the news of the election was made public. Could I provide him with background material? I could try.

My attempts were far from successful. About all I could offer was the fact my questioner already knew: that I had within a year or two received a couple of medals for scientific publications. Could I explain my investigations to the public? Only with difficulty, I had to admit. It soon developed that it didn't matter much. For the young man who was to represent me to the reporters hungry for a human-interest story had no desire to become a science reporter. He himself had never studied science, and he made it plain that he looked at all scientists with a jaundiced eye. I suggested that, in addition to studying the structure of the green coloring material in plants (chlorophyll) and the material that made blood red (hemoglobin), I had recently been investigating the blue blood of horseshoe crabs; there might be a story there. My official guide into the dread world of reporters shook his head; he saw only trouble in this suggestion. "Blue blood," he murmured; "too easily converted into an undesirable story about aristocrats at Harvard." As a greenhorn in the area of press relations, I could do nothing but agree.

Neither this conversation nor our subsequent ones were entirely satisfactory. By now I was thoroughly scared by the tasks that lay ahead. I was reluctant to dredge out of my past any anecdotes which might contribute to an interesting portrait. The young man was also scared. He had not been in office long. The reporters had given him a rather rough time in connection with some unfavorable story about the employment practices of the university. Furthermore, the tradition of extreme reserve that President Lowell had fostered made his job no easier. Only recently had Harvard had any designated official to answer questions of reporters for the wire services and the local papers. Indeed, the president had consistently refused to be interviewed or even photographed. Lowell's successor appeared to be ready to perpetuate the spirit of aloofness and would not even be on hand to be questioned on the day when the clamor for a story was at its height. The young man was in trouble, but I was far too nervous to be sympathetic.

I took the train to Philadelphia Sunday night. No one made any attempt to question me about my plans. Although the election was overdue and the Boston papers were on the scent, I was such a dark horse that no one bothered me. My lecture the next evening was to be one of a series celebrating the one hundredth anniversary of the publication of an historic paper in organic chemistry by two great pioneers in this field—Liebig and Wöhler. It was addressed to chemists only, a report on one phase of my own work. I knew it was far too technical to be of any use in connection with the brewing news story. I did not even make an attempt to relate it to any broader subject such as the history of chemistry or the role of the academic genius. As I look back now, I realize that with less fright and more imagination I could have delivered a lecture on which a reporter could hang a story. I did not even contemplate the possibility. I just waited alone for the blow to fall while I read the Monday morning papers in my hotel room.

I imagined the actual news release would be made just before lunch, when the Board of Overseers adjourned. At that time, my presence in a Philadelphia hotel would be made known to the newsmen in Cambridge. I was not surprised in the afternoon to see a small group of men in the hotel lobby apparently looking for someone. I started to play a sort of hide-and-seek game, which was easy since no one knew me by sight. Before too long I thought better of it and identified myself.

"We've found him," someone shouted and beckoned to several men some feet away. "Shall we shoot him first or interview him?" someone else asked. At that moment I was almost prepared to have the first alternative accepted in a literal sense. Thanks to an experienced publicity man from the University of Pennsylvania who suddenly appeared, some order was introduced into the scene. The president-elect of Harvard thus held his first press interview in a Philadelphia hotel before delivering an abstruse scientific lecture for which not even a press release had been prepared.

On my return to Cambridge, relations with the press did not ease. The young man wanted material. I had none. He suggested interviews with selected reporters; I refused. I was not ready to say anything about plans and policies and was most secretive about my personal affairs. The consequence was inevitable. A few enterprising newsmen wrote special stories based on interviews with a few people who had been spotted as old friends, including even my aged mother, who was by then living in Atlanta, Georgia.

A scrapbag of trivia was thus soon on hand, the contents of which kept coming to light for years as I traveled around the country and met with the local press. Did I fail the spelling section of the entrance examination for the Roxbury Latin School? Yes. Was I slow to start reading and writing? Not that I remembered. Had I acted the role of heroine in the school play? Yes, indeed. (It was, of course, a boys' school.) Had I started my career in chemistry by making soap for my mother? No. Had my father constructed a private laboratory for me when I was a boy? One might so designate the space provided and equipped with gas and water. As a chemistry professor, had I turned an egg into a rubbery mass and hurled it at the class? The transformation of the egg was a lecture-table experiment, yes; aggressive action against the audience, no; but I did enjoy lecture-table explosions when planned.

So the interviews would go. Just because there was nothing on which to build a substantial background news story when I was elected president of Harvard, I have been condemned ever since to confirm or deny inconsequential stories about my boyhood, my youth and my years as a professor. The results of the highly imaginative reporting of a few hard-pressed writers in 1933 will be with me to my dying day.

The proof of this last conjecture is afforded by a telephone call I received from the *New York Times* in 1966. The caller started asking questions about my past; these soon began to include almost everything to which I have been referring. I had to destroy a number of the anecdotes that might have been considered mildly amusing but were far from true. When he sighed with regret at the end of our telephone conversation, I could not refrain from asking if he was bringing a necrology up to date. My questioner admitted such was, indeed, the case.

CHAPTER 9

An Introduction to the English Colleges

As I HAVE ALREADY NOTED, my wife and I had planned to leave for Europe as soon as possible after the Corporation had acted. The sudden illness of our younger son, Ted, presented us with a distressing situation. Ten days before the election was to take place, he had developed a double mastoid. Surgery in those days was the only answer. Until a successful operation was performed, my wife could not think of leaving. Should I go alone? The urge to escape from what we both knew would be many embarrassments was great. After May 8 I would be a Harvard president-elect whose election still had to be confirmed by the Overseers. In theory, at least, the Overseers could refuse to consent. No one was really worried on that score, but the members of the Corporation agreed that it would be a good idea if I were not available in Cambridge during May and June.

For my own part, now that the uncertainty was more or less over, I had to think hard about the future. One problem already faced me. In March or April I had been asked along with a dozen other professors to meet with one of the Overseers, Henry James. He wanted to talk to us about the celebration of the Tercentenary in 1936. He reported that President Lowell had said he would be out of office long before that date and would have nothing to do with the preparations. We, as professors, were asked for suggestions. Whether we gave any, I do not recall. The significance to me of that meeting was Henry James' statement that nothing had yet been planned, though the great event was only three years away. I could expect that the Harvard community would expect me to formulate plans for the celebration almost as soon as I took office. Then, too, either Charlie Curtis or Henry Shattuck had mentioned casually that people might expect the university to try to raise some money in connection with the celebration. No one had suggested that I was under any obligation to organize a campaign. Still, I wanted to think over the possibility.

A visit to Oxford and Cambridge followed by a leisurely vacation trip in France semeed to be just what I needed. So, at my wife's urging, I started alone across the Atlantic. She was to come later, when our son was out of danger, and to bring the car with which we would tour a bit of England and much of France. The strain on her was great. I probably should not have gone. Yet had I postponed my departure, I should have missed a number of rewarding experiences in Oxford, for in May the academic year comes rapidly to a close. Furthermore, for a chemist about to undergo a metamorphosis, there were advantages in arriving in an English university unaccompanied by a wife. In 1933, even more than today, the life of the colleges was centered entirely about the male. Dining in hall in one Oxford college or another occupied the first week of evenings after my arrival. To take care of a visitor's wife at the time of the evening meal was a largely unsolved problem, I discovered, when several weeks later our son had recovered enough for my wife to join me.

President Lowell gladly furnished me with letters of introduction to the heads of a number of the colleges in both universities. He had many friends in English academic circles, and had made no secret of his admiration of the tutorial system and other aspects of English collegiate life. This was one reason I had thought it important to learn more about Oxford and Cambridge. Moreover, two of the masters of the Harvard houses had studied at Oxford and were apt to use their experiences there as a measure of all educational proposals.

In addition to my letters of introduction, I had my own sources of contact with Oxford. One of Britain's leading organic chemists, a man of about my age, Sir Robert Robinson, had been called to Oxford a few years before. I knew him, and our mutual concern with chemical problems provided a strong link of friendship. An older man, also an organic chemist, Neville Sidgwick, a fellow of Lincoln College, proved to be my real guide into the complexities of English higher education. He was a bachelor and had rooms in the college. As soon as he heard I was going to visit Oxford, he asked me to be his guest. When I told him of my desire to learn something about his university and mentioned the people to whom I had letters of introduction, he made a characteristic reply. "Those are fine gentlemen," he said; "as heads of houses they will welcome you and provide suitable hospitality. You won't, however, learn anything about Oxford from them because they don't really understand Oxford themselves."

Sidgwick then proceeded to start me on the right path, drawing on his thirty or more years of experience as a don. Before I knew it, I was embarked on a course of tutorial instruction in the government of Oxford University. Bits of scandal from the past and references to what one of his uncles who had been a don had told him made me feel that I had been permitted to peek into the family cupboard. The skeletons proved that academic men for decades, if not centuries, had been prone to fight with politically lethal weapons. Within a few years, I was to have occasion in Cambridge, Massachusetts, to recall this lesson.

Regarding Oxford as the model which, consciously or unconsciously, Harvard had been following, I was curious to discover how appointments were made in this university. I learned that each college was a self-governing community of scholars. In most cases the presiding officer, whose title varied from college to college, was elected by the other members of the community—the fellows. The vacancies in the fellowships were filled in the same way. There were many amusing stories about academic politics within a college, particularly when the fellows were about to elect a presiding officer. Since the position of vice chancellor of the university rotated among the heads of the colleges in a predetermined order, a young man who became the presiding officer of his college was certain to be head of the university before he retired. His tenure would be for only two years, to be sure, but an energetic vice chancellor could have a considerable influence on the policy of the university. Yet it seemed strange to me that such an influential post (the equivalent of an American college president) should be filled in such a roundabout manner. I soon discovered that to gain a real insight into the powers of the vice chancellor, I would have to find out who governed the university. And the answer was not forthcoming to anyone unprepared to become an active member of that society of scholars for at least a year or two.

One fact was clear. A large part of the teaching of undergraduates was carried on by dons who drew their salaries from the colleges and who were primarily college and not university officers. Certain colleges contributed far more members to the total teaching staff than did others. Apparently negotiations between the colleges enabled a student in one college to be under the guidance of a tutor in another. I was reminded that historically the university was the examining body, the college the teaching institution. Lectures by professors were relatively insignificant. Repeated meetings with a tutor and preparation for a general examination were the essentials of Oxford instruction, I was told. Quite different from Harvard, I thought, where the tutorial system had been simply added to the lecture system.

Sidgwick enjoyed pointing out the bewildering complexities of Oxford and took a certain pleasure in my obvious inability to arrive at a simple analysis of the relation between appointments made by the university and those made by a college. If I was trying to fit my new-found knowledge into the problems I foresaw in Harvard, I was sure to fail, or at least that seemed to be the implied conclusion of our conversations. Certainly the status of the men who were acting as tutors at Harvard was entirely different from that of the tutors I met at Oxford. The Harvard tutors were young men who hoped to be given positions as professors before too long. In Oxford they were for the most part older men who had secure and satisfactory places as life members of one of the colleges. They might leave Oxford for another university, of course, if a more attractive post was open. The question of promotion within the college to which they belonged, however, would never arise. Even in the spring of 1933, I saw how different were the basic suppositions underlying the two tutorial systems. A few years later these differences were to lead to a grave misunderstanding between the faculty of arts and sciences and myself.

I needed now to relate my intensive study of the oldest English university to the organization of the newer institutions. Fortunately, I soon met the vice chancellor of Manchester University, Sir Walter Moberley, one evening after dinner in the Lincoln College common room. He was quite ready to answer my questions about procedures in his university. The information I obtained from him enabled me to understand the over-all British system of "academical patronage." (Someone suggested I should read the early nineteenth-century essay by Sir William Hamilton that bears this title; I did, and subsequently appropriated the phrase for an essay of my own.) When, a few years later, Sir Walter became chairman of the vastly important University Grants Committee, he visited the United States in his new capacity and stayed with us in the President's House at Harvard. The friendship that started that evening in Lincoln College continued to be one of the most enduring and enjoyable links I had with the academic community across the ocean. The knowledge I acquired through Sir Walter about the appointment system at the English universities proved most helpful when I sought to change the Harvard procedures a few years later.

One of the important personages at Oxford to whom I had a letter of introduction was a former man of affairs who had been rather recently elected master of one of the colleges. After tea, as we strolled on the college lawn, my host remarked that he was glad to see me for many reasons. One was the fact that my name was so well known in Oxford because of an ancestor in the seventeenth century who had been vice chancellor. As I undoubtedly knew, his scholarly prowess had led his contemporaries to coin the Latin phrase: *"Conanti nihil difficile est."* I expressed my appreciation of my host's words without betraying that I had never heard of anyone with my name who was connected with Oxford.

When I returned to Sidgwick's quarters, I asked if he had ever heard of a Conant who was vice chancellor in the seventeenth century. The answer was in the negative. I was puzzled. Then I turned to the many-volume *Dictionary of National Biography* standing on the shelf in his study. There I found a half-page about the seventeenth-century scholar. The details of his life, including the Latin pun, were set forth almost verbatim as I had just heard them. The master had done his homework. When I told Sidgwick about my discovery in the *Dictionary of National Biography,* he was gleeful. "Very characteristic of the old humbug," he said. "This is the kind of man from outside Oxford whom they elect as the head of a college."

Lincoln College had become my Oxford base and continued to be so as the years went on and my friendship with Sidgwick grew closer. In Cambridge, Emmanuel College soon came to occupy a similar position; I was adopted as an honorary fellow. The reason was that John Harvard had been a student in the college (B.A. 1631–32, M.A. 1635). A few Harvard alumni at the time of World War I had made it a point to emphasize the seventeenth-century connection between the new and the old Cambridge. A John Harvard Fellowship had been founded and rooms in Emmanuel College set aside for a resident scholar. Of all this I had previously been ignorant. Before I had sailed for England, however, President Lowell had told me enough about Emmanuel College so that I was prepared for the welcome I received. Because I was an organic chemist and not a physicist, I had had no link with the famous Cavendish Laboratory where

Lord Rutherford was directing his younger colleagues in making one revolutionary discovery after another. In 1933 Oxford was more significant for an organic chemist than Cambridge. However, I had the privilege of becoming an honorary colleague of one of the pioneers in biochemistry, Sir Gowland Hopkins, who had a long connection with Emmanuel College.

In Cambridge I was as cordially received as in Oxford and royally entertained by many people. As the successor to President Lowell, I was something of a curiosity in both universities. Everyone seemed to have forgotten that President Eliot had been a chemist; therefore, more than one English don regarded my taking over the responsibility of the presidency of Harvard as a rather extraordinary experiment. In spite of the Cavendish Laboratory, the standing of scientists in the two ancient institutions of higher learning was far from high. What could a mere chemist do when faced with problems outside a laboratory? Very politely this question was put to me in one form or another as I was wined and dined at various high tables. I was not at all sure of the answer myself.

One reason for the interest in the new president of Harvard was connected with the recent changes in the undergraduate life at Harvard and Yale. President Lowell had established the House Plan in 1928; Yale had followed suit with its College Plan. The reforms seemed at first sight to be copies of the traditional structure of Oxford and Cambridge. The students lived in separate houses or colleges, with each of which a number of professors and instructors were associated. What would happen next? Would the houses and the colleges gradually become self-sufficient, independent entities as was the case with the colleges of Oxford and Cambridge? Or would they remain essentially residential units? The new Harvard president might provide a clue to the answer.

I recall a long conversation with Will Spens, the master of Christ Church College, Cambridge. He had made a specialty of academic politics. He knew the workings of his own university intimately since he had served a term of several years as vice chancellor. His visits to the United States had been frequent. On the basis of his experience, he predicted that the development at either Yale or Harvard (or perhaps at both) would lead to a pattern similar to that which had so long characterized his own university and Oxford. I thought his prophecy most unlikely. I pointed out that the present arrangements in the two English universities were the result of a long history. During the eighteenth century the colleges had been everything, the university hardly even a degree-granting device. Then came the drastic reforms of the middle of the nineteenth century. The independent financial resources of the colleges began to be tapped to support the university as a teaching organization. As he well knew, the present health of Oxford and Cambridge rested on a partnership between those who put their own college first and others whose prime loyalty was to the university. The growth of experimental science had been of the first importance in shifting the balance away from the colleges, since no single college could successfully maintain a research laboratory unless it was tacitly admitted to be, in fact, a university institution.

All of which Spens readily conceded. But he foresaw a time when the new American houses and colleges would obtain their own endowments and become powerful. I had to admit that if financial independence came to the Harvard houses or the Yale colleges, there would be a new turn in American academic history.

In the course of our conversation, Spens may have gained an insight into the premises of many Americans who had been nurtured on the German university tradition. I certainly came to see more clearly what the English university tradition meant to a Cambridge don. What was at issue was not methods of instruction but a way of life. The British college was a corporate living entity with a long past. The fellows were a self-perpetuating body which commanded prime allegiance. (As one of the dons said, "If the choice is between one's own family or one's own college, the college must come first, sad as this may sound.") The undergraduates were not admitted by the university but by the particular college, though this fact was often glossed over when one spoke of the entrance requirements of Oxford or Cambridge University.

I am reporting on Oxford and Cambridge of the 1930s, it must be remembered. There have been many changes in higher education in Great Britain in the last three decades. But the fundamental nature of the colleges of Oxford and Cambridge had remained essentially unaltered. And it is these colleges before World War II and their influence on American institutions that I am now considering. Their effect on the growth of American academic life in the formative period is evident from a glance at the history of American higher education.

Unlike German universities, but like Oxford and Cambridge, colleges and universities in the United States award the bachelor's degree. Even the origin of boards of trustees and the office of college president, so characteristic of our colleges, can be traced to the influence of English university graduates in the early colonial days of the seventeenth century. To be sure, by the end of the nineteenth century little similarity could be found between the organization and methods of instruction in Oxford and Cambridge and American institutions. Yet the existence of an English as well as a German component in our university tradition cannot be neglected. Years before Harvard and Yale built residential colleges and before President Lowell's introduction of the first tutors and the idea of general examinations, education in an Oxford or Cambridge College was recognized by Americans as something quite special. It could perhaps be defined best in negative terms. The objective was not to become a specialist. The intellectual experiences during the college years were for the purpose of broadening one's view, exciting curiosity about different aspects of the life of the mind and, above all, learning how to educate oneself. Listening to lectures might be stimulating, meeting with a tutor ought to be helpful, but access to the library was the essential element in a university education. At least this was the theory which I had heard expounded by a few members of the Harvard faculty who had studied in an Oxford or Cambridge college. I had come to England to learn more about it. My reception had been so cordial that I soon became converted to the way of life if not to the instructional methods. I was on the point of becoming an Anglophile.

During my many meetings with academic men, I had difficulty at times in answering a question as to my status. I had been elected president of Harvard by one governing board, I explained, but the confirmation by a second board still remained. A cable from Cambridge, Massachusetts, in mid-June announcing favorable action by the Board of Overseers relieved me of the embarrassment of having to give a long reply to a simple question.

Needless to say, I often received considerable advice as to what I should do when I took office. Only one concrete suggestion has remained firmly imbedded in my mind. At one small gathering, I was greeted by the exclamation, "Oh, you are the new president of Harvard; I understand you will be all-powerful and, unlike an English vice chancellor, can do exactly what you like." My protests against this caricature were brushed aside as my acquaintance hastened to his conclusion. "If you have the authority I am told you will have, I give you one piece of advice: Draw your salary and stay right here in Europe!"

CHAPTER 10

Initial Problems

ON SEPTEMBER 5, 1933, I formally took over the responsibilities of the office of president of Harvard. Not that there was much formality involved. I walked across the Yard from the house at 20 Oxford Street we were still occupying to University Hall and climbed the stairs to the president's office on the second floor. The secretary of the Corporation, Francis W. Hunnewell, came down from his office on the third floor. President Lowell was on hand to wish me well. We shook hands all around, and I was ready to start the laborious process of finding out what was on the minds of the deans of the various faculties, leading professors and others involved in the affairs of Harvard University.

There was to be no inauguration. With a tercentenary celebration just over the horizon, it seemed foolish to stage the kind of elaborate academic gathering which in those days usually marked the entry into office of a new man. We all agreed that a private Harvard family party involving not more than a hundred people in addition to the members of the two governing boards would suffice. Such a meeting in the faculty room of University Hall was scheduled for the afternoon of the first regular meeting of the Board of Overseers.

There would be no reporters and no photographers. That decision pleased the president of the university and the older members of the Board of Overseers. Two or three of the younger members registered a protest, however, suggesting that the new president and his advisers were living in the nineteenth century as far as publicity was concerned. Actually, they were a century off in their calculations, according to a report of the occasion in the *Harvard Alumni Bulletin*, dated October 13, 1933. Under the heading "J. B. Conant Installed President," it described the ceremony of Monday, October 9, as reproducing "as nearly as possible the one which took place when John Leverett was inaugurated as President of the College." That date: January 14, 1707.

The contrast with Lowell's inaugural in the fall of 1909 was striking. I had not the slightest desire to try to emulate President Lowell's oratorical success in addressing a large gathering out of doors. Since I had no plan for reforming the college or the university, I was grateful that I had a good excuse for not making an inaugural address.

It has been often said that in 1869 Eliot undertook to change a college into a university and succeeded. In the 1930s it was said by a few that Lowell had been endeavoring to rescue the college from the university, but it looked as though his successor were going to reverse the trend. Such oversimplifications of Harvard history, which depicted me as "a university man like Mr. Eliot" and a lukewarm advocate of the cause of the college, were not particularly helpful, though I do not deny they contained a grain or two of truth. Compared to President Lowell's clear vision of what he intended to do, however, I had relatively little to offer, even after a summer of cogitation. I was quite ready to applaud with all sincerity what my predecessors had accomplished.

I was especially enthusiastic about the founding of the Society of Fellows, which had been one of the last actions taken by the previous administration. The donor of a generous endowment was to remain anonymous for the time being. Actually everyone soon knew it was President Lowell himself.

The use of the word "fellows" at Harvard is most confusing. Some wit has commented that, like the word "justice," it is used for the highest and lowest ranks. Thus, just as we have the Justices of the Supreme Court and justices of the peace, so we have the president and fellows of Harvard College and the holders of fellowships in the graduate school. The senior fellows of the Society of Fellows might be said to be on the level of the president and fellows, whereas the junior fellows are essentially like the holders of scholarships and fellowships.

The senior fellows were to consist of two ex officio members (the president of the university and the dean of the faculty of arts and sciences) and five chosen by the Corporation. The Corporation had decided before I took office that if Lowell as president emeritus was willing to serve, he should be one of the five; another would be Charles P. Curtis, a member of the Corporation; the three professors were to be John Livingston Lowes, Alfred North Whitehead and Lawrence J. Henderson. Of these, Whitehead and Henderson had worked closely with Mr. Lowell in planning the Society of Fellows.

The terms of the gift provided that the junior prize fellows should be selected "for their promise of notable contribution to knowledge and thought, by such methods as in the opinion of the Senior Fellows shall seem most likely to measure their future capacity. . . . They shall devote their whole time to productive scholarship and preparation therefor, free from academic regulations for degrees. They shall have all the privileges of any instruction given in the university, but shall receive no credit for courses and shall not be candidates for any degree."

Rooms had been provided in Eliot House; a weekly dinner of senior and junior fellows in these rooms became at once an important part of the scheme. The first six junior fellows included three who later became professors at Harvard and achieved international fame. They were: Garrett Birkoff in mathematics, Willard Van Orman Quine, philosophy, and Burrhus Frederic Skinner, psychology. I was entitled to attend the dinners, of course, as well as to participate in the selection process. Charlie Curtis, however, suggested before I had ever sat down to the first dinner that two Harvard presidents in any gathering were one too many. I agreed and appeared rarely. I never ventured to explain my absence to President Lowell, as it would have raised too many questions. He indicated occasionally that he regretted my absence.

As I have already recorded, in spite of an initial coolness, the president emeritus was as cordial as he could be. A letter he had written in June (which reached me before my return to America) reaffirmed what he had said to me at dinner in his house that night in May. He expressed the hope that I would strike out on a new path unlike that of my predecessors. Nevertheless, he felt there would be no harm in describing his own method of administration. What followed was a curious defense of the way he had carried out his duties. He claimed he had not had the qualities that President Eliot had had for detailed current administration of the faculty of arts and sciences, such as judging the proposals of the departments for appointments and promotions; he had not done it well, he said, for he had not studied the individual cases enough. After the war, Clifford Moore had become dean of the faculty of arts and sciences and had taken over the general administration; he had done it far better. Since then no details of administration had come to the president's office. He had cast the details and responsibility upon the deans and had allowed no one to interfere. Enclosed was a letter from the Director of the Museum of Comparative Zoology listing the members of the National Academy of Sciences according to their present university affiliations. Harvard led with forty; California and Yale were next with eighteen each. Chicago and Johns Hopkins followed in that order. The enclosure ended with the statement that "the showing is not painful to the Harvard eye"—a sentiment with which the president emeritus must have heartily agreed.

Actually, what my predecessor had told me about administrative procedures in May had been far more valuable than this letter. At that time he had stressed the importance of seizing the initiative (he was clearly afraid I would not). "Don't give up your right to preside at the meetings of the faculties," he had said with much emphasis. Then he proceeded to tell me about President James Rowland Angell's first year at Yale. He, Lowell, had advised Angell to insist on presiding at the first faculty meeting. Angell had not followed the advice. As a consequence, a proper relation to the faculty had never been established. When later Edward S. Harkness had offered a magnificent gift for the building of one or more colleges, the Yale faculty had insisted on considering the proposal. The debate had gone on for weeks until, in disgust, Harkness had come to Harvard, where the offer was accepted. The president of Harvard, unlike the president of Yale, had been able to act promptly.

The story made a deep and lasting impression on me. A few months earlier, as a professor and chairman of a department, I would have resented the implications. As a president-elect, I reacted quite differently. I accepted wholeheartedly the moral of the tale, thereby starting a line of thought which would eventually get me into no little trouble.

A few days before our dinner with President Lowell in May, I had learned from several members of the Corporation that there was trouble in the Law School which I should have to face. The internationally famous dean, Roscoe Pound, and the faculty were feuding. Someone suggested that one reason for the disarray was the fact that President Lowell had left everything to the dean and was never even seen by members of the faculty. With this bit of gossip fresh in my mind, I asked President Lowell about his relation with each of the faculties of the professional schools and elicited the information that he had not presided over the law faculty for years. "That was probably a mistake," he said, and urged me to start by taking the chair at the first meeting.

The subject came up again that spring at an informal meeting with one or two members of the Corporation. Therefore I was almost propelled into making a decision when I met with Pound for the first time in September as president of Harvard. I asked when the faculty met and announced I would be there to preside according to the statutes of the university. "We meet every Tuesday at lunch," was the gruff reply, "and you will soon get sick of coming." The prophecy was correct, yet I stuck with the task and in so doing was exposed to the sharp give-and-take of the most quarrelsome group of men I ever encountered. Whether my presence was of any advantage, I do not know. At least I came to know quite well in their fighting mood a number of eminent legal scholars with whom I otherwise should have had only a bowing acquaintance.

I soon discovered that the symbolic value of the president of the university's being in the chair at a faculty meeting might be great, but that the dean had the real responsibility in the professional faculties. To be sure, by tradition the presiding officer appointed all the committees; yet no president would think of appointing a committee without consulting the dean. He might have some influence, but the power was in the hands of the dean. The important administrative decisions were made in conferences between the president and the dean of a faculty. All the deans who were in office in 1933, except the dean of the Law School, were glad to have the president preside at a faculty meeting.

What President Lowell had been thinking about primarily when he told me the story of Harkness' proffered gift to Yale, however, was the faculty of arts and sciences. In this body the president of the university was not only the presiding officer but the person expected to introduce most of the new business. The stories about the forty years of Eliot's presiding had become legends. He was firm in his convictions and powerful in the presentation of his views, but eminently fair, people said. When his proposals were defeated, as they were more than once, he always took his reverse calmly and without harboring animosities (or so, at least, was the legend). Whether his successor had really tried to carry on the tradition was open to question. The old-timers said that the debates of Eliot's day had gone. One professor told me shortly after I became president that he had long ago stopped attending faculty meetings, since he did not want to intrude on the president's private business. The remark was bitter but not without foundation, as shown by Lowell's own evaluation of the way Harvard had reacted to Harkness' offer: it had never come to a vote in the faculty.

The all-powerful body in the faculty of arts and sciences was the Committee on Instruction, consisting of the chairmen of the departments. Since they were appointed by the president, and since the budgets depended in the last analysis on presidential decisions, the organizational pattern was firm and clear. The dean of the faculty (like all the deans appointed by the Corporation) was essentially the president's chief of staff.

Those who complained about the lack of free discussion were referring to those legislative matters that eventually required a vote of the faculty; they did not refer to appointments which, by tradition, were in the hands of the permanent members of each department. The chairman discussed each case with the dean, and eventually the recommendation went to the president and, in the case of permanent appointments, to both the Corporation and the Board of Overseers.

Neither budgets nor lists of appointments were even considered in a faculty meeting. Every professor holding an appointment without limit of time had a double function. He was acting as a member of a deliberative body when he discussed educational issues and voted in a faculty meeting. He was acting as an adviser to the Corporation, by way of the chairman of his department, the dean of the faculty of arts and sciences and the president, when he voted for the promotion of one of his colleagues to a professorship. It is important to bear the double pattern in mind. During the first year of my administration it was only the first, or legislative, function of a faculty member that appeared to need re-examination. Three and a half years later it was the second function connected with appointments which created so much trouble that a basic reconsideration of procedure was forced upon me by a large number of angry men.

It has been necessary to devote so much space to the organization of Harvard as it had developed by 1933 in order to illuminate several significant events that were to occur in the next twenty years. The first was a reform of the faculty of arts and sciences which was my response to the criticisms that, in recent years, everything of impor-tance had been railroaded through the faculty by way of the Committee on Instruction. Soon after taking office, I suggested that perhaps the faculty had become too large to be serviceable as a forum for debate. As person-to-person discussions with the older members of the faculty continued, the possibility of a change in procedure grew. After a few months' exploration of the idea with some of the more influential members of the faculty of arts and sciences, I decided to incorporate it in my first annual report, dated January 1934.

"Where the faculties are small," I wrote, "they function well as legislative bodies; where they are much larger than one hundred, their size, for many reasons, makes the transaction of business difficult." Therefore, I went on to suggest, "it would seem worthwhile for the larger faculties to consider the possibilities of having a council of about sixty members elected on some representative plan. If provisions were made for rotation in office in this body, essentially all the members of the larger faculties would serve in the course of a few years. Such a council might then function as all faculties did a generation ago and the smaller faculties do today."

The scheme was frankly borrowed from the New England practice of recent years. The large town meeting had given way to a small body of elected representatives who met as a group and functioned much as though they were all still town meeting members. Indeed, the *Harvard Alumni Bulletin*, in commenting on the change which was instituted in the spring of 1934, spoke of it as "The Faculty—Town Meeting Style." It was not to survive for long. The meetings went well and some changes in educational policy were accomplished. Yet in the fall of 1939 the faculty voted overwhelmingly to abandon the idea. To be sure, the vote reflected a mood of bitter resentment. Administrative decisions to implement a new appointment policy had just led to an outburst of criticism. It is only fair to say, however, that there was some truth in the allegation that the absence of regular faculty meetings open to all had prevented some dissenters from airing their complaints. What had looked like a good invention had failed.

Meanwhile, another encounter with the faculty, which confronted me in the fall of 1933, was to have a more durable outcome. It was in regard to faculty retirements. The tradition about retirements in Cambridge could almost be summed up in the phrase: "Harvard has no retirement age." President Eliot had retired at seventy-six after completing forty years of service as president. President Lowell had retired at the same age. Several eminent professors who were still active were in their seventies. The Corporation was well aware of this fact. The members also knew that my predecessor had asked a professor of economics to retire on reaching the age of sixty-six. This was considered an exceptional case, though quite within the rules of the pension plan. The question was: Should the Corporation fix a definite retirement age?

After several meetings a decision was reached. Harvard should have a flexible policy, but not as flexible as it had been in the past. Each case would be presented by the president to the Corporation. Three possibilities would be considered: the man in question might be asked to retire at sixty-six, according to the published pension rules, or he might be asked to stay on to sixty-eight, or—if he was highly distinguished and in good health—to continue on a year-to-year basis, but under no circumstances beyond his seventy-sixth birthday. The last provision seems strange today; in the 1930s, however, the idea of a fixed age for retirement of academic people was just starting to be promulgated in various institutions. Across the ocean, Oxford and Cambridge had been wrestling with the same problem. The story of the head of one of the Oxford colleges who died in office at the age of one hundred was, perhaps, apocryphal but symbolized what had been the academic tradition.

At the first meeting where retirements and pensions were discussed, one of the younger members of the Corporation suggested that the president of the university was *sui generis*, and his case should be treated separately. The senior fellow disagreed. Looking at me in a pleasant, fatherly way, he said something to the effect that the only thing he held against me was my age. I was forty. If I stayed on in office until I was seventy-six, as had my two predecessors, my term of office would be for thirty-six years. "And that is too long," said Mr. Perkins. "A president of a college after a few years sets his course and is unshaken on it if he is any good. The world, however, doesn't stay on one course; it goes off in another direction. The results could be bad."

I agreed at once, and no exception for the president was incorporated in the rules. What is perhaps equally important, I made a vow to myself that I would never let the situation arise. As a professor, I had examined the pension rules. I had found that while sixty-six was the earliest age at which a man on permanent appointment could be asked to retire, a professor might choose to retire at sixty. I made up my mind then and there that sixty would be the upper limit for me, though I was not at all sure I would survive the occupational hazards of a college president until the distant date of 1953.

It all seems obvious now. It was not obvious in 1933. Indeed,

President Lowell said to me more than once, "You must remain in office until 1969, when you will be seventy-six as I now am. If you do this, there will have been only three Harvard presidents in a hundred years. That will be a record for any institution! Furthermore," he added, "twenty-four years, which is all I have had, is too short a time; I came to the position too late in life." I could hardly contradict the president emeritus. Therefore, only to myself did I say that twenty years would be the maximum for me. I was giving no hint to the alumni or anyone else that I had thought about the end of the task I had taken on. Rather, I wished to create the impression that people would have to bear with me for years to come. So I delighted in telling a story about the roads in a Canadian province which had not yet been modernized for automobile traffic. Leaving the city and heading across the prairie, the traveler saw an enormous sign which read as follows: "Pick your rut carefully; you will remain in it for the next hundred miles."

It was all very well to make rules and regulations applying to members of the faculty who would soon reach the age of sixty-six; the real problem was what action, if any, should be taken about those who were already over sixty-six. The group included some eminent scholars. Among them, two in particular, Professor George Lyman Kittredge and Professor Frank W. Taussig, had many friends and admirers among the alumni. Professor Kittredge's course on Shakespeare had become legendary; Professor Taussig, while never held in such high regard by any large group of undergraduates, was counted as the foremost American economist. What would be the reaction when it became known that these men had been asked to retire? There might be a storm; we all recognized the possibility. Nevertheless, the president was authorized to proceed and do the best he could. Fortunately, both Taussig and Kittredge were wise and understanding men. They both recognized the need for a definite upper limit to the term of active service. In individual conversations, we explored the possibility of the matter becoming a subject of public altercation. Both professors would be seventy-six within a year or two, and each agreed to announce his voluntary retirement without reference to our conversation.

All went according to arrangement. When Professor Kittredge's forthcoming retirement was announced, some reporter for a Boston paper, suspecting that the new president might have been at work, tried to worm out of the Shakespeare scholar an admission that his retirement was not entirely voluntary. He failed. "Having reached a certain age, I have decided to retire," said Kittredge, "and that is all there is to it." There was no public discussion of the retirement age. Gradually over the course of the next few years, the news of the establishment of a fixed policy spread through the Harvard family. By no means all who were over sixty-six wished to stay until seventy-six. Therefore, from time to time, retirements were announced of professors who were in their late sixties or early seventies. Once the policy had been in effect a few years, the danger of controversy was passed. I shall always be grateful to Professors Taussig and Kittredge for their cooperation. A few words from the latter spoken in a different tone to the reporter could have added an unpleasant load to the burdens of the new president.

Up to this point, I have said little about the great depression. Yet the initial problems I was to face as a new university president were to a considerable degree a consequence of that catastrophe. One cannot appreciate the nature of many of the questions which had to be answered after 1933 without realizing the impact of the events in the immediately preceding years.

I had been almost immediately aware of the stock market crash of October 1929 because I was a trustee, together with one of my sisters, of a small inheritance left by my father, who had died a few years earlier. The holdings included, in addition to stocks and bonds, an apartment house in Boston. The financial uncertainties of the years after 1929 were forcefully brought to my attention, therefore, in my fiduciary capacity. Thanks to good advice, the inheritance survived not only the first crash, but even the more eroding effects on real estate of the early 1930s.

Some of my friends were not so lucky. They had bought stocks in the soaring market of the late 1920s on small margins. The first crash destroyed all they had invested. I remember one professor of chemistry who had been building up capital for his old age by acting as a consultant and obtaining high fees for his services. Early in the 1930s, he told me that before the crash he had thought he was "well fixed for life"; now he had almost no savings left. Since I had not attempted to "play the market," the increasing seriousness of the depression had no effect on my personal finances. Indeed, the depression days were affluent days for professors in institutions which did not cut salaries. The cost of living was low. Aside from my worry as a trustee, I could read the news of the grim years of 1930, 1931 and 1932 with considerable detachment.

To be sure, as a member of the Board of Scientific Directors of the

Rockefeller Institute for Medical Research in New York, to which I had been appointed in 1930, I was reminded of the financial pressures of the times. Elaborate plans for the extension of the buildings of that highly important research center had been drawn. Dr. Simon Flexner, the Director, had presented them in some detail either late in 1930 or early in 1931. I remember with what disappointment he announced a few years later that these plans had to be laid away for an indefinite period of time.

In the summer of 1932 a Harvard faculty committee was called together on an emergency basis. The deepening crisis, we were told, made it necessary for Harvard to consider cutting budgets. The closing of the Widener Library in the evenings was proposed and met with our approval. The athletic budget, about which we were not consulted, was in process of drastic reduction as the net income from the sale of football tickets seemed about to disappear. In general we received the impression, however, that thanks to President Lowell's prudence, Harvard was more than solvent. Unlike many other colleges and universities, there was no likelihood of salaries being cut. We gathered that some members of the Corporation, not the president or the dean, were responsible for our being called together. It was rumored that these members thought the faculty did not realize the gravity of the national situation. If for no other reason than to remind the professors of the kind of United States they were living in, some budgetary cuts were advisable. At the very least, there should be earnest talk about such matters.

Of course, I had not the least suspicion of what lay ahead in the next twelve months. I could not imagine the banks closing nor, for that matter, my being elected president of Harvard. Like the other professors on the emergency committee, I hardly needed a reminder from the Corporation that the depression was continuing and, according to the newspapers, daily getting worse. There were large numbers of unemployed. Budgets in other universities were being pruned. More and more students were finding it difficult to pay their bills. Family allowances were shrinking. We were disturbed by the plight of many undergraduates. During the winter of 1931–32, the number of families unable to supply their sons with money enough to meet expenses had been increasing rapidly. Scholarships in all institutions were completely inadequate both in number and in amount. In Cambridge, students had been turning in increasing numbers to the dean's office for aid or to the employment office for jobs.

Some people had suggested that the easiest way to meet the

difficulty was to put student waiters into the recently established Harvard houses. President Lowell, however, was reluctant to adopt this course; he did not like the idea of some students being served by others. Fortunately, among the effects of the depression was a great decrease in the cost of food, so that the dining halls showed an unexpected profit of some $40,000. President Lowell allocated this windfall to start a plan of student employment. With this start, a scheme was launched which continued throughout the depression years. Part-time clerical jobs around the administrative offices and in the library were created. In the year 1932–33, some 383 students applied for these jobs, and roughly 70 percent were given employment during the course of the academic year.

This way of helping the financial situation of college students had been spreading throughout the academic world as the intensity of the depression mounted. One of the consequences of the New Deal legislation that followed rapidly on Roosevelt's inauguration on March 4, 1933, was to make money available to the colleges through one of the alphabetical agencies to take care of part-time employment for college students. Before I had been in office many months, I learned that Washington had proposed to allocate federal funds to provide jobs for 100,000 students. It was expected that the federal expenditure would be $5 to $7 million in 1934. The money would be distributed through the state agency of the Emergency Relief Administration (ERA). The authorization was to be up to 10 percent of the enrollment of the college as of the previous October—that is, 1933. Harvard and a number of the privately endowed Eastern universities and colleges considered the possibilities of applying for these funds. After much discussion with the dean of Harvard College and other officials, and exchanges of information with other institutions, in March 1934 we decided in the negative, saying that Harvard appreciated the offer but, without passing judgment on its wisdom as a national measure, we found that we did not need to take advantage of it, since sufficient funds from the college's own resources were at hand.

Only because President Lowell had created a financial base for our own student-employment plan could we say to the federal government in March 1934, "No, thank you very much." That at least one member of the Corporation would have opposed taking public funds on general principles is clear from a letter I received just after the decision to decline the proffered assistance. I need quote only a few sentences:

There is growing pressure which one can read about every day in the *New York Times* for federal aid to all sorts of education on a great scale.

Once the federal government begins spending any considerable amount of money in this way, it must inevitably follow that it will seek to control the method of expenditure and it would not be long before such a system would extend to influencing the curriculum and even the personnel. These are not fanciful objections, I think, but are based on experience of the past.

The date of the letter was March 1, 1934. Eighteen months later, the Regional Supervisor of the Civilian Conservation Corps, addressing a Harvard summer school audience, said that the CCC camps might become a permanent part of the American system of public education. Such declarations by New Deal officials were sending chills down the spines of both public school administrators and prominent citizens.

It is amusing to note that seven years later, in March 1941, Harvard applied for and received $80,000 from the National Youth Administration for student part-time employment. There was no comment in the *Harvard Alumni Bulletin* about this application, and no letters were published from alumni. Apparently by 1941 the fear of federal money had largely disappeared.

The mood of 1933 is hard to recapture in 1968. Yet I must make an attempt to convey to those readers who have no personal knowledge of the depression some idea of how people felt in that crisis year. I can do no better than quote from an address made by Walter Lippmann at a meeting of the Associated Harvard Clubs in Cleveland in May 1933.

At the end of February, we had reached a paralyzing deadlock in our affairs. The federal government appeared to be impotent; the executive had lost his hold upon Congress; the party leaders in Congress had lost their hold upon the members of Congress. Public opinion was distracted and disheartened; there was neither direction nor unity in public life, and the result was a general conviction among the people that they were at the mercy of blind and ruthless economic forces which no one could understand or control. They came to believe that those forces were unmanageable by any conscious policy, and they saw that if this were true they were being pushed irresistibly towards a complete collapse of credit and established values.

This sense of hopeless impotence produced a great panic in which men, acting on the impulse of each for himself and the devil take the hindmost, tried to save what they could from the wreck. They demanded their money from the banks. They demanded gold for their money. At the climax of the panic in the last week of February, the paralysis of government had become so aggravated by the paralysis of the mechanism of exchange that the business of the country was brought virtually to a standstill. No highly industrialized nation has been subjected to greater potential dangers than we were at the end of February. We had a government unable to act and a people divided among themselves in the midst of a universal breakdown of the machinery by which great urban populations are sustained. The crisis was one which had to be surmounted without delay. It was not possible to let nature take its course and trust, as in previous great depressions, that the process of adjustment through liquidation of debts, fixed charges and rates would restore a working equilibrium. . . . The condition of the farmers and of the unemployed wage earners had become so desperate that a policy of laissez faire could not be contemplated. There is a limit to the endurance of a democratic people. In February we had reached that limit.

"There is a limit to the endurance of a democratic people," so Walter Lippmann had said. Although he had continued with reassuring praise of what Roosevelt had accomplished between March and May, yet as the months went by and prosperity had not returned, the question of the future of democracy in America remained in doubt. Whether one was a liberal or a conservative, young or old, one was worried.

It was a sober group of seniors and alumni who celebrated President Lowell's last commencement in June 1933 (I was in England). The traditional class reunions were carried out on a highly restricted basis. The prominent graduates were feeling poor; some envied the Harvard family. While the salaries of professors had not been cut, the income of many of the prominent alumni had almost disappeared.

A member of the class of 1933 at Harvard, speaking at his commencement on June 20, expressed an opinion which seems to have been widespread among undergraduates in the fourth year of the depression. "We have been forced gradually to unlearn a lesson," he said. "We have been forced to forsake reluctantly the teachings of the Golden Age. Our four years of college have coincided with the dismal years of the depression. Many of our members have been forced to abandon their studies. Others have been sorely pressed to meet expenses. Some, who never contemplated it, have earned their way. And now we all stand at the end of a road and look forward to what?"

CHAPTER 11

The 300th Anniversary Fund

M Y FIRST MEETING WITH the Corporation fell in September of 1933. It threatened to be an ordeal. The prospect of presiding over the same group of six men who only a few months before had been evaluating me like a potential race horse was unsettling.

We assembled in the usual meeting place, the office of Henry L. Shattuck, the treasurer, on Milk Street, Boston, promptly at 10 A.M. Mr. Perkins' first words, gaily uttered, removed my worries. "Now, fellows," he said, "we have a brand-new president; let's raise hell with him." He proceeded to do just the reverse; he acted as though I had been presiding over Corporation meetings all the years he had been a fellow. Francis Hunnewell, who had served long and well with President Lowell as secretary of the Corporation, had procedural matters so well in hand that I need not have worried on that score.

When the treasurer had finished his business about investments, the docket was in order. First came a mass of routine appointments; then it was my turn to present some ideas that I had been mulling over since June. I outlined what was eventually to become the basis for the 300th Anniversary Fund. Remembering President Lowell's admonition to seize the initiative, I was quite specific as to what I thought should be the next step in the development of Harvard. What we needed now, I said, were men, not buildings. An era of building had been completed. If we were to try to raise any new money in the near future, it should be used for scholarships and professorships.

120

Without debating the merits or demerits of my proposal, Perkins raised at once his grave doubts about the possibility of success in any undertaking to obtain funds. The burden of his remarks was that the country was in a most serious situation. No one could tell what would happen; Harvard's finances were in relatively good shape because of my predecessor's foresight and prudence; yet we had had to make many drastic cuts in many budgets. Was it wise to stir up the faculty by even thinking about new funds and a 300th anniversary campaign?

Grenville Clark was more sympathetic to new departures and more optimistic. If not at that meeting, then at one only a little later, he urged the desirability of bold planning. All agreed, however, that before my proposed program could be accepted by the Corporation, faculty sentiment had to be sounded. Moreover, they predicted, with budgetary cuts present or impending, the first reaction of almost every member of the academic community would be: "If Harvard is to seek new money, some must come to my department; we have been the hardest hit by the depression."

I recognized the validity of the objections. After all, I had only ceased being a professor some six months earlier. I knew the hungry departmental voices. Indeed, I had, not so long ago, been ready to shout with other chemists for fair treatment by the administration. Nevertheless, I suggested, the many separate demands might cancel each other out. The amount of money that could be raised at best would be small. Was not the wisdom of using it for purposes which would benefit the entire university quite clear? So it seemed to me. I had some supporters, for I had tried the idea out informally with most of the Corporation members before this meeting. I pointed out that the Tercentenary was coming on us rapidly. If we were to use the celebration in any way to raise new money, we had to complete our plans rather fast. On this last point there was complete agreement. It was further agreed that an exploration was in order.

For that purpose, a small, secret, informal committee was formed. Not for the last time, a former professor of the Business School, Donald K. David, was recruited to lend a helping hand. He was one of my oldest friends and certainly my most loyal and helpful one. A letter to him dated November 18, 1933, shows that within two months I must have convinced the Corporation as to the desirability of at least exploring the prospects of a campaign. For one of the questions on which I asked his opinion in that initial letter concerned "the organization of the campaign both in regard to general committees, executive secretary, chairman." Another question was how the Dental School campaign, to which the Corporation had been committed before I took office, could be merged with any others that might be launched. A young professor in the Business School was to be asked quietly to reserve time to help Donald David. We were obviously afraid of getting the faculty's "wind up," since I wrote: "I have not told anyone here yet of what is up, and I shall try to keep as few people informed as possible." The letter started, however, with the sentence: "I have written Mr. Clark and the other members of the Corporation about our plan." The new president was not trying any end runs around the Corporation. The Board of Overseers was another matter. The members could be informed if and when plans for a campaign were firmly fixed.

Before the calendar year 1934 was far advanced, a faculty committee was appointed. There was no final announcement about a campaign, but the veil of secrecy had been removed. The committee was to consider what should be the objectives of a 300th anniversary fund campaign if it was decided to launch one. On the advice of the secret group of which Donald David was a member, I had agreed to divulge my plans to the faculty committee and take my chances as to whether the professors would come up with other goals. As I had first proposed to the Corporation, the specific targets were to be: first, new funds for National Scholarships, and second, funds for a new type of University Professorship. Of these, the first, which was nearest to my heart, is discussed in the following chapter.

The basic idea of the University Professorships was to give the president and fellows flexibility in the appointment of outstanding scholars. The endowment of each position would be so large that the income could pay a handsome salary and provide research money as well. My original conception of a University Professor, as presented in my second annual report, written in January 1935, was expressed in terms of increasing the scholarly potential of the university as a whole. I spoke of "University Professors with roving commissions whose teaching and creative work shall not be hampered by departmental considerations." A year later, after working with deans about budgets and presenting the scheme to them, I could see how the original idea would also provide flexibility in a system which could otherwise easily become rigid.

Although in the fall of 1933 the depression had weighed so heavily on the mood of the nation that the Corporation was loath to authorize even an exploration of the possibility of asking for new money, two years later people had begun to be more optimistic. The Corporation was willing to authorize a campaign but no intensive drive. What was most important from my point of view, my double target had been approved by the informal faculty committee. On October 21, 1935, the president and fellows adopted a statement entitled "The 300th Anniversary Fund of Harvard University," and cleared the way for a money-raising effort. After explaining in some detail the intention behind the fund itself, as well as the concepts of the University Professorships and National Scholarships, the final section, carrying the heading "Why New Money Is Needed for These Purposes," summarized the current financial situation in these words:

The finances of the University do not permit these new plans to be carried into effect without the aid of new funds.

The University is in sound financial condition, but, in spite of careful financial management, there has been a considerable shrinkage of income from investments in recent years. Expense budgets have already been reduced and there is no way of making further economies without abandoning or crippling necessary or valuable work that is under way. At the present time, the balance of free University income remaining after the payment of ordinary operating expenses amounts to less than 1 per cent of the aggregate expenses of the University, so that virtually all income is now mortgaged for what must be carried on. Some of these existing claims on income are legally inescapable, being embodied in the special terms of deeds of gift. Others are less formal but hardly less binding—such as commitments for the continuation of salaries, the repair and upkeep of plant and the maintenance of budgetary allowances in reliance upon which long continuing research projects have been started. If the University Professorships are to be maintained, and if any considerable number of the National Scholarships are to be made available, it is essential that new money be found.

The following extracts from the memorandum sent to all alumni will explain what was proposed.

This memorandum is an attempt to state briefly the fundamental reasons why we believe new funds should be obtained to support University Professors . . . an important aspect of the matter is to have the funds as free from restrictions as possible, and large enough to provide not only an excellent salary but also ample research funds ($5,000 to $10,000).

In any university today there are two great obstacles to stimulating teaching and imaginative research. The first of these is a lack of flexibility in the organization which manifests itself particularly when new appointments or promotions are to be made; the second is the present separation of a university into a multitude of special departments which have all too little contact with each other. . . .

There are a number of mature scholars and scientific investigators who are not today members of any university staff and who would probably be loath to accept academic positions because of a feeling that their intellectual activities might be too rigidly confined within departmental limits. Such men may be carrying on important research in their present positions in research institutes or as private scholars, but their influence would be incomparably greater if they could be brought into an academic community. They would then be in a position to transmit their knowledge to a steady stream of students and inspire a younger generation to follow in their footsteps. . . . Thus, both directly and indirectly, these men now removed from the current of youth would take their proper places in the great educational process and impress themselves more definitely on the whole current of thought of the nation. All this would be possible if University Professorships were open to attract such men into the academic fold. A professorship "without portfolio," free from departmental restrictions, and with ample salary and research funds would appeal to men with broad imagination who now regard the teaching profession with only slight interest. . . .

It is the essence of the proposal that such University Professorships be free from departmental restrictions. They should not be assigned to any faculty or created with reference to any special subject. The Corporation should be left free to use the money for the outstanding scholar who is available whether he be found within the present faculties or somewhere outside. When or where he is found, the chair should be fitted to him rather than he be invited to fit himself into a chair.

For the time being at least, the demands of the many component parts of the university had yielded to an effort designed to benefit the entire Harvard family. The big question in 1935, however, was how the alumni would respond. The fears for the personal fortunes of those who had retained some degree of affluence were diminished. The stock market had not taken another dive; the banks had not been closed again. The temper of the country did not seem entirely adverse to a money-raising effort. The criticism of the university from conservative quarters had, however, increased. As the presidential election of 1936 approached, the tension between New Dealers and anti–New Dealers mounted. Harvard was blamed for the active part some of its professors and recent graduates had been playing in President Roosevelt's alphabetical agencies. Though many more Columbia professors were active in Washington than Harvard professors, the wrath of many was focused on Harvard.

I shall never forget an incident at the Harvard Club of New York dinner which I attended in January 1935. As we at the head table were preparing to take our seats, an elderly gentleman with drooping white mustache and a ruddy face came up and faced me. Speaking loudly above the hubbub, he leaned across the table and declared, "I want you to know that I and my friends *hate* the Harvard Law School." That declaration of alumni hostility was hardly a good omen for the success of the 300th Anniversary Fund. In fact, funds were to come in more slowly than had been hoped, and the realization of the plan for the University Professorships (as well as the National Scholarships) had to proceed gradually. Yet in my report to the Overseers dated January 8, 1940, I was able to say that we were fortunate

in having been able to secure for the first appointments eminent and stimulating scholars. We now have two University Professors and one University Lecturer who serve as connecting links between different departments of knowledge. Professor Roscoe Pound has been giving instruction in both the Law School and the College (Department of Government) for two years. Professor Werner Jaeger, who has just joined us, is both a historian of philosophy and a student of many other phases of the culture of the ancient world. Mr. I. A. Richards's concern with "basic English'" is of interest to the department of English and to the Faculty of Education. The work of these men will each year demonstrate the value of appointments which transcend the usual academic barriers—barriers which nowadays separate all too rigidly both educational and scholarly activities in any large and complex university.

It is interesting to note that in the current catalogue of the university, a whole section is entitled "University Professorships." The vote of the president and fellows of June 19, 1935, is referred to as the origin of these professorships, though I still stubbornly claim them as my invention. The catalogue goes on to state: "The non-departmental character of the appointments is indicated by the use of the title University Professor, without specification of subjects." Among the present incumbents are Professor Ivor A. Richards, Hamilton A. R. Gibb and John F. Enders, who are all University Professors Emeriti. Those professors who are now active include: Paul A. Freund, originally of the law faculty; Paul H. Buck, the former provost and professor of history; Edward M. Purcell, Nobel prize winner in physics; Edward S. Mason, professor of economics; Merle Fainsod, professor of government; Edwin O. Reischauer, former professor of Far Eastern languages.

As I mentioned earlier, in retrospect it seems strange that no member of the Corporation when they were looking me over, or after my election, had spoken seriously about raising money. No one had suggested that one of the prime jobs of the head of an endowed university was that of seeking more endowment. There are two reasons for what in 1968 must seem an inexplicable omission. First of all, the bank closings in March and April 1933 had so frightened people that the very thought of a college asking for new funds had been driven from their minds. Second, President Lowell was so proud of his success in tucking away sums of money for a rainy day that now that the rain was pouring down, he came close to boasting publicly of his prudence. Incredible as it sounds, at a small private dinner of the two governing boards in his honor in the first winter of his retirement, he said that Harvard needed no more money and probably never would. With my scheme for a 300th anniversary fund in the back of my head, I could hardly have agreed. Yet I was not going to protest out loud. Fortunately, one of the elder Harvard statesmen present at the dinner persuaded the president emeritus to omit all references to finances from the published version of his remarks.

In spite of the depression and the temporary closing of the banks, Harvard was in the black—a fact which did not have the same connotation for all the deans. Under the Harvard system of bookkeeping as it then existed (and continued to exist until at least 1953), each faculty had its own budget. "Every tub stands on its own bottom" was the phrase used by a predecessor of President Eliot in the first half of the nineteenth century. Translated into the budgetary practice of 1933, Harvard's policy was one of decentralization. Every faculty and most of the research organizations and museums had their own endowments, and each was expected to live off the interest of its endowment, together with student fees in the case of the degree-granting faculties. Instruction in the undergraduate college and in the Graduate School of Arts and Sciences was given by members of the faculty of arts and sciences and those on one-year appointments in the same faculty. There was no dividing line between an undergraduate and a graduate instructor. The Graduate School of Arts and Sciences was not a separate budgetary unit. Nor were the separate departments so considered.

My chief concern was with appointments in the faculty of arts and sciences. There seemed to be no system of over-all planning for the future. I had thought from the first that the faculty should be strengthened by calling some outstanding scholars from other universities. The department chairmen, who were quick to sense the mood of the new president, were ready to suggest names of those who might be considered. Since the entire budget had a surplus, there seemed to be no financial reason against going ahead and calling a few new full professors. This had been done in the winter of 1934. In spite of this, the next year's budget (1934–35) was still in the black. About halfway through the first year, however, Kenneth Murdock, the dean of the faculty of arts and sciences, who had held the position only a few years, and the financial vice president, John W. Lowes, called my attention to the fact that there must be some limitations on what even Harvard could afford. They spoke particularly of the young men who were on temporary appointments but were hoping before long to be promoted to permanent positions with a considerable increase in salary. If the ambitions of all these young instructors were met, the budget of the faculty of arts and sciences would be heavily out of balance. At that moment Lowes, in pointing out the potential deficit, made a wise remark which should be inscribed in red on a placard to hang in university administration offices: "If you count men, not dollars, and project the count into the future for the lifetime of all permanent appointments, a true picture of the budget will stand forth sharp and clear." The important words are "project the count into the future for the lifetime of all permanent appointments." Young men may be appointed to life positions at a salary satisfactory to them at the time. Before they are ready to retire, however, they will be at the top of the salary scale. A dollar budget balanced in terms of the salaries of today may be potentially out of balance because, in a decade, many of those on relatively low salaries will be entitled to much larger compensations. My acceptance of Lowes' bit of wisdom was to keep Harvard's finances in order for some years to come.

CHAPTER 12

The National Scholarships

I N THE CURRENT CATALOGUE of Harvard University, the section on Harvard College contains the following entry:

The National Scholarships were established in 1934 in order to enable young men of outstanding ability and promise to come to Harvard, no matter what their financial circumstances may be. The stipend is sufficiently large, if necessary, to meet nearly all of the student's essential college and living expenses. Successful applicants who maintain honor records will continue to hold their scholarships throughout their College course and, in many cases, throughout graduate study in a Harvard graduate school.

Anyone familiar with college scholarships will at once recognize that the awards described in this statement are somewhat unusual. The stipend is said to be large enough to cover all essential expenses; the scholarship can be held throughout college and in a Harvard graduate school provided the recipient maintains an honor record. Another feature which was novel in 1934 is described in a paragraph following the one I have quoted: "Since the National Scholarships are regarded as prizes to be competed for by all students, whatever their financial circumstances, the stipends will vary with the resources of the recipients."

This last feature was, at the time the plan was developed, called "the sliding scale." Purely honorary scholarships at Harvard were well known. Some years before, the John Harvard and the Harvard College scholarships, which carried no stipend, had been established. No one applied for them; they were given to those whose grades for the preceding year were at a certain level. To have one's name printed in the catalogue as a holder of one of these scholarships was to have a mark of high academic distinction recorded. It was also to have one's financial situation registered as that of a student who needed no assistance. On the other hand, the holder of the National Scholarship might be rich or poor; what was received from the college would be a matter known only to himself and the scholarship committee. Being listed as a recipient indicated only high standing as a scholar; it told the public nothing about a person's need for funds.

My original plan for the National Scholarships (or Fellowships as I first spoke of them) involved establishing a set of sliding-scale awards for incoming freshmen from a group of Midwestern states. If Harvard was to be a truly national university, I declared in my first annual report, we should attract to our student body "the most promising young men throughout the whole nation." We should be able to say that any man with remarkable talents may obtain his education at Harvard whether he be rich or penniless, "whether he comes from Boston or San Francisco." The Harvard alumni who lived west of the Alleghenies cheered when they read these words.

Indeed, the whole idea of assigning some new scholarships to a group of Western states was, in part, an answer to the restlessness of the Western Harvard alumni. For some years they had been complaining about what they claimed was Harvard's exclusively Eastern orientation. As a professor, I had been aware of the discontent. It had been brought forcefully to my attention again by a few leading Western alumni as soon as I was named president. The scholarship proposal was thus at first expressed in rather narrow Harvard terms. It was not until the Tercentenary was over that I was to broaden the argumentation in terms of the national interest.

The members of the Corporation liked the idea in general; the flexibility, the large maximum award and creating new scholarships in the Midwest appealed at once. Everyone granted the importance of recruiting more students from outside New England, which had always provided the vast majority of the student body. Thomas Nelson Perkins, however, expressed his initial skepticism in a trenchant question. How did I propose to select those incoming freshmen who would be recipients of the great honor? What criteria did I have in mind? The potential for success in collegiate work, I answered. We would hope that all or almost all holders would graduate *magna* or *summa cum laude*. I hastened to concede that we would miss many future leaders of the nation. There were qualities of great importance that were not measured by marks in courses. What other criteria, however, could one use in choosing outstanding high school graduates?

"All right," Perkins answered, "but can you make a fairly certain judgment about a freshman's chances of even academic success during a four-year course?" I replied that I felt sure we could and attempted to clinch the argument by suggesting that my belief could be put to a test. If the Corporation would authorize me to reshuffle certain scholarship funds, I could set up some sliding-scale awards in a few states. We could start in the fall of 1934 and in four years we would have some evidence as to whether my confidence was justified. We would have at least one group of seniors in 1938 whom we had picked to be high-ranking seniors when they were incoming freshmen.

The idea of a trial of the selection procedure appealed to Mr. Perkins and the others. They were ready to give me my head on a temporary basis. Therefore I was empowered to proceed at once.

The process of devising a mechanism of selection was soon under way. The first step was to consult the dean of Harvard College, A. Chester Hanford, and the college scholarship committee. At a luncheon at my house I put my proposal before them; I repeated Mr. Perkins' challenge (without giving the source). Could we make the choice with sufficient certainty? I wanted the college to bet heavily on the recipients. If the scheme was successful, it might change the whole attitude of the academic community toward financial aid to students. We all knew that, in spite of the honorary scholarships (or perhaps because of them), holding a scholarship was in many people's eyes a badge of poverty. These new scholarships were to be awarded only to those who were expected to be the top-ranking scholars of the class on graduation. The question was: Should we now gamble on the ability of the committee to choose potential winners? I warned that if the first recipients turned out to be mediocre students, the demonstration would have to be abandoned. If such was the outcome, the whole scheme would have done more harm than good.

The dean and the committee members all liked the proposal. They responded to my questions by asking me to appoint a subcommittee of Wilbur J. Bender and Henry Chauncey, then assistant deans, to look into selection procedures in other institutions. I could not have put the fate of the idea into better hands. These two young men were able to look at examination procedures with a fresh eye. They consulted those concerned with scholarships in Yale and Princeton. They were particularly impressed with what Carl Brigham had been doing at Princeton. The Scholastic Aptitude Test, which he had been instrumental in developing and which was already offered by the College Entrance Examination Board, seemed a promising device. In the course of a few weeks, the subcommittee reported that they believed a satisfactory selection procedure could be devised and proceeded to outline exactly what it should be. It consisted of requiring each applicant for the new scholarships to take the new Scholastic Aptitude Test as well as some of the orthodox types of subject-matter examinations. The results of personal interviews by someone from the college as well as the recommendation from the school were to be given great weight.

The report was endorsed by the full committee. Though it was already winter, we decided to proceed with the announcement. The awards would be open for the time being only to those entering Harvard from the old Northwest Territory—the states of Minnesota, Wisconsin, Michigan, Illinois, Indiana and Ohio. That we were embarking on an experiment to test our ability to choose "worthwhile young men" before entry into college was made quite clear. Though only a few months intervened between the announcement and the last date for filing applications, we received 250 applications the first year.

We were able to scrape together funds enough to award ten scholarships. A few years later, thanks to new gifts, the number of states had grown to sixteen and the number of new recipients to thirty-one. Of these, I noted in my annual report for 1936–37, ten prepared for college in private schools, twenty-one in public high schools. Slightly more than half came from communities of under 50,000; eight had attended schools in towns with populations of 2,500 to 10,000. In presenting these figures, I reported that:

It is becoming increasingly clear as we proceed with our scholarship plans, that we are providing opportunities for certain youths who would otherwise not have been able to attend any institution of higher learning. Those of our staff engaged actively in the selection of scholarship holders who have travelled in the different states interviewing applicants, have been impressed with the large number of able youths throughout many sections of this country whose financial resources are too scanty to allow them to proceed with a first class education.

In the same annual report, I justified the decision to have the maximum stipend "high enough to take care of the student's total expenses" by pointing out that probably three-quarters of the families in the nation received an annual income of $2,500 or less. (At this time, there had been no real recovery from the depression.) In view of such figures, hardly anyone could question the inadequacy of a scholarship that covered only a half or a quarter of a student's total expenses, nor could anyone deny that the learned professions suffered from their inability to recruit talent from all economic levels. My report continued:

In the past the danger that the capable boy without money would be eliminated was to some extent avoided by the opportunities afforded for working one's way through a university. In many localities these opportunities are now rapidly diminishing; furthermore, we are coming to realize at what cost to health and well-rounded development the poor boy has all too often obtained a higher education. With the increasing emphasis on the importance of having a student's scale of living commensurate with physical well-being and the growth of a well-adjusted personality, the need for scholarships and other forms of aid becomes more pressing.

I attempted to answer the critics who were protesting that Harvard was trying to rob the Midwest by bribing the most promising high school students with fabulously high awards, and quoted Dean Hanford on the subject as follows:

Our experience so far has also led us to believe that the National Scholarship plan has very important social implications and that Harvard College is rendering a worthwhile service to the nation by widening the opportunities for higher education. . . . It is possible that a university will be criticized for embarking upon a plan which it may be claimed attracts able students away from institutions in their own sections of the country. Our experience shows that the number of high ranking, all-around students is large enough to give each institution its share and that there are a large number of promising boys who are financially unable to attend a college even in their own section. A large endowed university has a very special social obligation to widen the opportunities of education regardless of residence, birth and financial circumstances. By attempting to maintain carefully and rigidly the sliding scale principle of adjusting the stipend of a scholarship, unfair competition can be avoided.

The last sentence had particular significance. It reflected Dean Hanford's concern lest a high school student accept a Harvard National Scholarship only because the sum of money attached was larger than that offered by Yale or Princeton. Our ancient rivals had been busy recruiting in the West years before Harvard had announced its National Scholarships. By interchange of information with these institutions, it was hoped that the amount of money which was involved would not be the determining factor in a potential freshman's decision to accept a scholarship in one college rather than in another.

A letter I had written as early as 1936 to an alumnus in San Francisco gives contemporary evidence as to how Dean Hanford and the scholarship committee were thinking as the experiment got under way.

Frankly, the main reason why the Midwestern states were chosen rather than those of the Far West for the initial experiments in this plan was simply because that section was not too remote from Cambridge to make the expense of personal interviews prohibitive, it contained a very large number of College Board Examination centers, it had a large population—particularly of high school seniors, and at the same time was far enough away from Cambridge to be consistent with the ideals of this scholarship policy. The essence of the plan is, of course, to increase Harvard's representation in the very places where it is weak. . . . There is considerable interest in this plan even among Massachusetts graduates, for, although it may be a very long time before any National Scholarship is awarded to a Massachusetts man, yet graduates in this state feel that their own sons will benefit by the broadening contacts with outstanding men from other parts of the country.

Another letter written in the same year to Frederick Lewis Allen of *Harper's Magazine* indicates that I was having difficulty explaining the new policy:

Incidentally, if I may say so, I think you have overlooked the really novel aspect of our scholarship scheme. . . . The principle which I think you have overlooked is what we call the sliding scale with full indemnity at the top. In short, hitherto scholarships have usually been of such amounts that they could be given only to boys who had some other way of providing part of their expenses. They were not large enough to tap new areas of the population. Furthermore, the amount of the scholarships was not graded according to the financial status of the applicant. The more brilliant the boy, the larger the sum of money. This was the old policy. The new policy is to make the award on merit, everything considered, and then to adjust the stipend according to the need. The stipend, if necessary, is large enough to provide for all demands during the nine months of college. The further aspect which is novel here but not entirely novel in this country is to award the scholarship for a period of years after the initial tryout of one year. I trouble you with this explanation merely because your letter indicates that we have failed to drive home to the alumni the important aspect of our scheme. Perhaps we should claim more credit for the novelty, at least in this country. As far as England is concerned, of course, we are merely reproducing here what has been done at Oxford and Cambridge for a few years although the sliding scale is really a comparatively new thing there.

In 1936 the Harvard scholarship committee had developed in cooperation with their opposite members in Yale and Princeton a special one-day scholarship examination. A Scholastic Aptitude Test was given in the morning and objective achievement tests in various fields in the afternoon. By April 1937 just over two thousand candidates took this new one-day examination in the various College Entrance Examination Board Centers throughout the nation. Of these, over half were applying to Harvard and Yale. The examination was so well received by many colleges that it began to be used for admission of those who were not applying for scholarships. By April 1938 twenty-eight institutions were involved; somewhat more than four thousand candidates wrote the examinations, of whom twelve hundred were not candidates for financial awards. The record seems to show that Harvard's interest in the use of objective tests for selecting national scholars was an important factor in promoting the use of these tests for general admission purposes. My own interest in the new type of examinations certainly was aroused by the report of Bender and Chauncey and its outcome. Eventually it would lead to my playing a part in the establishment of the Educational Testing Service.

I must emphasize that the procedure for selecting Harvard National Scholars could only be introduced because the whole admission policy of Harvard College had been drastically remade in the previous decade, under President Lowell's administration. I had been a member of the faculty during the reform, and indeed I had served on one of the committees. Before the reform, admission to Harvard College had been based on success in the college entrance examination given under Plan A or Plan B. The former was the plan that had been in effect when I entered the college in 1910. The examination papers were the type that came to be called "essay examinations," in contrast to the "objective" type developed in the early 1920s. According to Plan A, the candidate aimed at obtaining fifteen credits. Passing an examination in a definite field, such as elementary French or advanced French or chemistry, yielded two credits, except for Latin and Greek, which benefited from a protective tariff supported by the professors of classics, who were fighting a rear-guard action: success on the examination in elementary Latin or Greek yielded four points each. Plan B differed in requiring only four examinations in those subjects specified by the college in question.

At a time when admission officers at Princeton, Yale and Columbia were already considering the new Scholastic Aptitude Tests, no one at Harvard in a position of influence showed interest. When in 1926 the College Entrance Examination Board offered the SATs for the first time, of 8,040 who took the test, only 536 were headed for Harvard as compared with nearly 1,300 headed for Yale, almost the same number for the University of Pennsylvania, and just under 1,000 for Princeton. The use of the new-type test obviously was not being encouraged at Harvard in the 1920s. Yet the faculty were well aware that they faced some of the same problems that faced their contemporaries in other Eastern institutions.

The large increase in enrollment in grades 10, 11, and 12 of the high schools since the close of World War I had opened a promising field from which an alert admission officer might pick talented candidates. (An interest in athletic prowess on the part of football-minded alumni was not without its importance then and for the next three decades.) The high schools, however, no longer were willing to consider themselves as preparatory schools for college. Changes of curricula were making it difficult for a boy to get ready to take the college entrance examinations. The teachers in the schools, both private and public, were in no mood to be dictated to by the Ivy League colleges. The whole trend was against strengthening the instruction in mathematics, science, Latin, Greek, French and German in the public high schools of the country. Only in the large Eastern cities, particularly New York, Boston, and Philadelphia, would the boy from a low-income family be able to prepare for Harvard in a selective public school such as the Boston Latin School. As a consequence, the student body of Harvard College in the early twenties was rapidly becoming a far from well-integrated collection of youth from the private preparatory schools and those from the public schools in certain cities.

The Harvard answer put forward by a special committee in 1927, of which L. J. Henderson had proved to be a highly influential member, became known as the "upper-seventh plan." What was provided was admission without any examination for those who stood in the upper seventh of the graduating class in those schools judged by the admission committee to be unable to prepare their college-bound students for the orthodox College Board Examinations. The all-important limitations excluded would-be candidates who went to school in New York and Boston and nearby communities. The beneficiaries of the revolutionary reform were supposed to be those who lived in towns and small cities. So they were, in fact. The proportion who entered Harvard under the upper-seventh plan was never large, but the scheme enabled some promising youths to enter who otherwise would never even have tried. That our national scholars were in part coming from the smaller communities for which the upper-seventh plan was devised was demonstrated by the figures in my 1936–37 report, which I have already cited.

The significance of the upper-seventh reform lay in the fact that the scholarship committee to which I turned in 1933 was not restricted in its deliberations by faculty votes requiring all entering freshmen to have passed this or that examination. In theory, entry into Harvard was already open without any examination to a certain group of boys. If it had been otherwise, I would have had to have a faculty vote approving the details of the selection procedure. I am sure that when the faculty approved the upper-seventh plan, any possibility of a future connection with a new scholarship scheme was far removed from anybody's mind.

The fact that one needed to argue for scholarships in 1933 must seem a curious fact to many readers. I must admit it was my stock in trade for the first few years of my presidency. In my speech to the annual dinner of the Harvard Club of New York in January 1934, the proposed new scholarships played a considerable part. The speech was not a success, my friends told me; I was too obviously scared. I had stuck to reading from a text. An address to the Associated Harvard Clubs meeting in May went better. Again the main theme was the elimination of artificial barriers—geographical or financial—in our educational system.

The following November I addressed the annual meeting of the Middle States Association of Colleges and Secondary Schools—my first formal presentation of my ideas to an audience of educators. I had been given the formidable task of speaking on the topic of "The Function of the Secondary School and College in Educating for Social and Cultural Leadership." After splashing the audience with many obvious truths not very well expressed, I struggled in the waters of defining leaders and culture, and finally emerged on dry land by a reference to one more truism, namely, that our future leaders ought to be "recruited from the ablest material." From then on, I could make what had become a standard speech. The questions are, I said: "How are we to choose the ablest for higher education, where is the education to be given, and how financed?" One out of every four students graduating from the secondary schools of the country entered a college or university, I said. (The figure is more than double that today.) Obviously a selection process was at work. I raised the question whether the selection occurred in such a way as to serve the best interests of the country and concluded it did not. I gave it as my opinion that we should aim to have the scholarship funds of the country used in such a way as to enable the high school graduates of real ability to enter our universities irrespective of the financial status of their parents.

With the rashness of a green college president, I plunged into the question of the curricula of the schools to what was offered in the colleges. I said I had the feeling that it would be well to recognize that there were many students who had high ability in mathematics but little ability in the study of foreign languages and vice versa. Such a difference might well be recognized in planning the course of study two years before entering college (I was expressing a point of view I had held as a professor of chemistry; it was based on no substantial evidence, and before long I abandoned it). As a forecast of my subsequent thinking, the following sentences are worth recording:

It seems impossible that we shall ever return to the day when it is felt essential that everyone who is going to college shall have studied two years of algebra, geometry, Latin, French and German. But I cannot help wondering if we have not in some quarters gone too far in making such subjects optional. If all the students are not subjected to a certain minimum of mathematics and languages, can we make an intelligent decision about the advisability of each individual's pursuing further this or that branch of study?

The question was an extremely cautious protest against what I had already found was going on in some schools as part of the progressive movement. I was a bit bolder when I declared that "an insufficient training in mathematics and languages would have serious consequences for those very youths whom we all agree should be the guiding lights of the future intellectual development of this country." In the next sentence I stumbled backward into the nineteenth century by speaking of "insufficient mental discipline"—I was soon to drop this set of words like a red-hot poker.

All in all, it was the speech of a person who really did not know what he was talking about but who had one conviction, namely, that large scholarships should be granted to enable high school graduates of "real ability to enter our universities irrespective of the financial status of their parents." The point I was attemping to make was understood and well received by many in the audience. I particularly recall one speaker from the floor who called my attention to Thomas

Jefferson's educational philosophy. At once, I made a mental note
of the relevance of the cited quotation. From then on, I was a Jeffer-
sonian, and a year later I was repeating the quotation in an address
at the fiftieth anniversary of the founding of Bryn Mawr College.
"Thomas Jefferson," I said, "writing in 1815 to Cabell about Albemarle
Academy, soon to be the University of Virginia, formulated an educational policy which I believe should be our guide in the development
of the liberal arts colleges in the future. He wrote of the importance
of 'culling from every condition of our people the natural aristocracy
of talents and virtue and of preparing it by education at the public
expense for the care of the public concerns.' "

When the attention of one of the top officials of the National
Youth Administration in 1935 was called to my remarks, he was not
enthusiastic. Asked about my proposals for more and larger scholarships, he replied that all the scholarships provided by private institutions could only be a drop in the bucket of the educational needs of
the country caused by the depression. He was, of course, completely
right. However, I was annoyed by the comment at the time. A New
Dealer had brushed aside my attempt to tie the need of Harvard to
the welfare of the nation.

CHAPTER 13

Concerning Academic Ceremonies

To most people an academic ceremony conjures up visions of a solemn, short procession of professors wearing gorgeous gowns with strange hoods hanging down their backs, followed by an almost endless parade of youth wearing gowns of drabber hue. There are memories of a beautiful sunny June day, of an audience ready to applaud, of speeches, of a rather tiresome ritual and, finally, of the handing over of a document to youth after youth as they move across the stage. Certainly the brightest memory is that of the pleasure of friends and relatives as they offer congratulations. The day stands out as the marker of the accomplishment of an objective. Even the honorary-degree recipients feel they have received a well-earned tribute.

Quite frankly, I envy those who cherish such uncomplicated benign memories. For me, the thought of academic processions has quite other overtones. In the first three or four years of my service as president of Harvard, the academic ceremonies in which I played a part were more than once hazardous events. There were no calamities, but there were unexpected troubles. Concern with the weather and the details of plans for escorting and seating highly honored guests is standard for all colleges at commencement time. I do not propose to inflict on the reader an account of my reactions year by year to such difficulties, which are so familiar to all college presidents. Rather, I present some rather unusual events connected with a few academic gatherings over which I have presided in the course of twenty years.

139

The tales I have to tell point up the minor hazards of a university president's official life. They carry no moral, but I hope they may provide a degree of entertainment. To set the tone, I shall start with an anecdote from New Haven.

As the story goes, President Angell of Yale (one of the wittiest men I have ever known) was in process of awarding an honorary degree to President Ernest M. Hopkins of Dartmouth College. The two men faced each other on the platform in Woolsey Hall. Angell was about to pronounce the official words awarding the degree, and an assistant was in the act of placing a hood over Hopkins' head, when a man in the front row of the audience had an epileptic fit. The proceedings were suspended; in the noisy confusion that followed, Hopkins is alleged to have said, "I am sorry to be the cause of the death of a prominent Yale alumnus." "That is quite understood," snapped back Angell. "We are used to protests about honorary degrees, but this is the first time we have had one so promptly."

The first Harvard ceremony that caused me difficulties involved a protest not about an honorary degree but about the supposed presence in the audience of an alumnus who, as a matter of fact, was absent. The date was June 1934; Hitler had come to power in Germany a little over a year before. Already the Nazis had made evident that their offensive anti-Semitic words were becoming the basis for action. Furthermore, the reality of a totalitarian grip on education was daily becoming clearer, as the news about purging the universities reached the United States.

Ernst F. S. Hanfstaengl of the Harvard class of 1909 was said to be a close personal and political friend of Adolf Hitler. A news dispatch from Berlin in April stated that the chief marshal of the forthcoming Harvard alumni festivities in June, Dr. Eliot Cutler, had named Hanfstaengl as one of his aides. It must be understood that the afternoon ceremonies on Commencement Day in Cambridge were entirely in the hands of the alumni; a member of the class celebrating its twenty-fifth reunion was elected chief marshal in midwinter by the directors of the Alumni Association. The chief marshal then appointed a number of his classmates to the honorary post of aide. Those who understood the implications of what had been going on in Germany since March 1933 were disturbed by the prospect that a personal friend of Hitler's would be a commencement aide. Even the slight honor involved was resented.

When it was learned through the press that Hanfstaengl had arrived in New York in early June and that he would attend the various events of his class reunion, the disquiet of some alumni reached my desk in the form of letters; a few critics made statements to the press. Whatever one might think of Hitler or of Hanfstaengl, however, it was perfectly plain an alumnus had every right to take part in a twenty-fifth reunion. I notified my correspondents that Harvard would not consider taking any action to interfere with such a right.

One of the events on the schedule of the twenty-fifth-reunion class was a reception by the president of the university two days before commencement. The time allowed was short; the affair was rather formal. The members of the class, their wives and children were welcomed by Mrs. Conant and me as they entered the ballroom of the President's House. Each alumnus was identified by a badge. Hanfstaengl was in about the middle of the line which filed past us. As I shook his hand he said, "I bring you greetings from Professor Hoenigschmid of Munich." My response was cold; I did not return the greetings. I had received many kindnesses from the professor in 1925. But knowing his political orientation then, I guessed in 1934 that if he was on intimate terms with Hanfstaengl, he was probably an ardent Nazi. (I later learned my suspicion was correct.)

Leaving the professor's views aside, I had another good reason for making our conversation as short as possible. I had on my desk a letter from Hanfstaengl dated May 24, Berlin; he released it to the press two weeks later. It contained an offer of a scholarship. At the Corporation meeting the day before, we had decided that a consideration of the offer would be postponed until the first meeting in the fall. The reception line was no place for me to transmit this information to a man whose every movement was followed by the press.

That the press was interested is shown by an incident on commencement afternoon described in the *Harvard Alumni Bulletin*:

[Hanfstaengl] was relentlessly pursued by newspaper reporters and photographers. He attended most of the exercises held by his class but kept out of the public eye as much as possible. He was not seen in the Yard during the Commencement proceedings but the next day was at the boat races in New London.

Some of Hitler's enemies apparently [and mistakenly] assumed that Hanfstaengl would be at the meeting of the Alumni Association in the Sever Quadrangle on Commencement afternoon, and they seized the opportunity to make a demonstration while the exercises were going on. President Conant had almost completed his address, when feminine voices were heard shouting and screaming in the seats at the Quincy Street side of the quadrangle. In the confusion it was impossible to hear all the words uttered, but enough was audible to make it plain they were protests against

Hitler, Hanfstaengl, and the German government. Aides and police hurried to the spot and found two young women handcuffed to the structure supporting the spectators' seats. The handcuffs were locked to the timbers; it was necessary to tear them down in order to remove the disturbers who continued their harangue till at length they were carried out of the enclosure. In the meantime, President Conant showing no sign of perturbation ended his address, and the alumni chorus sang one of its numbers on the program.

A little later in the afternoon, two young men were found handcuffed to the fence around the Massachusetts Avenue side of the Yard where they attracted a large crowd too. They, too, were taken into custody by the police.

At the request of Harvard, the case against those arrested in the Harvard Yard was not pushed. The seven arrested in the square, however, were convicted in a jury trial, which they demanded, received a stiff sentence of six months at hard labor, but were pardoned by Governor Joseph B. Ely.

The protesters on commencement afternoon had achieved one end. They had given vast publicity to Hanfstaengl's relation to Hitler —a relation, it is important to note, that Hanfstaengl never denied. When the Corporation met on September 24, the item with top priority on the docket was Hanfstaengl's letter to me from Berlin, which had been acknowledged but remained unanswered. It read as follows:

DEAR PRESIDENT CONANT:

Unfortunately there is still some doubt whether or not I can attend the unique—alas—never returning twenty-fifth anniversary of my class.

It is my profound conviction that my years at Harvard have since given me incalculable advantages, not the least of which consist in a knowledge of America and the world and in the spirit of discipline and fair play inculcated on the sporting field of Harvard.

American energy, character, and idealism personified in men like Benjamin Franklin, Emerson, Longfellow, James, Eliot, Higginson, and Roosevelt have ever been an inspiration to me. I have decided, therefore, as a modest proof of my loyalty to double the sum of my class subscription. I should like this donation of $1,000 to be known as "the Dr. Hanfstaengl scholarship."

This scholarship is to enable an outstanding Harvard student, preferably the son of one of my old classmates, to study in Germany in any field of art or science. It is requested the scholarship be assigned for work covering one year, six months to be spent in Germany's art center, my native city of Munich, the remainder in any other German university.

I do hope that I may be in a position to renew this scholarship in coming years. This, to my mind, would fittingly symbolize my perennial love and affection for Harvard, Boston, and New England. It would, moreover, constitute an additional factor in the important process of intellectual, scientific, and human interchange between the United States and Germany, without which there can be no true insight, no true understanding, no true progress.

I should be very happy indeed, Mr. President, to hear from you in which manner you contemplate awarding this scholarship.

Sincerely yours,
ERNST F. SEDGWICK HANFSTAENGL

The decision to accept or refuse had to be made that day. The press was waiting for the story. In June we had announced that the question would be decided at the first meeting of the Corporation in the fall. The meeting was now at hand.

I could well imagine that the people in Berlin thought that the new president of Harvard would be open to their approaches. In 1925, at a time when anti-Germanism was strong in America, he had come to Germany with his wife for a visit of many months; he had made a number of German friends; the first few months he had been in office as president of Harvard, he had attended a ceremony in Boston at which the German Ambassador had transmitted an academic award to Dean Roscoe Pound of the Harvard Law School. In reply, Pound had spoken well of the government in power in Germany, and the president of Harvard had remained silent. (I had refused to be photographed with either the ambassador or the dean, but this negative gesture was probably not reported to Berlin.) What may have been noted by the German cultural authorities was the absence of any Harvard representative on the Emergency Committee for the Refugees, which functioned in the summer of 1933. (As a matter of fact, the nonparticipation of Harvard was a consequence of the interregnum in the presidency.)

Since I might have been expected to have determined policy, Berlin might well have concluded that I was not disturbed by what was happening in German universities. Hence, an offer of a scholarship by an alumnus might have appeared to be an appropriate way of opening communications. Whether my suspicions were correct or not, the demonstration commencement afternoon now meant that the Corporation's action was bound to be regarded by the public as a judgment on the Nazis. Such considerations were evident as we considered my draft of a reply.

I was quite certain that I knew more about Germany and the

Nazis than any other member of the Corporation. I was not only strongly anti-Nazi, but I was convinced that Hitler's henchmen were trying to use Harvard as an American base to spread approval of the Nazi regime. Therefore, without referring to the responsibility I had as the man who would sign the letter, I argued for the flat rejection of the proffered scholarship by all seven of us. To me the answer was clear and simple. Hitler's followers had violated the freedom of the universities; professors had been fired, curricula tampered with. Irreparable damage had been done. Irreparable was too strong a word, Mr. Perkins said. I agreed and removed the adjective. Otherwise my draft was approved. The letter was dated September 24 and addressed to Hanfstaengl in Berlin:

DEAR SIR:

At a meeting of the President and Fellows of Harvard College held today your offer of a travelling scholarship, to be known as the Dr. Hanfstaengl Scholarship, was considered. I am authorized to say that although the Corporation appreciate your generosity as a Harvard alumnus, they have voted to decline your gift. We are unwilling to accept a gift from one who has been so closely associated with the leadership of a political party which has inflicted damage on the universities of Germany through measures which have struck at principles we believe to be fundamental to universities throughout the world.

Since your offer was made public and has been the subject of discussion, we deem it proper to make this letter public.

The public reaction to our letter was favorable. The Boston *Herald* for October 5, 1934, ran a long editorial which, after some flattering words about the "still untried young man at the head of Harvard," asked what were the German measures to which the Conant letter referred? The answer was given in four excellent paragraphs. The impact of Nazism on German cultural life was neatly summarized. Turning to Hanfstaengl, the writer of the editorial said that as an individual he was negligible, as a symbol all-important, and that my letter crystallized the resentment directed toward the government of which he was the symbol.

The next stages in the Hanfstaengl affair bordered on the ridiculous, as had, indeed, the protests on commencement afternoon against the presence of an individual who was actually not on hand. An ingenious holder of a Harvard A.M. and a Ph.D. from Freiburg entered the scene. He wrote to offer a scholarship of a thousand dollars to finance a year's study in Germany "along the lines suggested by Dr. Hanfstaengl," adding that it was a pity to rob some deserving student of a year's study in Germany because of Dr. Hanfstaengl's political convictions.

We could hardly refuse this offer out of hand. I asked for consultation and brought in the dean of Harvard College. The upshot was a second, more detailed letter from the professor in which the sum involved was raised to $1,500. The phraseology made it clear where he stood and provided us with a reason for declining the offer. The would-be donor wrote that "this scholarship is given to replace the one offered by Dr. Ernst F. S. Hanfstaengl" and ended his letter by expressing his wish "to restore to some deserving student the privileges of study in the New Germany which Dr. Hanfstaengl had in mind." The secretary of the Corporation answered on behalf of the president and fellows that the Corporation declined the offer because of its explicit identification with Dr. Hanfstaengl's letter.

In reporting the action, the *Harvard Crimson* added an interesting bit of information. It appeared that in October a German newspaper had printed a story revealing that the author of the new proposal had cabled Germany telling of his offer and saying he wanted to "put his services" at the disposal of the Nazi press agency. In the same German newspaper article, a cable from a Harvard professor was made public which condemned the Corporation's action in refusing Hanfstaengl's scholarship. Everyone knew the professor named in the *Crimson* article was strongly pro-Nazi. Therefore there was no surprise but considerable amusement when the *Crimson* of November 23 was read.

What the enterprising undergraduate reporters had discovered should have ended all discussion of Hanfstaengl and his scholarship. The only reason it did not was because of the kind of error which can occur in the best-run fund-raising activities. In early 1935 a letter went to all alumni of Harvard College asking for subscriptions to the 300th Anniversary Fund. Among the thousands of recipients of the letter was none other than Dr. Ernst F. S. Hanfstaengl. From Berlin he replied promptly to ask whether the letter he had just received meant I had changed my mind. My face was red. My answer was lame. By 1935, however, the sentiment in the United States had become so anti-Nazi that there was little publicity of my "clerical error." Not many years later, the news reached us that Hitler had become disenchanted with his close friend, who had barely escaped from Germany with his life.

The hazards of academic celebrations continued after the Hanfstaengl case was closed. On two occasions, the anniversary of the founding of a famous German university caused the president and followers of Harvard College to make decisions that were not well received in certain quarters. The first was the celebration of the founding of Heidelberg. The question was: Should we send congratulations and a delegate? I had composed the letter which expressed the Corporation's opinion that Hitler and his followers had damaged the universities. Should we have any truck with these damaged institutions? They were still under Nazi control. The case for a sharp refusal was easy to make. Many members of the faculty thought we should do just that. (Like voting on honorary degrees, sending Harvard delegates was by tradition in the hands of the governing boards, not the faculty.)

On the other hand, some of us had the Tercentenary Celebration very much on our minds. In September 1936 we were proposing to have a meeting of renowned scholars and scientists from all over the world. We thought there should be some academic men who were still in Germany among them. Not all the eminent professors had been forced to leave. No one was talking openly about war in 1935. Even if one despised the regime in power, should not one be ready to build a scholarly bridge between two nations? We weighed the pros and cons and sent greetings and a delegate to Heidelberg. The public announcement brought down a sharp shower of abuse. No one seemed to remember our letter to Hanfstaengl.

The next round was after the 300th Anniversary. It was a request to participate in the celebration on May 14, 1937, of the two hundredth anniversary of the founding of the University at Goettingen. Remembering the reception of the decision about Heidelberg and with the news from Germany increasingly distressing as anti-Semitism ran wild, we decided to slap the German officials gently. The secretary of the university wrote that while we had hoped to send a delegate, "the president and Fellows find themselves unable to do so." The letter enclosed a greeting which was hardly warm and friendly. In part, it read as follows:

The Two Hundredth Anniversary of a celebrated Society of Scholars cannot but be an occasion of significance to the learned world. That significance is especially marked in the case of a university whose services to the extension of knowledge have been as brilliant as those of the University of Goettingen. The contributions of your great teachers during the past centuries, and the direct benefits which American scholars have gained as their personal disciples, exemplify a function which knows no geographical or political boundaries, and the fruits of which are beyond all calculation. It is our earnest wish that all universities may survive the vicissitudes of these troubled times, and that the peoples of all countries will not fail to recognize that in the freedom and fraternity of the scholarly world lies the surest hope for the preservation of all that is best in our civilization.

If I threw discretion and good maners to the wind, I could recount not a few cases when the Board of Overseers disagreed with the Corporation's decision to award an honorary degree to a controversial figure. The Board of Overseers has the final word. In only one case in my time was the question raised whether it was final. A member of Franklin Roosevelt's Cabinet, Henry A. Wallace, was chosen by the Corporation to receive an honorary degree of doctor of laws in June 1935. There had been no objection by the Overseers' committee to which such votes were first referred. Nor had any voices been raised at the full meeting of the board. Therefore I wrote and asked if the proposed recipient would honor us by his presence. He replied he would. Then, unfortunately, he took upon himself the task of coming to a New England city and delivering himself of an attack upon New Englanders.

The anti-New Deal sentiment in the Board of Overseers, which had been growing for the last year, found expression at the next to the last meeting of the year. Some wanted the offer of an honorary degree withdrawn. I expressed as forcefully as I could opposition to any such action. Both as a matter of principle and practicality, I considered the idea impossible. Several speakers agreed. After a certain amount of spleen had been relieved, one member rose to make a suggestion. The board had many standing committees, he noted. One of ancient vintage was the Committee on the Happy Observance of Commencement; why not place the matter in their hands? The ensuing laughter finished the matter. Commencement proceeded without disturbance, including the afternoon meeting at which Secretary Wallace, among others, spoke.

The academic ceremony toward which my gaze had been directed ever since I first talked with members of the Corporation was the Tercentenary Celebration. It has been described in *The Tercentenary of Harvard College,** a volume of 492 pages prepared with loving care by the director, Jerome D. Greene. My major contribution to what was hailed as a truly great occasion was in the choice of the director. Greene had been secretary of the Corporation in the last years of President Eliot's administration. Then he had entered the investment business and had prospered. During the early days of the depression,

* Cambridge, Harvard University Press, 1937.

the firm of which he was a member failed. He was left with almost nothing, forced to sell a lovely house and grounds. He never complained and, indeed, never referred to his days of prosperity. He was a true gentleman, conservative in matters of taste yet a liberal on all academic questions. He made no attempt to hide his worship of President Eliot, to whose views on almost all subjects he subscribed. I had met him only once or twice, but knew of him by reputation. I also knew he was available at an appropriate salary for an academic post.

About the middle of the first academic year I was in office, the members of the Corporation overcame the caution I have earlier described and authorized the planning of a 300th anniversary campaign. Who should head it? I suggested Jerome D. Greene. "Not for a money-raising effort," said Mr. Perkins, who knew him well since he had been a member of the Corporation when Greene served as secretary. "But if you want someone to plan and run the festivities," he added, "he is the man for you. He will do a hand-painted job." As usual, Mr. Perkins was right—he did. Greene took office in May 1934 and in the fall became the secretary of the Corporation as well as director of the Tercentenary Celebration.

Greene's first task was to win the confidence of the Tercentenary Committee, composed of alumni, some faculty representatives and members of the two governing boards; it had been in existence some years and since the election of a new president had been waiting for guidance. In a couple of meetings Jerome Greene had learned all that the members had to contribute. In describing the preparations for the year-long celebration in his final report, he modestly referred to the conclusions of the Tercentenary Committee as the basis for the plans. As I was in and out of the discussions, I can testify that Greene himself provided most of the ideas. And what is even more to the point, he saw to it that they were carried out.

According to the director, the basis for his plans were the following conclusions of the Tercentenary Committee: (1) The emphasis should be laid on exhibiting the resources of the university of today rather than on the retrospective aspects of the anniversary. (2) The celebration should be the occasion for rendering services appropriate to the functions of a university, namely, the holding of summer schools, conferences and institutes, culminating in a special gathering of distinguished scholars representing various fields of learning, who should present the results of their research at a conference. (3) One day of the celebration should be largely given over to the alumni.

(4) The period of the concluding ceremonies should include September 18, 1936, the date on which had been convened in 1636 the General Court which on November 7 had reached the vote to establish Harvard College.

From the point of view of the historian, November 7, 1936, would have seemed more appropriate. The difficulties of a day in November were apparent, however. The university would be in session; the weather would be uncertain; an outdoor ceremony comparable to commencement would be a hazardous undertaking. As a concession to meticulous scholarship, the director proposed to start the Tercentenary Year on November 7, 1935, with a meeting in Saunders Theatre at which the Tercentenary Historian, Samuel E. Morison, would speak. The conclusion would be three days of continuous ceremonies, September 16, 17 and 18, 1936.

In March, 1936, to keep the spirit of the Tercentenary Year going, the president was to deliver a speech to a second meeting in Sanders Theatre. The date, March 20, was the date of President Eliot's birthday; but much as I revered the memory of Mr. Eliot, I decided to direct my remarks entirely to the future. I addressed myself to a question which today, as I write, is still being asked: What is the special function of a privately endowed institution?

If I had had more experience with state universities and their presidents, I might well have banished any thought of asking and answering such a question. What I said, I would not retract today. But I certainly would balance my conclusion by recognizing what were the special functions of a state university. As it was, my emphasis on the freedom of a board of trustees of a private college or university to launch new undertakings, as contrasted with the administration of a state university which must seek appropriations from a state legislature, was not well received in certain academic circles.

Mr. Greene, in planning the midwinter Harvard family party on President Eliot's birthday, had expressed the hope that I might use the opportunity to make the equivalent of an inaugural address. "You were not publicly inducted into office," he pointed out with some sadness, "and have never presented a full-length account of your ideas." To some degree, I was ready to respond as Jerome Greene desired, but at a later date. I knew I had a far more significant speaking engagement ahead, namely, as the orator on the final day of the ceremonies. That speech required real preparation. I was by no means enthusiastic about accepting the assignment. Against my reluctance and my doubts about my adequacy, however, Jerome Greene, backed by the Corporation, raised the unanswerable question: Whom could he invite to be the main speaker, if not the president of the university? I bowed to the inevitable.

From the first of July on, there could be no doubt that Harvard was holding a birthday party. The university was put on view. Special guides conducted tours through museums, laboratories and libraries. It was our endeavor to show through Harvard's Tercentenary the significance of three hundred years of academic history. To that end the summer was given over to a series of conferences and special sessions arranged by the various professional faculties. These conferences were attended by graduates of the various schools and by many visitors.

The Tercentenary Conference of Arts and Sciences, held during the first two weeks in September, was designed to bring together all the varied activities characteristic of a university. Invitations to participate were sent to more than ten thousand members of the faculties of fifty-four universities and colleges in this country; in response over two thousand members of the academic community of North America assembled in Cambridge. The papers presented by seventy-one specially invited scholars were divided equally between the four quadrants of the modern learned world: the Arts and Letters, the Physical Sciences, the Biological Sciences and the Social Sciences. The symposia which were the focal points of the conference were arranged to cut across the conventional lines of academic interests. Those who prepared the program sought to bring to bear on a single large problem the diverse points of view of widely separate academic disciplines. It was the verdict of the participants that the attempt was successful.

The audience, composed as it was largely of professors in American colleges, needed no special meeting such as this to be convinced of the essential unity of the learned world; but to the public at large the symposia served to symbolize the common tradition the universities have preserved for nearly a thousand years. They served also to demonstrate what in those days was rarely appreciated by those unfamiliar with academic affairs, namely, that however separate and lonely individual investigators may appear, they are in reality close neighbors. The conference was in a sense merely a reunion, as it were, of old friends—a renewal of intellectual ties which had their origins many centuries ago. The joint labors of these scholars proved once again that it is because of specialization that knowledge advances, not in spite of it; and that cross-fertilization of ideas is possible only when new ideas arise through the intense cultivation of special fields.

Although the papers presented were but little concerned with the direct application of knowledge, they nevertheless were reported at great length in the daily press. The accounts thus published were admirable. Everyone rejoiced in the widespread interest aroused by this Conference of Arts and Sciences. Here was conclusive evidence, it could be said, that this country prizes the triumphs of the mind for their own sake, as well as for their utility. At least this became one of the favorite themes of the new president of Harvard.

Our success was largely due to the international scholarly fame of the participants in the conference. The list of speakers had been carefully drawn by a faculty committee a year before. We realized that those who were invited, if they had not already received honorary degrees, must be offered the degree at the time of the celebration, which would be a few days after the close of the conference. Thus the list of sixty honorary degrees had to be approved by the two governing boards during the winter. I had the challenging task of writing the short citation which I was to pronounce in handing over each of the degrees. As I read the list over thirty-odd years later, such names as Sir Arthur Eddington, Arthur Holly Compton, Jean Piaget, Bronislaw Malinowski, Carl Gustav Jung, Ronald Aylmer Fisher, Friedrich Meinecke and Étienne Gilson strike me. It was a distinguished group, representative of the international world of scholarship, which honored us by their presence. The names of Hans Kelsen, Peter Debye, Werner Jaeger, all residents in the United States, are reminders of what the Nazis had already done to German scholarship. Black shadows surrounded all the gatherings; in the year 1936 the probability of still another European war was never far distant from our minds. The three or four Germans who had been permitted to attend spoke to each other cautiously when they spoke at all. In the background for those who were concerned with such materialistic goals as raising money was the knowledge that the depression was by no means over and the Tercentenary Fund campaign was going badly.

The three Tercentenary days were dedicated to the delegates, to the alumni and to the academic ceremonies, in that order. Universities all over the world were invited to name a delegate. Oxford, Cambridge, the University of Paris, and John Harvard's alma mater, Emmanuel College, Cambridge, for historical reasons were asked to send someone who would take a speaking part in the exercises on one of the days. These special delegates, as well as the recipients of honorary degrees, were entertained in a way which was unusual for the time. Well over a hundred guests with their wives were invited for three days by families in Greater Boston. The amount of work in making such arrangements can be imagined. The director's office carried a share of the burden. A ladies' committee headed by Mrs. Conant was involved for many days with the many details. This rather Napoleonic scheme for mobilizing the "proper Bostonian families" on behalf of Harvard's hospitality was the product of Greene's imagination. It was enormously appreciated by the visitors. No one expected it of New Englanders, more than one academic man from the West admitted. The proverbial chill of Boston seemed to have been dissipated for at least a spell of favorable academic weather.

President L. D. Coffman of the University of Minnesota spoke on the second day of the celebration on behalf of all the American universities. After pronouncing the conventional words of congratulations and praise, he reminded Harvard that New England had moved West. Speaking of the Harvard men on the faculty of his university, he observed that "many of them become quite human again, even democratic, and sometimes socially minded after they have spent a few years with us." He expressed the opinion that it would be for the public good if there were a few other institutions rivaling Harvard in every respect, some of them state universities scattered across the country. Other state university presidents may well have shared President Coffman's slight annoyance with Harvard's ambitious plans for a year-long anniversary celebration. If so, the hospitality with which they were welcomed and the tone of the ceremonies changed their attitude. So I was told by several well-placed observers.

To accommodate the crowds for the speeches, the space between the Memorial Church and the Widener Library was filled with chairs. A temporary platform was erected on the south side of the church. Such an arrangement came to be known as the Tercentenary Theatre and has been put together for every Commencement Day since.

Early in the planning, we had decided that the final day would follow the pattern of commencement. The morning would be academic, with everyone in cap and gown (except the members of the governing boards, in formal attire with tall silk hats). The afternoon would be at the disposal of the Alumni Association. Whatever might be arranged later as to the speakers at the morning and afternoon exercises, there could be no doubt that one person should be invited, namely, Franklin Delano Roosevelt, a Harvard alumnus and the President of the United States. As early as November 7, 1934, I wrote President Roosevelt; a letter from the director of the Tercentenary Celebration followed a week later. On receiving a favorable answer from the White House, Greene and I took it for granted that the distinguished speaker of the day would be the President of the United States and that he would address the alumni gathering in the afternoon. Yet I foresaw there might be difficulties. Hostility to the President was mounting. The Tercentenary Celebration would be followed in less than two months by a presidential election. What the sentiment among many alumni would be when the New Deal placed its record before the electorate was easy to imagine.

Nearly a year and a half went by, and then trouble began. The directors of the Alumni Association at their winter meeting in 1936 voted to ask President Emeritus A. Lawrence Lowell to be the presiding officer at the afternoon Alumni Association meeting which would conclude the Tercentenary Celebration. Greene and I applauded the invitation. Mr. Lowell, however, was less than pleased when he discovered that Franklin D. Roosevelt had already been invited to attend. He said, in fact, that he would not preside over a meeting at which President Roosevelt spoke.

The president of the Alumni Association, Judge Learned Hand, argued with Mr. Lowell most effectively. He pointed out that it was unthinkable to have the President of the United States present and not have him speak. The morning session was to be strictly academic and not an appropriate occasion. Therefore a speech by President Roosevelt in the afternoon was inevitable unless there was to be a public scandal. Mr. Lowell let himself be persuaded, but insisted that if he was going to preside, he would arrange the program as he saw fit. Thereupon he wrote a curt letter to the President of the United States, to which the recipient took such strong exception that he turned to his close friend Professor Felix Frankfurter for advice on how best to answer.

I regret that the ensuing correspondence has been published. In my opinion, it is unworthy of both the president emeritus of Harvard and the President of the United States. Moreover, the tone of Lowell's letter, which seemed to be that of a schoolmaster telling a pupil what to say (or rather what not to say), can only be understood if one remembers the reason for his annoyance. He had been placed in a position of having to introduce a man whom he despised to an audience which he loved.

An "Illumination of the River" the evening of the second day of the celebration was a combination of a fireworks display and a nautical journey of the university band on a large lighter decorated with Japanese lanterns. The start was the public landing on the Charles River Esplanade; the point of debarkation, the Weld Boathouse. It was a gorgeous evening show, and the Great Day lay ahead. The weather forecast was favorable, and everyone went to bed with anticipation of the great events to come.

Except for tension about my Tercentenary Oration, I was without a worry as I donned the traditional president's gown in my house and then walked to the Massachusetts Avenue entrance of Widener. I paid no attention to the heavily overcast sky.

Confusion before an academic procession starts is traditional. Scholars put on their robes and wander about greeting friends and disobeying instructions. I was in the middle of the confusion in the lower hall of Widener, welcoming guests, when suddenly I looked at the gown on the person whose hand I was shaking. There seemed to be water on it. Involuntarily I reached forward, swept my fingers over the front of the gown and drew back my hand in horror. "Your gown is wet," I exclaimed. "Yes," the guest replied, "it's raining; didn't you know it?"

I soon discovered from Greene that the weather forecast was most unfavorable. A hurricane had unexpectedly changed its course. The rain would become heavier toward noon, but there might be a short break in the storm before that time. There was no time for consultation. Greene urged that we proceed with the morning exercises as planned. The President of the United States had arrived and was ready to be moved from the shelter of the Memorial Church to the open-air platform where all specially invited guests were to assemble.

We went through with the morning exercises according to schedule. It drizzled, and the tall silk hats and the gowns got wetter and wetter. The audience did not flinch, however, though some put up umbrellas. Three-quarters of the way through the program, there was a brief letup. I delivered my oration, which was extremely well received, probably a tribute to my audacity in delivering it on a rainy day. (The text is presented in the appendix.) The sixty honorary degrees were conferred without undue haste, although a particularly heavy downpour marked the last few minutes of the ceremony. The meeting was formally concluded with the singing of the familiar metrical version of the Nineteenth Psalm and Bishop Lawrence's benediction.

The idea of a solemn, dignified procession from the platform to Widener was abandoned. By now, the rain was coming down in force. The President of the United States, who had sat through the ever-increasing rain without showing a sign of annoyance, moved back into the Memorial Church. The academic dignitaries with their dripping clothes almost ran to the protecting shelter of the Widener Library. Robert Blake, the head of the library, was given grateful thanks from many renowned scholars for providing Scotch whisky in abundance.

In spite of the rain, luncheon was served as planned. The alumni gathered under canvas in the Memorial Hall Delta. The dignitaries were entertained inside Memorial Hall in the vast room which had once been the undergraduate "commons." All thoughts of proceeding with the Tercentenary Theatre had been abandoned. A hurricane carries with it a certainty that cannot be defied. Only a small fraction of the morning's audience could be admitted to Sanders Theatre, which held only a few more than a thousand.

The alumni meeting was called to order by President Lowell as President of the Day just as though there were no such thing as bad weather. I had asked if I could be both the first and the last speaker on the program. I explained that I felt under obligation to report on the money-raising campaign just ended. I would also like to follow the precedent of 1836 and move to adjourn the meeting for a hundred years. "I understand," Mr. Lowell said. "It is difficult to combine the offering with the benediction."

He arranged the order of speakers so that my report on the Tercentenary Fund came first. It was followed by a carefully timed message from the University of Cambridge delivered over the radio by the chancellor, who was the Right Honorable Stanley Baldwin, Prime Minister of the United Kingdom. Then came the reading of a letter from the Right Honorable William Lyon Mackenzie King, Premier of Canada, and an address by Judge Learned Hand, president of the Alumni Association. Unexpectedly, President James Rowland Angell of Yale threw in an observation, in a short speech, which has become part of Harvard folklore. He reported that on his way to the ceremonies a few minutes earlier, he had heard a dripping alumnus remark: "This is Conant's way of soaking the rich."

The President of the United States was to be the next speaker. Everyone in the audience was curious as to what he would say. Greene, Judge Hand and I, who had not forgotten the difficulties in persuading President Lowell to preside, were equally curious as to what he would say in introducing President Roosevelt. He simply stated that Harvard had given four sons to the presidency of the United States—two Adamses and two Roosevelts: "Gentlemen, the President of the United States."

President Roosevelt, who knew he was facing a predominantly hostile audience, began with a subtle yet bold defiance. I rely on my memory rather than the printed record since I had every reason to remember the words he said:

> A hundred years ago when Harvard was celebrating its two hundredth anniversary, Andrew Jackson was President and Harvard men were sore afraid. Fifty years ago, when Harvard was celebrating its two hundred and fiftieth anniversary, Grover Cleveland was President and Harvard men were sore afraid. Today, I am President.

He stopped, standing boldly, not finishing the rest of the sentence. What was implied was clear. The audience responded to his audacity by an immediate outburst of applause. The remainder of his speech was not political and quite suitable for the occasion, thus relieving any worries that the Tercentenary platform might be employed as a rostrum for an electioneering speech.

The meeting closed with the passage of the motion I had asked permission to propose. I moved that "this assembly of the alumni be adjourned to meet in this place on September 18, 2036." In putting the motion, the chairman, President Lowell, said a few courageous words which were far better than an oration:

> Before putting the motion, I want to say a word in its favor. If I read history aright, institutions have rarely been killed while they were alive. They commit suicide, or die from lack of vigor, and then the adversary comes and buries them. So long as an institution conduces to human welfare, so long as a university gives to youth a strong, active intellectual life, so long as its scholarship does not degenerate into pedantry, nothing can prevent its going on to greater prosperity. In spite of the condition of many things in the world, I have confidence in the future. Those of you, therefore, who believe that the world will exist one hundred years hence, and that universities will then be faithful to their great purpose, will say "Aye"; contrary-minded "No." It is a unanimous vote.

CHAPTER 14

Promotion and Tenure

MY CONVERSATIONS with the members of the Corpora-
tion before my election had made it evident that if I became president
of Harvard, one of my first concerns would be with appointments to
the various faculties. I had misgivings about what seemed to be the
criteria for choosing members of the teaching staff of the faculty
of arts and sciences. I had expressed the view that every permanent position should be filled only by an outstanding scholar and
teacher.

Just before Christmas, 1933, Dean Kenneth B. Murdock and I had
a conference about the general principles which should apply to the
reappointment or promotion of junior members of the faculty. In a
memorandum summing up our conclusions, I stated that I would be
loath to recommend anyone for a fifth year on an annual appointment.
I also expressed the view that a second three-year term as faculty
instructor should not be offered unless the department felt that within
the next year or so it would be ready to make a recommendation for
promotion. As to assistant professors, I wrote that after a lapse of six
years (two three-year terms) at this grade, a reappointment would not
ordinarily be favored. Then I added a caveat which, without my knowing it, pointed to trouble ahead. Referring to the appointment of
assistant professors, I said, "As long as conditions remain as unfavorable as they are for placing men, it may be necessary to continue such
appointments. We do not feel prepared to take the heroic step of

putting them [i.e., the assistant professors who had served two terms]
on the street." A few years later, I felt it was necessary to take just
such a step in connection with some of the younger men on the
faculty of arts and sciences, with results that could only be described
as a faculty rebellion. It might have come sooner if I had followed
more diligently the policy set forth in the memorandum. For I subsequently discovered that in 1933 there were already a number of
instructors who had been serving on annual appointment for more

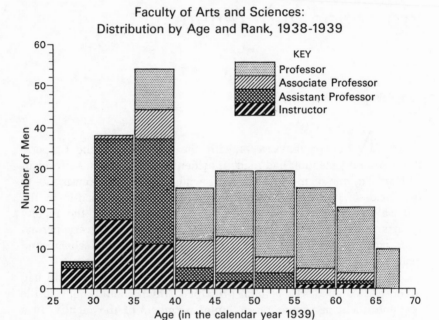

Faculty of Arts and Sciences:
Distribution by Age and Rank, 1938-1939

than the suggested limit of four years. The significance of what later
came to be called the "up-or-out policy" was not realized until I decided to apply it in the winter of 1936–37.

In the meantime, the preparation for the Tercentenary and the
organization of the 300th Anniversary Fund had distracted my attention from what should have been my first order of business. The
appointment of the distinguished mathematician, George Birkhoff, as
dean of the faculty of arts and sciences in 1935 forced a more careful
appraisal of the situation of the younger members of the teaching
staff. It was at that time that the admonition of the financial vice
president of the university, John Lowes, had a major impact on my

thinking. He had said, in effect, count men rather than dollars in forecasting the future. When one surveyed the roster of the faculty of arts and sciences with the age and rank of each member clearly stated, one saw trouble ahead. The nature of the trouble was best shown by examining a chart which showed the distribution by age and rank of the members of the faculty of arts and sciences. Such a chart for 1938–39 is reproduced on page 158; it was published in November 1939 in the *Harvard Alumni Bulletin* when the storm about the administration's promotion policy was at its height. The first charts I drew up by hand myself in 1936 were not dissimilar. Particularly revealing were those that showed the disproportionate number of young men on temporary appointments in certain departments.

In publishing the chart for 1938–39, the editors of the *Bulletin* had the following explanatory words about the past, present and projected future of the faculty of arts and sciences.

From 1924 to 1933 the income of the Faculty of Arts and Sciences increased nearly eight-five per cent. This enormous increase was due partly to the prosperity of the 1920s and partly to the increase in tuition and in the number of students. From 1933 to 1939, however, the income of the Faculty increased only three percent. . . .

During the period of prosperity, as indicated by the augmented budget, there was a natural temptation to expand the teaching staff, particularly at the lower academic levels. In the 1920s there was every reason to believe that, by taking a group of promising young men into the service of the University, teaching of freshman courses and tutorial work would be much improved at a period when it was most needed. The gain to instruction by this expansion of the staff cannot be doubted by anyone.

On the other hand, without realizing it, the University had become involved in a very serious personnel dilemma. When the depression struck Harvard, as it did about 1932, and the interest rate fell, it became apparent that it was time to take sober stock of the situation in each Faculty. The diminution in the University's financial prospects, it was hoped then, would be temporary; no one wished to economize by releasing young men from the staff. Hence the problem of facing the future tenure of these young teachers was postponed.

When President Conant assumed office in 1933 he was obliged to face a worrisome condition. As the difficulty was carefully studied by the president and his advisers, it became more and more apparent that there was a group of deserving and very able young men in the University to whom there was no commitment but who had natural hopes that they might find permanent positions on the Faculty of Arts and Sciences. This excess of younger men was particularly apparent in some of the larger departments which, because of increased undergraduate interest in their subjects, had found it necessary to enlarge their programs of freshman instruction and tutorial work.

The extent of this change in the composition of the teaching staff may be illustrated by noting that in 1924–25 the number of permanent members of the Faculty (professors and associate professors) was about equal to the number of non-permanent members of the staff (assistant professors, Faculty instructors, and instructors); whereas in 1933 the number in the non-permanent staff was more than double the number in the permanent staff.

A moment's consideration of these figures demonstrates one incontrovertible fact. It is abundantly clear that a system of promotion which would work well when the number in the non-permanent ranks was no more than equal to those in the permanent ranks was bound to fail when those on temporary appointment had more than doubled in comparison to the older men. Annual appointees were marching forward with a strength of about thirty per year, three-year appointees with a strength of about twelve per year, and permanent appointees with a strength of less than five per year.

The "worrisome condition" the new dean and I faced in 1936 could not be better stated. It would have been well if the administration had had at hand some such lucid statement of its predicament to give to every faculty member, young and old. As it was, we had nothing comparable. Indeed, neither Dean Birkhoff nor I fully understood at first all the implications of the task we had undertaken. We were groping our way toward a first formulation. The best we could think of doing in the fall of 1936 was to show the charts to department chairmen and explain these graphic ways of setting forth the personnel problem of the faculty. Some understood, as did also certain senior members of the faculty. A number, however, were less than happy about the diagnostic picture and rather resented talking about long-range plans. What was obviously called for was either drastic surgery or a massive increase in the number of associate and full professorships (permanent appointments).

Unfortunately, the prospects of raising new money were slight. The 300th Anniversary Fund was not prospering. All signs pointed to the difficulties of financing any large number of new permanent positions.

The only other possibility was to continue those who held annual appointments or three-year assistant professorships at the same rank and salary year after year. In which case, in five years some forty men between ages forty and fifty would be holding temporary appointments. That they would be satisfied with such positions was extremely unlikely. As chairman of the department of chemistry, I had had a little experience with young men holding appointments for three years. I was firmly of the opinion that by the time an individual was approaching middle age, he should have an appointment without limit of time and enjoy a commensurate salary. The memorandum I had written so soon after taking office was based on such a belief. I had emphasized the need for permanent, well-paid positions for faculty members beyond a certain age. Within a few years such a doctrine would be accepted by almost everyone, but not in 1933, nor by 1937, when my troubles became public.

The Oxford-Cambridge tradition was quite otherwise. A person might stay on as a tutor in the universities without ever becoming a professor. A variety of arrangements with a college might provide for his living expenses. Since the tutorial systems of the English universities had been President Lowell's model, I am sure he would not have agreed to the fundamental premise in my thinking. It was going to take more time and far more trouble than I had imagined to shift the almost unconscious attitudes of most members of the faculty.

John Lowes and I had agreed so thoroughly that we had never stopped to spell out the divergence of our joint view from what I might call the Oxford attitude. This attitude is exemplified by a question that was to be raised frequently by those to whom I endeavored to explain the significance of the charts. Granted that Mr. X cannot be promoted because there are no permanent, well-salaried positions available in his field; why can he not be permitted to stay on indefinitely on annual appointments as long as he functions satisfactorily as a tutor? My answer was, in effect, that no American college would be in a happy state if there were two groups of teachers of approximately the same age, one holding professorships, the other annual instructorships. To which one of the doubting chairmen might have said, if he could have looked into a crystal ball, "But if you try to put into effect the policy which is based on your premise, you will make Harvard College a most unhappy place."

No one ventured such a prognosis, although one chairman at least came close to some such prediction. He tied it, however, to the sensitive topic of the political views of the younger men, which indeed was to play some role in the crisis that ensued. The application of the policy to the department of economics resulted in Dean Birkhoff's sending in March 1937 letters to two young economists, Dr. J. Raymond Walsh and Dr. Alan R. Sweezy. They held three-year appointments which were expiring. The letters informed them that they were being recommended for two-year appointments, at the conclusion of which they would not be considered for further appointments.

The existence of these letters soon became public. Since both Walsh and Sweezy were officers of the recently established Teachers Union, a story of sensational value for the press was at hand. One evening during the April recess, the news office was faced with the alternative of issuing a statement or remaining silent while the next day's papers played up a story that Harvard had "fired" the two officers of the Teachers Union. The decision fell to me, and I assisted in composing a press release. As things turned out, the release was totally inadequate, and I would have done much better to have directed the news office to remain silent.

The release stated that Dr. Walsh and Dr. Sweezy "have been offered two-year concluding appointments as instructors in economics at Harvard. Their cases present no unusual features; decisions in regard to these men by the department of economics and the administration have been made solely on grounds of teaching capacity and scholarly ability. There has been no departure in this case from the principles laid down in a recent report of an Overseers Committee or the department of economics." The release then quoted from the report in question, which stated that views on controversial public issues should be left aside in considering a new member of the faculty. The phrase "concluding appointment" was left unexplained; there was not a word to instruct the reader about the new personnel policy at Harvard.

To large numbers of the Harvard community and almost all of the general public, the entire press announcement was taken to mean that the two gentlemen in question were being dropped because of their inadequacies as teachers and scholars. The protests were soon heard loud and clear. That the president had not only stumbled but put his foot in a hornet's nest was more than evident. I tried to right the public record by issuing a week later a long statement to the Board of Overseers. In it was said what should have been said seven days earlier. I pointed out that not everyone in the junior ranks could look forward to promotion to a permanent rank; that it was no kindness to a young man to keep reappointing him if there was no future for him in the university; that the decision in the case of Dr. Walsh and Dr. Sweezy did not mean they were not good teachers, but "simply that in the opinion of those within the university best qualified to

judge, there are others among their contemporaries of greater potentialities."

Whatever the merits of the declaration, it came too late. The publicity about what came to be known as the Walsh-Sweezy case had
aroused misgivings among the younger members of the faculty. On
May 18, 1937, I was called on by a committee of nine professors from
several faculties bearing a petition addressed to them by over a hundred members of the teaching staff (chiefly assistant professors or
instructors). The petitioners had asked the committee to inquire not
only into the specific case of the two instructors but into related matters that bore on criteria and methods of making promotions. The
group asked me to name them as a committee to make the investigation desired by the signers of the document. I really had no choice
but to do so. Thereupon, they all accepted, though one of them with
reluctance. He was my former teacher and long-time colleague, Professor E. P. Kohler. He gave as the reason for his reluctance his conviction that since the problem concerned the faculty of arts and
sciences it should be put before that body. His opinion was quickly
challenged by one member of the group, who correctly stated that
according to Harvard practice appointments and promotions were
never regarded as faculty business.

I doubt if the question was ever raised in the committee's deliberations; Kohler died before the first report was written, thus making
it a Committee of Eight, as it came to be called. When the issue of
faculty power over appointments was raised in the fall of 1939, I
believe everyone had forgotten Kohler's doubts about the wisdom of
a group that included three members of the law faculty investigating
a troublesome affair in the faculty of arts and sciences. Who actually
chose the members of the original group of nine, I never knew.

The Committee of Eight rendered its first report on May 24, 1938,
with the promise of a second report to come shortly. The first report
dealt only with the terminating appointments of Drs. Walsh and
Sweezy. The committee concluded that the department of economics
had misunderstood the administration's ruling of 1936 restricting the
number of instructors to be promoted. Therefore the committee recommended that Drs. Walsh and Sweezy be offered three-year appointments as instructors with the understanding that the department
might recommend advancement at any time during the three-year
period. I felt that the report overemphasized the extent to which misunderstandings may have affected the recommendations of the department as to promotions. I challenged the recommendations. I

was quite prepared, however, to leave the matter to the judgment of the other members of the Corporation.

The Corporation met for a whole day in the President's House. There had been a number of changes since I was elected president. Homans and Perkins had died; Curtis had resigned. Shattuck had become senior fellow. A Boston banker, William H. Claflin, Jr., had been elected treasurer; the two new fellows were Charles A. Coolidge of Boston and Henry James of New York. The seven of us went over the report in detail. I was authorized to forward the Committee of Eight's report to the Board of Overseers with a letter stating that "the Corporation regrets that it is unable to follow the recommendations contained in the report." In the same letter, I pointed out that the committee had found there was no foundation for "the suggestions made in some quarters last spring that the terminating two-year appointments given to Drs. Walsh and Sweezy were influenced by antagonism to their economic and social views." The report, prefaced by my letter to the Board of Overseers, was released to the press on June 1, 1938.

I, indeed, had been gratified at the committee's finding that neither the department, the dean nor I had been prejudiced against Drs. Walsh and Sweezy because of their active participation in the labor movement. A committee of the American Association of University Professors which made an independent investigation a year later came to the same conclusion. The president of the university, how-ever, was severely censured for linking what the writers considered the separable questions of promotion and reappointment. It was, of course, the inseparability of these two questions which was the es-sence of the personnel policy that had followed from Lowes' analysis. Clearly the idea was so novel that an outside committee of professors had not understood it.

To say the members of the Committee of Eight were unhappy about the Corporation's rejection of their recommendations would be an understatement. They continued with their work, nevertheless, and in March 1939 the second and final report was completed. From my point of view, it was an excellent document. The analysis of the present system was very much to the point. The proposed reclassifica-tion of personnel was based on a tacit acceptance of the "up-or-out" principle. The recommended rank of faculty instructor, for example, was defined by a five-year term with no reappointments. The rank of assistant professor was to be abolished, and the first permanent rank was to be associate professor. The budgetary limitation on both temporary and permanent appointments was clearly recognized. And although the principle of counting men not dollars was not mentioned, the distinction between short-term and long-term budgeting was brought out clearly. The recommendation of a dean's fund and a president's fund to introduce flexibility in the budgeting procedure was a forerunner of a scheme to be developed shortly, which was to be basic to the policy after 1941.

In the summary, the underlying assumptions of the committee were spelled out. They included the following: the revenues available to the faculty of arts and sciences in the near future would not increase; the appointive power would remain in the governing boards, with nominations ordinarily initiated by the departments; permanence of tenure would be granted to those in the upper ranks; the existing system of tutorial and course instruction would not be substantially altered. The committee noted that a large increase in endowment, the transfer of the appointive power to the faculty, or a division of the faculty into junior and senior groups would invalidate many of the conclusions. The committee expressed no opinion as to the wisdom of such conceivable changes. The spring of 1939 seemed to mark the end of the long disturbance. The tranquillity was deceptive.

The Overseers had received a printed copy of the committee's second report without any comments from the president. A few weeks later (May 22, 1939), I sent a special report to each member. In it I stated that the report of the Committee of Eight had been discussed in several meetings of the members of the faculty of arts and sciences. "In addition to this method of canvassing faculty opinion," I informed the Overseers, "I have asked all who have doubts as to the wisdom of the Committee's recommendations to write me and set forth their views." I reported that in view of the results of this canvass I had no doubt that a majority of the faculty endorsed the committee report. Therefore, after talking the matter over with the Corporation, I had decided to adopt the recommendations as a guide to general policy.

I might have added that since I had asked Professor W. S. Ferguson, one of the members of the Committee of Eight, to become dean of the faculty of arts and sciences, and since he would therefore be administering the new policy, I had every reason to think that the difficulties of applying the new rules and procedures could be harmoniously overcome. Such were my thoughts; I did not realize, however, that it was one thing for a faculty member not to challenge the committee's recommendation in an open meeting and quite another to sit by silently when the application of the recommendation to one's own department meant saying good-bye to some younger friends. I also misjudged the reception of my way of canvassing faculty opinion. I had presented the committee's report for discussion not to a faculty meeting but to four separate groups corresponding to the four major areas of learning—physical science, biological science, the humanities and the social sciences. There had been no votes.

The reasons why I had not presented the report to the faculty for formal debate and approval were well understood by the members of the Committee of Eight. Indeed, the Harvard tradition that matters of appointment were not the business of a faculty had been acknowledged in the report itself. There was nothing in writing to define the powers of the faculty and governing boards in matters of appointment. One might say the tradition was part of the unwritten Harvard constitution. I would have been well advised to let this tradition stand without any amplification or interpretation in my special report on the subject; instead, what I did was to try to make explicit and definite the distinction between the power of a faculty in regulating educational policy and the nominating power of a department when considering appointments.

"A department," I wrote, "is but a committee of the faculty and the rules and procedures of such committees can be regulated only by vote of the faculty or its authorized agent, the faculty council. However, when a department makes recommendations to the dean on matters of personnel, it is not acting as a faculty committee but as an informal group to whom the administration has turned for advice. The procedure in such instances is clearly a direct concern of the administrative officers." These sentences were read with strong disapproval by many faculty members, as I was to learn as soon as college opened in the fall. Before describing the explosion which they triggered off at the first faculty meeting in October, I must explain why my adherence to the Harvard tradition was so dogmatic as to be almost blind.

President Lowell, it will be recalled, had impressed upon me the importance of keeping the initiative and not letting administrative power fall into the hands of the faculty. When it came to choosing a dean, for example, he had told me he never allowed a faculty meeting even to discuss a candidate, let alone vote on the appointment or even on a nomination to the governing boards. He canvassed the opinion of important faculty members individually. Only in the Medical School, he said, had the faculty any power of appointment. The reason was an old agreement which had been made with an essentially independent Medical School and the Harvard Corporation in President Eliot's day. As a consequence, the professors voted on each appointment—a very bad procedure, he insisted, which should not be copied by other faculties.

To my surprise, in my first talks with Dean David L. Edsall of the medical faculty, I found that he and some other older members were as disapproving of the voting procedure as had been President Lowell. Examination of the records failed to reveal the agreement to which I understood President Lowell had referred. What the dean proposed was that I should announce at the next medical faculty meeting that in the future there would be no voting on a new appointment (only the occupants of full-time professorships were involved). I should say that I would welcome a full discussion in a meeting of all full professors of any nomination put before us by an *ad hoc* committee, but that the judgment of whether the recommendation should be forwarded to the Corporation would be mine in my capacity as president of the university. This bold suggestion, the dean assured me, would be welcomed. There had been some split votes in the past, which had reflected not the merits of the candidates but the successful electioneering of their friends. After talking with the more prominent members of the medical faculty, I agreed to do as the dean suggested. With considerable trepidation, I met with the faculty of medicine and made the announcement. It was well received. The new procedure seemed to work satisfactorily.

My experience with the medical faculty and President Lowell's powerful advice reinforced the opinion I had formed as a professor in the 1920s. At that time there had been some talk about how faculty members in all American universities should have the powers of Oxford and Cambridge dons, and the power of the college president should be drastically reduced. I had been completely unsympathetic. I felt that my claims for support for my research would fare much better with administrative officers than with any faculty committee. Thus, by 1937 an accumulation of prejudices and experiences had precluded my thinking seriously of following the idea Professor Kohler had put forward that day I met with the nine men bearing a petition. It is easy to see now, thirty years later, that it would have served the cause of academic peace if I had quickly buried my adherence to what I firmly believed was sound doctrine. Yet I can hardly imagine my taking the petition of the younger men to a faculty meeting and asking for advice. What would have been the outcome is hard to say.

The new dean of the faculty of arts and sciences, Professor

Ferguson, a distinguished historian and a highly respected member of the faculty, brought into office with him as assistant deans a young historian, Professor Paul H. Buck, and a mathematician, Professor W. C. Graustein. These three gentlemen and the outgoing dean met with department chairmen during May and early June 1939. As the Committee of Eight had predicted, there were many difficulties in applying the new policies to individual cases. Thinning out the ranks of those on temporary appointments was wise in theory but fraught with difficulties in practice. It was almost too late to perform such an operation.

As soon as I returned to Cambridge in September, I heard rumors that at the fall meeting of the faculty of arts and sciences one or more professors would air their discontent with the actions of the new dean and the policy of the president. According to the scheme which the faculty had adopted in 1934 at my suggestion, the major business of the faculty was generally conducted by an elected council and only one meeting of the full faculty was scheduled for each term. The latter had become perfunctory as the faculty council proved its effectiveness.

There was to be nothing perfunctory about the meeting of October 8, 1939. One hundred and thirty-five members were present. The actions taken the previous June were at once referred to by several speakers; sharp questions were directed to the dean, who was attending his first faculty meeting in that capacity. As president, I, of course, was in the chair. Dean Ferguson, who had been forewarned, read a memorandum of several pages in which he set forth the actions of his administration. He pointed out that all the decisions reached in the spring had been made jointly by the administration and each department concerned. Usually, he said, the department had been unanimous; in no department was there more than one dissenting opinion. The administration, he declared, was not open to the charge of having proceeded hastily or ruthlessly. All assistant professors who failed of appointment to the permanent staff were given at least a year's extension or a year's notice.

The challengers were not satisfied. On a motion by one of them, the meeting was adjourned to the next Tuesday. At the adjourned meeting 158 were present. The discussion of the application of the Committee of Eight recommendations continued. The meeting grew more and more into an attack on the president of the university for his failure to keep the faculty informed of the development of the new policy. The chairmen of the departments of English, government and biology demanded a reversal of the decisions of the spring which affected adversely the young men in their departments. Finally, an old friend of mine moved that "Further discussion of personnel administrative problems be deferred until the dean, after discussion with representatives of all departments, writes a report." The motion was adopted without debate.

By this time the debate had been picked up by the press. Dean Ferguson released his entire memorandum. The discontent focused on the recommendation of the Committee of Eight that the rank of assistant professor be abolished. I had noted in my report to the Overseers in May that while I had accepted this particular recommendation of the Committee of Eight as a guide to general policy, I had not agreed to it as a binding commitment. "In general the proposal seems to me wise," I wrote, "but any department of the faculty will be free to argue any particular case for the appointment of an assistant professor. In those cases in which it may seem best to make such appointments, I shall have no hesitation in recommending such action to the Governing Boards."

The dean was ready to report to a meeting of the faculty on November 7, 1939. The omens were not favorable. Members of the Committee of Eight who were on the dean's side reported increasing hostility on the part of a number of departments, some of whom were in a bitter mood. It looked as if some compromises would have to be made in individual cases, which was done a few weeks later. What disturbed me and some of my advisers most was the announcement by a professor of government that he would move that the faculty elect a committee of ten to examine the role of the faculty in the government of the university and report back. Such a motion obviously was put forward by those who thought the president should have consulted the faculty from the start and who objected strongly to my attempt to make definite the limited power of the faculty in matters of appointments. Much of the unpleasantness in the last meeting had pointed in this direction.

I consulted with a number of persons, indicating that the dean and I were prepared for a knockdown fight if necessary. Dean Wallace B. Donham of the School of Business Administration, on hearing of our intent through mutual friends, came to see me in alarm. For the first time during the controversy, he said, he was deeply worried. The issue which was now being raised was at the heart of the Harvard system; I had lost the confidence of a majority of the faculty of arts and sciences; if I let this loss of confidence result in faculty action that jeopardized the long-standing faculty–governing boards relation, I would be doing Harvard a great and perhaps permanent disservice. "The only thing for you to do," he said, "is to admit frankly and openly at the faculty meeting that you have made mistakes (and you have made mistakes) and ask the faculty not to attempt a revolution in the Harvard constitution because of your own errors. In my experience," he added, "if one admits a mistake to a faculty group, they will usually rally in support."

I did not like the advice at all. I had no stomach for apologizing to the faculty, particularly when I was under violent attack. I had made mistakes, beginning with the unfortunate press release of April 1937—that I had to admit to myself at least. To follow the course Dean Donham suggested was another matter. Yet I agreed with him completely as to the consequences of the election of a faculty committee to examine the government of the university. After considerable soul-searching, I finally decided that the dean's advice was wise, and entered the faculty meeting determined to follow it if a suitable occasion arose.

The audience was the largest ever—223. In response to the speakers who had blamed the existence of the faculty council for the failure in communications, a motion was passed 140–6 abolishing the council. The action was certainly a slap in the face of the president but raised no constitutional issue. The council had been my own invention; in destroying it, the faculty might be in part giving vent to its collective resentment. The next item on the docket was quite different. This was the motion to elect a committee to examine the role of the faculty in the government of Harvard.

Before the debate on this second motion had started, I said that as president of the university I wished to make a statement. I pointed out the grave implications of the motion. I agreed that the situation which had arisen in regard to promotion and tenure had greatly disturbed the members of the faculty. That I had made errors which were largely responsible for the current tension, I admitted. I asked the faculty, however, not, on account of my mistakes, to take a hasty step which might affect Harvard adversely for years to come. When I had finished, there was silence. Someone moved the motion be laid on the table; by voice vote, which sounded unanimous, the tabling motion was carried. Dean Donham was proved to have been right.

The question of a shift in the appointive power from the governing boards to the faculty was never raised again during the remaining fourteen years of my administration. If I had argued against the disturbing motion, I have no doubt it would have passed; the mood of the faculty that afternoon was close to being vindictive. A profound change might have started; though it can be argued that conservative forces would eventually have regained control. But the moral of the story for all new college presidents is clear: when you receive sound advice, however unwelcome, make the most of it and do so as rapidly as you can.

CHAPTER 15

Making Life Appointments

HARVARD WAS NOT ALONE in the late 1930s in having trouble about the tenure of faculty members. In 1937 a committee of the American Association of University Professors made public a report on its investigation of a complaint of Jerome Davis, associate professor of practical philanthropy in the Divinity School of Yale University. The purpose of the committee, the report stated, was "to ascertain whether the action of Yale University in terminating the tenure of Professor Jerome Davis or any facts connected with it constitute a violation of the principles of academic freedom or of academic tenure, or an abridgment of the civil rights of teachers as those are understood and maintained by the American Association of University Professors."

Yale was absolved of the charge of violating the principles of academic freedom. With respect to tenure as distinguished from academic freedom, Yale was severely criticized for consuming an excessive length of time in assessing Professor Davis' qualifications for a permanent position. (Twelve years had elapsed between his first appointment to an associate professorship and the decision that he should not be permanently retained in any position at Yale.) Sound principles of university administration require a reasonably prompt decision concerning fitness for a permanent connection with a faculty, the committee declared.

The council of the Association in reviewing the investigating committee's report endorsed the declaration. Expressing its own view, the council stated that the termination at so late a date of the services of Professor Davis was not justified and should be deemed a violation of the principles of academic tenure, "which must be maintained if freedom of teaching, of research, and of expression of opinion off the campus is to be a reality for members of the faculties of our institutions of higher learning." What the council did not point out was the significance of the investigating committee's finding that at the time Davis was first appointed the traditions at Yale lent support to the view that repeated appointments to the rank of associate professor implied a kind of indeterminate tenure not to be ended lightly or without "due process." It also failed to note that the current statement on academic tenure of the Association was completely silent on the length of time a faculty member might be allowed to continue in a temporary status.

In the statement adopted by the Association on January 10, 1941, the omission was rectified. It was declared that after the expiration of a probationary period teachers or investigators should have permanent or continuous tenure. The same document declared that, beginning with the first appointment to a full-time instructorship or higher rank, not more than seven years should elapse before a decision was made as to promotion.

The Harvard practice by 1941, following the recommendation of the Committee of Eight, was to allow a maximum of three years in the rank of annual instructor and five years as faculty instructor with no reappointment (a total of eight). What part the second report of the Harvard Committee of Eight played in bringing the council of the Association of University Professors to their formulation, I never knew. What is evident from the record is that in the early 1930s the academic world was far from ready to accept wholeheartedly the doctrine of "up-or-out," however politely it might be phrased. To the general public, if a young man was not reappointed, he was considered to have been fired. By 1941 the relation of tenure to appointment had been clarified. The acceptance of the idea of a probationary period for those who were starting their academic career was beginning to be accepted in many institutions. Today it is the exceptional university which does not accept it as a premise of the personnel policy of the institution.

At Harvard the application of the explicit tenure and promotion rules was greatly facilitated by a brilliant invention of Professor Graustein. Starting with one of the recommendations of the Committee of Eight which dealt with budgetary procedures, he developed the idea of a "revolving appointment fund." The committee had written in terms of dollars; Professor Graustein (who was a mathematician) wrote a bugetary memorandum without the dollar sign. Using what I have called the "Lowes principle," he showed how the administration could look forward to making regularly spaced appointments in the different departments. The objective was to ensure that each department knew when a permanent position in that department could be filled. The Committee of Eight had pointed out that the budget of the faculty would permit about seven new permanent appointments each year. Graustein showed the way by which these life appointments could be distributed among the departments without creating too great inequities. At the start, some departments would have to "borrow" permanent positions, so to speak; others would have to "lend" a few to a revolving fund; the arithmetic was in terms of men and not dollars.

In sending a copy of Professor Graustein's memorandum to a member of the Corporation on November 24, 1939 (seventeen days after the crucial faculty meeting), I wrote that "This scheme, if carried through with consistency, patience and wisdom over a period of years, will not only alleviate a temporarily distressed situation resulting from the overcrowding of the faculty ranks during the era of expansion, but will put us in a better position than we have ever been in."

The explanation of the Graustein idea to the departments was not easy. The prestige of Dean Ferguson as well as the effective work of the two younger assistant deans helped. Perhaps the uncertainties of the war period were the most powerful positive factor. Although Pearl Harbor was still twenty-four months away, World War II had already started when the last and most painful phase of the Walsh-Sweezy troubles ended. It was in the winter of 1939–40 that the immediate readjustments in each department budget were made; by the opening of the following academic year (1940–41), when some longer-range decisions had to be made, the probability of the United States' entering the war was foremost in everyone's mind.

Dean Ferguson insisted on being relieved of his administrative duties on February 1, 1942. The burden of making the new personnel policy work fell on his successor, Paul Herman Buck. I could have found no better man for a delicate task; he soon won the confidence of all factions of the faculty. The procedure which soon became standard was as much Dean Buck's creation as anyone's. He and I worked together as partners smoothly and effectively for the balance of my administration. All administrative decisions about the college were his or at least joint decisions of both of us.

By January 1945 I could report about the Harvard procedure for making life appointments and introduce a new invention, the *ad hoc* committee. In my annual report for 1943–44 to the Overseers, I wrote as follows:

It is a truism to remark that the position of this University or any other is determined from generation to generation by the quality of its faculties. Every year, even in wartime, the President and Fellows elect to life positions on our twelve faculties some dozen or so individuals. . . . After a little more than a decade of experience with such matters, including a stormy passage through a period of drastic reform in our largest faculty, I am convinced of two things: first, that there cannot be a uniform procedure for making life appointments applicable to all parts of this complex University; second, that nine times out of ten the normal forces working within any special segment of the University make for a good appointment, but against an excellent appointment. And it was Mr. Lowell who said, "The surest way to ruin a university faculty is to fill it with good men."

No board of laymen such as the Corporation or the Board of Overseers can hope to act as a specific check and balance on such matters. The Overseers can and do insist that evidence be produced to show that as far as possible a searching canvas of the situation has been made. You can and do demand that all things considered the man named is the best person both within and without the University who could be obtained to fill the position in question. All that our junior members of the staff who hold temporary positions can in justice ask is that their claims to promotion to a permanent position be weighed without prejudice against the merits of those who might be available from outside, and, if the decision is unfavorable, that they be given sufficient time to obtain a position elsewhere. Towards this goal we have steadily been working in recent years in all faculties of the University. . . .

Fifty years ago the permanent appointments in the Faculty of Arts and Sciences were recommended to the Corporation by the President of the University after informal consultation with a few professors. As the size and complexity of this Faculty increased, such a procedure became unworkable and the standing committees of the Faculty known as Departments or Divisions came to play a predominant role in the making of appointments. Recommendations for both temporary and permanent positions, with few exceptions, originated in the department concerned and were subject to review only by the Dean and the President before going to the Governing Boards. Within the last few years this practice has been changed and now all recommendations for permanent positions are reviewed by an *ad hoc* committee appointed for the special purpose of considering the merits of the department's choice as well as the qualifications of possible candidates outside of the University. The committee may find that in its opinion someone other than the person named by the department is the best qualified candidate. In that case the new name is sent to the department for careful consideration. Eventually the Governing Boards have before them the careful judgment of both the faculty group and the *ad hoc* committee. It would be a rare case when the Corporation acted favorably in the face of a strong negative from either the department or the committee.

These *ad hoc* committees are appointed by the President after consultation with the Dean of the Faculty of Arts and Sciences. As a rule there is only one member from the department concerned; the other members being drawn either from related departments or faculties or from other universities. The presence of at least two scholars from other institutions is of great importance in gaining a broad survey of the field and the maximum objectivity in passing judgment. The President of the University presides and the Dean of the Faculty of Arts and Sciences introduces the evidence which often includes the verbal testimony of members of our staff.

The procedure for making life appointments in the faculty of arts and sciences which I thus described in my report was first employed in the academic year 1942–43. In that year *ad hoc* committees were set up to consider departmental recommendations in biology, English, government and romance languages. The next year, four junior members of the faculty were given life appointments (starting at the rank of associate professor) and one scholar was called from another institution and made a full professor; all five appointments were passed through *ad hoc* committees over which I presided. The records for the year 1944–45 show the promotion to associate professorships of five members of the faculty and the calling of two at the same rank and one other as a full professor. I think it fair to say that after a total of twelve life appointments had been made as a result of recommendations of *ad hoc* committees the new procedure had become accepted practice. It remained so for the remainder of my term as president of the university.

From the evidence I have already presented, it is clear that my experience with the medical faculty had played a significant part in shaping my ideas about life appointments. Another powerful influence was my secondhand knowledge of the practices in the universities of Great Britain. The first time I visited Oxford as president of Harvard, I started inquiring about the way in which professors were appointed in that ancient institution. My curiosity soon took me to an

Harvard President James B. Conant with Prime Minister Winston Churchill, who visited Harvard in 1943. (*Harvard University News Office*)

Little "Bryant" Conant, age eight, in Union Army cap. (*Photograph by his father*)

The author with his grandmother, Jan Breed Bryant, in 1897.

James Scott Conant, the author's father.

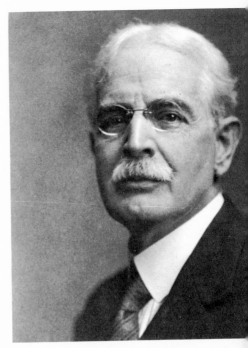

Professor Theodore William Richar the author's father-in-law.

Professor Conant in his Harvard laboratory, 1928.

Miss "Patty" Richards in 1920, before she became Mrs. James B. Conant.

The author with his mother, Jennet Bryant Conant, and sisters, Esther Conant and Marjorie Conant Bush-Brown.

President Conant during the Harvard Tercentenary, 1936. (*W. K. Vantine*)

President Franklin D. Roosevelt, Class of 1904, at the Tercentenary Celebration. (*UPI*)

President and Mrs. Conant greeting Governor and Mrs. Leverett Saltonstall of Massachusetts during the twenty-fifth reunion of the Class of 1914.

President Emeritus A. Lawrence Lowell (left), President Conant and Reginald Fitz, university marshal (right), leading an academic procession, 1938. *(Boston Herald Traveler)*

The author with his son Ted, St. Briac, France, 1935. *(Mrs. James B. Conant)*

James B. Conant, mountaineer, in the Canadian Rockies before an ascent of North Twin, 1938. *(G. Morris Taylor)*

Theodore Richards Conant and James Richards Conant with their father in 1936.

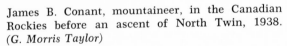

Dr. Conant as he departed on a special scientific mission to Britain in 1941. With him are Frederick L. Hovde (left) and Carroll L. Wilson. (*Wide World Photos*)

A meeting of the S-1 Executive Committee in California, 1942. Left to right: H. C. Urey, E. O. Lawrence, J. B. Conant, L. J. Briggs, E. V. Murphree, Arthur H. Compton.

Members of the wartime rubber survey committee: Karl T. Compton, James B. Conant and Bernard Baruch, chairman. *(Harris and Ewing)*

J. Robert Oppenheimer, Dr. Conant and Vannevar Bush at a meeting in Boston, 1948. *(Walter R. Fleischer, Harvard University News Office)*

Leading figures of the Manhattan District Project. Front row, left to right: Leslie R. Groves, Vannevar Bush, Enrico Fermi, K. D. Nichols, George B. Pegram, L. J. Briggs. Back row: Charles Thomas, James B. Conant, Arthur H. Compton, E. V. Murphree, Crawford H. Greenewalt. Picture was taken at the inauguration of Compton as Chancellor of Washington University, St. Louis.

The author with Secretary of State
James Byrnes in Moscow, 1945.
(*UPI*)

President Conant with Generals
George C. Marshall and Omar N.
Bradley, who received honorary
degrees from Harvard in 1947.
On this occasion General Marshall
delivered a speech announcing
the European Recovery Plan.
(*Harvard University News Office*)

Mrs. Conant arriving in Frankfurt in 1953 is greeted by her husband, the U.S. High Commissioner for Germany.

The author being received at the White House by President Eisenhower after his appointment as U.S. High Commissioner for Germany. (*Wide World Photos*)

Senator Joseph McCarthy (left) questioning Dr. Conant at a hearing of the Senate Appropriations Subcommittee, 1953. Seated next to the author is Glenn Wolfe, Executive Director, U.S. High Commission for Germany. *(UPI)*

With Chancellor
Konrad Adenauer
in Bonn, 1954.
(*USIS Photo Unit*)

The three Allied High Commissioners at the final meeting of the Allied
High Commission, 1955. Left to right: André François-Poncet, Dr. Conant,
Sir Frederick Hoyer Millar. (*USIS Photo Unit*)

At the dedication of the James B. Conant Laboratory, Harvard, 1959
Left to right: Arthur Fleming, Secretary of Health, Education and Welfare; Dr. Conant; Konrad Bloch; Nathan M. Pusey, president of Harvard
(*Harvard University News Office*)

With granddaughter Connie, Christmas, 1957
(*Theodore R. Conant*)

Dr. Conant and Mrs. Conant with Willy
Brandt, the Lord Mayor of Berlin, 1965.
(*Aufnahme der Landesbildstelle Berlin*)

Reporting to President Kennedy as vice chairman of the President's Committee on Youth Unemployment.

Being greeted by President Pusey in the Harvard Yard during the fiftieth reunion of the Class of 1914.

inquiry about what went on in such newer universities as Manchester and Birmingham. References to what had been written in the nineteenth century about selecting future professors made me aware of the parliamentary reforms of Oxford and Cambridge. I was thus led to make an amateurish study of the history of appointments. In particular I became intrigued by a paper published in the *Edinburgh Review* of 1834 by Sir William Hamilton. The title, "Academical Patronage and Superintendence," I purloined for the address I was to deliver at a Lincoln's Birthday Convocation at Williams College in 1938. (It was subsequently published as one of the Occasional Pamphlets of the Harvard Graduate School of Education.)

As a historical discussion of the appointment of professors in universities, the paper was satisfactory. As a speech before an alumni gathering, it was a disaster. The best that could be said of it was remarked by an old friend who was present: "At least the Williams College alumni can feel that they have heard you make an important address."

The speech exhausted the subject as well as the audience. Starting with Oxford and Edinburgh in the 1830s, I ended by comparing the newer English universities, the German universities before 1933 and the American institutions (both privately endowed and state supported). I quoted Hamilton's verdict that the "history of universities— in truth, of all human institutions, lay or clerical, proves by a melancholy experience that seminaries founded for the common weal, in the furtherance of sound knowledge, are, if left to themselves, if left without an external and vigilant, an intelligent and distinterested supervision, regularly deflected from the great end for which they were created, and perverted to the private advantages of those through whom that end, it was confidently hoped, would be best accomplished." I also quoted from the German theologian, Schleiermacher, who in connection with the founding of the University of Berlin had written in 1808 that nobody "would be inclined to accord a university the exclusive choice of its teachers. Universities are, one and all, so infamous for a spirit of petty intrigue that were this privilege once conceded, everybody would anticipate disadvantageous consequences."

If the listeners were still awake, my concluding paragraphs may have stirred their interest. The controversy about the appointments of Drs. Walsh and Sweezy had only recently been in the news, and other colleges had had their troubles. Summing up the history I had reviewed, I gave it as my opinion that trustees, however appointed, represented the general public. "Their function," I said, "is to maintain the balance of power between those within the academic walls and those without."

Amplifying this theme, I suggested that

We must never lose sight of two historical facts: one, the origin of the universities as independent guilds of masters or masters and students; the other, the apparent necessity of counterbalancing the inherent freedom of action of these guilds by some outside force, be it an official governmental representative as in Germany during the last century, or a body of curators functioning continually, or the power of the state acting occasionally and drastically as in England. Companies of scholars have not made an enviable record in the matter of self-direction over a long period of years. On the other hand, directive powers from without have repeatedly become autocratic and tyrannical—they have all too often abolished freedom of inquiry . . . the statement the Hitler regime has suppressed the German universities may not be an overstatement.

One reference to the current British practice makes evident the origin of the idea of using *ad hoc* committees. "The system," I wrote,

consists of either standing committees (usually containing an outside member) as in Oxford or Cambridge, or internal *ad hoc* committees in the newer universities. In the latter case, however, the Vice Chancellor, in a sense a curator (or at least a permanent responsible official), acts as presiding officer of the committees and thus exercises to some degree the same function as the representative of the government under the German system [which is that of choosing from a list of nominees made by the faculty].

Many of the chairs at Oxford and Cambridge were filled by the decision of a committee of academic men appointed as future electors before the chair was vacant. Such standing committees were apt to include several scholars from outside the university. I had been told the arrangement worked well. Therefore I incorporated the idea of outside members into my proposal for *ad hoc* committees at Harvard. The scheme, however, was fundamentally that used by the newer universities, which I had first heard of from the vice chancellor of Manchester in 1933. The information I had received was waiting in the back of my head, so to speak, for an opportunity to be of service. The opportunity arrived after Messrs. Ferguson, Buck and Graustein had succeeded in bringing order into the Harvard picture.

It is hardly necessary to underline the importance of the Graustein formula. But it must be remembered that this formula assumed either a static faculty budget (in terms of life appointments) or a slow and ordered growth. If an institution is set on a course of rapid and unplanned expansion, each new permanent appointment is not likely to be scrutinized with the same care as was premised by all of us at Harvard in the war and postwar period. If a department and the university administration believe that within five years not one or two but perhaps a half-dozen or more life appointments can be made, then it is not a serious matter if one decision turns out to be very bad. Since in the last fifteen years most American universities, private and state-supported, have been operating with what might be called an unlimited expansionist philosophy, the Harvard story I have related is obviously of limited relevance.

A basic assumption shared by faculty and administrative officers alike twenty years ago was solvency. The manpower budget had to be drawn for a decade or more so that the total dollar budget of the institution would be in the black. Except for an emergency year or two, a university operating deficit was unthinkable. The sources of funds were limited; new departures meant finding new donors.

All that has changed. The enormous sums of federal money which have flowed to the leading universities seem to have generated a totally new climate of opinion. I became forcefully aware of the change very recently when I served as a member of "The Select Committee on the Future of Private and Independent Higher Education in New York State," appointed by Governor Nelson Rockefeller of New York and chaired by McGeorge Bundy, the president of the Ford Foundation. We were asked to advise the Governor on how state money should be employed to assist the private colleges in New York State. We heard from the college presidents about their budgetary problems. They were markedly different from those I had encountered thirty-five years ago. The whole framework of discussion had altered. Expansion was assumed. If the hoped for growth was to continue, help from the state was needed. We so recommended.

As late as 1953, when I left Cambridge, I could not have imagined asking for taxpayers' money to support any Harvard activity. The passage of time has made my point of view completely out of date. Such being the case, a reader may wonder what is the relevance of the 1940 Harvard answer to budgetary and personnel problems. I can only reply that I wonder myself, but having undertaken an autobiography, I cannot avoid devoting some pages to a problem which was at one time of prime interest not only to people in Cambridge but to the entire American academic world.

CHAPTER 16

A New Degree for Schoolteachers

THE HISTORY of patented inventions is replete with examples of accidental experiences which have determined the focus of an inventor's interest. The situation as regards social inventions is no different. An example is afforded by the origins of the degree of master of arts in teaching established at Harvard in 1935.

If the Graduate School of Education had not been on the verge of serious financial trouble in 1933, I should not have spent much time as a new president on its problems. One or two conversations with a dean or department chairman usually sufficed in those first months in office to acquaint me with the prospects of that part of the university. If the dean of the faculty of education had been confident of his ability to balance his budget, I would probably have had only a *pro forma* review of his problems.

In that case my prejudices against professors of education would have lain dormant for a period of years. I would not have entered into an exploration of the reasons for the existence of a separate school and faculty of education. I would just have accepted the current arrangement as one of a number of situations which I had inherited but for which I had no special enthusiasm.

The budget of the School of Education in 1933 was, for the moment, in the black. The school had accumulated a surplus which stood to its account. But it looked as though lean years lay ahead. The endowment was tiny. As was the case in most schools of education

180

in those days, the chief source of support was the fees paid by school-teachers who were taking afternoon and evening courses. President Lowell, seeing the school prospering in the days of the 1920 boom and accumulating a surplus, had raised the question as to whether this type of part-time education was really worthy of a Harvard graduate school. Requirements for the degree of A.M., Ed.M. and Ed.D. had been raised as a result of his inquiry, and the enrollments had consequently fallen off.

But what had not been anticipated was the depression. Now the forecast for the future was discouraging, assuming no great recovery in the economic situation. Harvard had priced itself out of the market. The cost of a Harvard degree in terms of hours or dollars spent was too high to meet the competition of neighboring institutions.

My first reaction might well have been to suggest to Dean Henry W. Holmes that we close the school. As a chemist, I had acquired strong opinions about schools of education. I had heard from my friends who were professors in Midwestern universities that they could not place their graduates in public high schools unless several courses in education had been included in the programs. Such a "protective tariff" set up by state laws at the instigation of professors of education was generally denounced by all who knew of the situation.

It was not only chemists in state universities who took an unfavorable view of faculties of education. Many members of the faculty of arts and sciences at Harvard were unsympathetic, if not hostile, to the courses in education given by their colleagues in the faculty of education. President Lowell was generally believed to have been far from enthusiastic about the School of Education. Indeed, one of the stories which had been circulating as he left office was to the effect that he had declared to a confidant that he had left two kittens for his successor to drown. One of them, it was generally agreed, was the Graduate School of Education.

Instead of a direct attack on his school, however, at my first interview with Dean Holmes, I suggested we might explore without prejudice the question of the basis for the existence of the school with special reference to the training of teachers. Dean Holmes, an affable person who was, perhaps, too ready to agree with a new president, was quite willing to undertake the task of proving that courses in education were worthwhile. As to state laws, he refused either to support or condemn them, but said there they were—Harvard could not change them. If the state requirements were not met, a person trained at Harvard could not get a position in most states. (Nearly thirty years later, I was to hear a similar argument from the deans of many schools of education, but always coupled with the statement that the instruction provided by professors of education was important, if not absolutely essential, for a future teacher in an elementary school or a high school.)

So in the fall of 1933, after I had been in office only a few months, I started on a course of discussion about elementary and secondary schools and the preparation of teachers for such schools. I recall challenging Dean Holmes by asking to see the final-examination questions in several of the required education courses. After a quick look at them I ventured to say that I could answer most of the questions without taking the course. "Perhaps," Holmes replied, "but you have been horse shedded" (an old New England village expression for being briefed by the elders before or after church).

Our talks went on over a period of at least a year. I gradually began to give ground as I learned more about the tasks facing a teacher in a high school which was not selective and, therefore, quite unlike the school I had attended—the Roxbury Latin School. The curriculum of a Latin school was also put on the agenda for examination. This time it was Holmes who asked the skeptical questions and I who made an attempt to justify having spent six years studying Latin. We thrashed over the old mental-discipline arguments and the pros and cons of progressive education, for which neither of us felt any great enthusiasm.

In discussing the Roxbury Latin School I also emphasized the democratic tradition of that school, and indicated my interest in the desirability of having in the student body of a school or college a considerable variety in terms of family background. The Roxbury Latin School was free for children of families living in Old Roxbury. Those who could pass the admission examination were enrolled without expense if they came from that part of Greater Boston. Dean Holmes must have recognized my antiaristocratic bias and played on it for all it was worth.

As I have mentioned, I had not been in office long before I became immersed in promoting the idea of the National Scholarships and the University Professorships. The future of the School of Education was only distantly related to these two projects, with one important exception: The bright students I was looking for on the other side of the Allegheny Mountains were certain to be graduates of public high schools. Dean Holmes did not miss the opportunity to point out the connection between my desire for outstanding students from the public high schools and the education of teachers for the same schools, which was the concern of his faculty.

In December of 1933, I was invited by the president of the University of Chicago to receive an honorary degree at the midwinter convocation. I had never met Robert M. Hutchins and was most anxious to do so, as he was relatively new in office and had already obtained national prominence. During a pleasant visit in which I discussed many problems that were on my agenda, I mentioned the School of Education. Bob Hutchins told me that they had abolished theirs and that Professor Charles H. Judd was the man to tell me what to do.

So I returned to Chicago a couple of months later for a long talk with Judd. What he had to say made a deep impression. Apparently, until the reforms he had put through at Chicago, the students in the School of Education received instruction in academic subjects as well as education from members of the faculty of education (a scheme which was in effect in a number of large universities as late as the 1960s). Such an arrangement was all wrong, Judd declared. The instruction in the academic fields should be exclusively in the hands of the subject-matter departments. The professors of education should be statesmen in a profession.

Actually, at Harvard, instruction in subject-matter fields was given in courses offered by members of the faculty of arts and sciences. The decision as to what courses were required and the passing grade in each course, however, was settled by the faculty of education. As presiding officer at the midwinter meeting of the faculty of education, I had witnessed an altercation as to whether a C in a certain course could be allowed or not, since in the Graduate School of Arts and Sciences a B or an A was required. With this experience fresh in mind, I knew what Judd was talking about. I added a consideration of the Chicago Plan to the list of topics Holmes and I were discussing.

Almost exactly a year from the day I had been elected president of Harvard, I wrote a memorandum to Dean Holmes pointing out that, in fact, we were preparing future schoolteachers in two quite separate parts of the university—the Graduate School of Arts and Sciences and the Graduate School of Education. I went on to suggest: "The question of following the lead of Chicago should be seriously considered. This would involve the taking over by the Graduate School of Arts and Sciences the direct responsibility for the training of secondary school

teachers with the cooperation of the Graduate School of Education."
I then proposed a committee (giving names) "to discuss the possibility."

Holmes agreed to the appointment of an interfaculty group. By
the beginning of the next academic year our discussion of a reorganization of the education of teachers had proceeded so far that Holmes
was writing that he had no "institutional objection" to the establishment of a degree of master of arts in teaching to be awarded by the
faculty of arts and sciences. However, he thought it quite possible
"that the departments would rather have the School of Education
'carry the ball' and there are clear advantages in that because we are
the only group which really care about training teachers more than
anything else."

During the first year of our discussions, Dean Holmes had brought
in a younger member of his faculty who was eventually to have a
profound influence on my thinking—Professor Francis T. Spaulding.
He presented with great skill the case for professors of education and
courses in education. He was not notably enthusiastic about my idea
of following the Chicago lead, but he recognized the desperate situation of the school and Dean Holmes' responsibility. Therefore he
registered no dissent.

I had started off promptly in my examination of the status of the
School of Education, but other urgent matters soon slowed down
the pace of my inquiry. In a sense, I never did get a satisfactory answer to my skeptical questions about education courses. The immediate issues of what to do about the organization of the school and the
budget forced into the background the more basic queries as to the
value of courses in education.

As so often happens in administrative work, the exigencies of
day-to-day matters and competing demands on my time resulted in
something less than a quick consideration of the Chicago Plan. It
was not until February of 1935 (a year after I had come back to
Cambridge with Judd's ideas fermenting in my mind) that I invited
eighteen people to lunch "to explore the possibilities of cooperation
between the faculty of arts and sciences and the School of Education
to establish a joint program for the training of secondary school
teachers." In April I appointed eight committees to explore the matter
more fully. The committee from the faculty of education consisted
of Dean Holmes and Professor Spaulding, "with power to add a specialist when desired." From the faculty of arts and sciences, seven
committees of three members each—representing seven departments

—were created, with the dean of the faculty of arts and sciences, K. B. Murdock, an ex officio member of each.

In a letter to Dean Holmes announcing the composition of these committees, I wrote that it was my understanding that they would meet to consider the possibilities of establishing a joint program in each of the seven fields. If the discussion reached a point where it appeared that something was likely to develop in the way of a constructive report, I would be glad to hear from him or Dean Murdock before the matter was brought to the attention of either of the faculties. If he was so fortunate, I added, as to be able to get a satisfactory report from each of these seven committees within the next eight months, we would then undoubtedly need a smaller executive committee from the two faculties to work out the details for the whole plan.

In my annual report for 1934–35, which was published in early January 1936, I discussed the two methods of providing graduate training for teachers in elementary and secondary schools. The prospective teacher could either enroll in the Graduate School of Arts and Sciences, with the intent of obtaining a degree of master of arts after one or two years of work, or he could enroll in the School of Education. In the latter case he or she would be a candidate for the degree of Ed.M. The course of study in the School of Education involved devoting a considerable amount of time to the study of material concerning the educational process. In addition, the prospective candidate for the Ed.M. was required to take certain subject-matter courses given by the faculty of arts and sciences.

My conclusion was that it would be desirable to combine the two roads to the teaching profession. I argued that such a combination would retain the advantages of both of the present procedures: the departments of the faculty of arts and sciences should set the standards and examine the candidate's knowledge of the subject matter; the School of Education would have charge of the study of professional material and practice teaching in some one of the co-operating schools. If the committees then at work on the subject arrived at a solution along the general lines I had indicated, candidates for a new degree would be recommended jointly by the faculty of arts and sciences and the faculty of education.

In the fall of 1935, the two faculties, meeting and voting separately, recommended to the governing boards the establishment of a new degree: "Master of Arts in Teaching." The Corporation was requested to "create an administrative board empowered to administer this degree and to recommend candidates for it to the two faculties." The board was to consist of four members of the faculty of arts and sciences and three members of the faculty of education, the president of the university being a member ex officio. The necessary votes were passed by the president and fellows of Harvard College (the Corporation) on November 18, 1935, and consent to these votes was given by the Board of Overseers on November 25, 1935.

What the official records do not show is the amount of personal effort I had put into the task of "lobbying" among the faculty. My initial hostility to professors of education (which had been largely allayed by the untiring efforts of Holmes and Spaulding) was typical of the faculty of arts and sciences. Unless the elder statesmen could be won over to at least a neutral position, there was no chance of a favorable vote when the proposal for a cooperative degree came before the faculty.

One seat of academic power was the administrative board of the Graduate School of Arts and Sciences. For years, a group of scholars had met together to regulate the details of conferring the degrees of A.M. and Ph.D. The new proposal trespassed on their prerogatives. How would it be regarded? I still remember the considerable trepidation with which I met the board. Professor Kittredge, the Shakespeare scholar, was the most influential member. To my surprise, his questioning showed a sympathetic attitude. Indeed, the reception of the idea was in general all that I might have hoped. Of course, there had been informal earlier discussion among the members; I had not sprung the proposal on them at the meeting. Still, the questions showed that some of the details had not been previously understood.

Why the administrative board favored the joint degree so promptly is hard to say. In part, it reflected the desire of the older men to give the new president, a former faculty colleague, a chance. Such an attitude was apparent in the first few years—the honeymoon period which lasted through the Tercentenary Celebration in 1936. In part, the presence on the board of my old chemistry friend, Professor Kohler, was probably a factor. Kohler was a respected colleague and a quiet but skillful advocate of a scheme which he believed ought to be given a trial. And this was about as far as his commitment went. Perhaps, however, my diagnosis was accepted on its merits. It made no sense having two competing ways of training teachers, particularly as one way—that under the complete control of the faculty of education—was highly suspect in the other faculty.

As an ex officio member of the board for the new degree, I kept in close touch with the developments during the first two years. Indeed, I took the time to preside at a number of the meetings. In reporting to the Overseers in 1937, I was able to say that the number of candidates for the new degree was not large but the program was going forward satisfactorily. Each year marked a greater degree of cooperation between the two faculties, and some of the earlier difficulties involved in any new enterprise were gradually eliminated. Anyone who read my annual report for 1937–38 would have concluded not only that a new degree had been invented, but that the Graduate School of Education now had the full backing of the president of the university.

As I have pointed out earlier, the success of the National Scholarships underlined the importance of the public high schools throughout the country. I had thus been led to a conclusion about the structure of American secondary education which was quite foreign to my outlook when I took office as president. Dean Holmes had laid the groundwork for my changed point of view. It now remained for his young colleague, Professor Spaulding, to build on this belief. This he was able to do because of the many long discussions we had about educational matters as we traveled to some New England cities to speak to the local Harvard Clubs.

The reason for these journeys was the need of funds for the Harvard Graduate School of Education. The establishment of the degree of master of arts in teaching had in no way improved the financial situation of the school, nor had the completion of the 300th Anniversary Fund drive, since it had been agreed that the money raised on the occasion of the anniversary would be used only for the two projects which had university appeal, namely, the National Scholarships and the University Professorships. In the years immediately after the Tercentenary, the various deans had been asked to consider whether they should embark on money-raising enterprises. Dean Holmes had felt quite inadequate when faced with the need for explaining the purposes of his school to an audience of Harvard alumni from which might come potential donors. He had therefore asked Professor Spaulding to speak for him.

Almost from the start, Spaulding and I got on well together. He was no "yes-man." At the same time, he was a realist and quite ready to take the education of the new president of Harvard as one of his assignments (though, needless to say, this was never admitted openly). The qualities were already apparent that made him later so successful, first in the Education Branch of the Information and

Education Division of the Army under General Frederick Osborn and then as Commissioner of Education in New York State. He had the rare combination of being approachable and open-minded without being in the least uncertain as to his views. He liked an argument, but not for argument's sake. He was as critical of some of the fuzzy thinking of professors of education as were some of the rest of us. At the same time, he had a disarming quality, and one could find oneself heartily disagreeing with the man and still continue to like him and even to admire his tenacity.

He brought to our conversations the points of view about education which had taken shape shortly after World War I. They might be labeled the orthodox views of more forward-looking schools of education. He was not a "progressive educator" in good standing. As I was to learn some years later, he by no means saw eye to eye with the leaders of Teachers College at Columbia. In short, he was an independent thinker, and, what was most important from my point of view, he knew whereof he spoke. A survey of public education in New York State, which he was just completing, made him an expert on the present status of public secondary schools. How much I learned from my close association with Professor Spaulding is best illustrated by an incident that occurred sometime in 1936 or 1937; it is worth recounting because of the light it throws on my changing appraisal of secondary school problems.

A potential donor had been steered in my direction by some alumnus because of his reported wealth and his special views about secondary education. After a long talk, in which I tried to interest him in the Harvard Graduate School of Education, he ended only by expressing a great interest in me personally. In several subsequent conversations and some correspondence, he kept returning to an idea of his that Harvard should establish a selective secondary school for highly gifted boys and that I should play a key role in the management. In those early days of fund-raising, I attempted to accommodate the realities of the Harvard situation to the wishes of even an eccentric man of wealth. It was almost inconceivable that Harvard University would be willing to take on the running of a secondary school even if it was well endowed. Still, it was not entirely out of the question. Some schools of education did have campus schools attached to them. Therefore I explored with Professor Spaulding the possibility that the desires of this potential donor might be fulfilled, assuming that at the same time he would add some endowment for the graduate school itself.

Although nothing ever came of this idea, my hour-long conversations with Professor Spaulding about such a hypothetical school (which he did not favor) were revealing. In a letter I wrote to him in December 1937, I exhibited quite clearly my educational prejudices at that time. I insert the letter here at length because it sets forth without ambiguity a point of view which, in retrospect, seems to me so conservative as to be almost reactionary:

Continuing this process of thinking out loud, as it were . . . I agree that it is impossible to support the study of the older disciplines in the secondary schools on the basis of their use in college. I quite agree that except for the language requirement, which is purely an artificial one on the part of the Harvard College faculty (though one with which I agree perfectly), a student could enter Harvard without having studied any of the older disciplines, and if he was a boy of high composite academic ability, would undoubtedly do very well if he concentrated on such subjects as economics, history, government, anthropology, fine arts and probably a good many others. . . . The deficiencies in his secondary school education would only come to light at the end of his college career if as one of these "ill-prepared students" he decided he wished to become a scholar. The handicaps of his early education would be appalling.

I do not see how one can make very much headway as a student . . . of history and literature without a reading knowledge of Latin. I do not see how a person can go very far in any branch of science without a thorough understanding of mathematics, and if the underpinning was bad in school, probably the necessary calculus and so forth would not have been taken during the college years. I know that a man cannot be a research chemist without a reading knowledge of German. It is hard to acquire it as the *first* language in college.

I agree that it may be argued that the chances of any given boy of high composite academic ability desiring to be a learned man in science or literature or history are too slim to make it worthwhile exposing a whole flock of students to Latin and a modern foreign language and a heavy dose of mathematics at the school level. However, these subjects seem to have played a useful part in the education of a great number of people in the past and to have developed useful habits of work, and they have been helpful in conditioning the intellectual muscles, as it were, of a variety of men and women. If they are to be given up entirely in our schools, it seems to me we are cutting off at the base much of our supply of cultured and learned men and women. If the tendency urged by some were to go to its logical conclusion, a knowledge of Latin would be as rare as that of Arabic and our understanding of the genesis of Western civilization as little diffused as that of Islam. I confess that I would rather see a good many students suffer a little overexposure to the older disciplines in school than face this possibility. I suppose that is the real issue between those of us who favor the older disciplines on what we consider realistic grounds and those who would abolish them in order to improve pedagogic procedure. . . .

A practical question soon intruded itself in my academic debate with Spaulding. Not for the last time, Spaulding received an attractive offer to leave Harvard. He was well aware of the financial plight of the school. He naturally wanted to know what the future had in store for a professor of education at Harvard. What sort of school was going to be developed?

The question was directed to Dean Holmes. He, in turn, reported his alarm that Spaulding might leave us. He recommended strongly that Spaulding be made dean in his place, feeling, he said, a younger man could do the job better than he could. As a result, I placed Spaulding's name before the Corporation with enthusiasm. I took the occasion to spell out the financial problems, suggesting that the Corporation must now be prepared to say that the School of Education, like the Dental School and the Divinity School, could run a limited annual deficit to be covered by the unrestricted funds of the university. If this were done, the new dean and I would do our best to obtain temporary funds to decrease the deficit each year and get an endowment, the income from which would eliminate the deficit. A second alternative would be to agree to the slow liquidation of the School of Education, which would mean that Spaulding would not only refuse the deanship but would soon leave the university.

The Corporation accepted the first alternative. With due formality and gratitude, Dean Holmes' resignation was accepted. Spaulding was appointed dean by the Corporation, and the appointment was confirmed by the Board of Overseers. Following the Harvard tradition, I did not consult the faculty either as a body or individually except in a few instances. Though Holmes was sure the appointment would be welcomed, one faculty member wrote a letter of indignation at the arbitrary way I had proceeded; which protest, I may add, was also in the Harvard tradition. My next job was to try to win confidence for Spaulding among the leading members of the faculty of arts and sciences. One step in this direction was a dinner in December 1939, at which Spaulding performed brilliantly, disarming his potential critics in the faculty of arts and sciences by his frank approach to their differences of opinion. In short, the omens were good for an increasingly close cooperation between the school of which he would be dean and the faculty of arts and sciences.

With Spaulding as dean of the Harvard Graduate School of

Education, I had an adviser whose educational philosophy was quite different from what mine had been at the time I had taken office. We had come to an understanding on the M.A.T. I had been converted to the importance of the School of Education. But on the question of the high school curriculum we were far apart, as the letter I have quoted on the preceding pages proves. In that letter I had made no reference to differences in ability among students. Yet a recognition of such differences was the real key to our disagreement. I was directing my attention to those who were going to college; such students were not Spaulding's prime concern. My thinking was tied to the National Scholarship scheme; his thoughts were largely centered on the youth who attended high school without any intention of entering college. I was still not ready for an exchange of views about the education of those who did not have the ability or desire to study the subjects I thought important (foreign languages and mathematics). Nor did I trouble myself much about the advantages and disadvantages of selective high schools. Spaulding's and my disagreement about the suggestion of establishing a school operated by Harvard illustrates that I had not come very far toward an understanding of "public schools as instruments of democracy." What was to become a favorite phrase of mine would have seemed almost meaningless.

Not that Holmes and Spaulding were anything but devoted believers in public schools, but they were not emphasizing one characteristic of American education—the locally financed school district, with provision for terminal as well as college-preparatory education in one high school. Indeed, I am not sure to what degree they would have felt a single high school serving all the youth of a community was superior to two separate schools, one for vocational education, the other for those preparing for college.

In the meantime, I had been evolving my own brand of social and educational philosophy. There was no novelty in it. As compared with the then current "New Deal" point of view, it might be called reactionary or, at best, founded on an outworn myth. I decided to try it out on a California audience in March 1940. I had been asked to be the Charter Day speaker, a great honor which I took very seriously. I spent a considerable part of the summer working on the manuscript, which I headed with a question: "A Free Classless Society: Ideal or Illusion?" Speaking as an educator, I said that if we accepted the ideal of a free and classless society, then "our concern must be at every point in the educational system to provide true democracy of opportunity, to have all careers open to the talented." I went on to declare that educators by tradition think in purely intellectual terms, and I for one would do nothing to lower the standards of those institutions dedicated to finding and developing academic brilliance. (The Harvard National Scholarship scheme was clearly in my mind.) But I added, "This form of ability is only one aspect of the talents of mankind which can be useful to the nation. The skill of the artist and artisan are of equal significance for our national life. The possibility of careers open to the *talented of all types* must be provided."

The unorthodox words in this quotation are "of all types" and "artisan." Few, if any, college presidents of either private or state institutions would have used those words in those days. Their use by me manifests the extent of Spaulding's success in making me understand the challenges facing the public schools.

I ended the Charter Day Speech by asking: What choice have those who teach our youth? My answer was: "None, but to hope that the American ideal is not an illusion, that it is still valid; none, but to labor unremittingly for a type of education which will every day quietly loosen the social strata; none, but to believe that through the functioning of our schools and colleges American society will remain, in essence, classless and, by so doing, even in days of peril, preserve the heritage of the free."

A letter I wrote to Spaulding about the speech spells out my unfolding thoughts about the relation of schools and colleges to American society:

You are quite right in thinking that I am using the word "class" to mean hereditary class or caste. This being so, classlessness and social mobility are synonymous. I feel that I am justified in using the word "class" in this sense because it is so used commonly by Americans as evidenced by the quotation at the beginning of my third paragraph, "There are no classes in the United States." This is an expression which I feel a great many Americans in the past and even today would have subscribed to. In so doing, they would have passively equated the words "caste" and "class." Since words on the whole are what custom makes them, I think that it is not distorting meaning to use the word "class" in this discussion in this sense.

Spaulding had heartily subscribed to the educational implications of my speech. I, of course, was pleased. In my letter I raised the question with him whether it would not be possible to develop in connection with his School of Education the thought that perhaps the first duty of the public educational system in America was to provide for social mobility. I suggested that putting the emphasis on providing opportunity for talented people ahead of education for citizenship had its advantages. I agreed that both concepts were exciting and important, and I hoped we could discuss the relation of the two.

I do not recall whether we did or not. Before many weeks had passed, the fall of France had so altered the situation that the fate of the Harvard School of Education was no longer in the forefront of my thoughts.

CHAPTER 17

The Mountains

THERE ARE COUNTLESS EXAMPLES of the assistance that a president has received from graduates of the institution of which he is the executive head. Indeed, I have devoted the best part of another chapter to the account of the alumnus as benefactor. I could fill several more chapters by enlarging on the same theme. The benefits—thousands of them—which would thus be recorded would be, of course, benefits to the institution. I should now like to record a rather special case of the activity of a Harvard alumnus which influenced not the course of Harvard history but the extracurricular career of the president of his university.

In the summer of 1937 the Conant family traveled across the continent (by train, of course) in order to enjoy a vacation in the Sierra Mountains. My wife and I, our two sons, Jim and Ted, aged fourteen and eleven, and C. Colmery (Gib) Gibson, who had just graduated from Harvard College, constituted the party. The cottage we had rented was on Fallen Leaf Lake, California, not far from Lake Tahoe. I planned to take some short walking trips in the nearby mountains and do some trout fishing, a sport I had just taken up; the boys would find many companions, as Fallen Leaf Lake was a summer colony of academic people among whom we had several acquaintances. Furthermore, Gib would be prepared to see to it that the boys had a pleasant summer. On the first or second day after our arrival, our son Ted came down with measles, a state of affairs which placed his brother in quarantine as far as other children were concerned. It is no part of this story to recount in detail how two cases of measles, following one after the other, ruined the vacation for my wife and our two sons and altered completely the kind of help we had anticipated from Gib.

One day after we had settled into making the best of a bad prospect, I had an unexpected caller. He introduced himself as Francis P. Farquhar, a Harvard graduate of the class of 1909, a resident of San Francisco. He said he had heard that I liked mountaineering; he wished, therefore, to invite me to join him and a few of his friends on a pack trip in the High Sierras which they were planning for some weeks later. He explained that what was proposed would involve a considerable amount of walking at an elevation around six to eight thousand feet. He mentioned casually that we might try to climb a peak.

At this point, I registered a protest. I had to make it plain, I said, that while I had done a great deal of walking up and down hill in the mountains of New Hampshire, including what we called "climbing," I had never been on one of those expeditions which involved using a rope; I never expected to risk my neck in any such affair. I had a strong prejudice against mountain climbing of the sort one read about on alpine climbs. Farquhar, who was a subtle persuader as well as a stubborn man, said something to the effect that we would do nothing dangerous, but he might bring a rope along in case some of the party wanted to do a bit of rock climbing. So I accepted the invitation with many thanks.

The trip started at Parcher's Camp, twenty miles from Bishop on the east side of the mountains. The supplies were loaded on a pack horse, and there was an extra horse for the benefit of anyone who might find the long uphill walk over the pass too tiring. In addition to Farquhar and myself, the party consisted of three men; one was a young man who had a reputation as a rock climber, the other two were about my age or perhaps a little older. We all appeared to be in excellent condition, and little use was made of the spare animal. After reaching the top of Bishop Pass, we traversed one of the routes in the Sierra Mountains that runs to the west of the highest peaks. We camped every other night or so in a different spot. The scenery was magnificent, the fishing too good, if anything. The skies were cloudless day after day as we slowly moved southward at an elevation of about eight thousand feet.

On the third or fourth day, Farquhar showed his hand. We had just arrived, he said, at a point from which climbers started the ascent of one of the highest peaks of the range, North Palisade, which loomed up as we looked eastward. It was an easy climb if one took it slowly, he said, and added that he and the youngest member of the party had made the climb and knew the way. It seemed a pity not to use the opportunity since the weather was so gorgeous. It would be necessary to rope up for the last few hundred feet, he admitted, but there was nothing difficult about climbing as a member of a party which was roped together; or so he assured me. So, after a practice "climb" over some boulders, I agreed with some reluctance to go along.

The first day involved nothing very different from what I was familiar with in "climbing" above the tree line in the Presidential Range in New Hampshire, except there was no clearly distinguishable trail. One just went up and up over small rocks and around large ones, the view getting more spectacular with every step. At an elevation of eleven thousand feet, we bivouacked for the night (we had carried only the minimum of supplies, a blanket apiece and a few extra clothes). One of the great advantages of the high mountains of California in the summer, of course, is that one can sleep in the open almost without fear of rain. The bed was hard rock, but I slept well nonetheless. We were all up at dawn and, after coffee heated over a small campfire, were ready for the real climb, which was to be a new experience for me but not for the others.

We roped up, with the young expert rock climber in the lead position. Before long, we started up what looked to me like a sheer vertical cliff; I experienced my first pang of anguish. The leader, however, agile as a goat, found a series of footholds and handholds one above the other; he made himself secure, or so he claimed, in a sort of niche. The second man followed literally in his footsteps while the first man kept the rope tight around his own body and kept gathering it in as the second man moved upward. By such a maneuver, I had been told, the man in motion was protected against a serious fall. When it now became my turn to be the actual climber, my skepticism as to the protection afforded by the rope and the stance of the man ahead was equaled only by my mounting fear. I was soon introduced to what my friends called a "chimney," a narrow crevice in the rock which was like a real chimney insofar as it went straight up toward the open sky.

As all who have climbed as a member of a roped party are well aware, progress is slow. Each increment of the climb is the length of the rope between the members. Each man must try to find a secure place for his feet and often for his hands when his time comes for moving upward; the one ahead is tense and minding the rope; the others, except the climber, are in theory relaxed and awaiting their turns. There was nothing relaxed about my attitude; I was almost as frightened when I was standing still as when I was climbing. Whether I looked up or down, what I saw only increased the feeling of terror which I was struggling to overcome. As we approached the top, I seemed to be succeeding in my internal wrestling with incipient panic; I was beginning to enjoy the effort to overcome my fear.

Several years later, an experienced guide in the Canadian Rockies told me that in his opinion the people who were enthusiastic climbers were those who had to fight off at least a small degree of fear in the "stiff pitches" in every climb. He illustrated his point with a story: A girl he had once guided had shown no emotion on making the most hair-raising traverses or looking down many thousand feet from the narrowest of ledges. When the climb was over, she expressed the view that there was no fun in climbing; the alleged sport was not for her.

It must have been well toward noon when we all stood on the top of the northern peak of the Palisade Range at an elevation of 14,254 feet. I was still suffering a bit from fright and wondering anxiously how it would be going down. Otherwise, I was in excellent shape; in terms of muscular fatigue, the climb had not been taxing. My fellow mountaineers, however, began talking about their feelings of dizziness, exhaustion and even nausea. Mountain sickness, a consequence of the elevation, was the verdict. Farquhar exclaimed, "This is one of the highest mountains in the United States." Which observation, coupled with the fact that all my companions had made the transition from sea level to fourteen thousand feet within a few days, afforded an explanation of their present misery, but no remedy. I was frankly worried. We could not make the descent, I knew, without a reversal of the procedure by which we had ascended. I was counting on the others to guide and sustain me, if necessary, by the techniques of mountaineering, which to them were almost second nature. And here was the whole crew acting and talking as though they could barely move. They were unworried by the prospects of climbing down the chimney, but perhaps were too sick to make the trip. I was completely healthy, but ignorant and scared. For a short time, I kicked myself in silence for ever having agreed to make the climb.

The symptoms of mountain sickness, however, seemed to grow less as we rested and turned our attention to the view, which was a different order of magnitude in its splendor from anything I had ever seen. I kept my eye on the young man who had jumped around with so much confidence as he led us up the chimney. He seemed to be completely restored within the space of half an hour or so. I was then certain we could get back to our bivouac spot before it was too dark. The others soon indicated they were ready to start; we roped up again and headed down a truly frightening route. I did what I was told to do. Nobody took a misstep, and there was no occasion when any one of us had to rely on the supporting tension of the rope. Indeed, I have no doubt that the youngest of our party, at least, could have gone up and down the peak without being roped to anyone.

The loss in altitude of some three thousand feet seemed to make a great difference to all the other members of the party. I did not notice the difference because I had spent several weeks on long walks from Fallen Leaf Lake at an elevation of seven to ten thousand feet. I had become conditioned by taking exercise at these moderate heights, and for that reason had not suffered from mountain sickness when I had ascended to fourteen thousand feet. The phenomenon was well known; my friends should have known better than to plan a trip to the top of one of the Sierra peaks without some days of prolonged exercise at somewhat lower altitudes. All of which was discussed at length as we prepared hot soup as an evening meal and got ready to sleep at the same spot where we had spent the night before.

Everyone was feeling better. The climb had been a great success, we all agreed. I joined without reservation in the acclamation. Indeed, if I had but known it, the twenty-four hours which had just passed marked a quantum jump in my psyche. I was ready to become an irrationally enthusiastic mountaineer.

I had no further opportunity to explore the High Sierra Mountains that summer. Before we parted, however, I learned from Francis Farquhar about other Harvard men who were interested in climbing. I was thus led to an acquaintance with some of the leading mountaineers. From one of them, I heard of the Canadian Alpine Club and its two-week encampments designed for both experts and novices in mountaineering. I was assured that I would be welcome. Therefore I sent in my application for a place at the 1938 camp which was to be established in Jasper Park in the northern Canadian

Rockies. I was told by my friends the opportunity was unusual as this portion of the mountains had hitherto been accessible only by a pack train. Now an automobile could take a person and his duffel to the temporary camp to be located at the base of the Columbia ice field, a vast expanse of ice and snow that was the source of the North Saskatchewan River. From it emerged snow-covered peaks. Since I had never climbed on ice or snow, the experience would be most rewarding.

I enlisted the companionship of an old friend, Philip A. Johnson of Norwich, Connecticut, whom I had first met in Washington in 1917 and with whom I had tramped the trails of the New Hampshire mountains for a week or more almost every summer since the early 1920s. He, too, had little experience with climbing in ice and snow and readily agreed to keep me company. Thanks to a letter of introduction from one of the Harvard alpinists, we were cordially received at the camp and given an opportunity to join a red-letter excursion. A trip was planned up the glacier to an overnight temporary camp on the ice field set up as a base for tackling one or more of the snow peaks. Phil and I were not at all certain we were sufficiently experienced to rate membership on such a climb, but our doubts were politely pushed aside. Therefore we joined a party of some fifteen men and women who climbed up to the base camp; we roped up when we passed through a portion of the glacier. Each of us carried a sleeping bag, essential as a very minimum of protection against the cold, which was all too evident inside the tents when the sun went down.

Our experiences have been described by the leader of the party, Captain R. E. Gibson, an experienced member of the Canadian Alpine Club, in the *Canadian Alpine Journal* in 1938:

> Living on a snow field was a novel and most interesting experience to most of our members. The problems of cooking, sleeping and washing required some rather drastic readjustment of one's usual habits. The absence of any water makes washing an almost unheard of luxury; this is somewhat of a trial to the fastidious but a boon to the lazy! There were many amusing incidents. On one occasion one of the men had his plate handed back to him by one of the ladies and was told to go and wash it again in the snow—he meekly complied. The man in question was Dr. Conant, President of Harvard, who related the incident with much glee.

The second day out the party was split in two; Phil and I were assigned to the group to ascend North Twin, a handsome snow-covered peak 12,085 feet high. First came a two-hour trip over the snow field and then the climb. We made a start before daybreak to be certain the snow surface was still frozen hard. For the actual climb, we roped up, but, except in one or two places, all proceeded at the same rate, quite different from the rock-climbing procedure. It all seemed not only easy but unterrifying, that is, all but the traverse of a ridge just before the top. Here I was glad that I was joined by a rope to an experienced party of mountaineers. One looked straight down on either side a distance of many thousand feet.

I had been the last man on the rope coming up and was now told I must be the first man going down. I did not relish the assignment, but there was nothing to do but take the first step on the downward journey as boldly as I could. When we reached the relatively level ice field (more accurately, a snow field), our only trouble began. The surface was no longer hard. The summer sun of a perfectly clear day was in the process of leaving its temporary mark. In places, one sank in the soft snow well above the knees. The guide, who was now ahead, kept probing with his ice ax to find spots which had not yet thawed. In spite of his skill, we were forced to proceed extremely slowly as we waded through soft snow almost to our waists.

We finally made it to the tents from which we had started long before dark. Being ignorant of alpine conditions, I had not been worried. But our guide confessed, when we were all safely at the base camp, that if snow conditions had been uniformly as bad as the worst we had encountered, our progress might have been so exhausting that some of us could have been forced to halt. A freezing night on the ice field with the possibility of a change in weather and a party containing some inexperienced hands was a prospect our guide had not fancied.

He was one of the group of Swiss guides whom the Canadian Pacific Railroad had settled near Banff some years before. One or two of them were engaged by the Canadian Alpine Club each year for their annual camp. They were a wonderful group of men. Following such an experienced mountaineer was an educational experience in itself. They made difficult climbs with the expert members but were also available as instructors for novices. As I benefited from the instruction we all received incidental to the climb, I looked back with ever-increasing regret at the opportunities I had neglected on my European trips to learn about mountaineering from Swiss guides in their native land. But in those days, though I took a long walking trip with a friend, I was too timid to hire a guide. Now I was starting to try to be an alpinist at rather too late an age. All of which is evidence of the "breakthrough" in my thinking brought about by a Harvard alumnus who was bound his college president should, like himself, be a real mountain climber.

The Canadian Alpine Club camp which I joined in the summer of 1939 was located in the Ice River valley at the foot of the Vaux Glacier not far from Field, a station on the Canadian Pacific Railroad in British Columbia. The weather was not good. Nevertheless, I learned much about climbing. The following letter to my wife is testimony to the extent to which I had succumbed to the allure of high mountains.

Today is a day off in camp. Yesterday, I climbed Mt. Vaux (pronounced Vox) about 6,000 feet above the camp; it is a snow peak. The long climb started at 5 A.M., and we returned to camp at 5 P.M. The party consisted of a mixed crowd of graduating members, a couple of old-timers and two Swiss guides. We traversed a snow field which was in good condition after some mild rock work, slid down the snow couloirs on the way home—"glissading" they call it. Lots of fun. I have tried fishing today without any luck. We are in a great cirque of rocks with ice and snow above. The weather has been bad here and was when I arrived; it has been raining off and on for three days. Yesterday was clear but there were clouds on the lower mountains, which made the view interesting since we were above the clouds. Today started to be bright but now is overcast with high clouds and it looks like rain. The big climbs are not available as there has been too much fresh snow. I couldn't make them anyway as they are too difficult, but the camp is a bit gloomy. . . . Otherwise, everyone is happy. This is a very beautiful, wild spot and I am enjoying it all immensely. I hope to get in one or two other climbs of peaks just over 10,000 feet if possible. Vaux is 10,891 feet high; the camp is at 5,200 feet. All of the climbs are long. I have met many old acquaintances here and everyone is very cordial. I hope to send this letter out before I go. The trip is ten miles by horse, fourteen miles by car over a very bad road.

A second letter from the same spot is of some interest because it reflects my reactions to climbing in my third year as a true mountaineer.

I am on my way home this afternoon via Zinc Gulch, Lake O'Hara, Lake Louise and Banff.

The climb yesterday was the best yet—a peak of no significance, but a view and a climb rated A-1 by even the old-timers. A subsidiary peak (Martin's, we call it) of Goodsir—it rises 10,500 feet approximately as a rock ridge. The trip was long even from here, though we were a slow party due to the lack of experience in rock climbing. There was plenty of rock climbing, though none of extreme difficulty and the rock is good, which in this country is rare. After this climb I feel I can, given time, tackle any but the "stunt" climbs, in which I have no interest. I am glad I am so well conditioned, however, as the climb is not for anyone who is soft.

A third letter is really concerned with human nature rather than with the mountains. Since it reveals something about the writer's reactions to events beyond his control, my wife, who has the custody of these letters, insists that it should be included.

Here I am waiting at the end of the trail for an auto to take me to Lake Louise. There are four other "Alpinists" here also waiting. We walked over a twelve-mile trail this morning, had a sandwich lunch here and are now hoping the promised car will arrive. Another beautiful day, clear but very warm.

Yesterday was an amusing study in human nature as well as providing an opportunity for a little exercise and some glorious views. There was an auxiliary camp high up in Zinc Gulch from which, as a base, Mt. Goodsir (the major climb) and Zinc Mountain (said to be minor) can be attacked. The first party from this camp went up Monday afternoon and was supposed to climb Zinc Mountain and return yesterday. The second party was to replace them, the amateur guide to stay and take this second party up Zinc. The attack on Goodsir with two Swiss guides and a group of climbers was scheduled for tomorrow. I went along with the second Zinc Gulch party to see the place and then to walk out to the base here today. My plans went through as per schedule, but, alas, not those of the others. When we (three ladies, a boy and myself) arrived at about 5:30 P.M. yesterday at the Zinc Gulch camp, the climbing party had not appeared! When they got in about 7:30, they still had a long hike back to the main camp (about 2½ hours since their bedding had already gone down with the horses. They are a tired and mad crowd. It seems Zinc Mountain was not easy and they had a very weak sister, a *man*, on the trip. As I heard the gossip while they drank hot soup, the gentleman, a Dr. ———, was most unpopular. In spite of much talk about his rock climbing at the campfire, he had apparently gone to pieces on the ridge and had to be dragged down by the ladies! They were furious. The amateur guide struck. Abetted by his wife, who was boiling in several senses of the word, he said he would not try Zinc Mountain again and certainly not with the party that had been set up. He was going back with his weary gang to camp. At which news, a redheaded young English girl (very English) from British Columbia went into a fret. What was she to do the next day? Take a walk around the camp and enjoy the view, was the answer. This brought further very unbecoming rage and quite a nice little tantrum. A Miss Guest from Philadelphia, a seasoned climber who was one of the returning footsore climbers, said she would stay and take charge of a mild ramble, but not a climb. The English girl, who knows nothing about the mountains, was all for doing absolutely impossible things based on reading of her map. The conversation was amusing, but everyone except the girl kept their tempers and was firm. So we saw the defeated climbers off (defeated since they had failed to reach the top). The party, I am told, reached camp about midnight. Whether they burned Dr. ——— at the campfire or not, I have not heard.

About 6 A.M. I heard male voices. This seemed strange since Zinc Gulch is off the beaten track, to put it mildly. Then, into my tent popped Henry Hall of Cambridge, Massachusetts, and the famous Captain Rex Gibson. They had just returned with another man and a Swiss guide of their own from a very successful expedition to the Coast Range. They arrived in the camp at Ice River at 8 P.M., arose at 3 A.M. this morning and were up with us for breakfast and an attack on Goodsir. All of which has apparently irritated the climbers of the Alpine Club who have been waiting for a week to climb Goodsir. Now they are going to be beaten to it by this new gang. Of course, it is not a first ascent, but the implication (if Hall and Gibson succeed) will be that the Swiss guides and the climbing committee have been overconservative in holding back so long and waiting for the snow to melt.

And finally as I came down the trail alone early this morning after stopping to admire the view, I heard a female English hail! The redheaded girl was off in a huff and back to the camp to give the management a bit of her mind! No ordinary views for her. So you see, climbing mountains is not without human interest. All of which probably doesn't entertain you much, but has entertained me no end. If the auto ever arrives and we get to Lake Louise, I shall mail this letter there. . . .

The first thing Henry Hall asked me was: "What have you climbed? I said, Mt. Vaux. "Good," he replied, "that's a major peak; now you can get into the American Alpine Club." Honor of honors, to him!

By the time another twelve months had passed, Europe had been at war for many months. The Conant family had planned a vacation in Glacier Park and in the Canadian Rockies. With the fall of France, these plans were postponed, so we thought. In fact, they were abandoned. The war engulfed all four of us in one way or another.

As far as rock climbing was concerned, I had one more chance. In June 1940, in between my trips to Washington on government business, I arranged for a little rock climb with my son Jim, who was just graduating from Exeter, and one of his teachers, a skilled mountaineer. We proposed to climb up the side of Mount Washington from the Pinkham Notch camp over one of the well-known rock climbs. We were roped together in orthodox fashion and climbed one man at a time according to the accepted custom. There were no difficulties. As we unroped and prepared to descend by the usual path, I thought how relatively easy it would be to keep up my newly acquired interest so near to home.

And then I leaned forward to pick up my knapsack and suddenly I was in trouble. My back had misbehaved in a painful manner. I crept down the path looking like a lame man and feeling that I would never straighten up. I did eventually after much doctoring, but my days of real climbing were over. I was never again to be roped up. The American Alpine Club elected me, but the implied promise of my sponsors remains to this day unfulfilled. When I hear real climbers talk about their climbs, I feel that I am almost one of them, at least at heart. I am still full of gratitude to Francis Farquhar and have enjoyed his friendship for many years.

PART III

THE WAR YEARS

CHAPTER 18

Speaking Out as an Interventionist

THE FIRST SUNDAY in May 1940 fell on the fifth. As usual, Mrs. Conant and I were at home to the members of the faculty and their wives at 17 Quincy Street, the residence of the president of the university. We soon found ourselves discussing the events of the past four weeks. The European war had taken a new turn. The months of inaction—the phony war—had come to an end. Just a month earlier the British and French had mined the Norwegian waters. Two days later, on April 9, the Germans had landed troops in Norway. Although the Norwegians had fought back desperately and an Anglo-French expeditionary force had been sent to assist in the defense of Norway, the counterattack had failed. On May 3 the British and French troops had withdrawn; the Nazis remained in complete control of Norway.

The question in everybody's mind that Sunday afternoon was what would happen next. The expected air attack on England and France in September of the preceding year had not taken place. The prophets of gloom who had foreseen the destruction of Britain's cities from the air as soon as Great Britain declared war on Germany had been proved wrong. That is, they had been proved wrong so far. The attacks from the air had been confined to the distribution of propaganda pamphlets. A joke which had been circulating all winter epitomized the American reaction to the suspended state of tension across the Atlantic. A British flier, the story went, who had been charged with dropping pamphlets on a German city returned to his air base with the confession that he had failed to cut the binding threads around his package; the entire tightly bound bundle had left the plane. The base officer was horrified. "Don't you realize," he said, "the parcel might have hit someone and caused an injury?" The anecdote was considered funny in early 1940; I don't doubt it was told in England as well as the United States. The disastrous campaign of the Allies on the Scandinavian peninsula now put the European war in a different light. The time for jokes was past.

One of the older professors who was taking tea with us that Sunday asked how the British could be so stupid. They had mined the Norwegian waters, but failed to provide adequately for the defense of Norway against an attack by the German armed forces. The question was purely rhetorical, of course. Like most of us, the professor had his own sources of information, which he undoubtedly thought far superior to those of any others present. No one spoke up to defend or explain the Anglo-French strategy. Everyone was unhappy at this evidence of the weakness of the Allies. Yet if anyone saw in the debacle a forerunner of far worse things to come, he held his peace.

Instead, more than one of us repeated the optimistic predictions we had been hearing for the past months. It was the general opinion of those who were "well informed" that the German Army was no match for the French. Allied intelligence was said to have become convinced of the inadequacies of the leadership of Hitler's ground forces. "Someone who really knew" had reported that the Allied high command was just waiting to destroy the Germans "like rats in a trap" as soon as the Maginot Line defenses were attacked. As my contribution to the conversation, I repeated what I had heard Professor Heinrich Bruening, the former Chancellor of the Weimar Republic, say a few days earlier. Referring to Chamberlain's remark that Hitler had missed the bus, Bruening had said that in his opinion Chamberlain was correct; if Hitler had invaded Holland in the fall, he might well have succeeded; now it was too late.

I remember this discussion about the war so clearly because it was to be almost the last one to end on an optimistic note for some time to come. On Friday, May 10, the long-awaited German attack of the Low Countries started. By Sunday the Germans were across the Meuse. The following day a large section of Rotterdam was destroyed from the air. This first example of what air power could accomplish in minutes if unopposed was intended to teach a lesson. It did. The Dutch Army surrendered on May 14. The country was overrun. The efforts to stop the Germans by opening the dikes had failed. In the meantime, the Maginot Line was proving to be something less than impregnable.

The annual meeting of the Associated Harvard Clubs was scheduled for the weekend of May 18 in New York City. Speakers from the university were to present various aspects of Harvard academic life at a large Friday evening meeting in the Metropolitan Opera House. It was planned as a highly significant occasion. We in Cambridge knew how difficult a New York audience was to please. The citizens of New York had heard the most distinguished speakers time and time again. My role was merely as presiding officer—I might say ringmaster. Nevertheless, when I took the one o'clock train for New York on Friday afternoon, I was as apprehensive as though I were to make my first bow before an alumni gathering. With the war news changing almost hourly (and continually for the worse), how was a meeting centering on Harvard to attract and hold a crowd?

I had been sharing my worries over the telephone with my New York friend and classmate, Arthur Calvert Smith. He had long been my private source of information about the attitudes of the New York alumni. He was already scheduled to move to Cambridge in the fall to act as my special assistant and editor of the *Harvard Alumni Bulletin*. A trusted guide and friend was thus to be given an official status. Now we had an immediate problem. What, if anything, should I say in New York about the terrifying events in France?

In my remarks, I did refer, of course, to the shadow of a totalitarian state sweeping over the map of Europe. But I did *not* take a stand on the issue which was starting to boil to the surface. I was neither an interventionist nor an isolationist. Without dwelling on the European war, I talked about Harvard and matters academic. Not so, the alumni. They talked only about the war. Their sources of news were in many cases direct wires from London and Paris. Indeed, one prominent New York banker spoke almost as though he were himself the French Government. "We may have to declare Paris an open city," he said, "and make our stand along the Loire!"

In person-to-person conversation, or in discussions in small groups, I had an opportunity to sample alumni opinion throughout the two-day meeting. Over a thousand attended the meetings. I never heard even a slightly favorable word about the Germans. If a poll had been taken, I am sure the result would have shown that those present were pro-Ally and anti-German by at least 99 to 1. When it came to prophecy, however, opinions covered a wide range. Some assumed the war was nearly over, with Germany triumphant over France and Great Britain. To be sure, such extreme pessimism was the view of only a small minority. The extreme optimists remembered the Battle of the Marne; they predicted the German "Blitzkrieg" would yet be halted; they were also few in number. The vast majority seemed numbed by the news. They did not want to try to foresee the future; least of all did they wish to consider the effect the unexpected events would have on the future of the United States.

I must have talked at some length about the altered European situation and the policy of the United States with several hundred persons. Many of them were people with whom I was on terms of intimacy; with them I could speak frankly. There was no question but that these people, like myself, were pro-Ally. Yet some were so isolationist that their isolationism almost forced them to consider any accommodation with Hitler. I recall the response of one business friend to whom I suggested that the United States might have to intervene if France was conquered and Great Britain stood alone. "Be realistic," was the sharp reply. "If Germany wins the battle now in progress on the continent, the war is over. The United States has got to learn to live with the victor in spite of what the English may wish to do. As a matter of fact, they will soon make peace themselves." I admit I was shocked. Such a statement was to me not realistic but totally unrealistic. I was convinced that one could not do business with Hitler. Furthermore, I knew my knowledge of Germany was a better basis for a prognosis than his.

As an opportunity to learn how important people were sizing up the European tragedy, the meeting of the Associated Harvard Clubs was a great success. No one was bored because nobody had put more than a small fraction of his attention on the object of the meeting. A few alumni may have been interested in what was said by the professors who spoke, though I doubt it. Mayor La Guardia took a sharp poke at his Harvard friends in his words of welcome. "You Harvard men are wonderful the way you all stick together," the Mayor said. "You are all loyal to one another under all circumstances except when one of you happens to land in the White House." Many of his listeners were veterans of Theodore Roosevelt's campaign for the presidency; all knew that for a considerable percentage of Harvard College graduates Franklin Delano Roosevelt was *that* man in the White House, the traitor to his class. The audience appreciated the jibe. There was too much truth behind it for my taste. Some of us had hoped this New York gathering of the clans might serve to soften the bitterness against certain professors who had been prominent in supporting the New Deal. Yet what we witnessed was the start of another bitter fight among citizens all equally certain they knew the correct answer to the number one question of the day. And though neither side suspected it, the new issue eventually would drain away much of the hostility of Harvard men of my generation toward the President of the United States.

Many prominent Americans who made the defense of America the top priority in their thinking were already rallying both pro– and anti–New Dealers to their standard. They were saying it was time for all farseeing men to stand up and be counted. As I left New York, the question in my mind was: Should I be counted? In Calvert Smith's opinion as well as that of at least one member of the Harvard Corporation, Grenville Clark, the answer was an unqualified yes. A committee was at that moment in process of being formed by William Allen White, the well-known author and editor, and Clark Eichelberger, national director of the League of Nations Association. It was to be called "The Committee to Defend America by Aiding the Allies." An invitation to join had arrived just as I had left my office. On returning to my desk in Massachusetts Hall on Monday morning, I telegraphed to White as follows: "Am making an exception to my general rule not to serve on committees or sponsor movements not connected with education because of the paramount importance of your committee and my intense feeling that your aims are right. I am glad, therefore, to join your committee."

The news grew worse. Brussels fell. By the end of the week, King Leopold III of Belgium was so hard pressed as to believe he had no alternative but to capitulate. The British were retreating toward the beaches at Dunkirk. A telephone call from White over the weekend offered me the chance to speak over CBS the evening of Wednesday, May 29. White would introduce me. I accepted without hesitation and immediately telephoned Calvert Smith, who came up to Cambridge on Monday to help in the preparation of the speech.

We had advice from Eichelberger, and we borrowed freely from the arguments Grenville Clark had used in a letter to the *New York Times* ten days before. As it finally emerged from the labors of Smith, Dave Little (the secretary of the university) and myself, the speech was a call for action. Write or telegraph the President, Congressmen and Senators, I urged. Let them know you believe that the United States should take every action possible to ensure the defeat of Hitler. At the moment, I said, the entry of the United States into the war did

not seem necessary or wise; for the present, we were no better prepared to render aid as an active belligerent than we could render as
a nonbelligerent; actions short of war, if immediate and effective,
might suffice. I warned, however, that if the United States continued
to be confused and dilatory, our aid might come too late; in that case
the possibility of war under highly unfavorable conditions would soon
confront us; our previous fears of war might well have made inevitable our engagement in the conflict without the support of powerful
nations. The pacifist would then, indeed, have dug the grave of liberalism. Among the measures which could be taken at once, I listed: (1)
the release to France and England of "army and navy airplanes and
other implements of war"; (2) the repeal of laws now preventing
American citizens from volunteering for service in foreign armies;
(3) the control of exports with the intent to avoid leaks to Germany;
(4) the cooperation of our Maritime Commission with the Allies in
"every possible way under our present laws" to expedite the sending
of supplies and munitions.

I confess I was proud of the speech as an honest, hard-hitting
document. I liked the bit about the pacifist and liberalism in particular. I thought a short paragraph toward the end especially effective;
it went as follows:

At this moment, today, the war is in effect veering toward our shores.
The issue before the United States is, I repeat: Can we live as a free,
peaceful, relatively unarmed people in a world dominated by the totalitarian
states? Specifically, can we look with indifference as a nation (as a nation,
mind you, not as individuals) on the possible subjugation of England by a
Nazi State? If your answer is yes, then my words are in vain. If your
answer is no, I urge you as a citizen to act.

The incoming mail the next few days proved the address was a success. Overnight I had become one of the leading interventionists. From
that time on, until Pearl Harbor, I devoted more and more time and
energy to trying to convince others of the correctness of my diagnosis
of the dangers facing the United States.

However, this was not my first statement about the European war.
Nor was it the first evidence of my deep emotional involvement in the
cause of stopping Hitler. The winter months in 1925 that my wife and
I had spent in Germany had enabled us to get a glimpse of the troubles
plaguing the Weimar Republic. A summer vacation in the Black
Forest in 1930 had continued our education, and for the first time
we were brought face to face with the "man on the street," who was
responding so favorably to Hitler's speeches. We had followed the

news in the critical years of 1932 and 1933 with care; we thought we knew what Nazism was really like. Actually, of course, even the most severe judgment we could pass on the Nazis as late as 1940 did not begin to envision the potential barbarity of the regime. The horrors of the "final solution" still lay in the future.

That Hitler meant gangster rule, the suppression of individual freedom, ruthless anti-Semitism and armed aggression had seemed to me clear from the start. The Harvard Corporation in 1934 had refused Hanfstaengl's gift. Yet we had endeavored to keep open communications with German university scholars. Several were invited to the Harvard Tercentenary Celebration and received honorary degrees in 1936. As the true nature of the new government became clear, more and more German scholars had sought refuge in the United States. By 1940 we had filled a number of permanent positions at Harvard with distinguished refugees.

During the Munich days I had hoped the British would stand firm. I judged Chamberlain and his associates to be making an almost criminal error. Yet what right had a citizen of a nation deeply committed to isolation and neutrality to pass a verdict on another country's refusal to risk a war? Like many others, I was tortured by such questions. A year later, when even Chamberlain had come to see Hitler's true intentions, I was almost ready to urge a belligerent status for the United States. But at this time I contented myself with a one-man minor operation. On September 28, 1939, I wrote the following letter to Alf M. Landon, who had been the presidential candidate of the Republican Party; it was released to the press on October 4, 1939:

MY DEAR MR. LANDON:

I am venturing to write to you as the official leader of the opposition party concerning the current debate on the so-called neutrality bill.

I am personally strongly in favor of a modification of the law so as to permit the sale of implements of war to France and England. I believe that if these countries are defeated by a totalitarian power, the hope of free institutions as a basis of modern civilization will be jeopardized. To depart from our historic policy, and by so doing handicap those who are fighting for ideals we share, seems to me inconsistent and unwise.

But I am not writing you primarily about the outcome of the present debate. What concerns me most is the current denial of the democratic process inherent in the statement of the problem. As the discussion has developed, it appears to be taken as a premise that the only matter before the country is how to keep the United States out of war. This attitude is the natural result of twenty years of persistent agitation. To my mind it introduces an emotional element into the situation which is potentially very dangerous—equally dangerous as the opposite emotion, war hysteria, against which we are quite properly daily warned.

A clearheaded, realistic discussion of all possible eventualities would seem best suited to guide the decisions of this country. If every phrase must be chosen so as to avoid the charge of being a warmonger, a blanket of censorship has been cast on public debate. Should we not discuss openly and freely all phases of the international situation in the light of the best interests of this country? Should we not examine without fear the advantages and disadvantages from our own selfish point of view of every aspect of foreign policy? Must we not assume that a democracy can make a rational choice on matters of war and peace as on other phases of national policy? If not, war has already defeated democracy on this continent. This is to me the vital point.

The issue before Congress is in effect that of selling arms and munitions to belligerents who can come and get them. The question is, is it to the long-run advantage of the United States to sell these arms or not? The question is not, shall we declare war? No responsible person is now urging us to become a combatant. From time to time as the war progresses, other vital problems with respect to our foreign policy will arise. Let us deal with each in turn. Let us not be afraid to face any issue but have confidence in the cool judgment of the country, based on national self-interest and expressed through the democratic process.

What I referred to as the "current debate" had started as soon as President Roosevelt, on September 13, had called Congress into special session with the purpose of considering the neutrality legislation passed a few years earlier. Senator William E. Borah of Idaho had spoken over the radio at once against any changes in the legislation. On September 23, Hamilton Fish, a member of the House of Representatives from New York, had delivered a blast against all who were in favor of the modification of what came to be known as the "arms embargo." He declared that the paramount issue before the country was to prevent the United States' being "eased into war" by the "warmongers."

My letter to Landon received considerable publicity. It marked me as being strongly against the isolationists, but as yet I was not even a part-way interventionist. I had gone far enough, however, to receive plenty of negative comments on my letter. The undergraduate newspaper, the *Harvard Crimson*, said I had earned an unenviable place in the "road gang which is trying to build for the United States a super-highway straight to Armageddon." Being criticized by the *Crimson* was nothing new. The fact that the editors disagreed with my letter to Landon did not interfere in the least either with my weekly meetings with them or with my discussion of the war with students who came in on Sunday afternoons to tea. At that time, Mrs. Conant and I were at home to the faculty the first Sunday in each month of the academic year, at home to students the other Sunday afternoons.

I recall many discussions with students during the winter of the phony war, 1939–40. My own position I did not attempt to conceal, but at the same time I did not directly attack the isolationists. The dispute over the arms embargo laws had ended in November 1939 with the passage of a new Neutrality Act. The sale of arms to belligerents was authorized on a "cash-and-carry basis." Those of us who had feared that London would be subjected to devastating bombing from the air had been wrong. All was quiet on all fronts except the Soviet-Finnish one. Still, the strong probability that the phony war would someday become a real war was in everybody's mind. And the minute such a premise was admitted, conversation with young men of fighting age turned to a consideration of what the United States ought to do if Germany appeared to be winning. I tried to keep a discussion going by acting more or less like the chairman of a meeting, urging those present to speak their minds. Mrs. Conant joined with me in these efforts after those who really wanted tea had left the dining room and joined the circle in the living room.

What would those present be willing to fight for? This question in one form or another was tossed about on more than one occasion. It was all very hypothetical, of course. Nobody could be sure another Munich was not in the offing. Maybe there would be a settlement without further fighting. Very few cared to speculate on the consequences of vast land battles on the European continent as in the 1914–18 war. Indeed, the rapid success of the German armies in Poland in September had made a repetition of the world war unlikely. Looking back, it is hard for me to realize how great was the ignorance of all of us about modern military matters, including the role of the airplane, the tank and the submarine. We talked not about tactics and strategy, but rather about the United States' part in international politics.

On one occasion, when all present seemed to be certain there was no conceivable danger to the United States which would warrant their fighting, one youth spoke up in favor of the Chinese, who had been under attack by Japan for years. Perhaps he would be willing to fight for China if by so doing he could be of any service. I think one or two students agreed with him. No sooner had their somewhat idealistic point of view about the Far East been expressed than a cynic spoke up to suggest that fighting for China was an idea to be espoused with safety since there was not the slightest chance that such a sentiment would ever be put to the test, whereas similar views about England and France might be.

My most vivid memory of those student discussions is one occasion when the British Empire was attacked by apparently all hands present. Not only was the colonialism of the past heartily condemned, but the whole social and foreign policy of the British Government was about to be torn to shreds completely, when I intervened. Remembering the strong upper-class English accent of one of the late-comers I had greeted a few minutes before, I said, "Wait a minute, gentlemen. I think there is a representative of Great Britain here with us this afternoon, and I think it only fair to hear his views." At which the man in question spoke up at once and said, "I agree with everything that has been said. I would rather live in England under Hitler than under Chamberlain." I gasped and asked, "Where did you study in England?" "At the London School of Economics," was the reply. To myself I said, "That is what comes of extreme left-wing criticism of our capitalistic society: a student decides the government is not worth defending."

How the discussion continued after this surprising testimony from the former student of the London School of Economics, I have no memory. The incident was to me only one manifestation of the disillusionment of young people. It merely proved that the disease was not confined to the United States. Those Sunday afternoons had given me an insight into the way many of the younger generation were thinking. I thought I understood their point of view and in a way sympathized with it, yet I was 100 percent against it. At all events, I decided to incorporate a defense of the younger generation in a speech I made to the Jewish War Veterans in New York on June 12, 1940, as follows:

We are here today to honor the tradition of individual freedom. It is therefore appropriate for me to say a word or two in defense of those who do not agree with us, particularly those of the younger generation who are strict isolationists or ardent pacifists. These young men are ready to fight only to repel actual invasion. Some hesitate even to endorse strong measures of preparedness. Apparently they would run the risk of fighting too late and ill equipped rather than have this country enter a war for any purpose except defense of its geographic boundaries. I believe they are wrong. But let us be chary of passing harsh judgment upon them. Let us above all not accuse them of lack of idealism. Nothing could be further from the truth. Many are, rather, suffering from overexposure to one particular ideal, a noble one but not always sufficient: the ideal of peace.

In short, the errors of the youth of today, if they be errors, are symptoms of their idealism. Furthermore, having been bred in an atmosphere of freedom, they passionately desire to be independent in their thinking. These young people reject the old clichés. They decline to be rubber stamps. Their emotions and their thoughts have been conditioned by the turbulent times. Perhaps this is well, for they will enter a world which promises to be no place for weaklings. And let me emphasize that whatever may be the faults of our young men, they are no weaklings—they are tough-minded. With a few exceptions they cannot be converted by preaching or exhortation. For that I honor them. And so must you who honor the tradition of sturdy individual thoughts. Facts, not phrases, guide their thinking. With deeds alone, not words, the divergent thought of youth must be encountered. We must evolve a program for the individual that will make our great tradition a reality to each coming generation.

In defending the younger generation, I drew heavily on what I had discovered by talking with Harvard students in the preceding months. Not all those who had come to tea those Sunday afternoons had been isolationists. But there had been few, if any, who were prepared to go even as far as I had in my letter to Landon. The fear that the United States might be tricked into the war by Great Britain, coupled with dogmatic pacifism, was the predominant note. After May 10, when the Germans attacked the Low Countries, discussions about the war and America's possible involvement had a new flavor. With the defeat of France becoming daily a growing probability, the question of the United States' involvement had lost its hypothetical nature. The *Harvard Crimson* published on May 21 a document signed by hundreds of students stating that the signers were determined "never under any circumstances to follow the footsteps of the students of 1917." The *Crimson* in an interpretive statement explained that it was not an "ironbound pacifist ukase but an expression of a belief that the way in which America drifted toward war in those years was unintelligent and unworthy of our nation."

Thirty-four members of the class of 1917 quickly composed an answer (probably at the meeting of the Associated Harvard Clubs in New York). It was published on May 31. The authors denied they had been misled. They had fought for principles. In other words, these veterans of the world war gave the lie to all the propaganda that had been built up in the 1920s about how the Allies and certain New York bankers had deceived the American people in 1917. They knew and I knew how the investigation of the munitions industry headed by Senator Gerald P. Nye had poisoned the interpretation of recent United States history. By publicizing the way the British had financed the purchase of supplies in the United States in World War I, the impression had been fostered that there had been a sinister tie between American financiers and those who manufactured arms and ammunition. Yet the disagreement was only in part one between the middle-aged and the young. There were many of my contemporaries, particularly in the Midwestern states, who would have agreed with the *Harvard Crimson* rather than with those who claimed to speak for the class of 1917.

Living up to my newly acquired role as an interventionist, I wired President Roosevelt on June 5 as follows: "Venture to wire you personally in support of views set forth in my radio talk of May 29 particularly urging that all planes which can be spared without endangering our security be released quickly to Allies."

I must have been moved to send this message by a telegram I received from White on June 3 saying he was delighted with the reception my talk had received; he added that semiofficially he had been assured that two hundred planes had left Newfoundland two days before. (They were planes which the British were buying, of course; they were not the property of the U.S. Government. The concept of Lend-Lease lay in the future.) White added that "Washington is feeling impulse of our work."

On June 10 the President of the United States went further than he had before. In a speech in Charlottesville, Virginia, he stated that the United States would rearm and extend to "the opponents of force" the material resources of the nation. We interventionists were enormously encouraged. I wired the next day to White suggesting that the Committee to Defend America by Aiding the Allies should do all in its power to get an immediate favorable response from the country to the President's statement; I further suggested that telegrams and letters be sent to Congress urging "passage of all legislation necessary to implement this statement." What I had in mind specifically is not now clear. Perhaps it was the repeal of those provisions of the Neutrality Act which were still in force and prohibited the extension of loans and credits to belligerents. If so, I was getting ahead of the official policy of White's committee. Or rather, I should say, ahead of the chairman's position.

I became a member of the policy committee of White's committee and was in almost constant communication with other members. As evidence of the way my thoughts were running, I quote from a letter of July 15, 1940, to Clark Eichelberger:

I feel strongly that between now and August 15 your Committee should concentrate its efforts on sounding a general note of alarm about the future of this country in case Great Britain is overwhelmed. I think a copy of your excellent *Primer of American Defense* should be in the hands of every voter. Is that an impossible ideal? Couldn't you get money enough to have a tremendous distribution of this document? I feel that a great deal of public speaking should be directed in the next few weeks to warning the people and waking them up. I am glad that the military training program seems to be on the way towards accomplishment, but additional support on this point will do no harm. Indeed, if this act is to be put into force with the full power of public opinion, it is necessary that the whole country be made aware of the peril which threatens us. In all this publicity and speaking, it seems to me that the importance of keeping England going and the significance of the British fleet can be stressed without coming down to specific measures.

I do feel in this introductory period, however, that emphasis should be placed on the fact that England is like a beleaguered fortress. We are now witnessing the first frontal attack. I believe it would be important to emphasize the point that while some people believe that it will be carried in this first assault and predict its downfall by August 15, we of the Committee feel otherwise. We have confidence. By repeatedly sounding this note during the next month it will then be possible if England holds out until then to return and say, "See, we predicted she would resist the first attack. You predicted she would fall. We were right. England is now in for a siege. What shall we do about it?" When August 15 or thereabouts has come around, if the situation in England has not deteriorated to any great extent, I believe the time will come for a second type of publicity campaign coupled with the introduction into Congress of the legislation which your special committee, I hope, is going to formulate. At this time should not a second primer be issued which would have for its fundamental motif some such thought as this: "A month or six weeks ago the defeatists in this country said England cannot withstand the first fierce German assault. In the last six weeks, a drastic onslaught has taken place. (Then give here some startling figures of the number of raids, tons of bombs, etc.) In spite of this England still holds firm. It has been demonstrated she can withstand a frontal attack, but can she stand a siege? The answer is: Yes, for some months, but clearly not forever. She must stand until we are ready from the point of view of our defenses. We cannot be ready until September, 1941. Hence we must see that she stands the siege. To this end the following legislation must be enacted at once as a matter of national defense." Then open up on your modified neutrality act and, if public opinion seems favorable, the opening of the American ports to the British fleet. Personally I hope that some *quid pro quo* on the part of the British would be forth-coming such as turning over to us on some basis the British bases on this side of the Atlantic, but this is a problem of international politics in which I cannot feel competent even to express an opinion.

In July I was invited to join a group of interventionists which later came to be known unofficially as the Century Group. Francis P. Miller of Fairfax, Virginia, and Professor Henry P. Van Dusen of the Union Theological Seminary were the leaders in organizing the first meeting on July 11, which was to be a strictly private discussion among like-minded people. No statement would be issued. Such an assurance was of first importance. Thirty interventionists headed by Miller had published a statement on June 10 which I could not have signed. These extremists declared that "the United States should im-mediately give official recognition to the fact and logic of the situa-tion—by declaring that a state of war exists between this country and Germany."

I agreed with the signers that "Nazi Germany is the mortal enemy of our ideals, our institutions and our way of life." I did not agree that anyone should advocate a declaration of war. At this point in time my views were those of William Allen White, who declined to sub-scribe to Miller's statement. "By advocating the declaration of war, you get four jumps ahead of my group," he wrote.

For reasons which will be evident in the next chapter, I did not have time to attend the dinners of the Century Group, which were held in New York City. Since, however, the membership in this highly informal group involved no subscription to a public statement, I was glad to keep in touch. When on September 3 President Roosevelt announced the destroyer-base agreement with Great Britain, I knew that the Century Group had been successful in their efforts at the White House. The British would get the old destroyers, the United States would receive permanent rights for air and naval bases in Ber-muda and elsewhere in British possessions along the Atlantic Coast. Though I had been completely on the sidelines, I could join with some fifty others to sign a public statement giving unqualified endorsement of the President's action. The list of names included all shades of inter-ventionist opinion. Its publication showed that anti-Roosevelt and pro-Roosevelt men even in the heat of the election campaign were united in their support of a specific "aid to the Allies" move.

Traditionally the president of Harvard has made a short address on the first Tuesday of the academic year at the morning chapel services, and the opening of the college year on September 24, 1940, made it necessary for me to speak my mind once again. What I said in this case was certain to be news unless I avoided the subject of the war in Europe. And I had no intention of doing that. I remember discussing with Calvert Smith the use of this occasion to sum up my views about the current danger. He said I was trying to cover too much ground. When he saw the completed manuscript just before delivery, he admitted he had been wrong. I certainly put my heart into the preparation.

"We are members of an academic family," I said, "which can count a total of seventy-five college generations of four years each; many of these have lived through periods black with the smoke of war. . . . Yet even against this background of three centuries of human vicissitudes, it is, perhaps, not an overstatement to declare that the present college year opens under the shadow of a threat never before present in our history. . . . The possibility must be reckoned with that the course of the development of all institutions of learning may be drastically altered by events which are perhaps close at hand.

"What is the worst possibility which confronts us—war?" I asked. "So many people think," I continued, "but I venture to disagree. War is not the worst possibility we face; the worst is the complete triumph of totalitarianism. Such a triumph might conceivably include this republic among the victims as a result of military reversals. Or we might become in essence a dependent state through a policy of appeasement under the coercion of a Nazi system which controlled the seas."

To emphasize my judgment of the degree of danger, I then referred to the sweep of Mohammed and later his followers against the crumbling Byzantine Empire. Of course, I conceded I might be wrong. Then I jumped to another analogy. A messenger trying to warn a sleeping town of an impending flood might be wrong. (The story of the Jamestown flood in the days of my youth had made a lasting impression on me.) The inhabitants, hearing him shouting that the dam had broken, must make a quick decision. Is the messenger an alarmist? A not dissimilar decision, I suggested, was now before the United States. Those who felt we were going too fast had the right and duty to say "stop"; those who fretted at the delay were entitled to try to convert others to their views. Clearly, I was in the second group. I did not, however, carry this address to its logical conclusion, which was war with Germany if that was the only way of stopping Hitler. Rather I reverted to my proper role as an educator and spoke about the necessity of individual effort and the need for universities to preserve the ideals of tolerance and individual freedom.

Somewhat more than a month later, I spoke over a national radio hookup arranged by the Committee to Defend America by Aiding the Allies. On this occasion I did voice the logical conclusion of my chapel speech. Stepping far beyond the declared goals of the White Committee, I expressed the opinion that we must as a nation subscribe to "all possible aid to the Allies without reservation." It then became purely a matter of strategy whether at some later time active belligerency was required, I stated. I chose my words carefully, hoping to appeal particularly to the younger generation.

> The citizens of 1940 are the trustees of the future of these United States. We shall be rightly condemned by posterity if we needlessly become involved in war and squander life and treasure. But we shall be yet more guilty in the eyes of our descendants if we fail to preserve our heritage of freedom—if we fail because of timidity or lack of farsighted resolution. The decision is momentous. Those who feel as I do believe the future of human liberty is at stake.

The combination of my chapel talk and my radio speech of November 20, 1940, touched off a blast of undergraduate criticism. The quiet days of six months earlier when I could discuss hypothetical questions about war with students were gone. The *Crimson* attacked in force. My office was picketed (an operation which received little national publicity since commercial television did not yet exist). The *Harvard Lampoon* published a cartoon of the president of Harvard beating war drums. Between the halves in the Yale Bowl at New Haven, I was burlesqued in a skit staged by the *Crimson* and the *Lampoon*. A student with a big "1941" on his back lay down on the field reading a book when a figure appeared attired in cap, gown and mortarboard and wearing the sign "Conant." He began to annoy the student by parading around him with a wooden-bayoneted rifle. After a short interval, the student reluctantly took the gun but then turned to prodding "Conant" with the bayonet and chasing him around the field. Finally "Conant" was presented with a large retort and removed from the scene on a cart, presumably back to the laboratory. If I had been present, it would have been difficult not to show my embarrassment. Fortunately, at the last minute I canceled my plans to attend and took to my bed with a heavy cold.

The Yale game skit, the picketing, the editorials in the *Crimson* could be ignored. By today's standards, one might almost say there had been no protests. A petition from the undergraduates was another matter. A document signed by a considerable number of students was presented to my office. It was received with all courtesy. On my return from a trip to Washington, I sent off at once a letter to the leaders of the group. Since today communications between college administrators and students have become of special interest to academic and nonacademic commentators, I inflict on the reader the full text of what I wrote on December 2, 1940.

DEAR MR. BARNES:

I regret that I was away from Cambridge when you and other students presented a statement concerning my recent radio address.

I sincerely welcome the free expression of views on the most important question facing this country today. My remarks on the evening of November twentieth, towards which I take it your statement was directed, were in effect a call for discussion on what seems to me the fundamental issue. And certainly there is no more appropriate place for such discussion to be carried on than within this University, whose breath of life has been, for three centuries, controversy and debate.

May I point out, however, that one phrase in your statement—that referring to my remarks as a declaration of war—is inaccurate. The question on which I asked for discussion was not whether this country should declare war. There are many qualified observers who feel that active belligerency at the present time would not serve our purpose in aiding Britain as our first line of defense. The question I put forward for debate was whether or not a defeat of the Axis powers was essential for a continuation of our way of life. My own position I made clear. I hope this issue will be debated by the students of this University and of all colleges and universities of the country.

On one point we are in complete agreement. You emphasize that I was speaking as a private citizen. I stated this specifically in the opening sentence of my remarks, because I believe as you do that no individual or group of individuals can voice the opinion of this University on controversial public issues.

Very sincerely yours,

Many people besides this group of undergraduates disliked my radio address of November 20. The alumni had by this time, however, become somewhat used to my stating publicly my views about stopping Hitler. After the May 29 broadcast and my well-publicized remarks to the Jewish War Veterans in June, those with isolationist views had marked me as a dangerous man. I had now moved far away from the "short of war" position of the White Committee. I certainly was not speaking for all the members. I was saying too much for some, too little to suit others. But I had discussed the short radio address which worried the students with some members of the Century Group in New York at a luncheon a few days before the delivery. They had agreed with what I proposed to say.

As a member of the Boston group of the White Committee, I shared in the discussions of future strategy when I could. I was unable to be on hand to greet White himself when he came to Boston on November 24, and sent a letter of apology by Calvert Smith expressing the hope we could soon sit down together to discuss the future of his committee. I raised the question "whether it would not be better to start a debate now on whether the country is prepared to bring military aid to Great Britain if it becomes apparent that such aid is necessary." The fundamental issue I suggested was whether "we can continue our free way of life in a world in which the Axis powers have succeeded in forcing Great Britain to negotiate peace as a result of a stalemate."

A reference in the letter to the recently formed "America First Committee" indicates that we were all beginning to be worried about the effectiveness of this rival pressure group. The members seemed to believe that a Europe dominated by Nazi Germany could live at peace with the Americas dominated by the United States. We did not. Both groups appeared to admit that a decisive defeat of the Axis powers would not be possible without military assistance by the United States, which as a minimum would involve the use of naval and air forces.

In an October draft of a proposed policy statement, White seems to have suggested endorsing the granting of war credits to Great Britain. The response in my letter was strongly negative. I was at that time a long way from the subsequent "Lend-Lease" point of view. I wrote that I was opposed to any further experimentation with credits or loans. I wanted some sort of *quid pro quo* for material aid. I shared the suspicion of many adherents of the America First group, I admitted, who feared that we might be called upon to make "undue sacrifices to protect the British Empire." I expressed the hope that some formula could be devised like the destroyer-base exchange of the summer. However, I conceded this point of view might be considered as "hard-boiled and cruel."

These remarks illustrated a difference between some members of the Century Group and myself. Their early insistence that the United States declare war stemmed from an Anglophile attitude I could not share. I was as opposed to British colonial policy and as suspicious of the long-run objectives of British foreign policy as any Midwestern farmer. I knew the English dons and admired many of them, but I had no strong ties to Oxford or Cambridge—only seventeenth-century historical ones. I was aware of the subtle flattery of which the British were masters. My New England caution about our distant overseas "cousins" was to influence my point of view in several matters in the war years. When it came to the surface, it always surprised my truly Anglophile friends. A trip I made to England in 1941, which I shall describe shortly, left me with a great admiration for Great Britain in its "finest hour." These sentiments plus gratitude for the courage of the British in standing alone served to balance my original anti-British prejudices.

The White Committee in November showed signs of splitting in half. Therefore, in the interests of unity, I prepared a long draft of a statement which the committee might issue. I sent a copy to Mr. White for use in the meeting of the committee on November 22 and talked with him about it by phone several times. I was, of course, only one of many who submitted ideas. Mr. White had the advice of several active members of the committee and had consulted the President and four Cabinet officers. He and Eichelberger sent a telegraphic copy of the much-revised statement to me at Cambridge. He listened patiently when I suggested certain changes in the course of a telephone conversation. As finally issued a few days later (November 26), it followed in general the line I had been pushing (with much advice from Grenville Clark and some of the Century Group).

A Congressional debate was called for on the question of whether or not the United States could afford to permit the British Commonwealth to be defeated and the British fleet either destroyed or surrendered. One of the main points in my draft was incorporated: "The lifeline of both Great Britain and the United States is the sea route from the Western Hemisphere to England. Under no circumstances must this line be cut; the United States must be prepared for whatever measures are necessary to assist in maintaining it. The United States should supply Britain with all possible merchant vessels. . . ." A more controversial point in my draft was omitted. It read as follows: "The convoying of ships from the new world to Great Britain will be an increasingly serious problem and can only be met eventually by the United States' undertaking the convoying of merchant ships at least part way across the Atlantic through an extended neutrality zone or making available additional destroyers." I was many months ahead of the committee and the administration in advocating such a statement in public, although the idea itself was far from novel.

Even without the inclusion of an advocacy of convoys, the issued statement was too strong a dose of medicine for some members. President Henry N. MacCracken of Vassar in a letter to the *New York*

Times challenged the committee's statement that the United States would assume responsibility for maintaining "the so-called lifeline between Great Britain and the United States." This could only mean the use of warships and an act of war. He still believed in aid short of war. Therefore he resigned from the committee. Obviously, the new statement was hardly compatible with the original slogan: "All aid to the Allies short of war." Since I had always insisted that war might be an eventuality, the isolationists' hostility to me personally was tempered by an admission that I was at least frank.

Large numbers of people throughout the country were in sympathy with the isolationists. The fear of war was the determining factor in their minds. On the other hand, the success of the British in the air in September was widely admired. More and more it was realized that Great Britain was not going to follow France; she would fight on. The *sympathies* of a large portion of the population were on her side. Giving substance to our sympathy was a different story; at this point latent anti-British sentiment and fear of war united. No one except a pacifist, however, could object to the intensive defense effort then under way.

Harvard University as an institution was in several ways involved. The president of the Alumni Association, who was ardently pro-Ally, agreed that a special meeting of the alumni in Cambridge might be called to enable me to report on the current status of the university's activities in the defense effort. So what was in theory a homecoming day for alumni became, in fact, an enthusiastic gathering of potential interventionists. By a strange coincidence, the day was Saturday, December 7, 1940; exactly a year later the Japanese were to strike at Pearl Harbor. Speakers in the morning and afternoon sessions in Cambridge reported on various aspects of Harvard's defense activities. I had to make the major address at the evening dinner in the Harvard Club of Boston.

"You gentlemen, several hundred strong," I said, "have come to renew your acquaintance with the university and to participate in a symposium on Harvard and the national defense. A meeting such as this is heartening to all who are anxious as to this country's future. Here is no evidence of a weak indifference to their fate by the people of this land. On the contrary, your interest is symbolic of the true spirit of a free people concerned at one and the same time with the future of their schools and colleges and with the defense by force of arms of the integrity of their country." (I certainly joined together a considerable number of themes in this one sentence.) I then went on to list and describe the university's activities in the days of "national emergency." For whether one likes the phrase or not, I maintained, "it is an emergency of unprecedented scope which has confronted us since the Battle of France was lost last June. It is an emergency which brings us here tonight."

My report to the alumni mentioned that the ROTC units were functioning; the faculty had granted academic credit for those enrolled in aviation work; fair rearrangements had been made for those students who were called into active service with the National Guard or members of the Officers Reserve Corps; the impact of Selective Service was still slight. The story of the plans for a Red Cross–Harvard hospital was new. I could tell it with relish, as the idea was strictly my own.

The origin was my almost overpowering emotional reaction to the success of Hitler in the preceding May and June. At that time heavy bombardment of London and other cities with an invasion to follow seemed likely. As citizens of a neutral state, Americans could not legally aid the Allies. There was no law to prevent assistance to the sick, however. Many well-informed observers predicted outbreaks of epidemics in the bombed cities. Could not Harvard set up a public health unit to help in preventive measures? I raised the question with Dean C. S. Burwell of the Medical School and some of the professors in the School of Public Health. Of course, I queried the British through their embassy officials. As a result of lengthy negotiations, we decided to pool our resources with the American Red Cross, our resources consisting of the money I raised personally and the readiness of a couple of professors to go overseas on a somewhat dangerous mission. By the time I reported to the alumni meeting in December, I could say that Professor John E. Gordon of the Harvard School of Public Health was to be the head of a hospital which was in progress of construction, near Salisbury.

There were few if any dissents from the tone of the "homecoming" meeting, which is important evidence of the swing of opinion among college graduates along the East Coast. I have no doubt that in the middle of the country no such assembly would have been successful. President Hutchins of the University of Chicago, for example, was an extreme isolationist. On the West Coast, on the other hand, President Robert Gordon Sproul of the University of California was as much an interventionist as anyone except the extremists. As in so many cases in my lifetime, California sentiment was more that of the Northeast than of the Plains States.

Not long after the alumni meeting, I decided to write a personal letter to President Roosevelt. The move was inspired by Grenville Clark and Calvert Smith, who were worried about the apparent lethargy of the United States. My letter was to be a sort of trial balloon. It was sent on December 16, 1940. "As a private citizen," I wrote, "I am much disturbed by the defeatist attitude in certain quarters." I hoped the President would tell the country just how the defeat of Great Britain or a compromise peace would "jeopardize the future of free institutions." In the closing paragraph I wrote:

It may be that in the near future you will receive a letter along these lines with many signatures of which mine may be one. I am venturing to send you this more or less personal note because time is pressing and I feel so strongly on this issue. But for your bold stand during the crucial days of last spring and summer, Great Britain now would be in the position of France. I believe the American people will respond as readily to your leadership at this time as they have in the past.

By a strange coincidence, on the day the President received my letter (December 17), he suggested at a press conference a plan to aid Britain that was destined to be far more effective than any of us imagined. He spoke of eliminating the "silly, foolish, old dollar sign" from American assistance. You would not offer to sell your hose to a neighbor if his house was on fire, he said; no, you would lend it to him.

I doubt if I realized that this press conference was held for the purpose of broaching an idea which was to be the basis of the Lend-Lease legislation to be introduced in Congress on January 10, 1941. The President was moving, but keeping his plans to himself. In a fireside chat on December 29 he called for making the United States the "great arsenal of democracy." I was enthusiastic about the radio address. Some of my friends were more reserved in their appraisal. I analyzed the difference in opinion in a letter to Grenville Clark on December 31, 1940:

Fundamentally, I think we differ on the question of timing. Also, we probably differ on our judgment of the mood of the country, and what is possible and not possible at the present moment. For example, I thought the President's speech was much better than "pretty good." I thought it was magnificent and went as far as it was possible for him to go. I am not saying that a certain amount of private pressure could not be kept on the White House to see that he goes farther still, but publicly I think the efforts of all of us should be to back the President. It seems to me quite conceivable that within a few weeks he may come forward with a plan or plans which will involve direct belligerent action on the part of this country. . . . I am very anxious to avoid a split of public opinion on a hypothetical and, to my mind, largely strategic issue, namely, when, where, and how should we join in taking belligerent action against the Axis Powers. I believe that in three weeks or a month the issue will be made plain one way or another, either by Mr. Roosevelt's suggesting naval convoys, or by a direct appeal from England for planes and men to operate the planes, and our naval forces, or by some overt act of the Axis Powers themselves. We should all be prepared to bring the President assistance when he takes the step that is not "short of war." Until then, I think the main point is to keep the country in the present mood, which to my mind has changed rapidly and can be described as a growing realization of the importance of the country pledging all its efforts to defeat the Axis Powers. It takes time for a democracy to move, and we must be patient, or so it seems to me. I have been very encouraged by the responses to the President's speech in the papers. I should not have dared hope for as good a press and popular response. If this is only one of a series of appeals to the country, as I believe it is, then it's important to keep the waters moderately calm and untroubled until the President has played his entire hand.

In his annual State of the Union message on January 6, 1941, the President warned that isolationism was impossible. "Swift and driving increase in our armaments," he declared, were necessary; weapons must be provided both for our own defense and for those fighting abroad. A few days later legislation was introduced in the House (H.R. 1776) which became known as the Lend-Lease Bill. The executive branch of the government was to be authorized to lend the British what they needed "to enable them to fight for their liberty and for our security."

The premises on which the bill was based had already been made clear by President Roosevelt. He had told his national radio audience that there was danger in any course, but far less if America did all it could to support the nations defending themselves than in waiting for the attack by the Axis Powers. That there would be such an attack if Britain was defeated was part of the argument, of course.

The isolationists denied the validity of such reasoning. The leaders of the America First Committee were for the most part ready to endorse aid to Britain but wished a guarantee that such aid would not be a step toward America's involvement in the war. The situation as they saw it in the first months of 1941 was a stalemate. Hitler had lost the air battle over Britain; an invasion of England by Germany was, therefore, impossible. Even with all the aid we could give,

Germany could not be defeated. Why did not the President recognize the realities? Perhaps he would if the interventionists would stop urging him on to take steps which were bound to lead to war. The President's flat rejection of the idea of a negotiated peace disturbed them the most.

The opposition to H.R. 1776 mobilized by the America First Committee was massive. The string of prominent Americans who appeared before the House and Senate committees kept the debate going full blast for nearly two months.

As honorary chairman of the New England branch of the Committee to Defend America by Aiding the Allies, I was wholeheartedly a supporter of the Lend-Lease Bill. I had taken no public part in the controversy, however. Furthermore, I had never been one of the inner circle of those who determined the day-by-day policy of the White Committee. With the exception of my collaboration with Lewis Douglas in preparing an open letter to the President in late December, I had been relatively inactive. Therefore I was surprised (and pleased) to receive a message asking me to be one of three rebuttal witnesses before the Senate committee considering the Lend-Lease Bill. The other two were to be Wendell Willkie and Mayor La Guardia.

Who decided to place me on the stand, I never knew. I suspect that the reasons behind the choice included a realization that if I subsequently made a trip to England my open support of Bill 1776 would assure me an overwhelmingly cordial welcome. The only persons who knew what was scheduled for me in February were close to the President or to Henry L. Stimson, the Secretary of War. (Indeed, the plans for my visit were not released to the press until I was actually on board a ship on February 15, 1941.) Therefore, the fact that the message asking me to appear before the Senate committee of February 11 came from John J. McCloy, Assistant Secretary of War, was not without its significance.

Never was a witness better briefed than I. When Calvert Smith heard the news of my forthcoming appearance along with Willkie and La Guardia, he began again to worry. Ever since he had moved to Cambridge following my radio address in May, he felt increasingly the burden of responsibility for my interventionist speeches. He never wrote them; they were my own; but he always went over the various drafts with care and suggested many important changes. Now I was to be subject to cross-questioning by some isolationist Senators without benefit of anyone to help me in my answers. What could be done? First, a carefully prepared statement; second, a rehearsal. Smith wrote out the most disturbing questions he could think of, and we considered how I should reply.

Smith had been preceded as a tutor by no less a person than the President of the United States. I had been asked to call on the President on Saturday morning, February 1, to obtain his instructions about a mission to England to start scientific interchange with the British. But I could hardly get Roosevelt to talk about the purposes of my forthcoming trip. Rather he wanted to outline the political strategy behind the Lend-Lease Bill. He was well aware that I was going to be one of the rebuttal witnesses and obviously hoped that I would follow his lead in giving my testimony. There was nothing inconsistent between what he said and my own thoughts. Neither of us was ready to discuss the next steps beyond the passage of the bill; therefore I only had to listen. But it was a bit annoying that I could hardly get him even to ask me to undertake the task for which I had been chosen.

The President told me why he was appointing John Winant as Ambassador to Great Britain. He would get on well with the Labour Party, he said, and added that it was almost certain that that party would be in power when the war was over. To handle the negotiations about supplies, which would increase in complexity after the Lend-Lease Bill passed, he was sending over Averell Harriman. He would see that Winant knew of my mission. So, after an hour's talk, I left well prepared for my ordeal before the Senate but without even a scrap of paper (or the promise of one) authorizing me to share official United States military secrets with the British on an exchange basis.

The encounter with the Senate Foreign Relations Committee was not as terrifying as I had imagined. With my opening statement and the questions, my testimony occupied about an hour and a half. To anticipate a hostile question which might be raised as to my competency as a witness (as compared with Colonel Charles A. Lindbergh, who had appeared as a witness bolstering the isolationists' point of view), I opened as follows:

It is a privilege to appear before this committee in its hearings on the vitally important bill which now concerns you. On many of the points which have been discussed in connection with this bill, I make no claim to be an expert witness. I am neither a military strategist nor a student of constitutional law; nor am I familiar with the intricacies of international law. I presume that I have been invited to appear here today because, speaking as a private citizen, I have on several occasions given expression to my views on the nature of the present peril which confronts us.

I come before you quite frankly as a partisan—a partisan of the free way of life. To me the real issue before the country is the preservation of this way of life, of the integrity of the individual. To me the fundamental premise of our American civilization, the premise of Catholic, Protestant and Jew alike, is a belief in the dignity of the individual. Our freedom to hold this belief is, in my opinion, gravely imperiled by the success of the armed might of the Nazi state. For it is this belief, the belief in the dignity of the individual man, which is denied, condemned and ridiculed by those in power in totalitarian lands.

I then went on to deal with what I thought was the isolationist's best argument, though I did not say so. I suggested that the real difference between those of us who would have this country pledge itself to ensure the defeat of the Axis Powers and those who urged a compromise peace was not a difference primarily in appraisal of military or economic eventualities.

It is a complete disagreement on the character of our peril—a disagreement in our appraisal of the true nature of the Nazi state. We are miles apart, we members of these differing groups, in our estimate of the danger to this free country arising from the revolutionary anti-Christian philosophy which is the basis of the Nazi strength.

If this were an imperialistic war in the old sense of the word, as some claim, then those who advocate what they call a negotiated peace would have perhaps a plausible case. But I believe it can be demonstrated that this present war has in it many of the characteristics of a religious war. It is being waged by an army of picked men fanatically devoted to a philosophy which denies all premises of our American faith. Hitler's soldiers are proponents of a literally soulless creed. And they are well armed by modern science. They are hard to stop by force of fighting; impossible to stop by fair words or bribes, by talks of trade or by a negotiated peace. The argument today between two groups of loyal, sincere American citizens seems to me to come down to this diagnosis of the Nazi state. If those of my belief are wrong, not only this bill but any aid to England is unnecessary. If those of my belief are right, our only hope as a free people lies in a defeat of the Axis Powers.

I concluded on a note I had been repeatedly sounding since May:

It has been argued that the passage of this bill may lead to war. The bald fact is that any step we take, or even failure to take any step at all, so long as Hitler is in the ascendant, may lead to war. To support a line of action which might bring this nation into armed conflict is a terrific responsibility for any group of individuals to bear. To my mind, however, there is one responsibility more terrible. It is the responsibility of acquiescing in silence to policies which might lead to the wiping out on this continent of the free way of life. A needless war, an unnecessary war, is a national crime. But fear of war cannot be the sole basis of national policy if we as a people would be free.

The free way of life was not won on this continent by timidity nor by defensive tactics. It was not gained here, nor has it ever been advanced elsewhere, by men who, quailing before an uncertain future, were hesitant and confused in action. For the best interests of the future of these free people, in my opinion, the Congress of the United States should pass this bill.

In the questioning which followed my prepared statement, Senator Vandenberg said: "You are asking us to pledge ourselves to achieve a conclusive victory over Germany. Suppose it required us to go to war to do it. Would you go that far?" I replied without hesitation, "I should if it were absolutely necessary as the last step."

CHAPTER 19

Once Again a Chemist
in National Service

O<small>N FRIDAY, JUNE</small> 14, 1940, Dr. Vannevar Bush, the president of the Carnegie Institution of Washington, telephoned. The last time I had talked with him had been at a small informal luncheon on May 24 in New York after a meeting of the Committee on Scientific Aids to Learning. He and I, together with Dr. Frank B. Jewett, the president of the National Academy of Science, Dr. Irvin Stewart, the director of the committee's studies, and another member of the committee, Bethuel M. Webster, a New York lawyer, had shared our extreme worries about what was happening on the European continent. The German Army in the course of only two weeks had reached the Channel. We all had agreed it was high time for America to wake up; our unanimity of opinion was one of the factors that had led me to make my broadcast on May 29 on immediate aid to the Allies.

Now Bush was calling on a different but not unrelated matter. He referred at once to our conversation in New York, but wasted no time commenting on the rapidly deteriorating situation of France and Great Britain. It was unnecessary to remind ourselves that the British forces had been evacuated from Dunkirk and that the occupation of Paris was imminent. What concerned Van Bush was a vague proposal for a new governmental committee which had been tossed about at the luncheon meeting, a committee to answer the question of how American scientists could assist in the accelerated defense effort.

234

"The idea," said Van over the phone, "has now been given form; there will be a National Defense Research Committee appointed by the President. Will you be a member?" he asked, and then added that he would be chairman, with Dr. Karl T. Compton, the president of the Massachusetts Institute of Technology, Dr. Jewett and Dr. Richard C. Tolman of Cal Tech, the other scientific members.

I congratulated him on moving so rapidly to implement the idea we had discussed only a few weeks before. Of course, I would be glad to be appoined a member of his committee, I told him, and, subject only to my duties in Cambridge, would devote as much time as possible to the undertaking. I agreed to be in Washington for the first preliminary meeting of the committee on the following Tuesday, June 18. Before hanging up, Van explained that the Commissioner of Patents, Conway P. Coe, as well as a representative of the Army, Brigadier General George V. Strong, and of the Navy, Rear Admiral Harold G. Bowen, would also be members. Effective liaison with the armed forces, so necessary for the work of the committee, would be provided by the membership of these representatives.

Just how Van Bush operated to bring his ideas about organizing science for the defense effort to fruition, I have never known. According to Robert Sherwood* and James Phinney Baxter III,† Harry Hopkins played an important role. Whatever was done was done effectively without any publicity and with speed. On June 15 the President wrote to each of the prospective members of the committee. In his letter (which I have no doubt was drafted by Van Bush), the President announced that he was creating a National Defense Research Committee (NDRC) which would be attached to the Advisory Commission of the Council of Defense and under the chairmanship of Dr. Vannevar Bush. "I am happy to appoint you a member of this committee," wrote President Roosevelt, "for I feel sure that you can greatly aid in its deliberations and thus contribute substantially to an important aspect of national defense." The President went on to say that "if through the activities of this new committee, the efforts of American scientists throughout the country are effectively oriented in aid of the armed services in the serious problems which today confront them, an important piece of work will have been accomplished."

Whether the concluding sentence was the product of the President's thinking or that of Bush, it can only be regarded in the light of

* *Roosevelt and Hopkins*, New York, Harper & Brothers, 1948.
† *Scientists Against Time*, Boston, Little, Brown, 1946; Boston, M.I.T. Press paperback edition, 1968.

history as a vast understatement. Leaving aside entirely the new weapons and devices for which the NDRC through its subcommittees was largely responsible, forgetting (if one can) the contribution of the NDRC to the winning of the war, it is clear that the creation of the committee marked the beginning of a revolution. The mode of the committee's operation instigated by the chairman in the summer of 1940 has had a transforming effect on the relation of the universities to the federal government. The pattern set has made the postwar world of American science entirely different from that of the prewar years. The essence of the revolution was the shift in 1940 from expanding research in government laboratories to private enterprise and the use of federal money to support work in universities and scientific institutes through contractual arrangements.

I remember exactly when I learned of the new idea. It was during one of my first talks with Bush in my capacity as a member of NDRC. I recall saying something to the effect that, of course, we would have to build laboratories and staff them with government employees. "Not at all," Bush replied. "We will write contracts with universities, research institutes and industrial laboratories." He pointed out that such a procedure had already been used by the National Advisory Committee on Aeronautics of which he was then chairman. I shall never forget my surprise at hearing about this revolutionary scheme. Scientists were to be mobilized for the defense effort in their own laboratories. A man who we of the committee thought could do a job was going to be asked to be the chief investigator; he would assemble a staff in his own laboratory if possible; he would make progress reports to our committee through a small organization of part-time advisers and full-time staff.

I could see that the consequences of this way of mobilizing science to assist the Army and Navy would be profoundly different from what I had known in World War I. As I have already recounted in an earlier chapter, in 1917–18 the great bulk of the Army's scientific research was performed by chemists and physicists who had just put on a uniform. No permanent corps of scientist officers had as yet been formed. Now it was different. By 1940 what had been in 1917 a temporary set of laboratories, pilot plants and proving grounds—the Edgewood Arsenal outside of Baltimore—had become an integral part of the Army organization. I had imagined, as war drew near, that many of my scientific friends and, perhaps, I myself would once again put on a uniform. It was not to be. Bush's invention insured that a great portion of the research on weapons would be carried out by men who were neither civil servants of the federal government nor soldiers; they would be employees of a contractor.

Dean Don K. Price in his excellent book, *The Scientific Estate*, has written:

> . . . until recent years, our military services thought that civilian scientists in military laboratories should conduct their research only pursuant to "requirements defined by military staff work." This notion was exploded as it became apparent that what scientists discovered by unrestricted research might be of greater military importance than the things the military officers thought they wanted—in short, that the means might determine the ends.*

In an earlier book, Price wrote the following about the policy of the OSRD, which after June 1941 was the over-all agency of which NDRC and the medical research committee were parts: "The Office of Scientific Research and Development had been a tremendous success because it competed aggressively with the military research agencies. It brought in private scientists, gave them full authority, went directly to high political officers (from the President down) on disagreements with military officers, and used judgment in deciding which weapons to try to develop." †

Price's estimate of the policy of OSRD was correct, but the relationship between civilian scientists and military men was determined in the first days of the functioning of NDRC. As soon as the subcommittees were appointed which were to be concerned with specific problems, pains were taken to ensure liaison with the appropriate branch of the Army and Navy establishment. Our independence was never resented and our help was often solicited. Ideas that originated within the NDRC organization were more than once greeted at the start with skepticism, but usually discussion and the exhibition of the evidence on which the idea was based were successful in bringing about the desired cooperation. Indeed, I recall certain instances in which the degree of enthusiasm for an NDRC proposal by either the Army or the Navy was stimulated by the interest shown by the other branch of the service.

The success of NDRC as a war agency was undoubtedly due to what Price calls the ability of the committee "to compete aggressively with the military research agencies," but it must be remembered, first, that the existing government laboratories were overburdened with problems and, second, because we in NDRC were building no new

* Cambridge, Harvard University Press, 1965, p. 65.
† *Government and Science*, New York, New York University Press, 1954.

permanent facilities, our success seemed in no way to threaten the existing arrangements once the war was over.

There was a certain symmetry in the way Bush had put the committee together: two college presidents, one—Karl Compton—an ex-physicist, the other—namely, myself—an ex-chemist. To each was assigned the task of organizing his former professional colleagues in research groups to help the Army and the Navy. The president of the National Academy, Frank Jewett, director of the Bell Telephone Laboratories, was a highly important, indeed obvious, choice. To him fell the lot of calling on many engineers in industry and in the universities. Dr. Richard Tolman, a professor of physics at California Institute of Technology, was the fourth scientific member. Motivated by strong anti-Nazi feeling and deep apprehension about the military posture of the United States, he was already at work in Washington on defense problems. Both Compton and I were clearly on the committee because of our visibility as presidents of M.I.T. and Harvard. To be sure, our scientific backgrounds and our acquaintance with the leading scientists was important. So, too, was our administrative experience. If Bush had been looking primarily for a chemist and a physicist, however, he might have appointed any one of half a dozen other people.

I hardly need point out that my own affairs in 1940 and 1941 would have taken a completely different course if Bush had not asked me to participate in the undertaking entrusted to him by President Roosevelt. I should have been busy as the president of Harvard and an active member of a committee of the American Council on Education concerned with the relation of higher education to the federal government. No doubt my participation in the attempts to have Congress pass a draft law might have been solicited by the leaders of the Plattsburg group. I might well have been offered the position of the Director of Selective Service, as was at least one other college president. I believe such a suggestion was placed before Roosevelt in the fall of 1940. His comment, I was told, was to the effect that he didn't think this was the proper place in the emergency for Conant. One can only imagine that the President was well aware of the importance of Bush's committee and had in mind my role in the undertaking.

Bush's invitation returned me, in a sense, to the field of chemistry. When I had closed the door of the Converse Laboratory behind me in May 1933, I had thought my career as a chemist was over. Of course, I assumed I might continue my interest in the investigations of some of my friends; possibly I might express an opinion or two. (In fact, my close friend, Professor A. Baird Hastings, a biochemist at the Harvard Medical School, insisted on putting my name on a scientific paper published in 1941.) I further assumed I would continue from time to time to revise my textbook of organic chemistry if I could persuade one of my friends to become a co-author (which I did). I never dreamed that I should be placed in a position of being involved in recruiting chemists for research teams and making rulings about such matters as how the individuals involved fitted into the machinery of federal government. I could not have imagined a role as chairman of a committee of physicists and one chemist planning for the construction of an atomic bomb, which was in fact my assignment by Bush in 1941. I might have imagined that the government would someday ask for advice about synthetic rubber, since I had with Professor Bridgman investigated the use of high pressure to produce hydrocarbon polymers. But it would never have occurred to me, I am sure, in 1933, as I contemplated the end of my career as a chemist, that the President of the United States would nine years later, in 1942, ask me to be *the* chemist to advise him about synthetic rubber.

NDRC had come into existence almost overnight at a time when many people looked at the future with a fear that in retrospect may be hard to comprehend. I must ask the reader to remember that France was out of the war; England stood alone. The Battle of Britain had not yet been fought; many experts prophesied the destruction of the British Air Force by the Germans as soon as Hitler's planes were finished with their part in conquering Western Europe. For all that anybody knew to the contrary, an invasion of England might be only weeks away. What would then be in store for the United States if England, like France, Belgium and Holland, succumbed?

This question was taken with the utmost seriousness by the members of the National Defense Research Committee at the first informal meeting held in Washington in Dr. Bush's office on Tuesday, June 18, 1940. The mood was anything but relaxed. Either Karl Compton or I raised a question in the informal conversation taking place around the table. What, if anything, could the committee do when it was officially organized about helping the British? A federal statute made it a crime for any individual American citizen to assist the war effort of another nation. Karl, as a member of a defense committee, had explored that question in Washington at my request in September 1939, at a time when everyone thought the conquest of Poland would be at once followed by an attack on France. We were now asking whether an official American committee could take any action that would be illegal for an individual. The question was to be answered ten months later by the passage of the Lend-Lease Act, but any such legislation was in June 1940 beyond imagination.

There was not only the question of legality to be considered, General Strong, the Army representative, said, but also the question of military security. Without any ifs and buts, he declared that anything we did to assist the British would be the equivalent of helping the Germans, since it was only a matter of time before Great Britain shared the fate of France. If we gave the British any secret equipment, it would soon fall into German hands; the security of the United States would be jeopardized. Indeed, General Strong continued, the War Department had already had some difficulty along these lines. The White House had urged that certain items be shown to the British, and the responsible officers had to maintain that the development was not yet complete—a statement the General implied was not strictly true.

Such a forecast of the immediate future by a top-ranking Army man was by itself enough to frighten anyone. Its impact on my thinking as a member of W. A. White's committee was to make me more concerned than ever to promote the doctrine of "immediate aid to the Allies." As regards the plans of NDRC, whether we communicated with the British or not seemed to me at the time of secondary importance. Hurry as we might, there was little that the scientists could do which would have any bearing three or four months hence on the status of the rearmament program. According to what we had just heard, by the end of that time there would be no free and independent British nation with whom military men and scientists could talk.

I imagine that some around the table—in particular Compton and Bush—might well have had somewhat different thoughts. They may well have heard rumors of what certain British scientists had already accomplished in devising means of detecting enemy planes. If so, they then knew that it was not so much a question of giving secret information as of receiving it. Nothing was said.

Before the activities of NDRC had much more than started, the Battle of Britain had been fought and won decisively by Great Britain, with two consequences for the defense efforts of the United States. First, confidence in the ability of Great Britain to survive was restored, and the path to an exchange of ideas about military technical matters could be cautiously opened; second, the Army and Navy became aware of the significance of what we later called "radar" in the victory over the Germans in the skies. The importance of physicists for weapon development was rapidly recognized. Compton and Jewett and the subcommittees they had organized became the center of attention of high-ranking Army and Navy officers. From that moment on (about mid-August 1940), there was no question of Dr. Bush's committee being ignored.

As compared with the speed with which the new committee was created, the rate at which the creation was given form and substance was frustratingly slow. First, there was a delay in drafting the Executive Order, which was not completed until June 27; then it took time to organize the committee and its various subcommittees; then came delays caused by the necessity of having to obtain from the Army and Navy a security clearance of all individuals who were to have access to classified information.

One decision of the greatest importance was made at the first or second informal sessions in June. Dr. Irvin Stewart, director of the Committee on Scientific Aids to Learning, a political scientist, was named as executive secretary. He was well known to Jewett, Bush and myself, since we were members of the committee whose studies he was directing. Indeed, the three of us had been involved in choosing him as the executive officer in 1937 when the committee was being organized. Stewart at that time was a member of the Federal Communications Commission. His work with the Scientific Aids to Learning Committee, of which I was chairman, had been concerned with evaluating various audio-visual aids which were just then being introduced into the classroom. The necessary reports had been almost all completed. Therefore it was natural for Bush to suggest that the committee might release Stewart with salary, at least for the organizing phase of NDRC, provided, of course, Stewart so desired.

We were indeed fortunate he was available, and it all worked out most satisfactorily. The initial difficulty of arranging for paying an executive secretary from federal funds on an emergency basis was circumvented by an understanding with the National Research Council and the Carnegie Corporation, both of which were involved in financing the Committee on Scientific Aids to Learning. Thus, for many months, the key man in the organization—the executive secretary—was financed indirectly by the Carnegie Corporation; all the members of the committee and its advisers served without compensation. Only much later did the question arise of creating a few salaried staff positions.

Consciously or unconsciously, the President and Bush had largely bypassed those bodies which had been set up over a period of twenty years for the purpose of being prepared to mobilize scientists in time of war. These were the divisions of the National Research Council which had originated in World War I. It had received permanent governmental status by an Executive Order of May 11, 1918, which empowered the National Academy of Science to establish the Council as a permanent body. President Roosevelt had expressed confidence in his letter to Bush that the National Academy and the Council would respond cordially to requests from the new committee for advice on broad scientific problems. At its first meeting, NDRC passed a resolution requesting the cooperation of the Academy and Council, especially through the physics, chemistry and engineering divisions. In spite of this vote, we must have all realized that in fact the subcommittees of the NDRC were going to take the place of the divisions of the Council as the leading agencies for research in the emergency days which lay ahead.

As soon as Bush had made it plain that I was to be responsible for organizing the chemists, I decided to enlist the services of two men I had known since the days of World War I. I asked Professor Roger Adams of Illinois and Professor Warren K. Lewis of M.I.T. to assist me. They would be the vice chairman of the subcommittee or division of which I was the chairman. This division had been officially christened by Bush as Division B (Bombs, Fuels, Gases, Chemical Problems). Lewis and Adams rapidly gathered around them a half-dozen or more young chemists and engineers and began parceling out the problems.

How necessary it was for me to surround myself with a powerful group with prestige became clear at the annual meeting of the American Chemical Society in Detroit on September 8 and 9, 1940. I first met with the chairman and half a dozen members of the chemical division of the National Research Council. The group was neither young nor highly distinguished. The period following World War I had not been a favorable time to recruit able men into a semi-governmental organization which had almost no power and little responsibility. Those of my generation who were ambitious had devoted their energies to their own educational and research activities, perhaps including being consultants for industry. They were not active in the National Research Council nor, I might add, in advising the officers of the Chemical Warfare Service who were struggling to keep Edgewood Arsenal alive.

The members of the group to which I was to disclose my plans were for the most part old acquaintances. They were friendly but worried; the possibility of friction was not far distant. I outlined what the NDRC was commissioned to do and how we had set up an organization. I explained that we would farm out research by contract with universities and industrial companies. I revealed a few of the names of those who were being brought in, including W. K. Lewis. Roger Adams, who had come with me, spoke briefly. Since it was already known that Bush and K. T. Compton were on the top committee, those who entered the meeting with doubts were convinced that it was best for the chemical division of the National Research Council to remain essentially inactive. I recorded in my diary that the elder statesman of the group was as usual "very gracious but clearly miffed at being by-passed on chemical matters."

The next day I met with the directors of the American Chemical Society and outlined our plans in general terms. I was assured of complete and enthusiastic cooperation, a pledge which was honored in full. Indeed, I was embarrassed twice in the following ten years by the cordiality with which the officers of the society invited me to make a major address. On one occasion, I received the Priestley Medal; on the other, I was the principal speaker at the formal gathering which marked the celebration of the diamond jubilee of the American Chemical Society in 1951.

It had not been hard to convince my fellow chemists at the Detroit meeting that Bush's committee was going to be the official approach for civilian scientists to the Army and Navy. But I was not able to overcome a latent hostility to the defense effort in some universities. None of these present at the chemical society meeting openly expressed any reservations about what Bush and I were doing. Yet I had already discovered by correspondence that the isolationist spirit in the Midwest was affecting the leaders of some of the institutions with whom we wished to write contracts. Of course, when Adams or Lewis or one of their associates approached a likely professor with a proposition to be the chief investigator of this or that problem, the man in question could easily refuse. He might claim to be too busy, though he might really feel either that the suggested investigation was too trivial or that the whole NDRC was part of a conspiracy to involve the United States in the war.

After Pearl Harbor everything was different. But before that event the NDRC was feverishly active for a year and a half of peacetime, working under a certain psychological handicap. We talked in terms of defense. Yet privately some of us made no bones about the fact that we believed the United States would sooner or later enter the war. Those who thought in the same terms as the extremists of the America First group were not likely to respond with enthusism to an invitation to associate themselves with the NDRC.

As far as I now know, there was no open challenge of our efforts. We did not as a committee figure at all in the interventionist vs. isolationist debate of 1940 and 1941. The fact that all the members of the committee were strongly pro-Ally and some of us were interventionists may have been a handicap to enlisting full support of the academic community at the start. If so, the hundred percent cooperation we received after war was declared has washed out the memories of any reluctance to give top priority to our requests.

It may be not inappropriate at this point to refer to the current criticism of certain universities for their close cooperation with the Department of Defense. I do not agree with the basic premise of those critics who say that since war is evil a university should have nothing to do with research on weapons or weapons systems. If such a point of view had prevailed in 1940, NDRC would never have been born. The question of what kinds of research an academic community should undertake in peacetime is another matter. Without implying any criticism of other institutions, I venture to reaffirm the postwar policy of Harvard University, according to which no contracts were made which involved secret research. I wrote in the annual report for 1946 as follows:

> At the moment not inconsiderable amounts of government money are being spent in the universities to support research, thanks to the vision of certain leaders of the Navy and the Army. Here at Harvard, for example, we have no less than twenty-eight research contracts with the Federal government involving the expenditure, over the two years 1946–47 inclusive, of something like three million dollars. These contracts are not to be confused with the special wartime contracts under which Harvard carried on so much research and development behind closed doors. The problems covered by the present agreements are essentially of a non-military nature and are not confidential or secret; all the results may be published freely. Although there have been no difficulties with the present arrangements, it would seem more appropriate for Federal money for basic research to flow through a civilian scientific channel. If the National Science Foundation is created by the present Congress, this will undoubtedly take place. This Foundation should be in a position to make substantial grants to universities for the support of basic research which has become so very expensive in these days. *Such grants would presumably*

be in no way connected with direct military projects. Indeed, in time of peace I think it highly inadvisable for a university to undertake the type of work which was done during the war, namely, secret research or development. All such research in peacetime should be done in government establishments or by contract with industry, according to my views. [Italics added in 1969.]

Clearly, the evolution of a proper relation of our educational institutions to the Federal government is no simple matter. We can easily imagine a situation where substantial subsidies from Congress would result in a degree of control by Federal authorities which would be unfortunate indeed. In looking into the future, however, it is important to think as clearly as possible about these matters. The answer to this problem cannot be summed up in a headline or a few clichés. Rather, it is one of those involved questions concerning human organizations in the modern world which needs careful analysis and constructive thought. Personally, I have no fear that a National Science Foundation such as has been suggested, administering funds for fundamental research and a limited professional scholarship program, would be inimical to the future of our universities. On the contrary, without such a Foundation, I doubt if our institutions for higher education can function with maximum effectiveness. I have likewise no fear that if the Departments of Commerce or Labor or Interior should follow the example of the Department of Agriculture and the Public Health Service in providing money for specific research projects in our universities, the freedom of inquiry of our professors would be jeopardized. Rather, I wonder if progress in many areas in the social sciences can be as rapid as desired unless funds are made available by some such method.

After the war was over and the accomplishments of the National Defense Research Committee were made public, many people were curious as to what had made the organization so successful. There were a number of factors. First of all, we had been able to proceed in complete secrecy. At the outset, we had adopted the security policy of the armed forces. Confidential and secret information was transmitted on the basis of the "need to know" principle. That is, no one had access to classified documents unless reading the document in question was clearly necessary for the work at hand. Second, the initial steps in creating the organization, including liaison arrangements with the armed forces, had been wisely taken at a time when the defense effort was just beginning and lines of command were still fluid. Third, we had ample funds (at first through the White House). Fourth, the key members of the committee served on a part-time basis (at least in theory); each one of us had a satisfying full-time job which we were slighting only because of the emergency;

none of us attempted to use his days in Washington to further his own career. Unlike many other wartime agencies, OSRD was not plagued by feuds; no one resigned or even threatened to, though there were heavy strains at times during the five years of NDRC's existence. The fifth and last reason for the committee's record of achievement is the most important—Vannevar Bush.

An understanding of the effective mobilization of American scientists during World War II may be gained by reading a little essay by Bush on "The Art of Management."* The author gives no hint of his own experiences in Washington during the war years. He addresses his remarks primarily to the subject of the management of industrial enterprises. A great deal of what he has to say, nevertheless, is an exposition of those principles that made him so effective as the organizer and chairman of NDRC. For example, he writes one paragraph on the art of listening, which he states is an important part of the art of management. He then adds:

> But it must be emphasized—and this applies to art in any form that is to be worth a tinker's dam, it must be utterly genuine. No pose, no sanctimonious attitude, no back-slapping or false humility will get across the footlights with an intelligent audience, and if the members of the organization are unintelligent, the case is hopeless anyway. This refers not merely to vice-presidents; it also applies to janitors.

When I read this paragraph, I remembered a memorandum Bush had addressed to the "Old Guard: Conant, Compton, Jewett, Tolman," marked "personal" and dated May 6, 1944. It read as follows:

> A few days ago there was an incident that made a great impression upon me. In the heat of trying to work out a matter I made a remark which injured deeply one of the men in this outfit for whom we all have enormous regard. Fortunately, he brought it up a few days later, I realized what I had done, and I made amends as far as I could. But it caused me to wonder.
>
> The stress at the present time is enormous, and I think that the entire organization is on edge. The suspense caused by the invasion is intense to us who know some of the elements. The manpower situation has driven us all to the verge of distraction. We are at the end of a winter when academic men normally look forward to respite, and there is no respite in sight. The excitement of broad innovation of new things has been succeeded by the trying job of moving them into use. Throughout the organization I think these factors enter to make our ways less smooth.

* Vannevar Bush, *Science Is Not Enough*, New York, William Morrow and Co., 1967, Chapter IV.

Yet we have an extraordinary record. I wonder if there ever was an organization, made up as ours is of individualists, that had a better record of freedom from serious strife. The same group that started are still with us. We have had internal disagreements, of course, but I cannot remember a single one that did not finally end amicably, and I cannot remember an instance where any valuable individual in our organization has been permanently injured. Our external relations with other agencies and organizations have sometimes been lurid, but they have been kept as internal affairs and we have never been part of the Washington strife as viewed by the public. I think it is a record to be proud of.

I write this memorandum because the incident, that I do not need to go into in detail, rests heavily on my mind. I urge that all of us watch the organization with care, take every step possible to untangle amicably the little incidents and frictions that are bound to arise, seek out the man who badly needs respite before he cracks, and see that he gets it, and in general attempt to hold the line and come through the present intense period in harmony. I will certainly attempt to do my part in this if any of you will tell me where you think I could head in to advantage.

The memorandum tells more about why Bush was a great mobilizer of scientists, a great chairman of NDRC, than could any words of mine. The reader who understands anything of the ways of men will agree with me when I say the United States was indeed lucky that such an extraordinary man had President Roosevelt's ear in that crucial month, June 1940.

CHAPTER 20

Mission to England

THE TRIP to England in 1941 was the most extraordinary experience of my life. I was hailed as a messenger of hope by the inhabitants of a beleaguered nation. I saw a stouthearted population under bombardment; I saw an unflinching government with its back against the wall. Almost every hour I saw or heard something that made me proud to be a member of the human race. Courage I have always admired greatly; tenacity and loyalty to avowed aims I place high among the attributes of a civilized person. One must search far to find striking examples in ordinary daily life. Circumstances of living in a democracy develop other virtues—tolerance, sympathy, respect for the individual, a desire to alleviate suffering. But only rarely is courage bred.

Great Britain under siege presented the spectacle of collective bravery, of stubborn loyalty to ideals. There was no doubt these people would rather die (and many did in each air raid) than be controlled as was the puppet French Government in Vichy. No one could tell you how the British proposed to survive as free men. But the will was there; there was no talk of negotiations, no faltering, no whimpering. Whenever I feel depressed about the quality of human beings, I recall with emotion the picture of England under fire.

Of course, it could be said that I found what I was intent on finding. As an interventionist, I had followed the news from England since Dunkirk with profound admiration of the pluck of both the fighting men and the civilians. Along with many other Americans, I had held my breath during those mid-September days when the Battle of Britain reached its heights. I had read stories from the newsmen and heard Ed Murrow's broadcasts. A very few returning visitors had told of what London was like during the long blacked-out nights of the fall and winter. I was prepared to see and hear what I did in fact observe, namely, a whole nation not literally under arms but participating in a strange way in a continuous air battle. Dr. Gordon's report of his experiences during his short trip to make plans for the Red Cross–Harvard hospital in Salisbury had made me envious. If I had only planned better, I might have gone with him and seen for myself what war from the skies on cities was really like. When I heard from Bush that he was planning to establish an NDRC office in London, I saw another chance. I suggested that I should go over for a few weeks to get the enterprise under way. At first Bush assented, but quickly changed his mind and was adamant against my going.

I knew there was no use pestering him with arguments. I put my case briefly in writing and went to work on Bush's assistant, Carroll Wilson. Wilson, a recent M.I.T. graduate, had come to Washington as an aide to President Compton. Through his wife, he knew the British well. I could point out to him why my knowledge of the English academic scene made me the appropriate member of the NDRC to head the first mission. He became convinced. His arguments were strong enough, indeed, so that Bush sought an ally in the senior member of the committee. Or so I surmise.

At all events, a few days before Christmas I received a letter from Frank Jewett sympathizing with my desires, yet arguing strongly against my taking the risk involved. He had had a similar opportunity in World War I and had ended by staying in the U.S.A. in spite of personal desires. I replied at once in a letter, pointing out that I was only proposing to be away six weeks at the most. Furthermore, the risks were slight. Anyway, neither as a member of the committee nor as head of Harvard was I irreplaceable. The very fact that I was a college president was a strong argument in favor of my proposal. I had been active as a private citizen in urging a more belligerent policy for the United States. On the theory that actions speak louder than words, I believed there was some value in having a man who had taken such a stand show that he was willing to take risks. The effect on some of the young people might offset any dislocation of Harvard affairs which would result if I never returned.

Jewett replied on the first day of the year, saying that "in view of the reasons you give and the feelings you have, I think you should go to London. I am going to Washington tonight, and when I see Bush tomorrow I shall tell him so." He had made some discreet inquiries, he wrote. He had talked to a young relative who had a good many contacts among Harvard undergraduates. There was no doubt in the mind of his informant that "at Harvard at least there is a lot of cynicism about the older generation which would be offset by something such as you are proposing to do."

Bush's decision to send a mission to London was the result of a series of events which started when the National Defense Research Committee was just getting under way. The idea of an interchange of scientific information related to war seems to have originated with Professor Archibald V. Hill, a physiologist of world distinction who was the secretary of the Royal Society. He came to Washington as France was falling and the outlook was black. He talked with some of his many scientific friends but soon discovered that what was lacking was not good will but official authorization. Returning to England, he was instrumental in having a British scientific mission headed by Sir Henry Tizard come to Washington toward the end of the summer. Sir Henry was Rector of the Imperial College of Science and Technology in London and also Scientific Adviser to the Ministry of Aircraft Production. As has been since revealed, he was one of a small group whose foresight and energy made possible the development of that radar network without which the Battle of Britain could not have been won. He brought with him a group of men and a box of secret documents. He was empowered to exchange with American authorities information covering a wide range of activities. There were delays caused by many complications; it was not until the end of September that the reluctance of the Army and the Navy was largely overcome.

That the outcome of the great air battle over England made the difference seems probable. The apprehension of the early summer gave way by autumn to a considerable degre of confidence in Britain's staying power. The necessary agreements were prepared by Carroll Wilson, whom Bush had appointed as the NDRC liaison officer. The British established a scientific office in Washington with Professor J. D. Cockraft in charge. The information exchanged showed the Army and Navy officers concerned with the development of weapons and equipment that we had much to learn from those who were operating on a battle front. Yet the United States had enormous potentialities for research on problems the embattled British were encountering. A procedure was needed by which at the research level knowledge could be transmitted on a day-to-day basis. Instead of a *quid pro quo* exchange, which in theory was the basis for the conversations at first, a close continuous cooperation would be in the best interests of both nations. The initial hesitation on the part of the full-time government officials in London and the military in Washington had disappeared by Christmas. It became clear that a permanent NDRC headquarters in London was a necessity. On January 20, 1941, the official invitation which Bush had been expecting since November arrived.

Opening the London office was more a diplomatic than a scientific mission. There were some highly unorthodox aspects to the proposed operation. In the first place, the NDRC staff was purely civilian; second, it was a recent creation; third, in many fields, of which the most spectacular was radar, the major American research and development effort was going to be in universities by means of the contract system invented by Bush. How could authorities in England have any confidence in an unprecedented organization which had sprung up overnight? How could they be sure any secrets transmitted would be tightly held? How could they be certain research tasks undertaken would be effectively and promptly carried on?

It was expected that there would be a flow of American scientists to England. Each would find his place alongside a British worker. A particular problem, such as the improvement of a microwave system, would be tackled jointly. After a few weeks, the American would return to his laboratory and carry on the work. The question of locating the place in the British organization where the American could work to best advantage was not easily answered. Nor was the organization with which our men were to cooperate easy to understand; the British scientific work was located in several rather separate departments (Admiralty, Supplies, Air Craft Production).

There was no doubt but that some American must be in London for at least a year's assignment, one who knew how American projects were administered and who would come to feel at home in London. Bush picked for the job Frederick L. Hovde, assistant to the president of the University of Rochester, who had been working in the NDRC Washington office with Carroll Wilson. He and Wilson and I were to be the mission. Wilson and I would return in a month or so after seeing that Hovde was well launched on this highly important business. Hovde was a former Rhodes Scholar, a chemical engineer by training and an excellent administrator, as his subsequent career as president of Purdue has proved. My responsibility was to knock on the doors to introduce him and, above all, to convey to our hosts a feeling that we in Washington knew what we were doing and could be counted on to put our hearts into an undertaking which was not yet officially a life-and-death matter for the United States.

The only route to London in the winter of 1941 was by air from Lisbon. Obtaining a place on the London plane, operated by the Dutch, was a matter of priorities tightly controlled by the British. Our party of three traveled on an American Export Line boat to Lisbon, where we were greeted by officials from the American Embassy, only to find that through a mix-up in communications Hovde and Wilson were without priority ratings. Lisbon was a mad place. Hotels were crowded with transient visitors who had nothing to do except to try to get out. There were only six planes to London a week, and when they flew, they carried only eight passengers per plane. At the time of our arrival bad weather had held up flights from England for a week.

We resorted to cables, and Hovde's and Wilson's predicament was solved without too much delay. However, it seemed best for me to use my top priority to get off as soon as possible. Unexpectedly, I found myself leaving the Lisbon airport in a plane carrying only myself, Ambassador-Designate John Winant, his adviser, Benjamin V. Cohen, and a Britisher connected with the Red Cross. Whether Winant had arranged matters because of a note I had sent to his hotel, I never knew. Perhaps I was just the beneficiary of a mistake in the confused plane-reservation office. If so, I was extremely lucky. What could be better than arriving at the British airport with Winant and his special assistant?

A tall redheaded young man introduced himself most agreeably at the airport. He was Brendon Bracken, a close friend of Winston Churchill and his parliamentary secretary. Almost his first words as I climbed into a waiting automobile with him and Cohen and the American Chargé d'Affairs, Herschel Johnson, were: "We were very much interested in reading your testimony before the Senate on the Lend-Lease Bill." This remark fortified my conviction that because of my interventionist activities I was the right man to go to London to start an NDRC office.

On the special private train to London, Ambassador Winant and the Duke of Kent, who had come to Bristol to greet the new American envoy, occupied a private compartment. The rest of us moved about informally. When the train stopped for an hour at Windsor, I watched

Mr. Winant being welcomed by the King on the station platform and whisked off in a car for a visit with His Majesty. I had tea with Bracken at his request. In the course of a long conversation about the war and American opionion of it, he said in a characteristic British offhand way, "The Prime Minister will be wanting to have you lunch with him at 10 Downing Street one of these days." Such an invitation was far more than I expected; I trust my reply showed my appreciation.

I have often wondered if Bracken, as the Prime Minister's chief adviser on public relations, had not acted on his own. After signing me up, he may well have decided to present his boss with an accomplished fact. The basis for my suspicion is that many years later Bracken told me Churchill was appalled at the prospect of having the president of Harvard to lunch. "What shall I talk to him about?" he said, according to Bracken, who recounted the story with glee. "He thought you would be an old man with a long white beard, exuding learning and academic formality. Instead," said Bracken, "you arrived wearing a tweed suit."

As I recall the luncheon in the bombproof basement dining room of 10 Downing Street, the beginning was awkward. The Prime Minister was not in a good mood. In fact, he was grumpy. I now realize he might have been showing resentment against Bracken's having trapped him into a luncheon with what he feared would be a boring academic snob. Or, more likely, his mood reflected a situation that was to come to the surface shortly, namely, his deep worry about the Lend-Lease Bill. For a few days later I received a letter from Calvert Smith, dated the day before my luncheon, in which he said the Lend-Lease Bill situation was discouraging. "I have been hollering about the proponents losing control of the situation to certain friends for two weeks, but I can't see that anything very effective is being done," he added. "The Wheeler forces [Senator B. K. Wheeler of Montana, a leading isolationist] have been conducting what amounts to a filibuster and have encouragement of a drop in the Gallup Poll from 58 per cent to 55 per cent support in the last reading. The other side of this is that feeling among proponents is getting pretty irate."

The guests at lunch were Professor Lindemann (Lord Cherwell), Lady Portarlington, an old friend of Mrs. Churchill, and a young man from the House of Commons and myself. The Prime Minister was quite late. Indeed, Mrs. Churchill had asked us to sit down at the table before he arrived. Our host seemed tired and was not ready to talk, so Mrs. Churchill did her best, which was very good. Given an opening, I took the opportunity to air my belligerent views about the role of the United States. I took good care to relate what I said to my appearances before the Senate committee. Whether the Prime Minister did or did not know of my testimony, I could not be certain, but the gambit worked. Mr. Churchill began to talk. He described with some joy the recent successful raid into Norway, when, as he said, they had captured some "Quislings." He then turned to the Lend-Lease Bill. In referring to what was going on in the United States, he rather let himself go. Perhaps his rising irritation as he spoke was unconscious, perhaps consciously put on for my benefit.

"This bill has to pass," he said. "What a state it would leave all of us in if it doesn't; what a state it would leave the President in; what a failure he would appear before history if this bill is not passed," he exclaimed. "What would happen in the United States if the bill was rejected? Would the President resign; if so, who would then become President, the Vice President?"

Whether Mr. Churchill really had his mind on what he was saying, I shall never know. The mere fact that he could make such statements even casually amazed me. Could he really have such profound ignorance of the American constitutional system? I made bold to suggest that the President of the United States was not a Prime Minister and we were not operating under a parliamentary system such as was in force in England. Emboldened by thus gaining the ascendancy for a moment in the conversation, I suggested that perhaps more than an arsenal of democracy was needed. The Prime Minister immediately shied off the subject. "We don't want your men," he said. "Give us the tools and we shall finish the job." I noticed then and later that Mr. Churchill had this way of quoting from his own speeches even in a casual conversation.

From this conversation and subsequent ones with him on two occasions, I became convinced that early in his relations with the United States as Prime Minister he had been warned, perhaps by Harry Hopkins, that any move on the part of Great Britain to suggest that the United States would eventually fight on the British side would be fatal to the continuing flow of the supplies which they so desperately needed. Up to this time I had thought that Wendell Willkie, in his testimony in favor of the Lend-Lease Bill before the Senate committee, had perhaps stretched a point. He had declared emphatically that no one in England to whom he had talked had suggested that the United States should enter the war. I now became convinced that Willkie was an accurate reporter. I am not at all sure, however, that Mr. Churchill and his associates were entirely frank. What they said may have been one thing, what they were thinking quite another. No responsible statesman is required to be completely candid. On this occasion, if the purpose of Mr. Churchill's rather vehement remarks was to worry me, he succeeded.

In fact, I was so disturbed that on returning to my hotel I sent the following cable to Smith: "American news very discouraging is everyone giving all aid rapid passage loan bill ask G. Clark lunched with Prime Minister today." To which I received a cable reply, dated March 7, which said in effect that the tide was swinging and the final passage of the bill without destructive amendments was expected within ten days. I don't suppose that I imagined that my message to Smith, with the implication that the Prime Minister was raising questions, would do any good. I was simply so upset by Mr. Churchill's troubled eloquence that I had to do something to relieve my feelings. A letter to my wife written the same evening illustrates my sense of frustration at being three thousand miles away from the scene of action:

6:30 P.M. (Thursday, March 6, 1941) Had lunch with Mrs. C., the P.M., Professor Lindemann and two others at 10 Downing Street in the basement! Very interesting. It lasted from 1:30 to 3:30. I can't describe it even in a letter going through the diplomatic pouch [undue caution]. At the end, Bracken came in. He is most cordial; so was the P.M. Bracken says the P.M. wants me to have lunch with him again before I leave! News from U.S.A. very discouraging. Why don't they pass the Lend-Lease bill? Why doesn't F.D.R. appeal to the country in another radio speech? Is the Committee to Defend America, etc. doing anything? All these questions will be too late but I can't help expressing my disgust and annoyance. (And not only *mine*, let me add.) . . . On the NDRC side we are making good progress and I hope have already started some things. It is a comfort to be able to do something besides talk to Senators! London has been very quiet—a few alarms but only one burst of gunfire Monday night about 12.

Another letter to my wife, written on March 8, gives a sense of the hectic life on which I was embarked:

The first week in London is over. I've seen everybody but the King and got the mission well started. . . . As I cabled you last night everyone has been most cordial. The mission seems to be getting off on the right foot as far as the British are concerned. . . . The study of human nature here is as interesting as anywhere else—perhaps a little more so. Our problem with our own naval and military attachés is also not without its difficulties. The job is really very important and I'm sure I was the one man to undertake it. The mission certainly has kudos enough here. I've been embarrassed by the cordiality of my reception. Sir John Anderson, Lord President of the Privy Council, Lord Hankey, Lord Simon (the Lord Chancellor), who is supposed to be my academic guide, counselor and friend, and the P.M. himself have been very cordial. . . . Yesterday I came down with a very mild case of the "flu." I am in bed for good measure and shall stay here (unless blown out) until tomorrow noon. Then I'm for a luncheon given for Bill Donovan [chief of U.S. Office of Strategic Services], then to Portan [the Chemical Warfare proving ground] with Robert Robinson by auto, back to Oxford again to see Sir Henry Tizard, and return to London. Next week is very jammed with events so I'm praying I shall have shaken off this virus by tomorrow.

Today has been the first clear day for some time and Hovde and Wilson reported at 6 that the night was clear and a moon coming up. So we figured we might have our first real Blitz (not very real by September–October standards) and at 8:15 sure enough the sirens sounded (that doesn't prove anything for they've sounded about twice a day since I've been here and no one pays the slightest attention). But about 8:30 the guns began to bark and you could hear the planes overhead very plainly. The waiter who was bringing me dinner assured me it was German planes and from the racket of the guns I believed him. Down in the dining room you probably would hear little—certainly not the planes; on the fourth floor (7 in all) opening on a large court, you hear the sounds overhead better than at a distance (i.e., planes rather than the guns). Here sounds one now! As though it were going to land in the courtyard! They say the noise of the guns is very comforting but I haven't learned yet how to tell a gun from a bomb. Probably I haven't heard any bombs, but I would swear I heard two in the last hour *whistling* (they do, you know) and then exploding, but there was no concussion in the room and only a slight shaking of the windows so I may be wrong. There must be some gun near by that goes off now and then with a sharp bark; it sounds very near—nearer than Hyde Park, I should think. As far as I can see, this is a game where no one knows the score unless the hit is so near or the hits are so many that all the possible spirit of curiosity has evaporated! Perhaps the doorman or the newspaper tomorrow will let me know whether or not any bombs were dropped within the hearing distance of Claridge's Hotel, or perhaps I shall have to wait for further instructions as to how to tell a bomb-burst bang from a gun's discharge. . . . This Blitz so far is a cross between fire-works at the Braves' field heard from Quincy Street and a thunderstorm in the "Massif Central" (do you remember it?) with sound effects only. I'll add a footnote in the A.M.

Sunday A.M. 9:30—Judging by the enclosed clipping from the *Times* I was not imagining last night—the noises were all real including the whistle. But I need more practice to be able to tell a bomb from a gun. I am sending the clipping just to emphasize how large a city London is and how small the chances are of being near a blast even in a raid (and then like the dancers in the restaurant in the news story you may be quite unhurt).

In a letter four days later, I brought my account of the raid up to date:

Since writing on Saturday the 8th, I have further news of the air raid. As I suspected, it was a real one. Six bombs dropped within a quarter of a mile of Claridge's. The worst raid on this part of London since October. Just as I suspected, however, those at dinner didn't know it was taking place. Hovde and Wilson were dining at Grosvenor House in the dining room which is in the basement and, what with the music and all, only heard a few thuds. So you see living through a raid "isn't such a bad business."

What I don't seem to have written home about was the massive destruction in parts of London, as well as the scenes in the underground shelters for those poor people who had been "bombed out." Not pleasant topics, either of them. Saint Paul's stood out as never before, almost surrounded by what once had been slum living quarters but was now gaping holes and masses of rubble. An evening visit to the air-raid shelters, which were largely converted parts of the subway system, demonstrated how "the lower-income groups" were taking the Blitz. These quarters were occupied night after night by men, women and children, crowded into the narrow, fetid, dirty corridors. The spirit of those who were thus "carrying on," as judged by their talk, was just as good as those who could afford private shelters or lived in steel-and-concrete buildings. The law of chance was the real protection.

I recall a night I spent outside of London in the main building of a private estate converted to the operating headquarters of the London, Midlands and Scottish railway system. Lord Stamp, the well-known economist and chairman of the board of the railroad, and Sir Harold Hartley, a longtime "chemical friend," were my hosts. In the morning, the news of the damage done to the railroad system by the raids of the previous night was analyzed. The necessary repairs and rerouting of trains was then ordered. I remember talking to Lord Stamp about the efficacy of air-raid shelters. He took an unfavorable view of public shelters for large crowds. He said he had his own shelter in his garden, which was quite adequate. "Does it give you full protection?" I inquired. "Yes," he replied, "against everything but a direct hit." Within a month or two came the news of Lord Stamp's death as a consequence of a direct hit on his private shelter.

Early in my stay I visited Oxford and Cambridge. When I arrived at Lincoln College, Oxford, my very old friend Neville Sidgwick greeted me with the exclamation: "Seeing you again is almost as good as peace!" I stayed in his rooms as I had during visits in peacetime. If the warmth of Sidgwick's welcome could have been converted into heat energy to raise the temperature of his quarters, my stay would have been pleasanter from the point of view of physical comfort; from every other point of view the two days could not have been better. I talked with old friends and made new acquaintances. No one had any idea of how Hitler would be beaten. That he would be, there seemed no doubt. Rather than talk about the fears and hopes related to immediate strategic plans (which were, after all, military secrets), more than one don was ready to discuss the terms of the eventual treaty when Hitler was beaten.

At Cambridge I occupied one of the rooms of Emmanuel College (John Harvard's college) since I was an honorary fellow. My visit included two events. The first was receiving an honorary doctor of science degree; the other was attending the Trinity College annual festivity. The honorary degree ceremony was simple. It was one of those days at the end of the term when the vice chancellor confers degrees on a multitude of candidates, one after the other. I was squeezed in at a proper moment. My escort was the senior tutor of Emmanuel College, Mr. E. Welbourne, because the master's wife had just died. We joined a group of some five or six others in academic costume and we walked over from Emmanuel to the Senate House at the appointed time. As we started to seat ourselves, one of our group who was unfamiliar with academic tradition inquired what was going to happen. I assured him I was only certain of one thing, which was that the orator who would present me in Latin would make a pun on my name. The prophecy proved to be correct. That evening, Professor A. V. Hill, the eminent physiologist (whom I mentioned in connection with his trip to Washington in 1940), handed me a slip of notepaper on which he had written the following:

J. B. Conant
Cambridge and Harvard

As arrows are in the hand of a mighty man,
So are the children of his youth.
Happy is the man that hath his quiver full of them;

> He shall not be ashamed
> When he speaks with the enemies in the gate.
> Psalm 127
> A.V.H.   14 March 1941

The next day I wrote on the other side of the paper:

This was given to me just after I received my Sc.D. at Cambridge in the Senate House by A. V. Hill. He said the quotation came to him as I was standing before the Vice Chancellor. He was obviously much moved by the symbolic link of this degree between Harvard and Cambridge. Cambridge is now speaking surely with the enemy at the gates if not in the gate, and her children are speaking in the clouds with bursts of deadly fire, assisted by many keen minds on the ground directing them as if by magic.

The last sentence reflected my recent visit to an underground radar center. My commentary proves that Professor Hill was not alone in feeling the emotional impact of the ceremony.

The academic community never seemed more beautiful or peaceful than that Friday afternoon, the day of the annual Trinity College festival. The famous Cambridge "backs" were at their best; a marvelous display of crocuses was in full bloom. The only signs of war were a multitude of Army trucks drawn up in a column in connection with some maneuvers. In the evening, well equipped with woolen underwear and socks (under my silk socks) and a sweater under a boiled shirt, I went forth. My dress suit was rented from Moss Brothers in Covent Garden. Over the formal clothes we all wore academic robes. It was my only chance to sport the scarlet gown of the Sc.D. degree. Professor Hill told me it was the first time he had worn evening clothes since the war began. As my host, he took me first to the services in the Trinity College Chapel which were held in memory of the donors. The attendance was small, the chapel icy cold. The ceremony was, nevertheless, impressive. We then adjourned to the great hall where the feast was held. The dinner was excellent considering that it was wartime. About three-quarters of the way through, an air alarm sounded; no one moved. My companions explained that only if a warning came of enemy planes actually overhead would it be necessary to interrupt the party to take refuge in shelters.

The sole speaker was the new master of Trinity, the well-known historian, Professor George Macaulay Trevelyan. This was his first appearance as master. He made an excellent speech covering the internal affairs of the college during the past year. He made special reference to Professor Hill, a former fellow of Trinity College, mentioning his services in connection with the war and the fact that he was one of the two Cambridge representatives in Parliament. Professor Trevelyan said that Professor Hill had brought as his guest one who was "more welcome here than any other man in the world," and he then referred to the president of Harvard University. I was quite overcome by Trevelyan's statement and, particularly, by the tremendous stamping of the audience in response. Trevelyan assured me this had not been prearranged. He himself was surprised at the ovation.

After dinner we adjourned to the Master's Lodgings which were in the process of renovation; upstairs a reception was in progress with ladies present, music and a great deal of handshaking and talking. The dean of Trinity College, Mr. H. A. Holland, an old acquaintance, was holding his own party in his rooms in another part of the college. About ten o'clock, I went over to his rooms, where I found a typical undergraduate scene—a mixture of seriousness and conviviality. The always-present drunken undergraduate was obvious, but not too obtrusive. From time to time I was asked to sing a solo, which I politely refused to do. Another group of undergraduates, apparently sober, or only slightly in a celebrating mood, hovered around me for nearly an hour, pestering me with kindly questions. America and the relation of the United States to the war were, of course, the topics. Some of the academic seniors, particularly the master of Trinity and Professor Hill, seemed surprised that the undergraduates were so attentive.

I thoroughly enjoyed the occasion. One pale youth representing an out-and-out pacifist point of view said that the war could never settle anything, ideas could not be beaten except with other ideas, and implied that it was better to have Hitler conquer England than have the war go on. The other undergraduates, though not seeming to share his views, tolerated these sentiments without interposing any objections. The leader of the undergraduates seemed to be a remarkable man who had been a member of a plumbers' union before he came to Trinity. He was, I believe, a product of the Welsh extension educational system. He was curious about the social situation in America and very anxious to come to the United States. All in all, Holland's party gave me a strange sample of opinion, quite different from what I had been hearing from other sources. I had been warned that there were a number of groups among the student body who were rather disaffected about the war. As my informant said rather bitterly, the students in Cambridge were divided into two classes: those who talked about war aims and those who were preparing to take part in the war.

The necessity of wearing full dress at the Trinity College party provided me with an anecdote of two parts which afforded Hovde and Wilson huge amusement. On Wednesday, March 12, I had been received by the King in Buckingham Palace at 12:30. The two of us chatted quite informally for a quarter of an hour before an open fire. The King was up to date on what was then a highly secret matter, namely, radar. He spoke of the recent introduction of a device for telling whether a spotted plane was friend or foe (IFF). Turning from science to politics, he defended Baldwin and spoke with some apprehension of the probability of the Labour Government's coming to power after the war was ended.

As I stepped out of the main entrance of Buckingham Palace, I was hailed by A. V. Alexander, the First Lord of the Admiralty, who offered me a ride. I was headed for Moss Brothers to hire the dress suit. I saw no necessity, however, to explain the complications of my wardrobe to a member of the ministry. Therefore, I simply said I was going to Covent Garden. "Well, take my car; my chauffeur will deliver you wherever you say." After the First Lord of the Admiralty had been dropped off at his office, I proceeded in his car to the well-known outfitters, where my credentials were regarded as suspect and I was forced to make the full deposit of twelve pounds in cash for the clothes I rented.

The second part of the story concerns my embarrassment over the awkward package of the formal clothes, which kept coming undone. A kind friend, Professor R. G. W. Norrish of Emmanuel, drove me in his car from Cambridge to the Prime Minister's residence, Chequers, on the Sunday morning following the Trinity festival. Getting in and out of the P.M.'s house without betraying that I was carrying a rented dress suit was a feat which I did accomplish, but not smoothly. The juxtaposition of royalty, a cabinet minister, a hired dress suit and the P.M.'s country house is a tale which, with a little embroidery, I used more than once after my return to Cambridge, Massachusetts.

The other guests at the luncheon at Chequers included the Ambassador, John Winant, Averell Harriman, who had arrived a few days before to take charge of the Lend-Lease operation, and an American Major General, Harry J. Malony. Mrs. Churchill and her daughter Mary were the only ladies present if my notes are correct. The atmosphere was relaxed. Since I was outranked by many grades by the Ambassador and Mr. Harriman, my role was entirely as a listener. The Lend-Lease Bill had been passed by the Senate a week before and by the House the preceding Tuesday. There was no reason for our host to show any of the uneasiness which had marked the small luncheon ten days earlier. Little if anything was said about Anglo-American relations. Instead, Mr. Churchill talked about the battles of the American Civil War. He was well posted on this topic, which he obviously relished. When the conversation turned to the Reconstruction period, Churchill remarked that the men who can win a war can never make a peace. Somebody suggested there might be *one* exception. No one followed this lead. Instead, the talk grew more general; our host declared that the only things that really made history were wars. "I am glad to hear you say so," said General Malony. At which all of us joined in a general denunciation of those who said, "War never settles anything" (a favorite phrase of the pacifists of those days).

As I attempt to recapture the spirit of that conversation from my notes made a few days later, I realize how nuclear weapons on the one hand and perhaps the strivings of the United Nations on the other have changed the content of our universe of discourse. Mr. Churchill and his guests knew only a Europe where national boundaries had been changed as a consequence of major battles every generation. Since 1945 there have been no such battles. The United Nations Charter outlaws the holding of territory conquered by force of arms. Was our denunciation of the pacifists' slogan in 1941 soon to become as obsolete as the trenches of World War I? My guess is that the history of the second half of the twentieth century will record that armed might continued to settle many issues. I doubt, however, if conflicts involving the geographic frontiers of nations will be considered of prime importance. As Mr. Churchill was to predict in his speech at Harvard in 1944, "The empires of the future are the empires of the mind." To me these words mean that the twentieth-century struggles over ideology, technology and markets have replaced the nineteenth-century concern over territorial claims.

I returned from Chequers in a car with General Malony. He spoke freely of what he had seen and heard while in England. He thought the chance of another big battle in the air was one in three. If it occurred, the Germans might win this time. Invasion might follow, as he was not impressed by the coastal defenses. Even so, he said, the invasion would not be successful. "These people won't surrender," he declared with emphasis; "they may all be killed, but they won't surrender." I had already come to the same conclusion myself. It had been reinforced by my experiences at Oxford and Cambridge.

The British climate and the wartime shortage of fuel now got the best of me for a second time. Writing again from bed—this time in the White Hart Hotel, Salisbury—on March 25, I recorded for my wife's sympathetic eyes the following:

This is the hell of a note (in more senses than one). If all goes well and I arrive in the U.S.A. per schedule, I ought to beat this [i.e., the letter] home. If I get stuck here or in Lisbon, it may serve a purpose. I can at least relieve my spleen by writing it. It is a bit absurd to be laid low by another germ within 15 days of landing—yet considering the climate, the facilities for keeping warm (outside of London), the pace I've been traveling, it was inevitable. How low I've been laid remains to be seen!

Somewhere last week, I picked up what is called "a throat" in this country. As far as I can tell, it's the equivalent of a "cold" but never reaches your nose! Perhaps it was the very cold, long day in Dover Monday (to inspect the fortifications). Last week was bad; no doubt of that—badly planned, you'd say. Harvard Club and committee of House of Commons Wednesday, both with speaking; Thursday, Royal Society, where I believe I recouped to some extent my reputation as a speaker. Dinner Thursday night with a group of earnest left-wing individuals led by Julian Huxley, where I had to do some of the talking. Luncheon Friday by a small group of chemists, where again I had to respond for ten minutes. In between committees, a visit to Woolwich Arsenal, etc. Not a moment—to cap the climax, a tough personnel problem about the Harvard–Red Cross unit came over the horizon. On arriving in Oxford (second visit), I told Sidgwick I had a throat and felt I ought to sleep in a warm room with a fire. I even suggested going to the Warden of All Souls residence where I had a standing invitation; Sidgwick didn't take to this hint at all! His spare room has a fireplace, so he had a coal fire built there and a collapsible bed put in. With the windows closed and the fire going, two hot-water bags and my blanket, I passed two fairly comfortable nights, God be praised. Did I write you of the one terrible night I spent with him in his "fireless" room after I'd had the flu? Well, I had a good time in Oxford, but the weather was not good. A bit of snow— a bit of rain. Temperature outdoors 35°–40°, indoors 45°–50°.

I dined with the Vice Chancellor (Gordon of Magdalen) and met a lot of people. Sunday evening I dined at All Souls. They made me a member of the Common Room for the duration of the war! (But if I ever availed myself of this privilege, Sidgwick would never speak to me again, I feel sure!) Lots of messages to you, as was the case in Cambridge. At least two people in both places spoke to me about not only your beautiful self but your beautiful clothes. . . . Anyway, writing this letter to *you* even if you never read it (for if I beat it home, you won't) makes me feel much better.

Saturday afternoon tea, I talked (too much) with a group of men centering around "Chatham House in exile" now at Balliol. International professors, etc., Sir Alfred Zimmern, Arnold Toynbee, etc.—Professor Charles Webster's friends. I was way out of bounds, but I'm bound to say I enjoyed the conversation, which covered the war and the future peace from A to Z and back again.

Monday, I left bright (but not very) and early with Hovde, who had come down Sunday in our own hired car with driver for Porton. Porton is the C.W.S. experiment station near Salisbury. I have had no luck with this outfit *in re* personal health. They'll all think I'm made of glass or am a tissue culture for virus infections! I passed up a trip here with Robinson on Monday the ninth because of the recurrent "flu" at Oxford, and here I was off again with a bad throat. I got through the day, however, with only a slight manifestation of huskiness in the voice and I hope only a slight manifestation of irritation due to subnormal responses. Robinson, who has been most friendly in fact, said they all marveled at the quick way in which I picked up the miscellaneous threads of their complicated researches and went to the heart of their scientific problems. But one begins to acquire all sorts of remarkable qualities if one lunches twice with the P.M. and that becomes well known—not to mention the King and the Lord Chancellor.

Last evening we all dined here at the White Hart. Col. Marriott of the C.W.S., military attaché at the Embassy, who is making the visit with us "threw the party." Before dinner I met Dr. Gordon, Dr. Beeson [from Harvard School of Public Health], and two regional public health officers in preparation for our inspection of the site of the Harvard–Red Cross Hospital today. Beeson had a look at my throat with the aid of my pocket flashlight and a long-handled spoon. Advised me to take it easy but couldn't very well advise me to cancel the inspection of the Harvard Unit the next morning. A couple of white patches (in my throat, not on the site of the Harvard Public Health Unit) he allowed were bacterial and might be streptococci (cheerful man). Anyway, I went to bed early. This A.M. I felt as though I had a cold but no nose symptoms (this is a hospital chart, not a letter!). Went out and visited the site, then to the office of Public Works in the Cathedral Close and inspected the plans. Then to bed. I canceled the proposed return to Porton and sent Hovde instead. No great loss. Beeson thinks my throat looks better (11 A.M.). If nothing worse develops out of this party, I shall be very satisfied indeed. Anyway, I'm getting 24 hours of rest which was probably in order! I hope it doesn't rain or snow tomorrow!

The Cathedral looks as beautiful as ever. I took a look at it this morning from the close, just before going into the office of Public Works. This town is as peaceful as when we were last here—only seven bombs through all the months! I imagine it is crowded—all towns seem to be —Oxford and Cambridge beyond words. The Harvard site is grand—on a rise just on the edge of the town. Beautiful country. If I were to stay here long (and out of bed and warm), I might easily become a sentimental Anglophile! It is hard to get this country in focus these days—such a mixture of war and peace, of the normal and the abnormal, of life and death. But of that more shortly when we meet. I'm sorry about the delay in returning but it just couldn't be otherwise. As it is, I shan't have done half of what I would like to. I've tried to cover so many fronts, all necessary. I believe I've done some good. I hope so. . . .

My visit to Salisbury had nothing to do with my NDRC mission; I went there on Harvard business. What that was I can best explain by quoting from a letter to me from Wilson Jameson, the Minister of Health, written in March 1941.

Before you end your visit to this country I should like to write you about the Harvard Unit which is being provided so generously by Harvard University and the American Red Cross.

As you know, when your welcome offer of help was conveyed to us by Dr. Gordon, we ourselves proposed, and you readily agreed, that such help should take the form of an infectious disease hospital and laboratory with all necessary staff and equipment. Our greatest need then was for such a unit and our need today is no less. It is true that we have been singularly fortunate during the past six months in respect of serious epidemic disease, but we cannot hope to escape so lightly during next winter. Trained epidemiologists are by no means numerous in this country, and the inclusion in the Harvard Unit of an epidemiological medical team assisted by public health nurses gave me the greatest possible satisfaction. You may rely on our using them to the full.

One of the best features of the project is that it fits so well into our own scheme of things. We have none too many hospital beds for cases of infectious disease, and the area in which the Harvard Hospital will be situated is one in which both civil and military demands are great and difficult to meet. The laboratory will be associated intimately with our system of Emergency Public Health Laboratories, and the epidemiological team will be used as though they were members of the staff of the Ministry of Health, in whatever part of the country disease has to be investigated and brought under control. . . .

May I say in conclusion that it is not merely the professional help of this advance party of the Unit that is of value. The very fact that these men have come to this country to work side by side with us in our time of trial stimulates and encourages all of us. The sooner the hospital and the rest of its staff are here the happier we shall be.

To complete the story of the Red Cross–Harvard Hospital, I must report that the hospital of 126 beds opened in September 1941. It operated under the direction of the three partners—the Red Cross,

266 / My Several Lives

Harvard and the British Ministry of Health—until July 15, 1942.
On that date the hospital was turned over to the Commanding General at the American Headquarters of the European Theater of operation. We had foreseen that there would be no need for Harvard
to be involved in the enterprise after the United States became a
belligerent. Therefore the Harvard Public Health Unit was dissolved
a few months after Pearl Harbor. In the ten months of its existence,
it had performed a worthwhile service which justified the trouble
and expense involved in mounting the undertaking.

Mr. Churchill was chancellor of Bristol University. In that capacity, he planned to confer honorary degrees on Ambassador Winant
and myself on April 12. I learned of the intended honor too late to
change my plans, and I was already "overdue" in the United States.
I regretted then, and subsequently regretted still more, the turn of
fate which placed me on a plane to Lisbon the very day the Bristol
convocation took place. As Mr. Churchill told the story when he spoke
at Harvard in September 1944, the Germans did their best to inconvenience him. A very heavy raid the night before kept most of the
participants up all night fighting fires. In the morning, with devastation all around them, they put on their robes over their fire-fighting
costumes and the academic ceremonies proceeded as if it were peacetime.

Two days before, I had called on the Prime Minister by appointment at 10 Downing Street to say good-bye. A meeting with a group
of high-ranking officers was just breaking up. A series of maps they
presumably had just been consulting were hung on the walls with
suitable coverings. Mr. Churchill insisted on my coming into the
cabinet room and sitting down as the military filed out. The topic of
discussion had been the impending disaster in Greece. The German
Army called in by the retreating Italians was overpowering all resistance. The Prime Minister was somber. "Here we are," he said,
"standing alone. What is going to happen?" What I replied, I cannot
now recall. I do remember the intensity of my feelings as I left
London with the immediate objective of telling my friends in the
United States how desperate was the British situation. In three days
I would be in New York, thanks to the recently installed flying-boat
service from Lisbon. I was prepared to give the isolationists some
frank talk.

Within two weeks I had an opportunity of arguing my case before
a select audience. Contrary to all precedent, the two-day spring meeting of the Harvard Board of Overseers was held not in Cambridge,

Massachusetts, but in Williamsburg, Virginia. Our host was John Stewart Bryan, the president of William and Mary and an Overseer of Harvard College. The transition from the tension of England under siege to the peaceful Virginia landscape and the uttterly relaxed attitude of the Board of Overseers was difficult to take.

I shall never forget sitting on the lawn of one of the great estates near Williamsburg, when we met one afternoon for a social hour. The discussion at first turned on Harvard affairs. Then a group slowly gathered around me asking about my trip. Like any traveler, I was eager to talk. I tried to be a reporter, not an advocate. My advocacy, however, was soon showing. There were some isolationists among the group; hardly a single member of the entire board would have been ready to go as far as I had in my testimony before the Senate committee. Before the conversation had gone far, I was asked a loaded question: How is England going to win this war? I had to answer: No one knew. Admittedly, she was standing alone. (Hitler's attack on Russia was two months in the future.) Such being the case, my questioner continued, why shouldn't all of us urge the British to come to terms with Hitler? At that point, I found it difficult to be polite, even more difficult to appear to be judical and relaxed.

One of the most distinguished members, a close friend of Herbert Hoover, asked a couple of questions, reflecting the ex-President's views as they had been appearing in the press and suggesting we could assist Great Britain better by staying out of the war and sending supplies than by entry as a belligerent. My answer was twofold. First, if Hitler thought this to be so, he would declare war on the United States at once; second, the supplies had to be delivered to the British Isles. To accomplish this without the full assistance of the U.S. Navy might soon become impossible.

My wife and I were surprised at how many of the Overseers and their wives with whom we talked thought the war might soon be ended by a negotiated peace. I assured them that to anyone who had lately been in England such an idea was utterly fantastic. People in the United States just didn't understand the mood of the British. I was willing to wager a good deal that no British Government could come to power which was committed to making peace with Hitler. Though they were subject to a continuous threat of air raids and many suffered directly from night bombing, there was no thought of compromise.

A few days after the Williamsburg meeting, President Roosevelt asked me to have lunch with him in his office in the White House.

There were just two of us eating a tray lunch. Although I was to report on my English trip, it was natural for me to refer to the Williamsburg meeting. As one Harvard graduate to another, I could not help bringing into the conversation my judgment of the attitude of certain prominent members of the Board of Overseers. The President, in turn, without the slightest rancor or other emotion, recounted the extreme neutralist sentiment of certain men we both knew well. This bit of gossip (it was hardly more) I used a little later as a peg on which I hung a letter to the President.

In the middle of May, I addressed a meeting of the Associated Harvard Clubs in Baltimore. As was usual at such meetings, I spoke for the most part about the college and the professional schools. In conclusion, I announced I would say a few words as a private citizen about the "momentous decision which confronts the country—the choice between peace and war." I proceeded to repeat the ideas I had put forward in my recent "When Shall America Fight?" radio broadcast. I maintained that, in spite of all our talk about being hard-boiled realists, about self-interest and love of money, we are at bottom a romantic, idealistic folk. Our great decisions had been taken on moral grounds. Two great ideals were battling in our national conscience, I suggested. One was peace, the other freedom. The same conflict had, until a short time ago, been going on in Great Britain, too. Just in time the British awoke; a world revolution of "vile import" was about to break over them; they held firm; now we all saluted their bravery, their gallant stand. Then I concluded with the following words, which were in a new key for me; they betrayed what the trip to England had done to my emotions.

Only slowly, very slowly, are we coming to understand the significance for our freedom of the battles now in progress. To be sure, we have cast aside all pretense of neutrality, we gladly give arms and ammunition, eagerly supply all instruments of war. But is this enough? Can we stop there?

In the very name of that human decency for which the British today are battling, in the name of human decency, can we, a self-respecting people, let another nation do our fighting for us? This is the basic issue, which must sooner or later burn through the mass of verbiage of rationalizations, which must destroy the wishful thinking that arises from our will to peace. Gentlemen, I have no doubt as to the ultimate decision of the American people, for I have no doubt of the firmness of our sense of moral values. We shall regain peace through defeating evil, and in the fight for freedom throughout the world we shall before long take our proper place.

As an argument, I would today give the entire conclusion a low mark. But at the time, the speech was a magnificent success. The applause was no mere response of loyal alumni to the statement of a Harvard president; people clapped too long and too loudly for anyone to doubt the sentiments of a vast majority.

Back in Cambridge a few days later, I wrote a letter to the President connecting my experience in Baltimore with our luncheon talk:

I am venturing to send you as an enclosure in this letter a copy of the concluding paragraphs of my address to the Associated Harvard Clubs at the banquet held in Baltimore last Saturday evening. There is no reason why you should take the time to read my remarks, but I thought you might be interested to know that this highly belligerent speech was received with tremendous applause by the audience. I think I have never addressed a Harvard group who responded to my final words with such an ovation. As you know, Harvard men come to the meetings of the Associated Harvard Clubs from different parts of the country and may be considered a fairly representative cross-section.

I was particularly heartened by this response in view of the somewhat lukewarm attitude which I encountered at the meeting of the Board of Overseers a few weeks ago and which I reported to you when I had the pleasure of lunching with you the other day.

The conversation at the luncheon with President Roosevelt was not confined to comments on the isolationists. The purpose was to report to the President on my work in establishing an NDRC office in London. Before long I found myself presenting a proposal which I had made to Harriman in London. The basic idea developed during a visit Hovde, Wilson and I had paid to a radiolocator unit (as radar was then called). In conversation with the officers in charge of the equipment, I learned of a worrisome problem. They were unable to recruit enough technically-minded men to keep the instruments in repair and functioning effectively. Why not recruit Americans? I asked myself. As I saw the situation, Great Britain had need of two types of men—one, essentially repairmen and service men and the other much more highly trained technical or engineering personnel who would be in a position to supervise and direct the operation of radio locators. It was this last group, relatively small in number, which might be recruited in the United States and sent to Great Britain to get practical experience with the apparatus and methods used to spot hostile aircraft. The question of whether United States officers and men could properly function in this way while the United States was officially neutral, in spite of the Lend-Lease Act, seemed an open question to those with whom I discussed the matter in London. I was advised by Mr. Harriman to take the problem up with the President on my return to the United States.

I suggested to the President that a group of men with specialized training be recruited, made officers in the United States Army and sent to England as observers, with special assignment to assist the British in every way except taking part in combat. The President appeared to be much interested in the suggestion. It appealed to him as being a practical method of getting ahead with the training of personnel and assisting the British. I learned later that he had that afternoon told the Cabinet meeting of our conversation about radio locators. He expressed the wish that some men well grounded in physics be commissioned as reserve officers and sent abroad as observers. The Secretary of War acted at once on the presidential request.

A few days later, Secretary Stimson asked me to come to see him about sending a group of reserve officers to be attached to the British Air Force. He told me the President had spoken to him about the matter and he had already authorized General Marshall to send as many as three hundred. The actual recruiting of the group was shortly thereafter placed in the hands of George Bailey, the president of the American Radio Relay League. Before Pearl Harbor, 350 went to England as Signal Corps officers; eventually the total was over 2,000.

In the course of presenting the idea of the Electronics Training Group, I found, to my astonishment, that the President was almost totally ignorant of the functioning of radar. Perhaps this was not strange since in the accounts which had been published of the Battle of Britain hardly a hint had been given of the use of electronic devices. In the official account published in late 1941, it was simply stated that "information regarding the approach of the enemy is obtained by a variety of methods"; the reader is left with the impression that what was involved was visual spotting by members of a vast volunteer civil observer corps supplemented by a listening device. Thus I found myself, in response to questioning, briefing the Commander in Chief on the new technique which had played the key role in the winning of the great air battle of the preceding September. As a consequence, the President went to his Cabinet meeting full of enthusiasm for my idea. Thanks to his orders to Secretary Stimson, the scheme got under way in a miraculously short time, demonstrating what could be done in Washington by a promoter who could make a case directly to the President.

But in a sense I had been out of channels—a grave offense in my own eyes as well as those of Bush and Stimson. No one had authorized me to instruct the President of the United States about the use of radar. As to my own project, it would have been more orderly if I had prepared a memorandum for Bush and asked him to place it in the President's hands. Bush would certainly have notified Stimson's office. The Secretary of War would not have been in the somewhat embarrassing position of hearing for the first time about a novel project within his jurisdiction through a verbal order from the President of the United States.

CHAPTER 21

Deputy to Vannevar Bush

W<small>HEN I RETURNED</small> to Washington in April 1941 from my trip to England, I found that Van Bush, Frank Jewett and one or two others were in the midst of a discussion of a possible alteration of the committee's status; in fact, preparations were well under way for the establishment of a new agency—the Office of Scientific Research and Development (OSRD), which I mentioned earlier. Bush was to be the head of the office, with the title of director. The National Defense Research Committee and a new Committee on Medical Research were to be the component parts of OSRD, which was to be placed within the Office for Emergency Management of the Executive Office of the President. The two committees were to recommend to Bush the placing of contracts. Irvin Stewart would continue his effective services, but now his office would administer the contracts originating in two committees—the NDRC and CMR. Indeed, it was to accommodate a medical research committee that the new agency was being created.

I soon discovered that while the other members of NDRC would be little affected by the proposed change, my own function would be quite different. Bush could not be both director of OSRD and chairman of NDRC (at least not on paper); so I was to take his place as chairman and Roger Adams was to succeed me as the chemist on the committee. I was hardly given a chance to protest the new arrangement, even if I had wanted to. The chances are that I was so preoccupied with reporting on my trip to England that I gave little heed to the implications of the shift in jobs. Though officially the responsibility for the research contracts dealing with defensive and offensive phases of gas warfare and other activities in chemistry was to be in Roger Adams' hands, I expected to continue to be in a position to be informed about what was going on. Since I had already unofficially delegated the supervision of all the research contracts to Adams or Lewis or their section chiefs, what seemed to lie ahead was not very different from my activities of the past ten or twelve months.

If such were my expectations in May and June 1941, they proved to be almost completely wrong. In the first place, the Japanese attack at Pearl Harbor brought the United States into the war as a nation united to a degree that surprised both interventionists and isolationists. In the second place, after Pearl Harbor, the volume and significance of the contractual proposals from the NDRC subcommittees increased so rapidly that a reorganization of the committee became necessary. In December 1942 the one and only major reorganization took place; it involved an expansion of the chairman's office by which I obtained a partner, Professor Edward L. Moreland of M.I.T., one of the nicest men I have ever worked with, and three staff members. In the third place, within less than a year I became the intermediary between Bush and the special committee in charge of research on nuclear fission and later an alternate to Bush when he was made chairman of the Military Policy Committee in charge of the production of an atomic bomb.

I shall not attempt to write of my nearly four years of labor as presiding officer of the NDRC. The accomplishments of the committee have been well set forth for the lay reader in James Phinney Baxter III's excellent book, *Scientists Against Time*. Even an attempted summary would be inappropriate. Moreover, as chairman, I was not in a position to share the week-by-week excitement as important developments progressed.

The scientific members of the committee were more fortunate. They and their vice chairmen, who headed the divisions and sections, were able to exercise their originality and scientific judgment. When differences of opinion arose about pursuing one line of inquiry rather than another, almost without exception the conflict was resolved in the division or section. Rarely, if ever, was any time at the meetings taken up with a consideration of technical details. Therefore my job as chairman was almost entirely administrative. The problems with which I had to deal (and there were many) were not so much problems in applied science as those which arose from the interaction of human beings working under high pressure. My experiences as a university president were far more relevant than those I had enjoyed when directing a team of investigators in the Converse Chemical Laboratory in Cambridge.

According to the official documents, I had one additional function. If the director of OSRD was absent or disabled, I, as chairman of NDRC, was authorized to exercise his duties and powers. Only once was I called on to act as director—for a short time when Bush was in London. Otherwise, this provision was ignored. But the additional duty which I found gradually settling on me was not mentioned in any of the official papers. It was a result of a decision by Van Bush which never found expression in any executive order; it amounted to my becoming deputy to Bush for matters connected with the production of an atomic bomb.

On December 22, 1941, the director of OSRD met with NDRC and told the members that henceforth they would have no responsibility for the uranium program. Frank Jewett, I recall, greeted the news with enthusiasm, and the others seemed to be of the same mind. The contracts on which they had been asked to vote hitherto had been presented by Lyman J. Briggs, Director of the Bureau of Standards, who had been chairman of the Uranium Committee by Roosevelt's appointment before NDRC was formed. No one felt he was in a position to challenge Briggs or to evaluate the reasons he gave for what was proposed. We knew that Bush himself was better informed than most of us. As a consequence, there had been an uneasy feeling that the normal procedures of the committee were not suitable for what was, at least historically, a special case.

Perhaps Bush had sensed this feeling, and therefore, when on October 9, 1941, he conferred with President Roosevelt and Vice President Henry A. Wallace, he laid the ground for a fundamental decision by the President. The decision was to the effect that the knowledge of what Briggs' committee was doing was to be strictly confined to the President himself, Vice President Wallace, Secretary of War Henry L. Stimson, Chief of Staff of the Army General George C. Marshall, Bush and myself. Perhaps it was Franklin D. Roosevelt's own concern with keeping the audacious uranium project as secret as possible which led to his order restricting a full knowledge of the project to so small a group. Whatever the motive, when Bush told me of the President's directive, I knew it was only a matter of weeks before I would be deeply involved in the atomic bomb project.

The enterprise had started in the fall of 1939. Alexander Sachs, an adviser to Lehman Brothers, had responded to the urgings of three physicists, Leo Szilard, Eugene P. Wigner and Albert Einstein. He presented to President Roosevelt the known facts about uranium fission. The potentialities of discoveries which had just been made, he pointed out, had tremendous implications for the United States. Roosevelt responded by turning the problem over to Lyman J. Briggs. He made him chairman of a secret advisory committee on uranium whose members were named by the President. Representatives of the Army and Navy were included. The committee operated under conditions of strict secrecy and with a small budget provided by the armed forces. Such was the committee which the President had asked Bush to take on as part of his responsibilities as chairman of the NDRC. Now with the formation of OSRD, the scene was set for giving research on the fission of uranium a berth quite independent of all other scientific efforts directed to military ends.

During the month or more that I had been away from the United States, much had been happening in the field of nuclear fission. A number of research projects of a basic nature were under way, supported by NDRC contracts voted in the fall. Discoveries of fundamental significance had been made in the early winter months by American physicists largely working outside the official framework of the advisory committee. Using the atom smasher which Ernest O. Lawrence, the Nobel prize winner of the University of California, had invented—the cyclotron— his associates in Berkeley had produced the hitherto-unknown element No. 94; it was christened plutonium. Before long, experiments with tiny amounts of material had confirmed what the theoreticians had surmised, namely, that the new element, like one of the uranium isotopes, underwent spontaneous fission. Already, though hardly enough of the element had been manufactured to be seen, more than one physicist in the United States and England had begun to whisper that the large-scale production of plutonium might prove to be the essential step in a scheme for releasing atomic energy.

During March 1941, when I was in England, Karl Compton and Ernest O. Lawrence had been in conference with Bush (who was still chairman of the NDRC), and the committee had voted money to support the work at Berkeley. A certain amount of skepticism, I believe, had been expressed around the table when the expenditure of funds for such a long-range project had been discussed. The initial presentation of projects by Briggs had been in terms of a self-sustaining chain reaction which would be a source of power. The idea was that if the spontaneous fission of a single atom of the rare isotope of uranium (uranium 235) could occur under circumstances which enabled the neutrons thus produced to cause the fission of other uranium atoms, the process once started would continue by itself. In natural uranium, no such chain reaction took place, as the bulk of the neutrons escaped or were absorbed by other elements before being captured by another atom of uranium 235. What was needed, the physicists concluded, was a way of slowing down the neutrons so that the chances of their capture would be increased. A moderator was required, which might be graphite or heavy water, or so said the physicists. What was proposed was to construct a lattice arrangement of natural uranium and graphite. Calculations indicated that if one slowly increased the size of the arrangement (soon to be called a "pile"), a point would be reached when more neutrons were produced than escaped capture; at that point in time, a self-sustaining nuclear reaction would take place. From then on it would be only a question of controlling the reaction by introducing bits of any element that readily absorbed neutrons without undergoing fission.

By the time I left for England, I was familiar with the outlines of the theory of the use of uranium for power. I understood that if the uranium 235 isotope could be separated from the far more abundant isotope 238, a pile could be constructed of much smaller size than one made with natural uranium. What I did not at that time appreciate was that a mass of uranium 235 beyond a certain size would by itself support a self-sustaining chain reaction of enormous power by virtue of the fast neutrons spontaneously released. In other words, an amount of U-235 beyond a critical size would be an atomic bomb. Somehow or other, perhaps because of the need for supersecrecy, the possibility of producing an atomic bomb had not been made evident to me, at least not in the discussion which Briggs had initiated in NDRC. Bush, of course, was aware of the potentialities of what was going on. But as late as mid-February 1941 I was in complete ignorance of the prospects of a bomb.

Concern with the investigation of the possibilities of uranium as a source of power was not on my agenda as I traveled to London. As I have explained, my job was really diplomatic rather than scientific. Except as regards gas warfare and the manufacture of conventional explosives, I entered into few discussions about technical matters. In part, my self-imposed restriction was a product of my strong belief in the "need to know" principle; and, in part, it was a consequence of my lack of knowledge of electronics. At that time, the development of short-wave radar sets was the focus of the most urgent questions facing American and British scientists, and I was not equipped to take part in any such discussions.

What I heard about atomic energy was the consequence of two accidental meetings. One was with a French scientist whom I met at Oxford. Before the fall of France, he had been investigating a possible chain reaction using heavy water as a moderator. He told me of his worries and disappointments at the lack of interest and support in his work. Since his complaints were clearly "out of channels," I quickly terminated the conversation and forgot the incident. The other was a luncheon with Lord Cherwell alone at a London club. He introduced the subject of the study of the fission of uranium atoms. I reacted by repeating the doubts I had expressed and heard expressed at NDRC meetings. I wondered if it was wise to devote the precious time of scientists, with the German threat so critical, to a project which could not affect the outcome of the war. "A chain reaction for power might have vast industrial potentials," I said. "Even for the Navy it might have uses someday, for example, in propelling submarines. But these are distant objectives—too distant for us to take them seriously in these frightening days."

"You have left out of consideration," said Cherwell, "the possibility of the construction of a bomb of enormous power." "How would that be possible?" I asked. "By first separating uranium 235," he said, "and then arranging for two portions of this element to be brought together suddenly so that the resulting mass would spontaneously undergo a self-sustaining reaction."

This was the first I had heard about even the remote possibility of a bomb. Since Cherwell was clearly conveying secret information to me without authorization, I pursued the topic no further. I assumed, quite correctly, that if and when Bush wished to be in touch with the atomic energy work in England, he would do so through channels involving Briggs.

The first weeks after my return from England were occupied with reporting to the President as well as to the NDRC as a whole and the chemical subdivisions separately. Furthermore, Harvard affairs, including the two-day meeting with the Board of Overseers, occupied a considerable portion of my time. Then, too, I felt that, because of my recent experiences, I was in a rather special position to promote the cause of the interventionists. It must have been at least the middle of May before I was brought up to date on the plans for the impending reorganization. And only after it was clear that I should shortly have a new position did Bush begin to take me into his confidence as he pondered on what to do with the Briggs Committee.

I learned that Frank Jewett, in April at Bush's request, had appointed a National Academy of Sciences Committee to review the uranium program (in complete secrecy, of course). The chairman was the famous physicist, Professor Arthur H. Compton of Chicago, a Nobel prize winner. The report was placed before NDRC at a meeting in early June. The emphasis was on a chain reaction as a source of power. The possibility of a bomb was only hinted at. Nowhere in the document was there any specific statement about how one started an uncontrolled reaction, such as Lord Cherwell had made to me in London. My reactions after reading Arthur Compton's report were almost completely negative. My skepticism, which was shared by Jewett, led to the addition of two engineers to Compton's committee, which reported again in July.

In the meantime, OSRD had been established. I was now in a quite different position from the one I had occupied before the reorganization. It was one thing to have reservations about an NDRC contract placed before the committee by Briggs, with Bush's implied blessing, and another as a new chairman of NDRC to have serious doubts. In the future, the recommendations were to be voted in a meeting over which I presided. In other words, since Briggs' committee was to be a division of the new NDRC, I had a responsibility for its welfare; if I had questions about its goals, it was clearly my duty to express my thoughts to the director in private conversation.

What worried me about Compton's first report, I told Bush, was the assumption that achieving a chain reaction was so important that a large expenditure of both money and manpower was justified. To me, the defense of the free world was in such a dangerous state that only efforts which were likely to yield results within a matter of months or, at most, a year or two were worthy of serious consideration. In that summer of 1941, with recollections of what I had seen and heard in England fresh in my mind, I was impatient with the arguments of some of the physicists associated with the Uranium Committee whom I met from time to time. They talked in excited tones about the discovery of a new world in which power from a uranium reactor would revolutionize our industrialized society. These fancies left me cold. I suggested that until Nazi Germany was defeated all our energies should be concentrated on one immediate objective.

After the victory there would be time enough for research programs in physics connected with nonmilitary industrial objectives.

Bush was faced with a momentous decision as to priorities. I think he rather welcomed my skeptical opposition. He had on his hands a number of excited physicists urging him to prod Briggs into a rapid expansion of his program. My emphasis on the overriding necessity of improving the immediate military power of the United States and Great Britain was, in a sense, a balancing argument. During July, Bush had a discussion with Vice President Wallace about the question of spending a large amount of government money on the uranium program. He thus paved the way for the crucial meeting with Roosevelt and Wallace on October 9, 1941, to which I have already referred. In the meantime, Bush enlarged the National Academy Committee and asked for another review of the situation.

The two new members of Compton's committee were the chemical engineer, W. K. Lewis, and a physical chemist who had transformed himself during the past year into the NDRC expert on explosives— Professor George B. Kistiakowsky of Harvard. The additions were made at my suggestion. I remember quite distinctly Kistiakowsky's reaction. I had been authorized to tell him of his forthcoming appointment to Compton's committee. He was well aware of the research work on separating uranium 235, but had been thinking in terms of power. When I retailed to him the idea that a bomb could be made by the rapid assembly of two masses of fissionable material, his first remark was that of a doubting Thomas. "It would seem to be a difficult undertaking on a battlefield," he remarked. A few weeks later when we met, his doubts were gone. "It can be made to work," he said. "I am one hundred percent sold."

My doubts about Briggs' project evaporated as soon as I heard George Kistiakowsky's considered verdict. I had known George for many years. Indeed, I had played a part in the 1920s in persuading him to leave Princeton and join the Harvard chemistry department. More recently, I had asked him to be head of the NDRC division on explosives which Roger Adams and I organized. I had complete faith in his judgment. If he was sold on Arthur Compton's program, who was I to have reservations? My reversal in attitude I kept to myself until the National Academy Committee made its report. Bush was assessing his own position during the summer of 1941 as he considered what recommendations he would make to the President. My role was only to lend a hand.

By the end of the fall it was clear that the proponents of greatly increased tempo for the nuclear fission program had won their case, but only because they had stopped talking about nuclear power and had focused their energies on the prospects of a bomb. Among the factors which counted heavily with Bush was the attitude of Arthur H. Compton and Ernest O. Lawrence, who had been urging their point of view upon him as early as March. I had relayed to him the animated conversation I had with these two gentlemen and Dean George B. Pegram of Columbia at Compton's house in Chicago in September 1941, at the time of the fiftieth anniversary of the founding of the University of Chicago. Lawrence was particularly vociferous about the need for mobilizing all scientific talent for the uranium program. I could not resist the temptation to cut behind his rhetoric by asking if he was prepared to shelve his own research programs and work full time on some phase of the proposed research. He was a bit taken aback, but agreed that if necessary he would.

More significant than the arguments of Compton and Lawrence was the news that a group of physicists in England had concluded that the construction of a bomb made out of uranium 235 was entirely feasible. With those considerations in mind, Bush had conferred with the President and Vice President on October 9, 1941. It was at this conference, as I mentioned earlier, that Roosevelt had directed Bush to confine the discussion of policy to a small group who later became known as the "Top Policy Group"—Wallace, Stimson, General Marshall, Bush and myself. An important element in Bush's decision was the belief of a number of physicists who were refugees from Nazi Germany that the Germans were already engaged in the development of a uranium bomb. I was inclined to discount many of the stories, which were obviously placed before Bush by Arthur Compton and his friends to influence his decision. Still, one could not dismiss them altogether, though the factual evidence was slight. The terrifying thought that the Nazis might make an atomic bomb within the next year or two could not be shoved aside.

I remember spelling out the catastrophic possibilities of a German bomb to Harvey H. Bundy of Secretary Stimson's staff. As the civilian liaison man with the scientists, Bundy came to see me in Cambridge a few days after Pearl Harbor. I was in bed with a heavy cold. We talked of the serious blow the Navy had received; we discussed the long job ahead for Great Britain, the United States and the Soviet Union. After allowing Bundy to spread the gloom as heavily as he wished, I said in effect that I was confident about the eventual outcome of the war except for one possibility, which was that the Nazis would produce an atomic bomb and use it. Bundy, as a confidential assistant of Stimson's, was entitled to knowledge about the Uranium Committee. He had had some knowledge of what was planned but had not thought seriously about the danger of the German scientists literally beating us to the punch. Bundy recalled years later how he left my bedroom that December day with a worry that overshadowed those caused by even the most pessimistic foreshadowing of the air, land and naval battles yet to come.

December 1941 was not only the month in which war came to the United States. It was the month in which the decision was made to proceed full steam ahead on the manufacture of an atomic bomb. In the last days of November, Bush sent the third report of Arthur Compton's committee to the President. This report, unlike the two earlier ones, was explicit about an atomic explosive: "A fission bomb of superlatively destructive power will result from bringing quickly together a sufficient mass of element U-235." Bush wrote the President that he was forming an engineering group to plan for a production plant for separating the U-235 isotope.

As the authors of *The New World*, Richard G. Hewlett and Oscar E. Anderson, Jr.,* point out, even in his third report as chairman of the review committee of the National Academy of Sciences, Arthur Compton made no reference to the possible use of plutonium. According to their account, the possibility of using element 94 as a substitute for uranium 235 had been considered in a draft of the third report but omitted from the final version. Hewlett's and Anderson's comment on the deletion is that it was "good tactics" because "Bush was primarily interested in a uranium 235 weapon." The omission left Compton free to urge on Bush in private conversation the need for getting ahead rapidly with the construction of a pile in which a slow-neutron self-sustaining reaction would occur. The fact that such a pile would generate energy was only of incidental interest. The reason for its construction would be the production of plutonium. Calculations indicated that as the slow-neutron chain reaction occurred, some of the predominant isotope (U-238) would be transformed into plutonium (element 94), which could be separated from the uranium by a relatively easy chemical process.

As soon as Bush had endorsed the Compton report and sent it to President Roosevelt, he proceeded with a drastic reorganization of the

* University Park, Pa., Pennsylvania State University Press, 1962, p. 48.

work on uranium. Meeting with Briggs and his committee on the day before Pearl Harbor, he explained the new arrangements placing me in the position of intermediary between the physicists and Bush. As Arthur Compton tells the story, after the meeting on December 6, he and Bush and I had luncheon at the old Cosmos Club on Lafayette Square in Washington.* I remember the luncheon clearly for a highly trivial reason. I started to drink my usual glass of milk by taking a large swallow, only to discover it was buttermilk, which I detest. My sputtering and short outburst of profanity amused Van enormously but rather shocked Arthur, I am afraid.

I also recall the subject of the conversation, and my memory coincides completely with Compton's account in his book. My skepticism about making any atomic bomb in time to affect the war was now some months behind me, but I raised serious questions about what Compton now proposed. He was talking about producing a new element, plutonium, which had not yet been seen except in microscopic amounts. Yet it was proposed to produce large amounts of plutonium by the operation of a pile. The contents of the pile would then be put through a series of chemical reactions in order to separate the plutonium from the uranium. To my objection that the chemistry of the element was largely unknown, Compton replied that intensive research would produce the necessary knowledge. Furthermore, he said, even if it turned out that plutonium was not as readily separable as he believed, or for some reason could not be used in making a bomb, the construction of a self-sustaining chain reaction would be a magnificent achievement; it would prove that the measurements and theoretical calculations were correct. The pile would produce energy in the form of heat. It would be a model for all subsequent devices for producing power from nuclear reactions. I never knew whether it was this near-certainty of demonstrating a slow-neutron reaction which settled the matter in Van's mind, or whether he was impressed with Compton's faith in the production of a plutonium bomb, against my lack of faith as a chemist. At all events, within a matter of weeks he agreed to Arthur Compton's setting up at Chicago a highly secret project, the first objective of which would be the construction of a pile using natural uranium and graphite as a moderator.

Once Bush had made up his mind, he proceeded with his usual drive. He asked that an Army officer be assigned at once to follow the research program. A few days later, General Marshall named Briga-

* Arthur Holly Compton, *Atomic Quest,* New York, Oxford University Press, 1956, p. 70.

dier General W. D. Styer to the post. It was settled that when construction work became necessary, the Army Corps of Engineers would assume the responsibility. Thus the groundwork was laid for what was some months later to be the Manhattan District, with General L. R. Groves in charge.

I could not attend the first meeting of the Top Policy Group on December 16, as I was still in bed with a cold. By the eighteenth, however, I was again in Washington and met with the expanded Briggs Committee, now completely divorced from NDRC and designated the S-1 Section of OSRD. I was now representing Dr. Bush. I told the group of the new arrangements and said that in the future there would be no need to worry about money. To summarize the changes which had taken place, I can do no better than quote from the concluding paragraphs of Chapter 2 of *The New World*:

Now the arrangements were complete. Back in October, Bush had won White House sanction for a full-scale effort to explore the possibilities for an atomic weapon. After a review by top scientists and engineers, he had reorganized the program and marked out the main lines of endeavor. A panel of the President's most trusted advisers had approved the preliminary steps. The time had come to act. . . .

To achieve this much had been slow and painful. It was easy for younger men to complain that senior scientists and engineers had been slow to comprehend the meaning and potential of fission. It was easy to blame preoccupation with security. While secrecy was imperative in a world already at war, it was sometimes misdirected and self-defeating.

But it was also easy to fail to appreciate the position of men who held high responsibility. No scientist, no engineer held as much as Bush and Conant. Conceivably, they might have moved earlier. But Bush had assumed a tremendous burden in June of 1940: the creation of an entirely new relationship between science and government in the interests of national defense. He had to think of personalities and politics as well as technology. He and Conant had to look at uranium in the light of the entire role that science might play in the emergency. They had to turn a deaf ear to blue-sky talk of nuclear power plants and think of weapons. They had to navigate between the Scylla and Charybdis of excessive pessimism and soaring optimism. They had set a course by the Pole Star of fact.

Two weeks after Pearl Harbor, all this was ancient history. The United States was at war. The goal Bush and Conant had seen so long was clear to everyone. Gone was the confusion of objectives. Gone too was the old day of leisurely research with its almost mystical faith that society could depend on the largely undirected, unplanned, and capriciously financed efforts of lonely toilers in the scientific vineyards. Gone was the hesitation, so pronounced just two short years before, to spend public money on the theories of a few research men. American science would never be the same. The United States would never be the same. The world would never be the same.*

The new organization of the Briggs Committee provided that Bush, as director of OSRD, would place contracts recommended to him by the S-1 Committee or by a program chief or the head of the Planning Board, though in any case I was expected to be informed. The head of the Planning Board (the group of engineers about which Bush had writen the President) was Eger V. Murphree of the Standard Oil Development Company; the other members were W. K. Lewis; L. W. Chubb, director of Westinghouse Research Laboratories; P. C. Keith, vice president of M. W. Kellogg Company, and George O. Curme of Union Carbide and Carbon. During the first months of 1942, the chief concern of the Planning Board was an assessment of two methods of separating U-235—one by gaseous diffusion, the other by the use of centrifuges. The three program chiefs were Professor Harold Urey of Columbia, a Noble prize winning chemist, Lawrence and Compton. Each was to be busy in the area over which he had jurisdiction, an electromagnetic method of separation of U-235 (Lawrence), the gaseous diffusion method (Urey), the refining of certain measurements basic to theoretical calculations and the construction of a pile at Chicago (Compton). Meetings of the S-1 Committee were attended by Murphree, General Styer and myself.

As news arrived during the early spring of 1942 from the three program chiefs and Murphree, Bush realized that sometime in May decisions involving very large expenditures of money would have to be made. The recurring question in my mind was how great a commitment would be justified in view of the other demands of the war effort and the inevitable uncertainties of the estimates of the program chiefs. To be sure, the uncertainties had been growing less as the results from various research projects kept coming in. For example, early in March, Bush was reporting to the President, in an optimistic vein, that new measurements enabled the theoreticians to estimate that the minimum amount of uranium 235 that would explode (the critical mass) if assembled rapidly would be between 2.5 and 5.0 kilograms. Such quantities were quite different from 100 kilograms, which was the upper limit of the range of values estimated by the committee of the National Academy of Sciences.

I had kept Bush closely informed of what was reported at each

* Hewlett and Anderson, *The New World*, p. 52.

meeting of the S-1 Section. He let it be known that he hoped he would be able to come to a decision before June as to which of the alternate methods were sufficiently promising to warrant the building of full-scale production plants. Alas, when the three program chiefs and I met with Murphree and General Styer on May 23, 1942, no such decision could be reached. After considering all the pros and cons, the group recommended to Bush that he ask the President to authorize a construction program based on the assumption that a start should be made in each of four ways to manufacture a bomb—these were three separation schemes (the electromagnetic, the gaseous diffusion and the centrifugal) and the production of plutonium in a pile. The total construction cost we estimated as $80 million and an annual operating cost as $34 million. The project, we believed, would yield a few atomic bombs by July 1, 1944.

I recall vividly the argument about the time schedule. "Why nearly two years' delay?" I asked. "Why is it not possible to speed up the construction?" To which Murphree, speaking as an experienced chemical engineer, replied (I remember clearly the words he used): "Doctor, you can't spend that much money any faster."

As things turned out, our estimate was overoptimistic by a year. We had, in effect, told Bush that since we could not decide on which of four horses to place our bet, all four should be kept in the race, though we thought they might be running neck and neck until the final lap. Indeed, such proved to be the case, except that the use of the centrifuge method was eliminated before long and the number of horses thus reduced to three.

The report of the May 23 meeting was no surprise to Bush as I had told him frequently how matters were shaping up. He shared my disappointment that no one method had been found to be sufficiently promising to justify giving it priority. He was quite ready, however, to present the report to the President with his endorsement, which he did. A summary of the costs and estimated time with an "O.K., F.D.R." in ink at the bottom of the page was placed in Bush's hands by the President. Subsequently this document was used by General Groves when necessary to prove to an incredulous high-ranking government official that what was contemplated was authorized by the President of the United States himself.

CHAPTER 22

Competing Schemes for
Making a Bomb

SHORTLY AFTER the report of the meeting on May 23, 1942, had been accepted, Bush dissolved the S-1 Section and created a S-1 Executive Committee consisting of the three program chiefs (Lawrence, Urey, Compton), Briggs, Murphree, and myself as chairman. In *Scientists Against Time,* Baxter speaks of the "OSRD-Army operation" as the phase of the program which opened at that time. From an administrative point of view, it came to an end on September 23, 1942, when the Top Policy Group meeting with General Brehon Somervell (Commanding General of the Army Services of Supply), General Styer and General L. R. Groves agreed to the appointment of a Military Policy Committee consisting of Bush as Chairman, with myself as alternate, General Styer and Admiral W. R. E. Purnell. It was to this committee that the Army officer in charge of the Manhattan District would report. After this meeting, I still continued as chairman of the S-1 Executive Committee, but as the Manhattan District took over more and more responsibility for each of the programs, I functioned more as an adviser to Groves than as chairman of a committee. One could say that by May or June 1943 the S-1 Executive Committee had ceased to function.

During the six months or so that the S-1 Executive Committee was active, I, as chairman, had the task of presiding at the frequent meetings; it was not always easy to bring to an agreement the small group of highly distinguished scientists who constituted this committee. Arthur Compton in his book *Atomic Quest* was kind enough to

286

give me high marks as a presiding officer. Since he was one of the three persons most involved, I am frank to say I cherish his words. As an illustration of the kind of problem with which I was called upon to act in a more or less juridical capacity, I insert the following quotation from Compton:

Late in April 1942, Harold Urey presented a strong argument before the S-1 Committee that we should use heavy water instead of graphite as a moderator for effecting the chain reaction. . . .

Although I recognized the validity of the argument that we could more readily bring about a chain reaction with a heavy water moderator than with graphite, the time required to produce enough heavy water to do the job seemed to me prohibitively great. I thus could not agree to reduce our efforts on the use of the graphite moderator. I did, however, support Urey in his motion for the establishment of a major plant for the production of deuterium [heavy water]. . . .

After this meeting of the S-1 Committee was adjourned, Urey continued with Conant his arguments for making an all-out effort to build a plutonium producing reactor using heavy water as a moderator. Conant called me back to Washington. He took his characteristic role of "the devil's advocate" and for several hours argued strongly the merit of placing our prime reliance on heavy water rather than graphite. As to certainty of achieving the chain reaction the argument was sound, but the best possible schedule for producing heavy water was not fast enough. My answer was, first, that the progress being made at the Chicago laboratory gave good basis for confidence in the success of a graphite-moderated reaction and, second, that while there was no limit to the amount of graphite available, we would have to wait so long for sufficient heavy water to be accumulated that the program would be seriously delayed. Conant was satisfied, and I went on to New York where I discussed the points with Urey until we were in agreement. The result was that our program at Chicago continued to concentrate its major efforts on the graphite-uranium pile.*

The first Army officer to be brought into the project on a full-time basis was Colonel James C. Marshall. On June 18, 1942, he was directed to form a new engineering district to carry out the Army's responsibilities in the development of atomic energy. During the summer of 1942, he and his deputy, Colonel K. D. Nichols, struggled with the problem of priorities. The director of every project in the giant defense effort wanted to have the first call on copper and steel and other construction materials in short supply. The War Production Board assigned priorities of different grades for each undertaking.

* *Atomic Quest*, pp. 98–99.

Colonels Marshall and Nichols were soon immersed in the fight for the highest priorities.

Since construction was in the hands of the Corps of Engineers, I had no responsibilities in such matters. But, as mentioned in an earlier chapter, I became involved in the government's planning of a vast synthetic rubber program. Therefore, I knew something about the battle of priorities and the difficulties any engineering project would have getting under way in short order that summer. As I heard of the colonels' problems, I could only be sympathetic and keep Bush informed of the delays which were threatening to negate all the S-1 estimates of June. Bush, in turn, communicated with Secretary Stimson. The upshot of informal discussions at the highest level was the replacement of Colonel Marshall by Brigadier General Leslie R. Groves on September 17, 1942, and the creation of the Military Policy Committee to which I have already referred.

With Groves in charge of the Manhattan District of Engineers, my role as chairman of the S-1 Executive Committee slowly changed. My status as alternate to Bush as chairman of the Military Policy Committee determined my responsibilities. First of all, I had to keep Bush informed of the progress of the different programs. To that end, General Groves arranged to inform me frequently about plans and new developments. By keeping me in touch with what was happening, Groves was, in fact, supplying Bush, as chairman of the Military Policy Committee, with the information he needed. As the meetings of the S-1 Executive Committee became less and less frequent, the decisions taken by Groves after consultation with a program chief became more and more important. All the decisions rested on the authority that had been delegated to the General as head of the Manhattan Project, which authority was subject to that of the Military Policy Committee. Since the members were kept currently informed, the meetings Groves called from time to time concentrated on vital issues and were almost without exception brief, informal and harmonious.

I am not attempting to write a history of either the S-1 Executive Committee or the Manhattan District. Several important books have been written about the atomic bomb, a list of which may be found at the end of this chapter. Anyone interested in a detailed account of what might well be called the Bush-Groves project will find in these volumes many stories well worth reading. One which is in all the books, I repeat for that very reason. Two others which are obscured in almost all the volumes by reason of the technical details, I insert to demonstrate how great was the gamble Bush took when he made his recommendations to President Roosevelt in May 1942. They both concern the manufacture of plutonium for use in a fission bomb.

When, at a meeting of the program chiefs in the fall of 1942, it was decided that Arthur Compton should attempt to build a pile, it was assumed that the work would be done outside the city of Chicago at a site picked by the university in collaboration with the engineers, called the Argonne Forest. In November, acting on his own responsibility and responding to the urgent proposals of the Italian physicist Enrico Fermi, the mastermind of his group, Compton decided to make the crucial experiment in the middle of Chicago. He started to build a pile under the west stands of the athletic grounds of the University of Chicago—Stagg Field. He recounts in his book, with considerable glee, the consternation of the members of the S-1 Executive Committee when he told us what he was doing at a meeting in Washington on November 14. "Conant's face went white," he writes with understandable poetic license. General Groves, who might have vetoed the experiment (so might have the committee by appealing to Bush), was disturbed, but took no action. I think we all felt that the construction of the pile was so far advanced that it was too late to call a halt.

On December 2, 1942, the pile became critical. That is to say, the addition of the last increments of uranium and graphite had resulted in the liberation of more neutrons from the entire mass than were being absorbed. If the chain reaction had not been controlled by the insertion of rods of a material which would absorb neutrons, the pile would keep on emitting neutrons and liberating energy. Compton and Fermi and the other physicists involved in the experiment had been quite certain that under no circumstances would the release of energy be at a rate which could not be controlled. There was no danger of an explosion. Nevertheless, there were those who in retrospect felt that Compton had taken an unwarranted risk. There is no doubt that in doing so he saved time (it would have taken somewhat longer to assemble the pile at the place originally chosen).

In his own account, Compton emphasized the importance of impressing a reviewing committee which was considering each of the competing programs.* The Chicago group was afraid the program for the development of a plutonium bomb would be either eliminated or given low priority. The demonstration that a self-sustaining chain

* *Ibid.*, p. 140.

reaction was possible would change the picture dramatically. They were right; it certainly did. The reviewing committee was actually in Chicago on the day in which atomic power was first released, and one member was present when Fermi ordered the last steps which made the assembly critical. Now there could be no doubt that nuclear fission under controlled conditions was possible. December 2, 1942, was to become a famous date in the history of science.

Within a matter of hours, Arthur Compton telephoned me. The way the story is usually told, I was in my office in Cambridge. Actually, I was in Washington in my quarters in the dormitory attached to the Dumbarton Oaks Library and Collection of Harvard University, where I had been staying several days each week since Pearl Harbor. I was waiting for news. Therefore I was not surprised when I heard Arthur say: "Our Italian navigator has just landed in the new world." My apprehension influenced my immediate question: "Were the natives friendly?" There was no prearranged code, but Arthur knew that I was asking whether everything had proceeded according to prediction. "Everyone landed safe and happy," he replied.

To make the next story understandable, I must first introduce the Los Alamos project. The S-1 Executive Committee had recommended to Bush that responsibility for the assembly of the bomb be given to Arthur Compton. In the fall of 1942, Compton had created a section of his division to be concerned with drawing detailed plans for carrying out the process by which a mass of fissionable material would suddenly become critical and explode. To help in the calculations, Compton had recruited Professor J. Robert Oppenheimer of the University of California at Berkeley. As an outstanding theoretical physicist, he had already helped Lawrence in designing the electromagnetic method of separating U-235. Now it was suggested that Oppenheimer turn his attention to the design of a bomb. This he did. Before long, Groves decided to recommend to the Military Policy Committee that a separate laboratory be set up in a relatively inaccessible spot near Santa Fe, New Mexico, in which all the research connected with the bomb design would be concentrated. The committee agreed and consented to the appointment of Professor Oppenheimer as the head of the group of physicists, which he was asked to assemble. In May 1943, on Groves' recommendation, the Military Policy Committee appointed Commander William S. Parsons as head of the ordnance research, which would be necessary before the bomb could be devised.

My story really starts at this point, but I must digress further to record the fact that one of my duties as the alternate chairman of the Military Policy Committee was to keep in touch with the research at Los Alamos. It was soon apparent that the physicists in the distant and highly secret spot needed more scientific contact with the other research programs than I as chemist was in a position to provide. Therefore Professor Tolman, one of the original members of NDRC, was asked to be a scientific adviser to Groves. He was most effective as a liaison officer; we two worked together from time to time to straighten out misunderstandings between Groves and Nichols on the one hand and either the physicists at Chicago or at Los Alamos on the other.

I now return to the story of plutonium. As I mentioned earlier, even after I had shed my skepticism about the possibility of making a bomb in time to affect the war, I still boggled over the program Arthur Compton was proposing in private conversations. I had serious doubts about how long it would take to develop a satisfactory chemical process for separating the plutonium from the contents of the pile. Arthur Compton in his book twits me on my pessimistic forecast as an "expert chemist." The mastering of a separation procedure did not, in fact, prove to be a bottleneck. From only traces of the new element (prepared by transformations brought about by the high-energy particles in a cyclotron), its chemical characteristics were discovered. Several alternate separation processes were worked out by the Chicago group. They were given a practical test on the contents of a pile constructed at Oak Ridge, Tennessee. A highly satisfactory procedure was then chosen by the Du Pont engineers for use in the enormous plant they were constructing at Hanford, Washington, for the manufacture of plutonium.

The product of the pile at Oak Ridge not only enabled the chemists to try out processes for the separation of plutonium; it provided enough of the new element to be seen with the naked eye. It must be remembered that the go-ahead signal had been given by Bush when all that was known with certainty was that the element 94, like U-235, underwent spontaneous fission. As Baxter points out in *Scientists Against Time*, "This much was known before money started flowing to the reorganized [uranium] work. Huge sums were committed on this portentous gamble before enough plutonium was produced to prove that more than two neutrons were emitted in the fusion—an . . . essential property if a fast chain reaction [i.e., an explosion] was to work."

The essential property to which Baxter refers was confirmed at once by experiments with the plutonium which reached Los Alamos from Oak Ridge. But now for the first time it was discovered that the plutonium as manufactured contained an isotope with undesirable nuclear properties. As a consequence, neutrons were being constantly emitted from the material. It could not be certain that two portions of the fissionable material could be brought together without a chain reaction starting before the total was well above the critical mass.

In all the arguments in favor of the plutonium route to an explosive, it had been assumed that the design of a bomb could be made irrespective of whether U-235 or plutonium made in a pile was the fissionable material. The assumption was now shown to be wrong. (Neither Compton nor Baxter in their volumes refers to this fact, presumably because the existence of a plutonium isotope was still classified information when these authors wrote in 1956 and 1946.) Now the whole story is public property. I quote from *The New World*:

> On Friday morning, July 21, 1944, Roger Williams and Crawford Greenewalt [of Du Pont] hurried to Washington for an urgent meeting with Conant and Groves. On Wednesday, they had learned from Charles A. Thomas [who was in touch with Los Alamos] that Oppenheimer had abandoned all hope of using plutonium in a gun type weapon. Thomas' report meant first of all that the possibility of developing a plutonium weapon during the war was now small. Unless the Los Alamos scientists could design an implosion weapon within a matter of months, all the work at Hanford might be in vain.*

The gun-type weapon was an arrangement by which one mass of fissionable material was fired in a gun at a target composed of the same material. The combination of target and bullet constituted a mass more than critical; therefore a nuclear explosion would occur. It was now clear that at least with the plutonium which was to be produced at Hanford the gun-type weapon would not be reliable enough to use. The quantity of neutrons being continuously emitted would cause an explosion to start as soon as the bullet came within a short distance of the target. But such an explosion would be too weak. The bullet and target would not be as close together as possible. Therefore the total mass of the combination would be less than the possible maximum.

An alternative weapon had to be found at once. Fortunately, a design was already at hand, but far from complete. It had been suggested some months earlier by a member of the Los Alamos staff, S. H.

* P. 302.

Neddermeyer. It was known as the implosion weapon. The principle was simple. A mass of fissionable material not quite critical would become critical if powerfully compressed. The compression was to be brought about by means of specially designed conventional explosives. To reduce this idea to practice, a whole new branch of the science of explosives had to be developed. To that end, Professor Kistiakowsky had been asked to relinquish his duties as chief of the NDRC section on explosives and move to Los Alamos in February 1944. Now in July the situation was desperate. Work on implosion received top priority. As a result of the increased activity, the design of an implosion weapon was complete before enough plutonium had been produced by Hanford for a bomb.

As I review the story from a distance of twenty-four years, supplementing my memories by copious reference to *The New World* and General Groves' *Now It Can Be Told,* I am impressed by the narrowness which separated success from disaster in the undertaking to make one type of ·bomb. If Arthur Compton had known that the plutonium produced in a pile would be different in a highly important respect from the plutonium specks made in a cyclotron, he might have been far less certain of a favorable outcome of the colossal gamble he urged on Vannevar Bush.

Another narrow escape in the plutonium program occurred in connection with starting operations at Hanford. For a few hours, the giant piles produced heat at the expected rate. Then they ceased to function. What had happened? Experts were rushed to the scene. The trouble was diagnosed as a "poisoning" of the chain reaction. A small amount of one of the products—the element xenon—was absorbing an appreciable amount of the neutrons. The phenomenon had not been detected at Oak Ridge because, contrary to General Groves' order, the small piles had not been operated continuously for a sufficient length of time. It was now decided that the capacity of the piles must be increased. This could be done by adding more uranium. At least a 25 percent increase appeared to be called for. I quote from the outstanding book by Stephane Groueff to conclude the story:

If the reactor had been built strictly according to the scientists' design, such a modification would have been impossible. There would not have been enough space or holes in the graphite pile for the hundreds of additional tubes required. Furthermore, the plutonium program at that late stage could not afford abandonment of the completed reactors and the construction of new ones.

Once more, however, the Project was miraculously saved, this time thanks largely to the stubborn insistence of Du Pont's engineers. They had allowed large margins and left extra space in the pile, despite the disagreement of scientists who thought such precautions were completely unnecessary and served only to slow the completion of construction.*

One can only conclude that luck was on our side. Yet when all allowance is made for lucky breaks, two facts stand out. The first is that the two responsible gamblers, Vannevar Bush and Leslie R. Groves, like all successful players, never flinched. If any or all of the three methods for producing an atomic bomb had failed, they would have borne the blame whether justified or not. Therefore they deserve the credit for the success.

I have in another chapter given my estimate of the significance of Bush's leadership in the entire OSRD undertaking. At this point, I want to emphasize how indispensable was the role of General Groves. I cannot imagine another man doing the job. It required a man of high intelligence, courage and drive who could get industrialists to perform miracles. I watched his handling of these men and marveled at his success in obtaining their cooperation. And let me emphasize that the mobilizing of industrial scientists and engineers was just as important as the mobilizing of physicists. Without the second phase of the entire operation—after the Manhattan District took control—the first phase, with all the brilliance of Lawrence, Compton, Oppenheimer, Fermi and the other physicists would not have yielded tangible results.

In dealing with Compton, Lawrence and Murphree, the General had no difficulty in establishing a relationship of complete confidence. The same is true of his dealing with Oppenheimer, who was, after all, Groves' own choice to head the Los Alamos project. To be sure, many of the scientists at Chicago, Los Alamos and at Columbia and other laboratories regarded the General with jaundiced eyes. This was in part, no doubt, a consequence of his far from tactful initial attempts to introduce himself as an engineer to a group of academic scientists. It was also in part a result of the controversy between the members of the expanding group at Los Alamos with the administrative officials in charge of accommodations. No one could understand that the General had to be prepared someday to meet Congressional scrutiny about expenditures. He knew that a committee of Congress that would not question budget items of tens of millions for technical equipment might raise questions about the costs of sidewalks. (When

* *Manhattan Project*, Boston, Little, Brown & Co., 1967, p. 308.

I was before an appropriations committee as High Commissioner for Germany in 1954, one Congressman said to me, pointing to money for tires, "This is an item I can understand.")

Richard Tolman often visited Chicago and Los Alamos and, less frequently, places where other research was in process. He was in closer touch with those in intermediary positions of responsibility than I. He heard the rumblings of discontent but did not sympathize with them in the least. I doubt if even he realized the existence of a spirit in Chicago which came to light in a strange episode that occurred in the summer of 1944 when Bush was in London.

President Roosevelt telephoned me one day from the White House. He said that in Dr. Bush's absence he was going to ask me to handle a human problem. A strange young man—a physicist, "a friend of Eleanor's," he said—had some queer ideas and it was important that I see him. I agreed to do so; the young man in question (let me call him Dr. X—I have really forgotten his name) appeared in my office at 1730 P Street at the appointed time. Behind closed doors he told me of his worries, which were, indeed, very deep. As a young scientist in the Chicago Laboratory of the Manhattan Project, he had in the course of a few months learned many things that not only disturbed but terrified him. What ought to be done to produce an atomic bomb quickly was not being done; the Germans were much nearer to the goal than we were; many methods that should be tried were not being tested; the Chicago process was about to be turned over to the Du Pont people so they could control the commercial uses; as usual, the military were close to the capitalists; poor Arthur Compton, a nice man, was helpless; he, Dr. X, was going to force the President to know about the almost treacherous situation even if it meant breaking Compton's neck.

Of course, the recent recruit to the staff at Chicago had been hearing the complaints of some of his seniors. With the exception of a very few, these men did not know the score. The policy of departmentalization, which was essential for security, meant that no one at Chicago except Arthur Compton was entitled to know of the state of development of the other processes for separating uranium 235. There must have been much loose talk about the inadequacies of the top management, namely, General Groves and Messrs. Conant and Bush.

The arrangements with Du Pont were absolutely essential for the Chicago route to the bomb. Yet some of the leaders of the Chicago group had wanted to do the job themselves under university auspices.

The idea that no industrial contractor was needed was nonsense. I remember Tolman expressing himself vigorously on this point.

As I listened to Dr. X's emotional outburst, I could reconstruct the conversations he must have been hearing. The scientists had asked detailed questions which Arthur Compton could not answer because he had not been kept informed about the changing status of the separate atomic bomb projects. He was satisfied because the few of us who were privy to the whole assured him that all the different routes to the desired end were being vigorously pursued. His satisfaction really was based on his confidence in the honesty and competence of Groves, Tolman, Conant and Bush. (Since I was only a chemist, my competence was open to challenge, but Tolman's was not; he was a recognized top physicist of the nation.)

Such confidence was not shared by most of the members of Compton's staff; they were skeptical and some implied they wanted more facts. But to give the facts would be to open up the entire technical undertaking to hundreds of people. Security would disappear. Not only the Germans might learn much of value, but certainly Congressmen would wish to be in on the secret. The day that happened, progress would stop. Anyone who has doubts on this score need only read Chapter 23, in which I recount how plans for making synthetic rubber fared when they were the subject of Congressional inquiries.

My attempts to calm Dr. X were of no avail. My assurance that all was well, he brushed aside. He wanted facts. I was not in a position to supply them. He left completely unsatisfied. I learned later that after his talk with me he returned to the White House, to which he had social access. Buttonholing one person after another, he told his story, but he did not succeed in seeing the President. His talk of the Manhattan Project and an atomic bomb was worse than meaningless to those with whom he conversed. He was judged insane, and the question was raised whether it was safe to leave him free to circulate among Mrs. Roosevelt's friends.

But the First Lady herself was convinced he was sane and that he had a real problem on his mind. She communicated at once with an old family friend, Bernard Baruch. He was as ignorant as the rest, but he promised to find out what was up. Because of our work together on the rubber survey in the summer of 1942, he telephoned me. He could say enough for me to guess the rest. I assured him that I knew all about the matter, including the details of the young man's complaint. There was no real cause for worry. I could meet with

Baruch and tell him a little but not much because of security regulations. "I don't want to know anything," Baruch said. "I just
want to know whether you are well informed and can assure
me all is well." I said I was extremely well informed and completely satisfied that all was being done that could be done. "Your
word is enough for me," he said. "You were right about rubber and I
am sure your judgment can be trusted. I shall tell the lady to relax."

When after Hiroshima everyone started talking about atomic
bombs, it was generally agreed that the secret had been well kept. Few
appreciated the efforts required to restrict the knowledge of what was
going on under the auspices of the Manhattan District. The complete
ban on discussing nuclear fission with anybody who was not officially involved in the S-1 work extended to my own office. Neither my
close associate as chairman of NDRC (Professor Moreland) nor our
staff had an idea of my function as chairman of the S-1 Executive
Committee. My secretary, who had been well trained in government
procedures, kept the file on S-1 communications entirely separate
from my NDRC file. Therefore one day in 1944 Moreland could
respond to a question from a high-ranking ordnance officer that
as far as he knew "Dr. Conant was in no way involved in any project
to manufacture a bomb of enormous power." Of course, he could
have made the same response if he had been privy to the secret, for
he would have known that by presidential order only specially selected
military officers were permitted to know of the existence of work on
an atomic bomb. But it was far easier to keep Moreland in ignorance.
He had no "need to know" and did not have to lie to a major general
who had asked what appeared to be a proper question.

The amount of bare-faced lying that was done in Washington in
those days is beyond estimate. Military secrets of all sorts were closely
guarded. One just didn't ask an old friend whom one met at the
Cosmos Club what he was doing. A statement that a person was
working for the government on a confidential matter was a sufficient
sign to change the conversation. In Cambridge, outside of the affairs
of the research laboratories at M.I.T. and Harvard, the atmosphere
was somewhat different. My close associate, A. Calvert Smith, never
asked me about my work in Washington. I think he assumed it was
concerned primarily with gas warfare. He had not the slightest suspicion of my relation to a vast, supersecret endeavor to make a bomb.
In one instance his ignorance saved him from what would otherwise
have been an embarrassing situation for anyone but an experienced
liar.

One evening in January or February 1945, the Mayor of Cambridge and I had a pleasant conversation during a dinner given by the president and fellows of Harvard College for the Mayor and city counselors of Cambridge (an annual affair in the interest of promoting good "town and gown relations"). In the course of our talk the Mayor asked me point-blank about a bomb of enormous force which he stated the government was constructing for use in the near future. I assured His Honor the story was a complete fabrication. I explained how easy it was for such fantastic stories to be started, based, perhaps, on some improvement in the art of high explosives.

The next day I reported to Groves that the Mayor of Cambridge seemed to have heard about the work of the Manhattan District. The General at once called in his security people, who made one of the few errors I have ever heard of their making. An officer was sent to Cambridge to query the Mayor about his knowledge of war secrets. The Mayor was infuriated and at once proceeded to my office. I was in Washington. Calvert Smith took the full blast of the complaint. "At the dinner the other night," said the Mayor, "I asked the president of the university about a new type of powerful bomb. He must have reported our conversation to the Army for I have been cross-examined by an officer; it is an outrageous breach of privacy."

Smith could honestly say that he could not believe I had made any report to the Army. If I had attached any importance to the Mayor's question, I would certainly have spoken to Smith about it, which I had not. He (Smith) thought it much more probable that one of the Mayor's political enemies on the council had overheard the conversation and had reported it to Washington. The Mayor agreed with the hypothesis and left satisfied. Or so Smith reported to me a week later when I paid a fleeting visit to my Harvard office. I listened and implied my agreement with Smith's hypothesis.

I silently looked forward to the day when I could tell him the truth and we could both laugh about it. Alas, the day never came. Calvert died of a heart attack which he suffered on a vacation away from Cambridge a few weeks after the war ended. We exchanged letters about my secret wartime work, now revealed to the world. I never had a chance, however, to talk to him about it face to face. If I had had the opportunity, I could have tried to express my gratitude for all his devoted work in Cambridge for five years. Only his standing in for me on many crucial matters had left me free to desert many of my Harvard duties in my own atomic quest.

My own family did not escape the poison of deception. My younger son, Ted, who has a great nose for unusual news, asked me one day in 1940 or 1941 about the prospects of using the fission of uranium for power. (Enough information had been published, before secrecy was clamped down, so that speculation about a uranium chain reaction was a subject of current gossip.) I dismissed the idea as pure moonshine. "Impossible" was my firm comment. After Ted's return from the South Pacific, where he had been a radio officer in the Merchant Marine, I was reminded of my prevarication some years before. My credit as an honest man, I was told, had been permanently impaired.

I had no reproaches from my wife, who had heard me deny more than once the possibility of what was made manifest at Hiroshima. She was hardly in a position to make much of my deceitfulness, for she had accepted as a fact of wartime that I could tell her nothing about my work in Washington with Bush or my travels from time to time. She later said she suspected something strange when she found a Santa Fe Railroad matchbook in the pocket of one of my suits when, as far as she knew, I had been no farther west than Chicago. A few weeks later after I had seen the first atomic bomb explode at Alamogordo on July 16, I broke security to the extent of telling my long-suffering wife that when the war was over I would have some highly interesting things to tell her, which were still completely secret. Reflecting her years of frustration, she replied rather forcefully that she was not at all sure she would be interested. As applied to the knowlege of many secrets of NDRC, the indifference she predicted might well have coincided with the facts. But not as regards the atomic bomb; there was no turning one's back then or later on this piece of news.

Whether or not the high degree of compartmentalization that was enforced was necessary or wise can be argued. The secrecy was penetrated by Soviet agents (but not by Germans as far as anyone can tell). Widespread gossip did not take place, a fact which warded off possible Congressional investigations. On the other hand, the unrest evidenced by my encounter with Dr. X was to a considerable extent a result of the secrecy with which every phase of the work was surrounded. Because hundreds of young scientists felt left out, a secret ballot on a vote of confidence would probably have yielded a negative verdict.

Being aware as I was of some of the hostility toward me, I at first asked to be excused from serving on the Interim Committee that Secretary Stimson appointed in May 1945 to consider the postwar policy of the United States in all matters connected with atomic energy. I wrote to the Secretary that I doubted if I was a proper man to serve on such a committee. There was growing restlessness among the scientists actively involved in the program, I reported. Therefore I was far from sure that I would be considered a proper representative of the scientists' point of view. I made no reference to a lack of confidence in those of us who had been determining policy. I did refer to what I had heard (largely from Tolman) in regard to the worries of the scientists about our future relation with Russia. Whether I served or not, I hoped the Secretary would favor having some of the leading scientists present their views to the committee.

I ended by yielding to Secretary Stimson's renewed invitation. The other members, in addition to the Secretary himself, were Bush, Karl T. Compton, Ralph A. Baird (Under Secretary of the Navy), William L. Clayton (Assistant Secretary of State), George L. Harrison (one of Secretary Stimson's close advisers) and James F. Byrnes as special representative of the President.

Whether I was serving on the Interim Committee in my capacity as chairman of the S-1 Executive Committee (which had not been active as a committee for a year), or as a member of the Military Policy Committee, I was never sure. Bush had been handling the negotiations with the British. I was strongly inclined to follow his lead in all discussions in the Interim Committee about future international problems. This would have been true if we had never discussed plans for the postwar world. Actually, an inspection trip to Los Alamos in the summer of 1944 had provided an opportunity for us to discuss at leisure and in complete privacy what the policy of the United States should be after the war was over. On the basis of our talk and subsequent conversations, Bush wrote a memorandum to Secretary Stimson on September 19, 1944, which he asked me to join him in signing. This was the first of several papers we sent to the Secretary, signed by both of us, in which we pointed out the totally new and alarming situation which would result if no U.S. policy was developed before the war ended and the knowledge of the existence of the bomb was made public. We advocated free interchange of scientific information with other nations, including Russia, under arrangements by which the staff of an international office would have unimpeded access to scientific laboratories, industrial plants and military establishments throughout the world.

These documents are the ones to which Alice Kimball Smith refers in her excellent book about the postwar revolt of the scientists in

1945–47 when she writes: "Although it is now evident that Bush and Conant deserve credit for more liberal thinking on the political implications of atomic energy and for calling official attention to them than their critics among the Project scientists have granted them, the documents confirm the earlier impression of close correspondence between each renewed effort on their part and agitation in Chicago."[*] As a matter of fact, the papers remained unknown except to Stimson and his advisers and General Groves until they were unearthed by the authors of *The New World*. Their interest today lies only in the evidence they provide of Bush's farsighted thinking about the postwar scene a year before the first bomb was ready to be delivered.

At the first meeing of the Interim Committee to which General Groves was invited, the question was raised as to how much we should tell the Russians about our progress. This question in turn raised another one, namely, how long would it take the Soviets to produce a bomb? The estimates ranged from four years to twenty.

In the meantime, the Interim Committee had appointed a scientific panel consisting of J. Robert Oppenheimer, Enrico Fermi, Arthur Compton and E. O. Lawrence. At a meeting with the panel, the committee considered further the question of what to tell the Russians. The answer seemed to depend on how many years were likely to elapse before the American monopoly would be broken. The scientists were for the most part of the opinion that it would be only a matter of a few years before the Soviet scientists would be able to duplicate what had been accomplished in the United States. General Groves, who was the only person present with a full knowledge of the enormous engineering feats which had been performed, inclined strongly to the twenty-year figure.

Later a panel of industrialists who were in one way or another involved in the Manhattan Project were asked for their estimates. Their guess was nearer to that of General Groves. As the discussion proceeded, it became clear that no firm prediction could be made. Such being the case, it was inevitable that as far as taking steps to release any information was concerned, the government had no choice but to act as though the secret of the bomb could be held intact for many years.

Bush had been urging since the middle of 1944 the appointment of a committee to advise the President through the Secretary of War on postwar atomic policy. He felt it was essential to draft legislation

[*] *A Peril and a Hope*, Chicago, Chicago University Press, 1965, p. 15.

to be placed before Congress as soon as the war was ended. He had been thinking deeply about the international scene, which he knew would never be the same again once the power of the new type of bomb had been demonstrated. I doubt if he foresaw the involvement of the Interim Committee in what, in retrospect, was the most important matter on which an opinion was to be recorded. This was the question of the use of the bomb against the Japanese. Yet concern with this question has become the hallmark of the committee and the scientific panel in the eyes of those who have written about the bomb. The scientific panel reported that "We can propose no technical demonstration likely to bring an end to the war; we can see no acceptable alternative to direct military use." The Interim Committee, with one member (Ralph Baird) dissenting, voted to recommend that the bomb should be used against the Japanese at the earliest opportunity.

I do not propose even to attempt a summary of the many views which have been expressed. *The Decision to Drop the Bomb*, by Len Giovannitti and Fred Freed,* is to be recommended to all who would like a readable account of a complex bit of political history. (The bibliography lists fifty-five articles and books dealing in whole or in part with the decision.)

Everyone who was in any way connected with advising Secretary Stimson about the use of the atomic bomb must have reviewed in his mind at one time or another the correctness of the action taken. Not a few have expressed strong misgivings. Some have felt that the enormity of the destruction was so great that the weapon should not have been used under any circumstances. (Those who hold this view should logically likewise condemn the fire raids; in a single night eighty thousand lives were lost in Tokyo and sixteen square miles devastated.) Others have felt that Japan was so near surrendering that the use of the atomic bomb was unnecessary to end the war. This argument opens up a whole spectrum of considerations, military and political.

As far as the advice of the Interim Committee is at issue, it must be remembered that on June 21, 1945, the date of our last meeting, the war did not appear to be coming to an end. The plans for an enormous invasion of Japan had been agreed on and the necessary steps were under way. It was a month later, at the time of the Potsdam Conference, that the signs of the rapid deterioration of the Japanese situation were so clear as to be unmistakable to those who

* New York, Coward-McCann, Inc., 1965.

were privy to the latest intelligence service. By that time the first test bomb had been exploded at Alamogordo (the Trinity Test), and the detailed arrangements had been made for the use of a bomb as soon as enough material had been produced. President Truman could have canceled the plans to drop the first bomb, of course, any time up to a few hours before the departure of the plane carrying the weapon which was to destroy Hiroshima. He did not do so; neither Secretary Stimson nor any of his advisers recommended such a dramatic reversal of the orders under which the military were operating. As I consider the information which was available to the Secretary, I find no reason to join those who censure him (at least by indirection) for not calling a halt to the operation.

My own misgivings have never been about the use of the bomb. I think the decision was correct. What has often worried me is the thought that if only this or that had been different, the first bomb might have been dropped in May. The initial estimate of the S-1 group in the spring of 1942, it will be remembered, was to the effect that a few bombs would be ready by July 1, 1944. By the end of 1943 everyone had forgotten their earlier optimistic predictions. Still, the hope that a bomb might be constructed within another twelve months or so was the motivating force behind many of us who were engaged in the project.

I remember a visit I made at Groves' request to one of the operations that were just getting under way. The pace was too slow to satisfy the General. My argument for speed was that the first bomb constructed would probably end the war. This was after the successful invasion of Normandy had shown that Germany was bound to surrender before long. The job of defeating Japan, however, appeared to be one which would take years and require a heavy sacrifice of American youth.

I also remember a conversation with Oppenheimer in the fall of 1944 in which we both looked forward to "bombs away by the first of May." The optimistic forecast was of short duration. I still recall my disappointment and frustration when I became convinced by Groves' figures that the summer of 1945 was the earliest possible date. I felt the difference between May 1945 and August 1945 was very large in terms of American casualties. And history proved that I was right. Later, after the war was over, I became aware of the profound political consequence of the date on which Japan surrendered. If, in fact, the war in the Pacific had ended in May, the postwar international situation would have been very different. The Soviets were not prepared to challenge Japan with military force before the summer of 1945.

I have never been one of those who thought the use of atomic energy for peaceful purposes held such potential benefits for the human race that we should all rejoice at the discovery of atomic fission. To my mind, the potentialities for destruction are so awesome as to outweigh by far all the imaginable gains that may accrue in the distant future when atomic power plants may exist all over the world. I conclude this chapter by a reference to my visit to Secretary Stimson's office on the day after I returned from the Trinity Test. George L. Harrison, who had acted as chairman of the Interim Committee when Secretary Stimson was absent, welcomed me with enthusiasm. "Congratulations," he exclaimed as he shook my hand, "it worked."

"Yes," I replied, "it worked. As to congratulations, I am far from sure—that remains for history to decide." As I write these lines in 1969, with American and Soviet aircraft and missiles poised to strike on a moment's notice, I can only regard my reply to Harrison as quite correct. The verdict of history has not yet been given.

BIBLIOGRAPHY

Batchelder, Robert C. *The Irreversible Decision 1939–1950*. Boston, Houghton Mifflin Co., 1962.

Baxter, James Phinney III. *Scientists Against Time*. Boston, Little, Brown & Co., 1946. M.I.T. Press paperback edition, 1968.

Compton, Arthur Holly. *Atomic Quest*. New York, Oxford University Press, 1956.

Giovannitti, Len, and Fred Freed. *The Decision to Drop the Bomb*. New York, Coward-McCann, Inc., 1965.

Stephane Groueff. *Manhattan Project*. Boston, Little, Brown & Co., 1967.

Groves, Leslie R. *Now It Can Be Told*. New York, Harper & Brothers, 1962.

Hewlett, Richard G., and Oscar E. Anderson, Jr. *The New World*. University Park, Pa., Pennsylvania State University Press, 1962.

Irving, David. *The German Atomic Bomb*. New York, Simon & Schuster, 1968.

Smith, Alice Kimball. *A Peril and a Hope*. Chicago, University of Chicago Press, 1965.

CHAPTER 23

The Rubber Survey

IT WAS SOME MONTHS after Pearl Harbor before the country was fully aware of the impending shortage of rubber tires. At the outset of the United States' involvement in the war, it was assumed that Great Britain and the United States would continue in control of Southeast Asia, from which natural rubber came. Even those whose duty involved daily concern with critical materials failed to realize for a few months the consequences of Japanese victories in the South Pacific. Everyone knew that steel and copper were critical materials. Everyone knew that gasoline might become one. To most laymen, however, rubber seemed such a common material that it was hard to imagine its being listed as a critical war item. Yet when people began to think about what the United States would be like if there were no rubber tires, panic started to mount.

In midwinter of 1942 Congressional committees began to be active in investigating possible shortages. Before long, an impending shortage of rubber made the headlines. The Congressional probes and newspaper reports soon made it evident that the United States Government had not been foresighted enough to stock a large amount of natural rubber. News about shortages of critical materials hardly competed with news from the battlefields. In early summer, however, the accumulated effect of the Congressional hearings had thoroughly alarmed the country. The two major committees involved were the Truman Committee to Investigate the National Defense Program and the subcommittee of the Senate Agriculture Committee headed by Senator Guy Gillette. I was later to discover that something like seventeen different Congressional committees had felt obliged to hear witnesses about the progress, or lack of it, of the U.S. rubber program. The printed hearings of these committees measured well over a foot and a half when stacked one upon the other. While even the most enterprising reporter never read more than a tiny fraction of them, the publicity of some of the hearings was sufficient to bring forth further articles and editorials. Those who were only too ready to find fault with the administration had here a fine opportunity. To criticize military operations in times of war would be considered unpatriotic, but to criticize the government for failure to take care of civilian needs was fair game.

During the debates about rubber for tires and gasoline for civilian use, there was an opportunity for those who enjoyed such exercises to pit against one another those who were considered "soft" and those who were "tough." The former were characterized by their solicitude for the welfare of civilians, the latter by their willingness to demand more and more sacrifices from the home front. Under Secretary of War Robert Patterson, who was a tower of strength for the war effort, was, on the issue of civilian needs, almost pathological; he suspected me, among many others, of being "soft."

As I read the newspapers in the spring of 1942, I gradually acquired an interest in rubber. Indeed, Roger Adams had pointed out shortly after Pearl Harbor that there was bound to be a shortage of rubber. He suspected the program for making synthetic rubber was not going as rapidly as it should. Therefore the question arose whether the NDRC should not intrude itself into the synthetic rubber research and development program. Adams became more insistent as time went on, but to no avail. I wrote him toward the end of May that "unless the National Defense Research Committee was prepared to go into the whole synthetic rubber program in an all-out way, we should certainly be sticking our hands into a hornets' nest without adequate protection or assurance that we could make a real contribution. . . . I believe the original policy to stick to instrumentalities of war is correct." In other words, it was the committee's view that matters of this sort should be handled by the War Production Board. When I wrote that letter, I little knew that I was going to be asked to stick my own hand into said hornets' nest.

A conversation with Frank Jewett, the president of the National Academy of Sciences, may have been one consequence of Roger

Adams' needling. I recall suggesting to Jewett that he offer the services of the National Academy to the President or some high official in connection with the tangled discussion about how to manufacture a rubber substitute. Jewett would have none of it; he said the Academy was there to be called on; it was not the function of the president of the academy to offer his good services or that of his colleagues.

The next I heard about synthetic rubber was a conversation with Vannevar Bush on July 16, 1942. Bush reported that he'd just had a call from Donald M. Nelson of the War Production Board; Nelson was thinking about appointing a committee of disinterested scientists to review the technical aspects of the rubber program. He had called Bush to obtain clearance for approaching K. T. Compton and myself. Bush and I talked the matter over at some length; we were in complete agreement, as was usually the case. It would be absurd for the War Production Board to set up its own committee. Such a committee would be regarded by the critics as Nelson's own creation; the report would be suspect from the start. The normal procedure would be for the War Production Board to ask the National Academy of Sciences for a report.

Bush so reported to Nelson; he further informed him that the president of the Academy had been sounded out and would gladly entertain a request. Of course, Bush said, it would be better if another high government official, particularly Jesse Jones, the Secretary of Commerce, would join with Nelson in making such a request. Nelson expressed the opinion that there would be no difficulty in getting Mr. Jones' cooperation. He then stated that he would take the matter up at the Cabinet meeting that very morning and discuss it with President Roosevelt. Bush finished the telephone conversation by commenting that it would be by far the best if the President himself created the committee; the report could then be forwarded through Nelson and Jones to the President.

On hearing from Bush about how the conversation had gone, I very much hoped if anything came of the proposal I would not be involved. A National Academy committee would not necessarily have included me, for Roger Adams, supported by one or two chemical engineers, could do the job quite apart from the NDRC.

But I did not succeed in bowing out. On Monday, July 27, 1942, (ten days after Bush's conversation with Nelson) the New York *Herald Tribune* published a strong editorial about the rubber situation. The writer of the editorial stated that since Chief Justice Harlan

F. Stone had refused the assignment of investigating the rubber controversy, Dr. Conant was the obvious man. I had the technical knowledge, wide administrative experience, was dedicated to the war effort and would undoubtedly accept the job if drafted. Furthermore, I was disinterested, which was true. My last contact with the synthetic chemical industry had been in May 1933. I had ceased being a consultant of the Du Pont Company when I became president of Harvard.

My old friend and adviser, A. Calvert Smith, who as secretary of the Corporation was holding the fort in Cambridge, read the editorial and called it to my attention in the course of one of our many telephone conversations about Harvard affairs. I asked him whether he thought I should accept if I was tapped for the task.

Smith's notes, which I now have at hand, show that I raised an interesting point. I must have had in mind the difficulties of my predecessor, President Lowell, in connection with the Sacco-Vanzetti case. He, together with the governor of M.I.T. and a retired judge, had been asked by the Governor of Massachusetts to advise on whether the death sentences of Sacco and Vanzetti should be commuted. Their report had been in the negative. As a consequence, a vast amount of criticism had descended on President Lowell. I suggested to Smith that the production of synthetic rubber had now become so highly controversial that my usefulness as the president of Harvard might well be over if I took a strong position. Smith replied that he did not agree. There would be criticism whatever I reported; he ventured the opinion, however, that 80 percent of the people would rise and cheer on reading any forthright document which laid out the facts. Anyway, he did not see how I could refuse if I was asked by the President of the United States. Smith put in a bid to be involved in the undertaking if it eventuated. He said he could obtain a leave of absence for a month or so from Harvard University. He knew I was more than busy with NDRC affairs, and he itched to be more active in the war effort.

We did not have to wait long. On Thursday, July 30, I had a call from President Roosevelt's secretary, Marvin McIntyre, asking me to come to the White House to see Judge Samuel I. Rosenman. He warned that I was going to be asked to investigate the rubber situation as a member of a committee of which Bernard Baruch was to be chairman. I immediately called Smith at Harvard to explain that our worries about my being chairman were unjustified. The President had turned to an old friend of his, an elder statesman about whom I had almost no information. I asked Smith what he knew about him.

He said he would try to check with some friends about Baruch's past activities.

Much as I had dreaded the possibility of assuming the major responsibility for poking into this "hornets' nest," I was a little bit disappointed that Baruch was going to head the committee; obviously he, and not I, would call the shots. Whether or not I could work with him was a question. The next day, Judge Rosenman gave me no choice but to try. He treated the matter as though it were settled. I was a natural for the job, he said. We had a little discussion about the third member. I think Rosenman wanted to leave the impression that I had some say in selecting my other colleague. We discussed the possibility of President Edward C. Elliott of Purdue, who had once been a chemist. There was something to be said for him on behalf of his geographical location, Rosenman suggested; the White House was anxious to have a wider representation of the entire country. However, I argued strongly for Karl Compton as I knew the job would be a tough one involving, perhaps, more than one confrontation with the chairman. I was certain that Compton and I would see things the same way; I might well need his powerful reinforcement.

As matters turned out, my worry about a conflict with Baruch was completely unjustified. After a little sparring, all three of us got on extremely well. Although I must say that my introduction to Baruch was not such as to allay my fears. The first thing he said to me when I met him at the Carlton Hotel in Washington was: "Well, you're not much to look at—that's certain." To which he quickly added in a courtly fashion that he never judged people by their looks.

The encounter was a day or two after I'd seen Judge Rosenman but before the committee had assembled even for a preliminary talk. One amusing aspect of my brief visit to the White House is recorded in the notes which Smith prepared in the early days of the rubber committee. Stephen Early, the President's appointment secretary, greeted me when I arrived in the White House to offer President Roosevelt's apologies for not seeing me personally. I said that I would not think of bothering the President; I quite understood; anyhow, I added, I could talk more frankly to Judge Rosenman (I had in mind that I might be able to talk myself out of the job—a false hope). Early's reply, which may have reflected White House reaction to my conversation with the President after my return from England, was to the effect that he would like to inquire when I had ever been reluctant to talk frankly to the President.

At the time, I thought the President was misguided in offering the investigating post to the Chief Justice of the United States and then turning to Baruch. It seemed to me that this was a job for a person who had some technical competence and could quickly assemble a team of disinterested experts. We had not proceeded far in our inquiry when I discovered how naïve had been my judgment. What was involved was not only a clash of technical opinions in regard to the feasibility of different processes, but also a clash of personalities. I soon came to understand that any investigators would have to examine conflicts within the Cabinet. That there was need for impartial technical opinion would become quite clear. However, it was natural for the President and Judge Rosenman (who was at that point Roosevelt's close adviser) to assume that if the quarrel among Jesse Jones, Harold Ickes, Secretary of the Interior, Donald Nelson and Leon Henderson, administrator of the Office of Price Administration, could be straightened out, technical matters would easily fall into their proper places. In other words, as the White House then viewed the scene, if Bernard Baruch could use his well-proven skill in manipulating human nature, there would be no difficulty in finding any number of applied scientists who could decide how to manipulate inanimate matter. I do not think I am falsely portraying the White House opinion as of the summer of 1942. The evaluation of the importance of scientists and technical experts was not high.

The evidence as to the basic hostility between members of the administration is a matter of record. Senator Ralph Owen Brewster of Maine in mid-February said that the Truman Committee would soon "blow the lid off the rubber situation in the country." He added: "I know that Donald Nelson and his associates in the War Production Board are far from satisfied with the way Jesse Jones has handled the synthetic situation." To prove his point, Senator Brewster went on to say that Leon Henderson had told him: "The whole synthetic program is only a gleam in Jesse Jones' eye." If so, the gleam had been well publicized; less than a month earlier, Jones had boasted that the United States would have "enough rubber for all war purposes for several years and enough left over to let you run your car about a quarter as much as you used to in peacetime." At least one Senator was not convinced; Robert A. Taft, always ready to attack the administration, assailed the President and his advisers for lack of foresight in providing production facilities for synthesizing rubber.

If I had followed the daily news more carefully or if I had had a more sensitive ear for political gossip, I would have been more prepared for the confusion we soon found. It was so public I cannot write "unearthed." Everyone knew that Ickes and Jones had a strong antipathy to one another. Ickes, as Secretary of the Interior, was also Petroleum Coordinator. Whether petroleum would be the sole raw material for making rubber was a question already being tossed around by the reporters. Jesse Jones as Chairman of the Reconstruction Finance Corporation had had the financial responsibility for the entire rubber program. A story went around Washington in early April that at a semipublic dinner in Washington Jones and the proprietor of the Washington *Post*, Eugene Meyer, had nearly come to blows because the *Post* had severely criticized Jones for the long delays in planning and building synthetic rubber plants. I was vaguely aware of still another disagreement which concerned the rationing of gasoline. Leon Henderson and Donald Nelson were in favor of the rationing; Harold Ickes was opposed.

It might seem strange that I, who had spent so much time in Washington since the fall of France, was so ignorant of the bitter quarreling that was going on. The atmosphere in which Compton and I had been operating was, in a sense, synthetic. We had been working hard on behalf of the United States Government, mobilizing scientists and assisting the Army and the Navy to write contracts for vast sums of money. The only personal conflicts we had run into, however, were at the levels far below that of Cabinet officers. Of course, there were plenty of disagreements on technical matters, some of which escalated into rival bids for power. But they were all resolved without either side taking the case to the public.

Since Karl Compton and I had been operating on the assumption that research and development work would be done outside of government-manned centers, we found nothing surprising in the absence of United States Government facilities for rubber research. What did strike us as amazing was the absence of any group of independent technical advisers to those responsible for the rubber program. The only person who was functioning, we soon discovered, was E. R. Weidlein, Director of the Mellon Institute of Pittsburgh; his recommendation to Jesse Jones that a technical division be established had been ignored. Perhaps those who considered the recommendation were thinking of the 1917 model, which would have meant the erection of buildings and the creation of a full-time technical staff. What Karl Compton and I were thinking of when we recommended in our final report the creation of two technical divisions were organizations, somewhat like the divisions of the NDRC, made up of a small group of impartial experts allocating research and development problems through contracts to universities, research institutions and industries.

I dwell on these organizational problems because one of the interesting points about the rubber survey was the fact that it exposed the lack of adequate scientific judgment available to the government. To be sure, this lack was accentuated by the personal animosities of at least two Cabinet members as well as considerable public disagreements among subordinates. In a word, applied science had not yet found a place in the structure of government except for the secret work of the Office of Scientific Research and Development.

Messrs. Jones, Ickes and Nelson might have justified their point of view by claiming that they had contracted indirectly with the research men by turning to the laboratories of industry, which they did. Such a plea on their behalf, however, would ignore the fact that the experts who were employed harbored loyalties to individual companies. In organizing the divisions of the NDRC, we had made it a point that those who recommended the contracts to the top committee were not employees of, or associated with, the contractors. All of which, in retrospect, seems obvious. But having lived through the turmoil of the rubber crisis and at the same time enjoyed the almost complete tranquillity of the NDRC operation, the contrast is vivid in my mind.

In July 1942 everyone was worried as to whether his own set of automobile tires would last through the conflict. If not, where could one obtain another set? No other aspect of the war so directly affected so many families. It was becoming increasingly clear that every effort should be made to conserve the rubber which was now at hand. This meant reducing the wear on the tires then in daily use. In turn, this might mean rationing of gasoline. Obviously, the less gasoline used, the less wear on the existing tires. Equally obvious was the resulting inconvenience to millions of citizens. Every family that owned a car was deeply apprehensive about what lay ahead. At the same time, they wondered if rubber substitutes could be manufactured quickly enough to provide tires before the present ones wore out.

Congress had tried its hand at answering this question. A bill known as Senate Bill 2600 was passed by the Senate and the House on July 24 "to expedite the prosecution of the war by making provision for an increased supply of rubber manufactured from alcohol produced from agricultural or forest products." It created a new agency to be known as the Rubber Supply Agency to be headed by a Director of Rubber Supplies. The new organization was directed to "make available at the earliest possible time an adequate supply of rubber which, when added to the rubber being supplied by other agencies, will be sufficient to meet the military and civilian needs of the United States."

To perform this duty, the agency was to provide the required plants and supplies. The Director was empowered to obtain all necessary material and was given priority over all other private plants engaged in making implements of war. By legislative fiat, the manufacture of synthetic rubber from agricultural or forest products was given preference over all enterprises scheduled by the War Production Board or the armed forces.

Judge Rosenman told me the President was going to veto the bill. It was preposterous to subordinate the procuring of scarce materials such as copper to the demands of a rubber program. What Rosenman did not tell me was that the President had allowed the bill to be passed in order to bring the whole crisis to a head. The legislative record shows that in neither the Senate nor the House was there anything approaching a quorum. The Congressional leaders must have known both that the presidential veto was in order and that they could not muster anything like enough votes to override it.

The crisis involved not only the demands of the synthetic rubber program but the merits of one type of manufacturing process over another. By specifying the manufacture of rubber from "alcohol produced from agricultural or forest products," Congress had made a far-reaching technical decision. As the President was to point out in his veto message, the government had already planned for the erection of two types of plants, those using farm products and those using petroleum. The processes involved were in a state of flux. There were many technical questions to be answered. What was needed was not new legislation but an examination of the facts. With this conclusion, the veto message ended with the announcement of the appointment of the Baruch Committee. In the meantime, the President declared the development of plans for the manufacture of synthetic rubber from both petroleum and grain would continue. Thus both the farm bloc, which had forced the bill through Congress, and those who backed the use of petroleum as a raw material were temporarily appeased. The veto message was released for publication on Friday, August 7, 1942.

Baruch did not wait for the official announcement of the appointment of the committee, which he knew would be made in connection with the forthcoming presidential veto. On Monday, August 3, 1942, Baruch, Compton and I met at Baruch's house in Port Washington on Long Island. Baruch had brought in Samuel Lubell, a writer, then active in the Office of War Information, and I had brought A. Calvert Smith. We covered a good deal of ground; most important, the responsibilities of the chairman, Compton and myself were defined. To me was assigned the review of the status of current plans for making rubber substitutes, including an estimate of production through 1944. Compton was to be responsible for statistical information and physical inventory as well as the reclaiming and saving of tires for civilian and military use. Baruch was anxious to get his hand on the subject of "critical materials," which had long been his hobby. His main responsibility, although it was not spelled out, was the politicians. He gave us his assurance that he would handle his friends, the Congressmen. He also announced that he would call on the heads of all the agencies concerned, particularly Messrs. Jones, Ickes, Henderson, Nelson and Joseph B. Eastman of the Office of Defense Transportation.

From the beginning, Baruch maintained that he was an old man and that he was not going to do any of the work. As these matters were being discussed, he said, according to Smith's notes: "I know Ickes. He has something in his mind. I'd like to play him against Jesse Jones. That's often a good way to get something done. I'll talk to Jesse. I'll tell him it's a God-given opportunity for him to get himself off the spot if he can. Then let me handle the Senators and fellows on the Hill. They're mostly good friends of mine—Truman, Gillette, Wheeler. I'll give a dinner for them some evening, and we'll all talk things over informally—get them into the picture. Very important. I'll do that sort of thing. You fellows will do the work. I've always been that way. I'm busy. And besides, I'm old."

Although there was still no assurance that we would actually be appointed, Lubell brought up the question of budgetary allowance and an office. Baruch said that we certainly were not going to work in the street and added that he could call the President in Hyde Park. If he did so, he could get the money; but he thought this would be a mistake. He told us that FDR would like nothing better than a chance to change the signals and leave him, Baruch, in the lurch. He obviously had little faith in the consistency of the President. He forthwith recounted a number of stories where the President had changed his mind to the disadvantage of Mr. Baruch.

The decision was finally made to call Judge Rosenman, and we overheard Baruch saying: "I'm not going to be chairman of this God-damn committee, Sam, and hang my hat in the street. And I damn well am going to have what I need in the way of a budget. I've got two fine fellows with me. They're good, practical men. I like them. We're getting some preliminary things out of the way now. . . .

"No, it will not do to have this committee named by WPB. And it would be a great mistake to have it in the message that Nelson asked for it. We aren't anybody's committee except the President's."

Overhearing this, I promptly stated that if it were a Nelson committee I wouldn't serve. Compton agreed. When the telephone conversation was over, Baruch repeated what Rosenman had said about
trying to pull Nelson into the picture—wanting apparently to keep
everybody happy and not hurt anybody's feelings—and said that he,
Baruch, had told him he wouldn't serve on any WPB committee. Compton and I reported we had both reached the same decision. "Good,"
said the chairman. "That's settled. The President won't be back from
Hyde Park till tomorrow, and we probably won't have an announcement till Wednesday morning, or possibly for the press conference
Tuesday afternoon—provided we get any announcement at all."

In talking over the expansion of the committee's staff, Compton
and I naturally thought in terms of technical people. Baruch thought
in terms of industrialists and bankers. Compton and I had no objection
to such an enlargement of the working group; indeed, we saw advantages. On the other hand, I doubt if either of us would have had
the perspicacity to realize how important it was to establish at the
outset a good reputation among influential people. I am sure it would
never have occurred to me to add a dozen or more well-known people
who were in no way connected with the industries related to the
rubber program. Among the people eventually invited by Baruch were
E. E. Brown, president of the First National Bank of Chicago; Clarence
Dillon of Dillon, Read & Co. of New York; B. K. Smith, president of
a national bank in St. Louis; Alvin Brown of the Johns Manville
Corporation and, most important, John Hancock of Brown Brothers.
Hancock, in effect, served as vice chairman. He labored long and effectively both at the hearings and, above all, in the writing of the final
report. With these appointments Baruch laid the foundation for excellent public relations with the banking and industrial community.

An amusing example of Baruch's skill with the press is illustrated
by an incident that happened shortly after the news of our appointment became public. Compton, Sam Lubell, Calvert Smith and I
arrived at Mr. Baruch's rooms at the Carlton Hotel for a meeting just
as he was putting on his hat to take a walk. Since it was a warm and
pleasant day, we strolled over to Lafayette Park and seated ourselves
on a couple of benches under the shadow of the equestrian statue of
Andrew Jackson. Just as we started to talk, an Associated Press man
who covered the White House appeared. He was well known to
Baruch, who greeted him with the sally: "What are you doing here?
Why aren't you back at the White House where you belong?" The AP
man countered by asking, "Is this the first meeting of the rubber committee?" "It is a meeting," Baruch said. "Do you know of any better

place to hold one? Now we've got some private things to talk about and you had better run along and leave us alone." To which the newsman agreed and added, "I am not going to send any photographers over because I like you."

The story appeared that afternoon about the Baruch Committee holding its first meeting on a park bench. Sam Lubell and Calvert Smith were identified as "experts," though they didn't know one hydrocarbon molecule from another. I am convinced, though I never aired the suspicion, that Baruch himself had tipped off the press in advance. At all events, the committee got off to a good start and was known as the "park bench committee."

Thanks to our private meetings, first at Baruch's home in Long Island and then in hotel rooms in Washington, we had lined up our procedure and the nature of our advisers before the appointment of the committee was made public on August 7. Just where we were going to hang our hats had not yet been made certain. I suggested that at least temporarily we might use rooms in the Dumbarton Oaks estate in Georgetown. This estate had been recently transferred to Harvard as a generous gift of the owners, Mr. and Mrs. Robert Woods Bliss. The necessary arrangements were made with the people in Cambridge who were administering the gift; although the rooms were used only intermittently, the beautiful gardens became a necessary part of our plan of operation. I think no acknowledgment of indebtedness appeared in the final report, but one was certainly in order. When Calvert Smith was guiding Baruch on a tour of the gardens, he explained that the property had only recently been given to Harvard together with a large endowment, the income of which would provide for the upkeep of the grounds. Baruch said: "That's interesting; I didn't think a fellow as smart as Dr. Conant would fall into the trap of having to keep up such an estate without a special endowment."

We usually met in the garden at ten in the morning or two in the afternoon. Since Baruch had a cold from which he continued to suffer for several weeks, he insisted on sitting in the sun whenever possible. Compton and I were always close to him. The other members sat in folding chairs on the stone terrace. Sam Lubell used a card table as a desk. The arrangement was about as secret as hiring Symphony Hall. Voices carried far over the quiet garden. But our interviews with more than two dozen important people were held in the most delightful surroundings.

Eventually the government procured working quarters in a suite of rooms in the center of Washington. They were spacious but not air-conditioned. As the weather continued hot and the traffic noise steady, the report was finally put together under highly disadvantageous circumstances.

Because of our preliminary discussions, we were in a good position to start to work immediately, which was essential considering the great concern about the rubber shortage. As Frank A. Howard says in his book *Buna Rubber; the Birth of an Industry:* "There was no longer any confidence in the national synthetic rubber program. What was to be done? The end of the President's veto message of August 6, 1942, provided the answer."* It read in part as follows:

I have set up a committee of three men to investigate the whole situation—to get the facts—and to report them to me as quickly as possible with their recommendations. . . . They will be equipped with adequate staff and will, I know, submit their report at the earliest possible moment. I am asking them to investigate the whole situation and to recommend such action as will produce the rubber necessary for our total war effort, including civilian use with a minimum of interference with the production of other weapons of war.

Mr. Howard, principal executive of the Standard Oil Company of New Jersey until 1945, goes on to say:

The appointment of the Baruch Rubber Committee was probably the most widely acclaimed action on the domestic front in the history of the war program. The public, the press, the Congress, Washington officialdom and the rubber, oil and chemical industries engaged in the rubber program breathed a sigh of relief which swelled to a gale of approval. To those of us who were actively engaged in carrying out the program, it was apparent immediately that this confidence was not misplaced. Almost before the ink on the announcements was dry, the Committee had organized itself and started its job.

My own contribution to the process of getting the facts as quickly as possible was to organize a staff. In addition to Roger Adams, I enlisted the services of H. F. Johnstone, a chemical engineer from the University of Illinois, W. L. McCabe from Carnegie Tech in Pittsburgh and two of my close associates from the NDRC, T. K. Sherwood of M.I.T. and Earl P. Stevenson of A. D. Little Company of Cambridge; they became known as the "four horsemen." Stevenson and Sherwood had the job of examining at once the plants which were in operation for making butadiene and talking with the technical people in the chief companies already in the program.

* New York, D. Van Nostrand Co., 1947.

That this action was appreciated is clear from the following comment in Mr. Howard's book:

The procedure of the Committee in its contact with Standard was typical. Dr. Conant telephoned to explain that he had selected a sub-committee under the chairmanship of Mr. E. P. Stevenson, a leading independent chemical engineer, to make the field studies on the butadiene problem. He asked us to arrange at once to receive this sub-committee and to assist them in their work.

The sub-committee began its work by meetings in New York with the members of our technical executive staff. It then proceeded to the central Esso Laboratories of Standard Oil Development Company at Bayway, N.J., for sessions of several days and from there to the Baton Rouge Refinery where butadiene and Buna rubber were already being manufactured and where the new plants, which were to form the design basis for the Government's principal program, were under construction. The members of the sub-committee interviewed the research leaders and engineers who were engaged in the rubber program, examined the pertinent laboratory data and pilot plants and took away with them copies of the important reports and engineering information.

The spirit and manner of conducting the study by the Baruch Committee disarmed criticism and stilled controversy. The Government officials and private interests concerned in the rubber program were quite certain in advance of completion of the Baruch report that it would clear away the mountain of doubt and confusion which had been built up during the preceding months and give at least a clear picture of the national synthetic rubber development.

Serving on the Baruch Committee was my second exposure to the chemistry of synthetic rubber. As I have mentioned earlier, in the 1920s I went each month to Wilmington, Delaware, to consult with the chemists in one of the research laboratories of the Du Pont Company. I remember so well my old friend, E. K. Bolton, who was head of the research activities, saying that one of the great possibilities for the future was the manufacture of a substitute for natural rubber. Actually, he was soon to find a far more profitable new development in the discovery of how to make the polymer which came to be known as "nylon." What then intrigued Dr. Bolton was the possibility of starting with limestone, coke and water and eventually producing a mass of rubber-like material which could be used in manufacturing automobile tires. I was asked to advise on one step of the complicated chemical process.

I am sorry to report I was not able to come up with any helpful suggestion. A younger chemist, however, whom I had recommended to the company, Dr. Wallace Carothers, succeeded where I had failed. He showed them how by a special trick a material could be produced which came to be known as neoprene. It was in composition quite different from natural rubber, for it contained a chlorine atom. It had many of the properties of natural rubber, however, and was far superior in its resistance to oil and chemicals. Far too expensive to be used in the 1930s for tires, it had already found considerable market, and I have no doubt the Du Pont Company earned many, many times over the investment in the research project on which I had once attempted in vain to advise them.

German chemists had been at work on the search for synthetic rubber since before World War I. The Germans were well aware that a British-Dutch monopoly of natural rubber might cause them to pay far too much for their automobile tires. Therefore a commercial objective, as well as a concern for national defense, stimulated the chemists of that country to continue all through the 1920s to look for a rubber substitute. One of their products, Buna-N, was competitive with Du Pont's neoprene. Indeed, when the Du Pont plant was put out of commission for a long period by an explosion, this German product was used as a replacement. Like neoprene, it had special qualities which made it valuable for special uses. Like neoprene, it was far too expensive to be considered in making automobile tires. However, the basic process of its manufacture was copolymerization. What is involved is the joining up of two *different* kinds of small molecules to make one very large molecule. The size and structure of the large molecule determine the properties of the resulting material, which is a rubber substitute.

Not only did Buna-N involve copolymerization, but it involved the manufacture of a substance which was to play a part in my discussions with Messrs. Baruch and Compton, namely, butadiene. The Standard Oil Company of New Jersey and its affiliates had acquired the patent rights from the Germans for the manufacture of Buna-N. In the 1930s they had also obtained the rights for a closely related copolymer called Buna-S; this material had promise for the manufacture of tires. Unfortunately for the understanding of Cabinet officers and the public, the possibilities of rubber substitutes were not exhausted by neoprene, Buna-N and Buna-S. There was at least one other product which conceivably might be used as a substitute for a rubber tire. This was called Butyl rubber, also a hydrocarbon polymer.

Buna-S and Butyl rubber were still being tested as ingredients of a suitable tire when the United States Government had to make decisions about setting up an industry to make rubber substitutes.

There were thus three or four possible synthetic rubbers available. There were also alternate processes for making the material to be polymerized, chiefly butadiene. Since neither the polymers nor the raw material (butadiene) had as yet been made on any large scale, those who were making the decisions under either Nelson, Jones or Ickes were faced with difficult alternatives. Clearly, this was the point at which ample adequate independent technical advice should have been available.

We found that often what was being argued was not how to make a particular rubber substitute, but whether the rubber substitute in question could be made into a suitable tire. Tire making was an art in itself. The know-how was in the hands of the rubber companies; it could not be reduced to any simple formula covered by a patent. There was no way in which the manufacturers of the basic raw materials such as butadiene could determine whether their factories could yield a successful product except by turning the product over to a rubber company for compounding into tires which could be tested on the road.

One can readily see that whether to start petroleum or ethyl alcohol was no simple decision, and whatever the raw material, a number of subsequent decisions had to be made about the process for the manufacture of butadiene, the copolymerization of butadiene and the fabrication of tires. It is no wonder the public was confused; it is no wonder that anyone who sought to reduce the confusion might pick on such an erroneously simple question as to whether the petroleum industry or the farmers should be the basic producers.

The background of scientific knowledge I have just sketched will help to explain not only what the rubber committee recommended but how we worked—and work we did, feverishly during the blazing-hot month of August. As an illustration of the way we operated as a committee, I will refer to our interviews with Jesse Jones and Weidlein, the chief technical expert for the program. In these and other interviews, almost without exception, Baruch, Compton and I were present and did most of the questioning. Ten or twelve other members of the group were almost certain to be on hand as well. A verbatim transcript of the interviews was available to all the group shortly after the interviewing had taken place. It is interesting to note, however, that, as in the case of Congressional hearings, the transcript often shows that the discussion was off the record; as a result, much of the most interesting material has been lost forever. However, the arrangement was in accordance with a decision made by Baruch. He told the press that our hearings were going to be not secret but private. "There is a great difference," he added, and he wanted that difference to be clear from the start.

In the end, the transcript was not made available, as far as I know, to anyone outside the group that had been brought in by Baruch. The President did not receive progress reports, but had to wait until our report was ready for publication. There were no leaks. The fact that the press was patient is a tribute to Baruch's good relations with newspaper owners and reporters and Sam Lubell's day-by-day handling of requests for information.

As the records show, our questioning of all the principals was polite but far from superficial. For example, the "chief" himself (i.e., Baruch) asked Jesse Jones how he arrived at the decision that 60 percent of the rubber was to be made starting with petroleum as a raw material and 40 percent starting with alcohol. Jones said that at the beginning all his people had been told that there was not much alcohol available except a little synthetic alcohol made by the Carbon and Carbide Company. On being pressed by Baruch, he continued: "When the Gillette Committee got started, the boys found some more alcohol and we were told along about the first of May that we could have a certain amount of it so we immediately tied that into the program; and on the twenty-fifth we were told we could have enough to make up to 200,000 tons of rubber."

At this point, Baruch said: "As I understand it then, when you started to make your synthetic rubber you were advised that there was no alcohol from which you could make it? So any alcohol process would have to be ruled out because of that." Jones replied, not entirely seriously: "I didn't know you could make it out of alcohol. I thought that all you could do with alcohol was to drink it!"

This interchange highlights an important fact. Ethyl alcohol can be made either synthetically, starting with ethylene, or by fermentation of foodstuffs. It is the same alcohol by either route, but the political implications of its source were all-important.

When the production of butadiene was first considered, alcohol by fermentation was synonymous with beverage alcohol. Shifts in the demands for alcohol quite apart from the possibility of its use as a starting point for synthetic rubber had led to proposals for the establishment of many new fermentation plants to produce industrial alcohol. Such a scheme was pushed by a Senate committee headed by Senator Guy M. Gillette of Iowa. As soon as the prospect of an expansion of the production of industrial alcohol from grain appeared, the question arose as to why a still further expansion would not provide a basis for synthetic rubber.

Several engineering studies had shown that it should be possible to erect new plants for the conversion of alcohol into butadiene more easily and quickly than to produce butadiene from petroleum. In consequence of these findings, additional plants using alcohol as a raw material were authorized at this time by Rubber Reserve. According to Frank A. Howard in his book on *Buna Rubber*: "The effect on public opinion of these wholly constructive but seemingly belated changes in the program was most unfavorable. They confirmed the growing impression that those responsible for the production of synthetic rubber were not themselves sure of what they were doing."[*]

The questions addressed to Dr. Weidlein were, for the most part, concerned with his role as technical adviser. As I pointed out earlier, all of us had been surprised to find that the government officials making such important decisions had had to rely on one man. He himself stated that his official title was still "Chief Technical Consultant to the War Production Board and Senior Consultant to the Chemical Division of the War Production Board and Adviser to the Rubber Reserve Company." He was a man of great experience, having served as a chemical adviser to the War Industries Board during World War I. As head of the Mellon Institute, he had been instrumental in developing many industrial processes, including some starting with oil and some starting with alcohol. He carried a heavy load of work in Washington, and he deserves a vast amount of credit for what he had accomplished under trying circumstances. The committee ended by feeling that probably the right decisions had been made. But there was no way for the public to know that such was the case.

Just before the committee adjourned one morning, the following interchange between Weidlein, Compton and Baruch took place.

MR. WEIDLEIN: And I can say this, you people don't know how peaceful it has been to do work since this committee has been set up; we have accomplished more in the last three weeks than we have accomplished in two months with a better feeling going around. It has at least allowed us to do some work.

DR. COMPTON: Do you think our best contribution to the rubber program would be to hold up this report as long as possible?

[*] *Op. cit.*, p. 203.

MR. WEIDLEIN: I do.

MR. BARUCH: On this note, I think it would be a good idea to adjourn, get lunch and come back at 2:15.

Before Stevenson reported to me at the conclusion of his visits to many plants, one question which had been foremost in my mind had been fairly well settled by the testimony I had heard. I had come to the conclusion that the government program as planned was not going to take an undue portion of critical materials. Moreover, the controversy about the use of fermentation alcohol or petroleum had almost vanished. One of the main jobs of the committee would be, therefore, to explain the nature of the decisions already made.

When I expressed these views to Stevenson, he fired a disquieting question at me. "How do you know that these processes are going to work?" he said. "Your committee would look pretty foolish if after the plants were built, it took many more months to get the processes to work; delays of this sort are a common occurrence in the chemical industry."

"Well," I replied, "I am counting on you people to make so careful an examination of what is already in existence and what is planned that you can guarantee to me that the plants will operate according to schedule." Not many days later, Stevenson returned with the necessary assurances. My task then was to convince the chairman.

I recall spreading out a diagram on the floor of one of the big rooms in Dumbarton Oaks; it showed the complicated layout of a butadiene plant. After a few minutes' scrutiny, Baruch said, "My God, Doctor, it'll never work. I've had plenty of experience in investing my money in industrial operations, and I know it takes time and often many changes before everything is proceeding according to plan." I assured him it would work and promptly. "I'll take your word for it, Doctor," he said, folding up the diagram. "That's what we are going to recommend."

As is often the case in my experience, collecting the facts was easier than putting down conclusions on paper. I still remember with a feeling of oppression the days and nights we worked over the report in the sweltering heat of those rooms in the center of Washington. There were many preliminary drafts. The report when printed amounted to seventy-five pages. It was dated September 10, 1942. The letter of transmittal formed an introduction summarizing all the important points:

We find the existing situation to be so dangerous that unless corrective measures are taken immediately this country will face both a military and a civilian collapse. The naked facts present a warning that dare not be ignored. We present herewith the significant figures:

Crude Rubber Position of the United States
(July 1, 1942, to January 1, 1944) in Long Tons:

On hand July 1, 1942 (stockpile)	578,000 Tons
Estimated imports July 1, 1942, to January 1, 1944	53,000 Tons
Total crude rubber	631,000 Tons
Estimated military and other essential demands July 1, 1942, to January 1, 1944, with no allowance for tires for passenger automobiles	842,000 Tons
Deficit that must be met by production of synthetic rubber before Januay 1, 1944	211,000 Tons

Unless adequate new supplies (natural or artificial) can be obtained in time, the total military and export requirements alone will exhaust our crude stocks before the end of next summer.

Tires on civilian cars are wearing down at a rate eight times greater than they are being replaced. If this rate continues, by far the larger number of cars will be off the road next year and in 1944 there will be an all but complete collapse of the 27,000,000 passenger cars in America.

We are faced with certainties as to demands; with grave insecurity as to supply. Therefore this Committee conceives its first duty to be the maintenance of a rubber reserve that will keep our armed forces fighting and our essential civilian wheels turning. This can best be done by "bulling through" the present gigantic synthetic program and by safeguarding jealously every ounce of rubber in the country. . . .

Discomfort or defeat. There is no middle course.

THEREFORE, WE RECOMMEND:

THAT NO SPEED ABOVE 35 MILES AN HOUR BE PERMITTED FOR PASSENGER CARS AND TRUCKS. (IN THIS WAY THE LIFE OF TIRES WILL BE PROLONGED BY NEARLY 40 PERCENT.)

THAT THE ANNUAL AVERAGE MILEAGE PER CAR NOW ESTIMATED AS 6,700 MILES BE HELD DOWN TO 5,000, A REDUCTION OF 25 PERCENT. (THIS DOES NOT MEAN THAT EACH HAS A RIGHT TO 5,000 MILES A YEAR; IT APPLIES TO NECESSARY DRIVING.)

THAT MORE RUBBER THAN NOW IS GIVEN TO THE PUBLIC BE RELEASED TO FULLY MAINTAIN, BY RECAPPING OR NEW TIRES, NECESSARY CIVILIAN DRIVING.

THAT A NEW RATIONING SYSTEM OF GASOLINE BE DEVISED, BASED ON THIS 5,000 MILES A YEAR TO SAVE TIRES.

THAT THE RESTRICTIONS AS TO GASOLINE AND MILEAGE BE NATIONAL IN THEIR APPLICATION.

THAT COMPULSORY PERIODIC TIRE INSPECTION BE INSTITUTED.

THAT A VOLUNTARY TIRE CONSERVATION PROGRAM BE PUT INTO EFFECT UNTIL GASOLINE RATIONING CAN BE ESTABLISHED.

The implementation of these recommendations depended largely on the good will of the owners and drivers of a vast number of automobiles. Clearly, the readers of the report must be convinced; only their cooperation could ensure that both the civilian and military needs would be met.

In answer to the question as to why the synthetic program was not yet in full swing, our report stated:

Why not earlier? Why so late? The answers to these queries lie in the past. These errors, growing out of procrastinations, indecisions, conflict of authority, clashes of personalities, lack of understanding, delays, and early non-use of known alcohol processes, are not to be recounted by us, nor shall we go into the failure to build a greater stockpile of crude rubber. We are concerned with the past record only insofar as it has seemed to us to cast light on problems of future administration.

To prevent a recurrence of these mistakes, this Committee asks an immediate reorganization in present method and the creation of a Rubber Administrator. This official will have authority over the policies governing the priceless stock of rubber now on our automobiles, the drivers of which are trustees of our national safety. He will direct the course of the technical and industrial development—wholly new to America—of the synthetic rubber production.

In the body of the report we recommended a complete reorganization and consolidation of the government agencies concerned with the rubber program. In so doing, we pointed out that there had been many adjustments and readjustments in the plans for making synthetic rubber. Some of these were inevitable; some appeared to be the result of bad administration. Referring to the shift to the use of alcohol in the spring of 1942, we suggested that a more adequately staffed organization might have recognized the changed situation earlier, and the program could have been altered a few months sooner. Among our recommendations was one calling for the establishment of a Technical Division under the immediate control of the Rubber Administrator. "It will be a matter of great importance," we said, "to have the Technical Division adequately staffed and provided with branches in charge of all the various phases of research and development."

We excluded research on the manufacture of butadiene from petroleum, which we placed in another Technical Division responsible to the Petroleum Coordinator.

One of our key recommendations read as follows: "The Rubber Administrator, acting on authority delegated by the Chairman of WPB, should have the sole responsibility for supervision of operation of all Government plants engaged in the production of rubber." Mr. Baruch, in his memoirs, reports that K. T. Compton and I had favored excluding the War Production Board from any committee program. According to his memory, we had urged that the Rubber Administrator be completely independent of WPB. It may well have been that we advocated an independent status for the Rubber Administrator, although of that I am far from sure. Anyway, in retrospect, one can see the force of the arguments against creating a rubber czar with completely independent powers. On the question of the allocation of critical materials alone, it was necessary to have a coordinating authority in the hands of Nelson or his successor. The President's veto of Bill 2600 was based largely on the impossibility of giving to the proposed Director of Rubber Supplies powers over raw materials and processes independent of the control of the War Production Board.

Our report contained not a word of direct criticism of any of those who had been making the decisions. However, the following statement was clearly aimed at Jesse Jones and Harold Ickes, though no names were mentioned: "The Committee finds a number of different Government agencies with overlapping and confusing authority over the synthetic rubber program. The conflict between the Rubber Reserve Company, a subsidiary of the Reconstruction Finance Corporation and the Office of Petroleum Coordinator has delayed and conflicted with the bringing in of new facilities for the production of butadiene from oil."

There was no such implied rebuke to Nelson, though Compton and I had argued for it. For a day or so we thought we had Baruch convinced. For my own part, I have often thought that it would have been useful if we could have found some way of expressing strong criticism of Nelson privately to the President and hinted at it in the public document. Instead, the public criticism focused on Jones, which was, to a certain extent, unfair. He felt aggrieved and so indicated in a letter to President Roosevelt three days after the report was out. Perhaps his basic justification was a statement he had made before a Congressional committee in March: "Any one of you," he said, "who foresaw the disaster to our fleet at Pearl Harbor and the fall of Singapore, please step forward."

The press reception of our report was highly favorable, with the exceptions of *PM*, a daily newspaper published in New York, and *The Nation*. I. F. Stone, writing in *The Nation* on September 13, recorded his dissatisfaction in the following words:

Regarded as practical politics, the report made it easier for the President to order nationwide gas rationing to save tires, a painful task on the eve of congressional elections. Regarded as scientific inquiry, the report comes to no conclusions which might hurt the endowment funds of Harvard or M.I.T. Regarded as a fortunate bit of public relations for Standard Oil of New Jersey, it takes the edge off the revelations of the Truman, Gillette and Bone Committees. Best of all from this point of view, while the report attempts to appease the farm bloc, it also leaves the synthetic rubber program exactly where it was, in the lap of the Standard–Mellon–du Pont interests.

Stone concluded:

The result is a program so lopsided that it invites disaster. The casual reader of the Baruch report may gain the impression that we cannot afford to jeopardize our synthetic rubber program by experiments. The truth is that every process in the program is more or less experimental, and that the program leans most heavily on those processes which have been least tried. The way to cut down the risk is to diversify the program so that the breakdown of one process will not affect too large a part of the program. The WPB, Jesse Jones and the interests which use them, have chosen instead to put most of our eggs in a few baskets. . . . We ought to try several grain processes in our butadiene program instead of concentrating on the cumbersome four-step Carbon and Carbide process on which we are depending for 242,000 tons. . . . This is not possible until we loosen the grip of the oil and chemical trusts from the synthetic rubber program.

The question remains whether or not Mr. Stone had failed to understand that alcohol from grain was the same chemical substance as the synthetic alcohol which had been planned as a raw material right along in one portion of the program. Such a confusion might have led to his erroneous estimate of the future. The year 1943, it is true, was a bad one from the point of view of those of us who had made predictions. By the end of 1944, however, the various plants were operating at an annual capacity of over one million long tons of synthetic rubber, chiefly Buna-S. We had endorsed the program which looked forward to an annual production of 705,000 long tons of Buna-S together with 172,000 tons of other synthetic rubber substitutes.

All of us who had worked on the Baruch Committee could be satisfied with our role as prophets, and we could take satisfaction in the fact that we had been midwives at the birth of a new industry which had come into being by an unusual combination of private initiative and governmental funds. The private initiative had included the pooling of patents and the cooperation of a number of companies with officials in Washington who, in spite of a lack of adequate technical assistance, had nevertheless come up with a satisfactory program. Before World War II the United States had been the largest importer of natural rubber; at the close of the war an industry was in existence which made this country the largest producer and exporter of synthetic substitutes for natural rubber.

The final report was presented to the President by Baruch, Compton and myself on Thursday, September 10, 1942. The conversation was short. The President, who had already been informed of the highlights, was greatly pleased. He promised to put the recommendations into force as rapidly as possible. As we left the White House, a reporter stopped me and asked whether I had anything to add. My comment was: "No—it is all in the report and it's a lot. Now for some sleep!"

CHAPTER 24

Peacetime Conscription

THE FACT THAT I was once a chemist largely determined my wartime activities with the NDRC and the Baruch Committee. Experience as a scientist and my acquaintanceship among chemists made me useful to Vannevar Bush. To be sure, the fact that I was a university president may have helped to the extent that the position carried a certain prestige which was recognized by the Army and Navy officers with whom I had to deal.

My connection with the movement to enact a military training bill in the summer of 1940, on the other hand, was based on quite different considerations. Grenville Clark, a leader of the Military Training Camps Association, enlisted my services because I was president of Harvard. He was not in the least interested in my scientific past. Indeed, it turned out that certain worries, which originated among my scientific friends, were a minor nuisance to those who were pushing Congress to pass a law authorizing the drafting of young men for military service. I intruded into their thinking the troublesome question of deferments or exemptions for special groups of men.

To a considerable degree, the people who were active in the Military Training Camps Association were the same as those who formed the William Allen White Committee. In those frightening days after the fall of France, the need to defend America by aiding the Allies seemed to be closely meshed with the need for strengthening the military forces of the United States. Thus in my speech to the Jewish War Veterans on June 12, 1940, I advocated a bill which had just been placed before Congress. Referring to the military manpower situation, I said: "Only one course seems possible: the adoption by the country of the principle of universal compulsory military training and service." I went on to outline the measure proposed by the Military Training Camps Association and stated, "I believe such a law is the only fair way to develop a potential fighting force of the magnitude required. I believe it is the only practical method for an industrialized free society to pursue. Let us hope a law for compulsory training and service will be carefully considered at once and acted upon this summer. Let us hope that Congress will stay in session for this purpose, and to consider other emergency measures which may be soon required."

In making my plea for the passage of a military service bill, I was echoing the position taken by Grenville Clark. He and I shared a deep apprehension for the future of the United States if the fall of France was followed by the fall of England, which in June 1940 seemed extremely likely to occur. I leaned heavily on his counsel in preparing my speeches. Therefore I accepted almost without question the proposed law which Clark showed me in draft form. What I was to question later, namely, the power of the local boards, I did not then know enough to challenge.

The one point I raised concerned the drafting of scientists and engineers. I argued that in a modern war those who constructed new weapons and improved existing models were as important as the fighting men who used them. Clark was convinced and added a new section, 7(c), to meet my objections. The section required the President of the United States to defer the induction into active service of those whose work in engineering, chemistry, physics, medicine or dentistry was found necessary to the maintenance of the "national health, safety or interest." The representative of the War Department with whom Clark was in almost constant negotiations, Major Lewis B. Hershey, at once opposed the introduction of Section 7(c), but Clark went ahead nevertheless.

How the famous Burke-Wadsworth Bill came into being is a strange story. When Clark and his friends started their agitation for the immediate passage of a draft law, no bill was before Congress. The War Department had its own plans for compulsory service, but those ideas were under official wraps. Neither the Secretary of War, Harry Woodring, nor the Chief of Staff, General George C. Marshall, were ready to push for legislation. The President was not willing to make the proposal of the Military Training Camps Association an administrative measure. Yet he was willing to let a nonpartisan pressure group do what it could to persuade Congress to enact a measure of profound significance for the future of the free world.

The first step had been the drafting of a bill. Then Clark had found two sponsors, Senator Edward Burke of Nebraska and Congressman James Wadsworth of New York. The details of the legislation which was thus formally introduced in the Senate and House on June 20, 1940, were the product of a handful of citizens. That is why my views about the necessity of giving engineers and scientists a special status were incorporated in the bill. As a matter of fact, it was a close thing. The day before Burke and Wadsworth introduced the Military Camps Training Bill, I received the latest draft; I looked in vain for Section 7(c) or its equivalent. I called Clark on the phone at once in great alarm. Once again I repeated my arguments, and to them I added a highly personal one. Relying on an early draft of the bill and my conversation with Clark, I had assured a committee of the American Council on Education two days before that the bill contained adequate provisions for protection against the draft of doctors and scientists, including those who were preparing for those professions. Because of my rather frantic representations, Clark at once reinserted Section 7(c). Therefore the copies which Burke and Wadsworth had in hand conformed to my desires.

I was one of the first witnesses to testify before the Senate committee in favor of the Burke-Wadsworth Bill. Without giving any hint that I knew of the opposition of Major Hershey, I said, "Section 7(c) of the bill provides very wisely, I believe, that military training and service be deferred for men whose work in engineering, chemistry, physics, medicine or dentistry is found to be necessary to the maintenance of 'the national health, safety or interest.' I understand the word 'work' covers not only those now engaged in those professions whose services are deemed essential to the national health, safety or interest but also those in training in our universities and schools for these professions. I think some such provision as this is essential. Not essential, mind you, to protect the universities or the schools, but to protect the country. In an age of mechanized war, it is unnecessary for me to stress the point that many scientists must be kept at their scientific labors if the production of effective instruments of war is to be satisfactorily continued."

I then explained why engineering, chemistry, physics, medicine and dentistry had been singled out, saying, "These are the minimum number of highly trained professions which are essential, absolutely essential for national defense. The first three are essential to the development of instruments of war. The last two are necessary for the maintenance of public health."

My dogmatic statement to the committee about what was essential for national defense reflects what I had just been learning as a member of the NDRC. I had seen only a few days before in the Naval Research Laboratory new methods for locating airplanes and ships, later to be called radar; they seemed to me as a chemist to border on the miraculous. I could already recognize how vital might become the role of physicists in the rearmament task.

George F. Zook, president of the American Council on Education, Dr. Guy E. Snavely, executive officer of the Association of American Colleges, and several university presidents testified in favor of the bill, including Section 7(c). In referring to that section, however, they emphasized the importance of defining the word "work" to include training. It was not scientists as such with whose deferments they were concerned, but the continuity of the educational process. Indeed, President Zook in his testimony stated that "we are clearly of the opinion that any deferment should be clearly selective on a qualitative basis and there should be no deferment of groups on a blanket basis. That, by the way, applies to the status of those deferred people in chemistry, physics, and otherwise, as well as agriculture and industry."

In their testimony before the committee, the Army spokesmen kept making the point that no specific designation of occupational groups in the law was necessary. The needed deferments could be made by regulation. If you once started naming even doctors or dentists, they said, let alone engineers and chemists, there would be no end to the list of occupations for which a good case could be made. I kept hearing the phrase "no blanket deferments." I might have known my case was lost.

Three weeks after I had testified before the Senate committee, Clark telephoned me that the phrase in Section 7(c) in which I was most interested was likely to be deleted by the Senate. I at once notified Dr. Zook by phone and wrote a confirming letter. I expressed my disappointment at the amendment to the bill. I said I still thought Section 7(c) as originally drawn should stand, or, better still, be amended by the insertion of the words "education and training."

I think the case for the special standing of these five professions: physics, chemistry, engineering, medicine and dentistry in the present emergency, can be clearly stated and openly defended. I think we should not shrink from proclaiming that a profession which requires a very long and expensive education is in a class by itself, and that when a large number of members of any such profession are essential to the national defense, then the profession is in a unique position. This point should be written into the Act of Congress dealing with the drafting of manpower for war. Other occupations necessary for defense, such as farming, and many technical employments are demonstrably of a different type *by virtue of the different length of time* and nature of the training.

In retrospect, I do not think my argument about the length of training was a good one. The next paragraph in my letter to Zook made more sense:

I understand that the War Department representatives have assured the sponsors that the aim of the section to which I refer will be accomplished. I have no doubt of the desire of the War Department to keep the men referred to in Section 7(c) out of combat units. I am wondering, however, whether there will not be a great temptation as the months go by for those officers in charge of these matters to promulgate rules and interpret regulations so that a similar but not the same aim as Section 7(c) will be accomplished. This similar aim to which I refer is the enrollment of men irrespective of their education or training or work in physics, chemistry, engineering, medicine or dentistry and *then their assignment to a university to complete their training* or to a research laboratory to continue their work. This similar aim might well appear to the military as being identical with the intent of Section 7(c) as written. *But in fact, it is very different and this difference is vital to our universities and to the country.*

I went on to say that, while both methods could serve to keep men in training for essential professions, one left the men under civilian control and the other put them under military control. "I trust you and your committee," I wrote,

will hammer on this point continually either while the bill is before Congress or, if Section 7(c) stands amended, before the War Department. My chief reason for hoping Section 7(c) will emerge unamended by the House and eventually by the Congress is that it cannot then be changed without due notice and a public hearing. As a War Department regulation it will be easy and natural, as complications increase, for such a regulation to be altered.

I admitted that at present nobody in the War Department wished to put men in uniform and then assign them to our medical, engineering and scientific schools for study. I expressed the worry that we might slide later into a situation where, by gradual changes in the rules governing the draft, we would end by putting all young men into uniform. "Administrative law has great advantages, and one of these is flexibility," I wrote, "but in the case at issue, it is this very flexibility I fear."

In early September I received a telephone call of distress from Dr. Snavely, Secretary of the Association of American Colleges. It appeared that in anticipation of the passage of the bill, a Civilian Advisory Board headed by Frederick Osborn had been appointed. He had been in touch with the Committee on Education and National Defense of the American Council of Education (of which I was not a member). He informed the educators at the first meeting that there was nothing in the bill that authorized the deferment of students. On transmitting this distressing information to me, Dr. Snavely suggested I might get hold of Representative Wadsworth and have the bill amended by the House before final passage. (The Senate had already acted.) I replied that it was much too late. As I had said in a letter to President Zook on July 27, I felt it necessary to bow out of the discussion of legislation about military service. As a member of the National Defense Research Committee, I could not jeopardize my relations with the armed forces by vigorously opposing the War Department position on draft deferments.

It turned out that I was able to perform a slight service for Zook, Snavely and the others in spite of my withdrawal. On Thursday, September 12, I happened to meet Osborn and told him of my troubles and the concern of educators. He confirmed that what I had heard about his opinion was correct. He did not see how any students could be deferred. I pointed out the possible significance of the words "or whose activities in other endeavors," which occurred in the section authorizing the President to provide for deferment. What would be the point of the inclusion of this phrase unless it was intended to cover education? Employment had already been covered by other phraseology. Mr. Osborn was inclined to agree with me. He reversed himself with the committee of educators and agreed that the law did authorize student deferment. All subsequent deferment of students under Selective Service in World War II, and later right down to the present day, turns on the interpretation of a half-dozen words which was suggested in our conversation.

In the debate over the Burke-Wadsworth Bill in the summer of 1940, the matters I have just mentioned were of relatively little significance. The basic issue was whether a draft law should be passed in peacetime. Those who were in favor had one view about the international situation created by the military success of Hitler's armies; those who were opposed had another. What I wish to emphasize is that a discussion of a measure affecting the liability of young men for military service may be fundamentally a debate about foreign policy. So it was in the summer of 1940 and again in 1941; so it is as I write these words in 1969. When public opinion is unanimous as to basic aims of American policy, as it was after Pearl Harbor, it becomes possible to handle even complicated details of conscription without a public turmoil.

The leaders of the Military Training Camps Association, while unable to obtain the endorsement of President Roosevelt for their measure in a presidential election year, did succeed in having Henry L. Stimson appointed as Secretary of War and Robert Patterson as Assistant Secretary of War in June 1940. Stimson accepted the position only on condition he could continue to support the efforts of his friends in the Training Camps Association. Therefore the official position of the President was at least not one of hostility to the measure. The candidate of the Republican Party, Wendell Willkie, was not opposed. Thus the bill was essentially a nonpartisan measure. The law as enacted in 1940 was due to expire in twelve months unless Congress decided on a continuation. A year later when its renewal was before Congress, the nation was still deeply divided. The isolationist sentiment against an extension was so strong that strenuous efforts of Stimson and leaders of both parties were necessary for the passage. The margin was a single vote in the House of Representatives.

In a long memorandum dated November 17, 1940, I reviewed the fate of Section 7(c) of the Burke-Wadsworth Bill. In the concluding paragraphs, I admitted that from the point of view of simplicity of operation the War Department might be well advised to provide for the induction into the Army of all men physically able and without dependents. I suggested that the Department might prefer to have chemists, doctors, dentists and research workers drafted and then reassigned in uniform to whatever tasks the Army saw fit. The fear had been repeatedly expressed in the past months that what I had been advocating was "class legislation"; it favored the rich and discriminated against the poor boy who could not afford to go to college. Actually, the Selective Service law might be designated inverse class legislation, I maintained, because "there is less likelihood that the university-trained man vital for defense in a civilian capacity will be kept out of the Army than a manual worker."

The last sentence now seems to me an extremely poor argument. The memorandum closes where I should have begun in May.

Another and better approach to the whole problem is that of the British. I personally hope this will be given serious consideration during the next session of Congress. I hope that educators and scientists can agree on the minimum number of professions in which there is such a shortage of men that it is imperative to have the practitioner deferred and the advanced student likewise. The British have a list of several thousand "Reserved Occupations." Anyone in these occupations above a specified age cannot even volunteer for the armed services, let alone be drafted. The list is predominantly that of manual workers. There can be no charge of class legislation.

From the records now available, it would appear that neither I nor any of the educators I consulted in the summer of 1940 knew of the British scheme. Or if we did, no mention was made of it. Not until November in the memorandum from which I have been quoting and in yet another letter to Clark (November 20, 1940) do I seem to have been aware of what had been going on in Great Britain. To Clark I wrote:

I am in favor of exploring the British approach. Frankly, they learned a lot from the last war about losing their scientific brains which hasn't been understood in this country either by the military men or by a group like your own. I am sure that very few men appreciate fully the *military* importance of science in modern warfare. I still stick to my guns, in short, though the army and the majority of college presidents are against me. If I had to do it over again, I should insert one more broad category to cover some aspects of the social sciences, but would first try to convert the sponsors of the bill to the British point of view. Then the bill would leave out all idea of a "necessary man" but would direct state and federal authorities to draw up lists of reserved occupations after suitable hearings and assign age limits to those occupations. I admit it would be a difficult task to sell such an idea to the American people.

When I was in England in 1941, I was able to find out how the scheme of "reserved occupations" was working. At the same time, I heard from my academic friends about the University Joint Recruiting Boards. What I learned I put into a lecture which was published in the *Bulletin* of the Association of American Colleges. "In retrospect," I wrote, "it seems clear that the British were wise beyond measure in establishing a list of reserved occupations, carrying through their scheme of enrollment of students under Joint Recruiting Boards, and establishing the Central Register."

The university people with whom I talked in Great Britain, whether scientists or not, were enthusiastic about the way these boards were performing. In each university community a board had jurisdiction over the drafting or enlistment of a university student in a scientific field. After consultation with the appropriate technical committee (e.g., in mathematics or engineering or chemistry), the board told an individual either that he should continue his studies or enter one of the services in a technical capacity, or, if he did not appear to be a "good bet" as a future scientist, that he should enter the armed forces in the ordinary way. In the winter of my visit, the authority of the University Joint Recruiting Boards had been extended. They were starting to pass on applications for deferment of university students (or those about to enter) who showed exceptional promise as potential officers. Such deferments would allow for a year or a year and a half of university study (in any field), but the man in question was obliged to join the Service Training Corps or the University Air Squadron.

The advantage of these boards as a device for keeping potential scientists and engineers out of combat as compared with any Selective Service scheme was clear. In the first place, the man in question had no option. If he was a successful science student, he could not even enlist. His freedom of choice had been taken from him. He hardly needed to be reminded that this was because his country was at war. The emotional consequence of the home front's being also an active front was something no American then or later could appreciate fully. In the second place, the decision about the science students' future was made by technically competent people. Personal favoritism could hardly enter.

The extension of the jurisdiction of the boards to nonscientists who were potential officer material was another matter; I was not prepared to praise this part of the system. Was a year or two of university study really beneficial to an officer as an officer? Was any scheme by which military officers came almost exclusively from university students satisfactory? Certainly it would not be in the United States.

As I wrote to Judge Patterson, the Under Secretary of War, in commenting on what I had seen in England, "If college men in this country were to be the main source of officer material, I think the social implications would be very bad indeed." I then added to my letter the following suggestion: "If one were to look forward to a five-year plan for a vast army, I believe the government should pick a likely group of boys at the 17th year level from all walks of life, arrange for two or three years of college training for them, and then make officers of them. But until or unless the draft age is lowered, such problems probably do not arise to plague us."

Perhaps I appended the last sentence because I believed the draft age should be lowered; or perhaps I knew that Patterson, like many of us, thought we should already be in the war, which would mean the lowering of the age limit. At all events, shortly after Pearl Harbor the law was amended to permit the drafting of twenty-year-old youths. Before another year was over, the lowering would go still further; eighteen-year-old boys would be called up in ever-increasing numbers. These youngsters, the field commanders maintained, made the best combat soldiers. What education beyond high school, if any, they should receive shortly became the number one question for college presidents.

CHAPTER 25

War Policy for American Colleges

A LITTLE MORE than a week after the news from Pearl Harbor had shocked the country, I attended two meetings in Washington. One had been called by the National Resources Planning Board to discuss the possibility of a manpower budget. The other was a scheduled joint meeting of the Executive Committee and the Problems and Plans Committee of the American Council on Education. In both, a variety of questions were asked, all related to the role of the colleges in time of war.

The units of the Reserve Officer Training Corps in the various colleges had been flourishing and were in full strength in 1941. Should the scheme be expanded? To do so would be one way of recruiting and training officers for a rapidly expanding Army. Since the colleges were compressing their four-year programs into two and a half or three years, it could be argued that placing ROTC units in a great many institutions would be the simplest way of quickly increasing the number of potential officers.

I expressed the view at both meetings that until we knew the needs we could neither plan our educational programs intelligently nor arrange for the deferment from the draft of students and recent graduates. Everyone was in agreement. A mammoth meeting of college presidents was held in Baltimore in early January. We asked the federal government for a comprehensive plan for the utilization of the colleges and universities in the days ahead. Such a plan was needed, the resolution asserted, to maintain "a continuous and adequate supply of men and women trained in technical and professional skills and in leadership to meet both immediate and long-range needs of the United States."

We might just as well have asked for the immediate unconditional surrender of Japan and Germany. Not only was no agency prepared to make the kind of analysis about which we spoke so readily, but the top officials of the Navy and the War Department had no intention of accommodating their plans to any general scheme. The calendar year 1942 was to be a year of confusion in educational circles. Proposals and plans were to be urged on governmental agencies. A committee of the American Council on Education would be appointed to cooperate with the Army and the Navy. Yet when the cards were finally down, it turned out the departments were not interested in the advice of educators.

I was one among many who spent his time and energy in what turned out to be a fruitless operation. Indeed, I was, perhaps, the leading spirit in one particular endeavor. However, I was not alone— I soon found a number of other college presidents who were thinking along similar lines. None of us realized we were beaten before we started. Indeed, we were so stubborn that we bounced back more than once when we were repulsed. The developments were not as simple, of course, as this capsule summary may indicate. The Washington jungle grew more tangled and dense as the months of 1942 went by. New vistas of hope seemed to open just as it became clearer and clearer that the demands of the fighting forces for very young men were threatening the enrollments of the colleges.

The final denouement was postponed until February 1944. Secretary Stimson records that at that time he had a choice of either abandoning the use of the colleges as training institutions for officers (the Army Specialized Training Program) or losing ten divisions from the forces that were necessary for the summer. The summer campaign, of course, was the invasion of France. Faced with such alternatives, the Secretary of War in fact had no choice. What all of us educators slowly came to realize was that essentially all the able-bodied youth of several age groups had to be mobilized for combat.

The eventual size and composition of our fighting forces (in terms of age) was something I doubt if any of us visualized as we argued and argued in the winter and spring of 1942. I doubt if anyone, even the President, the Secretary of War or General Marshall, foresaw what the situation would be like in 1944. The uncertainties in the first year of the war were not due to a lack of candor in the authorities concerned but to a lack of prophetic power. No one was wise enough to foresee what decisions would be required. No one could respond to the collective plea of the educators at Baltimore. For some months at least, there was neither a plan for using the colleges nor a clear statement that they might as well close for the duration, though Under Secretary Patterson came close to saying that to me in private conversation in March or April.

The Educational Policies Commission of the National Education Association and the American Association of School Administrators met early in January 1942 to prepare a pamphlet on *A War Policy for American Schools*. At the meeting I made suggestions reflecting my knowledge of the English system, and what I proposed met with favor. By the time of adjournment, we had formulated a policy along the following lines:

1. Approximately 10 percent of each age group from seventeen to nineteen were to be placed in a reserved category. Those so reserved would be able-bodied youth who had either intellectual promise along scientific lines or general ability and leadership or special characteristics likely to make the man a good pilot or flying officer.

2. The men in the reserved category would be under the control of special boards in each state. Each board would have attached to it one or more Army or Navy officers. The board would have power to allocate the men under its control to the armed forces as enlisted men or to schools or colleges for additional training or to an Officer Training Corps or directly for commissions.

3. The further education of those in the reserved category would be paid for fully by the government.

The third item had no counterpart in the British scheme, which otherwise might be regarded as a model; though in arguing for my original suggestion to the members of the EPC, I was careful to avoid emphasizing the success of the British University Joint Recruiting Boards.

In the preparation of my annual report as president of Harvard during the last week in December 1941, I had decided to expose cautiously my thinking about the use of colleges in training officers. I had no way of knowing that my ideas would be picked up, made specific and endorsed by the Educational Policies Commission on January 10. Therefore my proposal was tied to a discussion of the current question of whether the ROTC units should be expanded. In considering the objection that such an expansion would be "class legislation," I admitted it was true, unfortunately, that the college community was drawn largely from the more prosperous upper third of the nation. I raised the question whether, if a large bulk of the future officers were to be drawn from those drafted, the results would not be the building up of the officer corps from one economic group. Of those chosen from the ranks to be officers, would not the vast majority be college men? In order to broaden the base for the selection of officer candidates, I proposed that the most promising boys from all economic groups be selected on graduation from high school; their subsequent education would be at government expense.

In a letter to John J. McCloy, Assistant Secretary of War, a friend of many years, accompanying a marked copy of my report, I expanded the arguments for my proposal. I pointed out that at the present time a large number of capable youth were being drawn off from the age group sixteen to nineteen by the demands of industry. Unless the government watched the situation carefully, many potential officers would be lost to defense industries. Many would be in positions where they could quite properly be deferred from the draft.

In a second letter to McCloy, responding to one of his, I agreed that the Army's proposal to make all candidates for commissions in the future proceed from the ranks to Officer Training Camps was far better than the re-establishment of the Plattsburg Training Camps of 1917. There were military needs, on the other hand, which the Army scheme did not take into account. I mentioned the requirement for a thousand officers trained in electronics to man the new radio-locators. Such men, I said, could be turned out by our colleges in a year or so. Similarly Chemical Warfare Service officers could be specially trained in ROTC units. My scheme provided for the training in our colleges of both the kind of specialist officers I had mentioned and combat officers. The students would be taken into the Army at once as privates just as in the Army proposal.

I then introduced what should have been a telling argument: "Unless the Army takes some long-range plan such as I have suggested and makes it its own, I believe these men will be lost as potential officers. They will be lost in part to the Navy and very largely to industry. All the evidence indicates that the private school boys are headed for the Navy through the V-7 and V-5 programs and all the public school boys are going into industry before they reach the college level." I knew that the Navy through various schemes was already recruiting officers. The possibility of a joint Army and Navy reserve category, I thought, might appeal to the War Department.

I concluded with a paragraph in which I noted that my scheme had the advantage that it would utilize the colleges. I predicted that since some of the smaller colleges were going to be "up against it during the coming period," the War Department would hear a good deal more from the college presidents.

The prediction was, in fact, correct. My proposal met with a certain degree of favor among educators just because it did show a way in which essentially all the colleges could participate. My own worries were not at all about the Harvard enrollment. We had been asked to provide quarters for a number of specialized Army and Navy schools. Our dormitories and classrooms were certain to be filled; many of our professors were applying for leaves of absence in order to take commissions or enter war work as civilians. Harvard foresaw no acute budgetary problems. Most institutions had not been so fortunate. The presidents looked forward with dismay to the academic year 1942–43, when there might be little income from student fees.

I felt I had a certain obligation to present the case of these colleagues of mine since I had accepted the position of vice president of the Association of American Colleges and membership in the Problems and Plans Committee of the American Council. If I were not willing to support the legitimate claims of the institutions of higher education, I should resign from both positions. I did not do so. On the contrary, I began to be more and more involved in the search for ways by which the colleges could fulfill an important function in the mobilization of youth for war.

At the end of March, I decided to write directly to the President of the United States. I was emboldened to do so, I don't doubt, by Grenville Clark. He had declared in a memorandum to the President that my suggested scheme had great merit and should have consideration as an important segment of the major plan for the inventory and use of our manpower (on which Clark was working). In my letter to Roosevelt, I proposed that fifty thousand of each year's secondary school graduates be selected by special civilian boards in each state for induction into a Selected Officers and Specialists Training Corps. The government was to guarantee a year and a half of college education, all expenses paid. The allocation among the colleges might be on a quota basis, following as far as possible the student's preference. A national commander and staff should determine the further education of each member and the allocation to the different services.

My letter to the President emphasized the significance of full government subsidy of the men selected. Equality of opportunity, I said, was not yet a reality in the United States. Accidental factors, both economic and geographical, played far too large a role in determining who went to college; what I was suggesting was a wider base from which to select officers. The choice of young men on graduation from school irrespective of their financial resources would to some degree mitigate the inequality in our present system.

I also included an argument about which I was beginning to feel most keenly. Was it not unfair in time of war to ask a college student to make his own decision as to how he should best serve his country? What might be involved was a question of life and death; few high-spirited boys who realize the peril of their country would freely elect the safer course by staying in a university; yet we needed certain types of men with special talents developed through education. Shouldn't the promising youth be put under orders for further training so that their abilities could be used in the war effort?

The President did not answer for a month. I learned through Walter Lippmann, with whom I had been in correspondence, that Secretary Stimson was opposed. When the reply came over the President's signature, it set forth the policy already adopted by the Army and Navy, which was soon to be announced. An Enlisted Reserve Corps for the Army, with V-1, V-5 and V-7 volunteer programs for the Navy, provided education at the college level. It was expected that 160,000 physically fit freshmen a year would enlist in these college programs. Of these, some seventy thousand would go on to active duty. Those who could not meet the physical standards would be able to continue advanced studies. The President admitted that the system did not provide for those with good brains and no financial resources. However, he said, my scheme was too expensive. Furthermore, the subsidization of a certain group of students might cause resentment.

On reading the President's reply, I knew that I had failed. The essence of my idea was before the public through the publication of the Educational Policies Commission pamphlet. College presidents were well aware of the scheme through the American Council. I did not, however, broadcast the fact that I had placed my case before the President. Therefore I could not reveal his reply—which was, perhaps, a pity. The educators were demanding a national plan—an answer to the repeated request for information about what was to be the role of the colleges (if any). I was certain the scheme for a joint Army-Navy-civilian-scientist training corps was dead. There was no use in attempting to challenge the word of the President of the United

States even if I felt sure it represented not his own reaction but that of Army and Navy officers.

I suspected that one reason for the rejection was the suggested merger of the plans of the Army, the Navy and the Air Force. The Navy had been doing very well enlisting able young men in their college program (V-1). I could imagine that the admirals would refuse to abandon a line of procedure which worked well from their point of view, although it was draining off the best future officers of the Army. What Mr. Stimson subsequently wrote about this rivalry in his book, *On Active Service in Peace and War*,* indicates that my suspicions in 1942 were essentially correct.

As I talked over the defeat with some of my college president friends, a new idea emerged. Granted the Army and Navy would each have their own different college programs, why could not my original goal of broadening the base of selection be reached by another method? Why not urge Congress to establish fifty thousand "Military Studentships" to be awarded to needy students enrolled under the Navy V-1, the Army Aviation Cadet Corps and the Army Enlisted Reserve Corps? I have no recollection of just when, where and how the studentship proposal originated. The documents now available show that I incorporated it in a speech I gave in May which was later published in the *Atlantic Monthly*. The manuscript I sent to Harvey Bundy, Mr. Stimson's confidential secretary. Because Vannevar Bush and I had been having many talks with Bundy about scientific problems, he had become my channel of communication to the War Department.

I discussed the ideas in a letter to President Robert G. Sproul of the University of California on May 28, 1942:

I am writing you about some of the ideas we talked about when you were here. My scheme for a training corps recruited from the best high school graduates and combining Army, Navy and scientists was *not* accepted by the Army and Navy. As you know, they have put in their own rather vague schemes. One trouble with them is that they are going to miss a lot of good material, particularly in some areas. I have now fallen back on a second line of defense—namely, a scheme of military studentships or scholarships financed by the federal government but distributed locally. Walter Lippmann and Grenville Clark have urged me to go ahead and formulate this scheme, and try to get the Army and Navy to give at least a silent blessing, and then seek Congressional action. We are forming a small committee to draft a bill. [President E. E.] Day of Cornell has

* New York, Harper & Brothers, 1948.

agreed to act as chairman. King of Amherst and Gaines of Washington and Lee are joining. We should like to have you one of the number. I am having my assistant, Mr. A. C. Smith, send you the material anyway. All this is, of course, very confidential for the time being. Later we may come out in the open.

Similar letters went to the other college presidents whom Day and I were bringing into our conspiracy. A little later each received a copy of the first draft of a proposed bill which had been prepared by Calvert Smith with the help of a couple of Harvard Law School professors. An accompanying memorandum explained the purpose of the bill, section by section. The aim was to provide college education at government expense for needy students "of special worth and promise" who wanted to enlist in the Navy or Army or Air Force programs. There were similarities to my first proposal; fifty thousand able-bodied young men were to be chosen by a national board acting through state boards; the holders of the studentships were to be assigned by the national board on a quota basis to colleges, "having due regard for a student's preference." The difference was that no joint Army and Navy corps was involved; the program of study was to be determined from the outset by the Army or Navy or Air Force for each holder of the studentship just as for those who were paying their way and had joined either the Navy V-1 program or the Army Enlisted Corps.

President Day, as chairman of the informal group, and Calvert Smith, as secretary, worked hard during the month of June. For a short time it looked as if this bold, private undertaking might succeed. But on July 1 Smith wrote to the eight college presidents involved a letter which amounted to a confession of defeat. He reported that all the members of the group had agreed to support the general purposes of a bill if one was introduced into Congress. However, the War Manpower Commission had entered the picture. President Edward C. Elliott of Purdue, who had become in late April the educational adviser to the Commission, was becoming active. His position made him the key governmental figure. The proposed bill was in his hands. It was being considered along with other proposals. Smith's letter concluded with the statement that "in view of the negotiations now going on between the various departments of the government and also of the reluctance under the circumstances of the Army and Navy to give approval to the studentship plan, it has been decided wise not to go further for the time being in the direction of securing Congressional sponsorship."

What is strange to me as I now write is the absence of any trace in my memory of what must have been a keen disappointment. I can only conclude that, once I had interested Day in the proposal and left to him and Smith its formulation, I became absorbed in the ever-increasing claims of OSRD.

But I do recall with painful vividness even now my own and my friends' increasing involvement in the potential tragedy of war. The atmosphere was entirely different in the fall of 1942 from what it had been a year earlier. On all sides, one met people whose sons or nephews were in uniform; many were expected before long to be in combat. Our own son Jim was preparing in an ROTC unit at the University of Michigan to be a naval officer. (He later volunteered for the submarine service.) Even before the casualty lists had begun to lengthen, I was conscious of what countless families were soon to suffer. As president of Harvard I had undertaken to write a short personal note to the parents of Harvard graduates who had been killed in action.

Talk about deferring young men from the draft now had emotional overtones. The risk of death in battle could hardly be balanced against the nation's need for scientists. I found my annoyance with draft boards shifting to an annoyance with my chemical friends who thought all undergraduate majors in chemistry should be deferred.

Word of my changed attitude eventually got back to Charles L. Parsons, the secretary of the American Chemical Society, whom I had known for twenty years or more. About Christmastime (1942), he wrote inquiring whether it was true that my point of view had altered. I replied at length. My opinion about the necessity of deferring trained chemists had not changed, I said. Where he and I disagreed was about young men now in college. I expressed the opinion in my letter that "when the casualty lists begin to come in, I think there will be a justified reaction of public indignation against any wholesale deferment of students."

I also raised the question of whether there was a real shortage of chemists for war work. (I knew there was of physicists.) I suggested an impartial examination of the distribution of chemists among industries and research establishments. I had reason to believe many were occupied in activities not essential in time of war. If war work was suffering, then the government should try to remedy the situation by a distribution of trained men. I was not singling out chemists. I had been urging for a year that a manpower survey be made of each vocation and profession. (I might have added that such an inquiry had been asked by a conference of one thousand educators a month after war had come.) I could not resist the temptation to remind Dr. Parsons that he had not supported my efforts eighteen months earlier.

Referring to the fate of Section 7(c) in the Burke-Wadsworth Bill, I wrote: "I am sure if we had gone down the road of restricting the number of essential occupations to the very few then named, we would not have ended in the position of lumping together physicists and chemists obviously vital to modern war with architects, economists, osteopaths, psychologists and others, the essential need for whom is to say the least obscure." (I was referring to the guidelines being sent to local draft boards, which had become more and more inclusive as one pressure group after another had come into action.)

Whether the chemists could rightfully charge me with inconsistency is, perhaps, a question, but certainly my concern had shifted. I was no longer worrying about keeping some kinds of students in college; I was disturbed by the possibility that far too many would be thus protected. I had warned Bundy early in the year that the Army Enlisted Reserve might come to be regarded as a gigantic draft-dodging scheme. The War Department soon came to the same conclusion. Before 1942 was over it was announced that all members of the Enlisted Reserve would be called to active service as soon as they reached draft age. I was in no mood to quarrel with this decision, though I was still ready to suggest ways in which the collegiate resources of the country might be used by the Army.

In an address prepared for delivery at the inauguration in September 1942 of Everett N. Case as president of Colgate University, I had undertaken to discuss "The Role of a Liberal Arts College in a Total War." (A highly secret meeting in California of the committee in charge of atomic energy research prevented my being present at the ceremonies.) I referred to a statement made by the War Manpower Commission a few weeks before that "all able-bodied male students are destined for the armed forces." I assumed everyone accepted the principle. Therefore no thoughtful person connected with higher education would wish to see the colleges transformed into institutions where able-bodied young men were exempted from playing an active part in the gigantic struggle. I predicted that as the country became more and more actively engaged in the conflict, the climate of opinion would not tolerate any scheme by which able-bodied young men, of their own free will, were deferred from active military duty. I suggested that the government might have to order some young men with special talents (obviously I had scientists in mind) to positions which involved no combat duty. But if this was done, I felt it should be arranged so that the men thus singled out could not be accused of having voluntarily avoided the risk of war.

On the more positive side, I expressed the view that a limited number of promising high school graduates might be given a short period of academic work in our liberal arts colleges for the purpose of providing a basis on which selection for specialized training could be made. A nine months' college course in mathematics, physics, chemistry, English and American history would suffice. What I envisaged was certainly not the essence of a liberal education. Until the days of peace returned, the colleges would have to nourish the liberal arts tradition as best they could. "For the moment, the exigencies of war require that the liberal arts colleges take on a special and peculiar role. We must hold in suspense—hold in suspense, not give up—many of our educational ideals and our cultural goals. To the extent that we make the sacrifices now required, we shall hasten the day when we can once again return to our true mission."

One of my friends who read the Colgate address wrote to disagree. He argued the case for setting up in the colleges groups of exceptional young men to study the social sciences and the humanities in preparation for solving postwar problems. I replied that if he was thinking of students who were not physically fit (Class 4F), then I was ready to agree. But if he had in mind, as I thought he did, able-bodied youth, then I had three questions to put to him:

1. Would you yourself want to be one of these men?
2. Would you want your son to be one of these men?
3. Do you believe that such a group of young men who had stayed at their academic studies during the war would be in a position to exercise leadership in a postwar world full of returned veterans?

It seemed to me that the answers to these questions were emphatically "No." Nevertheless, I granted that ten thousand men, more or less, in the armed services would not affect the winning of the war.

I expressed much the same sentiments in my talk to Harvard students at the beginning of the new academic year in October. The government, I suggested, might well have to hold some in college or university for special training as engineers or medical men or Signal Corps officers, but the orders must clearly come from the government. If by next spring our forces were actively engaged on many fronts, no physically able young man would wish to be placed in a position of having consciously avoided the risk of war. I think these words spoken in Cambridge in the fall of 1942 were my last contribution to the public discussion of the use of the colleges in wartime.

On January 10, 1943, we at Harvard acknowledged the closing of the normal functioning of the college by holding a Valedictory Service in the Memorial Church. It was a service we announced of "farewell and Godspeed for some fifteen hundred undergraduates about to enter the armed forces of the United States." Many of those present had completed the requirements for the bachelor's degree but could not wait to participate in the commencement ceremony of awarding degrees in June; others were interrupting their college course. It fell to me as president of the university to make the address. It was no easy assignment. I thought of the occasion as one in which the university saluted all who were leaving Harvard to serve the nation in an hour of need. The realization that some of those to whom we were saying good-bye would never return was never far distant from the center of our thoughts. Quite unashamedly I invoked the past. I concluded as follows:

Formal education for the present you leave aside, but you will grow in wisdom nonetheless. New knowledge will come to you by virtue of the sacrifices that you will be asked to make. Having been ready to run all risks for freedom, you will comprehend it as those of us at home cannot. On some subsequent commencement day you will return with the understanding born of great events. On that occasion it will be said of you as of returning Harvard soldiers in 1865:

> Today our Reverend Mother welcomes back
> Her wisest scholars, those who understood . . .
> Many loved Truth, and lavished life's best oil
> Amid the dust of books to find her. . . .
> But these, our brothers, fought for her. . . .

Gentlemen, with anxious pride, Harvard awaits the day of your return.

As I relive twenty-six years later that valedictory service and see that church full of young men standing before me, emotions of pride and sorrow well up once again.

CHAPTER 26

The Debate over Universal Military Training in Peacetime

MY THIRD ENTANGLEMENT in the briars of military training was a consequence of my continued membership on the Problems and Plans Committee of the American Council on Education. In late February 1944, President W. H. Cowley of Colgate, Francis J. Brown from the office of the American Council on Education and I called on President Roosevelt in his office to urge the inclusion of seventeen-year-old boys in the Army Specialized Training Program. The Army and Navy had been out of step ever since the ASTP and the V-12 programs had gone into effect almost a year earlier. The Navy was accepting volunteers below eighteen; the Army was waiting until a youth was eighteen. The issue did not seem to me of vital importance, but I went along to accommodate Cowley.

The three of us soon discovered that the President was not interested in the point we were making. Rather, he said that as long as we were in his office he would like to get our opinion on a subject he had been considering for some time. He wondered what we would think of an act establishing a compulsory national service system. When the fighting was over, the government would have many empty camps on its hands. They would be excellent for housing those who would devote a year to national service. He had long thought a year of training was a good thing for every boy whether or not he met the physical standards for a combat soldier.

We were somewhat taken aback by President Roosevelt's unexpected and eloquent presentation of his case. We knew that bills providing for one year of universal military training had been before Congress for some time and the President was on record in favor of such a measure. I also knew that some members of the Training Camps Association had for years been advocating legislation to send all boys to training camps for a year. We had never discussed the subject in the Problems and Plans Committee. Cowley and Brown had no way of knowing my views. They may well have thought that I was among the proponents of universal military training. I feel sure the President did.

Actually, my immediate reaction was negative. I was certain that on educational grounds most of our colleagues on the committees of the American Council would be against any such scheme. Therefore, I mildly expressed my doubts and reservations, particularly about debating the issue while the war was going on. After a short discussion, President Cowley asked the President if he would like a memorandum from the Problems and Plans Committee of the American Council on Education. The President said he would very much like to have such a memorandum, and we left with our original mission completely unfulfilled.

Fortunately, I received a communication from the President a week or so later which gave me a chance to reaffirm in writing the doubts I had felt impelled to express in conversation. The President forwarded to me for comment a letter which had been sent to Mrs. Roosevelt from a sergeant in the Quartermaster Corps. The sergeant proposed universal compulsory training and service for one year; he also included a new scheme for recruiting and educating Army officers which seemed to imply the abolishment of West Point.

I suggested in my reply to President Roosevelt that the sergeant's suggestion seemed a bit impractical. Turning to what the President himself had outlined to us in our talk, I reaffirmed my doubts. I went so far as to hope he would not recommend that a law on this subject be passed while the war was still in progress and added that I was not convinced that a year of national service would be in the best interests of the country. If it should develop after the war was over that a year of compulsory military training was necessary for national defense, then I was prepared to support such a proposal. It seemed impossible now to debate this subject intelligently in view of the uncertainties in both the international and military situations. I felt it unnecessary even to hint that I was thinking about the Manhattan District Project. President Roosevelt would read between the lines easily enough.

Cowley, true to his promise, reported on the White House visit to a joint meeting of the Problems and Plans Committee and the Educational Policies Commission. The proposition to turn over for a year to the federal government the education of all male youths was like a call to battle to the assembled educators. Many of us were veterans of the arguments about the National Youth Administration and the Civilian Conservation Corps in the 1930s. The New Dealers had never understood the problems of the public schools. For the most part, from Justice Frankfurter and Harry Hopkins down to those in the lower echelons, they had shown little sympathy with the causes the National Education Association had sponsored. Certainly the leaders in the Training Camps Association, who were almost without exception private school alumni, could not be expected to value highly the merits of the American high school. Now we had to contend with an alliance which wielded two arguments, one educational, the other military. The discussion in the joint session was completely one-sided, centering on how best to formulate our objections to the passage of a measure authorizing a year of compulsory universal military training.

The memorandum was sent to the President, but the American Council on Education did not even receive an acknowledgment. We obviously had not reacted as the President had hoped. In August he proposed in a press conference that the American people should start debating universal military training. Mrs. Roosevelt contributed her bit by advocating a national service including women. The American Legion started a campaign to arouse public opinion on behalf of military training as an educational measure. In January 1945 the President in his State of the Union message called for the establishment of universal military training as an "essential factor in the maintenance of peace in the future."

It had been clear ever since the discussion of Cowley's report to the Problems and Plans Committee that almost all my educational friends were opposed to the enactment of a universal military training law while the war was in progress. It was equally clear that those who were urging such legislation believed their one chance of success turned on having Congress act before the fighting ceased. My own reason for opposing action was special, since I was privy to a secret that I could share with no one.

By mid-1943 the time schedule for completion of the first atomic bomb had been laid out. I added six months to the calculations to correct for overoptimism on the part of the scientists and concluded in my own mind that we would certainly have a bomb by Christmas

1945. That the bomb would revolutionize warfare was a premise among the few of us who were concerned with all phases of its development. If without any knowledge of the new weapon, a universal military training law was passed, it seemed to me inevitable that there would be a public outcry when the existence of the revolution in warfare became known. Would not the public and, indeed, the Congress itself feel that a vital element in the national defense—military training—had been determined under fraudulent conditions? Such was my deeply held conviction. But I could not mention my basic argument to anyone concerned with military training.

There were plenty of educators who were strongly against the President's proposal. Some of them who were against it on educational grounds felt that a year of compulsory service was so obnoxious that they would oppose a military training bill whatever the postwar situation. Others, like myself, were willing to keep an open mind about the military needs after the war was over but objected to the emotional drive to commit the nation to a course of action during a war.

President Donald B. Tresidder of Stanford, I discovered, felt strongly on this point. He and E. E. Day and I were the prime movers in writing a public letter to President Roosevelt in answer to his State of the Union message. The signers included the presidents of Stanford, Cornell, Harvard, Princeton, Tulane, Chicago, Missouri, Kansas, California, Indiana and Brown. The letter declared that "we challenge the necessity of urging the American people to act under the tension of war psychology in order to bring them to a decision which, it is said, they would not reach under normal conditions."

Our letter stirred up a storm, as we expected. The fraternity of college presidents was split wide open. Within a matter of weeks, fourteen presidents published an open letter in which they declared that the country was better able at this moment to make a wise decision on this important matter than it would be after the war was over, when we should be lulled by a sense of false security. Those who signed this letter included the presidents of Rutgers, the Massachusetts Institute of Technology, Johns Hopkins, Amherst, Yale, Northwestern and Pennsylvania.

A large number of my friends and acquaintances were astonished to find my name with those who were in opposition rather than among the fourteen who were in favor of legislation at once. More than one alumnus who had agreed with me in the days of the William Allen White Committee and the Selective Service Act wrote in puzzlement. How could I now be in opposition to a measure to insure a strong United States? My reply is illustrated by the following excerpts from a letter to a prominent Chicago Harvard man:

I am afraid the Chicago papers must have garbled the statement which I signed together with eleven other university presidents. I am therefore sending you the complete version. You will see that the proposition is directed not to the merits of compulsory peacetime military training, but to the question of when the subject should be debated in the country and how it should be considered.

There are usually two sets of arguments used by the proponents of immediate action: First, that compulsory military training is a "good thing" for American youth—with which, as head of a college, I slightly disagree. To my mind the expenditure of a billion dollars a year for the establishment of a federal system of education through military camps would be a great mistake and would do more harm than good. The second reason usually given in favor of immediate action is that military necessity requires it. Here I have an open mind as to the future, but am opposed to a discussion of the subject and action by Congress while the war is on. I feel that to enact a law for compulsory military training in peacetime first, and consider the other tremendous problems of national defense later, is to back into the defense program.

It would seem to me more logical for the Army and the Navy to sit down and digest the strategic and tactical lessons of the present war, outline a proposed system of defense of the country in terms of modern weapons and the men necessary to man them, and then see what the manpower, military and naval situation would be. If when such a total plan is evolved, it is clear that there is no way to man an effective national defense program except through compulsory military training in peacetime, then I am for it.

As I wrote to Tresidder in February of 1945, the proponents of a universal military training act seemed to be sweeping all before them. Public opinion polls indicated 70 percent of the electorate in favor of the measure. The same month, the House passed a national service bill and a few weeks later the Senate passed another and weaker version. Just before President Roosevelt's death, the Senate rejected the compromise bill and the issue was dead for the time being. In President Truman, however, the advocates of military training found at least as ardent a supporter as the late President. In his message to Congress in September, he announced he would soon have specific recommendations about military service. On

October 23 he delivered a message in which he urged Congress to enact a measure which would require all able-bodied young men to spend one year in military training upon graduation from high school or at age eighteen and then spend six years in a general reserve.

The war was over; the atomic bomb was no longer a secret. The prime reason for my unwillingness to endorse universal military training had disappeared. Nevertheless, I was not prepared to desert my friends who had been in opposition for so long without being moderately sure the role of atomic warfare had been taken into account by the military planners. Furthermore, the War Department faced real difficulty in continuing to keep an army of some sort in being. We had demobilized fast enough. Indeed, by November many were asking whether we had not been too precipitate in "getting the boys home." But it was not fair to ask those who had been through combat to stay as occupation troops, and parents were protesting against the continuation of Selective Service now that Germany and Japan had been defeated. What was to be done?

The advent of the bomb had had the expected effect on public opinion. The need for a large conventional army seemed to have disappeared. All of us who had been doubtful of universal service as an educational measure indulged in some wishful thinking during the weeks that followed Hiroshima. For example, in a letter to George F. Zook on August 25, I wrote: "I am inclined to think the atomic bomb blew up most of what was left of the force behind compulsory military training." I then went on to say that we still had a problem which deeply concerned all of us in higher education. How were we going to provide for our armies of occupation during the next two years? In this letter I was inclined toward the abolition of Selective Service. A professional army on a volunteer basis with much higher rates of pay might do the job.

The Problems and Plans Committee at a meeting in early September thrashed over many suggestions, including that of abolishing Selective Service. A committee of the American Council drew up a statement urging the President to appoint a commission to study the whole problem of national defense in view of the changed technical situation resulting from the atomic bomb. More discussions and more correspondence followed. Extracts from a letter I wrote to the Commander of the American Legion in October will show how the minds of many of us were turning over the old questions in a brand-new setting:

I am very glad indeed to answer your inquiry about my present stand in regard to the question of universal military training. One of the reasons why I joined with the others in urging postponement of this issue was my knowledge of the work on the atomic bomb. This reason, of course, I could not share with anyone. I felt sure, however, that this weapon would prove to be revolutionary in its effect on the art of war, and I believe it has, in fact. To my mind universal military training is now an obsolete question. What is needed is the appointment of an impartial board to examine carefully the plans for our national defense, which should include the most drastic overhauling of our Army and Navy, as well as a consideration of the dispersion of our industry. When that is done, we can see what is needed in the way of manpower and training.

Opinion among those college presidents who opposed hasty action on universal service crystallized rapidly in November. First we made public a statement signed by thirty-four college presidents. Then I testified before the Military Affairs Committee on November 20, 1945, on behalf of those who had issued the statement. What we advocated was:

1. The extension of existing Selective Service on a year-to-year basis, with an amendment limiting the period of military service of draftees to fifteen months.

2. The vigorous promotion of a new program of voluntary enlistment in the Army, with special emphasis on adequate pay, attractive retirement options and opportunities for vocational and other training.

3. The appointment of a special national defense commission to study in detail the problems of national defense and bring forward a comprehensive plan for our future military establishments and consider also such closely related matters as dispersal of industry, stockpiling of strategic materials and scientific research and developments.

4. The postponement of a decision on universal military training until such a commission had made its study and rendered its report.

The last sentence of the public statement, which I repeated in my testimony, was a firm pledge with no escape clause. We said: "If after thorough study, such a commission finds universal military training an indispensable part of our long-range national defense program, we would support it."

In December 1946 President Truman named a committee to study the feasibility of universal military training. It was an excellent body of men headed by Karl T. Compton. I was asked to testify before the committee, and I repeated what I had said in public many times. I was not enthusiastic about universal military training as an educational measure. I did not agree with those who said a year in camp would be a "good thing" for all youth. I was worried about the military planning for the future. I had questions about the function of ground forces in a future war. On the basis of the information now at my disposal, I would vote against universal military service if I were a member of the committee. I told the committee I had great confidence in them, and if they decided unanimously to favor universal military training as a defense measure, I would support them.

The Compton Committee, reporting in May 1947, did unanimously recommend universal military training. I kept my promise promptly and publicly supported the committee's recommendations. Furthermore, as a consequence of the request of a friend who was organizing a citizens' committee in favor of the Compton report, I joined with Day of Cornell and Tresidder of Stanford, who, like myself, had opposed universal military training, in signing a statement urging the passage of the necessary legislation to put the Compton proposals into effect. So once again I had shifted my posture, although I thought I had good reason for my long vacillation and my eventual shift. I was certain I had the excellent company of some other college presidents during the whole lengthy journey.

In spite of the Compton report and the labors of many, the bill authorizing universal military training was defeated. In the meantime, the Selective Service Act of 1940 as amended had been allowed to expire on March 31, 1947. For some months the United States was without legislation for building an army until events in Prague and the impending Berlin blockade demonstrated how dangerous was the postwar situation. Some of us began speaking about "the divided world in an atomic age."

Congress re-enacted a Selective Service Law, responding to the mood of the nation as the Soviet Union blockaded Berlin. President Truman signed it on June 24, 1948. Again there was no time for a careful consideration of this mechanism for raising armed forces. With Selective Service once again the law of the land, all the old questions about deferring students came up again. Once again Day and I and other like-minded college presidents were worried about colleges becoming draft-dodging institutions. We urged our friends to oppose blanket deferment of students. We felt all young men eighteen to twenty-two should be obliged to serve, although the age group was too large. The Army couldn't handle all males who became eighteen years of age in any one year. I suggested that the fair way of settling who should serve would be drawing of lots. In my annual president's report for 1948 (written in early January 1949), I wrote:

Concern is now being expressed lest the flow of well-trained professional men be interrupted by the drafting of promising college students for twenty-one months' service. Therefore, the suggestion has been made that all students preparing for certain professions such as medicine, dentistry, chemistry, physics and engineering be exempt. This has received relatively little support, however. For it is argued that while the members of these professions have special significance for waging a modern war (or preparing for one), it is equally important for the future of the nation to educate able young men for leadership in other professions including the management of industry. Those who favor some type of deferment for college students are therefore turning to a distinction based on aptitude for college studies without regard for the nature of the college work. For example, all those who make better than a certain score on some nation-wide aptitude examination might be deferred as long as they were in the upper third of their college class.

To my mind the difficulties of administering any such proposal would be great indeed. One hates to think of the responsibility placed on professors and on faculties by any scheme in which academic standing determines who is to spend twenty-one months as a private in a peacetime army and who is not. Under the present law the final decision is in the hands of the local boards, and widespread occupational and educational deferment of young men is bound to lead to charges of unfairness. There is all the difference in the world between passing judgment on whether a man who is already a trained scientist or engineer should be drafted in time of war and trying to identify the potential capabilities of freshmen and sophomores.

The same considerations apply to occupational deferments for those who because of their youth can have acquired only a few years of experience in any position however essential. To my mind, the only fair method of selecting among those who are of college age is by lot. There is a grave danger that all attempts to choose in any other way will lead to charges of favoritism and even corruption. The morale of the younger men of this country could easily be destroyed by what seemed unfair administration of Selective Service. Some may argue that as long as the numbers called are small it matters little who is deferred and who is not. That argument is fallacious, it seems to me. The principles established reflect the spirit with which the country wishes to approach the whole question of military service, and I submit this spirit must be one of scrupulous honesty and fairness. . . .

A strong case can be made, I believe, for distinguishing between youths of college age and older men. The former have not yet either proved their capacity for specialized education or gone far enough down a professional road to be classified as essential for civilian work. With these considerations in mind, the Association of American Universities has publicly recorded its opposition to any occupational or educational deferments for men under twenty-two years of age. To my mind this is a sound position and one that I heartily endorse. If this recommendation of an association of thirty-three of the leading universities, represented by their chief executive officers, is taken seriously, there will be no deferment for younger college students except to complete an academic year as now provided.

If necessary, the present law should be amended to insure a selection by lot of the members of the younger age groups who are to be called up each year. If a new law is passed making military training or military service of some type universal, the particular problem I have been discussing disappears. I am one of those who feel that the present act is in the nature of an unsatisfactory stopgap; but it would require far too much space for me to consider in this report the question of how our army, navy, and air force should be kept up to strength in these days of an armed truce.

My criticism of the Selective Service Law in January 1949 was based on the assumption that the United States was facing a period of relative peace. Those of us who were arguing for the acceptance of the principle of universal liability for service at age eighteen or on graduation from high school did not envisage the possibility that within two years the United States would be again involved in heavy military action. We were thinking of a relatively small Army. To induct all the eighteen-year-olds would be unnecessary and unwise. The problem at that time was how best to build reserves for the possibility of a war. Before the discussion proceeded very far, however, the Korean War began. In June 1950 it looked to many as though it might be the beginning of World War III. At all events, once again the United States was in a crisis which involved the expansion of the armed forces. Once again I became involved in the activity of a group of citizens. We named ourselves "The Committee on the Present Danger." A description of our activities is to be found in a later chapter of this book.

PART IV

_____

THE POSTWAR YEARS

AT HARVARD

CHAPTER 27

_____

The Harvard Report

A FTER PEARL HARBOR and until V-J Day in August 1945, Harvard was primarily a university at war. Before the academic year 1941–1942 was over, a gradual exodus of professors had begun. Some took commissions in the armed forces, some in civilian war agencies; almost without exception, the physical scientists were enrolling in one or another of the government-supported secret laboratories located in various institutions of higher learning. The number of graduate students rapidly diminished. One could foresee that it was only a matter of time before the War Department would complete its plans for calling to arms many if not all the young men of college age. (By 1944 the undergraduate enrollment was only 850 as compared with 3,500 before the war.) Special Army, Navy and Air Force schools had come into existence in many universities in the early months of 1942; Harvard had its share; no less than twelve such training courses, accommodating a total of three thousand men, were soon in operation and would continue in full force until the war ended. Young men in uniform swarmed over the Harvard Yard and into the buildings of the Harvard Graduate School of Business Administration across the river. A total of many thousands of officers were thus trained in Cambridge during the years 1942 to 1945.

In the fall of 1942, as Dean Buck and I contemplated the transformation of the Harvard scene, we wondered what should be the

363

role of the members of the faculty of arts and sciences who remained to carry on instruction in Harvard College. Even with the expected shrinkage in the size of the college classes, there would still be instructional tasks to be performed at the undergraduate level. But important as such teaching would be, it would hardly counterbalance the forces that were rapidly turning Harvard into an institution concerned only with winning the war. We thought particularly of those scholars who would be remaining in Cambridge but would not be connected with the service schools or government research. They could hardly help feeling somewhat isolated from their colleagues who were engrossed in matters affecting directly or indirectly the prosecution of the war.

The idea occurred to us that if the scientists could take time off from their research interests and normal duties to do applied research for the government, why could not a group of professors devote themselves to drawing plans for education in the postwar world? We decided that such a scheme was feasible and found the men who were willing to devote time to it. Dean Buck agreed to serve as chairman; in the spring of 1943 a committee of twelve came into being charged with writing a report on "The Objectives of a General Education in a Free Society." The members were chosen from the faculty of arts and sciences, with the exception of two professors of education whom I appointed because of my interest in furthering cooperation between the Graduate School of Education and those responsible for instruction in Harvard College. Since the committee was to consider general education at both the school and college level, it was clearly of importance to have the point of view of the School of Education represented.

A somewhat unusual feature of the project was a generous expense account. The idea was the result of a conversation I had with Cowley one evening in the old Cosmos Club in Washington. Though we were in agreement in general, there crept into our talk from time to time the difference in point of view between the head of a small college and the president of a university who had once been a chemist. We eyed each other somewhat suspiciously. Cowley said something to the effect that, of course, I wasn't really interested in the liberal arts tradition. At which I flared up and indignantly replied that I had just appointed a university committee to study and report on the subject. "Oh, yes," he said somewhat bitterly, "you appoint a committee, but what does that amount to? Have you done for that committee what you would automatically do for a research project in science, namely, finance the undertaking? Why don't you put up a handsome sum to make it possible for the committee to function properly?" "An excellent idea," said I. And on my return to Cambridge, after checking with Dean Buck, I asked the corporation at the next meeting to grant $60,000. We saw to it the favorable decision was well publicized in the academic community.

Though Dean Buck and I hoped for a document which would present a view of the total American educational scene, we were primarily concerned with a continuing problem in Harvard College. Ever since President Lowell had abolished the free elective system in 1910 and introduced the ideas of concentration and distribution, there had been almost continuous discussion of what courses or group of courses the faculty should require of a candidate for the bachelor's degree. It was generally agreed that a graduate of Harvard College should specialize in one subject and should also have an acquaintance with several fields. What fields? By what specific requirements should the acquaintanceship be assured? These were two questions still not answered satisfactorily after more than twenty-five years of experience. This was the essence of the Harvard problem which the committee set out to solve. Since Dean Buck was himself to be the chairman, I had no fear that this problem would be overlooked.

When I was a professor of chemistry, I had taken no part in consideration of the content of undergraduate instruction either at Harvard or elsewhere. I was aware of the recent introduction of survey courses in certain institutions to provide a student with a broad view of many fields of knowledge. What I heard about these courses was not favorable. Those who claimed to have some knowledge of their operation branded them as superficial. I was far from ready to endorse them, and no one on the Harvard faculty became a proponent of survey courses. There was no serious discussion of such a possibility at any of the meetings of the faculty of arts and sciences council at which revisions of the distribution requirements were debated. Even the term "general education," which was associated in many people's minds with survey courses, was not in favor in Cambridge in the 1930s.

As I read what was being written about undergraduate education and heard the topic discussed at meetings of educators, I evolved my own approach to liberal education. I had ventured to present it as part of the Tercentenary Oration.* I spoke of the

* See Appendix 1.

wave of anti-intellectualism which was passing around the world and the "weariness as we see an ever-increasing wealth of new knowledge poured at our feet by the scholars of the arts and letters no less than by the scientists." I then made a far from novel declaration, that "Intellectual anarchy in our schools and colleges has been more or less rife for the better part of a hundred years." To bring order out of this educational chaos was the mission of the liberal arts curriculum, I suggested, and gave my own specifications as to how this might be done. Speaking of the older classical tradition which had all but disappeared, I expressed the view that we must find its modern equivalent. I then said kind words for the historical approach which I was to advocate for several years. My conviction that a liberal or general education should be based on history provided an opportunity for expressing views about freedom of discussion and "absolutely unmolested inquiry."

My defense of tolerance and free inquiry was widely applauded. My belief in the possibility of finding a cure for our educational chaos by following an historical route found few supporters either in 1936 or thereafter. Indeed, in 1941, I had to report to the Overseers that my efforts at that time to promote the study of American history on an extracurricular basis had failed completely. One forward step had been taken by the publication of a reading list in American history which had been well received. But the hopes of stimulating undergraduates to benefit from this reading list had been disappointing. Six fellows in American history had been appointed annually— one for each house—to guide the reading of students who were interested. Practically no one was, except for some members of the freshman class each year. The scheme was abandoned after a two-year trial. By the time the European war began to color our thinking, I had given up all attempts to promote the study of American history as a basis for a general education.

As I write these words, I find it a painful necessity to admit not only that I retreated decades ago from my advocacy of an understanding of history as an educational basis "for a unified coherent culture suited to a democratic country in a scientific age," but that I have silently thrown overboard my assumption that a unified, coherent culture was possible in a democratic country. Using the word "democracy" in the American and British sense as implying a large degree of individual freedom, I long since became convinced that a pluralistic ideology must be the basis of a democracy.

In June 1939 a committee of the Student Council at Harvard

published a report on education which amounted to a vigorous attack on the requirements for a bachelor's degree. The authors claimed that the concentration and distribution rules and regulations failed to ensure that an undergraduate would obtain "an intelligible and broad view of the main areas of learning." What they advocated was the establishment of five new introductory courses (not survey courses) —two in the natural sciences, two in the humanities and one in the social sciences—which all students should be compelled to take. In commenting on the report in my annual report for 1938–39, I stated that while I was more than a little sympathetic with the criticisms, I was still uncertain as to the details of reform. I raised the question whether "any single program suitable for a heterogeneous group" could be devised.

A year later, I again referred in my annual report to the "interesting comprehensive report of the Student Council" and the current discussion of the undergraduate curriculum among members of the faculty and in the student body. The problem of continuing a general liberal education at the collegiate stage with ample opportunity for specializing in some subject seemed almost insoluble. I reported that "several steps have already been taken to provide wider fields of concentration, and a revision of the distribution requirements is at this moment being considered by the faculty. Since this question is still unsettled, I shall have to postpone until another year a detailed account of the modified Harvard College curriculum which is still being shaped on the anvil of debate." These sentences were written in early January 1941. Before my next annual report was presented, the United States was at war.

In reporting on the new wartime status of the university in January 1942 (annual report for 1940–41), I returned to a consideration of the tradition of the liberal arts college. I did not, however, carry out my promise of a year earlier to report in detail on a "modified Harvard College curriculum." What the dean and I had planned in 1941 had failed. A rather radical proposal developed under the dean's guidance in the Committee on Instruction (a committee of department chairmen) had proved to be unacceptable to the faculty; it had contained too many requirements to suit a majority of the members. Therefore, instead of a new curriculum's being shaped by debate, the attempt at reform had been rejected after a rather stormy session in which the administration came near being accused of having totalitarian tendencies.

In my report for 1941–42, I announced the appointment of the committee headed by Dean Paul Buck which was to consider the whole matter of the general education of the "great majority of each generation—not the comparatively small minority who attend our four-year colleges."

I then presented my own views brought up to date:

The heart of the problem of a general education is the continuance of the liberal and humane tradition. Neither the mere acquisition of information nor the development of special skills and talents can give the broad basis of understanding which is essential if our civilization is to be preserved. No one wishes to disparage the importance of being "well informed." But even a good grounding in mathematics and the physical and biological sciences, combined with an ability to read and write several foreign languages, does not provide a sufficient educational background for citizens of a free nation. For such a program lacks contact with both man's emotional experience as an individual and his practical experience as a gregarious animal. It includes little of what was once known as "the wisdom of the ages," and might nowadays be described as "our cultural pattern." It includes no history, no art, no literature, no philosophy. Unless the educational process includes *at each level of maturity* some continuing contact with those fields in which value judgments are of prime importance, it must fall far short of the ideal. The student in high school, in college and in graduate school must be concerned, in part at least, with the words "right" and "wrong" in both the ethical and the mathematical sense. Unless he feels the import of those general ideas and aspirations which have been a deep moving force in the lives of men, he runs the risk of partial blindness. . . .

The primary concern of American education today is not the development of the appreciation of the "good life" in young gentlemen born to the purple. It is the infusion of the liberal and humane tradition into our entire educational system. Our purpose is to cultivate in the largest possible number of our future citizens an appreciation of both the responsibilities and the benefits which come to them because they are Americans and are free.

I thus recorded my own views about general education. I let it be known, however, that I did not expect to be a party to the committee's deliberation, though like other members of the Harvard faculty I might be called as a witness. The announcement of the appointment of the commitee stated that the inquiry was expected to last for at least two years since it would consist of a "careful survey of the actual situation which confronts a nation committed to universal education at least through the high school years."

Dean Buck kept his committee at work with his eye on completing a manuscript early in 1945. His efforts were successful. The report appeared in book form in the early summer of 1945, after V-E Day and before V-J Day. In the letter of transmittal addressed to me, the committee stated:

Your instructions to the committee were as expansive as its name was long. We were urged to consider the problems of general education in both the school and the college. We were cautioned that the general education of the great majority of each generation in the high schools was vastly more important than that of the comparatively small minority who attend our four-year colleges. . . . In short we were directed not so much to make recommendations for general education in Harvard College as to venture into the vast field of American educational experience in quest of a concept of general education that would have validity for the free society which we cherish.

The letter of transmittal ended with a reference to the statement in my annual report for 1941–42 about the "primary concern of American education today" which I have just quoted. The committee did me the honor of saying that "such a concept of general education is the imperative need of the American educational system. It alone can give cohesion to our efforts and guide the contributions of our youth to the nation's future."

In a sincere and enthusiastic letter to Dean Buck written in June 1945 after I had finished reading the manuscript, I summarized what I thought he and his colleagues had accomplished. "You have," I wrote:

1. Produced a cogent, integrated, *and balanced* conception of education at secondary and college levels in this country.

2. Made it clear that your first concern has been not the welfare of Harvard nor the technicalities of this or that college program, but the great over-all job of making education serve the continuance of a free society on this continent *in the twentieth century*.

3. Acknowledged, therefore, the problem of the high and secondary school as more important from many points of view than that of the college. (To me this is significant to the country, and gives increased confidence and pride that Harvard continues in the vanguard. As Archibald MacLeish said: "Committed to one time and one time only—the future toward which the American Republic moves.")

4. With all the difficulties of a group product, attained through many pages a distinguished level of prose.

The fifth chapter of the report dealt specifically with the curriculum of Harvard College. This portion of the document was debated in the faculty of arts and sciences during the fall of 1945.

On October 30, by a very large majority, the faculty approved the recommendations with a few slight alterations. A new standing committee was authorized with responsibility for recommending from time to time modifications for the scheme, which was adopted on an experimental basis.

An editorial in the *Harvard Alumni Bulletin* in 1951 provided a layman's appraisal of the new departures in undergraduate instruction which were the result of the recommendations in Chapter 5 of the report:

After five years of testing, General Education is an experiment no longer. Beginning with the freshman class this autumn, the new courses become a required part of the curriculum. What this means, in essence, is that the system of concentration and distribution has been refined. Not only will a student be able to gain some mastery in a particular field of learning, but he will also have a chance to sample courses in other major areas and find that his samplings have some unity, order, and meaning. In a sense, therefore, this completes the cycle begun with President Eliot's revolutionary free elective system. The Harvard student now concentrates in a specialty. He also must distribute his interest among other fields of learning. This is where the reform introduced by General Education applies. It is now required of all freshmen and sophomores, beginning with the Class of 1955, to take at least three elementary General Education courses, one in each of three great areas of learning—the Humanities, the Social Sciences, and the Natural Sciences; the student must also include at least three more courses outside his department of concentration in order to satisfy the distribution requirement.

It is unnecessary to detail the rules regarding distribution. The important thing about the General Education program is its leavening effect upon the natural desire of every Harvard student to widen his intellectual horizon at the same time he is specializing. Here the possibilities are exciting and challenging. Consider the Harvard man of a decade ago. If he were concentrating in history, shall we say, he might find that his samplings of other fields would run to unrelated survey courses in philosophy, zoology, psychology, fine arts, music, or even German. Today the freshman can choose from among such courses as "Epic and Novel," taught by a great classicist; "The Ideas of Good and Evil in Western Literature," examined by an historian and a philosopher; an historian's interpretation of "Western Thought and Institutions"; or a physicist's exposition of "The Physical Sciences in a Technical Civilization."

These are ambitious ways to present material which has intellectual meaning. Obviously the subjects cannot be all-inclusive. But the effort has been successful because the program puts a premium upon good teaching and because it applies a sort of case system to the subject matter. These are not the great survey courses of old, depending upon a Merriman for their success. Instead of the once-over-lightly approach, a few crucial thinkers, experimenters, or historical epochs are selected for fairly intensive study. In this way the student begins to comprehend some of the principles of learning and recognize some of the events of history and thought which have had lasting effect upon Western Man.

With the execption of General Education A—the much-discussed substitute for familiar old English A, ancient bane of freshmen—a student will find at least two, and ordinarily four, courses to choose from in each of the three required fields—the Humanities, the Social Sciences, and the Natural Sciences. The experiment with parallel forms of elementary courses has been a great success: The students have an important freedom of choice; teaching methods and organization can be the subject of continued experimentation; and the classes themselves tend to be smaller. General Education has come of age, and it will without doubt continue to flourish, so long as it has good teachers and fresh approaches to the age-old problem of communication between teacher and pupil.

The committee in the course of its labors had called on many persons within and outside the university to come before it as witnesses. On two occasions I appeared. My general approach to many problems was well known to the committee members. Therefore my evidence consisted for the most part in specific answers to their questions. I had suggested to the committee the possibility of a new type of course on "The Advancement of Knowledge in Modern Times." The objective of the course, I said in a subsequent memorandum, would be "to show by examples chosen from a wide variety of fields the methods by which knowledge has been advanced in the last four hundred years. It would be assumed that these methods will be continued in the future and significant answers will be eventually obtained to questions now unanswered." The examples chosen, I wrote, "should be sufficiently simple to involve relatively little previous knowledge of the subject matter . . . they should illustrate the combination of logical analysis, careful observation and experiment and imaginative insight which has characterized the great advances in the past. As a secondary consideration, the examples might well be chosen to correspond to certain decisive periods in the development of the various disciplines."

At that time, I was making much of the distinction between "accumulative knowledge" and "disciplined and informed value judgments." The physical and biological sciences were, of course, examples of accumulated knowledge. But so, too, I claimed was archaeology. Therefore, in my outline of a three-term course of forty-five weeks, I allocated three weeks to the "beginnings of Classical

Archaeology." I also supposed that some time be spent on "political arithmetic in the Seventeenth Century and the development of statistical methods in the Nineteenth." The bulk of the time, however, was to be spent on studying examples chosen from the history of the physical and biological sciences.

The influence of my thinking on what the committee wrote was slight. On the other hand, the report influenced my own personal plans to a considerable degree. I volunteered to give one of the general education courses in natural science. The offer was accepted, and Natural Science 4 was listed under my name in one of the first announcements of the new plan. I justified my return to the lecture room by the argument that by enlisting as a member of the general education staff, I demonstrated my wholehearted support of the new scheme. I also had in mind that after my extracurricular activities of the war years there would be some advantages in positive proof that I could stay in Cambridge and devote myself to an educational task. Perhaps what really moved me was a desire to demonstrate a way of presenting science to laymen, on which I had been cogitating for several years.

As I began to consider my suggestion to the committee, my proposal appeared too ambitious. Therefore, in a second memorandum to Dean Buck in December 1944, I retreated to what became in fact a perfectly feasible outline.

The distinction between the case-history method and the more usual history of science course was not easily made. What was needed was a platform in order to explain in some detail just how I envisaged the use of historical material in giving a course in science to freshmen or sophomores who had no intention of concentrating in any field of science. Yale provided the platform by asking me to give the Terry lectures in the fall of 1945.

I used the three lectures to argue for my concept of how a college course "On Understanding Science" might be presented. (The lectures were published under this title in 1947.) When it came time to organize Natural Science 4, the manuscript of the Yale lectures provided the ground plan. I was fortunate in recruiting three young men to help, an astronomer, Fletcher G. Watson; a physicist, Thomas S. Kuhn; and a chemist, Leonard K. Nash. After several years in general education in the faculty of arts and sciences at Harvard, the group dispersed; the astronomer moved to the faculty of education where he is now the Henry Lee Shattuck Professor; the chemist has continued teaching one of the natural science courses as well as chemistry courses at Harvard; the physicist has become a philosopher and is now a professor at Princeton. In the immediate postwar years when we were all working on developing Natural Science 4, a number of case histories were written. Though I cannot say that their use at once spread throughout the United States, they have been used in other colleges than Harvard. Even today there is a small but continuing sale of the two volumes in which all the case histories are printed under the title *Harvard Case Histories in Experimental Science*, edited by James Bryant Conant, Harvard, 1948 and 1957.

My excursion back into undergraduate teaching lasted three years, though in each year portions of the course were handled by my younger colleagues. I enjoyed the experience enormously, particularly the lecture-table demonstrations. There is no doubt that if one has ever lectured to a sympathetic audience, there is a certain temptation to repeat the experience.

To reconcile my interest in Natural Science 4 with the demands on my time as a university president was not easy, although the nature of the student body in the immediate postwar years made the task less difficult than would have been the case under normal circumstances. The mature student body which filled our colleges in 1946 and 1947 was a delight to all who were then teaching undergraduates. I shall always think it was a fortunate accident that the start of general education at Harvard coincided with the existence of an unusual undergraduate body. Certainly in the case of my own course, I found myself facing in the first year an audience whose age and background were quite different from those of the normal freshman class. Therefore I must be cautious in claiming that I was once again for a period of years an undergraduate instructor. I had the privilege of starting an experiment under conditions which were quite special. For the opportunity, I have to thank in the last analysis the committee I had appointed in 1942. I doubt if any other college president has been thus a beneficiary of his own administrative act.

CHAPTER 28

Coeducation in Fact If Not in Theory

ONE OF THE MOST SIGNIFICANT events during my presidency of Harvard was the agreement of the Harvard Corporation with the Trustees of Radcliffe College. When the faculty voted to recommend the basis of this agreement to the Corporation in March 1943, a major step was taken down the road leading to coeducation. One might think such a radical departure from tradition must have been the consequence of a deep conviction held by the president of the college. It would be pleasant if I could record that such was in fact the case. Alas, any such picture of my part in the reformation of women's education in Cambridge would be completely false.

The last thing in the world that I desired when I took office was to open Harvard College to "young ladies." I recall being opposed to coeducation in 1933, a recollection fortified by a recent conversation with the wife of one of the professors who joined the Harvard faculty in the first year of my administration. She remembered a dinner at my house and a talk we had about coeducation; she had set forth the advantages, I the disadvantages; she had argued in favor of coeducational colleges, I had expressed strong views in opposition. She wondered what had made me change my mind. Changed circumstances were the best explanation I could offer; it would have been more accurate if I had said that I became slowly convinced that administrative awkwardness was too high a price to pay for the continuation of the prejudices of those who, like myself, wished Harvard to remain strictly a man's college.

374

At the time I entered Harvard as a member of the class of 1914, I am sure a large proportion of my classmates shared my negative opinion about coeducation. I had prepared for college at an exclusively male public institution. Those who came from the private preparatory schools were likewise products of a schooling of boys apart from girls. My ignorance of coeducation was complete. I only knew I was against it. Almost none of the girls I met at dances were Radcliffe students. I hardly knew of the college's existence.

The contrast with the Harvard of the post–World War II period is a striking example of the fact that undergraduate opinion changes. In 1946 or 1947 I was spending an evening with a group of students in one of the houses (at that period I started a practice of visiting each house once a year, giving a talk and answering questions). I raised the question: "How many undergraduates would like to see the new Harvard-Radcliffe arrangements given up?" "What new arrangements?" I was asked. "The presence of many Radcliffe students in the courses," I replied. "Until a few years ago," I explained, "the instruction was given, with few exceptions, in separate courses. How many would be in favor of a return to such a scheme?" I asked. Not a hand was raised. "That is interesting," I said. "When I was in college I doubt if any undergraduate would have been anything but opposed to the joint classes which you all seem to like." At this point, one of the group spoke up. "My father was in your class or near to it," he said. "He has told me about the conditions which then existed, but he says Radcliffe girls were different in those days."

In the first decade of this century, Radcliffe College had been chartered by the Commonwealth of Massachusetts as a successor to the Society for the Collegiate Instruction of Women, which had been formed in 1879. The promoters of the enterprise had at first tried in the 1880s to have Harvard take over officially the instruction of young ladies. According to Samuel Eliot Morison, "Harvard firmly declined to annex the Annex on condition of granting Harvard degrees to the alumnae. A sensible compromise was worked out by which the Harvard governing boards accepted visitorial power and consented to countersign women's degree diplomas on the condition that all instruction be given by members of the Harvard staff."*

Morison expressed the opinion that under its charter "Radcliffe had grown and prospered beside her somewhat supercilious parent"; he concluded his discussion of the education of women by declaring

* *Three Centuries of Harvard*, Cambridge, Harvard University Press, 1936.

that "no proposition to make Harvard College coeducational has ever been seriously entertained."

The official historian of Harvard in his rather complacent report on the status of Radcliffe fails to mention certain dissatisfactions with the Harvard-Radcliffe relationship which were present in the faculty. For example, one of the oldest and most distinguished scholars, Professor Kittredge, always voted "no" loud and clear when the faculty was called on each year to approve an essentially *pro forma* resolution about the certification of Radcliffe courses. He regretted that Harvard was in any way connected with the education of women. President Lowell made no secret of his lack of enthusiasm for the connection with Radcliffe which he had inherited. On one occasion he indicated to me that, as a young assistant professor, I had no obligation whatsoever to teach in Radcliffe.

My older colleagues in the chemistry department felt differently. So, too, did many members of other departments. They believed that the faculty of arts and sciences had a moral duty to provide instruction for Radcliffe students; they further believed that the courses given should be treated as seriously as the parallel courses in Harvard College. For those of us who were young and impoverished, the extra compensation provided on a per-course basis was sufficient inducement. But as my personal finances improved, thanks to a textbook and consulting fees, I was moved to turn over my Radcliffe course in elementary organic chemistry to a young instructor. Ada Comstock, president of Radcliffe, was not pleased. At that same time, a somewhat older faculty member in another field lectured me on the scandalous way we younger men treated Radcliffe. "You only look at it as a source of extra money when you need it," he said. "You have no interest in making the instruction as good as possible."

When I became president, I had talks with President Comstock from time to time. I admired her greatly, as did all who knew her; I came to have a great sympathy with her predicament. Here was a college president with a board of trustees and a student body but no faculty; she had no real control over the instruction which was offered to the students. She had come to rely on the devotion of a small group of professors who served on the equivalent of an administrative board and who endeavored to arouse interest in Radcliffe problems among their colleagues. She negotiated each year, so to speak, with the departmental chairmen about the course offerings. These negotiations, however, had no official basis.

The difficulties in the compromise which had been adopted in

President Eliot's day and which Professor Morison had praised were illustrated by a problem I took to President Comstock in the first year or two of my presidency. A few women were candidates each year for the degree of Ph.D. They fulfilled all the requirements for the Harvard degree; they did their research and wrote their dissertations under the direction of Harvard professors; yet the degree they received was a Radcliffe not a Harvard degree. The injustice was apparent. Why could not these young women receive a Harvard degree? So I was asked by some members of the faculty.

President Comstock, although well aware of the complaints, was unwilling to have the Harvard Ph.D. awarded to any of her students unless the Harvard A.B. degree would also be awarded to Radcliffe undergraduates. Yet we both agreed that it was hard to conceive of the governing boards' agreeing to a scheme by which women received the Harvard bachelor's degree. Such an arrangement would automatically open up the Harvard Alumni Association to women. Neither of us could imagine the alumni consenting to such a revolutionary measure. I abandoned my interest in justice for the few women who wanted a Ph.D. degree. Anyone who knew about advanced degrees knew that the Radcliffe degree was the equivalent of a Harvard degree. Why so much concern about a diploma and who signed it?

Far more troublesome was the basic arrangement by which Harvard professors, if they so desired, could offer courses. These courses were, with few exceptions, given in Radcliffe buildings. Indeed, in the 1920s a new chemical-physical laboratory was built on the Radcliffe grounds. It was in this building that I lectured to a class of some ten to fifteen who wished to study elementary organic chemistry. A Harvard graduate student was in charge of the laboratory work given in the various courses. He had his own little laboratory in which he was carrying on his own research as a candidate for the doctor's degree.

On paper the system looked ideal. The Radcliffe students were instructed by members of the Harvard staff. Yet the instructor was under a temptation to neglect his duty. As I knew from personal experience, it was all too easy to walk over to a Radcliffe building, give a lecture and rush back to a Harvard laboratory or library without waiting to answer questions. A friend of my wife's complained to her that she found it necessary to run several blocks after a lecture to catch up with me to ask for a further explanation of some point which I had not made clear in my exposition. Still, as long as there was an ample supply of Harvard professors and instructors who wished to teach at Radcliffe, the arrangement could be considered satisfactory in spite of its precarious foundation. The alternative which President Lowell was said to favor, namely, to cut the link between Harvard and Radcliffe, was impossible. The "Annex" had too many friends who would stoutly oppose all attempts to transform Radcliffe into a woman's college with its own faculty.

From time to time in the first seven years of my administration, a few professors spoke to me about the possibility of making the provision of adequate instruction some sort of official responsibility of the faculty. I always replied that it would be almost impossible to make any drastic changes because so many Harvard professors had a pecuniary interest in the present scheme.

The war brought to a head the latent difficulties in the informal arrangements by which members of the Harvard faculty staffed Radcliffe courses. After Pearl Harbor the young instructors and many of the older members of the faculty left Cambridge to enlist in the armed forces or take positions in the war agencies. The pool of available academic manpower on which Radcliffe had depended rapidly contracted. The whole situation was in a state of flux. Dean Buck (who now had the title of provost) and I had many talks. We were concerned not only with temporary measures to alleviate the current shortage of teachers for Radcliffe; we also examined the basic shortcomings of the system and wondered if we could not use the instability of the present to construct a more stable system for the future. I felt myself impelled toward coeducation as the only sound administrative arrangement unless Radcliffe was to be cut loose and transformed into an orthodox women's college.

The ingenious device which became the basis of the Harvard-Radcliffe agreement of 1943 was Paul Buck's idea. Persuading the faculty to adopt it was his accomplishment. Buck proposed that Harvard should accept the responsibility for providing instruction for Radcliffe girls in return for Radcliffe's turning over to Harvard all but a small portion of the receipts from tuition. Giving courses at Radcliffe would thus become just as much an obligation of a department of the faculty of arts and sciences as providing instruction for Harvard men. The burden or the privilege (depending on one's point of view) of instructing young ladies would be passed around within a department. The old scheme of extra compensation for giving a Radcliffe course was to disappear. At first sight this seemed to me to present an obstacle which could not be overcome. How could one persuade a faculty to renounce a tradition which had provided financial profit to so many professors in the past? An upward shift in the salary schedule was the answer—a shift of such an amount that no one on the faculty would receive less money after the new scheme came into effect than he had received before. To be sure, those who had not recently taken part in Radcliffe instruction would find their academic incomes increased. The significant point, however, was that no one would have his income lowered.

The justification for considerable increase in salaries (some 20 percent) was that the new burden on the faculty presumably meant everyone would have to teach more courses. The change in salary schedule was contingent on the adoption of the entire new plan. The faculty had to recommend it to the Corporation, which then would have to enter into a formal agreement with the Radcliffe Trustees.

The discussion at the faculty meeting was neither long nor acrimonious. Probably the scheme had been explained by the provost to many in conversation. There was no substantial disagreement; almost everyone saw the new relationship as a vast improvement on the old. Candor forces me, however, to record that the faculty meeting was small; many professors were on leave of absence; the war was then in a phase which involved an ever-increasing number of American boys in combat; the casualty lists were mounting every day. There was a certain sense of unreality in any talk about strictly academic affairs. Whatever may be the explanation of the ease with which the faculty was persuaded by Provost Buck to act in the spring of 1943, it is important to note that no one ever suggested that the action was mistaken. After the war was over, no faculty member suggested (at least publicly) that the old arrangement be restored. The pressure of faculty opinion was rather for the administration to push ahead along the lines made possible by the new Harvard-Radcliffe relations.

In the formal announcement of the agreement, it was explicitly stated that "Radcliffe students will continue to receive instruction in separate classes at Radcliffe." It was explained, however, that not only would Harvard and Radcliffe students continue to attend the same classes as they had in a few instances as a temporary wartime measure but that under the new arrangement more courses would be opened to Radcliffe students. "This does not place either college in the category of coeducational institutions," the official statement declared.

As the number of courses open to Radcliffe soared in the following years, two jokes began to circulate. According to one, Harvard was not coeducational in theory, only in practice; another was to the effect that Harvard was not coeducational, but Radcliffe was.

The initial plan, put forward with complete sincerity, provided for separate freshman and sophomore courses for Radcliffe students. I, for one, was not prepared in 1943 to face what I thought would be an enraged alumni body if all Harvard courses were opened to women. Just how rapidly the erosion of this plan occurred, I cannot now say. I leave it to some enterprising historian to examine the records to see when the last class for Radcliffe students only was a fact. A press release of October 21, 1947, announced that the "existing arrangements between Harvard University and Radcliffe College have been formalized." Most freshman classes in Radcliffe, it was stated, would continue to be taught separately from Harvard classes. However, "upper class and graduate men and women will share the same instructors in lectures and in conference rooms." The *Harvard Alumni Bulletin*, commenting on this news story, recalled that many years before a popular professor, "Copey" (Professor Charles Townsend Copeland), was alleged to have refused to give a course in argument at Radcliffe, saying, "How deplorable for women to become apt in argument. We can't obliterate a natural tendency, but why cultivate it?"

From the point of view of the departments, arranging to staff separate Radcliffe courses was an awkward business. It would be far simpler and easier to have all courses open to both Harvard and Radcliffe students. Experience in the immediate postwar years had shown that for upper-class students joint instruction was entirely satisfactory. The only real argument in favor of the restriction in the original plan had been the desire to avoid coeducation for the younger students. The question began to be raised quietly as to why this feature of the plan should be retained. Without any furor, it was slowly abandoned. Before long, all courses given under the faculty of arts and sciences were open to Radcliffe students. Whatever loyal Harvard men might say, the scheme was by all outsiders properly labeled as "coeducation."

The admission of women to the professional schools is another part of the story. The Graduate School of Education had been open to women for many years for the obvious reason that a large number of women wished to be schoolteachers. Agitation for the admission of women to the Medical School was started by a few members of the faculty in 1942. Before long, a considerable number of the leading professors were asking the dean privately what they could do to bring about the admission of women. The dean and I decided that the first thing to do was to appoint a special committee to report to the faculty. Eventually, the matter would have to come before the two governing boards, but what was needed at the outset was an indication of faculty sentiment.

Unlike most other universities, both private and public, there was no academic senate comprising representatives from all faculties at Harvard. The authority of each separate faculty stemmed directly from the Corporation. To be sure, the Harvard statutes had for years provided for a "university council" composed of the professors (of all ranks) in all the faculties. The function of the council according to the statutes was "to consider questions which concern more than one faculty." As a matter of fact, the council had met only once in President Lowell's administration. The matter for discussion involved, I believe, requirements for admission to the Medical School. According to Mr. Lowell, the law and medical professors began attacking each other so violently that the meeting ended in confusion. He never called another. There was one meeting in my service as president to consider pension plans. I never heard a suggestion from any professor that the university council be brought to life. Each faculty valued too highly its independence of other faculties to wish for the existence of an all-university faculty committee with any power.

On the question of admission of women to the Medical School, the special committee reported unanimously in favor of a new admission policy to the effect that the proportion of men to women admitted each year was to be determined solely on the basis of the quality of the applicants. The report of the committee was approved by the faculty of medicine on April 2, 1943, by a vote of 68 to 12. According to constitutional procedure, I brought the action of the faculty to the attention of the Corporation by presenting a communication of the dean of the faculty of medicine. I explained that neither the dean nor I was prepared to endorse the faculty vote, nor were we ready to oppose it. We both thought that there were no good reasons why women should be admitted; there was an excess of places in other medical schools for women; on the other hand, we had heard no good arguments against the change recommended by the faculty.

Two members of the Corporation were reluctant to agree to the admission of women to the Medical School. One of them at least had with reluctance accepted the Harvard-Radcliffe agreement; he made it plain that he had done so only because Provost Buck and I had endorsed the change. He objected to the fact that these moves toward coeducation were being made when so many faculty members were on leave of absence for war work. The function of the governing boards was to ensure that adequate consideration was given to any proposal for drastic alterations. The majority of the Corporation decided that the faculty of medicine might well consider the matter further. The formal record which I communicated to the faculty through the dean read as follows:

"It was voted that this board is unwilling at the present time to make the proposed changes in regard to the admissibility of women to the Medical School."

The twelve members who had voted in the negative at the faculty meeting were pleased; the majority were disappointed. During the next academic year (1943–44), a second special committee considered the admission of women and ended with a somewhat different formulation of policy. Women of superior ability were to be admitted in limited numbers. In this form, the policy was recommended by the faculty of medicine by the large majority of 56 to 3 in May 1944. The Corporation agreed in June; according to the established ritual, I communicated the vote of the Corporation to the Board of Overseers "that they may consent if they see fit."

The meeting of the Board of Overseers at which the admission of women to the Medical School was debated was the most amusing meeting I ever attended. According to a custom established long before I became president of Harvard, every vote of the Corporation communicated to the Overseers was referred to that Overseer who was chairman of the visiting committee for the school or the department in question. (The other members of the visiting committee were usually alumni and others thought to have an interest in that phase of the work of the university.) It so happened that in 1944 the chairman of the visiting committee for the Medical School was a retired surgeon and a gentleman of the old school, David Cheever. He held strong views about the evils of coeducation. He recommended that the Board of Overseers refuse consent to the Corporation vote. At some length and with formal eloquence, he explained why he could not agree with a majority of the faculty. He pointed out that the vote might be misleading because some of the leading members of the Medical School faculty were on leave of absence serving with the armed forces. The main thrust of his argument, however, was in nineteenth-century terms, reminding me of the strong opinions I used to hear from the opponents of the extension of the suffrage to women. He covered a wide range of arguments from the health of women to the revolutionary doctrines of the Soviet Union. The members of the board listened in respectful silence.

There was every reason to think that the motion to consent would be passed. Still, I could not be sure. The argument about the professors on leave of absence might appeal to many Overseers. I was worried lest someone would move to lay the matter on the table, thus postponing action for months. I did not wish to face the faculty of medicine with still another statement that for the time being the governing boards did not accept the faculty recommendation. Therefore I asked for the floor.

I made it plain that I thought the real issue before the board was the relation of the faculty to the governing boards. As to the substantive issue, I said I had heard no compelling arguments why Harvard should admit women and no convincing argument why Harvard should not. What the board had before it was a vote of the Corporation based on two votes of the faculty of medicine more than a year apart, each carried by a large majority. The Board of Overseers could, of course, take whatever action it saw fit. But in view of the record, if the Overseers failed at this meeting to consent to the Corporation vote, I should have to make a public statement indicating clearly that the board had blocked approval of a policy of the faculty recommended after two years of discussion. There was no response to my announcement; when the president of the board called for a voice vote, it was clear that I need not have worried; only a few negative voices were to be heard.

CHAPTER 29

The Second Rescue of the School of Education

MY INTEREST in secondary education as apart from collegiate education had been aroused by the problem of financing the Harvard Graduate School of Education. I have recounted the steps by which Dean Holmes and Professor Spaulding led me to an understanding of the importance of the aims of their graduate school. My invention of the master of arts in teaching degree (M.A.T.) was only a part of the story. The school had other functions to perform besides being a partner in educating schoolteachers. The work for advanced degrees by those who planned to be administrators, professors of education or specialists in a public school system were all significant undertakings. The need for guidance and hence for testing in the public high schools was slowly impressed upon me.

Reflecting my growing appreciation of educational problems outside of Cambridge, in my annual report for 1937–38 I undertook to discuss "certain questions concerning the secondary schools of the country." To many, it may be far from evident, I wrote, that the future of secondary education is a matter of "supreme national importance." Yet such I believed to be the case. If we wished the present type of society in this country to survive and to improve along "thoroughly democratic lines, we must," I said, "as a people, pay due attention to our schools." I added: "The economic, political and social implications of every aspect of public and private education, particularly at the secondary level, go to the very roots of our national life."

To illustrate my contention, I pointed out the profound changes which had occurred in the last forty years. The proportion of the population of secondary school age attending school had mounted from 30 to 65 percent between 1920 and 1936. In the same period, the primary function of the high school changed. "Instead of being concerned largely with boys and girls whose interests and abilities were such as to give them high aptitude for 'book learning,' the schools now include every kind and level of ability; the student body comprises youths with the widest possible range of ambitions. The schools must accommodate pupils the majority of whom would not profit from the type of education which was standard two generations ago."

I went on to consider the impact of these changes on the admission policy of Harvard College on the one hand and the training of teachers on the other. I reported the action of the Administrative Board for the master of arts in teaching in passing a resolution requesting me to appoint a joint committee of the faculty of arts and sciences and the faculty of education "to study the whole subject of the training of secondary school teachers with special reference to the training of teachers of English." (Such a committee was appointed and rendered a constructive report just before Pearl Harbor.) Continuing in the same vein, I suggested that it was not, perhaps, an overstatement to say that, by and large, American universities have avoided a wholehearted or systematic attention to public education at the school level. "There has rarely been in any institution a concerted attack by the faculties of arts and sciences and of education on the problems presented by the new conditions; yet such an effort is imperatively needed." The climax of my argument, clearly addressed to possible donors, followed: "There can be no question today that the study of education as a social process—quite apart from the training of teachers—is as important as the study of law or of business administration. Any university which wishes to do its share for the public welfare must have a strong faculty of education with the same degree of professional feeling as exists in other professional faculties."

The report from which I have been quoting was written in January 1939. The amount of space I devoted to secondary education and my strong endorsement of the School of Education were intended to support the efforts to raise money for the Harvard School. What I wrote reflects the indoctrination I had been receiving from Francis Spaulding (now Dean Spaulding) as we made the journeys I have described. As part of my own education, they have proved to be highly fruitful; as money-raising enterprises, they were all failures. Spaulding, it will be recalled, was persuaded to stay at Harvard in 1939 by making him dean and promising support in raising money for the school; the guarantee of $20,000 a year for five years as an addition to the budget also helped. Then came the fall of France. For a year, I was heavily engaged in starting the chemical division of the National Defense Research Committee. I nevertheless did what I could to interest potential donors. But schools of education in those days (unlike medical schools) were not thought of as requiring endowment. Who ever heard of giving money to a school for training teachers? Within more than one large urban private university, the school of education was a money-maker. It was not only supporting itself by the fees of part-time students; it was turning over to the central administration by one device or another considerable sums each year. Harvard, under President Lowell, had refused to cater to the needs of part-time students.

Spaulding and I worked together on plans for revitalizing the School of Education. The first item on our agenda was the development of a program in educational administration. In May 1940 I was writing to Spaulding that I assumed that he was working along satisfactorily toward "a solution of his administrative professorship." The solution to which I was referring must have been some attempt on Spaulding's part to interest an individual or a foundation in the program in educational administration. Another item involved a revision of the M.A.T. program. It is apparent from a memo of 1941 that, in desperation, we (Spaulding and I) were ready to expand the number of part-time courses which would increase the tuition income.

Shortly after Pearl Harbor, Spaulding obtained a leave of absence for the duration to become a colonel in the Army. Reporting to Frederick Osborn, who had been recently commissioned a general, he was responsible for the Education Branch of the Information and Education Division of the Army. In that capacity, he organized the educational program of the Armed Forces Institute. Another young man (really young) working with General Osborn was a Harvard A.B. of 1938 named Francis Keppel, of whom more later.

The war years were not happy ones for most of those who stayed on the job in Cambridge. In the case of the School of Education, my attempts to find an acting dean were not too successful. Finally, a professor of educational psychology, Phillip J. Rulon, took the position. Though he was a member of the committee which wrote the

Harvard Report on General Education, he did not develop good relations between his school and the departments of the faculty of arts and sciences. The hostility to the faculty of education was, therefore, at least as great as the war came to a close as it had been when I set up the M.A.T. a decade earlier. What Spaulding could have done in the postwar years, no one can say. Among the wreckage caused by the war years was the program for the master of arts in teaching degree. As I wrote to the Harvard Corporation in the summer of 1945 (just before the surrender of Japan), the program had never been given a fair test. As long as Spaulding was on the job, the scheme worked in spite of the fact that two faculties were involved. After his departure for the war, things started to go badly—so badly that in both faculties there was sentiment for abandoning the scheme and going back to the Ed.M. for teachers given by a single faculty.

Spaulding had been in favor of developing a five-or-six-year program for training teachers as part of the offering in Harvard College. Thus undergraduates would be encouraged to get a running start by taking courses in education in the senior year. But this was a minor issue. What depressed both of us was the lack of funds. Indeed, as we talked from time to time during the closing months of the war and I reported on my disappointment at the failure of several leads to new money, we turned over in our minds possible lines of retreat. In one of our conversations at the old Cosmos Club in Washington after V-E Day, the idea of giving up an orthodox school must have developed. For I find that on June 27, 1945, I wrote to Spaulding in great distress as follows:

> If we give up an orthodox school of education, won't your face and mine (and I am thinking particularly of mine) be very red in view of the hullabaloo I have been raising of the importance of schools of education and the need for a truce between faculties of arts and sciences and schools of education? . . .
>
> More serious than my red face—if we ran the swankiest of Brookings Institutes to study education at the school level, aren't we giving up our duty in abdicating from the training of teachers and school officers? Indeed, can we give up this training, or are we willing to give it back to the faculty of arts and sciences?
>
> In short, it seems to me that you have led an unsuspecting chemist out on the end of a very long limb and anything short of continuing a fairly orthodox school of education here with yourself as the head looks like sawing off the limb! Please think all this over. The more I think about it the deeper into difficulties do I get.

At the time I wrote this letter, Spaulding must have been already approached by the Board of Regents of New York State with the offer of the position of State Commissioner. As I explained in a memorandum to the Harvard Corporation on July 20, 1945, he was trying to balance in his mind what the future might have in store for him at Cambridge and in Albany. He had promised the New Yorkers a decision by October 1. Clearly, we at Harvard had a chance to make a counteroffer, and we must do better than we had in 1939, when we agreed to finance an annual deficit of $20,000 for five years.

After recalling the history of the master of arts in teaching, I stated that this degree was more difficult to attain than an A.M. or the old Ed.M., at least in terms of the time required. Yet I had to report that in terms of academic brilliance the type of student who enrolled for the degree was often not the equal of the student who enrolls for advanced work in one of the departments of arts and sciences. As a result, the M.A.T. candidates were not regarded highly by many members of the faculty of arts and sciences. These same professors who had no understanding of public high school problems insisted on what I regarded as meaningless requirements. I stated in the memorandum that, from my personal experience for several years as presiding officer of the Administrative Board for the M.A.T. degree, the faculty of education had been right 90 percent of the time in the negotiations about the requirements for the joint degree.

In the same memorandum, I record my own belief, which was shared by Spaulding and Paul Buck, that under normal conditions with certain readjustments the M.A.T. program would become popular and have high standing. What we had in mind was a five-or-six-year program as part of the offering of Harvard College. Such a program should be actively promoted at the college level and assisted by generous scholarship grants. In this way, a better type of Harvard College student, in terms of academic brilliance, would be drawn into public high school teaching than in the past. But for this to be accomplished there must be an ever-increasing sympathy and understanding on the part of the faculty of arts and sciences and, above all, a strong cooperative faculty of education led by a dean who was *persona grata* to the faculty of arts and sciences. Spaulding, I wrote, was "probably unique in meeting these requirements; without him it is hard to see how progress along these lines could be made."

I emphasized, however, that it would be putting the picture upside down to envisage the role of the faculty of education solely in terms of its work with the prospective teachers in the schools. No first-rate man will join a faculty of education, I stated, unless he is given a chance to do research and work with advanced students. Therefore we must provide for good graduate programs in educational psychology, history and administration.

I raised the question whether Harvard could afford to withdraw from the field of training men for professional educational work, to which my answer was in the negative. Then I outlined five conceivable alternatives, briefly summarized as follows:

1. Merge the members of the faculty of education in the faculty of arts and sciences, giving up the professional aspects of their work.

2. Turn the School of Education into something like a Brookings Institute for research in education, abandoning the A.M. in Teaching degree.

3. Continue along the lines to which we agreed when Spaulding became dean, with more emphasis on cooperation with the faculty of arts and sciences and with a strengthening of the School of Education's professional position.

4. Drift along in the present general direction, but without doing a good job or having a scheme for the future.

5. Return the School of Education to a completely independent position, give an Ed. M. to all comers, go in for heavy registration and low standards.

In presenting these alternatives to the Corporation, I made it clear that the first and second would be for me personally impossible; the retreat would be not strategic but disastrous. Number 3 was my choice, but it would cost money. The fourth possibility would happen, I prophesied, unless we were careful; and the fifth would solve the budgetary problems, but for me was unthinkable. Therefore it all boiled down to what funds we could commit from our unrestricted resources for the expansion of the School of Education. As I made clear in the memorandum, we (the Corporation) had to decide what should be done in terms not only of what was needed in the School of Education, but what was needed elsewhere in the university. I did not have to tell the members of the Corporation that the demands were large and many highly important areas of the university were short of funds.

To say that the Corporation was faced with a highly important decision at a most inopportune moment would be an understatement. When I wrote the memorandum in question, I knew—but few others did—that the war with Japan was almost certain to be brought to an end in a few weeks by the explosion of an atomic bomb. The postwar period of readjustment in all faculties started almost without warning when Japan surrendered in August 1945. What financial promises we could make to Spaulding if he stayed, I do not recall. I was certainly in no position to urge him to stay. So he resigned and accepted the position of Commissioner of Education of New York in the late summer of 1945.

Shortly after the resignation was announced, I wrote a letter to President Zook of the American Council on Education, explaining the situation in answer to a letter of his suggesting a successor to Spaulding. I said that we had not come to the point of even drawing up a list of leading candidates. The faculty was still at work trying to decide what type of school we should have with our limited resources. I went on to say that in the loss of Spaulding Harvard suffered a major defeat and I personally lost a battle, although I did not blame Spaulding for leaving us—quite the contrary. "After I canvassed the situation here very carefully with the Corporation," I wrote,

it became evident that it would not be possible to finance the type of school both he and I felt Harvard should have to meet the challenge of the present in regard to work in education. The truth of the matter is that schools of education are not attractive objects of gifts or bequests by wealthy individuals; nor do they awaken too much enthusiasm among the majority of those who support colleges and universities of the type of Harvard. As compared with fine arts, or music, a library or science, a medical school or a school of business administration, a school of education has tough going in a privately endowed university, whatever the president of the institution may think. Therefore, it is probable that we shall have to devise some specialized field of activity in which we can operate with our present totally inadequate plant and small endowment.

The letter to Zook reflects my discouragement and pessimism about the future of the School of Education. There was at least one member of the Corporation who would have gladly seen us withdraw from the whole enterprise, much as Yale did some ten years later. There were, however, at least two and possibly three staunch supporters of the school. They encouraged me in December to appoint a subcommittee of the Corporation (a very rare procedure) to meet with the members of the faculty of education. The faculty was asked to prepare a statement of future plans. By March 1946 such a report was at hand (multigraphed in purple ink and henceforth known as the purple memo). In May of the same year, I attempted to sum up for the Corporation the conclusions of the faculty of education. I wrote that while the plans are much less ambitious than those which Dean Spaulding and I considered some years ago, they nevertheless represent, I believe, a very constructive approach for the immediate future. Furthermore, as events have developed within the University within the last few years, I believe that the new ideas are sounder than the ones which Dean Spaulding and I discussed. They certainly have more novelty and are easier to carry out within the framework of the present University. They have, therefore, my enthusiastic endorsement.

What was proposed was a small school. The emphasis would be on the improvement of public education through the actions of school superintendents, state superintendents and high school principals. A carefully selected group of not more than a hundred full-time students would be working with a staff recruited largely from the social science disciplines; in particular, psychology, cultural anthropology and sociology were named. The work of this new staff would complement the offerings in school administration of the usual historical-philosophical courses. The novel feature of the plan would be a group of social scientists of the first rank directing their attention to education as a social process.

All of which, in retrospect, was far easier for the small faculty (a handful of men) to propose than for me as executive officer of the university to bring into being. A new dean to be recruited from one of the social science disciplines and proper financial support were prerequisites. I told the Corporation that I was appointing a committee drawn from the faculty of education and the new department of social relations (of the faculty of arts and sciences) to canvass the appointment of the new dean. I thus hoped to establish a closer bond between this department and the faculty of education.

The committee was appointed, and I was constantly in touch with it. I recall full well that, either before the appointment or shortly after, Professor Rulon, who continued as acting dean, expressed the worries of the faculty that their affairs would be run by the members of the social relations department. But Professor Samuel A. Stouffer, one of the newly appointed social scientists, told Rulon not to worry. He and his colleagues would be far too busy with their own affairs to attempt to intrude in the education faculty's business.

Whether the orientation to the newer social sciences was Rulon's idea or that of one or more of his colleagues, I cannot say. Certainly I was consulted more than once before the "purple memorandum" was drawn up. I am also sure that my enthusiasm for an outstanding social scientist as dean was as great as it would have been if the idea had been my own. I was to argue its merits for some years to come. The analogy I used was the revolution in biochemistry in the leading medical schools in the 1920s. I had witnessed the replacement of professors of biochemistry trained in the medical schools by professors of organic and physical chemistry educated in the graduate schools of a university. I could name names and show what a revolutionary effect such importation from a basic discipline—chemistry—had produced. I argued the same might be expected in a school of education.

At the close of the 1945–46 academic year, I could report to the faculty of education that the Corporation had accepted in principle their report. The Corporation had agreed to allocate from the unrestricted funds of the university on a dollar-for-dollar basis an amount equal to any new funds which might be obtained by a new dean. I added that I was going ahead to canvass certain foundations and individuals. The tone of this communication was optimistic. Indeed, as things turned out, overoptimistic. It was to be nearly two years before a dean was appointed. And when he was, the man chosen did not in the least fit the specifications we so easily drew up in 1946. That he subsequently proved to be a brilliant and imaginative leader of a faculty he recruited proves nothing about the correctness of the course we were plotting in accepting the purple memorandum. However, my attempts to steam ahead constituted an important part of my experiences with social scientists and educators.

For two years I was on the hunt for an endowment and a dean. The best I could accomplish was to obtain from the Carnegie Corporation a pledge of $300,000, to be spent at whatever rate was deemed advisable over a period of ten years. The Corporation agreed to match dollar for dollar the annual expenditure from this fund. (It was assumed that the search for endowment would continue.) Armed with high hopes and the generosity of the Carnegie board, I proceeded to try to persuade a leading social scientist to take the job of dean. In June 1947 I was writing to explain the prospects to a potential candidate (one of a group of four or five young "new" social scientists of rising reputation) as follows:

The present budgetary figure of $185,000 (exclusive of scholarships and items for which corresponding income is assured) could be very conservatively figured as being increased to $200,00 to cover all the present activities projected for a 5 to 10 year period; the tuition from the smaller student body which is planned might be $60,000 instead of the present $85,000; if the Carnegie money were spent on a five year basis, $64,000 annually would be available for new activities including the dean's own salary and budget; if temporary funds could be raised to finance a new project in which the members of the department of Social Relations played a key role, the Carnegie money could be used to cover a longer period of time up to ten years.

I shall not try to refresh my memory of the fruitless attempts to win the interest of an outstanding social scientist in the Harvard School of Education. I had hoped that the proposal for a close relation between the School of Education and the newly formed department of social relations might prove to be a sufficient lure. But such was not the case. After one or two flat turndowns in the first half of 1947, I developed a more ambitious scheme in the hope it would appeal to the newly established Ford Foundation. The scheme involved the financing at one sweep of the immediate needs of the Business School, the School of Education and the department of social relations. Needless to say, cooperative research projects involving all three academic entities were set forth. All to no avail.

On March 24, 1948, I wrote to Spaulding (now Commissioner Spaulding) that I was still "behind the 8 ball on this question of the future of the graduate school of education." My bad luck, I went on, had been "really enough to try the patience of a saint, and I'm a long way from being that!" I then referred to my failure to land a large sum of money which I had thought we had some chance of getting. Everybody seemed to like the basic idea, but I had to admit that I could not find a man "in the social sciences of 'A' grade who is willing to jump the fence into this unknown and somewhat uncertain pasture."

The next few paragraphs of the letter I shall quote in full:

Although I am not absolutely at the bottom of the barrel, I am so near it that I am turning to the possibility of a totally different solution, namely, of finding a man who would be acceptable to the public school group and who would be flexible enough in his point of view to work with our Social Relations group here in Cambridge. If they would then join the faculty and take an active part in the planning of the new staff (which must be recruited from very young men, I am convinced) and some of the research projects, we might make a start. The best we can hope for now is to build for the fairly distant future. We are not going to be able to make a splash by a lot of new work in a few years.

Two types of individuals would recommend themselves. One would be a young man who had made some reputation as a superintendent of schools or even as a school administrator and whom the profession would recognize as a coming man, provided he was sympathetic towards our program. The other possibility would be an older man who had the same characteristics but would use this as a concluding four or five year appointment, being ready to step out as soon as we could locate from the younger generation of social scientists the man who would fill the original specifications, or if our ship did come in by any miracle, would be willing to step out in favor of one of the social scientists of reputation who has turned us down. Julius Warren comes to my mind, for example, to fill this latter bill.

I shall be very grateful for your advice on the fundamental policy and for a list of names. I am sorry to trouble you, but this is a matter of great urgency, and I hope you believe of some importance.

What happened between the time I sent this cry of distress to Spaulding in Albany on March 24, 1948, and the first days of May, I do not remember. But, unless there is documentary proof to the contrary, I am going to maintain that Spaulding over the telephone urged the name of Francis Keppel. He knew him well and had a high regard for his ability. He had had a chance to observe his work with General Osborn during the war. Since his return to Cambridge to serve as Dean Buck's assistant, Keppel had been fully aware of our attempts to find a social scientist as dean. Equally important, the members of the committee on the lookout for a dean had come to know Keppel well. Therefore, in writing to Devereux Josephs, the president of the Carnegie Corporation, on May 11, 1948, to tell him of the appointment of Keppel as dean, I could say that "we have now found a satisfactory dean who I am sure will work most intimately with the Department of Social Relations and forward our general plans."

In a letter of June 3, 1948, to a long-time benefactor of the school, Mr. Lincoln Filene, I explained that Mr. Keppel's appointment was still confidential until confirmed by the Board of Overseers at commencement. The new dean, I wrote, was

a young man who made a splendid record in the war with General Osborn and Francis T. Spaulding who was then a Colonel in the Morale Branch. He is a splendid administrator and has great imagination. He is the unanimous choice of both the permanent members of the faculty of education and those social scientists who are in our department of social relations. This fact argues well, I think, for the close cooperation between these two groups on which, as you know, we plan to count heavily.

I did not add that Dean Buck had found Mr. Keppel of such great value that he was extremely annoyed at my stealing him away. I also did not mention the only worry I had, namely, that there might be some little trouble in selling Keppel to the public school people. Keppel's subsequent career proved that my worry was unnecessary. His personality assures that he makes friends on whatever task he is engaged. Nevertheless, I am inclined to think that naming as dean a young man without any degree beyond the A.B. and with absolutely no public school experience would have raised more questions among public school administrators than it did if I had not personally taken a hand in his introduction.

The fact that I was in a position to do so was primarily a result of my serving on the Educational Policies Commission, to which I had been elected in 1940. The Commission had come into existence in the depression years by joint action of the American Association of School Administrators and the National Education Association. The members were chosen for a five-year term by the two sponsoring organizations. At the time I joined, the chairman was Alexander J. Stoddard, Superintendent of Schools in Philadelphia. The secretary was William G. Carr, later the secretary of the NEA. Other members included President E. E. Day of Cornell, four professors of education, five public school administrators and a classroom teacher. During the war years, I was a faithful attendant at the meetings, which came about twice a year. A number of times I also attended meetings of the American Association of School Administrators at which, through my friends on the EPC, I met many school administrators. Therefore, by the time Keppel was appointed dean, I had a large acquaintance-ship among public school people, and because of my service on the EPC I was well regarded. I recall a meeting of the AASA at which I gave a luncheon for some of my friends in order to introduce Dean Keppel. I feel certain that my active sponsorship of the dean among school superintendents helped him in his first year in office.

As a matter of fact, in the first few years of his administration as dean, Mr. Keppel did not hew to the line laid down in my plea for funds. A small school was not established. While the emphasis on the social sciences which had characterized the "purple memorandum" was not renounced, the master of arts in teaching program was taken out of a neglected corner where it had been placed by the faculty. I recall how much pleasure I had in hearing Keppel report from time to time of his success in pushing forward this degree program. The pride of authorship is strong. I was delighted, therefore, to learn that my invention had been given a new lease on life. Indeed, before I left Cambridge in 1953, the dean told me the idea of a master of arts in teaching was being copied in several universities. And I might note that the revitalization was not accomplished as Spaulding had envisioned. The extension of the program into Harvard College, while not precluded, was not of the essence. What had been brought about was a cooperative effort between some leading four-year colleges and the Harvard School. Over the years, a type of student was thus being recruited into teaching and school administrative work who, in intellectual terms, was several cuts above the students of prewar days.

I shall not attempt to detail the many innovations introduced by Dean Keppel nor his success in winning friends among the kind of people who had hitherto looked askance at schools of education. As the years went by and Keppel's success became more and more apparent, I received more and more "kudos" as his discoverer. I never disclaimed the credit for making him dean. For even if the original idea was not my own, I did persuade him to take on a job which he knew full well a number had refused. He took a chance, and so did I. Though I never raised the endowment he should have had, I backed his own effective money-raising efforts during the five years we were together. On one point which is often mentioned, I never had the slightest doubts. Keppel had received only an A.B. degree. Some have marveled that without an advanced degree Harvard should have appointed him. There was no problem here for me. I had taken over some of President Lowell's antipathy to higher degrees. And neither the members of the Corporation nor the Overseers were degree-minded. Indeed, there was no difficulty in piloting the appointment through the two governing boards.

As dean, Keppel had a free hand. I was ready to give advice when asked, and in the first few years I may have been more active in consultations with the new dean of the School of Education than with any of the other deans of professional schools. Consciously or unconsciously, my recently acquired enthusiasm for bringing social scientists into the picture was transmitted. Some of the first appointments recommended after Dean Keppel took office were social scientists, and the trend continued. Indeed, it came to be a rather special characteristic of the school.

Though certainly not alone, Harvard was in the vanguard of a postwar movement to bring to the study of school problems men trained as social scientists not in schools of education but in university departments. The national implication of this movement is illustrated by a story. At a resort on one of the Virgin Islands in the winter of 1967, I happened to run into a former school superintendent. We gossiped a bit about the state of the educational world. He had current news from Washington. Reporting on both the Office of Education and the Office of Economic Opportunity, he said that, of course, the social scientists were now in the dominant positions. They tended to look down on those educators who had once occupied all the important positions in the Office of Education. When I asked how these social scientists had come into such positions of influence in educational matters, the reply was short and decisive. "Oh, Frank Keppel started appointing them when he was Commissioner of Education."

CHAPTER 30

Benefactors and Benefactions

AMERICAN COLLEGES and universities have grown and flourished because of the generosity of many men and women. To no small degree, the future of some institutions has been determined by the interest of the donor. The Harvard houses, for example, became a reality because of a gift of a Yale alumnus, Edward S. Harkness, who had a vision of an undergraduate college composed of a number of residential units. President Lowell quite independently had developed the same idea. When the two men met, not entirely by chance, the transformation of Harvard College in the late 1920s was assured. From the point of view of the president of Harvard, Mr. Harkness was the ideal benefactor; from Mr. Harkness' point of view, A. Lawrence Lowell was the ideal college president.

At first sight, one might think that the ideal gift would be a large, unrestricted fund, and, to be sure, such bequests have greatly aided Harvard College. From time to time, indeed, during my twenty years in office I spoke or wrote about the benefits that flowed from the increase in the general unrestricted funds of the university. In theory, if Harkness had said to President Lowell, "Here are many millions of dollars which can be expended in any way you see fit," the president of Harvard could have said, "Thank you very much; I shall build seven houses." In practice, it would not have worked out that way.

A university is composed of many hungry scholars grouped according to their appetites. If the possibility of new sources of financial nourishment were suddenly to appear, each group would claim a lion's share. A project of the president's would have to be considered by the president himself in competition with the other needs of the university, each of which would be ardently portrayed by highly vocal scholars. I remember after President Lowell told the faculty of arts and sciences that a donor had made possible the building of one or more houses, there were mutterings that it was a pity the money could not have been used for other, more pressing objectives. By which the mutterer meant, of course, the needs of his own department.

If Mr. Harkness was President Lowell's ideal benefactor, Mrs. Agnes Wahl Nieman of Milwaukee might be considered mine. The Yale alumnus made possible the realization of a plan the president of Harvard had been evolving for some years. The widow of the founder of the Milwaukee *Journal* led me, by the terms of her will, to recommend the creation of the Nieman Fellowships in Journalism—an invention of which I am very proud.

The will provided that the bequest, made in memory of Lucius W. Nieman, should be used "to promote and elevate the standards of journalism in the United States." When I first heard the news, I must admit I was disappointed. We had just concluded the far from successful Tercentenary Fund drive. The two projects close to my heart—the National Scholarships and the endowment of University Professorships—had not received the measure of support I had hoped would be forthcoming. The depression was still very much of a reality; every private college and university was hard pressed for funds. The last thing I should have thought of asking Santa Claus to bring was an endowment to "promote and elevate the standards of journalism." Here was a very large sum of money (the exact amount was still uncertain) which was tied up in perpetuity by what looked like an impossible directive.

How did one go about promoting and elevating the standards of journalism? By establishing another school of journalism? I hoped not. We had been having trouble enough in the last few years with a new School of Public Administration. It had proved to be no easy matter to fit a new academic entity into the Harvard framework. However, the possibility of establishing a school or department for training future journalists could not be discarded out of hand, and various ways of spending our sudden riches must be explored. Since no reference in the will pointed to any faculty or existing division of the university, no formal consultation with faculty members seemed to be required. Therefore, on my advice, the Corporation (the president and fellows) authorized me to seek suggestions on an informal basis from people within and without the university. Arbitrary as it may seem, I never heard the Corporation's decision challenged.

Let it be noted that it was the president and fellows—not the president—who made the crucial decision that the use of the Nieman bequest should be determined without formal action by any body of professors. The president was to explore with publishers, editors and professors the obvious idea of a school of journalism and any other schemes that might be forthcoming. He was to report back to the Corporation and make his recommendations. There was no guarantee, of course, that what he recommended would be accepted. The final action would be taken by the president and fellows of Harvard College. Thus the president was left free to come up with an idea, but the responsibility for its adoption would be that of seven men.

From the start no one seemed to favor establishing a school of journalism. There were already several such schools attached to both private and public universities. Some practicing journalists spoke well of them; some did not. Whatever might be a just appraisal, there seemed no compelling reason for still another.

As to other suggestions for spending the income of the Nieman fund, only two were put forward with any force. The department of English suggested the establishment of courses in writing which might be of special value for journalists; the director of the university library suggested a collection of microfilms of newspapers from around the nation. Of the two ideas, that of the librarian had the advantage of novelty and flexibility. A collection of microfilms could be as large or small as desired; it could be curtailed if better uses of the money were suddenly to appear. But I was not entirely ready to commit all the income from the new endowment to the augmentation of one of the resources provided by the university library. It would be hard to make a case that the existence of microfilms of many newspapers would "elevate and promote the standards of journalism." Some more imaginative scheme was surely needed.

Why not a fellowship scheme? I asked myself. Why not offer newspaper reporters the opportunity to take the best part of a year off and participate in the intellectual life of the university? I doubted if taking courses would be of much benefit. Certainly, I was not going to suggest the introduction of lectures about journalism nor suggest a program the completion of which would be marked by a degree. Indeed, one of the cardinal points in the plan developing in my mind was a firm prohibition against enrollment for a degree. I was already sufficiently familiar with what was going on in many institutions to be extremely wary of adding journalism to those studies in which after passing examinations one could obtain a special master's degree. Fortunately, journalism, unlike schoolteaching and school administration, was not yet caught up in the tangles of academic red tape. No newspaper owner or managing editor was going to ask a prospective employee about his degrees. Therefore the fellows I envisioned would obtain no tangible rewards for their year in residence. The intangible benefit obtained by listening to lectures and discussions would have to suffice.

I broached the idea to some members of the corporation, a few deans and faculty members. Some liked it, but no one reacted with enthusiasm. In the ensuing informal discussions, the details of a plan emerged. The recipient of a fellowship should have had at least three years of experience in journalism; the stipend should be the same as the man was earning on his newspaper; there must be a person in charge on a full-time basis supported by an advisory committee of professors. Such a man would be a "guide, counselor and friend" to the holders of the fellowships. He would endeavor to keep them in contact with newspaper work by inviting to Cambridge, from time to time, publishers, editors and columnists for an afternoon or evening session. The fellows would be free to listen to lectures or not as each saw fit. There would be no requirements for the completion of a paper and no examinations.

It was obvious that the fellowship scheme would work only if those who controlled the major newspapers wanted it to work. To give a man who had already proved himself to be of great value to a paper a year's leave of absence would be a sacrifice on the part of an editor. Did experienced newspapermen think enough papers would cooperate to give the scheme a fair trial? I put this question to several leading journalists in several cities. The answers were ambiguous. I recall a meeting at the President's House of three or four men who represented the Boston papers. After I had expounded my idea and been subjected to cross-questioning, the verdict was about as follows: "We have no better suggestion; you might as well try what you have in mind, though it will probably fail."

I reported the results of my exploration to the Corporation and made a cautious recommendation. Nieman Fellowships in journalism should be established, but only a portion of the income of the Nieman bequest should be earmarked to support them. The rest should be used for starting a collection of microfilms of daily newspapers as the director of the library had suggested. My recommendation was accepted.

In my annual report for 1936–37, I explained the creation of the new Nieman Fellowships: "New gifts for special purposes bring with them new responsibilities. Sometimes these responsibilities are such that the university accepts them with a heavy heart and some reluctance; in rare cases it refuses them altogether. But the recent Nieman bequest, though it places an additional problem at our door, can only be regarded as a great challenge to this particular community." (If I had been improperly frank, I would have written that, while I at first regarded the Nieman bequest with "a heavy heart and some reluctance," I had decided to regard it as a challenge.) I stated that "the plan is frankly experimental. The exact path of development cannot now be traced. Since no building is involved and no additions to our staff are required, the scheme is flexible and, if found impractical, can be modified or, indeed, abandoned in favor of some other project which may seem more promising."

A year later in reporting to the Overseers, I was far less cautious. There were two reasons for my change of mood. In the first place, contrary to the first gloomy prognosis, approximately four hundred applications had been received; second, I had been lucky enough to persuade Archibald MacLeish to accept the responsibility of heading the project. (Since he was to be responsible for the microfilm collection as well as guiding the nine fellows, we agreed he should carry the title of Curator.) He had brought the kind of enthusiasm that was needed to the novel undertaking. He saw the possibilities for the university and for the fellows in having weekly seminars on the role of journalism in American life. He rallied to his assistance professors in the Law School as well as in the faculty of arts and sciences. These academic men appreciated the opportunity of discovering the point of view of journalists; the journalists in turn welcomed the chance to debate current issues with well-known professors.

The tradition of an exciting exchange of views thus established in the first year by MacLeish was carried on by his successor, Louis Lyons. Without the insight of these two men the scheme might well have failed. Indeed, it is hard to think of the Nieman Fellows without Louis Lyons, for he continued as Curator through the difficult war years and well beyond my administration, retiring only after twenty-five years of service. The success of his administration may be measured by the fact that shortly after his retirement the former Nieman

Fellows raised a large endowment to supplement the original bequest. The increase in the number of fellows and the cost of living had made additional annual income a necessity. It was particularly noteworthy that several newspapers made substantial donations. The new endowment might well be considered as primarily a testimonial to what Louis Lyons had done "to promote and elevate the standards of journalism in the United States."

My indebtedness to Mrs. Nieman I have made clear. It is the indebtedness of an inventor to a person who challenges his ingenuity. What I owe as a college president to many other benefactors is different. I could not begin to list the men and women who during the twenty years of my administration came forward to make possible some new building or some new departure planned by a dean or director of a museum or head of a research institution. In spite of the years of depression and the years of war, the resources of the university increased; that this was so is largely due to the stimulation of interest of potential donors by those within the university who saw a need and obtained the Corporation's approval to raise the necessary funds.

Two examples will illustrate the kind of assistance I have in mind. One is the construction of Houghton Library in 1942 and the other the building of Lamont Library in 1949. To understand the significance of these buildings and illustrate the role of two understanding donors who responded to cries for help, I must explain the library problem which confronted me as a new president in 1933. For the immediate future, the Widener Library, which had been built just before World War I, was sufficient. It would not remain so long. The director of the library showed me figures to illustrate the way libraries grew. He told me what he considered to be the needs in the next two decades. To meet them, he believed we should start planning at once for another large library alongside of Widener—perhaps a tower of glass, he suggested. How we were to raise the capital required, he did not say. Since the question of providing library space could be postponed for a few years, the Corporation agreed that plans for a new building could wait until the Tercentenary Year was passed. The prospect of raising a large sum of money for a new university library remained, as did the threat of ruining the beauty of the college Yard by the intrusion of an enormous building. The less I thought about the growth of libraries, the happier I was in those early years of my trials as a university administrator.

Before the Corporation was faced with the immediate architectural problem of designing a new library building, Harvard had a new director of the university library. I had been fortunate in 1937 in being able to persuade Keyes DeWitt Metcalf to leave the Public Library in New York and come to Cambridge. He at once concerned himself with the plans for the future. In the meantime, what in 1933 had been a problem that could be postponed was now in 1937 one of urgency. The Widener Library was full. The new director presented a plan by which the building of another large library edifice was avoided—perhaps forever. With a great sense of relief, I welcomed it and encouraged its implementation.

The plan had several parts, each of which was to some degree independent of the others. The rare books and manuscripts were to be taken out of Widener and placed in a new building attached to Widener; this building would be so constructed as to provide constant temperature and humidity and thus ideal conditions for storing our valuable collection. A deposit library across the river not far from the Business School was to be a joint undertaking of academic institutions in Greater Boston. The less-used books would be stored in the building, whose construction would be relatively inexpensive since it would function only as a storage building. The third feature was the construction of underground stacks connected with Widener; the fourth and perhaps the most significant was the establishment of a library for undergraduates. When such a building was a reality, Widener would become a library for scholars. The nightmare of a vast new building in the Harvard Yard had disappeared. The planned shelf space would accommodate the growth projected for the next few decades and perhaps longer.

Mr. Metcalf not only drew up plans but before long found the ideal benefactors, who grasped his vision and responded with the necessary cash. I was able to report to the Overseers in January 1941 that the new building to house the rare books and manuscripts was under construction. A year later I was permitted to announce that the donor of this building, who had remained anonymous, was Arthur Amory Houghton, Jr., of the class of 1929.

The second ideal benefactor, Thomas W. Lamont of the class of 1892, had already been solicited by Mr. Metcalf before the entry of the United States into World War II. He was waiting in the wings until the close of the war would permit us to talk once more about the needs of the university. Toward the end of 1945, his gift of $1.5 million toward the building of an undergraduate library was announced. As a contribution to the Tercentenary Fund, Mr. Lamont had already endowed a university professorship. His willingness to make a large contribution toward the realization of the vision of the director of the library, therefore, was a second example of his readiness to respond to a specific request for funds. Quite apart from his generosity, I was personally in his debt for his constant support as an alumnus. He was a man of affairs who understood the academic mind. He was a conservative, but one who prided himself on his tolerance and his firm stand as regards the rights of professors to speak out on controversial issues. He was certainly not a New Dealer, but was miles removed from the Harvard alumni who complained that President Roosevelt's policies were being carried out by Harvard Law School graduates recruited for the purpose by Professor Felix Frankfurter.

It so happened that Mr. Lamont's generosity of spirit and his understanding of other people's intolerance were needed in connection with the placing of the undergraduate library in the Harvard Yard. Metcalf's first plan had envisioned that the library for undergraduates would be built outside the Harvard Yard. A small committee headed by the provost, however, reported in the fall of 1945 that much the best site was one on which stood a wooden frame house once occupied by Professor Palmer of the philosophy department. They recommended that the building be torn down. The Corporation agreed; the announcement was made that the new building would be erected "in the corner of the Harvard Yard opposite the Union." Almost at once, dissenting faculty voices were heard. What had been just another one of the old houses owned by the Corporation became a gem of architecture, a priceless heritage that must not be destroyed. Someone discovered that the author Richard Henry Dana had once occupied this dwelling. Overnight the building became the historic Dana-Palmer House; the Corporation was portrayed as a group with no interest in either history or architecture, ready to destroy the past to make room for the future.

The story was picked up by the daily press. One alumnus who read about the opposition to placing the undergraduate library in the Harvard Yard undertook to write directly to Mr. Lamont. His letter was such as would have annoyed severely a man of lesser stature. He placed the blame for the location of the new library on the donor, which was completely unjust. In writing me about the communication he had received, Mr. Lamont, who betrayed no sign of irritation, suggested that, instead of destroying the Dana-Palmer House, we might move it across the street and place it next to the Faculty Club. If this was done, he wrote, he was ready to provide the money needed to cover the expenses of both moving the house and reconstructing it as a guest house of the university. The Corporation welcomed the generous offer. Thinking we would still the protests, we announced that the Dana-Palmer House would be relocated on the other side of Quincy Street and would be made into a guest house for the university.

To our dismay, the new plan was subject to almost as much hostility by certain vocal members of the faculty as had been the original proposal. The vacant lot next to the Faculty Club, it was said, was a necessary part of the setting of the club. Until a few years ago, a wooden building had occupied the spot. Its removal during the war had relieved an ugly congestion; now the Corporation was proposing to crowd another house into too narrow a space. Furthermore, some argued that the move would cost great sums which the university had better spend on projects which were suffering from lack of funds. The fact that we had Mr. Lamont's promise to pay the cost was a secret we could not divulge as he had specified this second gift was to be anonymous.

While we were debating in a Corporation meeting what to do, a report came from the maintenance department that it was by no means certain that the Dana-Palmer House could be moved intact. There was a distinct possibility it would fall apart in the middle of Quincy Street. In that case, we all agreed, the matter would be settled. The historic dwelling would have disappeared, but by no act of vandalism by the Corporation. We concluded that efforts should be made in all sincerity and with due care to move the suddenly historic house. If successful, we would ask a committee of alumni to collect suitable New England antique furniture and pictures to make it an attractive guest house.

The move was successful; the house on the new site showed to much better advantage than before. A long addition which had housed Professor Palmer's library had been removed. The remodeling of the interior provided two stories of convenient bedrooms. University guests, who would be put up with no expense to them, could use the Faculty Club next door for breakfast and whatever other meals they desired. A Federal period house had been not only preserved but made more beautiful; everyone realized how sorely a guest house had been needed all those years. Thus ended a storm in an academic coffeepot.

By the time the Lamont Library, with its collection of 100,000 volumes, was opened for undergraduates, there were no thoughts for anything except Mr. Lamont's generosity. Only a few of us knew that the patience of an ideal benefactor had come close to being unduly tried.

The story of much of Harvard's growth in the period 1933 to 1953 can be told by substituting for the director of the library, the dean of the Business School or some other administrative officer and for Messrs. Houghton and Lamont, other men of wealth. What might be called "stimulated donations" enabled buildings to be built and professorships to be endowed. The stimulators were the deans and others authorized to speak for the university. Their persuasive enthusiasm was sufficient to enlist the support of potential donors.

In contrast to stimulated donations stand gifts and bequests from individuals who had made up their own minds as to what they wished to see endowed. Such persons might well be designated as self-directed potential benefactors. While the relation between the stimulated benefactor and the university is certain to be uncomplicated and happy, such is often not the case with a self-directed, would-be benefactor. I recall a well-substantiated rumor that in President Lowell's day a certain individual offered to endow a professorship quite handsomely, provided only that he himself would be appointed to the chair. President Lowell is alleged to have replied that Harvard professorships were not for sale.

A self-directed donor, as I am using the term, comes to the university with a clear idea of what he wants the university to do. More than once in my experience, the Corporation said in effect, "Thank you, but we are not willing to undertake what you have in mind." In the rare case where an individual's desire coincides with a recognized need of the university, the difference between a self-directed and a stimulated donor disappears. The meeting between Mr. Harkness and President Lowell is the classic example of such a situation. Usually the correspondence between the donor's ideas and the needs of the institution is not perfect, in which case long discussions are in order. In the first instance, it will probably be a dean or a museum director or a department chairman who represents the university. If the amount of money is large or the donor's ideas unusual, the case will soon land on the desk of the president of the university. (Or so it was as in President Lowell's day and in mine. I have made it a point not to know what has gone on in Cambridge since 1953.) The worst outcome of such discussions is a compromise that leaves a basic issue for settlement at a later time.

There are few generalizations to be drawn from a study of the wrecked hopes of people long since dead. Each case has its own characteristics. But there is one conclusion I came to after two decades of trying to adjust the mode of operation of some part of the university to a donor's wishes. From the point of view of the benefactor himself, it is a grave error to attempt to direct the expenditure of the income of an endowment beyond a relatively short period of time. No one can foresee what factors will develop in the course of ten or fifteen years which will seriously affect the scholarly work the benefactor has in mind when he draws his will. The wise donor, I believe, should provide that after a span of years—say, twenty-five at the most—all restrictions on the bequest should be considered void. I must admit that there are great difficulties in convincing either a donor or a stimulator of a donation (a dean or museum director, for example) of the correctness of my conclusion. Therefore I place in evidence a capsulated account of the Gordon McKay bequest to Harvard in support of applied science.

When Gordon McKay died in 1903, the value of his estate was estimated at something like $23 million. He proposed to leave it all to Harvard for the support of applied science; he charged the president and fellows, among other things, to "take special care of the great subject of mechanical engineering in all its branches." The size of the bequest was spectacular. If McKay had provided for the transfer of the capital to Harvard at once or even within a period of two decades, the history of instruction and research in the physical sciences and engineering in Greater Boston would have been quite different from what it has been. McKay, or whoever advised him, however, had the distant future in mind. The deed of trust provided that the bequest was not to be paid to Harvard until the death of the last annuitant (this proved to be no less than four decades later). In the meantime, Harvard would receive 80 percent of the accumulated income, to be paid annually and treated as endowment. The initial payment made by the McKay trustees in 1904 was a million dollars of accumulated income; thereafter the payments were to be annual. In 1904 a million dollars was a fortune; no one interested in science or Harvard could ignore the will of Gordon McKay. No one seemed to realize the full significance of the provision which was to delay the full payment to Harvard for so many years.

The uses of what seemed a very large endowment in 1904 soon became a matter of controversy. The basic question was older than McKay's will. Its origin can be traced to the 1890s, when leading Boston citizens began asking whether it was wise to plan for the expansion of both the Lawrence Scientific School in Cambridge and the Massachusets Institute of Technology in Boston. The talk of a merger which started was resented by many of the alumni of both institutions. The proposal received a new impetus when the possibility of using the McKay endowment to support a joint undertaking loomed over the horizon about 1905; the proponents and opponents squared off as for a knockdown fight. A. Lawrence Lowell, as a member of the Corporation of M.I.T., became a strong advocate; other Harvard men denounced the idea as being contrary to the wishes of the founders of the Lawrence Scientific School and Gordon McKay. After a few years the attempt was abandoned, only to be tried again after Mr. Lowell became president of Harvard in 1909. The Institute was at that time in process of moving from Boston to its present location in Cambridge. The time seemed ripe for a "complete cooperation in the teaching of mechanical, electrical, civil and sanitary engineering, mining and metallurgy in the buildings of Technology now under construction on the Charles River Embankment in Cambridge." (I quote from the agreement between the governing boards of the two institutions.)

In 1917, however, the Supreme Judicial Court of the Commonwealth held that the agreement was not in accord with the provisions of the will of Gordon McKay.* No further attempt was made to use the McKay funds to benefit M.I.T. Since then, the Institute's history has been that of a flourishing and expanding institution of the very first rank. It could hardly have prospered more if the decision of the court had upheld the agreement. The Gordon McKay will is only a passing incident in the success story of "Boston Tech," settled on the Cambridge bank of the Charles River.

The impact of the McKay trust on applied science at Harvard is quite another matter. I am prepared to argue that the Gordon McKay trust did more harm than good as far as Harvard was concerned. I leave aside entirely the two attempts at formal cooperation with the Massachusetts Institute of Technology, and base my contention on the effect of the fundamental fault in the deed of trust. By announcing to the world that Harvard would someday have a handsome endowment for applied science and then arranging so that the "someday" might be postponed for over forty years, I believe Gordon McKay did Harvard a great disservice. From the early 1900s until after the close of World War II, no effective appeal to support applied physical science at Harvard was possible. In the 1920s, when fund-raising efforts were being successful all over the country (including at Harvard), no one would have considered the situation of applied science

---

* The interested reader is referred to Henry A. Yeomans, *Abbott Lawrence Lowell*, Cambridge, Harvard University Press, 1948, Chapter XVII.

at Harvard. Everyone knew that Harvard had the McKay endowment, but since no one could tell how long the annuitants would live, no one could plan for the future.

When the time finally came in 1949 for the McKay trustees to transfer the final residue of the estate to Harvard, the value proved to be considerably less than earlier anticipated. What was more important, in the course of forty-five years the whole scale of academic expenditures had vastly altered. Furthermore, the president and fellows had been instructed in McKay's will to "take special care of the great subject of mechanical engineering in all its branches and in the most comprehensive sense," and mechanical engineering in 1950 was something quite different from mechanical engineering in 1903. To quote from the report of a reviewing panel in 1950: "Mechanical engineering, once concerned with relatively simple conversions of power, and the largely empirical alterations of the form of materials for man's use, now ranges over a vast scope of human effort. Airplanes, automobiles, modern mass production, intricate instrumentation, new metals and materials, are but part of the present day interests of mechanical engineers."

A five-man panel, headed by Dr. Vannevar Bush, was appointed by the Harvard Corporation shortly after we were notified that the responsibilities of the McKay trustees were at an end. Off and on in the 1920s and 1930s, the trustees had questioned Harvard's procedure in regard to the uses of that portion of the McKay money already received. Therefore the president and fellows decided that it would be wise to ask a group of distinguished applied scientists to review the whole situation and recommend how the income from the entire endowment should be expended in the future. The first conclusion of the panel was comforting and spelled the end of a period of discontent. "There is no doubt," said the panel, "that the present use by Harvard of income from the endowment is fully in accord with Gordon McKay's admonitions."

As to McKay's special concern for mechanical engineering, after pointing out the expansion of the field in words I have already quoted, the members of the panel wrote: "No one group no matter how endowed can treat mechanical engineering in the most comprehensive sense in all its branches. The attempt to do so would lead only to superficiality." The report continued with the guidelines for the future.

There must be selection even in this area. It would not be wise merely to scale down the extent of effort, and try to cover in some manner all that McKay wrote. Neither would it be justifiable to go to extremes and devote the entire income from the Endowment to one special phase of the original interest. In between lies reason. Specifically, the applied physical sciences should be further pursued with special emphasis upon the manifold ways in which mechanical engineering now enters them, and with the determination to cover a reasonable portion of the field very well indeed.

In 1950 the Corporation accepted the report of the Bush panel. In 1952 I could report to the Overseers that a single division of the faculty of arts and sciences had been created to correspond to the single unitary organization recommended by the panel. The new dean of applied science was quoted as saying, "It is our plan to accentuate the fundamental scientific and research aspects of engineering rather than to concentrate on highly specialized technological developments. The increased income from the Gordon McKay endowment furnishes an exceptional opportunity for such a program. Harvard will endeavor to keep abreast of the times in developing the branches of engineering which are modern and of current interest." To implement the desire to train engineers and applied scientists of the highest caliber, five special Gordon McKay fellowships for graduate study with a stipend of $2,000 each were created to attract top-ranking students to Harvard.

A new laboratory was in process of construction. In short, in 1952, after decades of living off restricted and uncertain rations, the applied scientists in the university were in a position to utilize the nourishment which Gordon McKay desired to put at the disposal of the university.

The moral of the tale needs no underlining. If you would hinder the growth of an educational enterprise, promise large sums for the future and tie up the gift so that it is many decades before its full benefits are received. Conversely, if you would promote the enterprise, see to it that the promised sum is made available without restrictions in not more than two decades, and preferably in a shorter time.

At first sight, the gift of Lucius N. Littauer, which eventuated in the endowment of a graduate school of public administration, seems to fall in the same category as the gift of Mr. Harkness. A self-directed donor found Harvard already prepared to carry forward the objective close to his heart. Actually, quite apart from the differences in the magnitude of the gift, the similarity between the cases is far from complete. President Lowell could speak for Harvard; as to undergraduate residential units, he knew exactly what he wanted. So, too, did Mr. Harkness. I never heard of the slightest disagreement between the two. Mr. Littauer was, perhaps, as definite in his desires as had been Mr. Harkness, but no one could speak for Harvard with either the clarity or authority of President Lowell. Mr. Littauer wanted to endow a new school which would bear his name. The school was to be a graduate school, comparable to the Harvard Graduate School of Business Administration, to train men for public service.

Before Mr. Littauer appeared on the scene, several Harvard programs for training public servants had been announced, starting with the Business School in December 1934. In May of 1935 a committee had been appointed on "University Training for Government Service" to coordinate the six separate programs which had come into existence. If the university committee had been able to function as a true coordinating committee, its chairman might have met with Mr. Littauer and detailed plans might have been drawn up at once. That nothing like that happened illustrates the difference between abstract concepts and reality.

Harvard in 1935 was concerned with training men for government service (an abstract idea), but rather than one real policy it had many. The Business School, the Law School, the department of government, the department of economics, all claimed to be able to present the most suitable course of studies to a young man who wished to prepare for a position in the federal government; so, too, did the Engineering School, the School of City Planning, the School of Public Health. There were certainly not a few who had been educated in all these branches of the university on the federal payroll in 1935. There were also chemists. The department of chemistry, however, was not interested in being listed along with the six schools and departments which announced something special to offer to those desiring to work for the government.

The academic stampede to gain an acknowledged position on the Harvard road to a career in Washington had been set off by Dean Wallace B. Donham's decision to expand the objectives of the School of Business Administration. As he frankly admitted privately, the depression and the New Deal had turned many young men's attention away from business careers. The same methods of instruction that had been successful in training men for business could easily be adapted to training for positions in government; so at least was Dean Donham's contention. It was not well received on the Cambridge side of the Charles River. My first introduction to a deep-seated distrust between most of the faculty of the Business School and a majority of the members of the economics department was in connection with reaction to the Business School announcement about training for government work.

The excitement about increased educational efforts directed to improving the quality of the Washington bureaucrats was one of those sudden gusts of opinion which have characterized American education all through my lifetime. They usually cause disturbances on many campuses. For example, one Harvard professor of government foresaw the immediate need for a large number of college graduates who had been instructed by professors of his ilk for a year or two. His colleagues in other departments foresaw a similar need, but for those trained in their disciplines. Thus economics, business administration, law and public health each felt they should be in a position to recruit and train more able young people to man the expanding New Deal agencies.

When Mr. Littauer made his offer of a generous gift, he threw a golden apple into a Harvard family already in disagreement. If he and the Harvard Corporation had been able to agree quickly as to what faculty or department was to control the new funds, negotiations might have proceeded smoothly. More endowed chairs and more fellowships in either the Business School or the Law School or the department of economics or government would have been welcomed not only by the recipient group but by the rivals, provided that the fortunate one was not designated as being Harvard's only way of training for government service. But the donor wanted a new school to bear his name. Clearly all who had been active in various programs must be heard. Therefore, as president, I stalled for time. I wrote in my annual report for 1934-35 as follows:

> For a number of years Harvard like other universities has been sending men into the government service—economists, lawyers, business administrators, scientists, doctors, engineers. Within the past fourteen months the business school has initiated a new program for training men for public administration, the government department has offered new courses for graduate students interested in practical work, and the economics department has increased its instruction along lines of interest to graduate students who might obtain positions of importance in government bureaus. It would be beyond the scope of this report to describe each one of these new developments and, moreover, such description would be premature.
>
> The splendid gift of Mr. Littauer for the establishment of a graduate school of public administration was received after the close of the year I am considering in this report, but since it profoundly affects our plans for the future I may be permitted to refer to it at this time.

The school which will be established through his generosity will supplant the Committee on University Training for Government Service which the Corporation appointed last winter. This committee was composed of the deans of the several faculties and the chairmen of the departments con-concerned with the different phases of training men for public service. It had made a start in working towards a series of unified programs of graduate study for those who were interested in entering the government service. . . .

The new school, which will be organized with its own dean and separate faculty, will be the focal point for all the many university activities which are concerned with training men for government service. Many members of the new faculty will also be members of our other faculties; there is no intention of duplicating in one part of the university work done elsewhere. Before proceeding with the plans for the new school, we shall await the report of a special commission which I have appointed under the terms of the gift. The commission, of which President Dodds of Princeton has kindly consented to be the head, is composed of L[eonard] D. White of Washington, D.C., W[illiam] B. Munro of Pasadena, California, and the following members of our faculties: Dean Donham, Professor Burbank, and Professor Lambie. These gentlemen will survey the whole problem of training men for government positions and the possibility of placing men trained by our university in responsible posts. Their findings will be of the greatest assistance to us in planning for the future.

The findings of the Dodds Commission included the advice to proceed slowly. The student body should be small and, initially at least, the emphasis should be on the further training of men already in government positions. The Commission recommended that before opening the new school Harvard should organize two "exploratory sessions" to which those familiar with government work would be invited. The recommendation was immediately accepted. A series of conferences was held in Cambridge attended by more than fifty officials drawn from the federal, state and municipal governments. To receive the advice of these many consultants, a new faculty was appointed consisting of a dozen professors drawn from the departments of government, economics and sociology of the faculty of arts and sciences and from the faculties of law and business administration.

As a result of all the discussions that took place during the winter of 1937, we moved further and further away from Mr. Littauer's original idea of a new school with a totally independent faculty. All the consultants agreed that we should endeavor to bring all the resources of the university to bear on the problem of training for government service. To that end, they almost as one man rejected the idea of a completely separate school with a wholly independent faculty and endorsed the idea of a faculty composed of persons who also held appointments in other faculties.

Close cooperation of the departments of economics and government could be furthered by housing the members who were concerned with public administration in one building. The idea appealed to Mr. Littauer; he increased his gift to provide specifically for the erection of a building to be known as the Littauer Center for Public Administration. The school was officially opened at the beginning of the academic year 1938–39; the Littauer Center was ready for occupancy in May 1939. Fourteen in-service fellowships had been awarded to a group selected from some 170 candidates, all of whom had had some government service. The seminars were also attended by graduate students in the faculty of arts and sciences. Within two years, the faculty of public administration voted to add to the Littauer Fellows (the in-service fellows) a limited number of high-ranking college graduates. In the spring of 1940 the faculty voted to recommend to the governing boards the creation of two graduate degrees in public administration. In his annual report, the dean explained the action of the faculty as follows:

This action represents the outcome of much thought and discussion. Initially, there was a great diversity of opinion. There were those who felt that the school should be entirely separate from the existing graduate schools, and that it should grant its own degrees. As the school was actually organized, the faculty was drawn from existing schools in the university, and the curriculum stressed a new method rather than a new content in the broad field of public administration. Our first energies were concentrated on the problem of developing the research seminars of the school, and it was thought best to postpone the question of separate degrees. There is now, however, a considerable body of experience which indicates that it is desirable for the school to have its own degrees.

The final outcome of the two-or-three-year process of evolving a Harvard Graduate School of Public Administration by no means pleased everyone. The members of the faculty of arts and sciences who had been appointed members of the new faculty were quite content, as they well might have been since they were the immediate beneficiaries of the physical plant made possible by Mr. Littauer's second generous gift. Members of other faculties were critical. So, too, were many outside the university. It was said that Harvard had taken Mr. Littauer's money and used it for the benefit of only two departments. The statement of the dean which I have just quoted

was an answer to such thrusts. They continued nevertheless. The idea
that the student body would be composed primarily of government
officials on leave of absence was well received in theory; in practice,
however, it proved difficult to recruit a sufficient number of such
individuals. Without the bait of a Harvard degree, it was thought
impossible. (The difference between the Littauer Fellows and the
Nieman Fellows is worth noting.)

I must admit that as I look back at the founding and development
of the Graduate School of Public Administration, I am happiest about
what was *not* done. If an entirely separate school with a separate
faculty had been established, Harvard would have gone down a road
which many institutions have traveled, but, to my mind, without
distinction. The rivalry between an essentially independent faculty of
public administration with its own buildings and the faculties of law
and business administration would have led to all sorts of undesirable
complications. The new faculty would have felt it necessary to gain
financial support by taking in a large student body and by appealing
for temporary gifts. Both would have required publicity of a rather
crass sort. In my opinion, the content of the courses given by such a
new independent faculty would have been thin.

Years later, I saw what such courses would have been like when I
examined graduate courses in school administration in many schools
of education. To make an art—administration—into a learned profession is a most difficult operation. The Harvard Business School after
many years' trial has succeeded primarily because of the imaginative
leadership and adherence to high standards of Dean Donham and his
successor, Dean D. K. David. Those who criticize most severely what
Harvard did with the Littauer gift seem to believe the equivalent of
the business school curriculum could have been developed in the
field of public administration. I doubted it in 1936, and my doubts are
stronger now. At all events, the decision *not* to have an independent
faculty made early in the exploration process settled the matter for
my administration. I am still of the opinion it was settled correctly
whatever present-day experts on public administration may say to the
contrary.

CHAPTER 31

ETS—An Educational Invention

THE EDUCATIONAL TESTING SERVICE is a nonprofit company located near Princeton, New Jersey. In 1966 it did nearly $25 million worth of business. Since one of its main activities is connected with the College Entrance Examination Board, the initials ETS are well known to school people all over the nation. Each year, not a few parents became aware of the Educational Testing Service through concern with the scores their offspring make on the Scholastic Aptitude Test (SAT) and the achievement tests prepared and graded by the organization.

Three separate testing enterprises were merged in 1947 in order to avoid overlapping and unproductive competition and in order to make available more resources for research and development; ETS was the result. An attempt in 1937–38 to bring about a similar consolidation had failed; the leaders in the testing movement were not then ready to join forces. After the war was over, it was suggested that another attempt be made. The successful merger was guided by the skillful hand of Devereux C. Josephs, at that time president of the Carnegie Corporation. Aware of my involvement in the prewar effort, he asked me to head a committee of educators to bring about what he had in mind. Because of my connection with two negotiations among testing experts, I became somewhat of a legend. Thus Henry Chauncey, the president of ETS, wrote me in 1961 when I retired from the Board of Trustees that the merger was my idea, "going back to 1937

417

or 1938. In 1946, it was put forward a second time. With the assistance of the Carnegie Corporation and after long negotiations in which you yourself took an active part, the merger was finally agreed upon."

President Chauncey was mistaken; a merger was not my idea in either 1937 or 1946. I was acting not as an inventor but as a promoter. If anyone is interested in naming the true inventors of ETS, he will have a hard time drawing up a list. Which illustrates an important point: if social inventions were covered by patents, the possibilities of litigation would be as endless as they are with the usual type of patent applying to new products, processes and procedures in the physical sciences.

I agreed in 1937 as a college president to lend a hand to the combining of several testing agencies because of my recently acquired enthusiasm for the Scholastic Aptitude Test. During the first year of my presidency, as I mentioned earlier, I turned to the Harvard Scholarship Committee to gain support for my idea of a new type of scholarship. Would it be possible to pick out from the applicants for admission to the college a few extremely able young men to whom we could award prize scholarships with reasonable certainty that the subsequent record of the recipients would be outstanding? To answer my question, a subcommittee was formed consisting of Henry Chauncey, then an assistant dean of Harvard College, and Wilbur Bender. The report of this subcommittee recommended the use of the Scholastic Aptitude Test.

As far as I can remember, my conversations with Chauncey and other members of the Scholarship Committee were my first introduction to what psychologists had been doing in the field of examinations since World War I. I had heard of the psychological tests used by the Army during the war, but the opinions about such tests were usually far from favorable. I was almost completely ignorant of what Professor Carl C. Brigham of Princeton had accomplished by developing a scholastic aptitude test which the College Entrance Examination Board started to give annually in 1926. It was hardly a new invention when we decided at Harvard to employ it as an instrument to differentiate among the incoming freshmen. Yet the more I learned about the use of the new objective tests and the more I became familiar with the concept of scholastic aptitude, the more I showed signs characteristic of a recent convert to a new religion. And it was a recognition of these signs that led half a dozen leaders in the testing movement to turn to me in 1937 when the question of a merger of testing agencies came up for discussion.

Like those of many converts, my beliefs included hopes that went too far. Looking back over the thirty-five years since my conversion, I recognize the almost naïve faith with which I embraced the testers. It was easy to see the limitations of the college entrance examination system which then existed and had existed during the first decades of this century. In reacting against it, I was too ready to see in two new concepts—verbal aptitude and mathematical aptitude—the keys which would unlock all doors to a more promising future.

An historian of American higher education is apt to overlook the extent to which professors of Latin and Greek dominated the scene in the closing decades of the last century. They were fighting a rearguard action, to be sure, but as late as 1910 few of them realized that almost complete defeat was just a few years around the corner. The traditions they defended stemmed from both Europe and England. In the European universities, as in the colleges of Oxford and Cambridge, it was assumed in 1900 that unless one had studied Latin and Greek to good advantage, one had not taken the first step toward becoming an educated man. To be sure, an indigenous American university tradition exemplified by the founding of the land-grant colleges in the 1860s and 1870s had injected into American higher education another virus which might be called an anticlassical strain. However, its influence was weak, at least on the East Coast. If my experience in 1904 to 1910 is representative, I would say that the defenses surrounding the study of Latin were holding firm, though those around Greek were crumbling fast. For example, a student in the Roxbury Latin School had to choose in his third year between German and Greek, and a majority chose the former.

If one elected Greek in school and was successful on the college entrance examination, one received a double credit as compared with all other subjects except Latin. The scoring of credits for admission to college in 1910 in favor of Latin and Greek exemplifies the deliberate influence of the College Entrance Examination Board on the curricula of the schools. Since each collegiate institution set its own admission requirements, the Board could not mandate the content of the curriculum. But the double credit for Latin and Greek was not without its effect. Some colleges required at least an elementary knowledge of both Latin and Greek. Harvard at that time required neither, but by an ingenious scheme favored Latin by awarding the S.B. degree to those who knew no Latin and the A.B. degree to those who did. One of my first attempts at reform in my first year or two as president was an effort to remove the restrictions on the awarding of the A.B. degree. When the proposal was debated in the faculty of arts and sciences, the classicists said little; it was the historians and the professors of English who spoke with emotion about the advantages of studying Latin. The proposal was roundly defeated. Another decade was necessary before deaths and retirements produced a faculty which could consider dispassionately an educational question involving Latin.

In the early days of this century, the nature of the examinations in all subjects was determined to a large degree by the examinations in Latin and Greek; at least such is my contention. The virtue of both languages, we were told in school, lay in the fact that in the process of mastering them one trained one's mind. A careful and thorough knowledge of the grammar was the backbone of what had to be learned by the student. French (which was also required of all Roxbury Latin School students) and even German (which was optional) could not offer the same mental discipline as did the two ancient languages; Latin and Greek also had the great advantage that no one knew how they had been pronounced in antiquity; therefore they could be taught entirely on a paper-and-pencil basis. But I doubt if I heard much discussion about the special significance of studying Latin while I was in school. All of us accepted the curriculum and the examination system without question. It was only later as a faculty member that I began to be aware of the arguments which sought to justify the emphasis on a knowledge of Latin.

The core of the requirements for admission to college in the days when I was seeking admission was composed of languages (six years each of French and Latin and three of German in my case). This fact, I believe, determined the type of questions found on all the examination papers; it also determined what those who read the bluebooks considered to be the correct answers. The study of ancient and modern languages in the school years established the idea that the main purpose of an examination paper was to test a candidate's knowledge of a restricted group of facts. The College Board annually published *Definitions of Requirements*. These syllabi were easily constructed for the languages and without much difficulty for geometry and algebra. Even ancient history, which was then the customary subject studied in the last two years of a preparatory school, could be made the basis for a syllabus; it was essentially a static field of knowledge. Physics and chemistry presented real problems. I first became aware of them when I served as a young professor in the 1920s on a committee of the College Board to prepare the chemistry paper for the forthcoming year. How much of the new discoveries and new ideas should be included? Was it fair to ask a question which could only be answered by a schoolboy who had been fortunate enough to have had an up-to-date teacher? Questions of this sort must have haunted the College Board committees preparing examination papers in the sciences all through the 1920s.

The annual revision of the *Definitions of Requirements* must have presented many problems. How these problems evaporated once the College Board, through ETS, established achievement tests I shall explain later. First, I must quarrel with the terminology of those who have labeled the examinations of the first decades of this century "essay examinations" in contrast to modern multiple-choice tests. The significant characteristic of those earlier examinations was not the long essay-type answer required in some instances. The hallmark was their relation to a carefully prescribed area of content. The student, of course, heard nothing about definitions of requirements or syllabi. But he was fully conscious of the existence of a field of knowledge; its boundaries, he knew, set limits to what he might find on the examination paper. His acquaintance with the content of the field was largely a result of his having pored over old examination papers. A bound copy of those given in previous years in each subject was essential as a textbook (though there was only one copy, carefully guarded by the teacher). Just how one should answer each question was gone over in some detail. Toward the end of the year, the class was given a full trial examination. One of the old examination papers was assigned to each student; bluebooks were distributed, and all concerned wrote as though their entry into college really depended on how they answered the half-dozen or so questions. The reader may recall how my participating in one of these trial runs led to N. Henry Black's taking me seriously as a would-be chemist.

Today it is easy to deride the entrance examinations of fifty or forty years ago on the grounds that the questions asked tested only rote learning. I have never felt that such condemnation was justified. The changes that came during the 1920s and 1930s were in people's ideas about what knowledge should be required by admission officers of the colleges. Once the unanimity among institutions about the place of Latin and either Greek or a modern language vanished, the whole relation of school to college altered. At least such is my considered opinion; though I must warn the reader that it is not the usual interpretation of recent academic history. As I see it, the dissatisfaction with the college entrance examinations began when college faculties became less certain that there was a well-defined package of academic skills and knowledge that entering freshmen in all first-rate colleges should possess.

After World War I, even those who looked with suspicion on the new psychological tests began to speak out against the entrance examinations, which were said to test only unrelated fragments of knowledge. Even in the foreign language examinations too much emphasis was placed on grammar, the critics claimed. Everyone knew that the preparation for taking the examinations could degenerate into a "cramming" course and often did; in such a course memory alone was involved. The words "comprehensive examinations" began to appear in the writings of the leaders in education about the time of World War I. President Lowell had advocated such tests early in his administration. He sought to pull together the four years' intellectual experiences of a graduating college senior by a set of comprehensive examinations. To assist the undergraduate in preparing for them, tutors were needed. Thus the tutorial system which he introduced at Harvard just after World War I rested on the premise that a certain type of final examination would mark the termination of a four-year college course.

President Lowell in the years when I came to know him spoke of his efforts in reform. The medical faculty, he said, was the first to understand what he was driving at, and passing a comprehensive examination was made a requisite for an M.D. degree. Writing a three-hour essay on "milk" was found to be an excellent way of stimulating a student to consider as a whole the knowledge he had acquired in biochemistry, physiology, pathology and other fields.

To make college entrance examinations comprehensive was another story; they were obviously quite different in many respects from the final examinations which President Lowell had introduced. As long as the questions asked on the examination paper had to conform to a syllabus, the content had to be restricted. Within the time allotted (one hour for most subjects, never more than three), a candidate could not be expected to answer more than six to ten questions. Yet a hundred would not exhaust the information covered by the syllabus alone. The examiners might endeavor to ask at least one or two questions which would tie together separate topics and at the same time test the candidate's capacity to use his knowledge in solving a problem.

I recall the way my ingenuity was taxed the one time I served on a College Board committee. Many other professors must have had a similar experience. The schoolteachers who sat on the examining committee were particularly impatient with the syllabi. For several decades the forward-looking headmasters had complained that the colleges were attempting to determine the curricula in the schools through the examinations of the College Board. Finally, in 1942, the Board ceased publishing *Definitions of Requirements*. By that time, however, the Scholastic Aptitude Test had gained so much prestige as to make the nature of the subject-matter examinations of relatively little importance.

The old-fashioned examinations were on the way out, not because some involved writing an essay, but because all were based on an old assumption in process of being discarded. I may call it the classical premise, which in the nineteenth century had been accepted as self-evident in Europe, England and the United States. In a word, it amounted to a definition of the knowledge that all educated men must have mastered before leaving school. Knowledge of ancient and modern languages and mathematics constituted much more than half the total content.

Once the classical premise was abandoned, the foundation of the college entrance examination system as it had existed rapidly disappeared. The schools would call the tune, each in its own right. Even within one school different pupils could elect different programs, each according to the headmaster entirely suitable for a future college student. What a heresy! In place of the uniformity among pupils and schools which acceptance of the classical premise ensured, academic chaos was the order of the day. The teachings of the ancient prophets were thrown aside; a group of modern successors came forward, each with his own analysis of education and each with his particular design for a progressive school curriculum said to be "suitable for the modern age." Teachers or administrators in secondary schools or colleges had to seek new supports for their pedagogical prejudices unless they tried to hold fast to the tottering classical premise. Some sought educational salvation in one direction, some in others. My own orientation was determined by my ignorance of psychology on the one hand and by Harvard's success with the Scholastic Aptitude Test on the other. The word "aptitude" seemed to me to be the key to the new revelation. I proceeded to try to make it my own.

A letter I wrote in February 1938 to the principal of a high school in Boston is clear evidence of the way my thoughts were running at that time. Replying to a letter of appreciation of my annual report for 1936–37, I wrote that the only hope I saw of solving the problems of a high school lay in the trend toward differentiation. "I do feel encouraged by the results which have been obtained through the testing and guidance movement. If we can discover methods of finding out the inherent abilities of our students at as early an age as possible and select education to suit them, perhaps some of the difficulties at least will partially disappear."

I had become a firm believer in what I thought the proponents of the Scholastic Aptitude Test had postulated. I equated "aptitude" with "inherent ability"; I thought the psychologists had shown the constancy of inherent abilities from childhood on. I was later to see the error of my oversimplification, but for a number of years my thoughts about education reflected what might be called a Calvinistic view of intellectual ability. If better testing methods could be devised, I saw no reason why the inherent abilities of each child could not be determined as early as age twelve. How many separate abilities or aptitudes there might be, I could not say. But if aptitude for mathematics might be taken as an example, a proper measure of it would enable one to predict for a junior high school youngster the degree of success in mathematics courses in school and college, irrespective of the efforts of the teachers. Such were my assumptions.

The advantage of this point of view for a college admission officer was obvious. Measure the various aptitudes of a candidate for admission and choose only those with the highest scores. Since there were several aptitudes, those who guarded the college gates would have to decide as to what would be an acceptable balance of aptitudes in a youth who sought admission. Low aptitude for mathematics might be offset by high performance on a verbal aptitude test. The significant fact appeared to be that the school record was of little consequence. Subject-matter examinations were of slight value. The aptitude, not the schooling, was what counted. In some such words, I would have expressed my educational creed after three or four years in office. If asked for evidence, I would have cited our success with the SAT in administering the National Scholarships at Harvard.

In the spring of 1937 the chairman of the Harvard Admission

Committee, Richard M. Gummere, talked to me about a plan for merging the forces of the College Entrance Examination Board with those of several organizations which were preparing tests or using them in connection with school and college problems. He knew my enthusiasm for the SAT (which he did not entirely share); speaking on behalf of a committee of the Board, he hoped I might be the spokesman for those in the testing movement who wished to move forward through close cooperation. More research was needed in order to prepare better tests. The proposition appealed to me as a man who had left a laboratory only four years before. I indicated my willingness to do what I could.

Benjamin D. Wood of the Educational Records Bureau was one of the early proponents of multiple-choice tests. He did not talk in terms of aptitudes (at least not to me). I think he would have been quick to see the fallacy of my naïve acceptance of the concept of "inherent ability" if I had ever spelled out to him my point of view in 1937 or 1938. He was one of those who favored a merger. I recall being tackled by George Zook, president of the American Council on Education, at an Atlantic City meeting of educators about my alleged interest in a merger; he warned me against Ben Wood, who, he said, did not speak for many test makers. I can still hear his rather plaintive voice as we hurried along the boardwalk, late for some important meeting.

In spite of the warning, I agreed to address the annual meeting of the Educational Records Bureau on October 28, 1937. I wrote to my educational mentor, Francis Spaulding, asking for help in preparing the speech. I was in "desperate need of advice and guidance," I said. The questions I asked in the letter betray my beliefs about many details of the educational process. In particular, one question reflects my hope that the acceptance of the concept of scholastic aptitude would open a new chapter in school and college relationship. Specifically I asked Spaulding whether or not he would agree that "during the education received in even the best school in four years, the scholastic aptitude of a given individual is not changed more than 10 percent."

No answer to this letter has survived. I cannot believe that Spaulding did agree; he must have pointed out the unwarranted assumptions that lay back of my belief in the constancy of scholastic aptitude as measured by the tests available. A sharp discrepancy between tests which could measure an aptitude (such as mathematical aptitude) and those which measured mathematical knowledge did not, in fact, exist. As I was gradually to realize, the most perfect mathematical aptitude test yet devised could measure only a *developed* aptitude; exposure to good teaching in mathematics as contrasted with no exposure in grades 9, 10 and 11 did make a difference in development.

I made my speech as promised to a gathering of educators assembled under the auspices of the Educational Records Bureau in New York. The text is of interest as a document showing my prejudices as of 1937. I spoke of two groups of educators; the one had "high hopes that if we can perfect our methods of education any boy, yours or mine, for example, can become a very reputable member of any learned profession he may elect." The other held that "if not at birth at least early in his school career each student is a bundle of definitely set capacities, and those aptitudes are highly resistant to change by external agencies."

To illustrate, I referred to a student studying a modern language in the last years of school or the first years of college. All would agree, I said, that "the rate of progress was dependent on two factors: (a) the effectiveness of the teaching and (b) the inherent capacity of the individual student for learning languages." The educational optimists, I thought, emphasized the first factor, teaching; the believers in the toughness of inherent capacity (aptitude) did just the reverse. "Most of us would vibrate in our view between the two extremes," I said and added: "Whatever one's average position, surely one would agree as to the need for tests which could unscramble the two factors of (a) capacity or aptitude and (b) the knowledge acquired. . . . We need accurate tests not only of what a student has mastered, but of how difficult it will be for him to proceed to master a given subject; at the college level the need for accurate testing of aptitudes is more important than the need for information about the acquired knowledge."

My concern with improving the existing tests and the devising of new tests was thus made clear. The speech was intended to put me on the side of those who not only favored testing and the use of multiple-choice tests but were arguing for cooperation between testing organizations. My concluding words were as follows:

I have only one final suggestion to make tonight. I hope it may possibly be a constructive one. Would it not be worth while to combine in one organization a number of our present testing and examining agencies? We have made only a start in this business of testing. We need to know how to break down this "composite academic ability" I have spoken of, how to develop predictive tests for all sorts of vocations and avocations. To do this requires investigation—a great deal of investigation—and the results of this should be available rapidly for all examining agencies. Furthermore, these agencies should be in close touch with the investigative work. In any such merger I should wish for an agreement that the independent functioning of certain of the present boards should be assured. There would need to be a constitution, as it were, that would prevent the new from devouring the old, or vice versa. The continued existence of the College Entrance Examination would be essential. Many colleges, including Harvard, need these examinations and I understand many schools agree as to their value. From my point of view such examinations are particularly necessary for the boy of somewhat less than the highest rating of "composite academic ability" for with such students this lack along orthodox academic lines must be offset by thorough training and careful education in suitable pre-collegiate subjects. . . .

I suppose that all through school and college we should endeavor by repeated testing to discover the development of a student's strong hand and judge him by that hand. At the same time we should endeavor to some extent to round out his intellectual stature by paying careful attention to his weaknesses. From all this it seems clear to me that we need to continue to have varieties of tests and examinations in school, between school and college, and in college. But I suggest that we should have a more intimate association of all those interested in this subject so that we might coordinate the activities, exchange ideas and direct a common program of research and study.

Those who had urged me to espouse the cause of objective testing and the merger of existing testing agencies should have been happy with my remarks. As an outsider manifesting enthusiasm for what the experts had been doing, I thought I had done quite well. But if the instigators of my intrusion into the prickly thicket of test makers thought that my presence would bring about a change, they were soon to be disappointed. The last months of 1937 and the first of 1938 were a period of private conferences and exchange of letters among Brigham, W. S. Learned, George W. Mullins (the secretary of the College Board), Ben Wood and George Zook. Before I realized what had happened, a quarrel among psychologists had ensued. Brigham published an article in *School and Society* in the issue of December 11, 1937,* referring to my address. He stated that "the present testing movement carries the germs of its own destruction and unless the proposed organization is set to develop a cure for these afflictions it will retard rather than advance educa-

* Pp. 756–759.

tion." I soon discovered that tests which superficially resembled the SAT were being used by Learned not to test aptitudes but to measure the extent of a person's knowledge of a given field.

Learned had been active for some years as a member of the staff of the Carnegie Foundation for the Advancement of Teaching in studying the schools and colleges of Pennsylvania. Using his own tests, he measured the progress of many youths in the schools and colleges subject by subject. He discovered that some high school seniors were more advanced in their comprehension of many subjects than were college sophomores—a result which when published was easily subject to misinterpretation. People began saying that Learned had proved that some schoolboys were better educated than many college sophomores. I remember President Lowell speaking harshly about Learned's work in 1934 or 1935. "I have known many schoolboys and many college sophomores," he said. "I am quite sure that they differ in their educational progress just as I know a fat boy differs from a thin one; and if anyone told me they weighed the same, I would say, 'There is something wrong with your scales.' There is something wrong with the tests Learned is using."

Looking at the scanty records that are now available, I conclude that Professor Brigham's quarrel with Learned was fundamental. They disagreed over what the new tests were designed to show; was it aptitude or achievement? Brigham's prestige was properly high. When he expressed doubts about the beneficial effects of a merger on research (as he did in December), to all intents and purposes he scotched the plan that the conspirators had been hatching. As far as I was concerned, my brief foray into the battle among testers was just one more among many unsuccessful endeavors. I never expected to hear about testing agencies again except as their activities infringed directly on Harvard affairs.

My expectations were wrong; I had not counted on the resilience of the idea of a merger. If a definitive history of the testing movement or even of the Educational Testing Service is ever written, it will have to treat in detail the immediate postwar activities of Learned, Henry Chauncey (who became associate secretary of the College Entrance Examination Board in the summer of 1945), Mullins, the new officers of the Carnegie Corporation, Devereux Josephs (president), Charles Dollard (second-in-command), as well as O. C. Carmichael of Vanderbilt, who became president of the Carnegie Foundation for the Advancement of Teaching. I was in no way involved until late in March 1946, when Henry Chauncey came to

Cambridge to see me. He explained what had been going on since the end of the war. He referred to a document prepared by Mullins and Learned, of which I still have a copy. It is dated March 21, 1946. The introductory statement by George Mullins is so illuminating that I shall quote almost all of it.

In 1937 I discussed with President Walter Jessup and Doctor William S. Learned of the Carnegie Foundation the possibility of bringing together a number of testing agencies either in a single unit or as co-ordinated independent units. After considerable discussion, the plan did not seem desirable from the point of view of the College Entrance Examination Board, and no further consideration was given to it.

More than three months ago Doctor Learned again discussed the matter with Mr. Henry Chauncey, the Associate Secretary, and briefly with me. He indicated that he was retiring soon and that it was the desire of the Carnegie Foundation and Carnegie Corporation to terminate the operation of the Graduate Record Examination and the Pre-Engineering Inventory Test and yet to find some way to have these tests carried on independently of the Corporation and the Foundation.

On February 5, at the invitation of President Devereux Josephs of the Carnegie Corporation, Mr. Chauncey and I lunched with President Josephs, Mr. Charles Dollard, the Assistant to the President, and Doctor Learned at the offices of the Corporation. President Josephs stated that the Carnegie Foundation and the Carnegie Corporation felt that they owed an obligation to the many universities that had cooperated with the Carnegie Foundation in these testing experiments and that it was their desire to find some way to carry them on for the service of the colleges and the universities; that the Carnegie Corporation and the Carnegie Foundation were interested, and they were also interested in seeing a large nationally recognized testing agency established. President Josephs felt that these ends might be achieved by incorporating the Graduate Record Examination and the Pre-Engineering Inventory in the College Entrance Examination Board. He asked me to indicate a method of procedure for exploring the possibilities, and I suggested that Mr. Charles Dollard visit Princeton and that he and Mr. Chauncey, after thorough exploration of all phases of the problem, draw up a plan. This was acceptable to all concerned.

At this luncheon we discussed briefly the revision of the Constitution and By-laws of the College Entrance Examination Board and the further revision that would be necessary in the event that the Graduate Record Examination and the Pre-Engineering Inventory Test became a part of the Board's activities. President Josephs spoke of my desire to retire from the work of the Board and, in this connection, said that he felt that the enlarged Board resulting from this merger would be fortunate to have Mr. Henry Chauncey assume the title of "Director." Mr. Josephs suggested that the term "Director" for the highest office and "Assistant Director" or

"Associate Director" for the second-highest office would be more in keeping with the nature of the organization than the terms "Executive Secretary" and "Associate Secretary" respectively. He also expressed the feeling that I should remain with the Board for a year or two, and suggested that an appropriate title for me would be "Chairman of the Executive Committee" or "Chairman of the Board of Trustees," depending on the form of organization.

Chauncey, in writing to thank me for my advice about the proposed merger (I have forgotten what the advice was), reported on an informal meeting of certain members of the Executive Committee of the College Board. In theory, all were in favor of "moving ahead to a larger and broader field of service, while at the same time they were reluctant to make the specific changes in the organization that would be necessary." He concluded that the College Board was not unlike a faculty and time was needed. However, he was optimistic about the eventual outcome of the proposed merger.

That more than optimism was required is evident from a letter of Chauncey's to Dean Henry Dyer, in charge of scholarships at Harvard. The pertinent section is as follows:

While we were working hard at the behest of the Carnegie Corporation to see how the matter could be presented at the April meeting of the Board (and as you know there were many complications involved, particularly those relating to the new Articles of Association and By-Laws) a meeting took place between Josephs, O. C. Carmichael, and Dollard, of the Carnegie Corporation, and Zook, Brumbaugh, and McConnell of the ACE [American Council on Education]. The later group raised a terrific storm of protest. They claimed that arrangements were being made which vitally affected them without their having due notice. . . . As I got the report from Dollard right after the meeting, the session was a stormy one. In fact, there was so much heli raised that the officers of the Carnegie Corporation decided that it would be inadvisable to proceed with the merger at this time, so that everything has been put off at least until the end of this year. In the meantime, the Carnegie Corporation proposed to appoint a commission to investigate the following problems: (a) What is the best disposition to make of the GRE [Graduate Records Examination]? (b) Is it advisable to have a national testing agency which would include all of the larger testing groups in the country? (c) If the answer to "b" is yes, what is the best way to bring about the formation of such an agency? What will develop is anyone's guess.

At this point, I entered the scene. In the middle of May (1946) Carmichael appointed me chairman of the commission which Chauncey had foreseen in his letter. The other members were: the presidents of Cornell, Brown, the University of Cincinnati, the University of California and the University of Minnesota; the dean of the Graduate School of the University of North Carolina; Alexander J. Stoddard, Superintendent of Schools at Philadelphia; and Francis Spaulding, only recently inaugurated as the Commissioner of Education for the State of New York. Mr. Stephen H. Stackpole, an officer of the Carnegie Foundation, served as secretary. Such a group of well-known educational administrators was regarded with considerable respect in those days. It was extremely likely that what we recommended would find acceptance in all the hostile camps.

The report was unanimous; we carried out the task which Josephs wished us to perform, recommending "that there be established the Cooperative Educational Testing Service," but we envisioned this new organization as "affiliated with the American Council on Education." Now it was the turn for the College Entrance Board to dissent. There were others also who questioned the report of our committee, among them Henry Dyer of Harvard and Paul Buck, the provost of Harvard University.

It would be wearisome to recount the negotiations which went on from the date of our report (October 4, 1946) until a letter from Josephs in February informed me that a modified plan had been approved by the CEEB and the members of the committee most concerned. Only the American Council of Education was holding out. Zook's stubbornness proved to be formidable, George Stoddard, the president of the University of Illinois, had to be brought into the picture as another spokesman for the American Council. He saw clearly the need for a merger. Finally, Joseph's persistence and diplomatic skill, as well as Chauncey's, succeeded.

On June 20, 1947, the secretary of the committee wrote to me as chairman that the representatives of the CEEB and ACE had come to an agreement. The Carnegie Corporation had already promised to contribute handsomely to the initial endowment. The Board of Trustees of the new Educational Testing Service met and elected Henry Chauncey as president. The new educational invention was ready to function, and function effectively it did, with a manifold expansion of its projects. On my return from Germany in 1957, I became a trustee and therefore can speak from personal knowledge when I testify to the importance of the research and development activities in support of which the merger had been originally conceived.

Since 1937 not only I but others have modified our views about tests and testing. The concept of aptitude as distinguished from achievement is no longer as clear-cut as it once was. What is assessed by aptitude tests is not an inborn set of dispositions but the resultant of the experiences of the youth in question. I long ago recognized the effect on the SAT results of differing school environments. And since I made a study of the schools in the big-city slums, I have begun to appreciate how much all test scores are influenced by the out-of-school environment—the home, the family and the neighborhood. Nevertheless the significance of the introduction by the College Board of multiple-choice achievement tests remains. These tests were so all-embracing that no syllabi for them could be written. This fact was of determining importance. (The *Definitions of Requirements,* as I mentioned, were abolished in 1942.) Since the end of World War II it has been widely recognized that for the purpose of predicting subsequent success (or lack of it) in college, both achievement tests and aptitude tests, as well as the school record, should be carefully considered. The new type of this test of the knowledge acquired (the multiple-choice achievement test) is a far better test than the old College Board papers because, instead of five to ten questions, there are now many items; the element of luck as to what a candidate would find on the examination paper, so great in the old days, has been largely eliminated. Today we have much better methods of assessing what a boy or girl has mastered during the school years than before the new-type tests were introduced. Though there are still critics of the new procedures, few school or college people would wish to go back to the days of fifty years ago. The establishment of ETS was part of an educational revolution in which I am proud to have played a part.

CHAPTER 32

Much Ado About Economics

M Y DISCUSSIONS with undergraduates when I was an assistant professor in the early twenties were largely confined to chemistry. I did have an opportunity, however, from time to time to learn of student opinions about other topics. In those days each faculty member was asked to serve as an adviser to a small number of students. He was supposed to give wise counsel on the choice of electives and thus help an individual construct a worthwhile program of studies. Regulations required that if any changes were made during the year, the consent of the faculty adviser must be obtained.

One day in the late fall, one of my advisees, a sophomore, called. He said he wanted to drop the introductory course in economics— a large lecture course with many sections. "What is the matter," I asked, "is it too difficult?" "No, indeed," came the answer. "The course is easy enough, but I just can't listen any longer to what I have to hear. I am a Republican, my family has always been Republican— down on labor and all that. And now I am supposed to pay attention to a professor who believes in free trade." He added with disgust that he suspected that all the section men were Democrats. The young man's views were definite; it was not for me as a chemist to explore the matter further. I signed the card which permitted him to drop the course. The sophomore departed, freed from the necessity of listening twice a week to heresy and arguing once a week with an instructor whom he suspected of being a Democrat.

For nearly a decade, I cherished the memory of the incident. I told the story more than once. Perhaps unconsciously I prided myself on being a professor of a subject in which differences of opinion could be settled by appealing to experimental evidence. (My views about the nature of science were in those days oversimplified.) After I left the comfortable chair of organic chemistry and became president of the university, I kept recalling my experience with my staunch Republican advisee for quite another reason. I realized that more than one alumnus with whom I talked could well have been the very person who had refused to continue to study Economics A.

My first year in office was the first year of the New Deal, it will be remembered. Criticism of Roosevelt's policies was mounting. At alumni meetings I met graduates who were anxious to tell me about what they regarded as the dangerous follies of the new administration. Many of the specific complaints were in the area of economics. Yet at that time I heard little talk about the way the subject was taught to undergraduates at Harvard. The few critical comments I did encounter, I could turn aside by quoting from a report of the visiting committee for economics of the Board of Overseers for 1933–34. The chairman, Walter Lippmann, had referred to the general impression that the selection of teachers of economics raised "acute issues over irreconcilable questions of public policy." But he had stated there was no problem at Harvard because the principle of free inquiry was so deeply rooted and because the criteria of scholarship were so high. In another report written in 1936, he reverted to the same question and wrote the following most helpful paragraph:

"In the task of recruiting a new member of the faculty, the question of his views on controversial public issues is now, and we believe should continue to be, left aside; insofar as it arises at all, the question is whether or not he arrived at his views by thorough scholarship and by intellectual processes which command the respect of his peers."

No one on the Board of Overseers challenged the statement. It stood for years as a comforting report of a distinguished alumnus about a department of the college. Only in 1950 when another chairman of the committee of the Overseers challenged the composition of the department of economics did I fully realize the extent of the protection Lippmann's declaration had afforded me for so many years.

As an example of the way in which the visiting committee's report of 1936 helped me, I may cite my correspondence with Ogden

L. Mills. As a former Secretary of the Treasury in the Hoover administration, he was in close touch with the banking and business community. As a member of the small group of the alumni who were
engaged in the Tercentenary Fund campaign, he was in a position
to hear critical questions raised about the college. More than one of
his friends had objected to what certain younger members of the
department of economics had said publicly in support of Roosevelt's
fiscal policy. Moreover, Mills had frequently heard the fear expressed
that unsound doctrine was being taught in the department of economics. He was a loyal alumnus, who was lending an effective hand
in the money-raising effort. He understood fully the nature of a
university. Therefore, I sent him a copy of the report of the committee
to visit the department of economics, which I thought would be of
help.

"I greatly appreciate your interest in this whole matter of academic freedom and am delighted you feel as you do," I wrote.
Referring to the question of choosing a new member of the economics
department, I suggested that it all came down "to picking a group
of clear-thinking scholars who are primarily scholars balancing the
inevitable tendencies to right and left, and then letting discussion
rage." I went on to say that while I should not appoint a geologist
who believed literally in the Genesis account of creation, I should
hesitate a long time before taking any action against a full professor
who came forward with this view. I was certain, however, that "his
colleagues would demand his scalp."

The system of visiting committees at Harvard evolved in President Eliot's day. I know of no other institution with exactly the same
arrangement. In theory, the purpose of the scheme is to provide the
Board of Overseers with consultants who evaluate the work of various
branches of the university. In practice, by the time President Lowell
took office, the visiting committees were often regarded as a device
for raising money. One member of the board was designated as
chairman of the committee to visit a particular professional school
or one of the departments of the faculty of arts and sciences. The
other members of the committee were, with few exceptions, not
members of the board. They were chosen, usually by the chairman,
because of their interest in the school or department and in many
cases with an eye to a possible financial contribution. In my day,
the members in most cases were the same from year to year, a practice which had its drawbacks and I believe has been altered. Since
theoretically the Board of Overseers functioned as a check on the

otherwise almost unlimited power of the Corporation, the president of the university was never consulted about the membership of the visiting committees nor their operation.

As a professor of chemistry, I had been usually invited to dine with the visiting committee in chemistry once a year. I knew that on one occasion shortly after World War I the chairman of the chemistry visiting committee, Mr. Edward Mallinckrodt, Jr., had risen in a meeting of the Board of Overseers and demanded that a drive for money to build the Fogg Art Museum and buildings for the Business School across the river be expanded to include the construction of a new chemical laboratory. The success of the subsequent campaign was in no small degree a result of both his activity and generosity. Therefore, as a faculty member, I regarded the Overseer who was chairman of the committee to visit the chemistry department as the equivalent of a tribune of the people. If necessary, one could appeal to him against any possible tyrannical acts of the president and fellows. On becoming president, my attitude toward the Board of Overseers visiting committees did not change.

The visiting committees during the twenty years I sat in the president's office were a strong, positive factor in ensuring the smooth running of the university. The annual short verbal reports made by their chairmen to the Board of Overseers often provoked discussions which were useful. The members of the board were thus informed about some of the matters that were agitating certain professors. If the report included criticism of the president of the university, I could at once reply. Frequently, an Overseer pleaded the case of a school or department for more money. My justification of the alleged niggardliness of the administration involved presentation of the sad story of the lack of free funds at the disposal of the president—a message I was anxious for all thirty members of the board to hear. Occasionally the chairman of a visiting committee in his remarks would touch on alumni criticism of the department or school in question. Since these complaints might have come to the attention of many other Overseers, an airing of the differences of opinion in a meeting of the Overseers could be highly beneficial. The meetings were closed, of course. However, the word would be passed around to the members of the visiting committee if anything of significance developed in the discussion of the chairman's informal verbal statement.

Once every three years, the report was formal and printed for public distribution. I made a point of commenting at some length on these printed reports at a meeting of the board. But in only one instance in the entire period of my service did I consider the questions raised by a chairman of a visiting committee of sufficient moment for me to prepare a formal written reply. I hardly need say that the subject was the department of economics.

In his public report dated November 27, 1950, the chairman of the visiting committee, Clarence B. Randall, declared that the most pressing criticism his committee had to offer was the lack of "balance with respect to the viewpoints of its members." He went on to state that "we have in the Department, for example, one or more Socialists, some zealous followers of British economist John Maynard Keynes, and some who advocate the extension of economic controls by Government. Some of these men are nationally known for their views and are both active and zealous in promoting them. But on the other side of the social spectrum, the Department seems to lack men of equal ability and zeal who hold opposing views and are prepared to teach them."

This was the beginning of an episode which illustrates a general academic problem of the 1950s. If Randall and I had started exchanging sharp words at an Overseers' meeting, the affair might have turned into a vendetta. But it so happened that Randall was one of my oldest friends. We had belonged to the same undergraduate club. When I became president, Randall was already a prominent alumnus, a high official of a large steel company, a public-spirited citizen of Chicago. He had repeatedly supported my endeavors. I often wished there were more loyal and effective graduates like Clarence Randall. After his election to the Board of Overseers and his appointment as chairman of the visiting committee for economics, we discussed more than once his growing concern with what he called the lack of balance in the department. Our friendship was not disturbed. His written report for 1950–51 came as no surprise. My printed reply (for private circulation) was in a sense part of a prearranged exercise in placing before the two governing boards Randall's indictment of the department (on one score) and my defense.

Two paragraphs in Randall's report (which was a public document) were as important as the criticism. They amounted to an appeal to any critics to keep their negative views within the framework of accepted university procedure:

It is not our purpose in making a report at this time to initiate controversy or to suggest that we view with extreme alarm any phase of the Department's work. We do have apprehensions, but our viewpoints have been fully expressed to the President and the Provost, both of whom have encouraged us at all times to be frank in such criticisms as we have had to present. . . .

No friend of academic freedom need fear the purpose which underlies our comment on this matter. We would be the first to insist that a professor must teach that which he honestly believes and we know that the fact that this differs from viewpoints which we may hold as individuals is altogether immaterial. This is too obviously right to need discussion.

My reply to Randall, like his report, was frank. I took over a year to prepare it. Though I did not publish it, I did expect it to be read rather widely by the faculty, the Overseers and their friends. The amicable disagreement between the president of Harvard and the chairman of the economics visiting committee had significance, I believed, because of what was being said by a small number of alumni whose approach was far different from Randall's. What they printed was not worthy of reply. Unlike Randall, they indicated no concern with possible dangers to academic freedom. Their outlook might be considered a more adult and yet venomous expression of the judgment of my advisee of the 1920s who suspected the professor and all the section men in Economics A of being Democrats.

I decided that in answering the visiting committee I could provide the basis for those who might wish to argue in defense of the Harvard department of economics. I ended by constructing a document which recorded the conclusions I drew from several months of talking with academic economists on three continents. It also included an attempt to classify economists in groups according to the methods they employed. I placed the empirical approach to specific problems, as illustrated by the *ad hoc* case studies of the Harvard Business School, in opposition to both the logical-deduction approach and the method of statistical aggregate analysis characteristic of economic theorists. But before presenting the consequences for Harvard of my methodological classification, I must explain why I was emboldened to undertake such a task. To do so requires devoting several paragraphs to my education not in economics but in understanding economists.

I started, as a naïve chemist, in supposing that the faculty of the Harvard Business School was composed of experts in applied economics while the department of economics in the faculty of arts and sciences was the home of the pure theorists. I was soon disabused of any such idea. In almost our first meeting, Dean Donham of the Business School told me that almost none of his professors were economists. Then I gradually came to realize that the two groups of professors whom I had imagined would be closely related in their research and teaching were, with one exception, far from enthusiastic about each other. Those in the school of Business Administration on one side of the Charles River and those in the department of economics on the other faced the urgent practical problem of the day—the depression—with quite different outlooks. In connection with Mr. Littauer's gift, I had had occasion to discuss the cooperation between the School of Business and the department of economics. The outlook was not encouraging. The one professor who seemed to be respected on both sides of the river was Sumner Schlichter, who held an appointment in both the Business School and the department of economics. I recall his diagnosis of the ills of the United States and other free nations. Long ago he stated (if I remember correctly) that a nation could not have both full employment and a currency free from inflation. It seems to me that the history of the last thirty-five years is evidence of the correctness of his view.

After the war, the successor to Dean Donham, Donald K. David, rather rapidly destroyed the curtain of suspicion and disrespect which had separated the Graduate School of Business Administration from the faculty of arts and sciences. His success with special courses of short duration for business executives was beyond question. As presiding officer of the faculty, I had an opportunity to learn through informative debates about the ambitions of the school. Thus I was aware of the methods of instruction which had been initiated under Dean Donham and carried forward to still more effective use under Dean David. The method has been described in a report by a faculty committee on *Behavioral Sciences at Harvard,* published in 1954. The following extracts summarize the essential element:

> The case method used at the [Harvard Business] School is based on the principle that one must learn by doing. It is aimed at developing the student's capacity to make sound decisions and to take action by making him act. The student is repeatedly placed in situations where as an administrator he must not only evaluate evidence and opinions but also act with responsibility. . . . The case method of instruction used so long at the School has emphasized the practical problems of decision-making in concrete realistic business situations. . . . Since the war, therefore, instruction at the School has stressed the fact that practical business problems involve not only substantive aspects in reaching a decision in the context of the community around us but also the administrative problems of getting a job done. . . . The instruction, almost entirely by the case method, not only utilizes the discipline of economics on which the School

was originally based, but has also begun the adaptation to problems of business administration of knowledge, skills and methods of analysis derived from all the behavioral sciences.

I should add that the case materials on which the instruction was based had been built up slowly and as of 1954 were estimated to have cost something like $2.5 million. That the case materials used by law students are a product of our judicial system and therefore essentially available without cost was a fact that both Dean Donham and his successor were fond of reminding the president of the university.

Undoubtedly my close friendship with Dean David has influenced my judgment. We had been young assistant professors together in the 1920s before Don David left the university for his success in the business world. I considered it a great triumph, as it proved to be, when I persuaded him to return to Harvard as a dean. Over the years, I had so benefited from his counsel that I could hardly be counted an unprejudiced witness when I brought the methods of the Business School into a discussion of the affairs of the department of economics.

To this digression about the Harvard Business School, I must add another before I return to the presentation of my reply to Clarence Randall. In 1938 John Williams was dean of the School of Public Administration, which was just starting. He was a conservative but forward-looking specialist in the field of money and banking and had served the Federal Reserve System with distinction. He suggested that, to fill one of the positions made possible by Mr. Littauer's gift, we invite Alvin H. Hansen of the University of Minnesota to come to Harvard. I did so, and Hansen accepted. According to a recent account of the teaching of economics in the United States, Hansen became an effective exponent of Keynes shortly after he arrived in Cambridge. I have heard it said by economists that his seminars in the Harvard School of Public Administration just before the war influenced young policy-makers from Washington.

I recall having first heard of Keynes and his famous book, *The General Theory of Employment, Interest and Money*, in the early 1940s. The book had been published in 1936. By the time of Randall's report as chairman of the committee to visit the department of economics, Keynes' name had taken on a symbolic value. Among economists, his book was controversial. To a certain type of businessman, it was like the proverbial red rag. In the eyes of many economically illiterate but deeply patriotic (and well-to-do) citizens, to accuse a professor of being a Keynesian was almost equivalent to branding him a subversive agent.

To be sure, Randall had not associated himself with such critics. He would be no party to anything approaching a witch hunt for unsound and dangerous economists. He had only asked for a balance of views. Nevertheless, the implication was clear that with Keynesian and alleged Socialists in the group, the roster of Harvard professors of economics was weighted by the emphasis that was placed on left-wing doctrines. Was this an accurate portrayal? I set out to try to find the answer to this question.

What I discovered, I told the Overseers in my printed reply to the visiting committee report, was as follows:

My examination of the status of economics in American universities today has revealed the fact that in at least fourteen major universities questions are being raised by persons who are not economists about the teaching of economics. It is a curious fact that at the same period of history in which there is a certain degree of national unrest about academic economists, one group of businessmen (the Committee for Economic Development) is closely associated with professors of economics in a series of investigations of vital problems. It seems a pity that the confidence that part of the business community has in at least some university economists does not receive as much publicity as do the attacks by others who claim our schools and colleges are teaching "collectivism." Not that any such charge is made by the Overseers Committee here at Harvard. What is criticized is only "that the Department as presently constituted lacks balance with respect to the viewpoint of its members." This is a reasonable criticism and warrants a careful investigation. . . .

At the outset of my inquiry the difficulties of formulating criteria for cataloguing the viewpoints of economists became evident. I tried the test of Keynesian and anti-Keynesian but soon discovered I was using a totally inadequate analytic tool; I became convinced that Keynes himself was an anti-Keynesian before he died. The Overseers report states categorically that there are "one or more socialists" in the Department. With this statement I must respectfully but firmly disagree and in so doing point out both the difficulties and the necessity of defining terms in the social sciences. The term "socialist" as used in countries where socialism is a live political issue means one who advocates by democratic political action "the nationalization of the means of exchange, production and distribution." It might be a good thing to have a socialist on the staff of a department of economics, but as a matter of fact there are no socialist professors of economics at Harvard today.

One could classify economists, at least theoretically, in terms of their political beliefs, but except for communists and socialists this is a very difficult matter in the present flux of political opinion. Furthermore, people's political convictions, like their religious beliefs, are often subject to violent change. Everyone speaks of the dangers of introducing political criteria into the consideration of academic appointments. If analyzed, I believe these dangers stem largely from the fact that political views do not represent a bias relevant to an academic intellectual discipline as does a philosopher's adherence to a philosophic doctrine such as idealism or logical empiricism. Political opinions are temporary, emotional, and subject to change under social duress; it is to avoid such duress that politics and religion are considered "out of bounds" in judging persons for academic posts in the United States in the mid-twentieth century.

The Chairman of the Visiting Committee in his report speaks of a "social spectrum." I have attempted to use this concept to classify present-day economists as radical or conservative without getting into the political quagmire to which I have just referred. I have had little success except that in a vague sort of way a number of informed observers have expressed the view that the leading universities of the nation were about equally radical or conservative as regards their departments of economics. But if the President is to direct a department or an *ad hoc* committee as to future appointments, he must have some more definite criteria as to a man's position in the social spectrum, and these I failed to find. For example, I find it difficult to decide whether advocacy of strengthening the Sherman Anti-Trust Act is radical or conservative. I ask myself was the Harvard Department a generation ago radical or conservative? In retrospect it seems conservative to many; forty years ago it was considered radical, as the free-trade point of view predominated. When I first took office, some discussion in the Board of Overseers indicated that there were those who used man's attitude towards organized labor as the touchstone of his radical or conservative outlook. This is no longer so. As a consultant to the Government, an economist may take a strong position as to need for immediate drastic action to offset a depression or control an inflation. In recent years such rather technical economic opinions have bulked large in some people's minds in classifying economists as being to the left or right. For example, if you confine your attention to fiscal policy in the immediate past, you would find two professors in the Harvard Department today to place in opposition to one another. But I have become convinced that no criteria of lasting value in terms of a social spectrum can be devised for the guidance of any body charged with responsibility for nominating candidates for appointment in a department of economics.

I concluded that as far as the types of economic theory and analysis presented to students are concerned, the Harvard department was typical of departments of economics in the leading universities of the English-speaking world. I agreed that in economics, as in other departments, there should be a balance as between fields such as labor, agriculture, money and banking. I pointed out, however, that "rigid insistence on having each field represented by a permanent appointment limits the number of candidates and tends to encourage the appointment of 'good' rather than 'excellent' men."

My classification of economists in methodological terms I tried out on a few members of the department. I was able to report to the Overseers that the department admitted its relative weakness in the empirical approach as compared with the Harvard Business School. However, steps had been taken to correct this lack of balance. Two professors of the Business School faculty were now giving courses in the department of economics. The departmental chairman had written me that he and his colleagues believed that their instruction would be improved if they had at least one member "whose major interest was what we might call the economics of enterprise." He then made a suggestion which had an all too familiar sound. An additional permanent professorship should be allocated to the economics department so that a new member might be appointed to make a "better balance." I noted this proposal from the department of economics in my statement to the Overseers and replied as follows:

To follow this suggestion would lead to no end of difficulties in the Faculty of Arts and Sciences; other departments would be quick to press for an increase in their quota of permanent places. But I am glad to report that much the same end can be accomplished because the Dean of the Business School has expressed his interest in a joint appointment. With his consent and with the concurrence of the Provost I therefore recommend that the Corporation agree to appoint one full professor of economics over and above the quota allowed by the schedule of appointments for the Faculty of Arts and Sciences established a decade or so ago. I further recommend that this professor hold an appointment in three faculties, namely, the Faculty of Arts and Sciences, the School of Business Administration, and the School of Public Administration, and that his salary be charged to the three faculties in such amounts as the President shall determine. Further, that the nomination for the new chair be made by the permanent members of the Department of Economics of the Faculty of Arts and Sciences and six members of the Faculty of the School of Business Administration appointed by the President after consultation with the Dean, the two groups to sit together as a nominating committee, and the name or names thus nominated to be passed on by an *ad hoc* committee as is usual in the Faculty of Arts and Sciences.

The directive to the nominating committee would be as follows: to submit one or more names of men of character, high scholarly distinction and first-rate teaching ability who have an understanding of business as it is actually operated. To that end, the man in question should have had contact as a scholarly investigator or consultant with the operations of industry and commerce; he should have an awareness of the positive role of business enterprise in a changing and developing economy. His teaching would be directed towards presenting to Harvard College students a realistic view of business management and its relation to the total economy. If this report is accepted by the two Governing Boards, I shall proceed with this appointment.

My recommendation was accepted by the two governing boards in early January 1952. I was not able, however, to proceed with the appointment. The candidate I had in mind when I wrote about the future so hopefully was Marion B. Folsom, a member of the Board of Overseers, a leader in the formation of the Committee on Economic Development and treasurer of the Eastman Kodak Company. I had had a number of helpful talks with him, and I knew he was in agreement with my diagnosis and my proposed remedy. When I made a closer approach to his becoming a professor, he demurred, claiming he wished to retire. Yet within a few years he was Secretary of Health, Education and Welfare in the Eisenhower administration. In that capacity, he enters my story once again.

When I left Cambridge in 1953, no progress had been made in finding an occupant of a chair of the economics of enterprise. Since I have made it a point of honor not to be informed about Harvard affairs since I retired, I have no way of knowing the ultimate fate of my proposal. I cannot help suspecting, however, that it was not immediately successful. For I had a number of occasions during the four years I was in Germany to talk with Clarence Randall, and he never referred to his report or my troubles with the department of economics. I leave the reader to conclude that my effort as an innovator in the field of economics was a dismal future. Perhaps my ambitious attempts as an analyst of the methodology of one branch of social science were at fault. Or possibly they were correct, and my error lay in suggesting that a single professor could embody both the deductive and the empirical approach to a treatment for the aches and pains of the economy of freedom. As I write, the patient still suffers. In spite of, or perhaps because of, the arrival of the dogmas of John Maynard Keynes in America, the opinions of economists still cover a wide spectrum.

The concluding paragraphs of my reply to the visiting committee's report may explain why I took such pains in the rebuttal of one particular criticism of one particular department of the faculty of arts and sciences. Suspicion of universities was in the air. Much of what was being said about left-wing professors was nonsense. I welcomed an emotion-free rational inquiry in these words:

Unfortunately, the public criticisms of professors in these days do not all conform to the restrained pattern set by this report. Rather the demands for "firing" or "muzzling" professors or censoring textbooks have increased in number and intensity in the last few years. I suppose all members of the two Boards are familiar with such irresponsible attacks and the rather violent statements about the teaching of economics emanating from more reputable sources. I mention these matters for they have a certain relation to the problem that a president of a university faces today when he must recommend action in a controversial area such as economics. The analogy with his distant predecessors' problems in theology comes to mind.

The existence of hostile critics and extremists makes it imperative for fair-minded men concerned with the future of education to thrash out their differences of opinion around a table. Over the last fifteen years the Department of Economics has been at fault in not attempting to meet the Visiting Committee in a spirit of wholehearted cooperation. The Board of Overseers has been at fault, I venture to suggest, by not widening the membership of the Visiting Committee to include more professional economists and more businessmen who have been working closely with university economists. But the situation is better in both respects than it was a few years past; in my opinion it can be still further improved.

In these critical days when economic decisions play so vital a part in determining national and international policies, it is unfortunate that an atmosphere of hostility exists to some degree throughout the country between the management of industry and academic economists. Whatever can be done here at Harvard to increase the understanding between men of good will within and without the University cannot fail to be of service to the nation.

CHAPTER 33

_____

Heresy or Subversion?

THE TITLE of this chapter might well be "in defense of academic freedom." Such a phrase summarizing twenty years of speech-making has a noble ring and would not be totally inaccurate. Yet it might be misleading. There is less unity in the story than words imply. The threats in 1934 were not the same as those in 1949. The issues to which I addressed myself at one time were different from those at another. For example, I am less certain now of the validity of the arguments I presented in the 1930s than I was at the time I made them. What had appeared as a black-and-white matter was transformed by world events in the late 1940s into a series of difficult questions.

In the preceding chapter, I noted that Walter Lippmann as chairman of the committee of the Overseers to visit the department of economics in 1934 had referred to the principle of free inquiry so "deeply rooted in Harvard." He was quite correct. President Eliot had boasted of the freedom of professors at Harvard. President Lowell in 1917 had taken a decisive position against certain Harvard graduates who were attacking a Law School professor because of his public statements. There had been a widespread acceptance among the alumni of President Lowell's stand. His subsequent analysis of the issue was generally welcomed. In his annual report for 1916–17, he had written as follows:

446

The gravest questions, and the strongest feelings, arise from action by a professor beyond his chosen field and outside of his classroom. Here he speaks only as a citizen. By appointment to a professorship he acquires no rights that he did not possess before; but there is a real difference of opinion today on the question whether he loses any rights that he would otherwise enjoy. The argument in favor of a restraining power on the part of the governing boards of universities and colleges is based upon the fact that by extreme, or injudicious, remarks that shock public sentiment a professor can do great harm to the institution with which he is connected. That is true, and sometimes a professor thoughtlessly does an injury that is without justification. If he publishes an article on the futility and harmfulness of vaccination, and signs it as professor in a certain university, he leads the public to believe that his views are those of an authority on the subject, approved by the institution and taught to its students. If he is really a professor of Greek, he is misleading the public and misrepresenting his university, which he would not do if he gave his title in full.

In spite of the risk of injury to the institution, the objections to restraint upon what professors may say as citizens seems to me far greater than the harm done by leaving them free. In the first place, to impose upon the teacher in a university restrictions to which the members of other professions, lawyers, physicians, engineers, and so forth, are not subjected, would produce a sense of irritation and humiliation. In accepting a chair under such conditions a man would surrender a part of his liberty; what he might say would be submitted to the censorship of a board of trustees, and he would cease to be a free citizen. The lawyer, physician, or engineer may express his views as he likes on the subject of the protective tariff; shall the professor of astronomy not be free to do the same? Such a policy would tend seriously to discourage some of the best men from taking up the scholar's life. It is not a question of academic freedom, but of personal liberty from constraint, yet it touches the dignity of the academic career.

That is an objection to restraint on freedom of speech from the standpoint of the teacher. There is another, not less weighty, from that of the institution itself. If a university or college censors what its professors may say, if it restrains them from uttering something that it does not approve, it thereby assumes responsibility for that which it permits them to say. This is logical and inevitable, but it is a responsibility which an institution of learning would be very unwise in assuming.

As a new president, I thought it important to make plain that I intended to adhere to the tradition established by my predecessors. For this purpose, I introduced into my remarks to the alumni on my first commencement afternoon in 1934 the following:

During his administration, and particularly during the stormy period after the war, President Lowell upheld with courageous vigor the principle of academic freedom. His stand convinced the alumni of this University and the people of this country that it was essential to maintain forever the proposition that members of the faculty are free to search for the Truth as they see it and express their considered views. Harvard, and all the other universities in the land, will forever be in President Lowell's debt for these services of his to the cause of academic freedom.

Today we are in a period of confusion, a period in which political and economic aims and purposes are subject to violent discussion. And political passions at times run high. Whatever be the outcome of the uncertain future which the whole world faces, the universities must stand firm by their principle which insures the right of free inquiry and free debate. No one can be certain as to the correct answer to the questions in economics and politics which confront the country today, but to keep alive Harvard's stimulating atmosphere we must see to it that these contemporary problems are earnestly discussed. So far as possible all sides should be represented among the permanent members of the staff—men of character, keenly intelligent, not propagandists but competent scholars, with radically different points of view. Harvard must continue to guarantee freedom to those who are here, and continue to attract representatives from the various camps. Only thus can we be of the most value to the country and worthy of our past.

I had written my speech without having any individual or any specific incident in mind. I knew only that there was an increasing suspicion of academic people throughout the nation. I was aware of a growing hostility toward at least one Harvard professor, Felix Frankfurter, a close friend and adviser to President Roosevelt. In a sense, I was stating a position as a defensive measure. I hoped that what I said would discourage any alumni who might be tempted to write me to complain about the New Deal sympathies of certain members of the faculty.

Most unexpectedly, the Governor of the Commonwealth of Massachusetts, Governor Ely, came forward as a live substitute for a straw man. In an address which preceded my remarks, he proclaimed it as his duty to speak against "ideas of government which are being instilled in every educational institution in this country in the minds and hearts of the young men who are to be the generation in control tomorrow." He asserted that those who believe in the traditional ideals of America should make themselves heard.

I had no advance knowledge of what the Governor was to say, but I could hardly have asked for a better foil. If I had been an experienced speaker, I would have grasped the opportunity for a collision of views. In fact, I was far too unsure of myself on my first commencement afternoon to refer even indirectly to what the Governor had said. I discovered later from a member of the audience that he and his friends thought I was in fact replying. In his judgment, I did not have the better of the argument. The Governor had received more applause than I had. My informant, though a dyed-in-the-wool conservative, was a reliable reporter. His appraisal of the alumni reaction added to my conviction that I had better continue to emphasize my advocacy of free speech for professors. Thus I was launched almost accidentally on a career as a defender of free inquiry. Any alumni who might be inclined to be critical were apprised of the fact that I would turn a deaf ear against demands to muzzle a professor.

As a matter of fact, by 1934 the doctrine that the rights of a teacher on permanent tenure were inviolable had been rather generally accepted, which had not been the case when President Lowell had written the statement I have quoted. I recall one of the Corporation meetings in my first year in which someone mentioned the discontent of many alumni with the assistance Professor Frankfurter was rendering the New Deal. He was active in recruiting young Harvard Law School graduates for the recently established agencies in Washington.

We all agreed that what was being said by a small group of reactionary graduates made little sense—it was only an outburst of resentment against Roosevelt. T. N. Perkins remarked, in his usual pungent terms, that "we couldn't fire Felix even if we wanted to," so everybody had better "shut up." His down-to-earth statement reminded me as a newcomer to the Corporation that the concept of permanent tenure had advantages for administrators as well as professors. The third statute of the university was a foundation stone of our whole enterprise. It read as follows: "All officers of instruction are subject to removal by the Corporation only for grave misconduct or neglect of duty." (The Harvard statutes are standing votes of the two governing boards; they can be altered only if both boards agree.) The official declaration applied, of course, only to those faculty members who held appointments without limit of time.

My oratory on commencement afternoon of 1934 left me little option as to what I should do the following winter when a politician introduced a teachers' oath bill in the Massachusetts legislature. I remember discussing the matter with the Corporation. Perkins thought any opposition to the proposed law was hopeless. Several states had already enacted similar legislation; the sentiment in the country was in favor of such steps. I would be fighting the inevitable. Furthermore, he implied the whole matter was a rather silly business. Grenville Clark strongly disagreed. He himself was worried about what had already happened. The idea of a teachers' oath was repugnant. Any limitation on the free speech of a professor would drive able men out of the universities. Mr. Lowell had made this clear. His advice was for me to rally the presidents of the other Massachusetts institutions in opposition to the proposed legislation. I ended by following Clark's advice.

Along with a number of other college presidents, I appeared before a committee of the state legislature to argue against the bill. Each in turn was cross-questioned in unfriendly terms about his attitude toward teachers who taught subversive doctrines. What did we mean by freedom for teachers? Could they say anything they liked even if it was treasonable? It was clear the committee had made up its mind to pass the bill.

Before the legislature acted, the *Harvard Alumni Bulletin* began to print articles and letters about the proposed law. Some correspondents denounced it; some ridiculed it; a few defended the measure. The fact that the Daughters of the American Revolution and the American Legion, as well as the Hearst papers, were in favor of teachers' oath bills was sufficient to condemn the legislation for many. To others, the requirement that a teacher swear loyalty to both the state and federal constitutions seemed no more onerous than taking an oath of allegiance in applying for a passport. Was it in reality a menacing first step toward a totalitarian society? Hitler's rise to power in 1933 was in everybody's mind; so, too, were the words and actions of Stalin and Mussolini. The fear of what might happen in the United States, however, could be cited by both sides in the debate.

One alumnus of the class of 1898 made fun of a prominent graduate who had written in support of the law. "Tom is all right," he wrote in a letter to the *Bulletin*, "but he doesn't go far enough. He gives teachers too much credit; they don't influence children so much as ministers and parents do. Every minister should be required to take the oath when he is ordained and every parent, as soon as he becomes one. Or better and safer still, make the oath a part of the marriage ceremony. That ought to save the country from the impending Communist revolution."

Whatever enjoyment the readers of the *Alumni Bulletin* might draw from the exchange of letters, the faculty was in no mood to treat the subject lightly. Professor Samuel E. Morison spoke for many of his colleagues when on two occasions he attacked the teachers' oath bill. In an article in the *Alumni Bulletin*, he drew on his knowledge as an historian to show the utter futility of attempting to control a person's attitude by demanding oaths. The members of the legislature, however, paid no attention to the views of the academic community. Perkins had been right. It was hopeless to combat the bill. As an expression of distrust of professors, the idea of making them take a special oath appealed to a large number of persons. No influential citizen had spoken out against a teachers' oath in a way to bring the issue to a real public debate. Only among the teachers themselves could one find vigorous opposition.

One of the speakers on commencement afternoon in 1935, President William A. Neilson of Smith College, used the opportunity to point out to the large alumni audience the objectionable nature of the law which had just been enacted. It singled out the teaching profession as a suspect group. He praised me for leading the fight against the bill and asked, "Where are the alumni?" He declared the "miserable and silly performances in the legislature" would never have occurred if the graduates of the colleges in Massachusetts had realized where their duty lay. President Neilson's remarks brought forth little applause. I heard later that many in the audience took strong exception to what he said.

When the college opened in the fall, the bill was law. What should Harvard do about it? I had assumed that every faculty member would take the oath whether or not he had favored the passage of the law. I was both surprised and shocked when I heard some professors say that they would refuse. The doctrine of passive resistance was no part of my treasured armory of liberal principles. Therefore I wrote a letter to all members of the teaching staff saying I was taking the oath and I hoped all other teachers would do the same. I reported that the act appeared to make it mandatory for the institutions concerned not to permit any citizen to teach who failed to take the prescribed oath. I added that "it is out of the question for Harvard University as an institution to consider not obeying the law."

Several faculty members disagreed. Their opinions were soon headlined in the local press. In answer to a question, I made a statement to the press which, translated into the lead story on page one of the *New York Times*, carried the headline: "Take Oath or Quit." The other Massachusetts college presidents were pleased, my liberal friends dismayed. One alumnus wrote to the *Bulletin* that: "Dr. Conant by 'dunking' his promising defense in a tub of tepid water has diminished one more of the few remaining hopes for the survival of freedom in America."

Grenville Clark made no bones of his strong dissent from my position. In the course of a faculty meeting I was asked to explain my letter. I said, in effect, that it seemed clear that the law intended to put the burden on the president of an institution to see that all the teachers did sign the oath. I was unwilling to do anything except carry out the intent of the law. Professor Morison asked at once what the professors who felt so strongly about the law should do. If refusal to take the oath did not seem the appropriate action, what did I suggest? I replied: "Work for the repeal at the next session of the legislature."

All but a handful of professors ended by agreeing with my view. There were a few troublesome cases, but none involved professors who by any stretch of the word could be considered radicals. They were either in the cranky New England tradition of Thoreau or impelled by religious considerations. All were willing to sign, but only if they could indicate their reservations. The Attorney General of Massachusetts, Paul Dever, an astute politician, proved to be accommodating. In a conference I well remember, he indicated that he didn't care what was written on the paper as long as the oath was signed. With this compromise, if it can be so designated, this particular affair was ended.

In March 1936 an effort was made to repeal the obnoxious law. Though I thought the action was premature, I rallied the college presidents once again. To my mind, we should have waited until a new legislature had been elected. It seemed unlikely that the present body would openly change its collective mind. My doubts proved to be well founded. Once again we faced a hostile legislative committee and made arguments in vain. The petition to repeal was rejected. In the meantime, the agitation against an oath for teachers was spreading. There were more letters in the *Harvard Alumni Bulletin*. A group in New York State succeeded in obtaining a hearing before a state legislative committee in Albany. Their efforts to repeal the New York law, however, were also unsuccessful.

The Social Science Research Council appointed a special committee on "Freedom of Inquiry in Teaching." The group met in my home in Cambridge. We recommended the preparation of a casebook, with special emphasis on what had happened in Germany. We also discussed the possibility of testing the constitutionality of a teachers' oath law. I think we all recognized that we needed to document our claim that the passage of a teachers' oath law might be a dangerous step. What had happened in Germany was our prime example. Thus in writing to a prominent alumnus, I said that I agreed it was unlikely in Massachusetts that any improper use would be made of the law just enacted. But I wrote that I was not equally optimistic about other sections of the country. I could imagine that in some state "very different from Massachusetts a potential dictator or a group of fanatics may succeed in passing a really unfortunate act and cite the Massachusetts bill as one step in that direction."

When in 1936 it came time for me to prepare my Tercentenary Oration, I was still under the influence of the debate about the loyalty of teachers. It was not only the passage of a bill aimed at teachers which disturbed me, but the justification of such a law. There seemed no doubt that reasonable people were frightened. Therefore, in my speech on the morning of the third day of the Tercentenary Celebration (as it turned out, in the pouring rain), I said:

For the development of a national culture based on a study of the past, one condition is essential. This is absolute freedom of discussion, absolutely unmolested inquiry. Since the seventeenth century, this has been achieved in the realm of religion. . . . Will the same conditions prevail in the future when political and economic problems are examined? Unfortunately there are ominous signs that a new form of bigotry may arise. This is most serious, for we cannot develop the unifying educational forces we so sorely need unless all matters may be openly discussed. The origin of the Constitution, for example, the functioning of the three branches of the Federal Government, the forces of modern capitalism, must be dissected as fearlessly as the geologist examines the origin of the rocks. On this point, there can be no compromise; we are either afraid of heresy or we are not.

These were fine words, and the audience applauded. I had no reason to re-examine them for a decade. In the meantime, an armed threat had been met on the battlefield and destroyed. The era of peace based on trust and collaboration of the victorious Allies which followed proved to be of short duration. By 1947 I, among others, was following the lead of the former Secretary of War, Henry L. Stimson. In October of that year in an article in *Foreign Affairs*, he wrote that while he had hoped that the Russians would be our friends, "those who determined Russian policy have chosen otherwise, and their choice has been slavishly followed by Communists everywhere." Then came a sentence which had implications for all of us who before the war had spoken in praise of academic freedom: "No sensible American can ignore this fact and those who now choose to travel in company with American Communists are very clearly either knaves or fools."

If one agreed with Mr. Stimson, the fear of one heresy—Communism—was quite a different matter from what I had had in mind in 1936. Fools or knaves—are either to be tolerated in an academic community? The reality of this question was not immediately apparent when I read and applauded what Stimson had written. A year later in my own book, *Education in a Divided World,* I was still repeating that we should have a "spirit of tolerance which allows the expression of a great variety of opinions." But I admitted we should be unrealistic if we failed to realize the difficulties that arise from the ideological conflict dividing the world, which, I prophesied, would continue for years to come.

For a page or two I did the best I could in formulating an answer to the "thoughtful and troubled citizen who wonders if our universities are being used as centers for fifth column activities." I attempted not to backtrack on what I had been saying for fifteen years about free inquiry and free discussions. At the same time, I wished to emphasize the danger in the Russian threat. I said if an avowed supporter of the Marx-Lenin-Stalin line can be found, "force him into the open and tear his arguments to pieces." I also said the government must see to it that those who are employed in positions of responsibility are persons of unswerving loyalty. Universities, however, I warned, were not government departments. The criteria for joining a community of scholars are not to be confused with the requirements of a federal bureau. I admitted that "the universities are certain to meet with many difficulties as they seek to preserve their integrity during this period of warring ideologies."

Within a year I was myself in the middle of difficulties emerging from the international tensions of the divided world. Two events occurred: In 1949 the Educational Policies Commission, of which I was then a member, issued a pamphlet on *American Education and International Tensions;* and a graduate of the Law School, a prominent member of the Maryland Bar, wrote me a letter protesting the attitude of Harvard toward extracurricular activities of professors "giving aid and comfort to Communism." In the pamphlet, I joined with the other members of the Commission in declaring that "members of the Communist Party of the United States should not be

employed as teachers." In my reply to the Maryland lawyer, Frank
B. Ober, I referred to President Lowell's annual report of 1916–17
and enclosed a copy. "We believe," I wrote,

that our way of operating the University is not only in the best interests
of Harvard but of importance to the entire country. . . . Since your comments go to the heart of the nature of a university and have broad implications, I have asked Mr. Grenville Clark, a senior member of the
Corporation and a leader in your profession, to write to you. I am sure
you will be interested in his account of the history and significance of
the traditional Harvard policy.

Clark sent a long letter to Ober, who in turn replied. The exchange
was printed in the *Harvard Alumni Bulletin*. There were several issues
involved. Mr. Ober had announced his decision not to subscribe to
the Harvard Law School Fund. Clark commented that such decisions
on the part of alumni were not new, but he added "that Harvard cannot be influenced at all to depart from her basic tradition of freedom
by any fear that gifts will be withheld." Citing a case in World War
I, he wrote:

I think it will be Harvard policy not to be influenced in any way "to
abridge free speech" by withholding of any subscription. And if $5,000,000
or any sum were offered tomorrow as the price of the removal of Professor [John] Ciardi or Professor [Harlow] Shapley [the two whose extracurricular activities had incurred Ober's dislike] or of initiating the
"closer watch" that you recommend, nothing is more certain than that
the Corporation would again reply that it cannot tolerate the suggestion.

Though the traditional Harvard position was well known, a
forceful restatement every generation was well worthwhile. This is
also true as regards what Clark called our consistent doctrine. His
formulation was as follows:

(1) Harvard believes in the "free trade in ideas" of Justice Holmes—
a graduate of 1861—which is no more than saying that she believes in
the principles of Milton's Areopagitica (1644), of Jefferson's First Inaugural (1801), and of Mill's "Essay on Liberty" (1859). She thinks that
repression is not wise or workable under our system, that wide latitude for
conflicting views affords the best chance for good government, and that
in suppression usually lies the greater peril. Harvard is not afraid of
freedom, and believes adherence to this principle to be fundamental for
our universities and for the integrity of our institutions.
(2) She believes that the members of the faculties, in their capacity
as citizens, have the same rights to express themselves as other citizens,

and that those rights should not be restricted by the University by trying to keep a "watch" on professors or otherwise.

(3) She believes that wide limits for free expression by professors are in the interest of her students as well as the teachers. The teachers have rights as citizens to speak and write as men of independence; the students also have their rights to be taught by men of independent mind.

Clark had taken many pains. He documented his points with more than one highly relevant episode in Harvard's history. I was delighted to have such a powerful brief on behalf of academic freedom placed before the graduates of the university. Nevertheless a new issue, namely the nature of Communism, had not been explored. Ober, in his reply to Clark, pointed to this fact.

The basic difference between us is that your essay on academic freedom completely fails to distinguish Socialism, or other unpopular radical issues, from Communism, which to most Americans means providing the fifth column for a foreign power plotting our destruction. Academic freedom, under your interpretation, would apparently permit a Harvard professor to advocate and to aid and abet Communism, in the same manner you would permit him to advocate any other cause. Your position must be due to your failure to recognize the implications of Communism and that one of the primary objects of the fifth column in the present cold war is infiltration of colleges, so that Communists can be close to scientific developments, corrupt the next generation and, incidentally, give prestige to front organizations. You would hardly say, if reasonable grounds on all the evidence indicates a professor is incompetent, or publicly leads a scandalous life—though not violating laws—he should be protected by academic freedom. Communism is not a lesser evil, and threatens national security. Your letter gave no assurances whatsoever that you are concerned about Communist teachers.

During the course of the correspondence between Clark and Ober, the pamphlet of the Educational Policies Commission appeared. Ober appended a reference to it in his concluding letter. He said he was glad that the president of Harvard had gone at least as far as stating that he would not employ a member of the Communist Party. There were many of my friends who did not share Mr. Ober's pleasure. To them, I had shifted to the wrong side of the argument. How could I reconcile what I had been saying for so many years with my signed endorsement of a document which flatfootedly ruled out the employment of a Communist as a teacher? My answer was essentially what we had stated in the pamphlet under the heading "Members of the Communist Party of the United States Should Not Be Employed as Teachers":

Such membership, in the opinion of the Educational Policies Commission, involves adherence to doctrines and discipline completely inconsistent with the principles of freedom on which American education depends. Such membership, and the accompanying surrender of intellectual integrity, render an individual unfit to discharge the duties of a teacher in this country.

At the same time we condemn the careless, incorrect, and unjust use of such words as "Red" and "Communist" to attack teachers and other persons who in point of fact are not Communists, but who merely have views different from those of their accusers. The whole spirit of free American education will be subverted unless teachers are free to think for themselves. It is because members of the Communist Party are required to surrender this right, as a consequence of becoming part of a movement characterized by conspiracy and calculated deceit, that they should be excluded from employment as teachers.

In the summary, the Educational Policies Commission explained the connection between the negative policy advocated for one category of teachers and its positive assertions for the future:

With the prospect of continuing ideological conflict, four main lines of strategy for American education are suggested:

(a) Young citizens should have an opportunity to learn about the principles and practices of totalitarianism, including those represented by the Soviet Union and by the Communist Party in the United States.

(b) Teaching about Communism or any other form of dictatorship does not mean advocacy of these doctrines. Such advocacy should not be permitted in American schools.

(c) The schools should continue with vigor their programs for giving young citizens a clear understanding of the principles of the American way of life and a desire to make these principles prevail in their own lives and in the life of their country.

(d) Members of the Communist Party of the United States should not be employed as teachers.

The accident of the dates of publication of the EPC statement and the Ober-Clark correspondence had placed me in an almost indefensible position. The charge of inconsistency was not easily answered. I attempted to explain my attitude to a meeting of one group of alumni a few days before commencement in 1949.

In this period of a cold war, I do not believe the usual rules as to political parties apply to the Communist Party. I am convinced that conspiracy and calculated deceit have been and are the characteristic pattern of behavior of regular Communists all over the world. For these reasons, as far as I am concerned, card-holding members of the Communist Party are out of bounds as members of the teaching profession. I should not want to be a party to the appointment of such a person to a teaching position with tenure in any educational institution. But with this single exception, which is the unique product of our century, I maintain that a professor's political views, social philosophy, or religion are of no concern to the university; nor are his activities within the law as a private citizen. I do not have to remind this audience that this is the traditional Harvard position and will be maintained in the face of whatever criticisms may come. Admittedly a university might be faced with a difficult problem if some member of the permanent staff should suddenly announce that he was a full-fledged member of the Communist Party, but no such problem exists here at Harvard. . . .

As long as I am president of the university, I can assure you there will be no policy of inquiry into the political views of the members of the staff and no watching over their activities as private citizens. Any suggestion that we should employ here a procedure comparable to that required by the necessities of secret government work and investigate the loyalty of our staff is utterly repugnant to my concept of a university. On this point I am sure you will all agree.

In a letter to a correspondent, I was more explicit. The issue, I wrote,

turns on a different evaluation of the nature of membership in a Communist Party in the United States today. I start from a premise that this is not a question of heresy; this is a question of a conspiracy which can only be likened to that of a group of spies and saboteurs in an enemy country in time of war. I am convinced from documentary evidence and from my own experience in connection with the atomic bomb project, which I cannot discuss openly, that card-holding members of the Communist Party today are not free agents. I have reluctantly come to the conclusion that they must be considered as essentially a group of persons who have declared war against American society and whose ethics are therefore exactly comparable to those of spies and saboteurs.

But Ober had come to exactly the same conclusion. He had stated in his first letter to me that "the vast majority of our people have gradually reached the conclusion that Communism is not a political movement—but is a criminal conspiracy." In the conclusion to his second letter to Clark, after applauding my participation in the EPC pamphlet, he expressed the belief that "appropriate steps to implement that policy are now in order."

It remained for Clark in his rebuttal, dated June 11, 1949, to rescue me from my troubles. He wrote:

You mention Mr. Conant's joinder in a recent report, one point of which is that a Communist Party Member is disqualified to teach. But you want to reach far beyond Communists. You want to discipline any teacher if, after hearing, "reasonable grounds on all the evidence" are found to doubt his "loyalty." These are slippery terms.

I affirm again that your plan implies an extensive system of detection and trial. Nothing of this character will happen under Mr. Conant. There will be no harassment of professors for engaging in open and legal meetings. There will be no apparatus of inquiry and "closer watch." The harm done by the effort necessary to discover even a single clandestine Party Member would outweigh any possible benefit. To go beyond that by searching for "reasonable grounds" concerning "loyalty," would still more disrupt Harvard or any free university. No greater mistake could be made than to suppose that because a proved Party Member, bound by Party discipline, should not teach, all professors are to be policed or watched. I know these to be Mr. Conant's firm convictions.

These were indeed my convictions. I could not have expressed them as well myself. The editorial page of the *Harvard Alumni Bulletin* for June 25, 1949, considered at some length both the Ober-Clark exchange of letters and the charges of inconsistency or worse leveled at the president of the university. After reporting that in a poll conducted by the *Harvard Crimson*, the student body was two to one in favor of allowing Communists to teach, and the faculty two to one against, the editors wrote a final paragraph:

President Conant had the answer to end all answers to the "iffy" question. Interviewed after receiving an honorary doctor of laws degree at the 18th Commencement exercises of Yeshiva University, New York, he was asked what he would do if a distinguished member of the Harvard Faculty walked into his office and announced himself as a Communist. Answered the President, "I would send for a psychiatrist."

CHAPTER 34

Are Private Schools Divisive?

In 1951 Australia celebrated the fiftieth anniversary of the creation of the Commonwealth. All manner of festivities were held throughout the year. Among many others, I was invited to attend a seminar on scientific research to be held in Canberra in July. I learned from Whitney Shepardson that the Carnegie Corporation was ready to cover the expenses for my wife and myself for an extended trip, Therefore I accepted the invitation. It would be our first trip to the antipodes.

In writing the vice chancellor of the National University, Professor D. B. Copland, I indicated that in addition to visiting the universities in several of the states and his own National University, I should like to look at some secondary schools. I explained that for a number of years I had had in mind a trip to Australia because of an interest in comparative education. I had been told that the educational systems in different Australian states reflected the influence of both British and American systems.

In early July, 1951, Mrs. Conant and I flew on a Pan American Airways Boeing "Strato" Clipper from San Francisco to Honolulu, where I spoke to the Harvard Club luncheon. Then we had a long, long flight to Sydney since airplane trips in those days were not what they were to become later when jets displaced the propeller planes.

Ten days in Sydney were followed by a week in Canberra, where the future of the new National University, which was just getting under way, was a constant topic of discussion. The seminar itself and related discussions about "Science in Australia" occupied only four days. My own contribution was a talk on "Science and Defense," which I fear was indeed a minor contribution and contained nothing new. In fact, any assistance I gave to the Australians in developing science would be difficult to pinpoint. But from my point of view, the rewards of the journey were great because I focused my attention largely on the schools. The Carnegie Corporation's investment, not for the last time, yielded tangible dividends for me.

One story about the expedition is not without its relevance. Dean Erwin N. Griswold of the Harvard Law School was also invited to attend one of the meetings. When we compared notes in June, we discovered that his journey was to be in the reverse direction to mine, his starting with New Zealand while mine would start with Australia. The one point where our paths would cross would be the Fiji Islands. We would fly from there in the same plane to Honolulu on our way home. And, to be sure, at the appointed day and hour, we met Dean Griswold in the waiting room of the airport. With him was a leading member of the American bar. After introduction, our new acquaintance said he was going over to a group of American girls who were on the plane from Australia, which Mrs. Conant and I were about to board, and tell them who the new passengers were. He returned with a smile, if not a grin. The young ladies had been in Australia modeling clothes. When he told them that the president of Harvard and his wife were to board the plane on which the dean of the Harvard Law School had already traveled, they shrugged their shoulders and one of them said, "It doesn't matter what your racket is, as long as you get a trip." I may add that this story served me well at alumni dinners for the next few years.

What I thought I would be able to study in Australia was the modification of the English pattern of education by the application of imported American ideas. I had had little solid information to go on, yet it turned out that my guess was entirely correct. Before we had been in Sydney, New South Wales, many days, I met Professor C. R. McRae, the director of teacher education at Sydney University. He was not only acquainted with American ideas but had been relying on them while engaged in the task of remaking the state secondary schools. He suggested that I should visit several schools, which I did.

I discovered in our conversation that each Australian state had its own educational system. In general they were alike, yet there were some differences. New South Wales was said to be the most "Americanized," and my newly acquired guide rather boasted of the fact. Later when I met some conservatives in Melbourne, the adjective was used with far from favorable overtones. The expansion of free, tax-supported schools in every Australian state was a relatively recent phenomenon. Within the memory of many adults, private schools had provided education for those over the age of fifteen. Now more youth were attending public high schools than private schools. To be sure, the total percentage of the fifteen-year-olds enrolled in any school was low by American standards—38 percent as compared with 88 percent in the United States (figures for 1950).

In each of the three Australian states I visited, private schools, both secular and church-connected, were flourishing to a degree unknown in the United States. People spoke openly of the dual system of education. Twenty to 30 percent of thirteen-year-old youths were enrolled in private schools in South Australia, New South Wales and Victoria, which with few exceptions were located in the metropolitan areas of Sydney, Melbourne and Adelaide. The famous English public schools, such as Winchester or Eton, were the prototypes. Yet the Australian private schools were not primarily boarding schools; they were day schools with a nucleus of boarders. The tuition had been kept relatively low; as a consequence, the range of income groups patronizing them was fairly broad.

Around each of the three cities I have mentioned were Church of England schools, Methodist schools, Presbyterian schools and Catholic schools. The existence of so many different kinds of private schools astonished me. I would not have been surprised to find the equivalent of the English public schools in addition to state-supported schools. But in England, as far as I was aware, the private schools were primarily boarding schools and were all, or almost all, Church of England schools. The idea that a considerable proportion of the youth of a community was distributed among a number of private schools, each connected with one of three or four branches of Christianity, appeared to me strange indeed. In the education of the sixteen-year-olds, I learned, the role of the private schools loomed still larger; in Victoria a considerably larger number was enrolled in private schools than in the tax-supported schools; in the other two states I examined, about half of the sixteen-year-old youths were to be found in private schools.

I was told that when free secondary education began to expand in Australia, the private schools were already in existence. It was assumed that there must be a separation of students into different types of schools with different programs. Expanded private schools would provide one type, the state schools another which would be more practical.

As I pondered on the differences between Australia and the United States, I came to realize as never before the importance of the American tradition of free common schools based on a long history; such a tradition was lacking in Australia. The concept of a public school as a binding force in a community was an American idea—a product of the special history of the United States. I became more convinced than ever that public schools had been significant factors in the development of the United States. If one started with the assumption that there might be as many separate schools as there were religious denominations, the concept of a high school to serve *all* youth in an area was destroyed.

I returned from Australia in late August 1951. One of the tasks awaiting me was the preparation of three lectures I had agreed to give in February 1952 at the University of Virginia under the Page-Barbour Foundation. I had decided, on accepting the invitation, that if my trip to the antipodes yielded the information I desired, I would use the Page-Barbour Lectures to compare the education of youth in England, Scotland, Australia, New Zealand and the United States. As I began to outline what I would say, I realized that I would not be able to avoid one highly controversial question on which I had not yet expressed an opinion. Should the American parochial schools receive public funds? The more I reflected on what I had found in Australia, the more I saw the importance of this question. What had been only a mild interest in the worries of some of my friends on the Educational Policies Commission was transformed into a deep concern. I thought I saw the dangers to the public schools if tax money were to go to support private schools of any sort. To be sure, no Australian state had as yet taken the step of authorizing public money for private schools, but there was agitation to that effect. I was acutely aware of similar agitation in the United States. The Catholic spokesmen, I had been told, had made it quite clear they would never support federal aid for the public schools unless the parochial schools were included.

In preparing the third of my Page-Barbour Lectures, I plunged boldly into the boiling waters of the old controversy about federal aid to parochial schools. My approach, however, was somewhat unorthodox in that I made no distinction between private nondenominational and denominational schools. I raised what I considered the basic question. I asked whether in the United States we wanted to move toward a dual system such as existed in Australia. I pointed out that many of the critics of the public schools seemed to favor a system in which a large proportion of our children would attend private schools. I granted that many sincere Protestants, Jews and

Catholics believed that secondary education divorced from a denominational religious core of instruction was bad education. I said I did not question the right of such people to organize their own schools and pointed out that the United States Supreme Court had settled the law on this matter in the famous Oregon Case of 1926. (The Court had declared unconstitutional an act of the state legislature which, in effect, would have compelled all parents to send their children to public schools.) I went on to say, however, that I did question the honesty of their tactics when some of the critics attacked the public schools in an attempt to undermine confidence in secular education. To each one who attacked our public schools, I said, I would ask the simple question: "Would you like to increase the number and scope of the private schools?" If the answer was in the affirmative, I would ask a second question: "Do you look forward to the day when tax money will directly or indirectly assist these schools?" If the answer to both questions was "Yes," then a debate on a vital issue could proceed.

In thus challenging the proponents of the use of tax money to support parochial schools, I took a new line. I argued in terms of the social function of the comprehensive high school, not against the denominational control of parochial schools. In asking the hostile critics "to show their colors," I made it clear I included those Protestant clergymen who had been "attacking" the public schools as "Godless" and yearning for the importation of the English system. I said I realized that in several English-speaking nations public funds were used to assist church-connected schools. But in the United States we believed our public schools should serve all creeds. I then added two sentences which were later to receive considerable publicity: "The greater the proportion of our youth who attend independent schools, the greater the threat to our democratic unity. Therefore, to use taxpayers' money to assist such a move is, for me, to suggest that American society use its own hands to destroy itself."

The press release of the third Page-Barbour Lecture contained these key sentences of my approach to an explosive issue. Somewhat to my surprise, no paper picked up the story. But as the winter went on, I decided to use some of the material for a speech scheduled for a regional meeting of the American Association of School Administrators in Boston on April 7, 1952. I felt sure that what I had to say about private schools and taxes would meet with the approval of a large majority of the audience even if my approach was novel. I also realized it might provoke strong negative comments from several quarters. Since the essence of my position involved lumping together private preparatory schools such as Groton and Exeter with parochial schools (Catholic, Lutheran or Jewish), I was fully aware that more than one Harvard alumnus would be greatly pained. Also, the trustees and headmasters of those private schools which sent many graduates to Harvard College might be offended.

As I judged the situation, these people had become allied without knowing it with the proponents of federal aid to parochial schools, though the last thing most of them wanted was federal (or state) aid. Therefore, with "malice aforethought," I included in my speech the following: "I cannot help regretting that private schools have been established in the last twenty years in certain urban areas where a generation ago a public high school served *all* the youth of the town or city." I suggested, however, that those of us who had such regrets should regard the founding of a new independent school in a locality as a challenge to those connected with public education.

Granted the "snob aspect" of some of these independent schools. Nevertheless, I feel sure in many cases they would never have come into existence if the management of the local high school had been wiser. . . . What is required is for those concerned to improve the high schools; public school administrators must recognize the validity of some of the criticism now directed against them in terms of the failure of the high school to provide adequate education for the gifted. The problem is especially acute in metropolitan areas.

The argument was sound and not unconnected with my consistent views about improving the curricula of public high schools. It was quite unnecessary, however, to have used the words "snob aspect," which irritated the headmasters of the private preparatory schools. Just how great was the irritation, I discovered in a meeting with some of these men and an official of the independent schools organization in the summer of 1952. In this meeting, while we agreed to disagree on some points, I do think I succeeded in directing attention to the fundamental questions. My lines of reasoning against federal aid for parochial schools—the practical issue for several decades—made it necessary for *all* private school people to decide where they stood. To this extent, what I had said might have done some good. On the other hand, it was implied by some of those in this meeting that it was a bit odd for the head of a private university to regret the founding of a private school.

The distinction between school and college, though quite evident in my speech, was not spelled out as it might have been. The failure to recognize the difference was seized on by many of my critics. As one highly dissatisfied prominent alumnus said to one of my co-workers in the Harvard administration, "Let me ask you one question: Is or is not Harvard a private school?" My stalwart supporter had to admit it was private. Then, said the critic harshly and triumphantly, what business has Conant "sounding off" against private schools?

An important section of my speech before the American Association of School Administrators* ran as follows:

> We desire on the one hand to provide through our schools unity in our national life. On the other we seek the diversity that comes from freedom of action and expression by small groups of citizens. We look with disfavor on any monolithic type of educational structure; we shrink from any idea of regimentation, of uniformity as to the details of many phases of secondary education. Unity we can achieve if our public schools remain the primary vehicle for the education of our youth, and if, as far as possible, all youth of a community attend the same school irrespective of family fortune or cultural background. Diversity in experimentation we maintain by continued emphasis on the concept of local responsibility for our schools. . . .
>
> If one has doubts about the ability of secular schools to promote the growth of moral and spiritual values, then these doubts must be weighed against the democratic objectives I have just listed. Similarly, if a family questions the ability of a high school to prepare a gifted boy adequately for university work, the family will have to balance these misgivings against the advantages to the boy of mixing with all sorts of people when he is young.

In this and other sections of my speech, I attempted to forestall certain counterarguments which I felt would be forthcoming. I was quite prepared for a vigorous attack from those who hoped for the eventual public support of parochial schools.

Though the newspapers had failed to find my lectures at the University of Virginia in February newsworthy, I was in no doubt that the essence of my speech in Boston on April 7, 1952, would be reported. So it was, though only short extracts of the address were printed. The headlines made it evident that I could expect replies from several quarters. Two of them read: "Dual System of Education Hurts U.S. Democracy, Dr. Conant Says" (Boston *Herald*) and "Conant Sees Peril to U.S. Education" (*New York Times*).

An Associated Press report of a meeting held the day following my address complicated somewhat the story but underlined the real

* The full text is given in Appendix 3.

issue. The convention of school administrators adopted the following resolution: "We respect the rights of groups, including religious denominations, to maintain their own schools so long as such schools meet the educational, health and safety standards defined by the states in which they are located. We believe that these schools should be financed entirely by their own supporters. We therefore oppose all efforts to devote public funds to support these schools either directly or indirectly." In a panel discussion, Professor John K. Norton of Teachers College, Columbia University, and several others expressed their concern at the increasing demand for funds for the support of nonpublic schools. A report of their remarks was combined with some of what I had said the night before. There were thus two stories, one following another, on the subject of the use of public money by private schools.

I did not have to wait long for the expected reply. Archbishop Cushing devoted the major portion of his Easter Sunday sermon in Boston to a highly unfavorable analysis of my address of six days before. Within a month news story after story recorded the dissatisfaction of Catholic groups and individuals with what I had said in Boston. They were joined by the heads of a number of Protestant private schools. The full text of my speech was printed in some local papers as well as in the *Harvard Alumni Bulletin*. A vigorous controversy developed which lasted several months. Those who disagreed were apt to take sentences out of context. I was depicted in the more violent attacks as being a totalitarian, as wishing to suppress all private schools. One cartoon had me pictured alongside of Hitler, Stalin and Tito with the caption: "Private schools threat to democratic unity, President Conant of Harvard. It's Been Said Before."

I made no reply to any of the assaults. Since I was in process of preparing the manuscript of the Page-Barbour Lectures for publication, I decided to make my rebuttal in the footnotes. Until the book appeared, I proposed to hold my fire. A number of people came to my defense, including Mrs. Eugene Meyer of Washington in a forthright, fighting speech before the annual NEA meeting in July entitled "Public and Private Education," and Rabbi Joseph S. Shubon of Temple Bnai Moshe, Brighton, Massachusetts, who on May 30 delivered a sermon on my behalf.

Since Rabbi Shubon's address exposed some of the misinterpretations which were current, I shall quote from it liberally. He declared that he had read my address several times and could not find any indication with which any profoundly religious man or true American citizen could find fault. Indeed, he congratulated me on reaffirming and reasserting the basic and imperishable foundations of American life and liberty. "It is pathetic," he said,

to see how a great address by a pre-eminent American scholar and university administrator could have been so thoroughly misunderstood and misinterpreted. Since President Conant's pronouncement was released to the press, there has been a barrage of criticism; with a great deal of that criticism one can sympathize, especially since the entire address was not made available to the reading public and since the slant given it seemed to emphasize secularism as opposed to religion and public school as opposed to private. It is clear, indeed, from a reading of the complete address which has appeared in the *Harvard Alumni Bulletin* that President Conant need take a second place to none in his respect for the highest teachings of religious and moral ideals. It is further clear that he has meant no insult to the private schools which have produced some admirable teachers in our country, as have many of the Church schools, but it is an incontrovertible fact that if we insist on an ever-widening cleavage between religious groups and the social and economic classes, we shall inevitably not be one nation but become many nations and thus become a household divided against itself, which cannot stand.

Rabbi Shubon then described his own situation as a graduate of the public Boston Latin School. At a class reunion, he embraced old friends of a diversity of origins and a variety of beliefs. "What would have happened," he asked, "if I had been educated completely in a Jewish Parochial School and my friends had never attended the Boston Public Latin? I would have personally been all the poorer and all the more limited in my vision and experience and all the less able to contribute whatever one may contribute, to the general welfare of the greater society of our beloved country."

In a nutshell, my argument had been that the multiplication of private schools, whether church-connected or not, was not in the best interests of the nation's future. In any given locality the introduction of one or more private schools alongside of a comprehensive high school tended to weaken the unity of the community. Since the nation would not benefit by the spread of private schools, there was no reason to promote such a spread by the use of public funds. Yet I would do nothing to interfere with the present status of private schools. My opponents said, in effect, that if I was opposed to the increase in the number of private schools, I must be logically in favor of their abolition. They claimed that either you are in favor of public support of private schools because they provide diversity or else you are in favor of closing them. To which logic, I could not agree.

Why had I decided to enter into this particular public quarrel? There is no doubt that my active participation in the isolationist-interventionist dispute of 1940–41 had increased my subsequent willingness to take sides on controversial matters. At the time of the Korean War, I was influential in forming the Committee on the Present Danger, urging a firm commitment to defend Europe. At the same time, I put forward a scheme for universal military service. Was there a difference between these activities, in which I was joined with at least a few other college presidents, and my expressing publicly my opposition to the spread of private schools? The novelty of my opposition to tax money going to private and church schools assured that I would be attacked from at least two sides. The private-school clientele as well as very many Catholics would be against me. If the hostility was then transferred to Harvard, damage to the university might result which would last as long as I was the head of the institution. Such a probability could not be lightly brushed aside. As one of my acquaintances said on referring to a much earlier speech he didn't like: "After all, no one would listen to you if you were not president of Harvard."

Of course, after firing my shots against the target I had so carefully defined, I could then withdraw from the field of battle. This, in fact, was exactly what I did and what I planned to do when I made the speech. As I have already mentioned, I had made up my mind shortly after taking office to retire from the presidency of Harvard soon after my sixtieth birthday. For that reason, I had refused an invitation from Dean Acheson in the fall of 1951 to go to Germany for a year as Ambassador in 1952–53. One couldn't ask for a leave of absence for a year when one planned to retire a year or so later. In strict confidence, I so told the Secretary of State in the fall of 1951. I had not, however, betrayed my intentions to anyone else except my wife. What I would do when I retired was not clear. I thought of writing about science and education.

In January 1953 President Eisenhower settled the matter for me by asking me to become U.S. High Commissioner for Germany. As I was departing, my book entitled *Education and Liberty*, based on the Page-Barbour Lectures, was published. In it I was able to record what were to be my last words about the storm I had stirred up. I developed my thesis much as I had in the Boston speech. Since I was anxious not to have the debate become one which turned on the issue of tax money for *church* schools, I stuck carefully to what I considered the important point, namely, why it would be most unfortunate if a dual system developed in the United States. I maintained that if the comprehensive high school in a community was replaced by a series of church-connected schools, something of great value would disappear. "By organizing our free schools on as comprehensive a basis as possible," I wrote, "we can continue to give our children an understanding of democracy. Religious tolerance, mutual respect between vocational groups, belief in the rights of the individual, are among the virtues that the best of our high schools now foster."

In *Education and Liberty* I carefully refrained from answering in detail the numerous attacks to which I had been exposed. With the aid of footnotes in which I quoted from *The Pilot*, the Boston Catholic weekly, I tried to do justice to those who disagreed. I made no mention of the fact that Archbishop Cushing had done me the honor of taking strong exception to my views in his Easter Sunday sermon, nor had I ever offered a public rebuttal to his attack. In this, my final statement, I had no intention of making a point-by-point reply to the denunciation of my speech by many supporters of church-connected schools. For example, much use had been made of the adjective "divisive," which I was alleged to have used. Actually, the word was put in my mouth by my critics. My claim that "the greater the proportion of our youth who attend independent schools, the greater the threat to our democratic unity" could be translated as "independent schools are divisive." But such a translation, which was frequently treated as my own statement, was not what I had said or written. To make much of this point, however, would have seemed like a quibble.

My views about private schools became one of the sticks with which I was beaten by those who opposed my nomination as High Commissioner for Germany. But the attack was short-lived. Once the Senate had acted favorably and I had left for my new assignment, my stand on educational issues was forgotten by most people.

On my return to the United States in early 1957, I once again became involved in discussions of educational affairs. The parochial-school question was not at that time in the news. I did not retreat from my position as set forth in *Education and Liberty*. On the other hand, I added no further fuel to the controversy.

At the federal level the old arguments pro and con federal aid continued. They were still going on in the early 1960s when I rejoined the Educational Policies Commission. The stalemate in Congress generally attributed to the control of the Rules Committee of the house by Catholic interests seemed likely to be permanent. Then the Johnson administration produced the ingenious bill which became the revolutionary Elementary and Secondary School Act of 1965. By focusing on the use of federal money to benefit the children, the way was opened for some benefits to accrue to those who attended parochial schools. The Catholic hierarchy supported the idea.

I happened to be attending the annual meeting of the National Association of Secondary School Principals in Miami when the news broke of the President's new proposals. The news stories gave an adequate account of the novel features of the proposed law. I was glad to count myself among the supporters of what the White House was proposing. In the course of my prepared address, I was able to insert a few words expressing my hopes that the bill would soon become law.

A day later at an informal question-and-answer session with several hundred people, I was asked how I could reconcile my enthusiasm for the new legislation with my long record of opposition to the use of taxpayers' money by private schools. I said, in effect, that it would not be clear until the bill was passed and in operation just how the students in private schools would benefit from the distribution of the new federal funds. My objection to the use of tax money to support private schools had always been based on my fear of atomizing our school system. I was particularly concerned lest the numbers and size of private schools would increase in a community in which a large proportion of the youth now attended a single public high school. I would have to wait ten years before I was ready to pass a judgment. If at the end of that time, the relative position of the public comprehensive high school the nation over had markedly decreased, then I would deeply regret the passage of the bill in question. On the other hand, if there was no such result, then I would think my present enthusiasm had been justified.

In 1967 I was asked by Governor Nelson Rockefeller to become a member of a committee of five to advise him "how the state can help preserve the strength and vitality of our private and independent institutions of higher education, yet at the same time keep them free." McGeorge Bundy, the president of the Ford Foundation, served as chairman; the other members were the president of Michigan State University, John A. Hannah; the president of Brandeis, Abram L. Sachar; and the president of Notre Dame, the Rev. Theodore M. Hesburgh. We decided to endorse the plea of the presidents of the private colleges and universities for state aid, but were faced with a problem because as we read the state constitution we felt such aid would be unconstitutional if given to an institution "controlled in part or in whole by a religious denomination." In stating that we were convinced that in the field of higher learning the rigorous prohibition was unwise, we sharply distinguished the elementary and secondary school from the four-year college and university. I was glad to find my colleagues agreeing with my old thesis that a distinction can be made between state aid to private schools (which we were not asked to examine) and state aid to church-connected colleges. What we said was:

The democratic argument for a single comprehensive public school system in each community simply does not apply, in our view, at the level of the four-year college and the university. The clear-cut tradition of this country is that there should be a wide variety of colleges and universities, supported in a wide variety of ways. Moreover, there has been a general recognition for many generations that privately controlled colleges and universities—if they are good—serve the public interest in a wider and deeper way than most private elementary and secondary schools. We intend no criticism of private schools; we are simply making the point that there is a pronounced and recognized difference between the public contribution of Columbia or Cornell and the public contribution of even the most distinguished of private elementary and secondary schools.

Since I had never objected to government money going to parochial schools because they were church schools, I could join in a recommendation that did not exclude aid to an institution of higher education. (We made it plain that we did not think assistance should go to a college whose "central purpose was the teaching of religious belief.") In thus separating the case against public assistance to private schools (including parochial schools) from the consideration of the case against public financial help for private colleges and universities, I was disagreeing with many who had endorsed my speech in Boston in April 1952. In a word, my concern then and now was with the future of the comprehensive high schools of the United States. I did not want to subsidize rival private schools which would draw away from the public school youth of a community and thus weaken the integrating force of the comprehensive public school.

PART V

THE POSTWAR

INTERNATIONAL SCENE

CHAPTER 35

Moscow, Christmas 1945

WITH THE END OF THE WAR, I disassociated myself as rapidly as possible from those activities which had required me to spend a large portion of my time away from Cambridge for five years. I had been serving the university on a part-time basis far too long. I retained an office in Washington for some months, but was rarely in it. Vannevar Bush lived in Washington and was thus on hand to advise President Truman on all problems connected with the atomic bomb. Therefore on V-J Day I signed off.

I read the papers and cheered silently when I thus learned of the joint declaration of President Truman, Prime Minister Attlee and Prime Minister King about the international control of atomic energy, issued on November 15, 1945. The heads of the governments of the United States, Great Britain and Canada had obviously been persuaded by Bush's hardheaded reasoning. Indeed, from what I knew of his line of thinking, he might have drafted the document. The newspapers had announced that he had been one of the few who had met together in Washington to hammer out a declaration.

Two basic decisions had been made. First, the three governments were to keep to themselves the engineering and industrial know-how pending the setting up of "effective reciprocal, and enforceable safeguards acceptable to all nations." Second, the United Nations was to be asked to handle the problem of preventing the use of atomic energy for destructive purposes while promoting its use for peaceful ends.

Ernest K. Lindley, writing in a *Newsweek* column on November 26, 1945, pointed out that there was nothing in the declaration which put Russia or any other nation "on the spot."

The declaration can be called "a stall," or a device for withholding the atomic know-how from the Russians, only if one assumes that the Russian Government (1) has evil intentions against the rest of the world, or (2) is so insecure internally that it dare not expose the Russian people to the contacts with the world which the effective international control of atomic energy would require.

The Russians, like the rest of us, will have to adjust themselves to the atomic age. It will not be easy for any of us. Messrs. Truman, Attlee, and King have proposed a way of beginning the adjustment which fuses prudence with vision.

When I read Lindley's article and similar comments in other journals, I could not foresee that within a month I would obtain a glimpse of how the Soviet Union was reacting to the three-power statement. Once again for a short period I would be acting as a deputy for Bush.

On Monday morning, two weeks before Christmas, I happened to be in my Washington office for a few hours. Word came that the Secretary of State, James Byrnes, was anxious to speak to me right away. When I went to his office in the old State Department Building, I was told an emergency had arisen. The Secretary was going to leave for Moscow on Wednesday. Dr. Bush was to have been one of the small party. He had just telephoned that morning to say his doctor had refused to let him go because he was not sufficiently recovered from the grippe. One of the main reasons for the trip was to talk with the Russians and the British about the problem of the international control of the atomic bomb. There must be someone in the American party who knew about atomic energy. I was the obvious person to substitute for Bush. Would I go?

My first thought was: "How in the world can I get ready to take off the day after tomorrow?" My second was: "What am I getting into if I go?" I explored the second question at once by pleading my lack of up-to-date information as to United States policy about the bomb. I had not been involved in any of the Anglo-American talks since the bombs were dropped. Nor had I been a party to the discussions of the American point of view. The Secretary at once showed me a "position paper," my first introduction to such a document. Some years later as a diplomat, I would come to regard reading "position papers" as a routine preparation for any meeting with the representative of another nation.

The paper Byrnes gave me to read was short and marked "Top Secret." A policy committee of four, including Bush, had been involved in its preparation. A supplementary paper was the product of three scientists whom I knew and in whose judgment I had complete faith. It was soon clear that the Secretary of State had adopted as his own a policy Bush had been developing for some months. In essence the position was that which had been formulated at the Truman-Atlee-King conference in Washington in November. I was familiar with it, thoroughly approved of it and therefore felt I could interpret it properly in negotiations with the British and Soviet representatives.

To make certain that I was on the right track, I checked by phone with Bush, who urged me to take his place. I was inclined to do so for the prospect was exciting. Before deciding, however, I telephoned Boston and talked with Dr. Roger I. Lee, the senior member of the Harvard Corporation and also my personal physician. I was well aware that my being away from Harvard on another public government assignment would not be welcomed by the members of the Corporation or by the deans. Another neglect of duty was likely to be the verdict. I hoped to forestall such complaints by putting the matter squarely before Dr. Lee. He agreed I had no choice but to accede to the Secretary of State's request. As far as my health was concerned, there was no time for inoculations; I would have to take a chance. A third telephone call to my wife, who was most understanding as usual, put me in a position to tell the Secretary I would go. The next day but one I would be back in Washington prepared to be one of his party.

On Wednesday, at the National Airport, a distinguished group was on hand to speed the Secretary of State on his way—General Eisenhower, then Chief of Staff of the Army, Dean Acheson, then Under Secretary of State, Justice Frankfurter and several others. The American mission was to be small. Charles Bohlen, later to be the American Ambassador in Moscow, was the organizing spirit; his command of Russian and his knowledge of the people in the Kremlin made certain that Byrnes would be in a position to argue effectively with the Soviet Foreign Minister, Vyacheslav Molotov (and we expected arguments). Benjamin V. Cohen was the Secretary's closest adviser. He had been a member of the Policy Committee which had prepared the paper I had seen two days before. In Paris the next day we were to pick up two senior Foreign Service officers, Freeman Matthews and John C. Vincent, to complete the group.

An overnight flight from Bermuda to the Orly Airport in Paris

was in those days sufficiently long to enable those who so desired to
stretch out in a bunk and have a fairly comfortable sleep. There were
four bunks on the special plane put at the Secretary of State's disposal; I was assigned one, which I gladly occupied. At the Paris
airport a complication arose that provided me with a precedent I
was to use to good effect eight years later when I was a traveling host
to the Chancellor of the Federal Republic of Germany. The American Air Force officer in charge refused to allow the plane on which
we had crossed the Atlantic to take off because visibility was too
low. Going on to Berlin as planned was out of the question.

There was much discussion between Byrnes, Bohlen, Matthews
and Cohen as to what should be done. The Secretary did not want
to be in a position in which he would have to meet the French
Foreign Minister or any of his staff. The Moscow meeting was taking
place without the French, who were not happy about their exclusion.
As long as he was in the United States-controlled airport, Byrnes
declared he was on American soil; no embarrassment with French
officials could occur. It would be best to get on with the journey
nonetheless. Therefore a smaller plane was found which the commanding officer of the airport agreed to clear for departure in spite
of the weather. In it, Byrnes and three or four others of us went to
Frankfurt, where we spent the night. The next day the big plane
arrived, and we boarded for Moscow via Berlin.

In Berlin the weather was still bad; the ground fog cut down
the visibility, but Byrnes decided to push on. Our stop in the Berlin
Tempelhof Airport (almost in the center of the city) was only long
enough to pick up two Russians—a navigator and a radioman. We
took off at once for Moscow. Our flight above the scattered clouds
appeared to be about to end as we came down to an elevation of
some five hundred feet. We looked out expecting to see a city; no
habitation was in sight. Bohlen went up to the cockpit and talked with
the two Russians. He reported that they could not find Moscow and
were in disagreement as to why and what to do next. We flew on
over snow-covered fields and woods, no villages in sight. What appeared to be aimless flying continued for about an hour, with Bohlen
going back and forth between the navigator's forward compartment
and Byrnes' seat. At last he announced to all of us that if we didn't
find Moscow in the next ten minutes, we would turn back; we had
gas enough for only an hour's flying in addition to what was required
for direct return to Berlin. Landing in the dark in the Berlin airport
was not recommended, but we would probably have to come to it.

A few minutes later, the plane made a rapid turn, and Cohen and I, who were sitting together, thought that the decision to return to Berlin had been made. We were mistaken; in a matter of seconds, a powerhouse and factories came into view and then Moscow itself.

We landed in a blizzard at an airport in the center of the city at 4:30 P.M. with no daylight to spare. Ambassador W. Averell Harriman and the official Soviet reception committee had gone to another landing field some twenty miles to the south, thinking the weather was too bad to allow us to use the main airport. The British Ambassador, Sir Archibald Clark-Kerr, welcomed us. Covered with fur from head to foot and standing in a snowstorm, he greeted me with the words, "I don't look much like an ambassador, but I am one." After the Secretary had said a few words into the waiting microphone, we all hastened into warm cars and were driven to Spasso House, Ambassador Harriman's official residence. Here we were made to feel at home and installed for the duration of our visit.

The conference was not scheduled to start until 5 P.M. on the day after our arrival (Saturday, December 15). Thanks to the hospitality of Kathleen Harriman, the Ambassador's daughter, I was able to make a tour of the city under her skillful guidance. Moscow was essentially still under war conditions. The rebuilding had hardly got under way before the winter snows had blanketed the city. My notes about my observations give a glimpse of what Moscow must have been like while the war was on.

Few cars; enormous numbers of people in the streets all carrying something. Most of them poorly dressed. Side streets show through doorways very simple style of living. Reminded me of French Canadian village as to the cultural pattern of living or is it just the snow? . . . A number of crippled ex-soldiers. Children everywhere on the streets. Looked well and well taken care of. Babies in better clothes than the parents. They take wonderful care of the children, says Miss Harriman. Went into a government shop where you can sell or buy clothes, jewelry, china, clocks, etc. Looked into other stores. No displays or almost none in windows. Moscow frightfully crowded as to living.

A few days later after another ride around Moscow and into the suburbs I wrote:

This is a police state, so we are told, and I have no reason to doubt it. However, no police are in evidence. All rather chaotic, as for example at the entrance to the railroad station. Very different from Germany even under the Weimar Republic. In the suburbs saw typical Russian village of "log houses." Terrific disorder and squalor everywhere—unfinished buildings not being worked on. There is an enormous job to be done here to make even a halfway modern capital of an industrialized nation. In ten years, it will look very different.

The conference meetings were held in Spridinovka House. For the most part, I had no role to play, since only toward the end of the conference did the subject of atomic energy come up. Therefore I sat in the background and listened to what must have been historic arguments, but, alas, my ignorance was so great that I probably missed the subtleties of the points that were made. The arrangements were such that each of the three foreign ministers had four of his staff sitting beside him around a table large enough to accommodate a total of fifteen. The American Secretary of State was always flanked by the Ambassador, Bohlen, Cohen and one of the experts, namely, either Matthews or Vincent or myself.

On the first day of the conference during the 9 P.M. break for vodka, I had a chance to talk with several members of the British delegation about a joint paper on atomic energy which was to be presented. The discussion was the first of several that unfortunately ended in a misunderstanding. I was having my first experience in diplomatic negotiating. As compared to my later experiences, the "staff work" at this conference was minimal. The papers which were to be our guide were few and brief and somewhat informally handled. Cohen and I had only one file for common use.

In my notes for Tuesday, December 18, the following occurs:

To the conference at 4 no break for Vodka! Put in paper on atomic bombs at the end. British quite miffed about it. A misunderstanding as Byrnes told Cohen and myself he had told Bevin he would put paper in today but have no discussion till tomorrow. British wanted to put off submission until tomorrow so that the "Ministries" in London could submit their views. Since, however, we modified the paper yesterday to meet the views of the British here and it largely repeats the three governments' declaration, doubtful if it makes any real difference. Nevertheless, it shows how easy it is to get "balled up" in diplomacy. The British had witnesses to Byrnes' conversation with Bevin; we had none.

Finally on Thursday, December 20, at 4:30 in the afternoon, the subject of atomic energy had been reached and I took my place at the conference table as an "expert." Molotov asked for more time to study the proposal. It was not until Saturday afternoon that I again sat at the conference table. We were all anxious as to what would happen; speculation among both the Americans and British delegations ranged widely.

Molotov was brief. To my utter amazement and contrary to all predictions by the staff of the embassy, he accepted the United States' proposals and suggested only that the proposed UN Commission be put under the jurisdiction of the Security Council instead of the General Assembly. The American-British-Canadian position, developed in the early fall, had become the American-British-Soviet position. There were no arguments, no need to consider any technical matters. As far as the success of the mission was concerned, I might just as well have stayed at home. Benjamin Cohen had ample knowledge of the field of atomic energy to be able to answer questions which the Secretary of State or the British might raise.

Indeed, from one point of view, it would have been better if I had been absent. After the Secretary had arrived in Moscow, the Senate Foreign Relations Committee had begun to be disturbed about what might take place at the Moscow meeting. Some members feared that the United States would give away some of its secrets in the course of the discussions with the Russians. My presence added to the worries of at least one Senator, a fact that was mentioned in a long cable about a meeting between the committee and President Truman. Why was there a "professor" in the group? Senator Tom Connally of Texas had asked.

If Bush himself had been able to go, there would have been no trouble. He had been the chief adviser to the President and the Secretary of State from the start. The sudden substitution of a college president whose past connection with the atomic bomb project was almost unknown was a disturbing factor. The Senators' apprehensions were based on a misunderstanding. Neither the President nor Mr. Byrnes had any idea of negotiating with the Russians other than to persuade them to accept the British-American proposal to create a United Nations atomic energy commission.

As I reread my notes of the Moscow trip, I am struck by the absence of any hint of the point of view toward the Soviet Union which was to be mine eighteen months or so later. I recorded my impression of a people who had until very recently been an ally. I was well aware, of course, that almost every item on the agenda of the conference dealt with issues that divided our hosts in Moscow from their guests. Indeed, I heard sharp words spoken by Molotov and knew that Byrnes was far from pleased by all that took place in the formal sessions and in private conversations. Yet on the particular issue which concerned me deeply, the control of the bomb, the Russians seemed to be ready to cooperate. The atmosphere, at least away from the conference table, was friendly. I was ready to believe that, in spite of the serious disagreements on many matters which I only vaguely understood, the wartime alliance could be continued in one form or another.

Contributing to my optimism was my conversation with the Commissar for Education. One of the younger members of the embassy staff who spoke Russian took me to pay a call on him. My reception was cordial, and the talk soon turned to the possibility of an exchange of pedagogic information between the Soviet union and the United States. The idea was put forward by the Commissar himself. "Exactly what I hoped; will take it up with N.E.A. when I get home," is the sentence in my notes. Nothing ever came of the suggestion, but my eagerness to "get on with Russians" is reflected by my recorded hope.

The Russian response to my presence as a member of the delegation also encouraged my optimism. At the first social occasion, a reception given by Mr. and Mrs. Molotov, the Foreign Minister rather floored me by his joking attitude about my being an expert on atomic bombs. "Do you have one in your pocket?" he asked. The same spirit was carried over to the state dinner in the Kremlin. Stalin and all the members of the Politbureau were on hand. According to custom, we were no sooner seated at the long table when the toasts began. Course after course of food was accompanied by toast after toast. Molotov started by toasting Byrnes, who, in turn, toasted Molotov. Since each toast had to be translated, even a short toast became a long one. Molotov, in toasting Benjamin Cohen as Mr. Byrnes' adviser, referred to another of the Secretary's advisers who was present but whose work was too secret to mention. I breathed more freely as I thought this meant I would not be toasted and therefore would not have to reply. After a few more rounds, however, Molotov said that now we had had enough to drink to enable us to explore secrets; he could now drink a toast to Dr. Conant, who, perhaps, had a bit of the atomic bomb in his pocket. The Conference had agreed on a UN Commission and he wished me success with it.

As all stood up to drink the toast, Stalin broke in, apparently in anger, although it may have been a prearranged scene. "This is too serious a matter to joke about," he said. "I raise my glass to the American scientists and what they have accomplished. We must now work together to see that this great invention is used for peaceful ends." After the appropriate pause, I responded with a toast to Russian science; I expressed the hope that the scientists of the three nations represented that evening, who had worked together to win a common victory, would cooperate equally effectively in the tasks of peace which lay ahead.

As I took my leave at the conclusion of the banquet, Stalin detained me for a moment to repeat his earlier congratulations; again he expressed the hope that what had been discovered would be used in peace for technical purposes and not in war. Fine words, but how much sincerity lay behind them? Were they to be taken as omens for the future?

Two things gave me pause. Attempts to obtain permission to refer in public to what Stalin had said failed. What was said within the Kremlin was never to be reported, we were told. More significant was an incident which occurred that evening after we left the table. We were escorted into another room to witness a special movie. It was an incredible film, allegedly about the war with Japan; there was no hint that the United States or Britain had ever been involved except for the attack on Pearl Harbor and the last minute or two when the ceremonies involving a Japanese and Russian general signing documents on the battleship *Missouri* were flashed before us. General MacArthur could just be seen nearly offstage as the film was ending. Was this an intentional insult? If not, what was the purpose of showing a crass nationalistic movie?

When a few of us assembled in the Ambassador's residence, these questions were raised with considerable indignation; they remained unanswered. What impressed me at the time was the complete lack of any channels by which our annoyance could be transmitted to our hosts. What we might do, someone suggested, was to write a statement of our feelings and throw the paper in the wastebasket; the next morning it would be read in the Kremlin.

Among the discouraging signs for one who, like myself, was pinning his hopes on Soviet cooperation was the evidence of Soviet experts in the British delegation. They were unanimous in private conversations that there was no chance the Russians would agree to any sort of inspection system. We must act as if there were a chance, however, one of them said; without inspection there could be no international control. Therefore, in spite of the unfavorable evidence I was accumulating in Moscow, I was not prepared to give up. Indeed, I framed a proposal for the Secretary which I thought might possibly serve to make the Soviets more ready to work with the United States and Great Britain in developing an international atomic energy authority.

The idea grew out of a long talk I had had with two American scientists who were members of the embassy staff. One was an agricultural expert, the other a meteorologist. They had both had the greatest difficulty finding anyone in Moscow who would talk with them. The Soviet Union was like a large American company with a policy of secrecy in regard to all technical matters, as was the case in the American rubber industry at the time of World War I. Neither Russian scientists nor officials would talk except after explicit permission from the front office. The three of us evolved a scheme for a Soviet-American interchange of scientists. After an encouraging discussion with Ambassador Harriman, I decided to present a memorandum to Secretary Byrnes.

I doubt if the paper I prepared and gave to the Secretary on December 26, 1945, was ever read by anyone of importance. As part of history, it has not the slightest significance. Since, however, it shows quite clearly my own attitude about American-Soviet relationships at the end of 1945, I include a large portion of it here.

It began with the following statement: "The three Governments are committed by their joint declaration on atomic energy to a free interchange of scientists and scientific information at once." I then suggested that there would be pressures within the United States for the implementation of this policy before the United Nations could render a report. (As a matter of fact, as U.S.-Soviet relations deteriorated in the next eighteen months, public opinion slowly moved in the other direction.) The memorandum went on to point out the difference between the positions of scientists in the Soviet Union and those in the United States. The analogy between an American corporation and the whole Soviet Union was said to be "fairly close when one considers the role of the scientist in Russia." A recent suggestion by an American that Russian physicists and American physicists should meet privately and informally to discuss the international complications of atomic energy was branded as totally unrealistic. "Soviet scientists could no more take part in such a discussion as private individuals than could an employee of the Du Pont Company discuss the manufacture of nylon on a personal basis." I went on to say: "Certainly in the field of atomic physics with all its implications for peace and war, it will be impossible for a Russian scientist to act as a free agent at a scientific conference."

Having laid down the limitations to the interchange of scientific information inherent in the nature of the Soviet Union, I concluded that "all arrangements must be made through official channels."

The balance of the memorandum set forth what at that time I thought was feasible. The third section, with the heading "Value of Scientific Interchange," leaves no doubt that I was assuming a post-war world in which cooperation between the United States and the Soviet Union would be the order of the day. The only debatable point was how such cooperation could be best attained. I wrote:

Personally I believe that everything that can be done to increase the flow of basic scientific information between Russia and the United States and the interchange of scientists will work for the benefit of both countries. It seems to me that the scientists in Soviet Russia occupy a very special position. They are the nearest approach to informed public opinion with high standing that exists in that country. They are bound to be more concerned with good relations with other countries if they have friendly contacts with the countries concerned. Indeed, it seems to me it is through the medium of science, education and the arts alone that we can build bridges of communication between the two countries. On all other fronts there is bound to be so much suspicion and misunderstanding as to make communication difficult.

For these reasons I hope that the State Department may take active steps to make definite arrangements with the Russian Government to promote scientific interchange. Specifically, I would suggest that an exchange of notes provide the following:

A. That the two Governments would sponsor each year gatherings of distinguished scientists. . . .

B. The two Governments would endeavor to see to it that . . . there are at least two distinguished scientists (members of the Russian Academy or the National Academy of the U.S.A.) working in the laboratory of a colleague in the other country for a period of a year.

C. The two countries would agree to arrange a limited number of tours of inspection of the laboratories concerned with basic scientific research (which in the United States would be limited to universities and research institutes).

D. The two countries would arrange through Scientific Attachés in their two Embassies to implement the above arrangements and to facilitate the flow of scientific information.

I believe that unless some such definite proposal were worked out between the two countries the United States will continue to be a loser by the arrangements. At present the barriers in Russia are much greater against our obtaining information than vice versa.

The concluding paragraphs of the memorandum reflect the worries then current about guarding the secrets of the construction of the atomic bomb. It was my attempt to educate the Secretary of State as to the difference between basic scientific knowledge and engineering designs. Many others were writing similar papers on the same subject at this time. I quote my own words largely because of the optimistic feeling they expressed at the end of 1945. Eighteen months later they would no longer portray my mood. My attitude toward the dwellers in the Kremlin was to undergo a transformation. The memorandum continued:

There can be no doubt that to some degree we shall be transmitting information about the technical details of atomic energy development when we allow Russian and American physicists to meet together. To be realistic one may as well attempt to estimate what the Russians will gain from such a procedure at the outset. It is my estimate that if the twelve outstanding physicists connected with the Manhattan District should sit down with twelve leading physicists in Russia, and without reference to any notes or diagrams, should talk about basic scientific problems there would be bound to be indiscretions which would be of value to the Russians. Assuming the worst, however, I do not believe the information thus transmitted would accelerate the Russian development more than six months; this is based on the assumption that if we gave them all our technical know-how and diagrams we would accelerate their development from two to four years. To my mind it is only a question of a year or two at most, however, before this much of our technical information reaches them anyway by one route or another. For example, a number of English scientists have about the same amount of information as that referred to above and the French have acquired some knowledge in this twilight zone as well. Furthermore, a considerable degree of this information which lies between basic scientific knowledge and engineering details will soon become widespread throughout the United States by the inevitable indiscretions of many people. As soon as this occurs it will only be a matter of time before it is picked up by an information service of another government. This being the case, on balance I think it advisable to arrange for regular scientific gatherings with Russian scientists, and to impress upon the American scientists who take part in these gatherings and who have worked with the Manhattan District, that they are still under an oath of secrecy in regard to all matters that have not been released.

I should like to point out that industrial concerns in the United States repeatedly meet a similar situation. They allow their scientists to attend meetings freely and to discuss the basic scientific information connected with their research and development but these men are trusted not to reveal the technical know-how, and the line between basic science and engineering in each case can be drawn. The analogy is quite perfect, I believe, between the atomic bomb project on the one hand and the development of several of the Du Pont products such as Nylon and Neoprene on the other. I have seen in both cases the scientists of this company operate without embarrassment in scientific meetings and without jeopardizing the interests of the company.

I venture to conclude by suggesting that the Federal Government will be able to maintain security concerning the past of the Manhattan District to the extent that the War and State Departments can together work out a positive policy in regard to the relations between the American scientists involved and their opposite numbers in other countries, particularly Russia.

I was never asked by Secretary Byrnes to discuss my proposals. I did not realize that the decision to place the problem of the control of atomic energy before the United Nations had already precluded the development of any arrangement involving only two or three nations.

When I returned from Moscow on December 28, 1945, I was still of good cheer. What I had seen and heard had not shaken my faith. I believed an international control of atomic energy was possible, although I knew any judgment of the intentions of the Soviet Union was not for me to make. I had listened to enough arguments about specific issues to realize that future good relations between Washington-London-Moscow turned on far more than plans for controlling the manufacture of the bomb. I had heard the British Foreign Minister, Ernest Bevin, a leader of the Labour Party, say to one of his staff that the Russians had to be told to stop acting like Tory imperialists. Yet I had heard no convincing evidence of Soviet intransigence in regard to European affairs which could not be explained on the theory that the Soviets sincerely believed Churchill had made promises about their future boundaries while the war was on.

Many Soviet apologists were then saying that Stalin and Churchill had made a deal. Poland, Czechoslovakia, Rumania and Bulgaria would be in the Russian zone of influence, Greece and Turkey in the British. If this was true, the wrangling I had heard in Moscow did not represent a postwar attempt of the Soviet Union to control all of Europe. In short, my hopeful views about the future had been little affected by the extraordinary experience of my Christmas visit to the capital of the Soviet Union. I was not alone in my optimism. An extract from an editorial in the Boston *Herald* for December 28, 1945, can be cited as evidence:

The agreement at Moscow on the establishment of a commission for the control of atomic energy "to the extent necessary to ensure its use only for peacetime purposes" is the most comforting news since the bomb fell on Hiroshima. For science has provided or will provide the means for adequate policing of all nations to prevent the manufacture of atomic bombs, and the will of all countries to avert a nuclear cataclysm is beyond question. Through the agency of such a commission, which "shall be accountable for its work to the Security Council" of the U.N.O., every nation may have the necessary assurance against a surprise attack by atom bombs. None will feel the need to prepare a similar offensive power. . . .

The great purpose of the Moscow agreement is the establishment of a world security against sudden death by atomic destruction in the hands of an unexpected and reckless enemy. If this can be achieved, it will not matter whether we share the "secret," which is after all only temporarily ours. For we shall have bent this enormous power more nearly to the uses of humanity.

In late November 1945 I had made a speech before the Cleveland Chamber of Commerce. After the usual disclaimer of being able to give a foolproof answer to the question, "What shall we do with the atomic bomb?" I ventured a prophecy:

As things stand today, only a highly industrialized nation with a large supply of scientific and technical manpower can build enough of these bombs to constitute a major military threat to another industrialized nation.

But my estimate is that the complete disclosure of all information to Russia, let us say, would advance the progress of her production of atomic bombs by two to four years. It is my carefully considered opinion that Russia without such knowledge would not be able to produce bombs sufficient for a major blow at an enemy in less than five years, nor do I think it would require more than fifteen.

During the coming months the question of when the Russians would get the bomb was to be much discussed. I stuck to the five-to-fifteen-year forecast, which was vague enough to be almost certainly correct. Actually, four years and a month elapsed after Hiroshima before the Soviet Union exploded an atomic bomb.

The Boston *Globe* had republished my Cleveland speech on December 12, 1945, just after the announcement that I was to accompany Secretary Byrnes to Moscow. The headline read: "Conant on A-Bomb Control: Inspector Corps Urged for World," which was not an inaccurate summary, though it highlighted the utopian implications of my views. What I actually said was:

One thing has been as clear as daylight to me ever since I first became convinced of the reality of the atomic bomb; namely, that a secret armament race in respect to this weapon must at all costs be avoided. If a situation were to develop where two great powers had stacks of bombs but neither was sure of the exact status of the other, the possibility of a devastating surprise attack by the one upon the other would poison all our thinking. . . .

By gradual stages the heavily industrialized nations must evolve a plan of interchange of scientific and technical data and a system of inspection and control of atomic bombs. Under the auspices of the United Nations Organization a corps of inspectors could be assembled, I believe, whose loyalty would be to the United Nations and whose honesty would be above reproach. These men, given free access to all parts of every industrialized country, would be the public accountants, so to speak, to guarantee to the world the status of the plants concerned with atomic energy in each nation.

Inspection would not be too acceptable either here at home or in Russia, I admitted. But given time and patience, such a scheme could be made to work. We might have to be content with a public report as to the number of atomic bombs in each country and the amount of material for their construction. But there was hope that "very soon the nations involved would agree to dismantle all their bombs and either store the essential material or use it in atomic power plants if by then such plants had been developed." An accurate and trustworthy report on the status of a nation under such circumstances would ensure that no surprise attack with atomic bombs could occur, for no nation would have any bombs.

I find it hard to realize now that I and many others ever believed what I subscribed to as the year of 1946 opened. My ascent into the golden clouds of irrational hope can only be explained by my honest appraisal of the world-wide catastrophic consequences of a failure to attain international control. Some scheme just had to work. And who is prepared to say my basic belief was wrong?

CHAPTER 36

Learning to Live in the Atomic Age

PRESIDENT TRUMAN in his *Memoirs** records his unhappiness over Secretary Byrnes' trip to Moscow. He says that on January 5, 1946, in a meeting in the White House, he read Byrnes a letter upbraiding him for his failure to communicate while he was in Moscow and reminding him that the President and only the President could make the final decisions. The letter ended with the sentence, "I'm tired of babying the Soviets."

Byrnes in his autobiography, *All in One Lifetime,*† gives quite a different version of his welcome by the President on his return from Moscow. He says that the letter of admonition was "never sent to me or read to me," and that a charge of babying the Soviets was the last criticism he ever expected to have leveled at him. The differences in the recollection of Truman and Byrnes in the mid-1950s may be regarded as symbolic of the public confusion as well as the tension about atomic energy affairs as the year 1946 opened.

On the one side were those who believed that all the United States had to do was hold tightly to the detailed knowledge and continue to build more and better bombs, thus assuring our military superiority over Russia for years to come. At the other extreme were those who maintained there was no secret; in a few years the Soviets would duplicate what the Manhattan District had accomplished; only

* New York, Doubleday & Co., 1955.
† New York, Harper & Brothers, 1958.

international agreement could ward off a nuclear arms race. A few concluded that the United States should give the Russians all our technical knowledge in exchange for the opening of communications with Soviet scientists. The majority, who looked with increasing apprehension at the possibility of a new kind of arms race, were more conservative and cautious. They would be ready to release information only if an effective international control system could be constructed. What would such a system be like and would the Soviets agree? On these two questions opinions differed; around these differences a vast amount of discussion, both private and public, was to take place in the next twelve months.

From the vantage point of what we now know about the Stalin regime, it is easy to portray all of us who advocate a conciliatory approach to Russia as softheaded. But even if Truman, Attlee and King had been gifted with prophetic vision and could have foreseen the obdurate stand of the Soviets, they would have had to proceed along the lines of their declaration. Public opinion in the three countries had been building up rapidly since the day the first bomb was dropped.

By the time Byrnes made his journey to the Soviet capital, the scientists who had worked in one or another of the laboratories of the Manhattan Project were forming an effective political pressure group. (Alice Kimball Smith has well described the organization of the scientific lobby in her excellent book, *A Peril and a Hope.** Editorial writers and columnists applauded and poured forth advice. After the three-power conference in Moscow the immediate issue for President Truman and for Secretary Byrnes was the American posture in the forthcoming United Nations meeting, at which time the Soviets would be voting members of a UN Atomic Energy Commission. When it came to formulating a detailed plan for international control, what would the United States contribute? Merely advocating inspection was not enough. What kind of inspection did the proponents of international control have in mind?

The Secretary of State decided he needed a committee to formulate American policy. On January 7, 1946, he asked Dean Acheson, then Under Secretary, to be the chairman. The other members were to be Vannevar Bush, General L. R. Groves, John J. McCloy and myself. Dean Acheson extended the invitation to me over the telephone. I was reluctant to serve, but Acheson assured me that the interference

* Chicago, University of Chicago Press, 1965.

with my duties at Harvard would not be great since the committee was not to be a full-time working body. I accepted and once again became entangled in affairs of state.

At the first meeting of Acheson's committee, we decided to appoint a panel to ascertain all the facts bearing on proposals for control and to prepare a report which would then be submitted to our committee for review and eventual transmittal to the Secretary of State. Acheson persuaded David E. Lilienthal to take time off from his duties as head of the Tennessee Valley Authority to serve as chairman. The other members he recruited were: J. Robert Oppenheimer; Charles A. Thomas, vice president of the Monsanto Chemical Company; Harry A. Winne, a vice president of General Electric; and Chester I. Barnard, president of the New Jersey Telephone Company. Thus came into existence the famous Lilienthal board of consultants.

The group went to work full time on January 28. An intensive course in nuclear physics and chemistry guided by Oppenheimer provided the scientific basis for their approach to the practical problem of inspection. The members of the committee worked long and hard. They ended with a high degree of unanimity. The report was ready on March 7. At a two-day meeting with Acheson, Bush, Groves, McCloy and myself, the panel's report received a thorough analysis directed to its possible revision.

The report opened by raising doubts about the first proposals for control. Many people had suggested immediately after Hiroshima that all nations should agree to outlaw the bomb and create an international corps of inspectors to ensure that no nation was in process of manufacturing a bomb. (My own thinking had been in this direction.) The inadequacy of such a concept, the panel stated, lay in the fact that the developments in atomic energy for peaceful and for military purposes were interchangeable. The only workable system of safeguards required international authority over every step in the process of constructing reactors or separation units as well as fabricating a weapon. The title of one of the sections of the report summarized the major conclusion: "Security Through an Atomic Development Authority" (the authority would be international).

Acheson, as chairman of the committee, said little. But Bush, Groves, McCloy and I had objections to raise, warning that the final report must contain a proposal that would appeal both to the American people and to the world. I for one was hardly ready to endorse a scheme based on the international ownership and operation of mines and manufacturing plants. Furthermore, I hated to see the step-by-step idea of the three-power declaration abandoned as it had been by the panel. The new scheme was to be put into operation all at once. The concept of testing the good faith of the Soviets by taking a little step first had been discarded.

The upshot was a request to the panel for another draft. On March 16 a revised document was at hand for another discussion. The section dealing with the specifics of the recommended action by the United States had been clarified and sharpened. Otherwise the report stood as originally submitted. After considerable discussion, we all approved.

The members of the Acheson Committee and the panel signed the letter of transmittal on March 17 and sent it to the Secretary of State. When I signed the letter, I hoped and believed my connection with atomic energy matters had ended.

I played no part in the formulation of the policy for the UN delegation. President Truman, much to everyone's surprise, had placed the leadership in the hands of B. M. Baruch. My guess was that Truman found that the suspicions of many Senators about scientists had to be allayed. A new figure with high prestige was needed to handle the human problems. My only contribution to Baruch's attempt to master the technical complexities of his new task was to suggest the name of Richard Tolman of the California Institute of Technology as chief scientific adviser. (Oppenheimer, who was the logical candidate, had refused.) On one or two occasions Tolman asked my advice. Otherwise I remained in the dark about what went on in the American delegation, though I gathered from the press that Baruch had placed before the United Nations Commission a document closely following the Acheson-Lilienthal proposal. After the UN Commission went into action, I lost all touch with the plans for the control of atomic energy.

Meanwhile in mid-July 1946, Dean Acheson had telephoned to say that President Truman would like to see me and would I kindly come to Washington. I suspected the President might offer me the chairmanship of the U.S. Atomic Energy Commission which had been authorized by the McMahon Act, passed and signed a few weeks before; my suspicion proved to be correct. The President in a few words expressed the hope that I would be chairman of the newly created agency. I was greatly tempted and asked for time to think the matter over.

Among the forces that impelled me toward the job was the state of the negotiations in the UN Atomic Energy Commission at that moment. It seemed possible that the UN would establish an Atomic Development Authority according to the plan proposed by the United States. And if such an international authority came into existence, the head of the American Commission might be transferred to the chairman's job.

Lilienthal records in his journal for July 27, 1946,* a conversation with Baruch in which Baruch explained why he was not pushing Lilienthal for the job of Chairman of the U.S. Atomic Energy Commission. He said he had urged the President that Lilienthal be "saved" in order later to become the head of the international agency. While my ambitions were not so specific, the attraction of the position rested on the assumption that the negotiations then in progress in the UN Commission would result in positive action. If such turned out to be the case, the Chairman of the American Commission, as the adviser to the President on all atomic energy affairs, would have a position of great influence on the future of the world. Dean Acheson, with whom I talked, seemed to be taking a moderately sanguine view of the UN discussions; he by no means regarded Russian adherence to the American scheme as totally impossible.

If I had thought of the position the President offered in terms of being head of a vast arsenal for improving and manufacturing weapons (which is what the job actually became), I doubt if I would have spent long in declining the appointment. Baruch, whom I consulted, was cautious in his advice. His prognostications about the eventual attitude of the Russians were neither completely negative nor positive. He and Acheson, however, both implied in the talks I had with them separately that being the president of Harvard was a good job and anyone who held it ought to be quite certain of what he was doing when he gave it up. That there were plenty of problems in Cambridge, I knew better than anybody else. It might not be as glamorous to tackle them as to engage all sorts of enemies in the thickets of Washington, but it seemed a more permanent undertaking.

After considering the proposition for a week, I wrote the President with a clear conscience that my reason for declining was the pull of the Harvard position. Actually, one of the factors that influenced my decision was my appraisal of the relative strength of the friends and enemies I would immediately encounter if I became Chairman of the Atomic Energy Commission. Of the support of Bush, Oppenheimer and the two Comptons, as well as General Groves, I could be

* *The Journals of David E. Lilienthal*, Vol. II, New York, Harper & Row, 1964.

certain. But how many others who had been part of the Manhattan District would view my appointment with favor? It was certain that a few at least would be hostile from the start. I had heard from Byrnes that Leo Szilard had expressed his lack of confidence in both Bush and myself. The incident involving the young physicist at Chicago recounted in an earlier chapter was proof that a considerable number of younger scientists in at least one large wartime laboratory had been highly discontented. At that time, for all I knew, the entire scientific and technical manpower of the atomic energy establishmens might have been just waiting until the war ended to become vocal in their condemnation of Conant, Bush and Groves.

What actually happened was not unrelated to my forebodings. Soon after the War Department introduced the May-Johnson Bill for the control of work on atomic energy in the United States, on October 4, 1945, almost all who had been involved in the wartime project were up in arms. Bush and I had been parties to the formulation of the scheme embodied in the bill. We both testified in its favor, as did General Groves. Indeed, it was Groves' strong support of the measure which brought to the surface the accumulated dissatisfactions among the scientists employed by the Manhattan Project. Their powerful lobby soon made its voice heard in both the Congressional halls and the White House.

In retrospect it is easy to see that the War Department was at fault in the way the official position was presented to the world. In the first place, two months were allowed to pass before President Truman told the public what he proposed to do about the weapon which had completely destroyed Hiroshima. In those sixty days far too many ill-conceived schemes had been put forward, and prejudices became hardened. In the second place, when the time arrived for Congressional hearings, the administration seemed determined to rush the bill through without adequate discussion. Only four witnesses were heard—all protagonists of the measure—Patterson, Groves, Bush, and myself. The administration appeared to rest its case when Congressman Andrew J. May, the chairman of the Military Affairs Committee, closed the first hearing on October 9.

To understand the fate of the May-Johnson Bill and the effect of my association with it on my own career, a brief review of history is required. I have already described the formation of the Interim Committee in the spring of 1945. One of the tasks urged upon it by Bush and myself was the drafting of legislation to be introduced in Congress immediately after the war ended. Secretary of War Stimson agreed that a draft should be prepared and gave the task to the Under Secretary, Robert P. Patterson. Patterson had brought in two lawyers, Kenneth C. Royall and William L. Marbury, who at once turned to Bush and Groves for the necessary information. Bush asked me to sit in on several conferences. Therefore, what became known as the Royall-Marbury draft was admittedly a product of conferences in which the top management of the wartime project had played a leading part.

To a few scientists the origin of the bill was an asset. Oppenheimer in his testimony after the May-Johnson Bill hearings were reopened said: "The bill was drafted with the detailed supervision of Dr. Bush and Dr. Conant, with the knowledge and the agreement of the former Secretary of War, Mr. Stimson. I think no man in the country carried a greater weight of responsibility for this project than Mr. Stimson. I think no men in positions of responsibility, who were scientists, took more responsibility or were more courageous or better informed in the general sense than Dr. Bush and Dr. Conant. I think if they liked the philosophy of this bill and urged this bill, it is a very strong argument. I know that many scientists do not agree with me on this, but I am nevertheless convinced myself."

Many scientists thought otherwise, and no small fraction of them aired their disagreement in the press. Stimson had retired shortly after V-J Day. My close association with Groves, as illustrated by my taking his side in more than one disagreement with Harold Urey, made me a poor witness in many eyes. I soon realized my usefulness to Patterson was at an end. Therefore I stood aside and let the battle over the May-Johnson Bill run its course.

A rival to the May-Johnson Bill was introduced in the Senate by Senator Brien McMahon of Connecticut on December 20, 1945. At once the dissenting scientists moved to McMahon's support. By the middle of March 1946 the administration had changed its mind. As President Truman makes clear in his *Memoirs,* he became convinced that the May-Johnson Bill opened the way to military control, and he was in strong opposition. He ordered Patterson to forget his previous stand and support the McMahon Bill.

As one who was present at the birth of the Royall-Marbury draft, I can testify that the main charge against the May-Johnson Bill was erroneous and unfair. The proposed law did not turn atomic energy affairs over to the military. But the bill did provide that "any active or retired officer of the armed forces" might serve as a member of the Commission as Administrator or as Deputy Administrator, "without prejudice to his commissioned status." To make it possible for an active or retired officer to serve, it was necesary to write into the bill certain exemptions from the provisions of the law regulating employment of military officers. Thus the bill provided eleven positions, any one of which (or all of which) might be filled by a military officer on active duty or retired. (The Commission was to be composed of nine members, one of whom would be designated as chairman; the Administrator and Deputy Administrator made eleven in all.)

It seemed to us when we were drafting these provisions that the possibility should be left open for an Army officer to serve in any of these posts. But the opposition soon fixed its attention on the position of Administrator, claiming that the Army intended Groves to fill this spot. The scientists could contemplate such a possibility only with extreme horror.

It is true that great power was given to the Administrator, "subject to the direction and supervision of the Commission." (Unlike the provisions in the McMahon Bill, which became law, the members of the Commission were to have no executive responsibility.) But the power to appoint the Administrator was the responsibility of the President subject to Senate approval. To claim that the May-Johnson Bill called for management of U.S. atomic energy affairs by a military man was completely wrong. Yet according to President Truman's *Memoirs,* such an oversimplification appears to have been the basis of his decision to kill the May-Johnson Bill.

I have never regretted my decision to refuse President Truman's offer of the chairmanship of the Atomic Energy Commission. The tempting possibilities of being involved in an international scheme for the development of atomic energy never materialized. On the last day of 1946, the UN Atomic Energy Commission voted to approve the American plan ten to two, with Russia and Poland in the negative. The negative vote of the Soviet Union meant the scheme for international control was dead. Any favorable motion in the UN Security Council was sure to be vetoed by the Russian member.

Whether my worry about the support I would have received from the scientists was justified or not remained a question in my mind. An incident in 1950 appeared to give substance to my feeling that by no means all the key scientific personnel in the Manhattan Project were enthusistic about my performance as deputy to Bush. This came about in connection with the presidency of the National Academy of Sciences.

Some weeks before the election scheduled to take place at the business session of the Academy, I was asked by the chairman of the nominating committee whether I would be willing to serve as president if elected. I was surprised by the suggestion and flattered, but by no means certain I should accept. I consulted by telephone several old friends, including Bush and Detlev W. Bronk, chairman of the National Research Council. Both urged me to accept; Bronk added he would be glad to give all administrative support possible from the National Research Council, an organization affiliated with the Academy. I pressed the chairman of the committee as to whether he and his associates were sure that the members of the Academy really wanted me to serve. He assured me they did. I had no way of discovering whether the disfavor with which I had been regarded five years earlier by some members still existed. I certainly did not want to become president of an academy whose membership was unfriendly. Therefore I decided not to attend the annual meeting, although, as far as I knew, there had never been any serious question raised in the past about accepting the recommendation of the nominating committee.

According to the customs of the Academy, the members of each section met together informally to canvass the names of those to be proposed by the section for election a day later. In this instance, so I heard later, the chemistry section decided to oppose my election and privately went to work to convert members of other sections to their views. As soon as my name was placed in nomination by the nominating committee at the annual meeting and the chair asked for other nominations (hitherto a *pro forma* action), Wendell M. Latimer, a California chemist to whose ideas I had not always lent a sympathetic ear, suggested there should be competition. He nominated Detlev Bronk, and the nomination was seconded by another chemist. Bronk, I am told, protested; but his protests were unheeded. The balloting showed a majority for him, and he refused to accept.

The meeting, I later heard, was in a "dither." Nothing like this had ever happened. Bush offered to get me on the phone, which, fortunately, he was able to do, while the meeting waited. He explained the situation, but named no names, so I was unaware until later that it was the chemists who had led the revolt. He then put Bronk on. Bronk said he couldn't take the job after having urged me to accept the verdict of the nominating committee and promising his support if I became president.

Without hesitation, I told him that the vote of the Academy meeting made it clear they wanted him and didn't want me. It would be impossible for me to function under those conditions, and I wouldn't accept the job even if he withdrew his name. He reluctantly agreed with my reasoning. Bush returned to the phone, and I told him to move in my name that the election of Detlev Bronk be made unanimous. "That is just what your friends said you would do," he said with evident satisfaction.

Bush returned to the meeting, and Bronk was elected president. His great success in that position (he was re-elected twice, serving until 1962) proves the majority of the two hundred academicians who voted that day in Washington were wiser than the nominating committee. Whether I might have done as good a job as Bronk can be questioned; certainly I could not have done a better one. Undoubtedly the spearhead of the opposition was personal, but I heard later that cogent arguments were used: I was too busy to give the position the attention it deserved; I had never been active in Academy affairs. Ironically, my absence from the meeting was cited against me.

Some of my chemical friends who did not attend the meeting were far from happy about what had happened at the section meeting. For my part, as the years went by, I was happier and happier with the outcome and soon almost forgot the incident. If I had been elected president of the Academy in 1950, President Eisenhower would never have sent me to Germany as High Commissioner in 1953, and I should never have spent ten highly satisfactory years studying American public schools.

The publication of the essential facts about the 1950 National Academy election in *Science* for April 21, 1967, spread a knowledge of the affair before the scientific world. The writer spoke of a feeling among chemists that I had been "excessively authoritarian" in dealing with some of my colleagues. He used the words "old vendetta." In a letter to *Science* a few weeks later (June 5, 1967), an old friend, Professor Joel H. Hildebrand, criticized the article severely. There never was a vendetta, he said. What the chemists wanted was a full-time president, and I was not in a position to play such a role.

When I turned my back to the prospect of a full-time involvement in the development of nuclear energy, I really felt I was freed from the atom and need not give the terrible prospects of an atomic arms race another thought. Again I was wrong. Soon after Lilienthal was nominated as Chairman of the Atomic Energy Commission (October 28, 1946), I received word from Bush, who was in touch with the White House, that the President would like to appoint me a member of the General Advisory Committee to the Atomic Energy Commission (a body provided for in the law establishing the Commission), with the thought that I might well be elected chairman. Bush supposed that, though I had declined the chairmanship of the Commission, I might well be willing to be chairman of the General Advisory Committee. I agreed and thought no more of the matter.

On January 1, 1947, Lilienthal and his associates took over the full responsibilities of the atomic energy establishment as provided by law, though he and the other commisioners had not yet been confirmed by the Senate. (An old feud between Senator Kenneth McKellar and Lilienthal delayed the action of the Senate for weeks.) One of the first acts of the Chairman was to make official the appointments of the members of the General Advisory Committee. Lilienthal in his journals speaks of giving President Conant his diploma. I was back in the atomic harness after all, for a term of five years.

A day or so before the General Advisory Committee was to hold its first meeting, Carroll L. Wilson, my old traveling companion to England in 1941, indicated he would like a private word with me. He had been nominated General Manager of the Atomic Energy Commission, and his name was before the Senate. I thought he might want to talk about my appearing before the recently created Joint Committee of the Senate and House on Atomic Energy to support his nomination (which I did on February 4). However, he referred to the fact that many people had spoken informally and privately about my becoming chairman of the General Advisory Committee. Now he had begun to wonder if I had sufficient time to devote to the work of the chairman of the General Advisory Committee; the demands in Cambridge must be heavy. Perhaps it would be better to have Oppenheimer serve as chairman. I at once agreed. The message clearly had come from Lilienthal, and I felt the Chairman of the Commission should have the man he wanted as chairman of the General Advisory Committee. As soon as the first meeting of the committee was convened, I nominated Oppenheimer as chairman. No one offered a rival candidate. He was elected by voice vote.

The records of the General Advisory Committee are still classified. I do not propose to discuss what went on in the many highly secret meetings between January 1, 1947, and August 1952, when my term came to an end. My only reference to the proceedings of the committee has been my testimony in 1954 before the Gray Board, which examined charges against Oppenheimer that originated in a letter of William Borden, a member of the staff of the Joint Congressional Committee.

The special board established by the Atomic Energy Commission consisted of Gordon Gray, former Secretary of the Army; Thomas A. Morgan, former president of the Sperry Corporation; and Professor Ward V. Evans of Loyola University. The hearings were held behind closed doors, and those who testified were led to believe their testimony was confidential and would never be published. In fact, the testimony was given to the press after the board's findings (adverse to Oppenheimer two to one) had been reviewed and reaffirmed (but not unanimously) by the Commission itself.

I was asked in a letter from Lloyd Garrison, Oppenheimer's counsel, to testify on behalf of his client. It so happened that I was planning to return from Bonn to Washington the end of April to defend my budget before the House and Senate committees. After clearing the matter by cable with the Secretary of State, I offered to appear before the Gray Board on April 18. Both the President and the Secretary of State were well aware that I was going to be a character witness for Oppenheimer, and neither objected. Indeed, the President went so far as to say that, of course, a man had to testify to what he believed, and if I thought Oppenheimer should again be given full clearance, I should say so.

Two portions of my testimony as recorded in the official transcript make my position in April 1954 quite clear. I opened in an aggressive mood that reflected my anger at the whole proceeding. The exchange between myself and Garrison went as follows:

Q: You have read the Commission's letter of December 23, 1953, which initiated these proceedings containing the derogatory information about Dr. Oppenheimer?

A: Yes, I have read it.

Q: Have you a comment to make on it?

A: Yes, I have. I would like to comment on it. I would like to comment on one section particularly. Somewhere in the letter it says that the substance of the information which raises the question concerning your eligibility for employment, referring to Dr. Oppenheimer, on atomic energy work, is as follows, and then later it says that it was further reported that in the autumn of 1949 and subsequently you strongly opposed the development of the hydrogen bomb; one, on moral grounds; two, by claiming it was not possible; three, by claiming that there were insufficient facilities and scientific personnel to carry on the development; and four, that it was not politically desirable.

Well, it seems to me that letter must have been carelessly drafted, if I may say so, because if you take those two statements together, of course, it would indicate that anybody who opposed the development of the hydrogen bomb was not eligible for employment on atomic energy work later.

I am sure that no one who drew that letter could have intended that, because such a position would be an impossible position to hold in this country; namely, that a person who expressed views about an important matter before him, as a member of the General Advisory Committee, could then be ineligible because of a security risk for subsequent work in connection with the Government. I am sure that argument would not have been intended. If it did, it would apply to me because I opposed it strongly, as strongly as anybody else on that committee, that is, the development of the hydrogen bomb. . . .

I should say I opposed it as strongly as anybody on a combination of political and strategic and highly technical considerations. . . .

If it were true that Dr. Oppenheimer's opposition to the development of the hydrogen bomb were in any way connected with a sympathy which he might have had with the Soviet Union, or communism, then surely many other actions and decisions which he was involved in over the period of years in which I was associated with him would have likewise been influenced by any such point of view.

The record is quite the contrary. I just call your attention to a few facts probably already before you—actions of Dr. Oppenheimer, participation in decisions, all of which were strongly detrimental to the interests of the Soviet Union after the close of the war.

I then proceeded to read into the record many actions and statements of Oppenheimer which I believed showed that he was not influenced by pro-Soviet and anti-United States views. A few minutes later, Oppenheimer's counsel turned to a letter I had written in March 1947:

Q: In March 1947 did Mr. Lilienthal as chairman of the Commission ask you for your opinion with respect to Dr. Oppenheimer's loyalty?
A: Yes. I recall that this was at the time when Mr. Wilson who was general manager, Mr. Lilienthal and the other members were up for confirmation in the Senate. I think that is the right time. I remember Mr. Wilson and I think Mr. Lilienthal coming to me, saying that we have been apprised that there are some things in the record of Dr. Oppenheimer which indicate association with alleged communists, some things of that sort, and we want to know whether you are prepared to make a statement in regard to his loyalty.

I am pretty sure I didn't examine the file. I am sure I didn't. I said that "I don't know about the past, but I am glad to put on record what I now believe, based on my knowledge of him since the early days of the war," and there is such a letter in existence. I have not seen it.

Q: I have it here, Dr. Conant. It was brought into evidence this morning. May I, with the board's permission, just read you the last two paragraphs. The first four of the letter have to do with a recital of your acquaintance with Dr. Oppenheimer and the circumstances of your writing the letter. Then you went on to say: "I can say without hesitation that there can be absolutely no question of Dr. Oppenheimer's loyalty. Furthermore, I can state categorically that, in my opinion, his attitude about the future course of the United States Government in matters of high policy is in accordance with the soundest American tradition. He is not sympathetic with the totalitarian regime in Russia and his attitude towards that nation is, from my point of view, thoroughly sound and hardheaded. Therefore, any rumor that Dr. Oppenheimer is sympathetically inclined towards the Communists or towards Russia is an absurdity. As I wrote above, I base this statement on what I consider intimate knowledge of the workings of his mind.

"At the time of Dr. Oppenheimer's entering the work on atomic energy, I heard that there was some question of his clearance by the security agencies. I understand that was based on his associations prior to 1939 and his "left-wing" sympathies at that time. I have no knowledge of Dr. Oppenheimer previous to the summer of 1941, but I say unhesitatingly that whatever the record might show as to his political sympathies at that time or his associations, I would not deviate from my present opinion, namely, that a more loyal and sound American citizen cannot be found in the whole United States."

You wrote that?

A: Yes, I wrote that. I have every reason to believe I wrote it.

Q: Dr. Conant, you formed your judgment at that time on your appraisal of Dr. Oppenheimer as a total man?

A: Yes. That was based clearly on my acquaintance with him during the Los Alamos project and this other period which I mentioned in which we discussed the whole question of the control of the bomb, which gave me a chance to explore many political problems which we would not have explored at Los Alamos.

Q: Having in mind the Commission's letter of December 23, 1953, to which we have referred on the one hand, and what Dr. Oppenheimer has done since March 1947 when this letter was written, do you have reason to modify or alter the view which you expressed about him in March 1947?

A: No. I would think on the contrary the actions and decisions which I put on the record here seem to me to make quite clear that he was party to many actions on the part of the General Advisory Committee which were strongly opposed to any Soviet policy. It makes more certain the statements I then made based on what was after all a shorter acquaintance with him.

MR. GARRISON: That is all, Mr. Chairman.

I have nothing of significance today to add to what I said in April 1954. My testimony before the Gray Board may stand as my final word about the actions of the General Advisory Committee as regards the development of the hydrogen bomb.

CHAPTER 37

The Committee on the Present Danger

T HE NEGATIVE VOTE of the Soviet member of the UN Atomic Energy Commision when the American plan was before the Commission had almost extinguished my optimism about the creation of an International Authority. Nothing happened in the next six months to strengthen my faith in the possibility of an agreement with the Soviets. There was no further action in the United Nations Atomic Energy Commission. Public attention turned from anxiety about the possibility of an atomic holocaust to another more immediate cause for worry.

President Truman on March 12, 1947, delivered a message to a special joint session of Congress that became the basis for the Truman Doctrine. Announcing that the British were no longer able to support the legal governments of Turkey and Greece with money and men, the President stated that the United States would take on the task. What he said in justification of the decision made history. After referring to the violations of the Yalta agreement in Poland, Rumania and Bulgaria, which the United States had in vain protested, he declared: "I believe that it must be the policy of the United States to support free peoples who are resisting attempted subjugation by armed minorities or by outside pressures." Pregnant words whose implications have reached to the present day.

My friends and acquaintances were divided as to the correctness of the President's diagnosis of the state of the world. I was inclined to accept it, though I had judged Winston Churchill's "Iron Curtain" speech in Fulton, Missouri, a year earlier (March 5, 1946) to be an error. At that time my mind was so fixed on the necessity for international accord on the control of the bomb that Churchill's eloquence seemed like rocking the boat. By the beginning of 1947, however, the record of Soviet intransigence in the United Nations Atomic Energy Commission left no doubt that on one issue at least the world was for the time being divided. What the President said about the terrorist activities of the Communists in Greece and Turkey made me lose almost all the hope to which I still clung.

The reception in foreign capitals of General Marshall's speech at Harvard on June 5, 1947, restored my optimism. (I had not understood its meaning when I heard it.) But the complete refusal of the Russians a few weeks later to join the European Recovery plan struck me as convincing evidence that President Truman had been right. The coup in Prague in February 1948 removed my lingering doubts. The book I completed in July 1948 I entitled *Education in a Divided World*. For me and almost all my friends, the cold war had started. We were living under an armed truce. Yet I made a clear distinction between the Nazi menace of 1940 and the present Soviet challenge. The former had been a direct military threat. The latter was an ideological and political thrust supported by military means.

According to my diagnosis of 1948, the Russian armies hidden behind the Iron Curtain were defensive troops to support political gains by the fifth column within another nation. I was bold enough to predict that, unlike Hitler, Russia would not take aggressive military action by invading a nation without an invitation from a *de facto* government. I admitted this was a bold prediction because of "the gravity of the situation in Berlin." The proper pattern for preventing the outbreak of another global war would seem to involve readiness to answer coercion by the use of force, coupled with willingness to negotiate at any time on matters of broad policy. I was in favor of a frank public discussion of the military situation as soon as the presidential election of 1948 was over. Since Russia might be ready to strike without warning in that part of Germany occupied by the Western Powers, our balanced strength should be equally ready for combat. How should this strength be deployed? The question needed answering.

Finally bringing in an old problem I had wrestled with since 1940, I wrote:

Keeping the Army up to strength seems the first requisite. If and when an overall strategic plan for the armed truce can be prepared and explained to the American people, another approach to the man-power problem must be attempted. The present draft law is surely only a stopgap; it merely postpones a real decision.

On March 17, 1948, Truman had asked Congress to introduce the draft once again. In September 1949 the Russians exploded their first atomic bomb. The arms race we had so dreaded in 1945 and 1946 had started. Nevertheless I still saw the Soviet challenge as I had described it in my book the year before.

Once the sixteen nations under the European Recovery Program have shown that they can prosper, their answer to the ideological and political thrust from across the Iron Curtain will be clear. Once our military answer to a possible military thrust from the same direction is definite and convincing, a real stalemate will be evident to all clear-minded men even in Soviet Russia. . . .

Even a fanatic believer in the Marx-Engels-Lenin doctrine may be able to see a road block when he meets it. If the sixteen nations prosper, the ideological thrust will be neutralized; if our balancing the Russian armies is evident, the stage is set for a frank talk with the Soviet rulers. And what should be the terms? A gradual demobilization on both sides; and the first step in this program must be a raising of the Iron Curtain. I recognize this is a great price for the Soviet rulers to pay, but we must play for the chance that they will eventually be willing to accede. From gradual and open demobilization one may hope in time to come to a gradual disarmament beginning, I hope, with the atomic bomb. But, as things now stand, that is a prospect at least five years away.

These hopeful sentiments became mere words devoid of content when on June 26, 1950, the North Korean forces suddenly invaded South Korea. What the immediate public reaction was, I know only from hearsay. I had been rushed to the hospital for an emergency operation the day after I had presided at the Harvard Commencement. It was not until the Korean War was nearly a week old that my wife allowed me to see the newspapers and summed up for me in her own words the actions of the U.S. Government and the United Nations. I never had a chance to form an opinion unbiased by the *fait accompli* as to whether President Truman had made the right decision. I like to think I would have been among the majority who applauded. Why the Communist attack had taken place while the Soviet representative on the Security Council was absent remains a mystery to me to this day. The fact that the United States' response, which I believe was inevitable, was made under a United Nations flag may have had advantages for the Soviets. My own guess is that the Soviets had not expected that the North Korean aggression would be effectively opposed. The fact that it had been altered the whole international picture. Clearly, the policy of the United States needed immediate examination.

A hospital bed is not a good place for anyone anxious to discuss foreign affairs. Cambridge is deserted in summer; I had few visitors and no opportunity of trading ideas. As soon as possible we moved to our summer cottage in Randolph, New Hampshire, and there one evening in mid-August an old friend provided me with a unique opportunity to hear about the Communist attack and its implications. At the home of R. Ammi Cutter (now a Justice of the Supreme Judicial Court of Massachusetts), I met another lawyer, Tracy S. Voorhees, who until a few months before had been Under Secretary of the Army. I had heard of him through Bush; I knew that they had been consulting during the winter on secret military matters. The conversation at once turned on the subject of the Korean War. Tracy Voorhees was not slow in demonstrating the alarm with which he regarded the situation. As I was to learn repeatedly in the years ahead when Tracy and I worked together, when he was alarmed about a public situation, he became the enraged citizen ready to argue his case to anyone who would listen.

I was all ears that night. What I heard reminded me of the cries of alarm in Washington and New York when France fell in 1940. No good words were said for the Secretary of Defense, Louis Johnson. It was more than implied not only that his economies had left the nation completely unprepared for war, but that as long as he stayed in office there was little hope. About the procurement of weapons I was completely uninformed, but Voorhees was not. He had much to say, and it was far from cheering news. About our atomic armament, I was myself well informed because of my position on the Advisory Committee to the Atomic Energy Commission. The subject, however, was too secret to discuss and was, anyway, irrelevant; no sane man would advocate the use of an atomic bomb now that the Russians had one of their own. As to the manpower situation, I was ready to believe the worst. The failure of the nation to develop an over-all policy, I had been attacking off and on for two years or more.

The more I heard from Cutter and Voorhees, the more worried I became. There was no doubt that they had solid grounds for their apprehension. If they were only half right, the nation was once again, as in June 1940, in extreme danger. Finally, as the time came for an invalid to go to bed, I suggested that they form a citizens' committee along the lines of the William Allen White Committee of 1940 or the Committee for the Marshall Plan which had been recently in operation under Judge Patterson. "Get a group of distinguished citizens together," I said, "draw up a program, put it before the public, get people to write Congress and, in general, respond to the gravity of the situation. From what I have just heard, I judge the country is asleep. You should wake it up."

"Would you be one of the leaders in such a committee?" Voorhees asked. I might, I said, but added that for some months I would be a semi-invalid and in a couple of months must have another bout with the surgeons. And so, with no commitment on the part of any of the three of us, a most profitable evening ended. Without being aware of it, we had just participated in forming the Committee on the Present Danger, which was to fulfill a useful function until the Korean War was over.

As the person who made the first suggestion (and who later produced the name of the committee), I might claim to be the inventor. And if in the field of social inventions it were possible to take out patents, I think I could justify my claim before a suitable tribunal. Yet with social inventions, as is the case with chemical, mechanical or electrical ones, it is not the inventor who usually makes the significant contribution; it is the person who takes the invention, develops it and makes it work. In this case it was Tracy S. Voorhees, the most public-spirited citizen I have ever met. Within a few days of our meeting, he was in touch with me through Cutter. How serious had I been in my suggestion? If he, Voorhees, would devote much of his time to organizing such a committee, would I be the equivalent of a chairman? Would I help recruit other members, particularly college presidents? These and similar questions and my answers were passed back and forth through Ammi Cutter. Before long, the idea began to take shape and the telephone became the standard method of communication.

Tracy Voorhees returned from his summer place in Sugar Hill, New Hampshire, to Washington right after Labor Day and in characteristic fashion went to work. He talked about the possibility of a citizens' committee with half a dozen important people, including John J. McCloy and General Alfred M. Gruenther. The responses were favorable. The importance of strengthening the ground forces in

Europe was stressed time and time again, requiring, of course, a new look at the Selective Service System, which I, for one, heartily favored. Tracy and I arrived at a number of decisions. I was willing to give as much over the telephone as could be desired, but I was not in a position to travel. I could write letters and call many people and explain what we had in mind. If Tracy would keep the records and pull the whole thing together, I would back his activities to the limit.

In retrospect, it seems strange that I was so ready to form an alliance with a man I had met only once and talked to face to face for only a few hours. When he was practicing law, Tracy Voorhees must have been a first-class advocate; he was most convincing; in a sense, he talked me into being essentially the honorary organizer of a committee before I quite realized what had happened. I can only say I have never regretted the series of decisions by which I became chairman of a committee that, in fact, was really Tracy's.

In September, Louis Johnson resigned; General Marshall became Secretary of Defense and Robert Lovett Deputy Secretary of Defense. The change was good news. The military situation in Korea had progressively deteriorated. By the middle of September the United Nations' Army was hanging onto only a small bit of territory at the end of the Korean Peninsula; the supply route was through the port of Pusan. In Europe the war had raised all sorts of problems. As I was to realize some years later when I was officially in Germany, many of the leaders of West Germany (the Federal Republic-to-be) were terrified that the Soviet divisions in East Germany would soon attack. If they had attacked, there was nothing to stop them. (So I was assured in 1953 by General Manton S. Eddy, who had been in command of the U.S. Army in Germany.) The new Secretary of Defense had inherited a formidable undertaking. He needed help; the question was: Would he welcome it? Tracy and I agreed that the committee could be effective only if it was welcomed (unofficially, but sincerely) by the administration.

William L. Marbury, the Baltimore lawyer whom I had met in connection with the drafting of the May-Johnson Bill and who was now a member of the Harvard Corporation, was one of the first we asked to join the committee. (He was an old friend of both Ammi Cutter and Tracy Voorhees.) In early October he and Tracy called on Lovett and unfolded our plans for a citizens' committee. He encouraged them to inform Secretary Marshall about what they had in mind. At this time the group of interested citizens had grown to six or seven, including Edward S. Greenbaum, another lawyer, who provided much valuable advice. By the time a draft letter to the Secretary dated October 24 and a statement were ready to be shown to Lovett on October 27, the number had increased to eleven, including Bush, who was to play a most important part, and Presidents James Phinney Baxter of Williams, Henry M. Wriston of Brown and Harold W. Dodds of Princeton.

The letter to Marshall, signed by the eleven prominent citizens, began as follows:

We are a small group of interested citizens who have been pondering the President's statement of September ninth that "The danger the free world faces is so great that we cannot be satisfied with less than an all-out effort by everyone," and the recent statement of the Secretary of State that we "must put our major effort at the present moment into creating strong North Atlantic defense forces." . . .

We are greatly heartened by your appointment as Secretary of Defense and by that of Mr. Lovett as your Deputy. But we are gravely concerned by a realization of the problems which you and all of us face to achieve in time adequate Western European defense.

We feel that bringing about in fact the "all-out effort" of which the President speaks will become far more difficult with the ending of the Korean War. We believe that even yet the gravity of the civilized world's peril is not adequately understood, and that it will not be easy to obtain action to take and carry out the hard decisions necessary.

We believe that a realistic defense must include not only a European army, but a hard core of American troops in Europe in strength adequate to raise the confidence and the morale of our allies to a level which will bring about their own full-scale effort to defend themselves.

After stating in these paragraphs what we thought must be done at once, we ended by offering our services in the following words:

We have felt that a useful purpose might be served by enlarging our group into a citizens committee wholly nonpolitical in character, acting without partisan or other criticism of the past. Specifically, we have thought that one way in which such a committee might be of help would be in strengthening the public support of such stern measures as may be necessary. We of course do not wish to involve you in any way whatever relative to this proposal, and write this letter only because we would not wish to proceed if you felt that it would not be constructive to do so.

General Marshall sent a short personal letter to each of the signers in which he said: "Your proposal is an undertaking of great importance." He suggested a meeting with him in Washington to discuss a possible public statement. Such a meeting was held in his office on

November 20. I could not be present as I was back in the hospital, according to schedule, for a second operation. The Secretary was cordial and welcomed the formation of the committee. On the subject of new legislation affecting the increase in the armed forces, he indicated that the Defense Department had not decided on a position but would within a few weeks. In the statement which had been sent to the Secretary with our letter, the point was made that:

We will have to maintain a very substantial U.S. ground force of several hundred thousand men under arms in Europe for a long period. This would, of course, be in addition to the strength required for our strategic reserve in this country and our military obligations elsewhere in the world. We believe that such a program will probably require universal two-year service of our young men both to train a manpower pool should war come, and to make possible rotation of personnel to maintain our requisite military strength.

Secretary Marshall made it plain that while welcoming the formation of the committee, he by no means agreed with all the points in the statement. One or two members of the committee recall the map in the Secretary's office showing the location of the UN forces in North Korea, which had now reached almost the farthest point in their advance. The position of large numbers of Chinese troops just over the Yalu River was also shown. Within a few days (on November 27, to be exact), the attack of these forces was to start turning General MacArthur's brilliant Inchon landing operation into a disastrous defeat. By the middle of December the news from the fighting front was once again extremely worrisome. It was more than time for the American people to wake up.

On Tuesday, December 12, 1950, we announced the formation of the Committee on the Present Danger at a press conference held at the Willard Hotel in Washington. I was able to be on hand. With Bush and, of course, with Tracy's assistance, I fielded questions as best I could. Our carefully prepared statement with twenty-five signatures was given to the press. The meeting was a success judged by Wednesday morning's papers. The headlines of the front-page stories in the metropolitan newspapers testified to the importance which the editors attached to our announcement. There was no question that Tracy Voorhees had succeeded in lining up a group of highly distinguished sponsors. Among the new additions were Julius Ochs Adler of the *New York Times*, Frank Altschul, the active head of the Council on Foreign Relations of New York City, Charles Dollard, president of the Carnegie Corporation, Presidents Frederick A. Middlebush of the University of Missouri and Robert G. Sproul of the University of

California, as well as Judge Robert P. Patterson, Robert E. Sherwood and John Lord O'Brian.

Bush's remarks were particularly effective. As reported the next day by Doris Fleeson, he said rather casually that he personally had no doubt that, "if the Germans had concentrated on making jet fighters instead of their terror weapons like the buzz bombs, they could have stopped Allied bombers from reaching their cities. Jets and improved radar screens now represent a mounting defense against atomic attack which has not had the attention it deserves. . . . While America has been building a television network, Russia has been building a radar network against the atomic bomb. . . . The power of the atomic bomb to prevent a world holocaust is therefore decreasing as it becomes increasingly possible for the Soviet Union to prevent it from reaching primary targets within her borders."

Bush's remarks were in support of the paragraph in our statement in which we said that in Western Europe the ability of the United States Air Force to inflict heavy damage on Russia's strategic centers had been the chief deterrent to a full-scale Communist attack. The time might come, continued the statement, when all of Continental Europe could be forced into the Communist fold, unless an adequate supplement for the atomic potential of the United States could be brought into existence. According to our view, the necessary supplement would be an Allied force "strong enough to furnish effective resistance to military aggression."

The nub of our argument was that the United States must make a powerful contribution of troops to the defense of Europe. Such a contribution, in addition to what was necessary in the Far East and a strategic reserve, would require a total United States armed force of at least 3.5 million men. To enlarge the number of men in uniform to anything like this figure, universal military service was the only answer. In addition to providing military manpower, we must expand far beyond the present goals the program for equipment and supplies. To do this, the committee declared, the nation would have to develop "the strongest possible organization to supervise our military procurement here and abroad." It would require submission to economic controls more exacting than those in effect in the field of credit, both government and private. A sharp reduction in government spending for nondefense purposes would also be required.

The statement ended with a strong call for action:

The doubt is not whether such a program is too arduous. The doubt is whether it is arduous enough. Certainly it is not nearly as drastic as the conditions which make it necessary. The price is high, but we believe it must be paid. It is, in our judgment, the only chance of averting a war of world dimensions, or of assuring victory if, in spite of all our efforts to maintain the peace, the Soviet Union insists upon precipitating World War III. We shall at the least have created strength which may convince the 14 men in the Kremlin that further aggression will not pay. . . .

The bitter fact is that our country has again been thrust into a struggle in which our free existence is at stake, a struggle for survival. We have no time to lose.

Shortly after the announcement of the formation of the committee, the president of Columbia University, Dwight D. Eisenhower became the Supreme Commander of the North Atlantic Treaty forces. A number of his fellow college presidents who were concerned with building up the military strength of the nation knew that the new NATO Commander needed no persuasion on this point. In late September he had spoken eloquently and convincingly to a private, closed meeting of some fifty leading citizens in New York. The gathering had been called by Harold Stassen, then president of the University of Pennsylvania, and six other college presidents. I was out of circulation and could not attend, but Don David, dean of the Harvard Business School, presented a memorandum I had written, setting forth the ideas which were to become the basis for the Committee on the Present Danger. Far more important in the light of subsequent events was what General Eisenhower said. He took a sharp position against a preventive war but in favor of a great increase in the military resources of the free world, particularly in Europe. He expressed agreement with the memorandum Dean David had read.

On January 6, 1951, General Eisenhower left for a short fact-finding trip to Europe, returning on January 27. The executive committee of the Committee on the Present Danger decided to use the occasion of his departure to issue another statement in which we declared that the basic question was whether the nation should support General Eisenhower in his "great mission." It is the firm conviction of this citizens' committee, we said, that "we cannot do less," and we recommended that as a nation we reaffirm our unity with Europe in the present danger; that we create with the utmost possible speed an army in being of ten to fifteen divisions—beyond our strategic reserve and our requirements in the Far East.

On his return from Europe, General Eisenhower addressed a joint session of Congress and made a radio broadcast to the nation. Tracy Voorhees and the other members of the executive committee decided that I should make a radio broadcast early in February putting the

committee squarely behind General Eisenhower. I started my address
as follows:

The United States is in danger. Few would be inclined to question
this simple statement. The danger is clearly of a military nature. On this
much we can all agree. The Congress of the United States has, with almost
no dissenting voices, authorized a vast program of rearmament and
mobilization. . . .

Now, if we are going to ask the youth of the country to serve two
years in the armed forces—as I believe we must—if the government is
going to ask this sacrifice of them, each one of us who supports this
program must be prepared to answer one simple question—why?

Why must we look forward to a period of austerity, of partial mobilization, of more weapons for war, fewer tools for peace?

The answer to these questions seems to me to be summed up in
General Eisenhower's recent statement that we must "build a secure wall
for peace."

The free world has entered a new period—a highly disturbing and
dangerous period.

I then proceeded to recall the signals which had announced the
arrival of this new stage in our history: first, the Soviets' explosion
of their first atomic bomb in September 1949; second, the attack
of the North Koreans; third, the entry of the Chinese Communists
into the Korean War and the "justification of this action in the United
Nations by the official representatives of the Soviet Union." Turning to
Europe, I put forward the thesis that the one deterrent to direct military aggression had been and still was the overwhelming destructive
power of the United States Strategic Air Force armed with the atomic
bomb. But as the years went by, I said, the deterrent power of our
strategic bombing would be met by an ever-mounting counterthreat—
the Russian threat to the industrial centers of Great Britain, the
United States and the continental cities.

I next used an old rhetorical tactic:

But at this point some listener may object. He or she may say it is
impossible to defend Europe against the vast manpower of Russia and its
satellites. This clearly is a question which only military men are capable
of answering with authority. General Eisenhower, whose professional competence no one can challenge, has just returned from an inspection of
the situation. If he believed Europe to be indefensible he would, as he
said, "recommend that we abandon the North Atlantic Treaty Alliance
and—by ourselves—attempt, however futilely, to build a separate fortress
against aggression." He made no such recommendation. Quite the contrary.
Such a recommendation, he said, was for him impossible. He reports, "In

every capital, there is growing a desire to cooperate in this mutual-security effort." The governments are taking measures to build up their defense establishments.

"On every side," General Eisenhower said, "I saw heartening evidence of a regeneration in Europe's spirit. Its morale, its will to fight, will grow with every accretion to physical strength. . . .

"The preservation of free America," General Eisenhower said, "requires our participation in the defense of Western Europe.

"While the transfer to Europe of American military units is essential . . . our major and special contribution should be in the field of munitions and equipment.

"The arrival in Europe of new American land and air units, though modest in protective influence by themselves, will certainly produce added confidence and accelerate the production of military force throughout the member nations.

"Success," he said, "is attainable. Given unity in spirit and action, the job can be done."

Continuing to wrap General Eisenhower's mantle around me, I asked what we must do at home and gave the General's answer: "We have to devise a scheme that we can support if necessary over the next twenty years or thirty years, whatever may be the time necessary as long as the threat, the announced threat of aggression remains in the world." The conclusion was the need for a system of universal military service, for which I argued at some length.

The address put a group of well-known people on record as to the importance of defending Europe by increasing the size and effectiveness of the ground forces. In particular, it put the Committee on the Present Danger on the side of those who were urging the sending of troops to Europe, an issue which became highly controversial shortly after General Eisenhower's final move to Europe as Supreme Commander.

On the last day of March, the Committee on the Present Danger issued still another statement directed to the fact that the Senate was about to vote on a joint Senate-House resolution concerning sending troops to Europe in support of the North Atlantic Treaty. We pointed out that it was the unanimous, professional judgment of our military leaders that the defense of the United States should be laid in Europe jointly with our Allies under the North Atlantic Treaty, that we must contribute our fair share of the ground forces to the joint army being created by General Eisenhower. We warned against obscuring the real issue by overconcern with the constitutional powers of the President and Congress (which at that time had been used as a red herring by those who opposed sending troops to Europe). The committee urged that the resolution before the Senate be passed and that both the Senate leaders and the President give assurances that Congress be consulted in advance as to any new long-range policy requiring the stationing of any large number of additional U.S. forces in Europe.

In early April the resolution passed the Senate, and four divisions were sent to Europe. I have always cherished the thought that the Committee on the Present Danger by its statements and the broadcasts of several members played an important part in shaping public opinion on this issue. If so, it was one of the two successes of our efforts.

The other success was in convincing the public and the Congress of the importance of supporting General Eisenhower's mission through a broad military and economic aid program. Early in April the committee set up what was in effect a new objective along these lines. It must be remembered that the Marshall Plan for economic aid to free European countries was coming to a close in 1951. It had been a great success; however, it had made Western Europe an even more attractive prize for the Russians. Since the Marshall Plan was exclusively economic in character and had done nothing directly to bolster Europe's military strength, the prize seemed almost ready to drop into the Russians' lap. The free nations of Europe were not yet in a strong enough economic position to enable them to establish a really effective independent defense. Their reliance must be on NATO. Moreover, the Marshall Plan left the European nations, including Great Britain, with a severe dollar shortage; the so-called "dollar gap" remained a problem.

The munitions industry of the NATO nations either had been largely destroyed during World War II or had become obsolescent. The military aid program for Europe at that time consisted primarily of the purchase of heavy equipment in the United States, which then had to be sent to Europe. Of course, insofar as such procurement relieved the European communities of paying for equipment, it amounted to economic aid.

Tracy Voorhees had been concerned with the problem of providing proper equipment for the armies of the free world even before the Korean War started. He was, therefore, in a good position to guide the activities of the Committee on the Present Danger as we undertook to outline what we thought was needed in the way of providing military supplies for the defense of Europe. It might be assumed, in view of the defeat which the United Nations forces had suffered in Korea in late 1950, that the committee would have been concerned with immediate problems facing the commander there. Such was not the case; we all felt that the battle in progress could only be fought with the equipment on hand and the troops which were called up from the reserves. Our whole concern was with the defense of Europe—a concern which had been made concrete by the appointment of General Eisenhower and his report to the American people.

On June 18 the committee issued a statement supporting President Truman's request for $8.5 billion of foreign aid for the coming fiscal year, most of which would be for military assistance. The committee stated that under the prevailing conditions military aid and economic aid were essentially parts of the same program to strengthen our Allies. The statement strongly urged that both military and economic aid be administered by one agency, which should be outside of the State Department. Our recommendations were supported by a detailed study of the "need, objectives and administration of foreign aid" made by a committee composed of Frank Altschul, R. Ammi Cutter, Goldthwaite H. Dorr, Paul G. Hoffman, Theodore W. Schultz and, of course, Tracy S. Voorhees.

During July and August 1951 the organization of foreign aid and the extent of this aid were the subject of public debate, in which the Committee on the Present Danger played an important part. For example, on August 3 its recommendation as to reorganization of the foreign aid program was presented to the House Foreign Affairs Committee. We pointed out that to make up for the heavy cuts which had been made in economic aid, such aid could be supplemented without adding to the appropriation by placing large orders for military equipment in European countries.

Reviewing the activities of the committee and its successes and failures in September 1951, Tracy Voorhees regarded the final appropriation by Congress of over $7 billion for fiscal year 1952 as a real accomplishment. Considering the inherent reluctance of Congress to provide funds for foreign aid and the fact that Marshall Plan aid had been only at the rate of about $4 billion a year, he may well have been correct. Certainly the emphasis on foreign aid from that point on in the committee's activities provided a central core for our support of U.S. commitment to the defense of Europe. That such support was necessary was evident from the way isolationist sentiment continued to be voiced. Sending American troops to Europe was no longer an issue; the Korean War had not spread, as some of us had feared it would. The "present danger" was much less obvious than it had been when the committee was founded. What we had to guard against was a lapse of public opinion into the mood of complacency which had been present before the Korean War began.

There was never any question but that ours was a temporary organization. The only question in the fall of 1951 was whether another year of activity would be in order. We realized that when the presidential campaign started in the summer of 1952 a nonpartisan committee like ourselves would necessarily have to reduce its activities. For the next twelve months, however, there was much to be done. Judge Patterson, who, alas, was killed in an airplane accident in December 1951, felt particularly strongly that the committee should continue. Such was the final decision. I should note that the committee had earlier made a decision not to try for the status of an enterprise to which contributions were tax-deductible. In spite of the difficulty of raising this sort of money, the committee had received $113,000 by the end of 1951.

In the spring of 1952 proposals for foreign aid in the 1953 budget were having a rough time. The members of the committee were aware of the necessity of continuing to talk to the American people about the importance of the defense of the free world. Tracy Voorhees himself testified as vice chairman of the committee before the special Subcommittee on Mutual Security of the Appropriations Committee of the House of Representatives in June. The burden of his remarks was that the proposed future reductions in the foreign aid appropriation would decrease our military strength to a degree far out of proportion to the amount of savings in U.S. dollars.

The subject of foreign aid both for military and economic purposes is far from simple. Those who were concerned had welcomed the analyses by the Committee on the Present Danger. I think it would be fair to say that without the activities of the committee it is extremely unlikely that as much money would have been appropriated for foreign aid as was in fact the case. A whole series of broadcasts completed by the members of the committee kept hammering on the same theme—the present danger and the need for America to wake up. Dr. Bush's voice was particularly heeded. What he had done in World War II was well remembered. Judge Patterson was another powerful advocate. But most important was the activity of the vice chairman, Tracy Voorhees.

CHAPTER 38

Selective Service—The Continuing Debate

T HE COMMITTEE ON THE PRESENT DANGER was completely
unsuccessful in influencing Congress to pass legislation to establish
two-year universal military training in 1951. But the arguments pro
and con the proposal we put forward so long ago are still being voiced
today. As one who has participated in discussions of Selective Service
off and on since June 1940, I propose to use the defeat of the committee's scheme in 1951 as a point of departure for an analysis of
certain recurrent problems.

As I have described earlier, toward the end of the war President
Roosevelt had proposed a scheme of universal military service, and
President Truman widened the concept, stressing the importance of
universal service for youth. I was one of several college presidents
in opposition. My opinions before August 1945 were based on my
conviction that after the first bomb had been exploded there would
be a demand in the country for a·new look at the entire military
program. President Truman had appointed a committee headed by
Karl Compton to study the problem—a move which I applauded. I
had stated that if the committee recommended universal military
training, I would support the recommendation, and I did so. Congress,
however, thought otherwise. A bill to provide for universal military
training was defeated in 1947. In 1948 another attempt by the proponents of military training had become entangled in a struggle in
Congress which involved the interests of the newly independent Air

Force as against the ground forces. The Air Force won. Congress added $822 million to the Air Force's appropriation, and the proposal for universal military training died in committee. The alarm over the situation in Berlin, however, resulted in Congress' enacting that year a Selective Service Act essentially like the original act of 1940 so worded that it would expire in two years, namely, on June 24, 1950.

About Selective Service I had my doubts. The system had many weaknesses, including the question of deferments and the placing of great responsibilities on the local boards. In *Education in a Divided World*, finished in July 1948, I had suggested that what might be needed was a scheme for enrolling every boy, when he reached eighteen or graduated from high school, in a national militia for a period of ten years. The local unit of the National Guard might be the medium for the training, to be accomplished in three or four years of summer camp and evening drill. I was thus in process of developing my own variety of a universal military training system. It was more military, perhaps, than what some advocates of universal training had had in mind.

In the book I had written:

As long as we in the United States are in complete ignorance of what is going on in Russia and its satellite nations, there can be no hope of relaxing the tensions of an armed truce. Security being what it is in a free country, the Russians must have an extremely poor intelligence service if they are not quite well informed as to our military capacity. We might as well be frank about it to ourselves and to them. . . .

. . . Since Russia might on short notice overrun Europe with her armies (which as far as we know may be mobilized to spring forward at any moment), our balanced strength should be equally ready to strike. How? With what? From where? These are some of the questions to which we need frank answers. And I cannot believe that this talk would in the least disquiet the dwellers in the Kremlin since they assume (according to Marx) that we will strike them in due course. When these questions have been answered in terms of a total diplomatic-military plan for action to offset the Russian challenge, then debate on preparedness will take a more realistic turn. Until that time comes, as the debates in Congress have made clear, we shall be lucky if we can keep our Army up to the strength required to carry out our acknowledged commitments.

When Tracy Voorhees and Ammi Cutter presented their alarming view of the military situation in August 1950, I had turned to my suggestion of 1948 and modified it to meet the new conditions. Enrollment in the armed forces for service, not enrollment in a national militia for training, seemed to be now required. On September 8, less than a month after my conversation with Tracy Voorhees, I was writing to President Wriston of Brown University about a forthcoming meeting of the Association of American Universities, which I would be unable to attend. Wriston was president of the AAU.

DEAR HENRY:

Sitting on a mountaintop between hospitals, so to speak, gives me a chance to be even more irresponsible with my advice than usual. . . .

I should like to urge that this coming meeting and the next few meetings provide a special opportunity for the AAU. The international situation presents the Association with a chance to show real leadership and the change of management of the American Council provides a chance for this leadership to be demonstrated in the American Council. Therefore, if my diagnosis be correct, I venture to suggest Adams [the president of the American Council on Education] might be asked to attend the meeting to discuss joint problems between AAU and the Council. I am prejudiced, of course, but I think he will prove to be much more sympathetic to both the AAU and the trend of the times than was Zook [former president of the Council]. (Not that I like the trend of the times, but at least I don't favor those who for the last five years have refused to admit it!)

What are the problems within the framework of the American Council which are the special concern of the AAU? There is first and foremost the impact of the mobilization program on university enrollment. Since I believe the sooner we have a million combat troops in Europe the better, I am naturally on the side of immediate action to raise the armed forces to 3–5 million men. Whether I am right or wrong, there is a good chance that in the next five years a considerable fraction of the young men of the country will be working for Uncle Sam and in uniform. What we need now, to my mind, is a long-range, sensible scheme for universal military service (*not* training). If a group of university presidents came forward with such a scheme within the next few months, it might be a matter of great importance. At the very least, they could show the inadequacies of present legislation.

Admittedly there are tough problems in this area. I won't burden you with my own thoughts in any detail. But could not the AAU agree almost at once on some basic premises such as:

(1) The times being what they are, we must reluctantly advocate that every male spend two years, or perhaps three, in government service between the ages of 18 (or on finishing high school) and 25.

(2) The able-bodied should spend the two or three years in military service; the others should spend the same amount of time in civilian government service at the same rates of pay.

(3) There should be no favoritism or special privileges in deciding

the type of service. *For those few* students who firmly commit themselves to spend at least four years in government service in uniform or out after graduation from specialized training in certain fields, the term of service may be postponed till graduation. The fields shall be medicine, dentistry, engineering, and what have you (here is where the difficulties come in!).

(4) The colleges and universities will try to work out programs for professional training and liberal education such that the two years spent in the armed forces will be as little disruptive as possible to the flow of educated men into the professions and positions of civilian leadership.

(5) To try to work out the details of what is implied in (3) and (4), a committee of the AAU will go to work with some full-time help (query: Who will foot the bill?).

Two weeks later, I had prepared the memorandum setting forth my ideas about universal military service which Dean David presented to the New York meeting and which was addressed to the meeting of the Association in Rochester in October. I sent a copy to General Eisenhower, president of Columbia, on September 22, accompanied by a letter in which I said: "You will see that I have ventured to intrude into affairs of which you know a great deal and I next to nothing. Nevertheless, the times being what they are, perhaps there is no harm in a private citizen's speaking out—at least in a private meeting. If you can persuade me that my drastic suggestions are unnecessary and unwise, I shall be more than delighted."

I learned much later from General Eisenhower that he was delighted with my advocacy of universal military service, starting at age eighteen. What I set forth in my memorandum corresponded closely to his own views.

In a second letter to Henry Wriston, dated October 6, (enclosing a copy of the memorandum which I hoped he would have distributed at the AAU meeting) I stated that Gardner Cowles had agreed to publish the memorandum in *Look* Magazine and that it would come out in about five weeks. On December 19 my recommendation appeared under the title "A Stern Program for Survival." It was answered in an article in the next issue of *Look* by President Woolsey Cole of Amherst: "A Reply to Harvard's Dr. Conant: A Total Conscription Will Hurt America." Cole had much the better of the argument. I had made a mistake in rushing into print. Between the time I had prepared the article and its publication, the Association of American Universities had held two meetings. The second was a special one held on December 4 in New York City to consider the report of a committee headed by President Gordon Gray of the University of North

Carolina to report on military service. A resolution on "Mobilization of Manpower" was unanimously adopted by the meeting.

The AAU document was significant in 1950; it has relevance for the debate over Selective Service still in progress today. Therefore I feel justified in reporting on it here in some detail. The resolution started with eight "whereas" statements, of which the most important was the estimate of the Defense Department that standing armed forces of from two and a half million to three and a half million men would be required. The principle of a system of universal training and service undertaken at age eighteen (or on completion of the twelfth grade) was endorsed.

The document went on to present two new and highly significant resolutions: "From those who have completed one year's service, the armed forces may select candidates to pursue Reserve Officer Training courses, on condition that they be obligated to serve an additional two years upon completion or termination of such courses." It was also stated that "at the conclusion of the period of basic training . . . an appropriate percentage of inductees shall be designated as eligible to suspend military service to take specialized training for professions and trades essential to the military needs of the nation."

The system of universal military service as presented by the AAU resolution became the system for which the Committee on the Present Danger was prepared to do battle. Our militancy did not go unanswered. Troops for Europe, UMS (Universal Military Service) and foreign aid were all parts of one package, and all three proposals were highly distasteful to the new isolationism which emerged at the end of 1950. The new isolationists rejected collective security; they, in fact, seemed to dislike America's European allies. They were "Asia Firsters." They desired unilateral action in world affairs and withdrawal from the United Nations. Domestic Communism, the "insidious forces working from within," they saw as a more potent threat to America's survival than foreign Communism. Excessive government spending was also a more potent threat to national survival, for such spending brought inflation, "creeping socialism," the extinction of free enterprise, and ultimately a bloodless Communist takeover. For all these reasons, the expensive proposition of stationing troops in Europe was opposed.

Many leading isolationists were men who had made their debuts on isolationist platforms in 1940 and 1941; among the best known were Herbert Hoover and Robert Taft. Hoover, in a nationwide radio broadcast on December 20, declared that the non-Communist world would be insane to commit its "sparse ground forces" against the ground forces of the Communist world. By air and sea power alone, the United States, without committing any troops to foreign soil, could "preserve for the world this Western Hemisphere Gibraltar of Western Civilization." America should arm its air and naval forces "to the teeth," for only this type of national defense would free the country from "the dangers of inflation and economic degeneration." A costly system of UMS was thus out of the question. America should cease to rely on the United Nations, which was "a forum for continuous smear on our honor, our ideals and our purposes." Moreover, America could also do without Europe, Hoover contended. "Even without Europe, Americans have no reason for hysteria or loss of confidence in our security or our future" if his policy were adopted.

Our efforts to counteract the new isolationist opposition had taken several forms. First, of course, there was the committee itself; then there was an effort to publicize UMS; my article in *Look* had been the initial and not well-aimed shot in this battle. But these were not all. Primarily through the efforts of a CPD member, President James Phinney Baxter III, of Williams College, the Association of American Colleges at its annual meeting in January 1951 adopted a resolution endorsing the universality of the obligation to serve the country. In addition, I presented the CPD's position on UMS to a special conference of the American Council on Education on January 19; and a couple of weeks later, at the request of Secretary Marshall, I submitted to him some suggestions on UMS for a speech he was to deliver to the American Association of School Administrators.

Voorhees and Bush represented our committee before a subcommittee of the Senate Armed Services Committee. We further publicized our advocacy of UMS through a nationwide radio broadcast over NBC which I made on February 7. This was the first of a series of radio broadcasts. Every Sunday from early March until I concluded the series on June 3, committee members spoke over nationwide radio in an attempt not only to support UMS and the troops-to-Europe issue but also to counteract the new isolationism.

I testified before the House Armed Services Committee on March 8. The Committee on the Present Danger favored UMS, I told the House committee, "on the assumption that a global war is not imminent, that we are not going to be engulfed in a global war in the immediate future, that the legislation you are considering is for a partial mobilization for a long period of time and not for a total war. . . ."

The Defense Department's proposed manpower policy was almost identical to the AAU proposal. Every physically fit eighteen-year-old would be liable for a maximum of twenty-seven months of service and training in the armed forces. The Defense Department, following the AAU, proposed suspending temporarily the active service requirements of up to 75,000 students so that they could complete their educations and keep the "educational pipeline from drying up." These students would fulfill their service obligations after graduation.

Congressional deliberation on UMS was slow and discouraging. Neither the bill in the House nor the one in the Senate was satisfactory to us, although both houses seemed to agree that universality, not selectivity, should be the basis of the assignment for military duty. But the House bill did not include the "feedback proposal" for 75,000 students, and it called for UMS at age eighteen and a half, not age eighteen. The Senate bill, on the other hand, called for the induction of young men aged nineteen to twenty-six before men under nineteen years old could be called for UMS, and it would authorize UMS for only a twenty-four-, not a twenty-seven-, month period.

The attack on the Committee on the Present Danger continued. We were that same old crowd, the new isolationists charged, those "same old salesmen."

"In days gone by," declared Senator Everett Dirksen, "we had the Fighters for Freedom, the Committee to Free [sic] America by Aiding the Allies, and so forth. Now we have a new committee. What is it? The Committee on the Present Danger . . ." Like its predecessors, Dirksen said, it "is selling us a bill of goods."

Many critics were vicious. The internationalist members of the committee, asserted Congressman John T. Wood from Idaho, are "whooping it up to draft eighteen-year-olds, send an army and unlimited supplies to Europe, and thereby hasten the day, so fervently hoped for by Joe Stalin, when we will have spent ourselves into bankruptcy." This was the same gang who sold us the Marshall Plan, he charged, which was "just a slick trick to force the American taxpayers to pay interest on foreign bonds held by international banker-racketeers of Wall Street . . . and to tax free enterprise in the United States to build up socialistic-communistic regimes in Europe and Asia which are committed to the destruction of free enterprise everywhere."

"It is time to think and talk and act American," he said, "and designate internationalists for what they are—potential traitors to the United States. . . ."

Certain liberals who saw the CPD as the direct lineal descendant of the White Committee and the Fight for Freedom Committee were critical of the committee's unwillingness to take hard stands against McCarthyism and General MacArthur. "Until the CPD is willing to descend from Olympus and mix in the fray," wrote Arthur M. Schlesinger, Sr., "it cannot do the job of the White Committee."

President Truman issued an Executive Order on March 31, 1951, which advised local draft boards to consider for deferments college students who had either superior academic standings or high aptitude test scores. The presidential order followed the recommendations of the Scientific Advisory Committee to the Selective Service System, headed by M. H. Trytten. The "Trytten Plan," favored by many academic people, was in sharp contrast to the position taken by the AAU and the Committee on the Present Danger. Therefore, a few days later I went on the air with Edward R. Murrow, a CPD member, to attack the Executive Order. It was undemocratic, I charged, and would establish a privileged class. I said I wanted to read a statement prepared by the Committee on the Present Danger "lest my language become too violent." After I had read the statement, Murrow asked me whether it would be fair to say "in wholly unacademic language" that the directive to which I objected "stinks." "Well," I replied, "I shouldn't disclaim that word."

The Congressional conference committee reported out a man-power bill in late May, and after Congressional enactment Truman signed it into law on June 19. S1, now Public Law 51, was entitled the "Universal Military Training and Service Act," but aside from the title our committee could derive little satisfaction from the measure. The first part of it simply extended the provisions of the Selective Service Act of 1948 until July 1, 1955. The second part prepared for the establishment of a system of UMS, but postponed the decision to put such legislation into effect. The act also authorized the creation of a National Security Training Commission, to establish policies and standards for UMS and to present these to the Congress not more than four months following the confirmation of the Commission's members. Congress had apparently given its approval to the principle of UMS, but it had also demonstrated its reluctance to enact such a program; and before any such program could become effective Congress would have to approve the Commission's recommendations.

The act "settles nothing," I told the Harvard alumni on commencement afternoon, 1951. "Instead of providing a clear-cut policy . . . the whole matter is left to the decision of the local draft boards."

Just before departing for a two-month visit to Australia and New Zealand in the summer of 1951, I sent a progress report to the members of the committee. Acknowledging the committee's "complete defeat" on UMS, I wrote that I still felt that the CPD had been a worthwhile attempt, and I urged the members to continue to support Tracy Voorhees, without whose "selfless and unremitting labors this committee could have accomplished nothing."

My annual report as president of Harvard for 1950–51 (written in January 1952) had a flavor reminiscent of the 1940s. I started by stating that "a year ago when I presented my annual report, the war in Korea had just taken a desperate turn. Some informed people believed that the conflict would assume global dimensions before many months had passed." I had suggested, however, that academic administrators should act on a hypothesis as to the future that would lead under any set of circumstances to the minimum of damage. This meant we should assume the Korean War would not become a worldwide conflict. We had thus proceeded, and, as a matter of fact, there had been no appreciable diminution of the number of students enrolled at Harvard. The Selective Service Law as then enforced provided essentially one year's deferment for all college students; in addition, local boards had been advised to defer students whose academic rating, as determined by rank in class or by scores on a national test, measured up to a certain standard. As long as the present law remained unchanged, I wrote, we should have a large undergraduate college.

In making these statements I am by no means expressing satisfaction with the situation that now exists. Quite the contrary, I am still convinced that it would have been far better if Congress last spring had enacted a universal military service law requiring every able-bodied young man to enter the armed forces at eighteen or on graduation from high school. (A limited number of future line officers and specialists to serve in uniform could have been provided by suitable training units in the colleges and universities.) But this is not the place to dwell on the serious shortcomings of the Selective Service Act and its administration. I should like to register, however, my disagreement with those who look with favor on the present scheme for the deferment of college students. A continuation of the policy that now seems to be officially accepted will mean either that many able young men will serve two years as privates after they have completed a long professional education, or else that they will receive occupational deferment when they get a job in a defense industry on graduation. The first alternative will involve drafting scientists and engineers into the Army, which seems a waste of trained manpower; the second will come to mean that student deferment in fact often spells total exemption from military service. Only if a man's tour of duty with the armed forces is over and done with before he completes his professional education can these unsatisfactory alternatives be avoided.

I thus was using my report as president of the university to set forth my analysis of a national problem whose solution gravely affected the university. There was an implied hope that the Selective Service Law would be replaced by a universal military service law. No such hope was realized. Nineteen fifty-two was the year of a presidential election. No new legislation could be contemplated. Before the new administration took office, President-elect Eisenhower offered me an opportunity to serve as United States High Commissioner for Germany. My concerns with military manpower, laws and regulations about conscription and deferments disappeared. I had other matters to think about during the next four years.

When I left the diplomatic service in 1957, I turned once again to educational problems, but not those of higher education. Therefore I have had no occasion to form opinions about the current relation of the colleges to the armed services. My information has come from reading the daily press and, from time to time, summary articles. Even on the basis of such limited knowledge, one is aware of considerable dissatisfaction with the Selective Service Law passed in 1967 by Congress. The probability of further legislation seems likely. Therefore an attempt to formulate a few generalizations drawn from the experience of nearly thirty years may have some value.

First of all, I would emphasize the difficulties of defining a policy which would apply in all varieties of international weather. A peacetime draft is quite different from mobilizing all the able-bodied youth for combat service, as was the case toward the end of World War II. The problems with which some of us educators wrestled in 1942 and 1943 are only distantly related to questions about conscription which arose in 1940 and 1941 or in 1948 and 1949, when the country was not at war. What is different is not only the magnitude of the mobilization but the attitude of the nation. During the seventeen months from the fall of France to Pearl Harbor, the country was deeply divided. One powerful group was hostile to the building of an army by a draft because they did not trust the President of the United States. The continuation of the compulsory military service law by only a single vote in the summer of 1941 is an historic reminder of the split within the nation. The parallel with 1967 and 1968 is obvious. Fortunately for those of us who were interventionists, the operation of the peacetime conscription law had affected very few families before the Japanese settled for us the isolationist-interventionist debate. I am convinced that if the period of disagreement had continued for another year and the enlargement of the Army had continued at full speed, evidence of youthful resentment would have taken concrete public form. The possibility existed that pacifist sentiment, which was strong in the 1930s, might have swung the balance toward complete isolationism.

Once United States soldiers, sailors and airmen were engaged in actual fighting, the mood completely changed. Induction took on a grimmer meaning. The whole country was on a war basis. As I recapture the point of view of the young men I knew in 1940 and 1941, I draw one conclusion. If large numbers are asked to prepare to fight and, if need be, die in defense of the United States, the nation must be at war or face serious outbreaks of disloyalty among the young. I am sure Selective Service was never intended to provide combat troops for military action that was less than an all-out national effort. On this point, I can speak with some authority as I knew so well those men who, like Grenville Clark, put the Burke-Wadsworth Law on the books.

The history of attempts to modify Selective Service has been one of a continuous but fruitless process. There were times, as I have described, when the reformers seemed about to succeed, but, in fact, failed. The latest unsuccessful effort was in 1966. President Johnson appointed a committee of twenty headed by Burke Marshall, vice president of International Business Machines. The report rendered in March 1967 was received with no enthusiasm by the President and was completely ignored by Congress for political reasons.*

In many ways, the conclusions of the Burke Marshall Committee were similar to those of the Committee on the Present Danger. The essential points were the abolition of student deferment, the limitation of occupational deferments, the registration and physical examination of all male youth at eighteen. One feature deserves particular mention, though it was rejected by the administration and a majority of Congress. The order of induction of those who had completed the

* Harry A. Marmion, *Selective Service: Conflict and Compromise*, New York, Wiley, 1968.

physical examination was to be determined "impartially and randomly."

The problem the committee faced was a consequence of the doubling of the size of the age group. There were more potential draftees than the Army could use. Unlike in the World War II years or 1950–51, there could be no thought of calling into armed service all able-bodied members of an age group. There had to be a choice. The same had been true when the draft was reinstated in 1948. The reason then, however, was that the projected size of the Army was relatively small. Now it was much larger, but the increase in the number of eighteen-year-olds had more than compensated for the expansion of the needs of the armed forces. In the peace years before the Korean War, I could argue for a lottery as "the only fair method of selecting among those who are of college age." The United States in 1948 was at peace but no longer in a relaxed mood; Selective Service had been re-enacted as a first step to strengthening our military posture. But I for one was not then willing to argue for putting all able-bodied young men into uniform. In those days of peace, to argue for an army of such a size would have been absurd. Some fair selective device was needed. So it was once again in 1967. But once again Congress disagreed.

Two generalizations can be made from this brief review. First, the over-all strategic situation of the nation, as viewed by those who determine foreign policy, is the basic factor. Second, the number of able-bodied young men available at any given date in the future must determine the size of the conscript force and thus the nature and kind of deferment.

A third observation, which is hardly a generalization, concerns the call-up of students. Student deferment has been a continuously controversial subject during the entire history of Selective Service since 1940. The logical time for military service is after graduation from high school. But public sentiment has been strong against drafting those as young as eighteen. The arguments of worried parents proved more powerful with Congress in 1951 than the reasoned opinions of the educators who supported the program of the Committee on the Present Danger. Closely related to the age of induction (or the order in which inductees are called up from a pool) are the worries of those whose job it is to maintain a steady flow of highly educated professional men. The question is essentially as follows: How serious is the interruption of a year or a year and a half in the education of the future engineer, scientist or research scholar, assuming the break comes between high school and college? Again and again in one form or another, this query has arisen. I have always answered it by saying the consequences of the interruption at that age would be relatively slight. Therefore I have argued since the end of World War II for universal military service even for those who were later to be highly trained professional men.

The point of view I have recorded in this chapter as the opinion of the Committee on the Present Danger in 1951 still stands as my best judgment today, with the important proviso that in the interests of fairness random selection be introduced to allow for the fact that not everyone needs to serve.

CHAPTER 39

_____

From Cambridge to Bonn

O N SUNDAY EVENING, December 22, 1952, I took the night sleeper from Cambridge to New York. The next day I was to lunch with President-elect Eisenhower and present a memorandum on behalf of the Committee on the Present Danger. What seemed far more important, I was to have a talk with José Luis Sert, the man who was about to accept the deanship of the Harvard faculty of design. I returned on the five o'clock train with both missions accomplished but already almost forgotten. My mind was focused on one fact: I had been offered the post of United States High Commissioner for Germany and had practically accepted.

Did I know what I was getting into? Events proved I did not. I expected one set of troubles and encountered another. I thought of facing hostile German audiences, of dealing with a government not yet sovereign, of the trials of diplomacy. As it turned out, my chief anxieties were to be the consequences of working for the federal government in the McCarthy era. It was not to be the Germans who would give me undue trouble; it was to be the Americans.

What I had not realized was that the American High Commissioner was responsible for a large establishment operating on a budget as big as that of Harvard University and also a system of courts; that with occupation nearing an end the whole enterprise was contracting, with many attendant personnel problems; that the Alger Hiss case still determined the atmosphere in Washington; that appearing before

Congressional committees to defend a budget was a more formidable undertaking than any I had yet encountered.

In part I had been misled by what I had heard eighteen months earlier. In the fall of 1951, Dean Acheson as Secretary of State had suggested I might take a year's leave of absence from Harvard to be the new United States Ambassador to Germany, taking office in early summer. Nothing was said about the existence of a High Commissioner's office with a vast number of employees, both American and German; it was assumed that the occupation would be over by summer. Certainly nothing was said about McCarthy; no mention was made of security risks and witch hunts. The pros and cons of German rearmament were the main topic of our conversation.

I had declined that invitation for personal reasons. But I was not entirely happy with the decision. In the next months, my wife and I speculated on what kind of experience it would have been to connect our German memories of 1925 with the realities of the present. We had almost made up our minds that if by any chance the opportunity again arose, I should seize it.

In the meantime, plans for ending the occupation of Germany had not proceeded according to the schedule Dean Acheson had predicted. John J. McCloy had been anxious to resign as High Commissioner, which he did in July 1952. Treaties providing for the full sovereignty of the Federal Republic of Germany had been signed but not yet ratified; the occupation continued. An experienced American diplomat, Walter J. Donnelly, had been moved from the position of High Commissioner for Austria to that of High Commissioner for Germany. The possibility of my being asked a second time to take the German post seemed to have disappeared. Shortly after Eisenhower had defeated Adlai Stevenson, I read that Donnelly was retiring from the diplomatic service. The post I once had been offered was open, but a new President and a new Secretary of State would choose the man to fill it. It seemed unlikely that my name would be considered. According to the newspapers, anyone who had been connected in any way with Dean Acheson was suspect to certain Republicans of influence. Would the ban apply to one who had been only asked to serve? Probably it would; still, I could not entirely banish from my thoughts the bare possibility that fate might give me a second chance.

A few weeks later, Tracy Voorhees and I were asked to lunch with the President-elect, some members of his future Cabinet and certain advisers at the Commodore Hotel. The luncheon was part of the daily schedule of the team preparing to take over the responsibility of government after the inauguration. The purpose of our appearing was to present a memorandum from the Committee on the Present Danger. Voorhees would make the actual presentation; therefore I relaxed as the meal ended. Suddenly General Eisenhower turned to his Secretary of State designate, John Foster Dulles, and said: "Foster, don't you want to talk with Jim about Germany?" "Yes" was the reply, and we both rose from the table and moved into an adjacent empty room.

I was quite certain what was coming and was ready with my answer. "What General Eisenhower and I have in mind," said Foster Dulles, "is your appointment as United States High Commissioner for Germany; after the treaties which are pending are ratified, you would be appointed Ambassador." How long would I be expected to serve? At least four years. "You would not be much good to us for a year until you have shaken down in the job," said Dulles.

Two matters troubled me, I told Dulles. The first was a question of high policy; I had grave doubts about rearming the Germans. How did such doubts square with the statements of the Committee on the Present Danger about the defense of Europe? asked Dulles. It might be a question of timing, I suggested, though I added I was far from having a fixed position. I only thought I should put my reservations before the Secretary. "Well, we don't have to agree on everything," was the reply.

I went on to my second and, for me personally, more serious question. I had incurred the wrath of many Catholics because of a speech I had made six months earlier about the use of tax money to support private schools. I was afraid it would be difficult to get my name acted on favorably by the Senate. "Such matters are in Brownell's* hands," Dulles told me. He said he would have him check on it and then telephone me the answer. "I don't believe there is anything substantial in such a possible objection," he added. After a very short private conversation with Eisenhower, whom of course I knew well as president of Columbia University, it was all but finally settled.

On the way to the train, I told Tracy Voorhees in strictest confidence what Dulles and I had been talking about. The idea of my going to Germany was received by Tracy with horror. His arguments, however, I hardly heard. I had made up my mind to accept before I had even been offered the job. I knew my wife felt much the same

* Herbert Brownell, Attorney General designate.

way as I did, so there would be no great decision to make when I got home. We could only speculate and wait for the telephone call. It came the next day. "You are hooked," said Dulles. "There is nothing in the objection you raised." We agreed that the public announcement would be postponed if possible until Monday, January 12, when the Overseers were scheduled to meet.

I had hardly hung up when Jack McCloy called to urge me to accept the job. He had been back of Dean Acheson's proposal of the fall of 1951, and I suspected that he had a finger in this second offer, though of that I am still not sure. At all events, he now wanted to impress on me the importance of the position at this particular juncture of world affairs. Donnelly's resignation had left the post unfilled for weeks. The ratification of the treaties signed in May (before Jack had resigned) was still hanging fire. The sooner I got to Bonn, the better. As to detailed information about the work of High Commissioner, he would be prepared to brief me when he came to Cambridge to give the Godkin Lectures on January 12 and 13. (The arrangements had been made months ago, which was a fortunate coincidence.)

Jack was never a person to let grass grow under his feet; having been assured that I would accept, he started taking steps to ensure prompt action by the Senate. Either he or his right-hand man, Shepard Stone, must have sent secret word to someone high in the councils of Chancellor Adenauer, which resulted at the appropriate time in a news story from Bonn to the effect that the arrival of the president of Harvard in Bonn as High Commissioner would be most welcome. As it turned out, the message from Bonn was to prove unexpectedly helpful.

The matter appeared to have been settled between the future Secretary of State and myself by our telephone conversation of December 23, 1952. All that remained was to guard the secret for three weeks, cautiously inform my relatives and close friends, arrange affairs at Harvard, have my name sent to the Senate as soon as General Eisenhower was inaugurated, be confirmed by Senate action, and I would fly to Bonn. Speed, McCloy had said in several telephone calls, was urgent. I was quite willing to agree. But we had not reckoned on the political weather.

The weeks immediately following the inauguration of the first Republican President since Herbert Hoover are a period of which those of us who are Republicans cannot be proud. The Republican Senators had been in opposition so long that they could not shake off the habit of challenging the executive branch of the federal government at every turn. Before the news of my appointment was public, the papers started to publish rumors about Senate objections to a number of Eisenhower's key appointments. There would be no perfunctory hearings before Senate committees, nor any rush to confirm whatever nominations the new President desired. The new Secretary of Defense was being questioned about his activities as head of General Motors. Senator McCarthy, as a prominent member of the party now in control of the Senate, was making unpleasant noises about the Truman-Acheson policy of putting people with dubious pasts into positions of power. The new administration was in difficulty from the start. At the outset, my name was not involved. By some miracle we succeeded in keeping the secret until January 12.

I had hoped that I would be the first to tell the Board of Overseers about my departure. I had looked forward to a full meeting and an opportunity to speak to the members about the somewhat complicated arrangement I had made for the balance of the academic year. It was not to be. A heavy snowstorm cut down the attendance; most of those living outside of New England missed the meeting entirely. And for most of those who did come, my speech was an anticlimax. A morning broadcast had broken the story. Only those who had not listened to the radio were surprised when I reported to the Overseers that the Corporation two weeks earlier had elected me as president emeritus from September 1, 1953, and granted me a leave of absence until that date. I added that in the president's absence the university would be administered by a committee composed of Provost Paul Buck, as chairman, and three members of the Corporation. I had promised to return to Cambridge for a day in June to preside at the commencement exercises since I would still be president of the university. This detail had worried the Corporation; the majority had insisted that no one of them as acting president should undertake the task of officiating at commencement. Because of the Godkin Lecture scheduled that very evening, the McCloys were staying with us in the President's House. My wife and I thus had a good opportunity to learn about the duties of the United States High Commissioner and his wife. Shep Stone, who came to Cambridge to hear McCloy's lectures and join in the entertainment, was particularly helpful in his diagnosis of many current German-American issues. I introduced the Godkin Lecturer, as was customary. My appearance as future High Commissioner on the platform with the past High Commissioner was an unusual circumstance, and Jack made a grace-

ful and flattering reference to my appointment in his opening remarks. I seemed to be launched on a new career under the best of
circumstances.

The editorial comment on my appointment was favorable. Only
one columnist struck a discordant note a few days later. The threat
of a Congressional investigation of the universities, he wrote, was
hovering like a menacing storm cloud over the academic world; this
was no time for the president of Harvard to resign; he should stay
at home and defend academic freedom. Many in Cambridge expressed
the same apprehension; I was leaving Harvard unprotected. In my
defense, it is only fair to say that when I had fairly jumped at the
chance to go to Germany, I did not know of the growing momentum
of the witch hunt Senator McCarthy and a few of his associates were
mounting nor of its ultimate impact on Harvard.

The first rumblings of open hostility to my appointment as High
Commissioner coincided with my final farewell to Harvard audiences.
The occasion was the annual dinner of the Harvard Club of New York
three days after the announcement of my appointment. For the
twentieth and last time, I made the concluding remarks. Winthrop
Aldrich of the class of '07, who had been named as the Ambassador
to Great Britain, was the main speaker. In introducing him, the
president of the club, Devereux Josephs, as toastmaster made some hu-
morous remarks about the collaboration between two Harvard graduates, one in London and the other in Bonn, which he noted had
already started in a huddle during the cocktail hour. To which he
added something to the effect that he was assuming the Senate would
confirm the nominations. I was hardly in a position to join the
laughter since my name had not yet been sent to the Senate by the
White House. It was not until a week later that I was officially nominated and my briefing by State Department officials could start.
McCloy's idea of the appointment being rushed through so that the
vacancy in Bonn could be speedily filled had found no place in the
timetable of the State Department.

By Monday, January 26, I had said good-bye to various Harvard
groups, including, of course, the faculties, the Harvard Fund Council
and the Alumni Directors. I arrived in Washington by night train,
ready to go to work for the United States Government as soon as
the Senate should see fit to place upon me their stamp of approval.
I was met by the head of the German Bureau, James Riddleberger,
who provided a temporary office near his own in the huge State
Department Building with which I had many associations. I recalled

how in the war days, when the edifice had just been completed, it was used for a variety of purposes. In a few rooms high up on one floor was the office of General Groves which I had visited so often. Then I was in government service by direct appointment of the President; I was serving without salary as Deputy Director of the Office of Scientific Research and Development. Now I was waiting in line, so to speak, to be cleared by the upper chamber of the legislative branch as suitable to be the chief of a mission overseas.

That the State Department was troubled about my case was at once apparent. Rumors of mounting opposition had been growing in the past few days. Drew Pearson had reported that the root of the objections was my attitude toward parochial schools. Moreover, there was Senator McCarthy, who could almost be counted on to raise questions about Harvard's reputation as being "soft on Communism." (Such charges against me as president of Harvard had been current ever since the end of World War II.) In a short talk with the Secretary of State, I reminded him of my anticipation of trouble with the Senate because of my opposition to public support of private schools. When he raised a question about an article I had written toward the end of the war that advocated a control of the reindustrialization of Germany, Italy and Japan, I pointed to the date. I said his predecessor had thought it no block to my going to Germany as Ambassador. Secretary Dulles responded that unless I was asked a point-blank question, I would do well not to refer to the offer of a position by the previous administration.

As I was rapidly discovering, the right-wing Republican forces in Congress were bitter about the past and strong enough to make a lot of trouble. For the moment, Senator McCarthy's hostility to me was under wraps. Just how this was accomplished, I never knew. Likewise, I never attempted to discover what some of my friends were doing who were in touch with influential Catholic leaders. By the time I was asked to appear before a closed session of the Senate committee, the adverse publicity, led by the Boston *Post*, was formidable enough to be worrisome. Moreover, my old friend and classmate, Senator Leverett Saltonstall of Massachusetts, reported that Senator Alexander Wiley of Wisconsin, chairman of the Committee on Foreign Relations, had responded in a far from cordial manner when my name was mentioned. He seemed to be in a mood to postpone a consideration of the nomination for many weeks. What swung him over to a helpful attitude, I am convinced, were the representations made to him by Jack McCloy and the attitude of Senator Saltonstall.

Lev arranged a lunch in his office for me to meet a half-dozen Senators. I was asked about my stand on parochial schools. I had with me a copy of *Education and Liberty*, which was just off the press, and answered by reading the relevant sections. All present apparently agreed with my ideas.

A final weekend in the President's House in Cambridge enabled me to relax and prepare myself emotionally for my appearance before the Senate committee the following Monday and Tuesday. The newspapers had made it evident that I would be questioned at some length.

At 10:15 A.M. on Monday, February 2, the Foreign Relations Committee met in executive session in the committee room in the Capitol Building. The chairman, Senator Wiley, announced that the citizens who had asked to testify would be heard first and that Mr. Conant would be present. In making the announcement, the chairman stated that the committee was departing from the usual custom of hearing the nominee first. The committee felt it would want to question Mr. Conant about the testimony concerning him and that he should have an opportunity to comment on that testimony. The chairman further announced that three persons had asked to be heard.

When I heard the chairman's statement, I knew I was in for a considerable ordeal. If a man has ever made provocative speeches or written on controversial issues, there is nothing like a hearing on his fitness for a government post to force him to probe deeply into his intentions. Those who opposed my appointment publicly and in private had directed their fire not only against my position about the financing of private schools but also against an article I had published in the *Atlantic Monthly* in May 1943, which carried the title "Wanted: American Radicals." The point of view was an extension of one that I had presented in a speech at Charter Day in Berkeley, California, in March 1940. I had portrayed a type of radical who would demand drastic (but constitutional) measures to make American society truly mobile.

John T. Flynn, an author of many articles about public affairs, was the first of the two hostile witnesses. He made the most of my use of the phrases "confiscation" and "a complete redistribution of property every generation." When he was interrupted by Senator Robert A. Taft, who asked whether I had advocated "confiscation," Flynn replied, "Oh, yes, he does that in plain language." At which Senator Taft calmly said, "I have read the article and he says this at the end of it." Then the Senator read from the article as follows:

The reader will undoubtedly derive the impression that I am sympathetic in my own personal views with the hypothetical gentleman I have just portrayed (the American radical). But I should like to make it clear that I am arguing for his introduction into the American scene not because I believe all his aims should be achieved, but because I believe his type of thinking would prove a most beneficial leaven. I urge the need of the American radical not because I wish to give a blanket endorsement to his views, but because I see the necessity for reinvigorating a neglected aspect of our historic pattern of development.

Putting aside the article, Senator Taft said to Flynn, in a not too friendly voice, "Doesn't that take a little of the edge off his advocacy of confiscation every generation?"

I was sitting along the wall of the committee room beside a man from the State Department who had shepherded me to the hearing. When Senator Taft directed the rather icy question to Mr. Flynn, my State Department guide whispered to me: "You are in; congratulations." I might have replied that a prominent Yale alumnus seemed more inclined to give me the benefit of the doubt than a few prominent Harvard alumni had been in 1943 when the article was published. But I held my peace.

My Boston speech about financing public schools had been referred to by Flynn. I was asked by the chairman about the phrase "divisive private schools." "I think the examination of the speech, which is in the record, Mr. Chairman," I said, "will show that I did not use the word 'divisive.' As a matter of fact, I never use it because I am never quite sure how to pronounce it."

The chairman responded that he had the same trouble. I then added that "this was one of those phrases that was picked up and used in the newspapers in attempting to summarize the contents of my speech." I went on to say that I had attempted to make the speech clearer in a book, *Education and Liberty*, which was to be reviewed the next Sunday. I asked to have the last ten pages of the book read into the record. My request was allowed, and I read three or four key paragraphs which concluded:

I know of no one today who wishes to suppress private schools. . . . But unwillingness even to consider advocating state or national action to suppress private schools is quite a different matter from being indifferent to their expansion. It is certainly a very different thing from acquiescing in the use of tax money directly or indirectly for the support of private schools. Public funds are used to assist private schools including denominational schools in England and Scotland. No one can object to an open advocacy of the adoption of the English pattern here in the United States.

Indeed, for those who believe that education divorced from denominational control is bad education, such an advocacy would seem highly logical. It is important for every American citizen to examine this issue as unemotionally as possible and see where he or she stands.

I then addressed the chairman, saying, "That is essentially my position. I think the issue should be discussed, and I have discussed it, I hope, as impartially and unemotionally as can be done by one who is deeply committed to the importance of our American public schools as schools for all."

The chairman, who obviously was trying to help me and, at the same time, to shorten the hearing, put his summary in the form of a question: "In a few words, do you want to say that your purpose, back of this article, is to see to it that public schools are improved in quality?" "And supported by the community," I hastened to add. Since Senator Wiley had decided to focus attention on a sentence I had read earlier, I was certainly not going to quarrel with this oversimplification of a complex matter. The sentence was as follows: "What is required is for those concerned to improve the high schools; public school administrators must recognize the validity of some of the criticisms now directed against them in terms of the failure of the high school to provide adequate education for the gifted."

I was not through with the Boston speech, however. As Senator Wiley asked each committee member in turn to take over the questioning, several asked me further about what I had said or now thought about private schools. For example, Senator Mike Mansfield asked, "Do you consider the private school system divisive and inimical to our democracy?"

My reply was: "No. As I indicated—perhaps you were not here—the word 'divisive' I never did use. I think what I have stated is that from my point of view I should argue with a parent to send his children to public schools rather than private schools, but I recognize that people, parents, might not have to agree with me. I would myself hope that a large proportion of the children of the United States would attend public schools rather than private schools, but I cannot even imagine doing anything to interfere with the rights of the people to organize private schools of any sort."

Senator Mansfield then asked two questions about my views on education which were directly relevant to my nomination as High Commissioner for Germany. The first was whether as High Commissioner I would regard it as "diplomatic and prudent" to suggest that a comprehensive public school system was needed in Germany.

My answer was "No." The second was as to whether I thought the present system of confessional schools in some German states was "incompatible with the ideals of a democracy." Again my reply was "No."

Two favorable witnesses had asked to be heard. One was Joseph M. Dawson, the executive director of the Joint Public Affairs Committe maintained by the major Baptist bodies of the United States to aid in upholding the Bill of Rights in the Federal Constitution. He testified that, while he appeared on his own responsibility, he was speaking in accord with the position of his committee. He expressed forcibly his opinion that my Boston speech "had been continuously misconstrued by the minority group now opposing Dr. Conant." It was asserted by this group, he stated, that I had attacked private and parochial schools, whereas I had clearly recognized the right of such schools to exist. He agreed with my Boston speech that a dual system supported by tax money would be a threat to our national liberty.

Mr. Dawson's appearance and his frank reference to the danger of federal money going to private schools is of interest. It shows that one group at least, as represented by one of their standing committees, was on the alert to oppose any measure that inclined toward using tax funds for private schools. Indeed, he testified that in his opinion if my nomination were to be decided on the basis of sectarian interests, it would mean that the whole incident was being used by "sectarian groups" to establish their doctrine that church institutions and church education have the right to tax support; which position, of course, "was contrary to the whole argument of President Conant's speech and his book that has just appeared."

The other favorable witness was Senator Saltonstall. He was not a member of the Foreign Relations Committee, but had asked permission to appear, as he said, "to present to the committee my friend, my fellow citizen and the leader of a great university." Speaking without a manuscript or notes, he made a handsome speech. No one could have been more generous in the appraisal of my past or more effective in arguing a case before his fellow Senators.

Senator Saltonstall had been a member of the Board of Overseers of Harvard for thirteen of the twenty years I had been president. Therefore he could well claim to know what he was talking about when he spoke of my services to Harvard. Of course, I was a controversial figure, he said. So, too, had been the other presidents of Harvard in the Senator's lifetime. He expressed the hope that any president of Harvard for as long ahead as he could see would be a controversial figure. After Senator Saltonstall had left the room and toward the end of the hearing, Senator Homer Ferguson of Michigan remarked: "As Senator Saltonstall said, they wanted a man who was controversial as president of Harvard, and there seems to be no doubt they got one when they got you."

I shall always be indebted to Lev Saltonstall for coming to my help by an act which was by no means likely to be applauded by all our fellow citizens in Massachusetts. The recently elected junior Senator from Massachusetts, John F. Kennedy, was quoted as saying he was in favor of my appointment to this particular post but would have opposed me if I had been nominated for the position of U.S. Commissioner of Education.

The State Department liaison officers thought the two-day hearing had gone well. The meetings had been closed, but, according to custom, the chairman, Senator Wiley, briefed the press on the main items. Since the chairman was by now almost one of my sponsors, the news stories on the hearing were for the most part favorable. By the evening of the second day any worry about my eventual confirmation had been completely dissipated.

I learned later that there was more reason to worry before my name had been sent to the Senate than I then imagined. There had been talk that the President might withdraw the invitation. Any such action made after two weeks of farewells in Cambridge would have put me in an impossible situation. I could not imagine President Eisenhower even considering a reversal. The Senate committee, to be sure, might conceivably decide in the negative. The administration could then bow to the wisdom of the Senators and withdraw the name. If the basis for an unfavorable report of a Senate committee were manifest hostility to me in Germany, those who opposed me on other grounds might have won. And I am convinced that some such plan was discussed. However, Jack McCloy's early private message to Bonn, which had resulted in an expression of warm welcome from high German quarters, had effectively blocked this line of action. Senator Taft had indicated in the course of the two-day hearing the importance he attached to the Bonn reaction. So, thanks to my friends, I seemed to be on the verge of official installation as a government official.

The Friday morning papers stated that while the Senate Foreign Relations Committee would report unanimously in favor of my appointment, action would be postponed ten days. The Senate was not to be in session the following week because of Lincoln's Birthday.

The State Department was upset by this development. The liaison people went to work. Various messages were sent to the White House and to Senator Taft, emphasizing the importance of filling the vacant position of High Commissioner at once. Secretary Dulles had already started a round of visits to foreign capitals and would be in Bonn in a day or two. The new High Commissioner should follow as soon as possible. (McCloy had hoped I could precede the Secretary by several days, which would have been much better.) As I waited, President Eisenhower was good enough to arrange for a short visit with him Friday afternoon. He was certain that, contrary to the rumors, the Senate would act on the nomination on Monday. I returned to my temporary office in the State Department Building not knowing whether I should have a few more days or a few more weeks of waiting ahead of me.

At six o'clock we heard from the liaison people on Capitol Hill that the report of the Foreign Relations Committee was about to be made the next order of business. At 7:15 word came that the Senate had adjourned for ten days. Before the small group following my case could assimilate what appeared to be bad news, the message came that just before adjournment I had been confirmed by voice vote.

Such rapid changes of fortune required that my own plans change equally fast. Although Saturday was not the usual day for a ceremony, and the Secretary of State was in Europe, it was decided to swear me in at 11:30 the next day, February 7, 1953, which was done with the minimum of formality. I returned to Boston by plane that afternoon.

I was to leave from New York by air on Monday. Because of the uncertainties of scheduling the last few days, my wife decided she could not complete her plans for departure until Thursday. So I set out alone. Two photographers wanted a picture of me shutting the door of the President's House for the last time. A reporter wished a few last words. All of this was a strictly local story. In New York, as I boarded the afternoon PAA plane for London and Frankfurt, I was photographed and interviewed, but the questions asked were bland. I was no longer a controversial figure.

In those days a transatlantic flight was long, but one could sleep in berths that were not too uncomfortable. In midwinter the traffic was light; I was the only passenger on the plane as it took off from London to Frankfurt. On arrival, I found myself surrounded with friendly but almost totally unfamiliar faces. I was to get to know them all very well in the next few weeks. The Deputy High Commissioner, Samuel Reber, headed the welcoming party, which included the chief of the United States Mission in Berlin, Cecil Lyon, the chief administrative officer, Glenn Wolfe, and the heads of the several divisions of the United States High Commissioner's Office in Germany. After shaking hands all around, I was escorted to the High Commissioner's train, which I was to come to consider almost as essential as a car and driver. The three-car diesel-propelled train included a dining car, in which we now all assembled for lunch as the train proceeded to Bonn.

Protocol required that I be met officially at the railroad station in Bonn, though the home of the High Commissioner's train was the little station of Mehlem a few miles up the river Rhine. That I had not yet met any German was hardly commented on as we sped north along the Rhine, a handsome trip which I was to enjoy many times. I had so much to learn about the High Commission and its problems that I almost forgot that I was in a sense an ambassador as well as High Commissioner.

On arrival at Bonn, I was greeted by Professor Hallstein representing Chancellor Adenauer. I shook hands and muttered a few words of German to the many reporters (both German and American) who were at the station. The next day, accompanied by the U.S. Chief of Protocol, William Schott, I paid my official call on the President of the Republic, Theodor Heuss. A day later, on February 12, 1953, a call on Chancellor Adenauer, a press conference attended by ninety, and a luncheon with the British and French High Commissioners made me feel almost like an old-timer. That afternoon I met my wife at the Frankfurt airport. It was a month and a day since Washington had announced President Eisenhower's intention of naming me High Commissioner for Germany.

CHAPTER 40

Problems in Bonn and Berlin

$\mathbf{N}$OTHING ILLUSTRATES BETTER the special position of the
United States High Commissioner for Germany than the fact that
on arrival in Bonn I presented no credentials to President Theodor
Heuss. He was not yet the head of a sovereign state. Strictly speaking, he was responsible to me as one of the three High Commissioners
who jointly ruled the Federal Republic of Germany. My call was a
matter of personal courtesy, not of diplomatic protocol.

My lunching on my second day with André François-Poncet and
Sir Ivone Kirkpatrick, the French and British High Commissioners,
was taken as the equivalent of a formal call, and thus I was accepted
by them as a colleague. Each month one of the three of us served
as chairman of the High Commission; in that capacity each of us
was in turn, in theory, the supreme authority in all matters affecting
the British, French and American zones of occupation. Since the
German Parliament had decided in 1949 that Bonn should be the
seat of the government, the offices of the three High Commissioners
were established in close proximity to that city. Before long, other
nations began to send representatives with the rank of ambassador
to establish relations with the recently created Federal Republic of
Germany. By the time the occupation was coming to an end, over
forty such representatives made up a sizable Diplomatic Corps.

If I had arrived in Bonn as Ambassador, not High Commissioner,
protocol would have required my calling on each member of the

Diplomatic Corps. I should have been the junior member, and my name would have been at the bottom of the list. For the status of an ambassador in a foreign capital is determined by the date of his arrival, not by the size or importance of the nation he represents. Since I came as High Commissioner, however, I was not a member of the Diplomatic Corps and could officially ignore all the foreign diplomats except, of course, my French and British colleagues. My privileged status, I realized full well, was soon to go. If the High Commissioners stayed on after the treaties were ratified, we would have to be metamorphosed into ambassadors.

That such a process would present a problem to the German Foreign Office became apparent only in the spring of 1955 when the full sovereignty of the Federal Republic was about to become a reality. The quandary in which the Foreign Office was placed is an amusing example of the tangles of protocol; it also underscores the unique status of a High Commissioner. When the three High Commissioners became ambassadors, where should their names be placed on the list of accredited diplomats? The answer, according to established custom, was at the bottom. Yet such a precipitous fall in rank was a bit unseemly, particularly for the French High Commissioner, who had represented his government from the first days of the military occupation.

According to the story which reached our ears by the diplomatic grapevine, the Chief of Protocol of the German Foreign Office decided to place his problem before the members of the Diplomatic Corps. He asked the Dean of the Corps, the Papal Nuncio, to call a meeting. There was a large attendance; the three High Commissioners, of course, were not included. On hearing the problem, the first reaction was almost unanimous that the custom established at the time of the signing of the Treaty of Vienna was sacrosanct. The principles established more than 150 years ago must rule. To add new names to the diplomatic list except at the bottom was unthinkable. One of the ambassadors is said to have remarked that he would gladly give his place on the list to Dr. Conant, but, of course, his government would object.

The matter seemed to be settled, when some one of the older men made an interesting observation on behalf of the present High Commissioners. As I heard the story, the speaker (whose name I never learned) pointed out that a number of the senior ambassadors had never been received by the President of the Federal Republic of Germany. They had been accredited to the High Commission; only later did the Federal Republic obtain the right to receive ambassadors. Therefore, if the principles of the Treaty of Vienna were rigidly adhered to, the names of several others besides those of the three High Commissioners would have to be placed at the bottom of the list.

The awkwardness of such a major reshuffle was at once apparent. There was an embarrassed pause; those who had spoken so strongly for adherence to long-established diplomatic usage began to have second thoughts. The strict constructionists saw the difficulties and retreated from their defense of the sacredness of protocol. The meeting finally adjourned without reaching a conclusion. The entire subject was thus left for the German Foreign Office to decide. The quite improper but obviously correct answer was to list individuals according to the date of their arrival in Bonn irrespective of whether they were accredited to the Federal Republic or not. The French High Commissioner would thus head the list; the British and American representatives would be placed as if they had been ambassadors on arrival. This eminently sound but irregular decision was made; I doubt if any objections were ever raised.

The distinction between an ambassador and a High Commissioner in terms of protocol is illustrated by this incident. In terms of day-to-day worries, the distinction can be best understood by referring to the large building program which had been required to provide office space and living quarters for the American High Commissioner's staff. When the consolidation of the governments of the British, French and American zones was first contemplated, it was assumed the headquarters of the Allied High Commission would be in Frankfurt. That city had been the headquarters of the American Military Governors, the predecessors of the American High Commissioners. The German decision to make Bonn the capital forced the American authorities to redraw all their plans. It would be out of the question to keep Frankfurt as the center of operation of the American High Commissioner's huge staff. Yet there were no buildings in existence in Bonn or nearby towns which could accommodate the large numbers who must be moved from Frankfurt as soon as possible.

An ample office building was rapidly constructed at Mehlem on the bank of the Rhine, a few miles up the river from Bonn. Another site was obtained in an adjacent small second-grade health resort named Bad Godesberg—a name that will live in history because Adolf Hitler occasionally stayed at one of the hotels on the Rhine and chose this town for one of the meetings with Neville Chamberlain at the time of the Munich crisis. This area, which was formerly occupied by large fruit orchards, was given over to an American settlement of many multifamily houses grouped around a clubhouse and including shopping facilities. A few single-family dwellings had also been constructed for the half-dozen or so top officials of the High Commissioner's staff. The High Commissioner himself was quartered in Bad Godesberg in a requisitioned German house with a lovely garden overlooking the Rhine. It must have been built for one of the retired wealthy industrialists who settled in this watering spot in the late nineteenth century.

By the time I arrived, the transfer of American headquarters from Frankfurt to Mehlem and Bad Godesberg was complete. Space had been assigned in the large new office building, and the families of the Americans had been taken care of for the most part in the new buildings of the American settlement. I soon discovered there still remained some troublesome housekeeping problems. A colony of several hundred Americans separated a mile or two from any German town gave an artificial and almost luxurious appearance to the complex. It was not long before both Germans and Americans began calling it the "Gilded Ghetto."

Our establishment was no more "gilded" than the settlements of various American Army posts scattered over the American Zone. There was, however, an important difference. Few, if any, Army wives in the isolated posts expected to meet any Germans. Their husbands were on military duty. Not so the majority of the civilian staff of HICOG (High Commissioner for Germany), whose jobs were involved very largely in doing business with Germans.

By 1953 a fair number of the senior officials of the American High Commissioner's staff were career Foreign Service officers. They resented living in a specially created, purely American community. The prewar Foreign Service tradition had called for a junior officer to live "on the economy," as it was called. That is to say, he and his family occupied a house or apartment in no way separated from the dwellings of the local citizens. Food and supplies were purchased at the local market. The necessities of occupation in a war-devastated, defeated country, however, had changed the basic premise. Even during the days when Frankfurt was still the headquarters, the American families did not live "on the economy," and some new housing had been constructed. The arrangements had not been as noticeable, however, as were those in Bad Godesberg, where the American buildings stood apart from any German settlement for all to see. And many critical newspaper writers had started to make unfavorable remarks. A few U.S. Congressmen had joined in.

By the time I had been in office a week, I could see that the headaches which were in store were in many ways not dissimilar to those I had faced in Cambridge in 1933. For example, it had been agreed before my time that the American settlement would be a more or less self-governing community. Separated from any group of German stores, it provided its own, rather inadequate American shopping center. How should the center be operated? Who would parcel out the living quarters? Who was to draw up all the regulations? Who was to listen to the complaints of the housewives? (This last question was all-important.)

With my background of experience with faculty meetings, I marveled at the boldness with which our chief administrator, Glenn Wolfe, faced the prospect of town-meeting rule of the American settlement in Bad Godesberg. I stayed in the background as much as possible. I recall one boisterous meeting presided over by some member of the staff who, I think, had been elected chairman. "This is worse than any meeting of professors," I said to myself. As might have been predicted, the scheme failed to work; within a period of months, the community meetings were given up. There was no letup, however, of the problems which could be labeled administrative.

A message from Washington in March or April disturbed the administrative staff greatly. A team of inspectors would soon be descending upon us. The idea that a few Foreign Service officers would be detailed for a period of time to serve as inspectors of a particular embassy was new to me, but not to the career officers on the HICOG staff. They did not like the prospect at all. The High Commissioner's office was not an embassy; the inspectors would not understand what had been done and why. I was urged to file a strong protest in Washington by "eyes-only cable" to the Secretary of State. After talking with F. A. O. Schwarz, a New York lawyer whom I had recruited as head of the legal staff, I decided to refuse to protest. As on many other occasions which were to come, Mr. Schwarz's advice was sound.

The inspectors arrived, and one of the first things they pounced on was the liberal use of automobiles. They demanded at once a restriction on the current practice of having many of the staff transported daily from their homes in the settlement to their offices in official cars with German drivers. Only the top officials were entitled to such a privilege in a normal embassy, the inspectors announced; public transportation must be used or the staff and their wives must take to bicycles. The wife of one of the inspectors, setting an example for her husband's directive, had an accident the very first day which resulted in a broken leg. While everyone was sympathetic, some felt there might be a bit of poetic justice in such an immediate demonstration of how the new harsh rules could affect the lives of the employees of HICOG.

I was never allowed to forget that the office of U.S. High Commissioner for Germany (HICOG) was the successor to the Office of Military Government of the United States Zone of Occupation (OMGUS), and that immediately after the fighting ceased Germany had been ruled by a four-powered Allied Council. In those days Berlin was governed by an Allied Kommandatura composed of four generals, each supreme in his own sector. In 1947 the attempt to restore some degree of health to the economy of the vanquished German nation foundered on the Soviets' refusal to cooperate in a merger of all four zones. On the immediate issue of the establishment of the reformed currency of the American, British and French zones as the currency of all Berlin, the machinery of four-power rule fell apart. The Russian representatives on both the Allied Council and the Kommandatura walked out, never to return. Berlin was blockaded. When in 1948 the Russians ended their stoppage of land transportation to Berlin, the four-power military rule was not restored. In Berlin the Kommandatura functioned with only three generals in attendance; the Soviet Sector was governed by a Russian general whose relation to the American, British and French military commanders of Berlin varied from time to time, but was never the basis of cooperation. The merged American, British and French zones were governed by the Allied High Commission, with each High Commissioner responsible for affairs in his own zone. With the establishment of the Federal Republic as the instrument of government in the zones of the three Western Powers, the Allied High Commission placed more and more responsibility on the Germans.

In 1950 the Korean War created a new situation. As a consequence of the fears generated by the invasion of South Korea, the American Army in Germany was greatly strengthened. The defense of Europe on the ground became the preoccupation of all who were looking toward the future. The premises of the thinking of all concerned with Germany had shifted.

Reflecting this shift was the physical separation of the High Commissioner's Office from the headquarters of the American General. At the outset, they had both been in Frankfurt, where the central office of OMGUS had been located. When the High Commissioner moved to Mehlem, the Commanding General moved to Heidelberg. Once a month I traveled in the High Commissioner's train to that ancient university city to meet with the top command. There were still some joint problems to be discussed in executive session. The chief purpose of my journey was to report on the political developments affecting the ratification of the treaties which would end the occupation.

The atmosphere in Heidelberg was still that of the days of military occupation. The largest hotel, for example, well equipped and with a gorgeous view over the Neckar Valley, was still under requisition. On several occasions, Mrs. Conant and I attended evening dinners as guests of the military officers. Military uniform was still worn on all occasions. The blue dress uniforms of all the officers contrasted with the black-and-white attire of the few civilian males on hand. As one looked around the room, one felt a part of an occupation force. We were witnessing the end of a period of American military history. We all knew that in a very short time, when the Federal Republic became sovereign, the hotel along with many other buildings would no longer be requisitioned. As Ambassador, I was never to attend such a party.

In preparation for the end of the occupation, new housing for the military in Heidelberg and certain other cities in the American Zone was under construction. The financing of the undertaking was one of the matters for discussion between members of my staff and the staff of the Commanding General. Another touchy topic was the disposition of the German war criminals; still another was the rate of restoration to German ownership of the requisitioned facilities. Some of the army officers who had been on duty since the first postwar years still exhibited traces of occupation psychology.

I recall one general saying something to the effect that, after all, the Germans had lost the war and therefore they had no right to complain of anything the Allies did. Strictly speaking, he was correct. However, we were not using such language to the Germans. We were looking forward to the formation of a German Army which would be marching shoulder to shoulder with Americans. (At that time we expected the German units to be part of a European Army; the idea died in September 1954 and was replaced by the scheme of making a German Army a part of NATO.) The spirit to which we were all officially committed was one of reconciliation. With the old-timers, the bitter anti-German attitude, however, did not perish easily.

A few sticky problems between the HICOG staff and some of the military men at Heidelberg threatened to be troublesome. Fortunately, General Charles L. Bolté, the Commanding General, proved to be a person with whom I found it easy to come to an understanding. On our first meeting, he said that he had heard rumors of a certain degree of feuding between his officers and some members of my civilian staff. He would do all he could to eliminate the sources of friction. I replied I would try to do the same.

On my side I found what might be called "categorical thinking" to be at times a block. By that phrase I mean those immediate re-actions to a proposal which are based on the status of the proposer, not the merits of the case. I found that some civilians who had once served in uniform were apt to bristle whenever a communication came from Heidelberg. "That is just what you would expect from the military mind," was almost the automatic first response. (Such reactions based on emotions generated by past experience are almost standard in academic circles. How often in twenty years had I ex-perienced someone saying behind my back, "What more can you expect of a chemist?") Since I have never had any unpleasant ex-periences with military officers and, in two wars, had many that were cordial, my reactions to Heidelberg as High Commissioner were all positive. If they had been otherwise, I would have been in trouble.

In a sense, the American High Commissioner wore two hats. He certainly had two official residences, one in Bad Godesberg, the other in Berlin. He was responsible for the American Zone of Ger-many and also for the American Sector of Berlin. In the latter capacity, however, he was bound to work closely with the American General in Heidelberg to whom the American member of the Kom-mandatura was directly subordinate. Quite properly, the control of Berlin as a military outpost rested with the military. The High Com-missioner, however, was deeply concerned with the rebuilding of that city, an effort into which a considerable amount of American money was flowing under the Marshall Plan arrangements.

Berlin had acquired a new importance in May 1952, after the signing of the treaties which provided for the rearmament of a sovereign Germany. Though the troops to be raised were to be not national forces but an integral part of a European force under the command of a European Defense Community, the Soviet Union objected violently. Indeed, the earlier merger of the French, British and American zones had met with no favor in Russian eyes, nor had the setting up of a government with jurisdiction over the three zones. When it was proposed to allow this government to raise an army, the Soviets replied with dire threats. The proposal to have German soldiers part of a European Army in no way softened the objections. Repeatedly the Kremlin declared that if the treaties were signed, traffic between their zone and the Western zones would cease. The threat was in process of being made a reality in the summer of 1952. The zonal boundary was turned into a barrier. Barbed wire, a death strip, watchtowers, sentries, soon made it all but impossible for anyone living in the Soviet Zone to leave. Except in Berlin, escaping from the rule of the Soviet puppet regime in Eastern Germany was a highly dangerous business.

Because it was no longer possible for an inhabitant of East Germany to consider an easy and peaceful departure, an increasing number decided they must leave through the one route which was still open. If they could get to Berlin, then by simply taking the subway they could without hindrance emerge in the American or British Sector and be free. The personal effects which could be taken were no more than a handbag or a few packages. But for those who were bent on fleeing, such considerations did not matter. Something like a panic began to form. Every day in the fall of 1952, more and more Germans appeared in the Western sectors of Berlin and stated that they had left their homes and wished asylum. A refugee center was established to which such people were directed. Those who were bona fide refugees were to be flown out and settled in one of the states of the Federal Republic. By February 1953 the daily arrivals at the refugee center in the American Sector began to run into the thousands. If the rate continued to increase, we might be faced with the prospect of a total of 300,000 refugees between March 1 and June 1.

James W. Riddleberger and the other State Department officials who had briefed me in Washington about my duties had taken no pains to hide their worries about the stream of refugees flowing into Berlin. I was advised to visit that city as soon after my arrival as possible. Therefore it was unnecessary for Cecil Lyon, the chief of the American staff in Berlin, and General Thomas S. Timberman, the American Commanding General, who were part of the welcoming party at Frankfurt, to urge me to come to their city. Within a week of my arrival in Germany, my wife and I had boarded the sleeping car of the three-car private train and made the first of what were to be many journeys through the Soviet Sector.

The departure from Mehlem was about 11 P.M., scheduled arrival in the American Sector of Berlin about 8 A.M. The trip was routine for the crew of the train and a few members of the HICOG staff who accompanied us. The necessary military papers in Russian to be shown to the Soviet officials at the checkpoint had been made out. I was assured that the inspection when the train came to the boundary would be a mere formality because this was the High Commissioner's train. When we woke up in the morning, we would find we were traversing the Soviet Zone, which we would continue to do until a few minutes before we reached our destination in the American Sector of free Berlin.

The predictions were correct. We got up as soon as it was light (which is not early in February at the latitude of Berlin). Our curiosity about the Soviet Zone was soon satisfied. There was nothing to see, only wintry fields under a cloudy sky. Someone pointed out to us the almost total absence of automobiles either on the roads or in settlements. We were later to discover that the Soviet Sector of Berlin was also characterized by relatively few cars. The train drew up to what had been one of the suburban stations of Greater Berlin before the war. Now it served only as a point of arrival and departure of the United States High Commissioner's train.

Waiting on the platform as we stepped off the train was the Lord Mayor, Ernst Reuter. His coming to meet me was a signal honor, for which I expressed my appreciation as cordially as I could. His valiant response to General Lucius Clay's leadership during the days of the Berlin blockade had made him a hero in the eyes of all Americans who understood the nature of the conflict with the Soviet Union. Cecil Lyon, General Timberman and a goodly number of civilian and American officers constituted the reception committee. We drove at once to the house which had served as the residence of General Clay in the blockade days and later of High Commissioner McCloy whenever he was in the city. It was a spacious, well-appointed private home in that portion of Berlin which had once been a fine residential section. A number of the nearby houses that had once been occupied by the leading Nazis had been partially destroyed by the Russians during the weeks when they alone constituted the occupying force. Such at least was the current story; some houses may, in fact, have suffered from bombardment from the air during the final days of the Battle of Berlin.

On that cold, bleak, overcast early morning, Berlin presented a fantastic, grim picture. Some snow lay on the ground; the sun, which presumably was just rising, remained hidden by heavy clouds. The houses we drove past were, for the most part, in ruins. Gaping holes showed where a bomb had accomplished a job of total destruction. There was no regular pattern of devastation—a few houses seemingly intact and then a ruin. So it was throughout the city, except in what had been the center where the government offices had stood and where Hitler had spent his last days deep in his bunker. Here, as far as the eye could see, were nothing but ruins and empty spaces. Mayor Reuter assured me that, compared with the mass of rubble and derelict military equipment which he saw when he came in 1945, Berlin was now a viable city. He might well be proud of the clean-up job that had been done, but, as he himself said, one was discouraged when one thought of how much remained to be accomplished.

The military overtones of the American presence in Berlin were clear. I was welcomed by a nineteen-gun salute and at once proceeded to review an honor guard. The American headquarters were a large group of buildings which had been built by the German Air Force. The rooms that had been occupied by American generals since the United States forces entered the city were now to be at my disposal. That I was responsible for one of three sectors of the "Outpost of Freedom" was borne in upon me in my first meeting with the staff. The future of the city was by no means clear. On that, all agreed. The trolley lines from the Western sectors to the Soviet Sector had been broken by the Russians only a few weeks earlier. Now the only through public transportation was the subway and the elevated trains. Almost the first question I heard at the staff meeting was: When will the Soviets seal off their sector completely? The second was: What will we do?

We had no real answer. One of the younger members present at this first meeting had just arrived in Berlin. He expressed a view which I must admit I held myself. Indeed, I was later to discover it was almost the standard first reaction of anyone at all responsible for the security of the city. "How in the world did we ever allow ourselves to be boxed into this situation?" he said. He then added words which closely duplicated the thoughts going through my mind: "There must be some action we can take to get out of this trap or at least improve our situation." Easy to say such words and think such thoughts. Within weeks, the young Foreign Service officer and I were to discover that one searched in vain for answers.

It was one thing to be briefed about the American position in Berlin in the State Department building in Washington. It was quite another to face the same set of facts presented at a staff meeting in the city itself. I found a stark sense of reality shaping my thoughts as I listened to the speculation about the future course of events. Varying estimates of the Russians' plans were put forward. Some of the staff were convinced the Soviet occupation officials were glad to see the numbers of refugees increase for two reasons. First, the larger the number, the more trouble it made for the Western Allies and the Federal Republic; second, those Germans who were so eager to leave the Russian Zone would likely be unruly citizens of a society being shaped into a Communist nation.

Other members of the staff assessed the Soviet view in different terms. They felt the Russian occupying forces would before long have to halt the exodus; too many young, skilled workers were being lost. The industrial potential of East Germany—the so-called German Democratic Republic—was being lowered. Either the access to the Soviet Sector from the Soviet Zone would have to be controlled by checkpoints or all traffic between the Soviet Sector and free Berlin must be stopped. Which option would the Soviets choose?

As everyone knows, the Russians did not take the final step of dividing Berlin by building the wall until some years later. By then I was back in America and deeply immersed in the study of American public high schools. But I could recall only too easily the threats of 1953 and our vain attempts to formulate counterthreats. As I traveled around the United States visiting schools, I often found myself answering questions about the building of the Berlin Wall. For the most part, I heard impatient criticism of the failure of the President (by then a Democrat) to order sufficiently strong counteractions. I could point out some of the difficulties confronting the Western occupying powers; short of starting World War III, there were few gambits open. To some of the more reckless proposals I could only reply, "We thought of that in 1953 and discarded it as completely unworkable."

At first sight one wonders why it took so long before the logic of a split Germany resulted in a split Berlin. The answer is to be found by noting the attitude of countless German families. People refuse to leave their homes and their possessions unless they are terrified of the consequences of not moving. It is an extraordinary fact that over a million inhabitants of the Soviet Sector of Berlin, who could have quietly moved to West Berlin via the subway, never stirred. The rapid building of the wall finally trapped them.

I remember one head of a family in East Berlin explaining in the winter of 1953 why he was remaining. "If we leave for the West, we would have to abandon all our furniture and possessions," he said. "I don't like the regime the Soviets are forcing on us, but I have a home and a job." The same thought must have been in many minds. "If I find the government too offensive," he added, "I can just take the subway with my family and leave on a moment's notice." When the time came, however, events moved too fast for all but a few. Those who left the sector after the wall was decreed, did so at risk of life and limb.

If my analysis is correct, the size of the refugee stream coming through Berlin in the winter of 1953 reflected a fear of the future more than a dislike of Communism. As evidence for my view I may cite the fact that the inhabitants of border towns were the first to register fright. When in the fall of 1952 the border between the Russian Zone and the American and British zones had been made tight by military means, they saw the German People's Army, under orders from the Soviets, erecting barriers and halting peaceful citizens who desired to cross what had hitherto been an almost unnoticed zonal border. What would happen next? The terror increased as the first attempts to escape across the border at many points were met not only by arrests but by shooting. The realization that only in Berlin was the border open gradually spread. Anyone who had become embroiled with the authorities for any reason was likely to leave while it was still possible through the only route still open. Tens of thousands of heads of East German families must have weighed the pros and cons of empty-handed flight each year from the summer of 1952 until the Berlin hatch was closed in 1961.

One of my first concerns on visiting Berlin was the refugee center. There each refugee was thoroughly questioned by a committee of several people. In order to receive financial help from the government of the Federal Republic, a person had to convince the committee, first, that he was not a Communist agent and, second, that he was seeking asylum because of the consequences of his political views. The examiners sought to discover the fraudulent cases, including people with criminal records, who were not accepted, or those whose only motive was economic. The line was hard to draw between a person who was moving in the hopes of getting a better job and one who had been so uncooperative with the local Communists that he had lost his position.

Together with Mrs. Conant and a member of the American Berlin staff, I sat in on several examinations during the first months of 1953. We heard the questions, the replies, and learned the verdict. As a way of learning what was going on in the Soviet Zone, the experience was revealing. Those Americans who had the task of following the examinations were satisfied of their adequacy. The Germans who succeeded in convincing the committee that they should be recognized as refugees were in all probability the people who deserved asylum.

The ever-increasing stream of refugees was a recent problem but by no means the only one which merited the attention of the new American High Commissioner. The physical reconstruction of the city was another; the creation of jobs, a third. Berlin before the war had been a manufacturing city, with a disproportionate number of white-collar workers, a consequence of the fact that it was the nation's capital and also because such businesses as insurance companies had employed many people. Now in 1953 an aging population of former secretaries and clerks was largely unemployed. To be sure, many persons were daily doing all sorts of physical labor which before 1945 would have been unthinkable. One saw women working over piles of rubble, for example. The ruins of a brick building were thus being converted into hundreds of thousands of bricks for new construction. A grinding machine first reduced the rubble to a uniform coarse dust, which was mixed with concrete and run into the necessary molds. There were plenty of people to tend the machines, sweep up the debris and do other unskilled work. What was in short supply were skilled workers. Here was the bottleneck of the efforts to rebuild Berlin.

Conference after conference between the American staff and the Berliners sought to speed up the renewal of Berlin as a self-supporting industrial city. Old industries were supported with funds; new industries were planned. As I worked with Mayor Reuter and the members of his Cabinet and other city officials, my admiration grew. I already had a high opinion of the inhabitants because of their courage and endurance during the blockade days. Those days were over. Other traits were needed. As one of the leaders of the Berlin workers said to me on my first visit: "We don't want to be regarded as heroes. What we want is jobs." And to make jobs, one had first to build buildings and make plans.

By the end of my four years in Germany I would still not be sure whether the progress I was seeing in the physical growth of Berlin was an American or a German triumph. At all events, it had been a constructive and exciting business in which I had had a part; I felt almost a Berliner myself.

CHAPTER 41

A Session with McCarthy

O NE CAN BRAND Senator Joseph McCarthy as a ruthless, effective demagogue who, like Hitler, used the "big lie" technique. In reconstructing the history of the early 1950s, however, one must not forget the impact of the Alger Hiss case and the Canadian spy trials. Since the end of the war, American public opinion had been literally of two minds as regards the Russians. Gratitude for the prowess of the armies which finally overwhelmed the Germans on the Eastern Front was mixed with fear of the ambitions of the dwellers in the Kremlin.

As I have already made evident, by 1949 I for one was ready to subscribe to the statement that membership in the Communist Party involved "adherence to doctrines and discipline completely inconsistent with the principles of freedom on which American education depends." Since I believed members of the Communist Party should not be employed as teachers, it was self-evident that they should not be government employees. At the beginning of the Alger Hiss trial I was certain he was an innocent victim of a vicious Red hunt not dissimilar to the one which had disgraced the Wilson administration at the close of World War I. After the conviction, it was hard to maintain that there was no possibility of Communists being in positions of responsibility. Careful security checks were certainly in order. Yet within a year I had occasion to find out to what damaging lengths the fear of Communism in Washington could be carried.

561

My first encounter with the atmosphere of fear in Washington was in early 1951. As chairman of the board of the recently created National Science Foundation, I found myself in the position of liaison officer between the White House and the board. An important decision was in the making. The President was about to appoint the first executive director of the Foundation. The name of Dr. Alan T. Waterman, Chief Scientist of the Naval Research Laboratory, had been all but agreed to when I received a call to come posthaste to the White House offices. There I met the man who was acting as special counsel to President Truman. He said in effect that the security check on Waterman was unsatisfactory; the appointment could not be made. I was flabbergasted. What could be wrong? Waterman had had access to all sorts of highly classified material in his work in the Naval Research Laboratory. I knew him well, as did Dr. Bush; it was unthinkable that the administration would balk at this late date.

"The trouble is with his wife," was the answer. "The file shows that Mrs. Waterman has been to the Soviet Embassy twice for tea." I almost exploded with annoyance. "Can such a trivial report block an excellent appointment?" I exclaimed. "It seems ridiculous." "So it may to you," President Truman's spokesman said, "but with the atmosphere what it is on the Hill, we cannot proceed with this appointment unless you can personally guarantee the man and stand ready to give full public endorsement." I gave the assurance, and the matter proceeded as scheduled. The words "with the atmosphere what it is on the Hill, we cannot proceed," remained with me; the incident I would never forget. "Against what follies must the executive branch struggle?" I thought. Two years later I was to discover for myself.

Of course, the Republicans had made the most of the charges of carelessness about Communist infiltration in the Truman administration. I did not like this aspect of the presidential campaign, yet I could not say it was all complete nonsense. The executive branch of the government had been in the position of trying to fight a battle on two fronts. On the one hand, the possibility of the existence of other Alger Hisses could not be denied. Some security checks were needed even if the introduction of them hurt the morale of government employees. On the other hand, an admission of apprehension would fan the flames of fear throughout the country. This in turn might lead to more Congressional witch hunts.

As long as I was viewing politics as a private citizen, I could enjoy the luxury of condemning both Communists and McCarthy

followers. Once nominated as a high official, my calm aloofness was
shortly to disappear. I could wish my party—the Republicans—had
not been so ready to give Senator McCarthy a free hand in 1952.
For it became evident within a few days of General Eisenhower's
taking office that, contrary to the plans and desires of the real leaders
of the party, McCarthy was going to continue his notorious activities
at full speed. He was going to cause no end of trouble for a number of
Cabinet officers and their staffs.

The overseas Information Service operated by the State Department had been one of McCarthy's targets. Though with Eisenhower's
election the man in charge in the closing days of the Truman-Acheson
administration was replaced at once, the attacks did not decrease.
Rather, they seemed to mount. I had hardly a chance to get settled
in Germany before I heard about cables from Washington dealing
with books on the shelves of the libraries operated by HICOG in the
public information centers in many cities (America Houses). I
soon learned that the head of the branch of HICOG responsible for the
Information Service was resigning. A new appointment there was
of great importance. I also began to hear of Foreign Service career
men and others in Germany who were either being moved by orders
from Washington or being asked to resign. In at least one case,
Senator McCarthy boasted that he was responsible for removing
the "security risk."

Some of the staff told me in strict confidence of their harassment
by the Department security officers. At least one career man complained (also in strictest confidence) of the failure of the Acheson
people to take his advice a year before. They should have gotten rid
of certain persons whose records were bad, he said. In short, the
reports that came to my ears were conflicting and heavily charged
with emotion. Even before my first return to the United States in
April 1953, accompanying Chancellor Adenauer, I knew the Department of State was in deep trouble.

My appearance with Chancellor Adenauer in Washington happened to coincide with a notorious visit to Bonn of Senator McCarthy's
two assistants, Roy Cohn and G. David Shine. A message warning
me about the impending trouble reached me just as I was boarding
the plane. Interestingly enough, it was sent through CIA channels,
as the regular State Department cable service was regarded as open
to those in Washington who were working with or for the Senator.
I found on my arrival in Washington that there were not only wheels
within wheels, as is usual in a complex government operation, but

that some of the wheels were spinning counterclockwise. Something approaching a state of war existed between the McCarthy forces and the majority of the Washington staff of the State Department. There was spying and counterspying going on. In the course of all these undercover activities, it was learned that I stood high on the list of those whom Senator McCarthy was "out to get." Yet nothing happened to me personally until I appeared before the Senate Appropriations Committee in June. A great deal was happening in HICOG which was causing an uneasy personnel situation to go from bad to worse.

Even if there had been no change in administration, even if there had been no Communist spy scare, the job of High Commissioner in 1953 would have been difficult. The reasons were inherent in the change from a High Commission office to an embassy. In 1952 approximately two thousand Americans were employed in HICOG; by July 1, 1953, the number was to be cut in half. While the reduction had been planned ever since the treaties were signed in May 1952, it was only after the responsibility was mine that many appointments were terminated. What came to be known as "operation RIF [reduction in force]" dominated the conversation in the American settlement. The uncertainty of the date at which treaties would go into effect added a most unwelcome variable. No one could be at all sure of the day when the special responsibilities which required an American staff would be terminated. News came that some of the high-ranking Americans were to be transferred against their wishes; there were rumors of resignation under pressure for alleged security reasons. This was the highly disagreeable situation I faced in May and June 1953.

A note I wrote for my own record on May 31, 1953, starts as follows: "Well, the HICOG part of the job has turned out so far to be the most difficult and least pleasant. Having inherited a large organization in process of contraction without a real head for nearly a year, the personnel problem would have been bad in any case. With the 'goings on' in Washington, a bad situation has become so bad as to be almost funny if it were not so tragic for some people."

Continuing, I thanked God for F. A. O. Schwarz "both as a friend and legal adviser." I also noted the "lucky break" that Tracy Voorhees of the Committee on the Present Danger had turned up in Bonn on a mission for Robert Johnson, the new head of the Public Affairs Program in the State Department. (Johnson soon resigned on account of bad health.)

In spite of these bits of good fortune, my entry was far from cheerful. My failure to quarrel openly with Washington's decisions about several men had led the American newsmen in Bonn to say in effect that the United States High Commissioner wouldn't defend his own people or his program. The general feeling among the reporters (a half-dozen able men) was that I was "too cautious and cagey." I recorded in my note that

this has not yet been reflected in the news dispatches but can be any time. The cocktail party at Boerner's [the new executive director of HICOG's information program] at which I was frank on all subjects except Senator McCarthy may have helped. The fact that Coblentz of the *Tribune* and Curry of the A.P. are on record as saying that my first two months were a success makes it difficult for them to reverse their field but they may do so. The situation is so reminiscent of the Walsh-Sweezy days at Harvard as to be comical. Even Roger Baldwin [head of the Civil Liberties Union] turns up again—a proponent of the downtrodden, this time a junior member of the staff [whose appointment had been terminated]. And now in a few days we return to Washington, face Congressional Committees on the budget and almost anything can happen.

The objective of my visit was to present the budget of the High Commissioner's office to the appropriations committees of the House and Senate. The hearing before the House subcommittee took two days; it was exhausting but not unpleasant. A similar hearing before the Senate Appropriations Committee was scheduled for a few days later. I knew McCarthy was a member of the committee, but those who thought they knew assured me I was not likely to be challenged since the junior Senator from Wisconsin was not in charge. Senator Styles Bridges was chairman of the committee. It was tacitly assumed the hearing would be closed as had been the sessions with the committee of the House.

Imagine, then, my consternation when at about 9:30 on Monday morning, June 15, 1953, just off a sleeper from Boston, I discovered the hearing was public. I saw cameras and klieg lights being put in place as I walked into the committee room with a half-dozen members of the Department's staff. A newsman whom I had known some years before greeted me. "I just dropped in," he said, looking at the cameras, "to see how you would do." That I was going to be put on the spot was clear. Hours of briefing by the staff of the State Department and HICOG had prepared me to answer all manner of questions about the budget and about Germany. But no one had suggested answers for the kind of question McCarthy was sure to ask. Of course

I had our chief executive officer, Glenn Wolfe, with me and also the head of the HICOG information service; it was on their knowledge that I would have to depend.

The notorious Senator was not present when the hearing opened, but within the first half-hour he took his seat. After my formal, prepared statement justifying the request for funds (some $14 million) had been filed and briefly discussed, Senator McCarthy opened with the abrupt question (I am quoting from the printed official record of the hearing): "Doctor, how much of this budget is to go for the information program of HICOG? Then he immediately went on with the following:

May I ask you this: Our committee has recently exposed the fact that there are some 30,000 publications by Communist authors on information shelves. Many of them in Germany. I am not speaking of the books that explain the workings of the Communist Party. I am not speaking of the books available to the employees of HICOG. We both realize that they must read those Communist books to know the Communist objectives. I am referring to the books by Communist authors on our shelves with our stamp of approval—some 30,000. May I ask what your attitude toward that is? Do you favor taking those books off the shelves? Would you favor leaving them on the shelves? Would you favor discontinuing the purchase of those books or the continuation of that purchase?

I was caught completely off base. I had not read the morning papers, nor had any member of my briefing staff alerted me. I discovered later (too late to be of service) that on Sunday, the day before, President Eisenhower had made some impromptu remarks at the Dartmouth College commencement exercises in Hanover, New Hampshire, denouncing book censorship. "Don't join the book burners," the President had said. "Don't think you're going to conceal faults by concealing evidence that they ever existed." The press had immediately made this into an attack on Senator McCarthy and his publicized demands for the purging of the books in the America House libraries.

I knew my first words of reply to McCarthy's question would be of great importance. Two thoughts flashed through my mind as I fumbled for an adequate answer. First, I myself would not want to claim that an American library arranged for the use of Germans— the inhabitants of a country we were trying to make democratic— should include all manner of books. Selectivity had to be assumed. My second thought was of the attitude of the Department. I was not a private citizen. I recalled the essence of one cable signed "Dulles" (though he probably never saw it). The message had said that, judging from the cables from Bonn and the news stories, it seemed that the HICOG employees did not understand that the Department expected cooperation with Congressional committees. I snapped to attention mentally and expressed what I thought was the official line, which was not far from my own private thinking.

My answer and the subsequent questions and replies for the next few minutes are printed in the official record:

COMMISSIONER CONANT. As I understand it, the whole book-purchase program has been arranged here in Washington in the past, and the question of what seemed to be the best authors to put on the shelves, from the point of view of our objectives, has been worked out here.

If I had that responsibility directly—it is clearly one that has to be delegated—I should have to examine each case pretty carefully to see who our Communist author was, what his point of view was, and whether the reading of that book by the Germans would do us more good than harm.

SENATOR MC CARTHY. Let's see what the point of view of the author is. The Communist is under Communist Party discipline, and the point of view is furthering the Communist conspiracy. There is no doubt about that, is there?

COMMISSIONER CONANT. With such a man, I would not want his books on the shelves.

SENATOR MC CARTHY. Such a man, I think—and every Communist—we can agree has the task of furthering the Communist cause; otherwise, he is not a Communist; is that not correct?

COMMISSIONER CONANT. Quite so.

SENATOR MC CARTHY. And one of your tasks over there is to fight communism. So I assume both of us know something about the Communist movement.

Let us get back to the question: Would you favor having on your bookshelves—you are asking for $21 million—would you favor using part of that $21 million to buy the works of Communist authors and put them on your bookshelves?

COMMISSIONER CONANT. The answer is "No."

SENATOR MC CARTHY. How about the 30,000 books that are on those bookshelves by Communist authors?

COMMISSIONER CONANT. I have no information as to that, sir.

SENATOR MC CARTHY. We will give you the information, then. Our committee has developed that there are some 30,000 by Communist authors, many of them in Germany. Would you favor removing from the bookshelves the works of the Communist authors?

Keep in mind, now, I am not talking about taking the books away from your employees, by Communist authors. I think it is necessary for them to read them. I am not talking about the books explaining the workings of communism. I am speaking about the books on the bookshelves, some 30,000, by Communist authors. Would you favor removing those from the bookshelves?

COMMISSIONER CONANT.   Do you mean by "Communist authors" a member of the Communist Party who is under instructions to further its cause?

SENATOR MC CARTHY.   That is right; either a man who has been proved to be a Communist, or a man who says, "I won't tell, because if I told the truth I might go to jail."

COMMISSIONER CONANT.   I would not be in favor of having books by Communist authors on the shelves. If they are already there, I would be in favor of taking them off.

SENATOR MC CARTHY.   You would not call that book burning if you took them off, would you?

COMMISSIONER CONANT.   I suppose you wouldn't, but I wouldn't suppose that you would burn them.

SENATOR MC CARTHY.   Then we both agree, I think, on that all right.

Because of my ignorance of what the President had said twenty-four hours earlier at Dartmouth, I was unaware of the fact that by this exchange I appeared to be clearing the Senator of the charge of being a "book burner."

After some questions about the subsidization of German newspapers, the questioning turned back without warning to the books. Again I quote from the printed record:

SENATOR MC CARTHY.   I understand that you have no objection to congressional committees exposing books by Communist authors on the information bookshelves, and you have no objection to the removal of these books by Communist authors.

COMMISSIONER CONANT.   I certainly would not object to a congressional committee investigating anything and making recommendations to the executive branch on any subject.

SENATOR MC CARTHY.   I think we will pin you down to a precedent because you are asking for $21 million, much of which is to be used for an information program.

You would not consider bookburning a rather vicious thing, if we insist that you do not have the works of Communist authors on your shelves over there to indoctrinate the German people?

COMMISSIONER CONANT.   May I once again be sure we are using the the words "Communist authors" in the same way, Senator.

SENATOR MC CARTHY.   By a Communist author I mean a member of the Communist Party.

COMMISSIONER CONANT. I agree with you that books by members of the Communist Party should not be on the shelves of the American Information Service in Germany.

SENATOR MC CARTHY. And you think they should be exposed and removed from the bookshelves?

COMMISSIONER CONANT. I think they should be removed. I am inclined to think that if they could be removed without too much publicity it would be much the best course.

SENATOR MC CARTHY. In other words, do you object to the publicity attendant to exposure?

COMMISSIONER CONANT. I think in a case of this sort, if it can be done without publicity it would be much better, in view of the way in which we are operating.

SENATOR MC CARTHY. Are you aware of the fact that the bookshelves have been stocked over the past number of years—and someone is responsible for that—and that they were not ordered removed until we did publicly expose them?

Do I understand you have some objection now to that public exposure?

COMMISSIONER CONANT. I regret the public exposure. I think it would have been much better, Senator, if recommendations were made to the executive branch and they could have been removed with the minimum amount of publicity.

SENATOR MC CARTHY. Do you realize they were not removed until they publicly exposed them?

COMMISSIONER CONANT. That would be a question between the Congress and the executive branch?

SENATOR MC CARTHY. You are advising us, Doctor. You are asking for $21 million for this program. I think we are entitled to know your thinking.

Do you object to the public exposure, realizing that they were on the shelves for a number of years, that we object to their being on the shelves? I did publicly, year after year, and they were not removed until we publicly exposed the Communist authors.

Having that in mind, do you now object to our public exposure?

COMMISSIONER CONANT. I certainly don't object to anything that congressional committees do, sir.

SENATOR MC CARTHY. That is going a long way.

The Senator had won this round. Only when the session adjourned for lunch did I find out what the silly questioning about burning books was all about. McCarthy could now tell the press that the former president of Harvard was in accord with his policy about books in the libraries of the Information Service. This portion of the hearings made the afternoon papers and distressed many of my liberal friends who were not working for John Foster Dulles.

There was still more to come in the morning session, however, and more newsworthy items than the exchange of views about removing books from libraries. Before many minutes had passed, the questioning by Senator McCarthy turned to the questions I most dreaded—those dealing with individuals. (McCarthy was now acting as though he were chairman. Senator Bridges had seemed bored, and at one point McCarthy rapped on the table and said: "Mr. Chairman, may I have your attention.")

Again I must introduce the printed record, both in my own defense and in order to portray what it was like to be grilled by a skillful prosecutor whose eyes were on the headlines:

SENATOR MC CARTHY. We have been publicly exposing over the past number of months, many unusual things that occurred before you were in the State Department, you understand. We are exposing individuals like Kaghan, who was over in your department. He was gotten in there under the old regime.

I gather, from what you said, you have some reservation as to whether or not we should publicly expose these men. The question now is keeping in mind that nothing was done until we did publicly expose them.

Do you object to our publicly exposing the Communist authors and the works by those authors that have been on our bookshelves, or do you think that is a good thing, or a bad thing to expose them?

COMMISSIONER CONANT. I regret the fact that you felt it was necessary to do it publicly. I don't think it is for me, working for the United States Government, to object or not object to what congressional committees do, any more than I object or not to what the Secretary of State does.

SENATOR MC CARTHY. Then if you object, let us take a typical case. Let us take the case of Kaghan. We called to the attention of your department the fact that Kaghan, who was head of your information section, had lived with a Communist, had signed a pledge pledging he would support Communist candidates, that he had written plays that were produced by the Communist fronts and that he belonged to Communist-front organizations. We suggested that that man be gotten rid of.

Two months later he was still there. We picked him up by the scruff of his neck then, put him on public exhibition. He was gotten rid of.

Do you regret now the fact that we did that?

COMMISSIONER CONANT. I do.

SENATOR MC CARTHY. Do you think we should have left him in your department?

COMMISSIONER CONANT. I think that Mr. Kaghan was under process of resigning for a lot of his own reasons when I got there.

SENATOR MC CARTHY. I can tell you that is not true. Mr. Kaghan did not resign for his own reasons. Mr. Kaghan resigned because he was exposed because of his Communist activities.

Do you know that he was resigning for his own reasons? Tell us when you learned it and what those reasons were?

COMMISSIONER CONANT. When I arrived in HICOG, Kaghan was a name to me, and in talking over the organization it was said, "Well, Mr. Kaghan, the Deputy Director, isn't going to stay with us very long; he is going to resign before the year is out." That was the general statement that I was given.

SENATOR MC CARTHY. Who gave you that statement?

COMMISSIONER CONANT. I would be inclined to think Kaghan himself did. But I would not want to swear to that.

I have a witness here saying that my memory is correct. It is one of those things, one of the problems I would have is to find a Deputy Director because the man who was Acting Deputy Director was going.

He was cleared, you understand. Of course you know. There was no question in my mind at that time of his being a person who would not be desired on the staff. He just made up his mind he was not going on.

SENATOR MC CARTHY. You say there was no question in your mind. Is there any question now, that he should not be discharged?

COMMISSIONER CONANT. Yes. I haven't examined the evidence. The State Department, who has the responsibility for this, may have.

SENATOR MC CARTHY. Do you know a man named Lowell Clucas?

COMMISSIONER CONANT. Yes. He is Information Officer in Munich.

SENATOR MC CARTHY. Do you think he is a good man for the job?

COMMISSIONER CONANT. As far as I know, I think he is a good man for the job.

SENATOR MC CARTHY. Have you examined the testimony of Clucas?

COMMISSIONER CONANT. Yes, I have.

SENATOR MC CARTHY. And do you think Clucas is a good man for the job and you will keep him on if we give you this $21 million?

COMMISSIONER CONANT. Yes.

SENATOR MC CARTHY. I think that gives us a fairly accurate picture, Mr. Chairman, of the type of information program we can expect.

Let me say this for the record: Mr. Clucas is one of the cases which I gave the Tydings committee some 3 years ago. His record is very clear. Mr. Conant just said that Clucas is the type of man he will have running the information program. He is the same type of individual as Kaghan, with the same type of record. I named him before the Tydings committee 3 years ago. I may say if he is the type of individual that Dr. Conant is going to have running the information program, teaching the German people how they should live, I think the committee certainly should have that in mind, and I will submit to all the members of the committee a more detailed picture of this man Clucas.

I am very happy to get your answer, Doctor.

COMMISSIONER CONANT. May I state, Senator, that Clucas, I have been informed by reliable authority, has had full clearance under the Public Law 402.

SENATOR MC CARTHY. Full clearance under the Acheson program. Alger Hiss had full clearance, Kaghan had full clearance. Every traitor that has ever been exposed has had full clearance. I am getting awfully sick to hear that someone is getting full clearance because Acheson's team gave him full clearance.

As you know, they gave every man that appeared their full clearance, except three, I believe, that they finally turned down.

COMMISSIONER CONANT. There are a good many cases where they did not give full clearance, I understand, from the history of HICOG, Senator.

SENATOR MC CARTHY. You say they did not?

COMMISSIONER CONANT. I understood there were a number of people that were not cleared and were never employed.

SENATOR MC CARTHY. I may say also, Doctor, we get rather weary in our committee having someone come before us and saying, "Sure, I was a Communist 10 years ago, but there is a presumption that I have reformed." I may say that when you have been a Communist, when you have been a member of a conspiracy, there is no presumption that you have reformed. The presumption is that you remain the same unless you can prove that you have reformed.

I would like to know if you think Kaghan was the right man to be in charge of that program?

COMMISSIONER CONANT. I think there is no question about his being the right man for the program. I think he proved that while he was in charge of HICOG in fighting communism and his effective work and the letters that came to me from Germans about him. From the evidence I had, I would say he was a very effective person against communism all along the front. There is no evidence that I have— and I admit I haven't gone into it in any detail with the FBI organization—that casts any question on his loyalty in the period that he was with HICOG.

SENATOR MC CARTHY. Doctor, you come before this committee and ask American money to continue a program and then try to give clearance to a man like Kaghan and say you have not gone into the case.

Do you not think you should not try to give him clearance until you have gone into it? Do you not think you should examine the evidence before you give him clearance? Otherwise, we cannot very well trust you to pick the right man to succeed him.

Take, for example, are you aware of the fact that his superior officer in Austria wrote a report on him pointing out his activities, pointing out that he played up in the papers over there all of the sordid side of American life, that he was overly friendly to the Communist cause? This was his superior officer. Does that mean to you he was a good anti-Communist?

COMMISSIONER CONANT. I have not seen that report and have no way of evaluating it.

SENATOR MC CARTHY. Then do you not think you should not give him clearance until you have seen it?

COMMISSIONER CONANT. We were speaking of a case that was past.

SENATOR MC CARTHY. There is nothing past, Dr. Conant, about the man that you have running your information program.

COMMISSIONER CONANT. He is out.

SENATOR MC CARTHY. That is very present.

COMMISSIONER CONANT. He has resigned and was on the point of resigning when I came there. You are asking me whether I think he was a man who on the record seemed to have been an effective agent against communism. I would say, from the evidence that I have looking back at this case, which is now closed because he has resigned, my answer is "Yes."

SENATOR MC CARTHY. It is not closed, Doctor, because his twin Clucas, is still there.

But just so that we have this on the record: Your testimony today is that Kaghan is the type of individual that you would be willing to have running this information program in the future, knowing his record as you do; you say he is the type of individual that you would select to run this information program in the future?

COMMISSIONER CONANT. I don't think I said that.

SENATOR MC CARTHY. Is that true, or not?

COMMISSIONER CONANT. Because, from the point of view of Kaghan, if you are talking about the question of what he did in HICOG in fighting communism, I would say "Yes." But in evaluating a man you've got to take his total personality and his executive ability and everything else. If you are talking simply to the question of this effectiveness as an anti-Communist person, the answer is "Yes."

SENATOR MC CARTHY. That he is the type of person you would have running it?

COMMISSIONER CONANT. That is right.

SENATOR MC CARTHY. Then I say—and this is definitely on the record—I feel and think that if you feel you should have men like Kaghan and Clucas spending money over there on the information program, I do not think this Senate should give you one penny. I think you have done infinite damage if you continue to keep men like that running that program, and they will continue to do damage.

I would like to be on the record for that right at this moment.

I may say at that point I have nothing against you for what has been done in the past, because they have been brought in under the old Acheson teams. But if you are going to insist on keeping men on of the Kaghan and Clucas strain, it indicates to me that any money we spend over there on that program will be worse than wasted.

I have nothing further, Mr. Chairman.

Halfway through the afternoon session, Senator McCarthy suddenly turned to the chairman and asked if the witness was sworn. On being informed he was not because it was not usual practice in such hearings, the Senator requested that I be sworn, which I duly was. Shortly afterward McCarthy spelled out the intended insult. He said: "You know right well that the only way to get the information is to supoena the witnesses and put them under oath and either make them tell the truth or refuse to testify or get them for perjury, as Alger Hiss was gotten by a different committee."

At another point, the Senator, speaking about the information program, said:

I feel that the idea of an information program, Professor [this was the only time he so addressed me], is excellent. I think we should try to get our version of the news into the Iron Curtain countries. I have made some comments today which you may think were a bit unfriendly toward you. May I say that I have no objection to you at all as an educator. I think you did a good job. I frankly think you are not doing a good job as High Commissioner of Germany. I do not think that is because of any deliberate attempt on your part. I think you are just one of those kindly professors who thinks that "God's in His heaven, all's right with the world."

A moment or two later, he continued as follows:

I may say, Doctor, I think almost your entire problem is a problem of personnel. You have in that information program now men who had to be acceptable to an administration that has been thoroughly repudiated, an administration which stood for something entirely different from what the new administration stands for. They could not be loyal to the old administration, loyal to its policies, and now be loyal to the new administration and loyal to the new policies unless they are complete hypocrites.

I just think that you have to have a housecleaning over there, and you have not had it yet. I know it is difficult to recruit good men, but I believe the progress over in HICOG has been slow beyond words. About the only men you have gotten rid of, as far as we know, are those that the committee has publicly exposed, and we just cannot run HICOG or any other department of government by committee.

But I may say this: We are going to continue, as far as I am concerned, picking up your men and exposing them unless you get rid of them yourself.

In pursuit of the policy he had just re-emphasized, he returned again, though it was getting toward four o'clock, to the so-called security question. He now turned his fire on Glenn Wolfe, and questions about Messrs. Clucas and Kaghan were repeated. Finally he signed off, and Chairman Bridges concluded the session with this statement:

The committee, Dr. Conant, and Mr. Wolfe, is disturbed, as you are well aware, by the rumors and the stories coming to it regarding some of the individuals who are administering the programs abroad. Senator McCarthy's questioning along those lines—Dr. Conant is new there—is evidence of the doubt in the minds of members of the committee and hardly a day goes by that some information is not furnished to us.

To appropriate money with a real satisfaction that it is to be well spent, requires confidence in the personnel, and we certainly hope that you are going to review the personnel in the key positions there in light of information which has been brought to your attention which you may not have been too familiar with before.

To which Mr. Wolfe replied by saying:

I have been responsible for the security program for 4 years. I have been very proud of that security program. We have checked and rechecked every individual, German and American, in the program. I am very proud of that program. You do not hear about it. You do not read about it, but I will stack it up against any security program any place. That is from 4 years' experience with the program.

The hearing was then recessed. Scheduled for the next day was the budget of the American High Commissioner for Austria. We assumed that the committee was through with Germany. Senator McCarthy, however, had other thoughts. During the next day he let it be known he would want to examine Mr. Wolfe further and desired the presence of Mr. Clucas.

Early the next day (Tuesday), a telephone call from Lev Saltonstall urged me to see the file on Clucas myself. He said that as a member of the Appropriations Committee he had been in and out of the meeting, but as soon as he realized what was going on he knew that he could be of no help. The less he said, the better. He did want to impress on me the importance of my knowing all the facts in the case. He had seen witnesses in trouble in the past because they had relied on the reports of subordinates. I immediately turned to Wolfe. Arrangements were made for two of us to see Scott McLeod, who had recently been appointed as the chief personnel officer in the Department with special reference to security cases. He welcomed us cordially and presented a thick file on Clucas, inviting us to examine it in a nearby room. We entered and he shut the door.

It was a small room with no windows and rather strange-looking walls. I at once made up my mind that this was no ordinary chamber. We sat before a table and together turned the pages. From time to time I would make noises that indicated I was intensely interested in what I was reading but gave no hint as to whether I liked what I saw or not. Within a few minutes, Wolfe wrote on a bit of paper, "I think this room is wired." To which I wrote, "I have so assumed from the start." Wolfe put the paper in his pocket and we continued our reading, making only a few innocuous remarks to one another until the job was finished. We returned the file to Mr. McLeod without comment. I have no idea whether my suspicion was correct. I can only say that from then on I acted as though it were.

The new security officer, Scott McLeod, had some Senators and Congressmen as his ardent supporters; however, he was regarded by most of the HICOG staff as a man who took orders only from Senator McCarthy. Even in the most confidential conversations in Bonn, I refused to take a position on these views. He had been appointed by the Secretary of State; he was on good terms with powerful members of Congress. As long as I was working for President Eisenhower it was up to me to play ball with the administration in every way. Before long this meant I had to welcome as a successor to Glenn Wolfe a member of the State Department Staff who was a friend of Scott McLeod. This I did, and I was well served. But I never forgot for a moment my suspicion of the wired room.

In my personal journal for Sunday, June 27, 1953, I find the following notation, written, of course, at home in Bad Godesberg:

The Department seems to have come to life on the issue of McCarthy versus personnel. This I think I can claim credit for (but I won't). It is a result of (a) my testimony before the Senate Appropriations Committee a week ago Monday when I stood firm on Clucas and even defended Kaghan; (b) my calling Jack McCloy Wednesday when I heard Wolfe was to be called back. I told McCloy he must see Dulles and point out that Wolfe should be judged on his whole record. Jack saw Dulles and perhaps went even further than I had urged; (c) my conversation with General Bedell Smith [the Under Secretary of State] just before I left Washington on Tuesday a week ago, when I said I was going to ask the Department to stand firm on Clucas. It was too late in the afternoon for me to see Dulles as Smith wished, so he (Smith) said he would talk with the head of the German Bureau and insist on a memo from McCarthy before he would order back Wolfe and Clucas or Ewing [the head of RIAS, the radio station in Berlin]. Now the Department, according to the papers, is standing on their unwillingness to spend the money to bring the witnesses back. I hope this is solid ground. I shouldn't have thought of it. We shall see.

Obviously what had happened after my talk with the Under Secretary was a decision to challenge McCarthy but not allow him a chance to raise the question of the right of a Congressional committee to examine anyone the committee saw fit. While the majority of the committee probably had little sympathy with McCarthy's search for hidden Communist sympathizers, they would have stood with him in the face of any intimation of lack of cooperation from the executive branch of the government. Pleading the interests of saving money was a clever stroke, and it succeeded. The question of bringing back employees of HICOG was soon dropped.

For a time I was in the good graces of the newspaper correspondents in Bonn. On balance, they judged my performance before the committee as satisfactory. The sickness of the staff, however, was by no means cured. There had been too many departures of prominent persons. Writing in August, Stewart Alsop in his column characterized Bonn as a "peculiarly depressing place for a peculiarly American reason." The Americans, he wrote, were suffering from a sort of paralysis and were substituting

dogma for policy and the official line for serious original thought. The chief policy advisers here were until recently three very able professional Foreign Service officers—John Davies, Charles Thayer and Samuel Reber. Now all three are gone, at least two of them victims of McLeodism, the State Department's dutiful imitation of McCarthyism. There have been, of course, plenty of other victims and victims designate, some well known, others purged under the cover of the reduction in force program, others still waiting for the ax to fall.

After a long column along the same lines Alsop included a paragraph of hope: "A serious effort is now being made it should be said to end the reign of stupidity. Stringent orders have been issued limiting such practices as wire tapping and the use of German

Nationals as informers against American officials. More important, High Commissioner Conant, after a natural initial period of uncertainty, has let it be known that he is prepared to back loyal subordinates to the hilt."

Wolfe and Clucas were not recalled. After a few months, Wolfe was moved to another post but with no indication from any source that he was a security risk or in any way one of those whom McCarthy was trying to expose. To be sure, as I have said, he was replaced by a friend of Scott McLeod who himself visited HICOG in both Bad Godesberg and Berlin. Within a period of months, the Senator from Wisconsin was dominating the news in his rough-and-tumble encounter with the United States Army. Since television coverage of this affair, which did so much to discredit the man and some members of his staff, was not available in Germany, we could not watch the day-by-day unfolding of the story. Then came the Senate vote of condemnation. What was once a name not to be tossed about lightly faded from the news. The last time I saw Senator Joseph McCarthy, he slipped unobtrusively into the background of a committee hearing while I was testifying as United States Ambassador on the German political situation. When the chairman polling the committee said, "Senator McCarthy, have you any questions?" the almost inaudible reply came: "None." I could hardly believe my ears.

Since a onetime victim is entitled to an opinion about a hanging judge even if the judge is dead, I must give it as my opinion that those who have said McCarthy was purely an opportunist were correct. From what I knew about him in his heyday and have read about him since, I am sure he was not in the least a fanatic anti-Communist. Almost by accident, he hit pay dirt. His demagogic skills and his utter disregard of the standards of truth and decency enabled him to exploit the rich vein he had discovered.

It is difficult to write about the last years of the Truman administration and the first years of the Eisenhower Presidency without giving a completely insincere politician too much credit. Those who were sincere in their exaggerated fears of Communism and their almost neurotic hatred of the leading figures of the Truman administration have had few articles written about them. Yet they included such powerful Senators as William E. Jenner of Indiana, Patrick A. McCarran of Nevada, Herman Welker of Idaho, William Langer of North Dakota, with William F. Knowland of California and Karl Mundt of South Dakota not infrequent allies. Without them the great and malignant opportunist, Joseph McCarthy, could have lied and shouted in vain. These men I never forget. Nor do I forget the fact that the trouble started because of the disloyal conduct of at least a few whom honorable men and the American public had once trusted. Whichever side one stood on in those days of inquisition, no one will now claim they were happy days.

CHAPTER 42

Traveling Host to
Chancellor Adenauer

CHANCELLOR KONRAD ADENAUER'S FIRST VISIT to the United States took place shortly after my installation as High Commissioner. Since several matters were on the agenda in which I was directly involved, I participated in the discussions in Washington.

Quite apart from the results of these discussions, the visit was a tremendous success from the Chancellor's standpoint. He was well received both officially and in a number of private gatherings. With an eye to the forthcoming German elections, the newsreel coverage of all events was more than adequate. Indeed, during the campaign in August 1953 the Chancellor and his supporters in the Christian Democratic Union (CDU Party) were to play on the theme "He is a friend of the Americans and they are friends of Germany because of him." One of the Bundestag members told me his campaign for re-election had consisted largely of showing a film put together from the many "shots" taken of Adenauer in the United States. The size of the vote by which, at the elections in September, the CDU gained a majority of Bundestag members was unexpected.

Whether the Chancellor attributed his success to his American trip, I do not know. But it might explain his willingness to accept a second invitation to America when Columbia University offered him an honorary degree at the time of the two hundredth anniversary celebration on October 31, 1954. This time the United States Government provided the transportation. An Air Force Constellation was put

580

at the Chancellor's disposal, and I became the official host. Under ordinary circumstances, my part in the expedition would have been perfunctory. The circumstances on the return trip, however, turned out to be far from ordinary.

The Chancellor had developed an appetite for traveling. He desired to see something of Iceland and Newfoundland on the way over, as well as to spend a day in Bermuda on the way back. The Chancellor's party totaled some fifteen. I was accompanied by my assistant, Allen Siebens. The stop in Iceland was just long enough to enable the government to welcome the Chancellor and provide a short trip to see the spot where the first parliament was alleged to have met in 930 A.D. From Iceland, we flew to Harmon Field, Stephenville, Newfoundland, where the Air Force had made all necessary arrangements for dinner and sleeping quarters for the entire group.

The next day the commanding officer and members of his staff briefed the Chancellor on the purpose of the base, the nature of the planes, how they could be fueled in flight and the area over which they could fly thanks to the refueling. It was a good show, backed by exhibits of planes on the field. The Chancellor was enormously impressed. He had had no idea of the air power of the United States. One of his close associates told me later that this stop at an American Air Force base had had an impact on the Chancellor's thinking not only because of what he heard but because the Air Force officers he saw were such outstanding professional men. "The Chancellor has formed a pattern in his mind," the friend said, "of the alertness and intelligence of a military officer; it will be hard for the new German Army," he added, "to meet the standards which the Chancellor has in mind as a consequence of his experiences on his trip to the United States."

The conferences in Washington and the Chancellor's visits to several cities in which I was not involved are no part of the present story. I again took up my duties as official host only at the conclusion of the Columbia University celebration. According to our carefully drawn plans, the Air Force plane would be waiting for us at Mitchell Field. The City of New York would be the host until the party was airborne. Former Ambassador Richard C. Patterson, Jr., chief protocol officer for the City of New York, met us as we all filed out of the cathedral where the convocation had been held. It was late afternoon. A procession of four cars, preceded by an escort of motorcycle police, left the Columbia campus with horns blaring and traffic giving us the right-of-way. The Chancellor was being given the proper send-off.

In the first car, the New York City representative, the Chancellor, German State Secretary Hans von Herwarth and myself admired the rapidly changing view of the city as the convoy swept down the streets and over the bridge headed for Long Island. Both the Germans expressed appreciation of what was almost a military escort. These were part of the city police force, we were told; when we reached the city limit, another escort provided by the county would take over and we would never notice the change, said our New York City host. We were driving along a parkway in the growing darkness when suddenly it became apparent to all of us that our police escort had vanished without a sign. The procession drove on. "There has been some mix-up," said Ambassador Patterson. "But it doesn't matter," he added in a reassuring voice, "the driver knows the way. Don't you, driver?" "No, sir, I am sorry I don't," came back the disconcerting answer. "Well, we will ask the other drivers then; just stop and go back and ask for directions," said our official host. Our chauffeur followed directions but, alas, without result; no one of the drivers had any idea of where we were or the way to Mitchell Field.

By now it was dark, the headlights had been turned on. We were lost and needed help. A passing auto was hailed and the obvious question asked. No one knew anything about Mitchell Field, but one of the occupants reported that a few minutes back, they passed a policeman standing at a crossroad. If we took a road to the right we would come across him shortly, which we did. Ambassador Patterson asked his chauffeur to speak to the police officer. "Just jump out and tell him we are an official party with the Chancellor of Germany and we want a police escort," he said. While the procession waited, our driver went over a few paces to where the policeman stood. He returned quickly and said: "Boss, I told the cop the Chancellor of Germany was in the car and we had lost our way. He wouldn't believe me; he thought I was kidding. 'Are you sure it isn't the Crown Prince of Ethiopia?' he said. But he did tell me how to find Mitchell Field."

Protocol was abandoned and, without an escort, we made our way to the field. The Constellation was waiting; we took off at once for Bermuda. On arrival a few hours later, the Chancellor was given proper attention by the Governor and his staff, while I spent the night with the American Consul.

The plans to have a leisurely visit in Bermuda's sunshine had been compressed because of the death of President of the Bundestag, the third-ranking man in Bonn, Hermann Ehlers. The funeral was to be held on Wednesday, November 3, in Oldenburg. The Chancellor said he absolutely must be present. We assumed he would speak, as such was the custom at German Protestant funeral services. The fact that Ehlers was the Protestant pillar of the CDU made his sudden death a particularly heavy blow for the Chancellor and added to the significance of his attending the state funeral. The timetable of our return journey had been suitably altered. A good night's sleep in Bermuda and at least six hours of sightseeing were arranged.

I was looking forward to seeing the Bermuda landscape, which I had enjoyed some thirteen years before while on my way to England to bring American aid to Britain's defense against the German power. The Chancellor at that time had been a prisoner of the Nazis. Now the head of the German Government, he was the guest of the Governor General of Bermuda, who officiated in the name of the Queen Elizabeth II. I ran over those thoughts as I went to bed that night.

A downpour awakened me. It had started raining before dawn and continued without letup until well after lunch. Siebens and I stayed indoors. The Chancellor saw almost nothing of the beauty of the island, although the time of departure was delayed as long as was possible for some sightseeing. When the heavy rain had ceased, we climbed aboard the Constellation and taxied down the runway. The pilot was just about to open up the throttle for the take-off when Chancellor Adenauer discovered he had lost his formal black overcoat. "I cannot attend the funeral without that overcoat," he declared in such plain and determined German that even I had no difficulty in understanding. Radio was brought into action. The airport and the various stopping places during the afternoon visits were searched. No overcoat, no clues.

"We can't wait any longer; we are two hours behind schedule now," said State Secretary von Herwarth, who had been pushed by Siebens on behalf of the Air Force pilot to make the declaration. "I will buy him an overcoat in Oldenburg before the funeral," he added. The plane again taxied to position and once again was poised to go down the take-off runway, when an automobile came rushing across the field. The Chancellor's overcoat had been found. With hardly a word of thanks on our side or explanation on the other, the all-important garment was taken aboard and we were really off.

An American air base on one of the islands of the Azores group was our breakfast stop. The adjusted schedule required our sleeping aboard the plane in transit. The Chancellor had been willing to undergo the discomforts of trying to sleep in a berth because of his desire to see Bermuda. I had a bunk as well. The rest of the party sat up and got what sleep they could.

We arrived at the Air Force base just at breakfast time. A short stop for refueling had been so scheduled as to allow the passengers a leisurely first meal of the day. An hour went by and then two, and I asked Siebens to find out what was wrong. After checking with the pilot and the commanding officer of the base, he reported the airplane radio was out of order and was in process of being fixed. Another hour and a conference with the base commander brought out the troublesome fact that what was out of order was not easily remedied. Unfortunately, no other plane was available. Ordinarily two extra planes were on hand, but the day before they had been dispatched on an emergency mission. We seemed to be plagued by bad luck.

We drove around a bit, visited a small church said to be the oldest in the Azores. The Chancellor expressed his admiration of what Salazar had done for Portugal. I rather gathered he envied him because as a dictator he was not worried by any assembly of politicians. The Chancellor said that Salazar was a highly intelligent man who knew what his country needed and was able to put into effect the necessary measures. We also examined the Air Force maps and talked a little about global strategy.

A few days later on thinking back on the many hours spent with Chancellor Adenauer on this trip, I gave myself low marks as a diplomat. A man with an instinct for international work or a well-trained Foreign Service officer would have used the time to draw out the head of the German Government. Early in the return trip, however, the Chancellor had shown no interest in discussing German politics, which, at that moment, was going through one of its crises. Therefore the one thing which was not mentioned as we waited for the radio to be repaired was the past, present and future of the German parties. The Chancellor was a reserved man. I leaned over backward to respect his privacy; my attitude looked at from the point of view of the interests of the United States was undoubtedly a mistake.

I hardly need say that I had an enormous admiration for the man. If before long I am able to write a full account of my four years in Germany, I shall have an opportunity to evaluate Konrad Adenauer's place in history. Meanwhile, I may simply record that I shall always count it my great good fortune to have seen as much of Chancellor Adenauer as I did. His vision of a European community, though it seems to have failed, was a noble one; it served well both the rehabilitation of the German people and the cause of freedom. I am sure the historians will rank him as a statesman in the same category as Roosevelt and Churchill.

Finally, the radio equipment was declared to be in good working order. We were three hours late, which meant we should arrive in Hamburg too late for dinner, but we would still be in plenty of time for a night's rest before the two-hour drive to Oldenburg the morning of November 3. I felt quite content when Siebens came down from the cockpit, where he had been visiting with the Air Force officers and announced that we were just passing over London and would land in Hamburg about half-past ten. Then, without warning, the scene completely changed. A crew member asked Siebens to go forward. He returned with a long face. The airport at Hamburg was closed by fog and was likely to remain closed at least till morning. Bremen was just closing. Within a few minutes we had to face the hard facts that we had only two choices—Munich or Paris—and we had better decide at once.

A general conference took place. For the first time, the German Chancellor's voice betrayed a worry. He would not land in France; there would be too many protocol problems. Who would receive him? How could he get away politely in the early morning to get to Oldenburg in time? Munich was ruled out. The train trip was too long. Even if a private train could be made ready by the time we might land (well after midnight), we could not get to our destination by 10:30 the next morning. We were in what appeared to be an impossible situation.

A thought suddenly occurred to me. I had been in a not dissimilar situation once before. On the trip to Moscow with Secretary Byrnes in December 1945, Byrnes had refused to enter Paris and had insisted on remaining in the American Air Force installation at Orly Field. As long as he stayed within the limits of the base he was on U.S. territory, he had maintained, and was under no obligation to be in touch with the French Foreign Minister or any member of his staff.

Why not stay in the United States portion of Orly as guests of the American Air Force? I suggested. The Chancellor liked the idea. A little calculation showed, however, that the two-hour drive from Hamburg to Oldenburg still might wreck the plan. The fog was unlikely to lift before eight or nine, too late to make the drive fit into a schedule which demanded the Chancellor's presence in the cathedral by 10:30. To ask for the postponement of a state funeral for even a few minutes was not to be considered. Bremen was much nearer; if we reached that city instead of Hamburg the next morning, we might get to Oldenburg on time.

So we radioed to the Air Force headquarters in Orly, stating who we were and whom we had on board. We landed in a heavy rainstorm with only a few minutes' warning and were met by an Air Force Major who was far from glad to see us. He said he was just making plans to send us into Paris to be put up as guests of the French Government at an excellent hotel. "I am sorry," said I in my capacity as High Commissioner, "this won't do at all." I explained our predicament and why we must be free from protocol so that our plane could take off for Bremen as soon as its airport opened up. "Please put us up in the officers' club," I asked. The Major replied it was impossible; the club was in process of renovation. There were no beds, only debris left by carpenters and plasterers. He was adamant in his refusal to let us stay under his jurisdiction. I was equally firm and ably seconded by Allen Siebens. "You must have a folding cot or two and some room or rooms where they could be set up," we said.

Reluctantly the Major led us to a building, the state of which was evidence of the truth of his story. Still, three cots were found. Two were opened up in one room for the Chancellor and his bodyguard, who was under German orders never to leave him under any circumstances. The other cot was set up for me in the midst of plasterer's equipment in another room. Siebens and Herwarth sat down with telephones and started an all-night job of changing plans, including the moving of the High Commissioner's train from Hamburg to Oldenburg. On it were my formal clothes, essential if I was also to attend the funeral. The other members of the party sat up in the plane all night.

The Chancellor looked at the accommodations with quiet amusement, said almost nothing and certainly demanded nothing, which was just as well, since nothing in the way of food or drink was on hand. In short, he was an excellent sport, making the best of a bad situation. Whether he could attend the funeral was still an open question. It all depended on when the fog would lift in Bremen. We left instructions to be called at any time in the early morning if a favorable report arrived from Bremen.

We were all in our plane seats shortly after 7 A.M. Siebens reported the train had been moved. The Chancellor's clothes were on another train in the Oldenburg station, which was to be reached by cars from the Bremen airport. It was going to be close, but the prediction was that the way would be clear by the time our plane arrived over Bremen. A delay in our departure from Orly due to local conditions did not quiet our nerves.

A little after eight we were airborne, and an hour later we landed at Bremen. Two cars and a few bewildered German officials were waiting. The Chancellor took off in his car, which in a moment disappeared from sight. He loved to drive fast, and this was an occasion when his passion for speed seemed justified. The driver of the car into which Siebens and I had been placed tried to keep up. We got a glimpse of the Chancellor's car as we rolled through Bremen with little regard for traffic. When we hit the open country once again, the lead car went out of sight. Not that we loitered. Our German driver was on his mettle. The road was paved with cobblestones, it had been raining. We bounced and slithered for the most dangerous three-quarters of an hour I have ever spent. As we pulled up at the Oldenburg station, I noticed the Chancellor had already arrived and must be in his train changing his clothes. I wasted not a minute. The formal clothes were laid out. As I climbed into them, I could hear over the radio in the train the funeral services, which had already started. Had we arrived too late?

Rushing out of the train through the station and jumping into the automobile, I headed for the cathedral, which we had passed a few blocks back in our hectic journey. With all the composure and dignity I could collect, I entered the cathedral. Just as I came in I saw the Chancellor of the German Federal Republic rise from his seat (which he could not have occupied more than five minutes), walk calmly and slowly to a position beside the coffin and start his funeral oration. My mission as host was ended. I had delivered the Chancellor to President Ehlers' funeral.

CHAPTER 43

_____

An Ambassador at Last

W HEN I CALLED ON President Heuss in February 1953, I was a High Commissioner. He assumed and I assumed that it would be only a matter of months before I called again to present my credentials as United States Ambassador. Actually, a little over two years went by before the Allied High Commission was abolished and the three High Commissioners became ambassadors. To explain the causes of the long delay would be to write the book I hope someday to write on German postwar politics. In it would be sketched the incredibly tortuous process by which the French and the German governments came to an agreement on how the Federal Republic of Germany would make a military contribution to the defense of Europe. Here I shall deal only with what might be called the death throes of the French resistance to granting West Germany a place among sovereign nations.

The idea of forming a European Army in which the German units would be incorporated went up in oratorical smoke in the late summer of 1954. Then followed what all trained diplomatic observers and knowledgeable newsmen said could never happen. Three new treaties were drawn up; a German Army was authorized; the Federal Republic was invited to join the North Atlantic Treaty Organization. One of the basic ideas in the former treaties, which had been signed in May 1952 (but never ratified by France), had been abandoned. There would be no automatic check on the possibility that a rearmed Germany could once again threaten the peace of Europe. The liberalization of the terms of German rearmament had not been the Chancellor's idea nor that of any important group of German politicians. It had been a consequence of France's refusal to pool her military strength in a European Army.

The new treaties were signed in Paris after a highly important conference of the occupying powers in London in October 1954. It would appear that at last everything was settled. But not at all. The diplomatic mills still had months of grinding ahead of them. Turning the pages of history of the year 1955, it seems as if the end of the Allied High Commission were so inevitable that everyone should have been patient with the recurring obstacles to final action. I can certify that it did not seem so to me and my advisers. We prepared to shift in a few days from a High Commissioner's office to an embassy, only to be confronted by one development after another, each of which threatened to jeopardize the ratification of the new treaties. The thought hung over us that once again the treaties would have to be re-negotiated—another London conference would have to be called.

The day before Christmas in 1954, the morning radio announced that the French Assembly late at night had voted 280 to 260 to reject one of the set of new treaties. The French Premier, Pierre Mendès-France, had put all the treaties on the block and had asked for a vote of confidence at the first meeting of the Assembly after the holiday recess. Remembering the rejection by the French Assembly of the old treaties, no one was in a mood to celebrate Chrismas Eve. Nevertheless the French High Commissioner, François-Poncet, and his charming wife, of whom we were very fond, had asked the Conants to a nondiplomatic dinner. As we were introduced to the other guests at this delightful, completely French party, not a word was said about the action of the French Assembly. I did allow myself one mild outlet of my pent-up resentment. A high-ranking French General said to me in perfect English, "Oh, you are the American High Commissioner for Germany. The Germans are a most difficult people." To which I replied, "To us Americans, all Europeans seem difficult people."

Mendès-France received his vote of confidence. The ratification process was back on the track, but before it could be completed the government fell. Then it was the turn of the German politicians to make trouble. This difficulty was of short duration; in March President Heuss signed for Germany and the French completed their ratification action. In my notes for Sunday, March 27, 1955, I wrote: "So it seems that at long last the Paris treaties are ratified." Yet a week later there is an entry indicating the date for depositing the treaties had not been settled and the French were being "difficult" again. In my ignorance I had not known that ratification followed by signatures of the heads of state did not bring a treaty into force. Copies must be deposited. To be sure, usually such deposition is only a matter of form and takes place at once. There was nothing usual, however, about a treaty involving Germans and Frenchmen. Bargaining about another treaty of an economic nature affecting the Saar seemed to be delaying the very last step of a journey which had been tiresome to say the least. The patience of Washington was wearing thin. With no advance notice, I was ordered to deposit in Bonn on behalf of the United States the two treaties to which the American Government was a party. The cable contained the proviso "assuming the Chancellor approves." The Chancellor was delighted when I informed him of my instructions. The British and French were notified but were not ready to join in a tripartite ceremony.

On the morning of Wednesday, April 20, 1955, I appeared at the Chancellor's office with the treaties and a twelve-line formal speech in German which I had learned by heart. Committing anything to memory has always been a painful task for me; the strain was worse when a statement in German was involved. I was so nervous that my hand was visibly shaking when I signed the necessary documents. This fact was noted by one of the American reporters in his dispatch, but the nervousness was taken as evidence of how deeply I was moved by taking part in this historic event. At the last moment, the Chancellor decided to deposit the copies signed by President Heuss.

Since the formal request to the German Government about my appointment as Ambassador had been already made, I was confident that, together with my French and British colleagues, I should be shortly received as an ambassador. The time for the ceremony had been set for Thursday noon, May 5, 1955. The protocol officers of the three High Commissioners and the Foreign Office had been in consultation. Each ambassador designate had been asked to arrive at the President's reception rooms in full evening attire. He was to be accompanied by four or five members of his staff, likewise in white tie and tails. The procurement of the requisite number of tall silk hats was a problem. A few of the group were forced to compromise by borrowing opera hats. We were all to assemble in the High Commissioner's office and proceed by car to the President's reception hall, arriving after the French High Commissioner and just before the British. A split-second schedule had been written out.

On Tuesday a worrisome message came from Washington. The

Senate Foreign Relations Committee had not yet acted on my name. What an embarrassing situation I should be in if my appointment as Ambassador had not been confirmed by Thursday noon Bonn time.

On Wednesday evening I talked over the transatlantic phone with Cecil Lyon, now the head of the German desk in the State Department. When he was chief of the Berlin mission in 1953, he had been most helpful to me, a neophyte in the Foreign Service. If there was anybody in the officialdom of Washington with whom I should not have spoken in anger, it was Cecil. Yet when he told me it was impossible for my appointment to be confirmed before noon the next day, my wrath boiled over. I more than implied it was all the fault of the German desk. I would be left diplomatically naked when the clock struck twelve noon. Cecil was distressed but powerless. I went to bed with thoughts of slaying the Washington bureaucrats so vivid as to make relaxed sleep impossible.

A meeting with the High Commissioner's staff the first thing in the morning was a cooling process. I was reminded that I would be Chief of Mission even if I was neither High Commissioner nor Ambassador. The drafting of the following cable, particularly the last sentence, gave a certain amount of satisfaction:

For Secretary from Conant. We are issuing at 10:30 A.M. today our time following statement: As the U.S. Senate has not yet confirmed the appointment of Dr. Conant as Ambassador he will not be able to present his credentials today. Dr. Conant will call on President Heuss today to present the personal felicitations of President Eisenhower on the attainment of German sovereignty and to say that his credentials will be presented with the usual ceremonies when his appointment has been confirmed. I am attending dinner this evening in my capacity as former High Commissioner. If asked by press will state that I am continuing here as Chief of Mission according to presidential commission dated February 7, 1953, with personal rank of Ambassador according to letter dated June 17, 1953. I have just told my French colleague of this awkward situation. He smiled and said he thought such a thing could happen only in France.

The reference to the personal rank of ambassador was a product of that morning's staff meeting. I had forgotten that in June of 1953 the Chancellor had expressed the hope that the three High Commissioners could be referred to as ambassadors, though in terms of diplomatic protocol they were not. The three governments had acquiesced. However, very little, if any, use had been made of the title. Now I could cling to it like a bit of stray clothing.

In strict terms, however, I had no place on the list of accredited diplomats, a fact which caused a slight and amusing embarrassment the following evening. The British Ambassador, as he now was, was the host for a dinner in honor of the French Ambassador, as he now was. The Conants had been invited on the assumption that I, too, would be a "real Turtle," to quote from Alice in Wonderland. The British protocol officer responsible for the seating was in a quandary; two of our friends, the ambassadors from other countries, were certainly full-fledged ambassadors.

Just how we were placed and in what order we went out to dinner, I cannot now remember. I do recall, however, our hostess' confusion and the friendly comments on our predicament.

On Saturday, May 14, I did present my credentials to President Heuss. Unfortunately, it had not been possible to arrange a formal call before the President had had to go to Bad Kissingen for a cure. He was quite willing to receive me informally in the hotel of this health resort. Therefore, accompanied only by my personal assistant, Allen Siebens, I flew in an Air Force plane to Schweinfurt. From there we drove by car to Bad Kissingen. I was welcomed without any ceremony by the President in a sitting room of the hotel, I handed him my credentials, and thus at long last became Ambassador Extraordinary and Plenipotentiary to the Government of the German Federal Republic.

A week earlier, Mrs. Conant and I had flown to Paris for a few days. A NATO meeting was to start on Monday. Sunday, May 8, we had a delightful luncheon with the Secretary and Mrs. Dulles on the terrace of the Trianon Palais Hotel in Versailles. The day was warm and sunny. Paris was looking its best. And with good weather, few if any cities in the world can compete with Paris in May with the chestnut trees in full bloom. During lunch, the Secretary reported that William Clark of Princeton, New Jersey, the former Chief Justice of the American High Commission courts in the American Zone, had insisted on being heard as a witness against me before the Foreign Relations Committee of the Senate. There had been difficulty assembling a quorum. We talked for a few minutes about Clark, with the result that on May 10 I sent the Secretary, at his request, a memorandum which became the basis for a libel suit in the United States in 1957.

What had happened in Washington at the hearing on my appointment as Ambassador is best recounted by quoting from a story that was printed in the Boston *Globe* under a Washington dateline of May 5, 1955. After reporting in the opening sentence that the Senate

Foreign Relations Committee had unanimously approved my appointment as Ambassador, the story stated that "the committee's action was tantamount to a tribute to Conant's role as a diplomat because it was taken after the committee behind closed doors had listened to an intense appeal from the former chief justice of Allied Courts in West Germany to reject Conant." Among the criticisms Clark directed against me were that as High Commissioner I had encouraged the release of German war criminals and I had failed to uphold the rights of American citizens.

The events which had so disturbed the former Chief Justice had occurred in late 1953. They revolved about the proceedings in the court in Frankfurt over which William Clark had presided since 1948, when he was appointed Chief Justice of the Military Government Courts in the U.S. Zone by the Military Governor of the zone. Before the war Clark had been a member of the U.S. Circuit Court of Appeals for the Third Circuit. His best friends admitted he was a judge with strong opinions sometimes expressed in unorthodox ways.

When the Military Governor was followed by a High Commissioner, the court system was continued and the courts' civil jurisdiction extended to include nearly all types of civil action, "thus furnishing a forum for the adjudication of disputes between members of the local population and of the occupation community as well as disputes involving only the latter." (The quotation is from J. J. McCloy's final report as High Commissioner.)

I had not been in office long before my legal adviser, F. A. O. Schwarz, told me of the troubles that were coming to a head in Frankfurt. The existence side by side of two legal systems was in itself an invitation to trouble. Disagreements were certain to arise over the jurisdiction of the American and the German court systems. Even before I came, the High Commissioner's legal staff was in disagreement on a number of issues with a group of American lawyers who had settled in Frankfurt for the duration of the occupation. The fact that the German legal system was so different from the American kept popping up in a way to confuse the American reporters who were attempting to record the growing break between Judge Clark and his friends on the one hand and the High Commissioner's Office on the other.

In October 1953 it became necessary to amend the legislation which was the basis of the authority of the HICOG courts. This I could do as High Commissioner. HICOG Law 37 was promulgated to prevent actions in HICOG courts against German officials by private citizens. I had been advised by Schwarz, as general counsel, and the legal staff that such an amendment of the law was necessary because a decision in the Court of Appeals, over which Clark presided, had cleared the way for calling a German judge and prosecutor before a U.S. court on a complaint by an American businessman.

The law as amended provided that action in the HICOG courts against German judges and other officials could only be instituted if authorized by the High Commissioner. What was made plain was that relations between the German authorities and the Americans were the responsibility of the United States High Commissioner and not the judges of the American courts. The Germans liked the change, of course. The American lawyers did not. Open warfare soon broke out. Within a month, charges against the High Commissioner and his staff were being aired in the *Stars and Stripes*.

The Association of American Lawyers in Germany claimed that the High Commissioner's Office had been guilty of wiretapping and appointed Judge Clark to head a committee to investigate. The Association passed a resolution demanding the repeal of Law 37. In support of this demand, the resolution declared that "the annulment of judicial decisions by executive fiats is repugnant to the concept of a separation of powers and an independent judiciary which we deem so essential under a democratic form of government."

Needless to say, our position in Bonn had not been taken without consulting with Washington. The people on the German desk were well aware of the public and private statements of Judge Clark. They agreed with me that the situation was intolerable. The Secretary of State himself decided to advise me to advise Clark that his appointment in the Foreign Service, which expired on January 8, 1954, would not be renewed and to request him to return to Washington for consultation. On receiving the messages, Clark turned his fire away from the High Commissioner and his staff and directed it toward Washington. In a statement to the press, he said that he had been fired by the State Department for failing to take orders; that he would ignore his dismissal and continue to hold court; that he had been ordered back to the United States for consultation, but he was not going to go. He was the Chief Justice of an independent court, he said, and added that it would take much more than locking the door to keep him from his bench.

The affair was now something more than local news for the *Stars and Stripes*. The United Press dispatch from Frankfurt on December 10, 1953, reported: "The U.S. courts in Germany are snarled in a unique legal tangle tonight with two judges trying to sit in the same chief justice's chair." What had happened was that we had been successful in persuading one of Clark's associates on the Court of Appeals to accept the position of Chief Justice. He was sworn in by me in Frankfurt. The picture of the ceremony which was published in the *New York Times*, I must admit, shows the High Commissioner with a rather self-satisfied smile.

The newly appointed Acting Chief Justice, Carl W. Fulghum, had announced that the next session of the Court of Appeals would be on January 18, ten days after the appointment of his predecessor was to expire. We hoped Clark would see the light and, after having made his protest, would follow the State Department order and return to the United States. He remained adamant. The backbone of the German desk now stiffened. I suggested in a letter to Under Secretary Smith that since the judge was going to spend the Christmas holidays in the Canary Islands, the United States Consul might pick up his passport and mark it as good for return to the United States only. The suggestion appealed to General Smith. The night before Christmas the decision was made to put the plan into operation. I was on vacation in Florence, but my deputy, Walter Dowling, said over the phone, quite correctly, that I was in favor of going ahead.

A year and some months had passed since the Department refused to reappoint Judge Clark and picked up his new passport good for Germany. In the meantime, his demands for a passport had merged with a general move on the part of a number of persons to modify the power of the State Department over such documents. If a passport was to be withheld, good and ample reasons must be given. Hence, Secretary Dulles' request to me at the lovely lunch in Versailles on Sunday, May 8. My reply, which to my surprise was later to become a public document, read as follows:

AMERICAN EMBASSY
BONN
May 10, 1955

MEMORANDUM
TO: *Secretary of State*
FROM: *Ambassador Conant*
SUBJECT: *Judge Clark's Passport*

Following our conversation on Sunday, and at your request, I am submitting my views about Judge Clark's passport.

It has been my position from the start that Judge Clark's application for a passport should be denied as long as the United States was an Occupying Power in Germany. The ground for the denial, I have suggested, would be that the Judge's irresponsible conduct and his public utterances have greatly embarrassed the United States as an Occupying Power in the past, and that there was no assurance that these incidents would be but repeated in the future. He was *persona non grata* to the United States Government, and the United States High Commissioner, who had the power to expel him, therefore has inherent power to refuse his admittance to a country occupied by the United States Forces. With the end of the occupation regime it would be my view that these objections cease *except* as regards his admission to Berlin which is still under occupation control. Therefore I would recommend the issuance of a passport marked with some such statement "Not Valid For Entry Into Berlin," and would suggest that any publicity emphasize the distinction between Clark's entering the Sovereign Federal Republic of Germany and occupied territory.

I have no doubt that Clark will make himself very objectionable to me as Ambassador, but this prospect I would not think was sufficient ground for denying a passport. If he libels the German Judges as he has in the past the Germans will be in a position now to take whatever action they think appropriate.

The memorandum I had supposed was confidential. But in connection wtih a litigation in the United States District Court about Clark's passport, it was introduced in open court. On reading it, Clark wrote to me at once. He charged me with libel and said I might think my statement was privileged but he could assure me it was not. There is no privilege, he wrote, if there is malice, and he stated that he could show malice in my case. From time to time, I received letters repeating the charge. I paid no attention to them. Just before I left Bonn in late 1956, Clark attempted to sue me in a German court. There was a certain amount of publicity, to which Clark was not adverse. But, as he must have known full well, a German court had no jurisidiction over an ambassador.

Then came what might have been a grandstand play. In February 1957 after my services as Ambassador were ended, I was to give three lectures at Princeton University. Clark planned to have me served with a court summons on the steps of the Princeton lecture hall. President Dodds got wind of the scheme and arranged to have me served in his house before the lecture. As a consequence, the only press story was a small item in the back pages of the *New York Times*. The suit was pressed by Clark. I was defended by the United States Attorney General's Office. I retained a Boston firm as a double protection. All agreed that the issue was whether or not a statement by an official made in response to a request from a superior officer was absolutely privileged. If the judge agreed, the suit would be dismissed.

If not, a jury trial would be in order to determine whether or not there was malice.

Before the court ruled, William Clark died on a trip to Ceylon. I understand that a decision by the Supreme Court has now created a clear precedent that such a memorandum as mine is absolutely privileged and the writer cannot be held to have committed libel irrespective of the question of malice.

CHAPTER 44

Concerning the Russians

T HE FOURTH HIGH COMMISSIONER for Germany, the representative of the Soviet Government, remains to be introduced. To meet him I had to travel to free Berlin and then by automobile to the Soviet Sector. His complete separation from the three High Commissioners of the Western Powers symbolized the failure of the attempt to govern occupied Germany on a four-power basis. A four-power control of air safety and of the Spandau Prison, which housed the German war criminals, were all that was left in 1953 of the first postwar arrangements.

There had been no attempt since the end of the blockade to convene a four-power council for all Germany. Nor had there been any effort to persuade a Russian general to occupy a vacant seat in what had been the four-power command center (Kommandatura) which had once ruled all of Berlin. The three Allied generals, each in command in his own sector, met regularly to determine joint policy. The same building was used as in the first days. But now only the flags of the United States, Great Britain and France flew when the joint meeting was in session. The fourth flagpole was bare.

The relation between the three Allied generals and the commanding officers in the Soviet Sector varied with the political weather. During my four years in Germany the fluctuations were extreme. In February 1953, the time of my first visit to Berlin, the skies were clear, but one could hardly say the sun was shining. Rather, many signs showed that a storm was brewing, the most dramatic being the ever-increasing stream of refugees—those people who were "voting with their feet"—who showed their distrust and loathing of the Soviets and their puppets. The American Mission nonetheless continued the formally correct diplomatic liaison with the top-ranking Soviet general, who was the Russian High Commissioner. I had been instructed by Washington to pay a courtesy call on General Vasili Ivanovich Chuikov, the Soviet High Commissioner, during my first visit to the former German capital. Since a member of the American staff met from time to time with an officer of the Soviet Mission, it was easy to make the arrangements.

At that time, the headquarters of the Russian occupation forces were located in Karlshorst, a suburban portion of East Berlin. Accompanied by the liaison officer of the American Berlin Mission, I drove to the Russian headquarters after luncheon on the second of my two days in Berlin. I was told that ordinarily the trip would be short; one could drive directly from the American Sector to Karlshorst without going into the center of the city. However, just as we were about to start, word came that the usual crossing point between the Soviet and American sectors had been closed. The action appeared to be part of those continuing activities of the Soviets which had so disturbed the American Mission. First, the electric surface-car line had been cut; now a number of access points for automobiles were being closed.

The news provided me with an opportunity to make a personal protest directly to the Soviet High Commissioner. I did not then realize how few would be such opportunities in the future. Since we were late, my first words after the formal greeting were those of apology for my tardiness. Speaking through my liaison officer, who was fluent in Russian, I explained that the usual sector crossing point was closed. Therefore I had been forced to take a long drive through the city. I added something to the effect that I regretted that the traffic between our two sectors was now restricted. General Chuikov at once replied that he was sorry; there had been no intention of causing me difficulty, and steps would be taken to remedy the situation.

The atmosphere was hospitable and friendly. We drank the appropriate toasts to our respective governments and to each other. The Soviet High Commissioner expressed the hope that our relationship would be as close as that which he had enjoyed with Mr. McCloy, of whom he spoke warmly. The cordiality did not surprise me. McCloy himself had told me that he had got on famously with the General.

Of course, those were the days before the signing of the treaties in May 1952. There were, to be sure, many problems in Berlin even then; access to the Soviet Sector was to some extent controlled; East German currency was different from that which circulated in the West. But no threatening steps to cut Berlin in two had yet been taken. It was perhaps a little strange that the Soviet High Commissioner said that he expected that our future relations would be the same as those during the McCloy regime. Perhaps the General was not himself enthusiastic about the new policy of reprisal which it was his duty to support. At least one West German writer familiar with East Berlin politics in 1953 has expressed the view that the Soviet High Commissioner and the high officials of the puppet regime did not at that time see eye to eye.

One result of my brief visit to Karlshorst was as pleasing as it was unexpected. By late afternoon word spread that the sector crossing was open once again. I was credited with this relaxation of a minor Soviet harassment, not publicly but in private conversation. I had told the story to a group of leading Berliners that evening at my house. They were quick to acclaim me as a man who had opened up a sector crossing. The story went the rounds. I had said nothing to the press representative with whom I met just after my courtesy call on General Chuikov. I reported only that our conversation had been social and that no matters of substance had been discussed. I had no intention of making a quite minor incident into a public challenge of the new Russian policy of clamping down on traffic between their sector and the other three.

The storm which was brewing in February became a reality in June. On the seventeenth of that month, the famous East Berlin uprising occurred. The workers vented their anger against the Communist regime. The East Berlin police were not able to control the situation. Russian tanks were finally ordered into the city. The protesters, armed only with stones and cudgels, were arrested or dispersed. The day all this happened, I was in Washington being cross-examined by Senator McCarthy. The French High Commissioner was in the chair and thus was spokesman for all three High Commissioners. Several of my staff later said I had been lucky to be out of Germany when the revolt took place. Otherwise I should have been under pressure from the American newspaper correspondents in Berlin and Bonn to take some immediate action to show sympathy with those who were defying the power of the East German Government and the Soviet authority. Yet action could be taken only by the Allied High Commission.

By the time I got to Berlin three days later, nothing had been done and nothing said by the Allied powers. As a concession to American opinion, I wrote a public letter to General Chuikov protesting the complete closing of all crossing points between the United States and Soviet sectors. Reaffirmation of the right of free circulation through all of Berlin was at best a mild gesture. And it came from only one of the three representatives of the Allies. Washington would have vetoed anything more drastic. A three-power statement was out of the question. London and Paris had little sympathy with the uprising. The British High Commissioner returned in a worried state from an interrupted vacation. He suggested that if the East Berliners were encouraged to insult the Soviet occupation forces, some of the West Germans might start making riotous protests against the American or the British or the French. Equating the legality of all occupying forces in Berlin may have been formally correct, but it in no way corresponded with the mood of the Berliners or the Americans in Berlin.

A fundamental issue continued to bedevil the Allied High Commission for months. The three governments were not of one mind as regards the uprising. The smoldering disagreement made a vigorous joint policy impossible. Without a policy, public relations are difficult, to say the least. The United States was continuing to work closely with the Berlin Government; American economic aid had been, and would continue to be, large. People tended to think of us as *the* occupying power. Yet any decision involving relations with the East Germans or the Soviets had to be made on a tripartite basis, a fact the newsmen continually ignored. All three High Commissioners received low marks from the press for their inaction during and after the revolt. The American High Commissioner in particular was judged to have fallen on his face. Given the temper of the times, the judgment was as inevitable as it was unfair.

The lack of understanding between the Russian occupying forces and the East German Communists may have been an important factor in the demonstrations in East Berlin. At all events, one of the results was the replacement of General Chuikov as Soviet High Commissioner by a civilian. Ambassador Vladimir Semyenov took charge. His office was moved from the military headquarters at Karlshorst to the refurbished Russian Embassy on Unter den Linden not far from the famous Brandenburg Gate, which then served as a crossing point between the British and Soviet sectors.

The new Soviet High Commissioner was completely different from his predecessor. He was a member of the Russian foreign service, a trained and experienced diplomat obviously under orders to pour oil on the waves. As an individual, he was charming, a lover of music and the arts; piano playing, he once told my wife, was his chief interest in life.

In early January 1954 the Berlin conference of the four foreign ministers took place. For three weeks the city was transformed. The offices of the American Mission were flooded by State Department personnel from Washington, including several "old German hands." The resident Berlin staff and the High Commissioner were courteously but firmly pushed aside. Similar if less drastic changes were made at the British and French headquarters. I do not doubt that if we had been able to talk on a personal, confidential basis with Semyenov, we would have discovered that he also had been forced to make many rearrangements in order to care for Mr. Molotov and a considerable number of his Moscow staff.

The conference marked the high point in cordiality between the Soviet and American High Commissioners. During those days the existence of a sector border was hardly admitted even in private conversation. Western officials and their families were encouraged to visit the Soviet Sector. Every effort was made by the Soviets to make the formal receptions which they gave gala affairs. Those when all four foreign ministers were present were occasions when the High Commissioners and their wives were expected to do what they could to make the evening at least pleasant if not gay. Since Semyenov spoke German, there was no serious language barrier. I remember one occasion when we had a long discussion on modern architecture. The new university building in Moscow, I had heard, was being built to conform to the previous style of official buildings. I expressed surprise that the Soviet Union was not in the forefront of modern thought. Semyenov defended the classical tradition. We agreed to disagree.

The most intimate attempts to come to an understanding with the Russians were the small dinners which each of the foreign ministers arranged for Mr. Molotov. Since we had arranged for Secretary and Mrs. Dulles to have a house to themselves, the Secretary was able to entertain the Soviet Foreign Minister at his residence. The return dinner was given at the Soviet Embassy. On one of these evenings when I was greeted by Mr. Molotov, he referred to our having met in Moscow in 1945. He had been well briefed, of course. Yet he seemed a bit confused. I feel sure he found something suspicious in the fact that I had come to Moscow with one Secretary of State as an expert on atomic bombs and was now serving as High Commissioner for another. Before the conversation went much beyond my confirming the date of our previous acquaintance, another guest appeared and my social visit with the Soviet Foreign Minister ended.

Although the Soviet officials were friendly, the conversation on social occasions was definitely sticky. There were so many subjects that one could not discuss and so many questions one could not raise. So we talked about such matters as fishing through the ice, which was a popular sport in Russia, I was told by the head of the American division of the Soviet Foreign Office. Even an experienced Foreign Service officer did not seem to do much better. I recall a long discussion of the difficulties of the Russian language among the American Ambassador in Moscow, one of the Soviet officials and a few others. As happened more than once, we were doing our best to pass the time while the Secretary of State and the Soviet Foreign Minister, with an interpreter, were talking business in another corner. When the Berlin conference ended, though I had spent hours on several social evenings with the Soviet officials, I did not feel that I had made any progress in knowing the Russians. But, after all, that was not my job. I was supposed to understand the Germans, and in that direction I had moved forward—the Soviets were somebody else's affair.

The Berlin conference had been conceived by the Americans and the British as an instrument to convince the French that the rearming of the Germans was a necessity and therefore the treaties establishing a European Army must be ratified. Such was not the aim stated publicly, of course. The purpose was declared to be a solution of the German problem. A vast amount of effort went into the drawing up of documents which were put before the conference; they outlined plans for the formation of a freely elected all-German Goverment. I doubt if few on the American side thought there was more than an off-chance that the public aim could be achieved. As to the unspoken one, only time would tell. In about six months the French Assembly rejected the treaties. The Berlin conference had been a waste of time and energy.

From the time of the Berlin conference until the ratification of the substitute treaties in the first months of 1955, all was quiet on the Berlin front. But once the Soviets were convinced that there was no longer any hope of a split among the Western Allies, the fair weather disappeared; the Russians permitted the East German Government to make trouble. The leaders of the so-called German Democratic Republic must have been restless under the long restraint imposed on them by their Soviet masters. They had been able to state their case in public, to be sure. But that was not enough; they wanted action. In the first week in April 1955 their desires were partially met. It was announced that the fees for cars and trucks using the auto-bahn in the territory of the German Democratic Republic would be raised tenfold. Since the road into Berlin from the Federal Republic was such an autobahn, the announcement amounted to blackmail. One of the lifelines into Free Berlin was threatened. All firms receiving supplies from the West or sending out manufactured goods were being forced to pay a special tax. The Berlin Government at once protested. Soo, too, did the Allied High Commissioners to the Soviet High Commissioner, who was no longer Mr. Semyenov but another Russian civilian, G. M. Pushkin.

Technically the Soviets had a strong position. It was customary to charge a fee for the use of an autobahn. The amount of the fee had been regulated by the East German Government. No one had raised any question before; why the fuss now? the Russians asked. It was not their affair anyway. Why didn't we address ourselves to the German officials responsible for the change in rates? Of course, they knew that from our point of view the German Democratic Republic did not exist. The last thing in the world any one of the three High Commissioners would do would be to communicate in any way with the regime which had been set up by the Soviets.

The exchange of notes was a useless exercise. So, too, was a meeting on May 20 between Ambassador Pushkin and the three former Allied High Commissioners, who had recently become Ambassadors. We met in the Russian Embassy in Berlin and argued for four hours. The experience was frustrating. We went round and round the same bush, the three of us maintaining that the Soviet Union was responsible for the traffic on the autobahn leading to Berlin even if control had been delegated to certain German agents. Pushkin kept making the same speech. He had no control over the traffic into Berlin. The military vehicles of the Americans, the British and the French were not subject to any fee; their passage to and from Berlin had not been in the least affected. Therefore we had no basis for our complaints. The government of the German Democratic Republic had control of all the roads in their territory; therefore he, the Soviet Ambassador, was not in a position to take any action about the fees. The whole matter was in German hands. It should be regulated by the Germans.

So spoke the Russian. To every argument of ours, he made one of half a dozen stereotyped replies. Clearly he was operating under strict instructions. At times his answers hardly fitted the questions. By refusing to be drawn into any real discussion of the issues, he protected his position completely. We finally gave up in disgust. With the minimum amount of cordiality, we took our leave. Each of us could report to his respective government that he had protested and argued quite in vain.

Three weeks before the meeting in the Soviet Embassy, I had urged Washington to lodge a protest in Moscow. Instead, the three ambassadors had been instructed to meet with Pushkin. To my mind, what was involved was important. Now that Pushkin had repeatedly said to us that the control of the roads was in the hands of the East Germans, it seemed to me some action should be taken to challenge his assertion.

I spoke to Secretary Dulles and Chancellor Adenauer during a visit of the latter to Washington in June. These gentlemen had many other matters on their minds and rather brushed aside my arguments. Their thinking was influenced, of course, by their mutual concern with the four-power meetings to be held in Geneva in a few weeks. They seemed inclined to wait and see if the Soviets and the East Germans took steps to carry their doctrine to a logical conclusion, which would be East German control of all civilian traffic in Berlin. Events justified their cautious attitude. No further regulations affecting vehicles on the autobahn were issued. Instead, the fee was reduced considerably after a meeting between unofficial representatives of the governments of Berlin and of the German Democratic Republic. The Berliners who were being taxed seemed content to live with the situation. The activities in the American Embassy now turned to discussions with the Foreign Ministry of the Federal Republic about methods by which a real threat to Berlin could be countered. Fortunately for me, such a threat did not materialize during my term of office.

My worries about the Russians and Berlin were not over, however. The most dramatic episode was yet to come. On Sunday afternoon, November 27, 1955, two Congressmen were driving through the Soviet Sector of Berlin in an American Army car accompanied by an Army lieutenant. The car, as was usual on such sightseeing trips, stopped by the large Russian war memorial known as the "Garden of Remembrance." The two Congressmen, Representative Harold C. Ostertag of New York and Edward P. Boland of Massachusetts, alighted for the short walk which takes the visitor to the center of the garden. On their return, they were detained by members of the East German police force for several hours. The reason given was the use of a radio telephone in the car, which the Germans claimed was contrary to the laws of the German Democratic Republic. The American Commanding General in Berlin, Major General Charles L. Dasher, Jr., sent a strong note of protest to the Soviet Berlin Commandant, Major General P. A. Dibrova. So far, the incident was minor, though there was a question as to whether the action of the police officers had been authorized in advance or was just a case of an excess of zeal.

General Dibrova's answer placed the affair in another category. He refused to accept the protest because he told Dasher that East Germany was sovereign and East Berlin was no longer occupied. The American General at once reported what had happened to the press. He repeated the words which Dibrova had used, and he stated that he was amazed by the Russian statement. He added that the stand of the Berlin Soviet Commandant quite possibly opened the door for other incidents.

The newspapers, of course, played up General Dasher's statement. I felt the attitude of General Dibrova should not be allowed to stand unchallenged. After a telephone conversation with Washington, agreement was reached with the British and French for a three-power protest. Each of the Ambassadors sent a letter to G. M. Pushkin, High Commissioner of the U.S.S.R. for Germany, which read as follows:

On November 29, General Dasher, the United States commandant in Berlin, called on General Dibrova, the Soviet commandant, to protest against an incident which occurred on November 27. This incident involved the unwarranted detention in the Soviet sector of Berlin of an American military vehicle of the Berlin command, and its occupants, including two members of the Congress of the United States of America.

I am informed that General Dibrova refused to accept General Dasher's protest and that in justification he made certain assertions concerning the applicability to this case of the laws of the "German Democratic Republic" and the relationship between the Soviet sector of Berlin and the "German Democratic Republic."

I must renew the protest made by General Dasher against interference with the freedom of Allied circulation in Berlin and against the grossly discourteous and threatening conduct displayed toward United States citizens by persons acting under Soviet authority and control. I do not consider the attempted justification of this incident to be acceptable.

As for General Dibrova's assertions, they are wholly inconsistent with the quadripartite status of Berlin. The position of my government as regards the status of Berlin, and its attitude to the so-called German Democratic Republic, are well known to you as a result of numerous communications on these subjects from my government to your government over a considerable period of time.

You will thus appreciate that the United States government must continue to hold the Soviet authorities responsible for the welfare and proper treatment of all United States citizens during their presence in those areas, including the Soviet sector of Berlin, which are subject to Soviet authority and control.

We had been moved to write this letter in part by statements of the East German Communists. The day after General Dasher's press conference, the First Secretary of the East Berlin Communist Party said that "the time will come when the Communists will take over the whole city." A day later the official newspaper of the party asserted that the occupation status of Berlin is now "nonexistent."

After sending off the letter to Pushkin, I decided to go to Berlin myself. I took the private train that evening. On arriving in the city the next morning, I scheduled a press conference for 3:30 that afternoon. I then drove around the city in the official car with the flags flying, the American flag on one fender, the Ambassador's flag on the other. We crossed into the Soviet Sector, with only the usual formal salute by the East German police. During the drive there was no evidence of the car being followed. Obviously no one wanted to challenge the High Commissioner's right to go anywhere he wanted in the entire city even if his car was loaded with radio telephones, which mine might have been for all anyone knew.

At the press conference, I explained that I had made a special trip to Berlin for two reasons. First, I wanted to consult with the staff of the American Mission. Second, I wished to provide visible evidence of the continuing interest of the United States in the welfare of the city. My presence, I said, underlined the position which my government had taken in regard to Berlin and which was set forth in the note I had sent to Mr. Pushkin the previous evening. I spoke words of praise for General Dasher and the Foreign Service officer who was the chief of the U.S. Mission in Berlin, Bernard Gufler. I expressed my full agreement with what General Dasher had told General Dibrova. Such support of the American General I thought necessary as some articles had appeared implying that he had spoken too freely at his press conference. I then read a prepared statement, which included the following paragraph:

I should never have imagined that the Soviet authorities would allow their agents the Volkspolizei [the East German police] to take such a discourteous and arbitrary action against a member of the United States Command here in Berlin and his guests. As to the position of my government in regard to the statement of General Dibrova, I should simply like to emphasize what is the significant point in the notes which the British, French and American Chiefs of Mission sent to Ambassador Pushkin last night. We said that the position of our governments in regard to the status of Berlin is unchanged. We insist that the quadripartite status of Berlin remain unaltered.

After I had finished, questions were in order. None were of much significance. One I fully expected never came. I was convinced I would be asked if I had driven into the Soviet Sector. It was largely in anticipation of this question that I had taken pains to drive around in East Berlin. I knew that if the question came and my answer was negative, the next day's papers would imply that I had not wished to challenge the Soviets' authority in their quarter of the city. After waiting in vain for the question, I decided to close the conference by a casual remark. So I simply said, loud and clear, that, of course, in driving around the city that morning I had included the Soviet Sector. I had hardly finished the sentence when the newsmen rushed to the telephones. A story was in the making.

The New York papers for December 3 made the most of what was, after all, only a gesture. The headline in the New York *Herald Tribune* was: "Conant Defies Reds, Flies U.S. Flag on Car for Drive in East Berlin." The news dispatch itself, when stripped to the bare bones, hardly justified the headlines. My friends in the United States were pleased. Official Washington was not. Several Congressmen wrote me expressing gratification. The only reference to the incident that I ever received from the State Department was a sentence or two in a letter from one of the assistant secretaries some days later. Speaking of the Berlin situation in general terms, the writer added that he was sure I was aware that decisions could only be made in Washington. I felt no reply was necessary.

The year ended without further incident involving either the Soviets or the East Germans. Indeed, in my notes for February 15, 1956, I find the following entry:

For the moment the worries about the Russians and the Pankow regime [the German Democratic Republic] are in the background. [They remained so for the balance of my stay in Germany.] The real excitement is on the German home front. . . . The former Western occupying powers and the Federal Republic are having a rather disgraceful squabble over "support costs" and in public. The German Minister of Finance is mostly to blame, but the matter has not been handled well on our side. Defense and State couldn't agree; the British are overeager, perhaps because they are in real financial trouble. Then the U.S. is about to have to take a position on further military aid and we have no position! The German Finance Minister has misled the German public and the Cabinet on the whole issue. Lots of trouble on this score too.

The last of my four years in Germany was full of what might be called the normal duties of an ambassador. If they were unusual, it was because of the unusual past. To be sure, negotiations about the status of American troops in the nation to which the ambassador is accredited are not the kind of diplomatic problems expected by most chiefs of missions. However, the knowledge that the Soviets were in a position to make real trouble anytime they so desired gradually became accepted as one of the facts of life.

I resigned my post, according to precedent, at the end of the first Eisenhower administration. After just four years in the Foreign Service, I turned my attention in early 1957 to American domestic problems. I followed with interest, of course, the news from Germany, particularly from Berlin. The two problems which had confronted me in February 1953 kept recurring. These were free circulation throughout all Berlin and free access to the city. The erection of the wall in July 1961 was an answer to the first; the second still remains solved on only a day-to-day basis. In 1953 the question of the future of Berlin was a symptom of the cold war. As I write, the question of whether the cold war is over is the most perplexing and yet the most basic of the many terrible questions with which the United States is faced.

PART VI

A LOOK AT

AMERICAN SCHOOLS

CHAPTER 45

Return from Diplomacy to Education

I F SOMEONE HAD TOLD ME when I was a chemist that in my old age I would devote a considerable amount of time and energy to examining the public high schools of the United States, I should have branded him as demented. I had no interest in secondary education and never expected to develop any. Even if a similar prophecy had been made in the first year or two of my Harvard presidency, I should have thought the prediction far from the mark. Only after Professor Spaulding had opened my eyes to some of the problems in American secondary education would I have agreed that it was not inconceivable that I might someday devote all my time to matters connected with schools rather than colleges or universities.

In earlier chapters I have indicated some of the steps I followed between 1933 and 1953 in broadening my educational concerns. Joining the Educational Policies Commission in 1941 was of crucial significance. I learned from the fellow members of the Commission about the realities of public education and the goals of those who were trying to develop schools which would provide education for *all* American youth. My book *Education in a Divided World*, published in 1948, was full of good words about American public schools. I had become convinced that the hostile and vocal critics were either misinformed or proponents of a dual system of schools.

In my second book about education, *Education and Liberty*, published in 1953, I had much to say about a unique type of secondary

613

school which had been developed only in the United States. Indeed, the last pages of the book might have carried the title, *A Defense of the Comprehensive High School*. The contrast between American public secondary schools and those in Australia, New Zealand and England was the main theme of what I had written. Such a contrast brings out clearly some of the characteristics of the American public high schools as they were organized in all but a few large cities. I knew that the contrast between American schools and German schools would be equally great.

My arrival in Bonn as High Commissioner made it necessary for me to spend at least a little time with German school people. A few who were familiar with the American scene and liked it urged me to explain to German audiences the nature of American public schools as well as the ambitions of forward-looking American educators. Therefore, from time to time, I spoke to meetings of German educators. I decided to translate portions of *Education in a Divided World* into German with the help of one member of the High Commissioner's staff whose job it was (among others) to write the High Commissioner's speeches in German. The title we chose for the little book was the German equivalent of *Equality of Opportunity*: *Gleichheit der Chancen*.

My exposition of American education and its goals suffered from at least one defect. My knowledge of American schools was all secondhand. As far as firsthand observations were concerned, I was better informed about Australian schools than American. As I became more and more worried about my lack of any direct acquaintanceship with the high schools I had been praising, the idea of making visits to American schools began to germinate. When my tour of duty as Ambassador was over, perhaps I could find some excuse for making at least a few such visits. If nothing else, I could satisfy my growing curiosity as to the degree of exactness in what I had been telling the Germans. I had not lost touch with my friends who were interested in the public schools.

During my official visits to the United States, either to accompany Chancellor Adenauer or to defend the High Commissioner's budget before Congressional committees, I had talked with William G. Carr, the secretary of the National Education Association among others. He had been secretary of the Education Policies Commission, and I had learned much from him, particularly during the preparation of a book entitled *Education for All American Youth* which the Commission had published in 1944. I was also in correspondence with John W.

Gardner, the new president of the Carnegie Corporation, who indicated that the Corporation was ready to finance any educational project I might have in mind when my term as Ambassador to Germany was finished. In the fall of 1955 I wrote Gardner that I probably would be leaving the diplomatic service after the elections in 1956 and was anxious to explore various possibilities for the future. I had not made up my mind what I would like to do. My interest in the public schools still continued; how to give concrete expression to this interest was a problem.

Shortly after the New Year in 1956, I had a long talk with John Gardner in his office in New York. We covered my future in an exhaustive way. I remember throwing out, not too seriously, the idea that perhaps I might simply retire, sit on the porch and contemplate the past. "You would soon get sick of that," was Gardner's comment, expressed with so much emphasis that it is the one bit of our conversation which has remained clearly in my mind. In essence, Gardner gave me what amounted to a blank check. He thought the Carnegie Trustees would, within reasonable limits, be prepared to finance whatever I proposed to do related to education.

Within six months an event occurred which forced me to become specific in planning for the future. I had to decide in August 1956 whether I wanted to leave the diplomatic life and re-enter the field of education.

While I was enjoying a leave of absence in our summer cottage in Randolph, New Hampshire, I received a message from the little North Country Inn, a mile away. Secretary Dulles wished to speak to me on the phone. (Since I was to be in New Hampshire for only a month, our own telephone had not been connected.) I drove up to the hotel and prepared to talk with Washington on the telephone from the hotel office (a far from private spot). I could not imagine what the Secretary of State had on his mind. Only a major catastrophe would cause him to consult an ambassador away from his post. I was quite unprepared for what he said. Without any introductory words, he stated: "The President and I would like to have you go to India as the United States Ambassador." I gasped and asked for time to consider the matter. There followed long discussions with my wife as we tramped the mountain trails. (Walking uphill and down, including climbing the northern peaks of the Presidential Range, has been for generations the only recognized sport in Randolph, New Hampshire.) The decision was not difficult. Neither of us had fallen in love with the diplomatic life. My relation with Dulles had been correct, but not such as to make me overdesirous of serving him for another four years. India did not attract me, though I was willing to accept the Secretary of State's judgment that the position of the United States Ambassador there was one of great importance.

In a few days, I said no and begged off from Dulles' urgent suggestion that I come down to Washington to talk the matter over with the President. I was somewhat flattered by the invitation, which seemed to indicate that the Secretary and the President thought well of my three and a half years in Germany. Yet knowing something of the intrigues in the State Department, I was by no means sure the proposal had not originated with one or more minor Washington officials. There were a number who appeared to be less than happy with my conduct of affairs. And I knew the *New York Times* correspondent, M. S. Handler, had not been cheering all my actions. It could be that without the President's knowing it, or even the Secretary's being fully aware of what was going on, I was being pushed out of my post by some of the "German hands." But this didn't matter. What the telephone call had accomplished was to emphasize the importance of our making up our minds about what to do and where to live after January 1957. For whether Eisenhower was re-elected or not, it was quite clear that my diplomatic life would be over in another six months.

Whether I invented the project of studying the American comprehensive high school right after Secretary Dulles' first telephone call or whether it was already definite, I cannot say. Certainly my lack of firsthand knowledge about American high schools had been worrying me. I do remember clearly that within less than two weeks I had a conversation in Randolph with Francis Keppel (then dean of the Harvard School of Education) in which I spoke of focusing my attention on the American comprehensive high school. He encouraged me and agreed that among the many problems facing the public school people, none was more important than the future of public secondary education. There had been ill-informed attacks. Yet no satisfactory answer had been forthcoming. The concept of a comprehensive high school serving all the youth of a community was not understood by the American public.

It was good fortune that Dean Keppel had planned to stop off and see me for a few hours on his way to a vacation in Canada. His visit came at just the right moment. After we had finished our talk as we walked through the woods, the essential elements of my project had taken form. His approval had encouraged me enormously; our exchange of views about procedure had gone far to settle my mind.

I tried to see John Gardner before returning to Germany in September 1956, but failed. We agreed by correspondence to meet in New York during the Christmas recess, when I should be taking a few days off from my official duties in Bonn and Berlin. At that meeting I put in writing my ideas about a definite project which I hoped the Carnegie Corporation would be willing to finance. I dictated to his secretary a long memorandum which started as follows:

What is proposed is a study of the education of the talented youth of a community in an American comprehensive high school (senior and junior high schools). The study would be conducted by me personally with the assistance of three or four collaborators. I would propose to be responsible for the findings and the conclusions. Any recommendations would be put forward under my own name and on my own responsibility. To be useful the project must be completed, including publication, in two years. The proposed date for starting the work would be October 1, 1957.

The memorandum then went on at some length about the judgments that might be made about the schools which were visited. These high schools were to be in Pennsylvania, New Jersey, New York, Connecticut and Massachusetts.

My Christmas trip to the United States had been short. In terms of the future, however, it had been most rewarding. On January 2, 1957, I was writing Gardner to thank him again for the sympathetic reception of my ideas and the hospitality of his office. I also recorded that since the meeting in his office I had talked with Dean Keppel and telephoned to William Carr. Both liked the basic idea and agreed to meet me and Gardner in New York on March 1 (when I was planning to be in the United States once again to deliver three lectures in Princeton).

A week later, I received a letter from the Secretary of State accepting my resignation as Ambassador effective at the time of my return to the United States to deliver the lectures at Princeton. The letter was brought by William C. Trimble, the new Minister (the second man in the embassy), who was dumfounded when I opened it and read him the contents. He had been told just before he was asked to carry the sealed letter that I was to stay on till spring, since I had agreed to accommodate my plans to the Secretary's convenience. His source of information was the high-ranking career officer in Washington with whom I had been corresponding. Either there was something less than perfect communication between the Secretary's office and the high official, or someone had at the last minute persuaded Mr.

Dulles to change his mind. This rather amazing performance, together with a subsequent delay of two weeks in the announcement from the White House, added to my suspicions that there might well be a difference of opinion within the State Department.

Whether my suspicions about the hauling and pulling in Washington were well founded or not, I was sincerely thankful for the decision. When I had rashly offered by letter to leave the exact date of my resignation open, I had not met with John Gardner or written my December memorandum, or talked about a specific project with Keppel and Carr. Now I was eager to plunge into the new work. Therefore I wrote on January 19 to Gardner, announcing that my ambassadorial responsibilities would end sooner than I had expected when we talked at Christmas. He considered it "great news" that I would be back permanently so soon. The press, he wrote, had tracked down the Carnegie Corporation's role in my future as soon as the acceptance of my resignation was announced. Therefore he had had to make a guarded statement. (I might have replied that since I did not as yet know the details of the project, guarded comments were all any of us could make.)

I did not realize at the time how lucky I was that Secretary Dulles and the State Department had not taken up my offer to remain in Bonn until spring. If they had, no real planning could have been done until June or July. This would have been too late to recruit co-workers from colleges or schools. Moreover, highly important decisions would have been so delayed that the actual operation would not have started until the beginning of 1958. That would have been after the Russian success with rockets. It would have seemed as if my study were a consequence of the public criticism of the schools which started after Sputnik. As it turned out, I could say that my investigation had been planned ten months earlier and was actually under way when the startling news was broadcast from Moscow.

The March 1 meeting took place as scheduled at the Carnegie office. (By this time, Mrs. Conant and I had left Bonn and were temporarily living in New York City, preparing to take a long trip to Switzerland before the summer.) In addition to John Gardner and James Perkins, the vice president of the Carnegie Corporation, and myself, William Carr, Francis Keppel, Henry Chauncey, president of the Eduational Testing Service, and John Fischer, then superintendent of schools in Baltimore, were present.

The group was unanimous that the study had to have a much wider geographic coverage than I had suggested in my first memorandum to John Gardner. The possibility of creating a study committee of educators and laymen which would visit the schools in question was discussed and discarded. The verdict was clear. I must visit many schools myself; a few trips to sample a few schools would not suffice. I could not complain. The whole idea of a study had originated in my mind because of my desire to obtain some firsthand information. Now it would appear that I was going to become directly involved in obtaining a great deal of information.

The comprehensive high school would be the focus of the study; on that we were all agreed. Yet we had some difficulty in defining the criteria by which we could distinguish the kind of school we had in mind. I had been much impressed by a book by Franklin J. Keller, *The Comprehensive High School.** He defined the phrase in terms of the curriculum. According to his view, a truly comprehensive high school had to offer a wide range of elective courses, including vocational courses. To his mind, such a school was to be found in the small cities in which there was one high school serving the whole community. The names of the schools he considered as truly comprehensive were a starting point for deciding what schools should be included in the projected study.

By the end of March the agreement of the Carnegie officers was at hand and the recruiting of a staff could proceed. My senior adviser I obtained as the result of a suggestion by Carr. He thought that Eugene Youngert, who was about to retire as principal and superintendent of the Oak Park and River Forest High School outside Chicago, might be willing to join the project. He had been a member of the Educational Policies Commission, and Carr was enthusiastic about his becoming the senior member of my staff. He could not have been more right. I was fortunate enough to reach Youngert by telephone in April just in time to persuade him to postpone a year's trip to Sweden. He was to be a tower of strength.

Thanks to Dean Keppel and his unusual assistant, Dana Cotton (who knows everybody and is an excellent judge of men), I got in touch with Nathaniel Ober, who had just been offered the principalship of a small high school in Connecticut. He came to New York in early April for an interview. Shortly after, he agreed to join the staff. My second bit of good luck. He was to be my traveling companion during the next year, and a more enjoyable and effective companion would have been impossible to find. He, as the younger man, and Eugene

* New York, Harper & Brothers, 1955.

Youngert, as the older experienced professional, could almost be said to have between them determined the nature of the final report. Reuben Gross, an assistant professor of history at Berkeley, and J. Bernard Miller, assistant principal of the Peekskill, New York, High School, completed the team.

By the time Mrs. Conant and I were ready to start on our trip to Switzerland (to be followed by a summer in New Hampshire), the plans for the study were complete. A well-balanced staff of four men had been chosen; plans for getting under way after Labor Day were completed; an office on the sixth floor of 588 Fifth Avenue had been rented; and, most important of all, the Carnegie Corporation had made a grant to the Educational Testing Service of Princeton, New Jersey, which would provide the "logistic support" of the enterprise.

All such matters as the terms of employment of the staff (including a succession of first-rate secretaries), travel accommodations and, eventually, negotiations with publishers were in both theory and practice in the hands of the Educational Testing Service. President Chauncey chose one of the ETS staff, John S. Hollister, to be the manager of the enterprise. From the day I first met Hollister in March 1957, I knew that fortune was favoring my undertaking. He entered with enthusiasm and energy into the adventure and with effective managerial skill took many worries off my mind. From then on he was for all practical affairs liaison man with the Carnegie Corporation, as well as a guide to all of us on many public relations problems. As one project after another was formulated, financed by the Carnegie Corporation, put into operation and terminated with a report, Hollister continued his imaginative and flawless services.

With full consciousness of my luck, I left New York with Mrs. Conant on April 19 on the S.S. *Constitution* for Italy en route to Switzerland. A vacation combined with visits to some schools and talks with some educational authorities in a few cantons and a visit to two universities occupied us until our return by air at the end of June. A preliminary staff meeting in the recently acquired New York office indicated the plans were progressing. I could banish all thoughts of both diplomacy and education until the fall. From that time on, I proposed to spend a large part of my time traveling. As I told my friends, I intended to devote a year to sharpening my prejudices about secondary education and a subsequent year peddling said prejudices all around the United States.

According to the schedule approved by the Carnegie Corporation, I had only the academic year 1957–58 to make my exploration. I personally visited, together with Ober and Youngert, no less than fifty-nine high schools, most of which had been recommended as among the best comprehensive high schools in the United States. For the most part, they were located in small cities in which a single high school accommodated all the youth. Our trips took us into sixteen states. (At least one member of the staff visited a total of 103 schools in twenty-six states.) Except for the existence of separate schools for Negroes in the South, we found no striking differences among the states. Therefore, when the time approached for writing a report, we ventured to generalize. Though we knew there was no such thing as a typical high school, we agreed that the title of the report would be *The American High School Today*, with the subtitle, *A First Report to Interested Citizens*.

The writing of the report was not completed when all the staff except Reuben Gross dispersed for the summer and prepared to take other positions in the fall of 1958. In September I acquired a new assistant, who was to be my right hand in my educational inquiries for the next five years—E. Alden Dunham. He, together with Gross and myself, struggled to produce a manuscript which went to the printer in November. The publication date was early 1959.

The timing was perfect. A wave of public criticism of the high schools which had started after Sputnik had reached its crest. School board members all over the country were anxious for specific answers to such questions as: "How should we organize our schools?"; "What should the high schools teach?" We supplied the answers boldly and categorically in twenty-one specific recommendations. We also reported on what we had found, but this portion of the book went relatively unheeded except for the main conclusion:

The number of small high schools must be drastically reduced through district reorganization. Aside from this important change, I believe no radical alteration in the basic pattern of American education is necessary in order to improve our public high schools. If all the high schools were functioning as well as some I have visited, the education of all American youth would be satisfactory, except for the study of foreign languages and the guidance of the more able girls.

Those laymen who had been criticizing the public schools most vigorously (and to my mind unfairly) cried "Whitewash." Carr and my friends on the Educational Policies Commission, as well as most public school superintendents and high school principals, greeted the findings and recommendations with considerable enthusiasm. The parents liked the book. For several weeks it was high on the bestseller list, an unusual distinction in those days for a book about schools. The reception by the professors of education was not so cordial. Some felt the recommendations were too conservative, if not plain reactionary. Perhaps the fact that a layman (for that was my status in their eyes) had ventured to intrude into their field of evaluating and recommending curricula had aroused some hostility. But, by and large, the professional educators endorsed the report, taking exception to only one or two of the recommendations.

My second book about high schools, *Slums and Suburbs,* was based on a further set of visits to schools in Philadelphia, Chicago, St. Louis, Detroit and the suburban communities surrounding these cities as well as New York and Boston. What I had to say about the suburbs attracted only limited attention, but my report about the slums was widely read and widely discussed. One phrase, "social dynamite," which I owe to Alden Dunham, has become nationally famous. I used it in describing what we now call ghetto schools. That was in 1961 (the publication date was September of that year).

The book reflected my sense of horror at what I had seen in the Negro slums. (Some reviewers wrote that I had written in wrath at the conditions which I found.) Among the concluding observations were the following:

> Social dynamite is building up in our large cities in the form of unemployed out-of-school youth, especially in the Negro slums. We need accurate and frank information neighborhood by neighborhood.
>
> Employment opportunities in the large cities must be promptly opened on a nondiscriminatory basis. Because of the attitude of management and labor this can be done only through the use of federal funds.

Neither of these recommendations was adopted. The social dynamite started to explode in 1966.

Two other recommendations were controversial from the start. For the record, I include them here:

> The answer to improving Negro education in the large Northern cities is to spend more money and to upgrade Negro schools, many of which are in slums, rather than to effect token integration by transporting pupils across attendance lines. Fully integrated teaching staffs are a necessity as well.
>
> Big cities need decentralized administration in order to bring the schools closer to the needs of the people in each neighborhood and to make each school fit the local situation.

I concluded *Slums and Suburbs* as follows:

I have sought to create a set of anxious thoughts in the minds of the conscientious citizens who may read these pages and who, while living in the suburbs, may work in the city. To improve the work of the slum schools requires an improvement in the lives of the families who inhabit the slums, but without a drastic change in the employment prospects for urban Negro youth, relatively little can be accomplished. Therefore, I close by urging that our large city educational problems be analyzed in far more detail than in the past and with a far greater degree of frankness. Neighborhood by neighborhood we need to know the facts, and when these facts indicate a dangerous social situation the American people should be prepared to take prompt action before it is too late.

The reception of the book was mixed. The reaction of the outstanding leaders of Negro education disappointed me. They were highly critical. While acknowledging my service in awakening the public conscience, they found my point of view unacceptable. My negative statements about transporting pupils, they thought, branded me as an advocate of the "separate but equal" doctrine. What I should have done was to emphasize the physical limitations of a major transportation scheme in a large city. Instead, I made the error of stating that it was my belief "that satisfactory education can be provided in an all-Negro school through the expenditure of more money for needed staff and facilities."

In retrospect, I realize I should have sought an alliance with those black leaders who found my book objectionable. If I had done so and had been successful in making peace, perhaps another public statement might have been helpful. Instead, I decided that, rightly or wrongly, I had become *persona non grata* for those who were in the midst of the problems of the urban schools. I turned my full attention to another field of education—the education of teachers.

Eugene Youngert was largely responsible for my undertaking a two-year study of teacher education. Consulting with a number of deans of schools of education and leaders in the national associations concerned with the education of teachers, Youngert succeeded in infecting them with his enthusiasm for my organizing a group of men to visit universities and teachers' colleges. We were to report our findings and recommendations for improvement of the process of recruiting and training future schoolteachers. I had been lukewarm to his proposal and agreed to consider it only if a half-dozen leaders in the field would ask me to make the study. Youngert assembled the group which proceeded to endorse the project. Carr, who was one of the members, carefully warned me that no matter what I reported,

the reaction which would follow would make all the other attacks I
I had received seem as nothing in comparison. The fall and winter of
1963 were to prove him right.

Before the second year of my inquiry had more than started, I
could see a report taking a shape which would be far from pleasing to
many of my friends. There was no question but that I should have to
write many pages critical of what was being taught by some professors of education. I could not endorse either the current certification
procedures or the efforts being made by schools of education to have
the responsibility placed in their own hands. I knew that in many
universities the members of the school or department of education
had been at war with the professors of the arts and sciences. The
professional educators were on the defensive. They hoped my report
would provide them with ammunition. I had begun to realize that it
would not. As I looked forward to the summer of 1963 when I expected my report to be published, I could see trouble ahead. Without
abandoning my interest in education, I needed a new project. I was
soon to find it, thanks to the Mayor of Berlin and the Ford Foundation.

A brief visit to Berlin in May 1962 proved to be a significant event.
Mrs. Conant and I had come to the city as guests of Ambassador Walter
Dowling, who had been the second man in the embassy when I had
been Ambassador. We met old friends, looked at the wall which now
split the city and met with E. Allan Lightner, Jr., chief of the United
States Mission, and some of his colleagues. They were deeply concerned about the future of free Berlin, which was no longer a place
where the Iron Curtain was transparent. Nor could the support of
this outpost of freedom now be justified by maintaining that it was a
"showplace of democracy." People were no longer free to come from
East Berlin to West Berlin. The special American Library which
the United States had built near one of the old crossing points from
East to West no longer served its original purpose. There were no
East Berliners who could come and read the books and newspapers
of the free world. What we saw and heard saddened and disturbed us.

Minister Lightner showed me a list of projects for strengthening
free Berlin as a cultural center for which he hoped Washington might
allocate funds. One of the items, the establishment of a Pedagogical
Center, caught my eye. I discussed it with the group and later with
the members of the city government responsible for schools. I learned
of the ambitious plan to make Berlin the leading city in Europe in the
field of education. An institution was to be created to which teachers
and school administrators and professors of pedagogy would come

from time to time to attend conferences and consult with the staff. As a focus for disseminating up-to-date information about secondary and elementary education, what was envisioned would no doubt be of great value.

On returning to New York, I prepared a memorandum about the proposed center for Shepard Stone of the Ford Foundation, who had asked for any thoughts I might have developed as a consequence of my short visit to the divided city. In the following weeks, Stone and I discussed in a tentative way the possibility of my going to Berlin under the auspices of the Ford Foundation to lend a hand in building the Pedagogical Center. News from Berlin indicated the city government was going ahead with an exploration of the scheme. In October I was asked to be honorary president of a planning committee. I agreed, underlining the word "honorary" and pointing out my inability to attend any meetings for some months to come.

As I talked with Stone, my interest in Berlin and my search for a new area of activity after July 1963 began to merge. The next step was a trip to Berlin which Mrs. Conant and I took to attend a German-American conference in November. Stone was on hand and proceeded to move rapidly to convert my flirtation with an idea into an irrevocable decision. He offered to have the Ford Foundation underwrite the expenses if we would move to free Berlin for a year or eighteen months. The Mayor of Berlin, Willy Brandt, agreed to have the city provide a furnished house. After a conference with Dr. C. H. Evers, the member of the Berlin Government responsible for schools, who urged me to come and help him, we agreed to take up residence not later than September 1, 1963. Then Mrs. Conant and I returned to New York.

As a consequence of my decision to move my base of operation across the Atlantic, farewell parties were in order. Of these, the pleasantest was a dinner in mid-May arranged by James Russell, secretary of the Educational Policies Commission, at the Century Association in New York. More than a dozen old friends who had served on the Commission with me over the course of more than twenty years were on hand. Russell presented me from the Commission a set of leather-bound volumes of the publications which had appeared during my various terms of membership. Without any introductions, others arose from time to time to say a few words about me and the Policies Commission. When finally it appeared to be more than time for me to express my thanks, I found I was indebted to almost everyone present for some kind words.

It was a delightful evening. My pleasure as the guest of honor was only marred by a thought which kept running through my mind. Some of the paragraphs in the forthcoming *The Education of American Teachers* (which was already at the printer's) would not please the majority of those who were being so cordial that evening. I felt I ought almost to apologize in advance. Yet I certainly did not want to spoil the atmosphere by injecting a sour note. I spoke of the still completely unsolved problems of the slum schools. Thus my conscience, troubled by what I knew lay ahead, was to some extent relieved by my harping on the lack of success of my endeavors. I said not a word about the education of teachers. Neither did anyone else, though I knew everyone must have had considerable curiosity as to what the report was going to say.

A few days later, Mrs. Conant and I flew to Berlin, returning to our summer house in Randolph, New Hampshire, for a vacation in August. The New York office was closed. My files were moved to the Educational Testing Service in Princeton, which kindly agreed to provide the equivalent of an American office with which I could keep in touch by post. Six years had gone by since I returned from diplomacy to education. The publication of *The Education of American Teachers* would mark the completion of six books on education since my return. One of my several lives was coming to an end.

CHAPTER 46

Reflections in Berlin 1963–1965

M RS. CONANT AND I had originally hoped to settle in a new house when we arrived in Berlin in May, but it became clear through correspondence during the winter that there would be delays. Therefore Mrs. Conant took a quick trip to Berlin in April to see how plans were progressing. She and the city authorities agreed on an attractive two-story house located just around the corner from the residence used by the Ambassador when he was in the city. The negotiations for purchase, however, were time-consuming. They were not completed until after we had arrived together in the city on May 23. The city provided hotel accommodations until the house was ready. The job of interior decorator was placed in Mrs. Conant's hands. She turned to a Berlin firm which in 1954 had redecorated for the United States Government the house that still served as the Ambassador's residence. For the second time, my wife and the decorator produced a most attractive house.

While the renovation was in progress, we flew back to the United States for a vacation in New Hampshire in the month of August. It was the eleventh of September 1963, therefore, when we landed in Berlin to take up residence in that city. The city government provided a car and driver; the Ford Foundation, a secretary. The members of the American Mission were most cordial and treated us almost as if I once again occupied an official position.

In the meantime, the plans for the Pedagogical Center had been

627

completed. The final meeting of the planning committee had been held as soon as I arrived on May 23. I had fully expected that on my return in the fall, I would find a director installed and ready to call on me for advice. But my expectations proved to be completely false. The appointment turned out to be a slow business. Time was consumed in locating the proper man. Then lengthy negotiations followed between the city and the prospective director, Professor Carl-Ludwig Furck of Hamburg. A final block appeared to be the unwillingness of the city to provide money in amounts which Professor Furck thought adequate.

At that point, I made my only substantial contribution to the creation of the Pedagogical Center. Acting in my capacity as educational adviser, I told the Mayor politely but firmly that if the necessary funds were not voted, the establishment of the Center would have to be postponed indefinitely—in which case I should be in the position of having to leave Berlin with nothing accomplished. I assured him that neither the collapse of the brilliant plan nor my own frustration would go unnoticed. To the delight of Dr. Evers, whose position corresponded to that of minister for school affairs in the city government, the Mayor replied to my plain speaking by seeing to it that a budget of adequate size was voted. This was in the fall of 1964. When we left in May 1965, the Mayor said that my presence in the city had made plans for the Pedagogical Center a reality. He likened my role to that of a "fleet in being" which never had to fire a shot, yet had been the decisive factor in a confrontation.

Whether my stay in Berlin was of much service to the city is a question. There can be no question, however, that the hospitality of the divided city served me well. The two years we spent there provided time for leisurely reflections. My inquiries into the training of teachers as a background for my consultations with the director of the Pedagogical Center caused me to examine in some detail the German system of state examinations. I had now a special reason to compare the American university tradition with the German.

Nowhere in the world does the novelty of the American approach to education stand out more clearly than in Berlin. On the other side of the wall, the leaders of the so-called German Democratic Republic boast of giving educational opportunity to all. The basis, however, is the rigid doctrine of the totalitarian state. In the free city itself the old European selective system still prevails; only a small fraction of the youth enter institutions of advanced education. But after talking with Dr. Evers about his plans, one realizes the impact of American ideas. He has already made significant changes in the extent and nature of secondary education. His objective is to increase the variety of educational experiences as well as to increase the percentage of young people who enter a university or an equivalent institution. Several new schools have been built which are not unlike a comprehensive high school.

The city and its history provided much to think about. Many factors conspired to make me prone to review past events. The process was assisted by playing host from time to time to American friends. I took them around the city in the car which was at my disposal, much as I had when I was High Commissioner. Every point of interest started a train of reminiscences. First of all, there was the isolated city surrounded with Russian troops. I had many reasons to recall the problem of keeping open the autobahn to the Federal Republic. Second, there was the wall. Its construction was after my time as Ambassador, but the cause of its erection, the stream of refugees, was a subject on which I needed no instruction. Third, the rebuilding of the city, by now well under way—the piles of rubble had gone—was a constant reminder that what we were seeing was the product of a modern war. The armed East German police who looked from watchtowers across the wall provided proof that the potentialities of yet a third world war were ever-present.

As I ticked off the dates of modern history in my mind, I almost always found myself starting with a picture of that placid world which started to go to bits just when I graduated from college in 1914. It seemed inconceivable that Americans could have ever been so aloof from international affairs and so self-righteous as we were then. The poor European nations, we said, had fought each other for generations largely because the ambitions of their crowned heads required it. Americans knew better, so we thought. The war between France and England on one side and Germany and Austria on the other had nothing to do with us.

When I had visited Berlin in 1925, I was most interested, as a chemist, in the great men of science who had been given wonderful opportunities for research in the laboratories of the Kaiser Wilhelm Society. (It was only after World War II that the appellation was changed to the Max Planck Society.) The outspoken monarchists were one of the disturbing factors in the Weimar Republic years. A biochemist who showed me his laboratory must have been one of them, for I can still see him showing me with pride a photograph of the opening ceremony of his institute. "There is the Kaiser," he said, pointing to the picture, "and there next to him am I."

The highpoint of my visit to Dahlem had been a call on the

chemist, Fritz Haber, not only famous for his scientific work, but notorious for having introduced poison gas into warfare. Whether in fact the idea of using chlorine gas against an enemy originated with Haber, I do not know. But, rightly or wrongly, he was credited with the innovation, which made his name anathema to my father-in-law, Professor Richards. I was particularly curious to meet Haber because of his pioneer work on the electrochemical method of studying certain oxidation reactions in organic chemistry. He paid me the greatest compliment an older man can pay a younger; he listened with interest as I spoke. If he was bitter about the ostracism of the German chemists by the International Union of Chemistry established by the victorious Allies, he gave no sign.

My interest in the German university had started as early as 1916. As I have explained earlier, I had hoped when I received my Ph.D. to enroll for a year in a German university, probably Berlin. The postponed visit to Germany in 1925 had been one of the molding influences of my life. Now I was in a position to place that experience in perspective. I could look at my first enthusiasm for German universities in a different light. I could superimpose on my youthful judgments as a chemist that of a university president. Futhermore, German higher education in the days of my official stay in Germany (1953–57) was already showing signs of being outmoded. In 1963 the demand for reform among thoughtful Germans was starting to be heard. My position as adviser to the city government gave me an opportunity to learn more about the German tradition and perhaps make a few generalizations about universities.

What had impressed me most as a young chemist was the way the whole university system in Germany functioned as an instrument for advancing scientific knowledge. The road by which a young man advanced from the status of a university student to a full professorship was characterized by almost ruthless competition. The steps were first a Ph.D. degree, then a *Habilitationsschrift* based on independent research in the laboratory of a famous professor, next a call to a professorship at one of the less famous universities, a series of publications and, if the aspirant was lucky as well as gifted, a call to one of the leading institutions. Finally came the ability to hire a group of research assistants. This last feature in particular had attracted my attention and had affected directly my career as a chemical investigator.

What I had completely missed in my first inquiry was the relation of the German universities to the professions. The reason was now clear. Historically, the training of all future professors had been quite separate from the training of lawyers, medical doctors, theologians and secondary school teachers. I had concentrated on this aspect of the functions of a university faculty. The power to award the much coveted Ph.D. degree was in the hands of the professors.

On the other hand, according to a doctrine established in Germany in the early nineteenth century, the state and not a university assesses the knowledge and potentialities of a future lawyer, doctor or schoolteacher; state officials decide who is entitled to be a practicing member of a profession. To be sure, the state examining board is made up of professors, but in operating as examiners these men speak on behalf of the state. For the future schoolteacher in Germany, for example, the state examination looms as large as does the entire college record for an American with similar ambitions. What in Germany has been for generations accomplished in the name of the state, in the United States is achieved in the name of the university or college. Of course, we have state bar examinations and the equivalent for licensing physicians, but as a matter of fact, the university diploma determines the status of a member of the legal or medical profession. In awarding a professional degree, an American institution of higher education is, in fact, acting as though it were a certifying agency.

In the mid-nineteenth century the German university tradition was assimilated in the United States by treating the course of study for a Ph.D. degree as a graduate program. The A.B. (or B.A.) degree, which had been awarded by American colleges for nearly two centuries, thus became a mark of the completion of the first step in a two-step process. At that time, a number of college presidents were busy placing the study of law and medicine on a graduate basis. Curiously enough, the applied scientists, particularly the agriculturists and the engineers, successfully resisted any such transformation of a professional undergraduate school to a graduate school. The S.B. (or B.S.) degree continued to be awarded by many American colleges for the completion of a rather tightly prescribed course of study even during the period when the free elective system was flourishing.

As the S.B. degree began to acquire a prestige almost equal to that of the degrees of bachelor of law or doctor of medicine, the A.B. degree became the hallmark of an undergraduate experience which was definitely not professional or vocational. Indeed, in the heyday of the free elective system, the contrast between a course of study leading to a bachelor of arts degree and one prescribed in a scientific school was as clear as the difference between day and night. In the one case, what the student studied was his own affair. In the other, the faculty had laid down the regulations for each year of study.

I cannot imagine how effective state examining boards could have been established even in the embryonic phase of American higher education. The political situation in the United States before or after the Civil War was such that neither the federal government nor the individual states could have been relied on to maintain standards of professional competence. In other words, American institutions of learning, unlike the German, had to accept early in their development the responsibility of attesting to the competence of a young man or woman who sought employment as a member of a profession or other organized vocation. As each new activity, such as school counseling, has been organized through a national voluntary association, the question has been raised almost at once as to qualifications for membership. It has been answered more often than not by the specifications of a program of courses leading to a new degree. One or more universities have usually been eager to expand by incorporating the new proposal in their offerings. The multiplication of the different types of degrees—particularly master's degrees—is a phenomenon characteristic of the growth of higher education in this century.

Thus it has come about that a program of courses leading to a particular degree is usually intended to fulfill two functions. One is to enrich the knowledge and enhance the skills of those enrolled. The other is to eliminate those who do not have the kind of talent which the leaders of a profession or vocation believe to be essential for success. The second objective is rarely set forth as crudely as I have phrased it. Rather, it is customary to speak of selecting those who would be worthy members of a profession. It is assumed that the selection must be made by exposing the candidate to courses, each of which terminates with an examination graded by the instructor. The standard is set by the faculty acting as a legislative body. For example, unless the grade is B or better, the course may not count for credit in many graduate faculties. When the appropriate number of credits have been registered on the student's record, he is recommended by the faculty to the trustees and receives what is usually known as a professional degree. However, it might more accurately be called a vocational degree, since there is no consensus in the United States as to what vocations are professions and what are not. At all events, for many careers, winning the degree is essential. The diploma is thus, in fact, a certificate of vocational competence.

Even a casual look at the American academic scene makes it evident that universities the country over differ enormously as to the range of the subjects which may be studied. Some do not have any graduate or professional faculties other than the one which awards the Ph.D. degree in conventional academic fields. Others offer many new varieties of degrees. How has this extraordinary diversity come about? In theory, it is a consequence of decisions made by boards of trustees. Actually the decision-making process is more likely to have been in the hands of a president or dean as leader of a faculty.

I have already explained in some detail how one new vocational degree (the M.A.T.) was added to Harvard's offering. The trustees (the members of the two governing boards) only acquiesced. Probably each expansion of each university has a slightly different history. In some cases outside groups may have initiated the step. The opinion of the alumni and of state legislatures (in the case of state universities) surely has often been a factor of significance. By and large, the forces urging expansion have met only one counter force, namely, that generated by financial considerations. Every additional course costs money. Yet I know how difficult it is to persuade the members of a faculty to balance the increased expenditures against the alleged benefits of what is proposed. If my experience is at all typical, it is equally difficult to get an outside group representing a profession (or vocation) to consider where the money is coming from to finance what is being urged.

As I listened to discussions of university reform in Germany, I was particularly interested when the issue came up as to whether or not an additional full professorship in a given field was to be created. Such an idea seemed revolutionary to the Germans. Hitherto one and only one professor had been appointed in each field. The object of reform was to reduce the autocratic power of the single professor and also to increase the size of the teaching staff. Both aims undoubtedly are worthwhile. Yet I reflected that in most American institutions what was needed was not an increase in the number of professorships of a subject, but limitations on faculty multiplication.

A faculty in most instances has a built-in expansion force. It exerts itself by demands for an increase in the number of courses offered. The time-honored process is as follows: A professor is called from another college or promoted to permanent rank in order to lecture in a certain field. After a few years, the professor develops a new interest and quite properly suggests he make it the subject of his lectures. The department agrees but then demands of the administra-

634   /   My Several Lives

tion the allocation of funds to hire another teacher to replace the professor who has undertaken his new self-imposed burden. The results are apparent if one examines the succeeding annual lists of course offerings over a period of years.

In 1936 I was bold enough as a new president to call attention to the expansion process. In an address on President Eliot's birthday (the one hundred and second anniversary), I referred to a remark in his inaugural of 1869: "It will be generations before the best of American institutions will get growth enough to 'bear pruning.'" I then stated that, in my opinion, the time for pruning had arrived. I suggested that the faculties "should endeavor to reduce the number of courses given and in many cases to condense the material now presented." I might have saved my breath. My words fell on deaf ears. The only check on the multiplication of courses in the faculty of arts and sciences and the professional schools was the budget. How such a check may operate in a privately financed university, I fully understand. How it works in a state university, I have never comprehended. The size of the appropriation of the state legislature must set the eventual limits. At all events, it seems to be a law of academic nature that every faculty and subfaculty (i.e., department), if healthy, is always hungry. Whether or not it is always wise to meet fully the demands for nourishment is a question to which my own experience as an administrator gives an uncertain answer.

One of the most significant changes in the pattern of American higher education since World War II has been the increase in the number of two-year colleges. I was fond of pointing this out to my German friends. I explained that these institutions, known as either junior or community colleges, are open to all high school graduates. When well financed, they offer a variety of courses. Some are vocational and terminal. Others parallel the freshman and sophomore courses in the state university. Those who pass these academic courses may transfer at the end of the second year to a four-year institution. Because the student lives at home, the cost of room and board is eliminated.

I was proud to have been one of the early advocates of this American innovation, the two-year college. Reflecting what I had learned as a member of the Educational Policies Commission, I wrote just over twenty years ago in *Education in a Divided World*:

The movement to establish more two-year free colleges locally has been gaining ground in the last few years. For these colleges to fulfill the desired function, however, will require genuine public support, not merely the educators' blessing. Before such support is forthcoming, there will have to be a rather complete change in public opinion. By and large, people think of colleges as four-year colleges or universities. The new status of a local two-year institution will require careful and repeated explanation in many states. Above all, the new institutions will have to be made as attractive as possible; if they are merely the colleges for the discards from other institutions, they will surely not succeed.

I then went on to advocate a new bachelor's degree (the bachelor of general studies) which would be awarded for a two-year program. (I have long since abandoned that idea and have accepted the associate in arts as the appropriate degree for the junior or community college.) Clearly more important than the degree was the type of education to be provided. As to that, I had the following to say:

These colleges should provide general education and vocational training of various types to accommodate a spread of interests and aptitudes among the students. There is no reason why the course thus offered—a combination of job training and education for a full life of civic responsibility—might not be superior to that provided in many a liberal arts curriculum in a large and crowded university. Those of us who believe the two-year community colleges are a significant step forward in the march toward our goal of equalizing educational opportunity have high hopes they will prosper in every state. But we realize that such colleges first must be accepted by the leading citizens of each locality, particularly by managers of industry. The present emphasis by employers on the importance of a degree from a four-year college could be quite disastrous if continued—disastrous, that is, for the development of the new educational picture in which the two-year college plays so significant a role.

I was still urging the same course when I published *Education and Liberty* in 1953. My ten-point "program for the future" included the following suggestions looking forward to the time when the "number of adolescents will be 50 percent greater than at present":

Do not expand our four-year colleges either as to number or as to size.

Do not expand the four-year programs in our universities, rather contract them.

Attempt to make a two-year college course (following the regular high school course) fashionable; to this end consider awarding a bachelor's degree of general studies to the graduates of such colleges.

Endeavor to create a climate of opinion in which the length of education beyond eighteen is *not* considered the hallmark of its respectability.

The book was published the same month that my confirmation as High Commissioner for Germany was under consideration before the Senate of the United States. I am sure that the heads of many small four-year colleges read the news of my imminent departure with a sense of relief. One disturbing voice would be heard no longer. As a proponent of the growth of junior colleges, I was not popular among college presidents. As a matter of fact, I doubt if anyone paid attention to my ten-point program. It was only when the increased size of the age group was actually upon us, that educators and politicians in other states began to take an interest in what had been going on in California since the end of World War II. Then and only then did the idea of public two-year colleges become attractive.

During the postwar period, when junior colleges were gaining in popularity and finally began to accommodate a considerable fraction of college-age youth, adult education was also being developed. Someday the provision of significant evening courses locally to part-time students may be the major undertaking of a community college. Whether, indeed, such is likely to be the case in a particular area will depend on the nature of the community. Part-time instruction is primarily significant because it makes possible the continuation of vocational education. For example, a person who had received an associate in arts degree some years before might start a course of study leading to a career as a public accountant. Such possibilities open up the prospects that the first exposure to college may be shortened to two years without necessarily curtailing the total time spent in expanding knowledge and skills necessary for success in many walks of life.

The two-year college may be regarded either as a prolongation of the high school or as the initial phase of post–high school education. The battle over this point has been going on in different states for no little time. What is involved may be more than the use of prestigious words. The control of appointments and the decisions about curricula under one system are made by local school boards, under the others by separate local boards or one state board. Probably both schemes may be made to work. The important point is that the two-year local college must be prepared to offer academic courses for those who wish to transfer to the junior year in the four-year course in a state college or university as well as a variety of vocational courses. The problem of staffing is, therefore, more like that confronting the administrator of a comprehensive high school than that of the president of a four-year college. Indeed, the question of how to recruit and train the teachers for the rapidly expanding two-year college is perhaps the number one item on the agenda for the future.

I offer no simple answer. Clearly the backgrounds of the staff of any one institution must be as assorted as are the goals of the students. Certain members (but by no means all) are facing the same instructional tasks as the teachers of freshmen and sophomores in a four-year college. This raises the question of whether in a state like New Jersey, in which an expansion of junior colleges is at hand, an effort could be made to create a voluntary association of college teachers with the objective of enhancing the prestige of those involved in teaching college students particularly in the first two post–high school years.

In an earlier chapter, I praised the professors of chemistry in the New England colleges in the 1920s as teachers. My nostalgic words betrayed my doubts about the recent fashion that requires all teachers of college youth to be engaged in the advance of knowledge. I would hope a distinction could be made between professors who were university teachers and those who were college teachers. Only the former would be in one way or another involved with candidates for the Ph.D. They would be the scholars active in research. The burden of advancing knowledge would rest on their shoulders.

The extension of the years of free education through the establishment of local two-year colleges has been the expression of a new social policy of the nation. Or perhaps I should say a further thrust of an old policy. For one could simplify the history of American public education in the last hundred years by noting the steps in the movement to make universal the opportunities hitherto open only to the well-to-do. First came the provision of elementary schooling at public expense; then came the free high schools and efforts to provide instruction for a wide variety of talents (the widely comprehensive four-year high school); lastly, the growth of the equally comprehensive public two-year college, the open-door college, as it has been sometimes called.

Looking back to the 1930s, when it was considered a bit bizarre to argue for more and larger scholarships, one realizes the revolution in the outlook of the American public. What was once a forward-looking proposition has now become a widely accepted premise. I refer to the idea that for the academically talented youth the entire cost of higher education should be paid through private scholarships or by the state or by the federal government. All the words that some of us wrote in the 1930s on behalf of the subsidy of promising students now seem to be only repetitions of obvious truths. This is largely because of the action of the U.S. Government at the end of World War II.

Early in the war, President Roosevelt had appointed a committee to consider the further education of veterans. As the war came to a close, this committee published a report entitled *Preliminary Report of the Armed Forces Committee on Post-War Educational Opportunities for Service Personnel.* It recommended that "a limited number of exceptionally able ex-service personnel" be selected on a competitive basis for higher education at government expense for up to three additional years of study. The House committee of the seventy-eighth Congress to which the report was transmitted did not like the selective features of the report. Many expressed a desire for a much simpler formula to determine the amount of educational subsidy a returning veteran should receive. In the Congress, sentiment began to solidify behind the proposition that the number of years of war service, not the ability of the veteran, should be the main factor.

Though I had taken no part in the preparation of the report, I was asked to do a little missionary work with the members of the House committee. I encountered hostility to any claim that there was a public interest in the higher education of able students. One War Department representative who took part in the discussion stated that those who wanted more education than that to which they would be entitled on the basis of length of service should pay for it themselves. That had always been the doctrine in the United States, he said, and he saw no reason to change it now. One Congressman went so far as to state that my argument in favor of more years of subsidized education for the bright student was socialism, which he was against.

I recognized an attitude that I had encountered more than once in pushing at Harvard my scheme of National Scholarships. The traditional way of obtaining a higher education in the United States was to work one's way through college unless one's family was at least moderately well off. As the difficulties of a student's finding employment increased in the depression years, it became accepted practice to borrow money for higher education. Various loan arrangements were developed by many institutions. Our experience at Harvard indicated that there was a point beyond which it was unwise for a student to borrow money. A youth who started his career with too heavy a debt was all too likely to end by failure to repay. On the other hand, the record of repayments of moderate loans was excellent.

To my mind, it is important to recognize the difference between different levels of education. When the two-year colleges become truly widespread throughout the nation, making free higher education available to all, there will be no national need for scholarships to support the college student in the first two years. Each four-year institution will have to decide for itself whether a four-year subsidy of certain of its students is desirable or not. For the academically talented youth who transfers from a two-year college, a subsidy will be needed in spite of the existence of tax-supported colleges. The expense of living away from home may be a formidable obstacle to the further education of many young people. The granting of substantial financial support to college juniors and seniors might well be tied to the plans of these students for graduate education because the principle is now widely accepted that the students in our graduate professional schools should be supported by the taxpayer. Whether the bulk of the money for such scholarships should come from the state or the federal government is a question. I shall not venture an opinion. Likewise, I shall not comment on any of the controversial plans for combining loans and federal scholarships to lower the financial barriers to the university education of talented youth.

As I see it, there is no conflict in principle between public support of post–high school education of all youth for two years and subsidizing the training of highly selected youths for as long as five or six years. A national social policy demands the first, a national need the second. The two ways of spending public funds to good advantage differ. Yet the improvement and expansion of the junior colleges and generous fellowships for research scientists, to pick but two examples, are all part and parcel of a vast total public effort. One may call it mass education or the provision of equality of opportunity. However it may be labeled, it has characterized the United States in my lifetime. The uniqueness of the effort can only be appreciated if one views it from another land. My stay in Berlin provided such an opportunity. I regard my visit, therefore, as an appropriate and rewarding climax to the years I have spent investigating educational institutions since I left the diplomatic service in 1957.

CHAPTER 47

Concluding Thoughts
in Uncertain Days

W HENEVER I HAVE MET an old acquaintance in the last two years, the first remark almost invariably has been, "Aren't you glad you are no longer a college president?" No such question would have greeted me in the past, even after the first disturbance at Berkeley in 1964. To be sure, clear evidence was then at hand that a campus could explode. The danger signs were apparent. But no one predicted that within two or three years a college president would be defined as a man in trouble.

Now anyone who reads the daily papers would have to conclude that educational administration is a hazardous occupation. The academic world appears to be afflicted with a crippling illness. Few institutions in the United States seem to be immune. Few nations with great traditional universities have as yet escaped. Institutions of higher learning have taken on the appearance of beleaguered communities where thoughtful, articulate young people, ready to question the basic assumptions of our society, are being misled by a small number of violent fanatics.

To my ears even the most raucous shouts of the dissidents are not completely alien sounds. What is different is the volume, the intensity of the noise, the number of attentive listeners and, above all, the attendant actions. What was hardly an audible whisper in Cambridge and Boston around 1910 is now a shout. And there is another difference. The radical speakers at Ford Hall in Boston half a century ago coupled their denunciation of wage slavery and capitalism with a picture of a bright socialistic future. Today the "new left" refuses to provide even a vague outline of what will be built on the ruins of the present when they, the radicals, have had their way. The hard core of sincere activists are essentially anarchists. A young rebel leader with whom I talked had much to say about the undemocratic structure of our universities, indeed of all American society. When I pressed for an opinion about taxation, concerning which I once expressed certain unorthodox opinions, I was made to feel the utter irrelevance of my inquiry. I should have expected the reply. My handful of radical acquaintances of decades past would have said, "Tinkering with tax laws is only treating symptoms of a sick society."

As I recall my many conversations with academic dissenting friends in the United States and England at the time of World War I, what is really new in the present situation stands out quite clearly. The leaders of the new left have decided that the best staging area for an all-out attack on society is the academic world itself. No such notion would have occurred to the radicals of fifty years ago. To them, the industrial arena was the target—there the forces of revolt would be assembled. The labor leaders would be in the foreground; the general strike, the most promising weapon. If it came to shooting (and in England in the 1920s, it was thought it might), the guiding brain power of a general staff might include professors. Only indirectly, however, would universities be involved. To be sure, in a crisis it was hoped that the sentiment of the students would be on the side of the rebels. What was envisaged, however, was totally different from the battle plans which now appear to guide the militant left.

The new tactic that has developed is suitable to any academic community in any land. Its effectiveness has been proved by repeated demonstrations in many places in the last few years. The successes have been widely publicized through television and radio. Words and actions have been compounded in a skillful way. The old doctrine of civil disobedience and the idea of passive resistance developed by Gandhi are usually essential ingredients of the mix. To obtain the support of those who are not anarchists, a local issue is provided. If one considers only the proclaimed goals of the rebels, no pattern emerges. Student demands at Columbia, at Harvard, the Free University in Berlin, in Rome or in Tokyo have almost nothing in common. If one starts from the assumption that specific student grievances are fundamental and are being aired for the first time, one misses the point of what has been happening.

If I am right, it is erroneous to consider the troubles that have disturbed so many campuses a global sickness of institutions of higher learning. There is no general failure of universities. There is no valid world-wide diagnosis. Every institution has its weak spots; every national system could be changed, probably for the better. I suggest, however, that dissatisfied members of an academic community who are not anarchists ought to be far more cautious about the alliances they make. Since disturbance leading to disintegration is the avowed aim of the new left, every protest movement among students employing the new tactic becomes part of the disruptive process. What would appear to be needed are countermethods to weaken the attractive force—the drawing power—of the anarchists. This means enlisting the loyalties of all who have not made the anarchist cause their own. Methods to attain this end would be obviously quite different in Japan, in Germany and in the United States. Knowing something about the history and present status of university work in all three countries, I am sure there is no universal panacea for academic ills. In short, the challenge of the radicals must be met community by community by directing attention to specific issues.

I have not in the preceding pages attempted to trace the evolution of the industrial society of the United States. Therefore I shall not venture to discuss any changes which may or may not be needed to fend off destruction through other than academic channels. But, as to the structure of society and its relation to universities, I would have to reply to the derisive remarks of the questioning students by saying: Of course the universities reflect the nature of the societies they are built to serve. Who ever imagined they didn't? Which is not to say that changes in American higher education are uncalled for. I have already mentioned several in the previous chapter. Now I can indulge in second thoughts to relate a few of them to what we have been hearing from those who follow the anarchists without fully realizing what is at stake.

Let me start with my advocacy of the two-year college. Addressing a discussion arranged by the Committee on Economic Development in 1967, I said:

Not long ago I attended, as a guest—a Rip Van Winkle from the distant past—a series of panel discussions on "Goals for American Higher Education." Two of the speakers represented college student organizations.

If their evidence has any validity, they and their contemporaries were far from certain as to why they had entered college. One said that all his contemporaries agreed that the education they were pursuing was "without purpose." Could not such a situation have arisen at least in part because the length of a span of years has come to be the measure of a liberal education? Does not our present pattern, which involves a high-prestige value for the bachelor's degree, postpone too long entry into a significant career for many youths? I suggest that all who are responsible for employment policy consider emphasizing the two-year associate of arts degree and de-emphasizing the B.A.

I am quite aware that reference to a career in business is particularly objectionable to the radicals of today, but what I am suggesting is not something to attract their sympathy, but something that might diminish the number of discontented youth in the next generation of Americans.

Ever since my study of the education of teachers, I have been disenchanted with what many institutions proclaim as liberal education. Professor Jeremiah Finch of Princeton accompanied me on a journey to many colleges characterizing themselves as four-year liberal arts institutions. We could discover no common denominator among the required programs, and all attempts I have seen to specify the content of a "good liberal education" have been failures. Perhaps it is a question of finding the proper label.

No doubt excellent courses have been provided in increasing number in undergraduate departments of universities with the aim of broadening the range of interests of the student. I venture the guess (it is no more than that) that such innovations in the last thirty or forty years have been particularly successful in engineering schools. If this be true, the explanation may lie in the fact that it was relatively easy to define what was lacking in the intellectual diet offered to future engineers. So much of a student's time had been taken up studying applied science and mathematics that no opportunity was left to explore other fields. In correcting the situation, attention could be focused on the humanities with a clear-cut purpose. A man who was to spend his life dealing with the application of the laws of inanimate nature needed to devote some time to understanding the vagaries of human nature. To this end, the study of history and literature can be highly rewarding. On the other hand, in considering the education of a young man or woman who has no vocational interest, it is not possible to be so definite about the objectives of a so-called liberal education. The content of a program to be recommended, therefore, becomes ill defined.

The patterns which were developing thirty years ago and were still in existence when Professor Finch and I made our travels are of questionable value. A package of so many courses (or hours' credit) in subject A, so many in B, so many in either X, Y or Z, can easily be regarded by critical students as mislabeled if it is marked "liberal arts education." To my mind, the old distinction between liberal and servile, if transferred to the academic world, might well read the difference between free and prescribed. The older I get, the more I think such an interpretation is fruitful. Yet I think of the hours that faculties have spent all over the country in the last thirty years determining what should be the *requirements* for a liberal arts degree. Perhaps the time has come to give up all attempts of a faculty to tell young men and women what they ought to study in order to be broadly educated.

One of the things wrong with higher education in the United States is that too many forces are at work prolonging full-time education. The anarchists and their present allies in the U.S.A., however, are not asking for a shortening of the college years. They are asking for a complete remodeling of the system. What they seem to have in mind is hardly novel, yet it may indicate the direction of the reform movement in the future. Not a few of the protesters demand the abolition of course examinations and course grades. Such a step would bring a college close to the actual situation which prevailed, at least at Harvard, about 1880. In those days there was apt to be a sufficient number of professors ready to give a C to any student who could write anything at all intelligible in the midyear or final course examination. Such a situation reduced the degree requirements in fact to nearly zero. A recognition of the almost anarchical state of affairs led President Lowell to introduce his plan of concentration and distribution in 1910. What he sought to cure was the attitude expressed by a saying current when I was young: "What you learn in college is not what matters; it is the friends you make."

I can imagine institutions of higher education in the United States freer even than Harvard before President Lowell's reforms. There would be no requirements for a degree, perhaps no degree at all. But in that case, let the present-day rebels note, a system of state and federal examinations, similar to the German system, would almost certainly have to be instituted for a large number of vocations. Unless the structure of our society is, indeed, completely revolutionized, the organized vocations and professions will continue to guard their ranks by setting up standards of employability. Young people will want jobs. Vocational examinations will be established.

Tutoring schools will arise to prepare students to pass these examinations. Indeed, it requires no great stretch of the imagination to envision a system of higher education in the United States comprised of two quite separate sets of institutions. One would offer opportunities to grow in wisdom at a rate as leisurely as desired. The other would be directed to equipping youth to enter vocations in as short a time as possible. I am not proposing the creation of such a dual system. But to open a discussion of possible solutions, I offer the scheme as my answer to student discontent in the United States.

I shall be accused of joining the radicals out of pure opportunism, I am afraid. Yet my advocacy of the community college and of shortening the time of training for a profession is not new. My suspicion of academic degrees probably stems from President Lowell's prejudice against the A.M. and Ph.D. The Nieman Fellows have flourished in large part because the scheme is devoid of counting courses and accumulating credits for a degree. Now I am suggesting a major change in the educational opportunities offered for high school graduates. Impressed by the failure of the present arrangements to win the loyalties of the youth, I suggest a drastic overhaul. The objective would not be proclaimed in terms of providing a better education, or even a more relevant education. The aim would be to place youth, as young as possible, in situations which appeared to be significant. Then I would pour money into facilities for providing part-time further education. The community college would be particularly important.

What my heresy amounts to is a suggestion that undergraduate instruction be re-examined with the idea that community colleges be given a more prestigious role than at present and that the significance of degrees be reduced as far as possible. The pattern of education beyond the high school that developed fifty years ago was suitable for a time when colleges were for only relatively few. It is questionable whether the same pattern is today satisfactory for mass education. Can it be that the fetish of upholding academic standards has misled us? The educational process should continue throughout life. The knowledge and the skills required in a vocation are something quite apart. Have we in the United States unnecessarily entangled the two? Has this come about by giving to our academic institutions control over entry to the learned professions and other vocations as well? I raise these questions humbly as possible working hypotheses for college administrators who almost daily struggle with problems which to an old-timer look almost beyond solution.

Related to the revolt of college youth have been recent changes in the picture of the education of the children of Negro families. Of all the books I have written, the one that most needs revision is *Slums and Suburbs*, written in 1961 and insufficiently revised in 1964. Yet it would be most difficult to bring up to date. Along with the revolt of youth has come an increased militancy of some of the more important Negro leaders. A new group has arisen which is no longer interested in an integrated society as a goal. They demand school systems in some of the large cities in areas inhabited by Negroes that reflect the concern of the citizens expressed in racial terms.

I myself have never given up an integrated school system as the ideal. Today, because of geographic considerations, 100 percent black schools are a necessity in some communities, but by bussing wherever possible schools with a mixed population should be provided. Therefore the improvement of the completely Negro schools is highly important, but must be considered only as an intermediate phase in the development of American public education.

In a recently published article about the comprehensive high school, I have suggested that the challenge of this type of school was a challenge to American society. A truly comprehensive school would include a wide variety of youth. As far as possible, the composition of the student body, in terms of racial background, would be mixed. Since I am not certain to what extent the leaders of opinion among the Negroes in the large cities would agree with my endorsement of the concept of the comprehensive school, I would be in a difficult position to provide yet another revised edition of *Slums and Suburbs*. Therefore I use this opportunity of reaffirming, first, my concern with the schools in the big cities and, second, my belief in the widely comprehensive high school as the eventual product of the development of public education in all parts of the United States.

The passage of the Elementary and Secondary School Act of 1965 amounted to still another revolution in American education. I have referred in an earlier chapter to the fact that Catholic opposition to the use of federal funds to improve the local schools was overcome. The change was accomplished by centering attention on the impoverished. The authors of the bill were able to devise a formula for distributing money appropriated by Congress which satisfied those who for a generation had quarreled over "federal aid" for public schools. What the bill provided, however, was not the general aid demanded for decades by the National Education Association. Instead, it was categorical aid, which is to say that the funds were designated to support specific programs. The program, although devised locally, had to be for the purposes named in the law. The debate over categorical aid versus general aid still continues.

One of the provisions of the law was aimed at improving the state departments of education. On this subject I considered myself something of an expert, or at least a knowledgeable commentator. In connection with my two-year study of the education of teachers, I had visited the departments of education in several of the larger states. I was shocked by what I found. Partisan politics more often than not dominated the scene. (New York State was an outstanding exception.) Mulling over my impressions, I decided to publish a little book about policy-making for educational institutions. A concern with the office of the chief state school official (often called the state superintendent) was one of its major themes. Therefore when the book *Shaping Educational Policy** appeared just after the presidential election, my comments about the role of the state and the federal government may have influenced to some degree those in the Johnson administration who were preparing the new legislation. I know that Francis Keppel, then United States Commissioner of Education, read the book as soon as it was published and commented favorably on my emphasis on improving the state departments of education.

Another person who read *Shaping Educational Policy* was John Gardner, at that time still the president of the Carnegie Corporation. His endorsement of one suggestion was to eventuate in what I may claim as my major social invention—the Education Commission of the States. In the concluding chapter of *Shaping Educational Policy,* I had criticized the haphazard interaction of forces determining educational policy in the United States. I knew from my travels that many states were considering such questions as the future of the two-year college without accurate information about what other states had done. What was needed, it seemed to me, was some way by which those who made policy in one state could communicate with their opposite numbers in other states. A meeting of all the chief state school officers was not enough. State legislators and representatives of state-supported colleges and universities and private institutions should also have some method of exchanging ideas.

Writing of the need for the development of a nationwide educational policy, I said, "Let the fifty states, or at least fifteen to twenty of the more populous states, enter into a compact for the creation of an 'Interstate Commission for Planning a Nationwide Educational

* New York, McGraw-Hill, 1964.

Policy.'" Such a commission, I went on to say, would be concerned with "drawing up of plans *not* with administration." Each state, I assumed, would be ready to listen to any conclusions of the Commission but, of course, would not be bound to follow its recommendations. As I pictured the operation of the Commission, the work would be done by special committees or working parties. Among the topics which, it seemed to me, might profitably be studied were: the junior college, vocational education and the education of the Negro. The Commission, of course, would have to consider problems of financing education and the role of state, local and the federal taxing authorities.

If John Gardner had not reacted favorably to my idea of an interstate cooperative body, I doubt if anyone would have paid much attention to the book. Gardner, however, believed in coupling ideas with action. He sent a copy of my book, in the late fall of 1964, to Terry Sanford, whose term as Governor of North Carolina was just coming to an end. Sanford liked the idea of an interstate compact. With Gardner's backing, he proceeded in the next twelve months to turn a rather sketchy idea into a definite proposal backed by many governors, the chief state school officers and not a few educators.

Governor Sanford introduced at once a highly important modification of my original suggestion. I had brought in the machinery of state government by proposing that the members of the Interstate Commission be appointed by the legislature in each state. Thus as a creation of a political body, the Commission might be expected to have more influence on legislators than would a committee of educators. Sanford proposed to make the governor the key man in each state. In a discussion with him early in 1965, I agreed to his modification. I recognized at once the significance of the change both from the point of view of getting the scheme under way and its long-range effectiveness. Sanford had many friends among the governors; he himself had made an enviable record by his support of public schools in North Carolina. Therefore educators, as well as politicians, were disposed to favor any recommendation he sponsored. In the first six months he talked with many people. By July he was ready to address the National Governors' Conference in Minneapolis. He asked me to join with him in presenting the idea of an interstate educational compact.

The meeting at Minneapolis was a great success. Governor Richard J. Hughes of New Jersey, chairman of the Committee on Human Resources of the conference, read a special report, copies of which had already been placed in the hands of all the governors. The conclusion was that the governors should give serious consideration to Sanford's proposal. From then on, events moved at an incredible pace and with unbelievable precision. I began to realize what a master workman had taken over the task of creating a new educational agency. The combination of Sanford's boldness, ingenuity and charm carried all before him.

I omit the successive steps by which the governors and educators from all fifty states were made familiar with the plan. A compact was drawn, and an Interim Steering Committee, presided over by Governor John H. Chafee of Rhode Island, was created which played an important part in overcoming a certain initial resistance to the idea. The Carnegie Corporation and the Danforth Foundation each made grants of $150,000 for an initial development period. The minimum number of states (ten) to put the compact into effect was soon reached. By the end of 1966, Wendell H. Pierce had been elected Executive Director and Denver, Colorado, chosen as the site of the Commission's headquarters. Financed by the states themselves, the organization appeared to be on the road to becoming a permanent feature of the American educational scene.

An annual meeting of the Commission, which I attended as a guest on June 26–28, 1968, gave me a chance to congratulate Dr. Pierce on what he had already accomplished. This included a publications program (a bimonthly magazine, a monthy newsletter and a series of reports). Particularly impressive was the fact that more than one hundred members of the state legislatures were present at the meeting. Many had come at their own expense. Some sixty of them were chairmen of the education committees of the upper or lower houses of their respective state legislatures.

"These are the men," I stated, "who determine day by day, or at least year by year, decisions in the legislatures of the many states. Their presence points a direction in which the Education Commission of the States may well move forward in the years ahead."

Governor Sanford had envisioned a body in which governors, state legislators and educators from all the states would come together to share their knowledge and discuss plans for the future. Today, from what I have heard, though the strengthening of the state departments of education has been progressing slowly, the prospects are bright for a useful role for the Education Commission of the States. I admit to a considerable degree of satisfaction. An inventor, like a writer, is not free from the pride of authorship.

Appendices

Four Addresses by J. B. Conant

1. Oration at the Solemn Observance of
the Tercentenary of Harvard College
Cambridge, Massachusetts, September 18, 1936

Such a gathering as this could come together only to commemorate an act of faith. This assembly honors a vision three centuries old and in so doing reaffirms an intent of perpetuating an ideal. A hundred years ago President Quincy, writing of the founding of Harvard, used these words: "On recurring to the origin of this seminary, our first feelings impel us to wonder and admire." From such admiration grew the celebration of the two hundredth anniversary; with no less reverential feeling the sons of Harvard have once again met here to mark the turn of another century.

The passage of a hundred years has enabled us to see more clearly the events which occurred between 1636 and the granting of the charter to the president and fellows in 1650. Thanks to the labors of the historians, we are able to appreciate more fully than did Quincy the spirit of the founders and to understand more completely the significance of their bold plan. And with the increase in our knowledge comes a more than proportional increase in our admiration. As you have heard, the Puritans' ambition was none other than to transplant to an untamed forest the ancient university tradition. They would be satisfied with nothing short of duplicating here in New England at least one college of Cambridge University. Carried forward by the strong tide of Puritanism, the enterprise was at first blessed with almost miraculous success. The goal might well seem to be in sight when, within twenty years of the founding, Oxford and Cambridge (then in the hands of dissenters, to be sure) recognized the Harvard degree as equivalent to their own. But many changes in both the mother country and the Bay Colony were yet to come. The enthusiasm for education in a new land waned, and even the second president of Harvard complained

651

of those who desired "to pull down schools of learning, or which is all one to take away the oyl from the lamps, denying or withholding maintenance from them." The acorn had been planted, the young tree was alive, but its growth was slow beyond the expectation of those who had brought the seed to a wild, new continent.

In the middle of the last century, in 1867 to be exact, the head of one of the Oxford colleges, an eminent scholar and educational reformer, saw no evidence that the university tradition had ever taken root in the United States. "America has no universities as we understand the term," he wrote, "the institutions so called being merely places for granting titular degrees." Taken literally, this harsh judgment is undoubtedly false, and yet I venture to think that it is not a gross exaggeration of the situation which then existed. The new spirit moving within the educational institutions of this country had not become evident to those outside the academic walls. Another decade was to pass before a university was opened at Baltimore, national in its scope, and proclaiming boldly that "all departments of learning should be promoted" and that "the glory of the University should rest upon the character of the teachers and scholars . . . and not upon their number nor upon the buildings constructed for their use."

We commemorate today the daring hope of a group of determined men—a hope the fulfillment of which was long delayed; delayed, indeed, until the lifetime of many now present here this morning. With feelings of gratitude we turn back through three centuries to pay homage to the faith that could see no obstacles and to ideals which are indeed eternal. But the real past which we salute is but yesterday. Harvard, together with all the other universities in this country, stands just beyond the threshold of a new undertaking. It is toward the future of our common enterprise that on this occasion we must direct our gaze.

The future of the university tradition in America—that is the problem that must concern all of us who are assembled here today. But what is this tradition; indeed, what is a university? Like any living thing, an academic institution is comprehensible only in terms of its history. For well on a thousand years there have been universities in the Western world. During the Middle Ages the air they breathed was permeated with the doctrines of a universal church; since the Reformation in Protestant countries these have undergone a slow and varied metamorphosis. But the essence of the university tradition has remained constant. From the first foundations to the present, four main streams have watered the soil on which the universities have flourished. These ultimate sources of strength are: first, the cultivation of learning for its own sake; second, the general educational stream of the liberal arts; third, the educational stream that makes possible the professions; and, last, the never-failing river of student life carrying all the power that comes from the gregarious impulses of human beings. All four streams are easily discerned bringing life to the English universities in the first half of the seventeenth century. For this reason Oxford and Cambridge flourished; and because they flourished, their sons who migrated to this strange land desired to cultivate the same sturdy tradition even in a wilderness.

The plans of President Dunster and his collaborators reveal clearly what the university tradition meant to the Anglo-Saxon world of the seventeenth century. Harvard's founders insisted on the "collegiate way of living," thus recognizing the importance of student life. They knew the educational values which arise from the daily intercourse between individual students and between student and tutor. Their concept of professional training was, to be sure, largely cast in terms of the ministry, but they envisaged also training in the law and medicine. The liberal arts educational tradition they transplanted *in toto* from the colleges which they had left behind. And finally, their zeal for the cultivation of learning is made evident by the reference in the charter of 1650 to "the advancement of all good literature, arts, and sciences. . . ."

Such, it seems to me, was the properly balanced plan of a university in a time when universities were flourishing; such, it seems to me, must be the idea of a university if institutions of higher learning are to fulfill their proper function in the times that are to come. But there have been periods of sickness, even of decay, in the history of almost every academic foundation. If one of the four vital streams I have mentioned either fails or swells to a torrent, thus destroying the proper balance of nourishment, then the true university tradition may perish. The cultivation of learning alone produces not a university but a research institute; the sole concern with the student life produces an academic country club or merely a football team maneuvering under a collegiate banner. On such abnormalities we need not dwell, but I should like to take a few moments to consider the disastrous effects of an overemphasis of either the liberal arts educational tradition or the element of professional training. This is a real danger at all times. For a university nourished exclusively from either one of these two educational streams always seems to the uninformed to be most healthy because they believe it to be most useful.

Let us consider, first, the situation created when the proper balance is upset by disproportionate concern with general education. In this case the stream of learning and research inevitably dries up; indeed, some have contended that it should. Newman defined his idea of a university as "a place of teaching universal knowledge, for the diffusion and extension of knowledge rather than the advancement." In his famous essay he recommended "a division of intellectual labour between learned academies and universities." (In twentieth-century terminology we should substitute the words "research institute" for "academy.") He believed that "to discover and to teach are two distinct functions." Newman's proposal amounted to eliminating one of the four vital ingredients evident in the life of the universities during their healthy periods. Unconsciously he was reflecting the condition of the English universities as he knew them before 1850 when they were still suffering from the long sleep of the eighteenth century. His proposition was in reality but a concise description of a disease. A few years later a prominent member of his own university, recognizing the condition as pathological, expressed himself in the following words:

The colleges [of Oxford and Cambridge] were in their origin endowments for the prolonged study of special and professional faculties by men of riper age. . . . This was the theory of the university in the Middle Ages and the design of the collegiate foundations in their origin. Time and circumstances

have brought about a total change. The colleges no longer promote the researches of science, or direct professional study. . . . Elementary teaching of
youths under twenty-two is now the only function performed by the university,
and almost the only object of college endowments. Colleges were homes for
the life-study of the highest and most abstruse parts of knowledge. They have
become boarding schools in which the elements of the learned languages are
taught to youths.

When we read this indictment penned before the completion of the
nineteenth-century reform of Oxford, we may well ask: If the intellectual
division of labor which Newman advocated and which still finds proponents
in our own time is to be desired, why were the English universities in
so unsatisfactory a condition? The accidents of time had destroyed the
ancient function of advancing knowledge and yet the institutions did not
flourish.

As further evidence, listen to what the Royal Commission of inquiry
into the condition of Oxford had to say on this subject in 1850. "It is generally acknowledged that both Oxford and the country at large suffer
greatly from the absence of a body of learned men devoting their lives
to the cultivation of science and the direction of academical education. . . . The presence of men eminent in various departments of knowledge would impart a dignity and stability to the whole institution, far
more effectual against attacks from without than the utmost amount of
privilege and protection." Attacks from without—the phrase has a modern
ring. Events proved that the Commission of 1850 was correct in its
statement; the changes which they advocated restored the confidence of the
nation in its two ancient institutions. They could not foresee, however,
the reluctance of certain sections of public opinion to welcome the restoration of the true university tradition. They did not realize how willingly
the public often follows those who argue for a separation of teaching and
research! No better illustration could be found than an article in the
London *Times* published in 1867. The writer endorses the general view
that "the university is mainly a place of education for young men just
before they enter upon life and should confine its whole administration to
this practical aim." (Please note the word "practical"!) "We are confident,"
the article continues, "that this view is the one from which Englishmen
in general regard the universities. It is a growing subject of discontent
among the public that the tutors and professors of both Oxford and Cambridge are becoming more and more absorbed in their own scientific
pursuits." And these remarks at the time when the two ancient universities
were undergoing that revolution which restored them to health and enabled
them to take the position of intellectual leadership which they now enjoy!
So shortsighted is often the popular reaction to matters of education.
Would the English public today wish to turn back to the years when the
professors and tutors rarely yielded, indeed, to the temptation to cultivate
sound learning and pursue new knowledge?

There is comparatively little danger, however, that in the years ahead
there will be any effective movement to turn the universities of this
country into boarding schools. The cause for apprehension seems to me
to lie in a different quarter. Even the most idealistic of those who lead
public opinion too often insist on examining educational institutions
through the dull glasses of immediate utility. To be sure, the promotion

of learning usually appears to be worth saving even when viewed through such an unfavorable medium. The most relentless reformers are at least partially convinced that at some time almost all research may be materially rewarding. There is, however, a growing demand for more and more professional training, and there is a tendency to stretch the word "profession" until it comprises every vocation. The utilitarian demand for specialized vocational training and the practical man's contempt for useless knowledge go hand in hand. When such influences gain control, an institution of higher learning supplies training, not education, and the promotion of learning is degraded to a vehicle for providing material well-being. The liberal arts conception of a general education disappears and with it the institution's most important contribution to the land. The universities of a country are the sanctuaries of the inner life of the nation. When they cease to be concerned with things of the spirit, they cease to fulfill their most important function.

If I am correct, then, in my interpretation of academic history, the future of the university tradition in America depends on keeping a proper balance between the four essential ingredients—the advancement of learning, the liberal arts college, professional training and a healthy student life. None must be neglected; no one must be allowed to predominate unduly. If this balance can be maintained, the universities of this country, privately endowed and publicly supported alike, will function both as instruments of higher education and as centers for developing a national culture worthy of this rich and powerful land.

Are we capable of evolving an American civilization commensurate with our opportunities? Surely this is the challenging question of the day. This is the question which transcends in importance even the most pressing demands of our troubled postwar period. Less than a century ago many people expressed grave doubts whether learning could be cultivated in a democracy. The last fifty years have proved them wrong. We can be proud of what has been accomplished in this republic, but only a start has been made. We must press on with all the earnestness and faith of those early settlers whose brave aspirations we honor by our ceremonies today.

A wave of anti-intellectualism is passing round the world. We see evidences of it on every hand but it is no new phenomenon. Before Harvard was founded Bacon referred to the "objections concerning the dignity of learning which arise from ignorance, appearing sometimes in the zeal and jealousy of divines; sometimes in the severity and arrogancy of politicians; sometimes in the errors and imperfections of learned men themselves." With these sources of objections we are all familiar. But the anti-intellectualism of the present is in part a protest—a most ungrateful protest, to be sure—against the benefactions of the learned world. It expresses a rebellion against the very triumphs of applied science, against the machines from which we would not be separated and yet toward which we feel a deep resentment. It is the expression of our weariness as we see an ever-increasing wealth of new knowledge poured at our feet by the scholars of the arts and letters no less than by the scientists. Intellectual anarchy in our schools and colleges has been more or less rife for the better part of a hundred years. "Will it never end?" we are tempted to cry in despair.

To bring order out of an educational chaos is the mission of the liberal arts curriculum of our universities—that is why it is important that this ancient tradition be not overwhelmed. Those of us who have faith in human reason believe that in the next hundred years we can build an educational basis for a unified, coherent culture suited to a democratic country in a scientific age—no chauvinistic dogma, but a true national culture fully cognizant of the international character of learning. In this undertaking the schools are involved quite as much as the universities, but the latter must lead the way. The older educational discipline, whether we like it or not, was disrupted before any of us were born. It was based on the study of the classics and mathematics; it provided a common background which steadied the thinking of all educated men. We cannot bring back this system if we would, but we must find its modern equivalent. Like our ancestors we must study the past, for "he who is ignorant of what occurred before he was born is always a child." In my opinion it is primarily the past development of our modern era which we must study and study most exhaustively and critically. We must examine the immediate origins of our political, economic and cultural life and then work backward. We must not, however, spread the inquiry over so wide a range that the average man will obtain only a superficial knowledge. It does not seem to me to be a step in the right direction to dip our children first in one barrel of tinted whitewash and then in another. The equivalent of the old classical discipline is not to be found in a bowing acquaintance with universal history and general science, and an exposure to scattered examples of art and literature. Our present educational practice, which insists on the thorough study of at least one discipline, is certainly sound.

For the development of a national culture based on a study of the past, one condition is essential. This is absolute freedom of discussion, absolutely unmolested inquiry. We must have a spirit of tolerance which allows the expression of all opinions however heretical they may appear. Since the seventeenth century this has been achieved in the realm of religion. It is no longer possible for some bigoted Protestant to object if any person within the universities or without expounds sympathetically the philosophy of St. Thomas Aquinas. It is no longer possible for a member of the Roman Catholic Church to take offense at a critical discussion of Galileo's trial. Statements believed to be erroneous are met openly and fairly by counterarguments. But there is no persecution; there has been an end to religious bigotry in this country, and there are no signs of its return.

Will the same conditions prevail in the future when political and economic problems are examined? Unfortunately there are ominous signs that a new form of bigotry may arise. This is most serious, for we cannot develop the unifying educational forces we so sorely need unless all matters may be openly discussed. The origin of the Constitution, for example, the functioning of the three branches of the federal government, the forces of modern capitalism, must be dissected as fearlessly as the geologist examines the origin of the rocks. On this point there can be no compromise; we are either afraid of heresy or we are not. If we are afraid, there will be no adequate discussion of the genesis of our national life; the door will be shut to the development of a culture which will satisfy our needs.

Harvard was founded by dissenters. Before two generations had passed there was a general dissent from the first dissent. Heresy has long been in the air. We are proud of the freedom which has made this possible even when we most dislike some particular form of heresy we may encounter.

In a debate in the House of Commons, Gladstone reviewed the history of Oxford and spoke of the lamentable condition of that institution during the reign of Queen Mary. Quoting a historian of that period, he continued: "The cause of the failure is easy to discover. The Universities had everything, except the most necessary element of all—Freedom: which by the immutable laws of nature, is always an indispensable condition of real and permanent prosperity in the higher intellectual cultivation and its organs." With this conclusion all who cherish our heritage must agree: without freedom the prosperity most important for this country cannot be achieved—the prosperity of our cultural life.

The university tradition in this country has been sustained through three centuries by the courage and sacrifice of many men. An ever-increasing number of benefactors have followed John Harvard's example. Patrons of learning have not only favored Harvard with their gifts but have established and aided other universities throughout the nation. In cities and states institutions have been founded and supported from the public funds. In all our colleges learned men have labored with little material reward to "advance learning and perpetuate it to posterity." Teachers of the young have so lived their lives that the coming generations might be inspired with a love of wisdom. All this devotion on the part of those concerned with higher education stands as a clear witness to the significance of what was here envisaged three hundred years ago. He who enters a university walks on hallowed ground.

If we attempt to sum up in one phrase the aim of higher education, we can do no better than to speak of "the search for the truth." A little more than a hundred years ago when President Quincy was exploring the Harvard archives, he came upon the early record book in which is the famous drawing of the Harvard seal as specified by a vote of the Overseers in 1643—the open books with the word "Veritas." Delighted by his discovery, Quincy restored "Veritas" to the college arms, but it was not until 1885 that this word found a permanent place upon our seal. To me there is an arresting symbolism in this bit of apparently accidental history. It is significant that the Puritan founders chose the word "Veritas," for this word is the touchstone of the real university tradition. And it is fitting that the original seal was finally readopted just when Harvard was developing into a great modern university.

When the Puritans wrote "Veritas" upon the open books, they had in mind two paths by which truth could be obtained: one, revelation as interpreted with the aid of human reason; the other, the advancement of knowledge and learning. Bacon expressed the spirit of the age which was to follow when he declared that a man cannot "search too far or be too well studied in the book of God's word, or in the book of God's work, but rather let men endeavor an endless progress or proficience in both." In the present century a French mathematician wrote: "The search for truth should be the goal of our activities; it is the sole end worthy of them. . . . If we wish more and more to free man from material cares, it is that he may be able to employ the liberty obtained in the study and contemplation of truth. . . . When I speak of truth," he continued, "I refer to scientific truth but also moral truth of which what we call justice is only one aspect. . . . Whosoever loves the one can not help loving the other." This same thought was expressed by President Eliot in an address in 1891 which stands as a challenge to our time. Speaking of a university as a "society of learned men," he defined their goal as "the incessant, quiet, single-minded search after new truth, the condition for both the material and intellectual progress of the nation and the race." The intellectual progress of the race—during the coming century of academic history what gifts will the American people bring to further this great advance? A hundred years from today the record will be read. With humility but with hope we look forward to that moment. May it then be manifest to all that the universities of this country have led the way to new light, and may the nation give thanks that Harvard was founded.

2. What Are We Arming to Defend?

Address before the Southern College Conference
Memphis, Tennessee, October 21, 1940

When I accepted an invitation to appear before this distinguished gathering of educators from all over the South, I had expected to speak on some subject connected with the work of the liberal arts colleges. That was last April; in terms of the calendar only six months ago—in terms of the problems facing us as educators and citizens, at least six decades past. As I think back to the date on which I received your kind invitation, I feel as though I were revisiting a country of tropical sunshine, as though I were journeying from the cold blizzards of some bleak plains in the far north to a carefree land of pleasant skies.

Let me ask you to retrace with me the long journey this country has taken since last April. I turn as a reminder to the back files of the *New York Times*. On April 30 the headline ran: "Isolation to Rule." But ten days later came the news: "Nazis Invade Holland." The climate of opinion begins to alter. As we turn the pages of the files for the month of May, we note that fourteen hundred students in one university have signed a petition opposing any aid to the Allies; we notice the first interest in a program of intensive rearmament. This interest mounts with each successive week and with each following month. In October the papers now record the registering of our youth for Selective Service, a large expansion of the Navy personnel and the construction of a two-ocean Navy authorized. From all sides, today, come demands for greater speed in rearmament.

And a Gallup Poll shows more than 70 percent of the country in favor of more aid to Britain.

Why has all this come to pass in the United States in these six months? Is this hysteria on our part, or is it an awakening to a menace that is real? It seems to me that in answering such a question one must merely attempt to evaluate the probabilities. First, the probability of the true nature of the enemy, who I believe is already pounding on our gates. Second, the probability of the future course of this enemy if he is successful in his present struggle with the British nation. I believe that we are witnessing today a phenomenon comparable to the sweep of Mohammed and his followers in their first successes against the Byzantine Empire. If that be so, our peril is real—and force alone can provide the answer.

Those who view the present as gravely as I do may of course be wrong. So a messenger might be wrong who rides frantically to warn of an impending flood about to engulf a sleeping town. "The dam is breaking, the river will rise!" So shouts the horseman as he gallops through empty streets. Those who hear him must make a quick decision. The man is an alarmist—no doubt of that; a propagandist, too. But is he right or wrong as a *prophet*? That is the point—that is what his hearers must decide. He says he has seen the dam breaking, but how can he be sure? Shall we assume he is right? Or shall we assume he is wrong and by doing nothing save ourselves a highly inconvenient dislocation of our lives on a black and rainy night?

The analogy is not perfect, but are we not in much the same predicament as the townsfolk I have just described? We have heard during the last few months from not a few experienced observers of the tragedy that has occurred in Europe. Their interpretations uniformly sound the alarm for this country. Shall we as a free people heed the warnings? To answer this question, each individual must weigh the probabilities, examine the evidence, participate in the debate by which a democratic nation must settle fundamental policy. Those who feel we are going too fast have the right and duty to shout "Stop!" Those who fret at the delay are entitled to try to convert others to their views.

Clearly, one decision has already been made, not only by the government but by a great majority of the people—namely, that we must rearm at once. All agree that we must not underestimate the danger which might possibly come to us from a triumphant victory of the totalitarian forces. We have passed a law for raising an army of a million men; we are frantically endeavoring to develop the production of ammunition and every instrument of war. But to my mind all this may well be not enough; not enough unless it assures the defeat of the Axis powers and thus frees us from the totalitarian threat.

In the last six months we have witnessed a drastic change in our intellectual and emotional climate. I fear it will be many years before the climate shifts again. Indeed, there are those who argue that the period in which we now live is normal and the years just gone, abnormal. Perhaps history will record that the many sincere people who believed that a war to end war could be fought and won, and that war as an instrument of national policy could be abolished by mere words, were suffering from a delusion peculiar to their age. It may be that for many generations yet we must reckon that force is the ultimate arbiter of all fundamental conflicts. The strength and vigilance of our police would indicate the necessity of armed might to keep the peace.

There may be an analogy between man's desire to abolish war and his desire to abolish death. For centuries alchemists sought the impossible—the elixir of life which would give to man eternal youth. Today we seek instead the maximum of health. Death is inevitable, but, thanks to modern medicine, many premature deaths are now preventable. In a sense the ills the human flesh is heir to are to some degree controlled. Perhaps it may be so with war. I wonder if the task before humanity is not that of minimizing war rather than abolishing it. In the last analysis, even if force alone will decide great issues, still the world may be so organized that the number of wars and their magnitude may be reduced rather than increased. That is a goal that we can all hold before us, though it is now a distant one. For the moment can we escape the bitter truth that only through fighting has liberty been gained in the past; and that only by the willingness and capacity to fight can freedom in the present be preserved?

If we as a free nation must be prepared to use armed force to maintain the basis of our independence, on what fronts shall we stand guard? Where are the true frontiers of the United States? Can we as a free people, even heavily armed, withdraw within our boundaries or be content to protect only the hemisphere in which we live? This issue, to my mind, underlies the fundamental questions now before the country. Can we, as Mr. Bullitt said, trust in the Atlantic Ocean as the French trusted in the Maginot Line? Above all, can we restrict our efforts not only in space but in time? Will we remain armed for a few years and then forget our previous alarms? Or are we willing to give a continuing pledge of our readiness to fight to preserve our way of life?

I believe it can be argued that we are now living in these days of terrific peril for the very reason that we were too shortsighted when we fought a war a generation ago. We thought then that by a relatively minor effort we could once and for all reform the world and then forever live disarmed in peace. To my mind, if this country makes that error again, we shall forgo not only the hope of peace, but the hope of maintaining the democratic and liberal way of life we all hold dear. Must we not accept the responsibility that, fully armed, prepared to fight if need be, and in collaboration with the others who hold our same ideals, we must organize a large portion of the civilized world in such a way that we may continue to prosper as a national unit and develop the potentialities of our nation?

In speaking before this audience in this place, I hardly need to press this point of view. The very history of the Mississippi Valley has proved that the people who dwell here in the South and West have in the last one hundred years been true exponents of American greatness. For two centuries before that time they had maintained their freedom by their willingness to fight the Spaniards and the French. It was they who made possible the Louisiana Purchase. They recognized that the destiny of this country lay in an expanding vision. I dare believe that the same spirit which made this country go forward in the adventure on this continent will once again be awakened to meet the challenge of these times.

But it is not with foreign policy or material rearmament that I wish to deal tonight. These matters touch only indirectly the most important function in defense which most of us here assembled this evening can perform. It is our task in our colleges and universities to try to think through the implications of all that has happened in these last six months, to evolve a philosophy of action for the dread days ahead.

I have been discussing up to now essentially strategic problems. I have not yet come to grips with the fundamental question which a skeptic might push home. We are arming to defend ourselves either on our own frontiers or on a larger area against the totalitarian states. We are arming to defend ourselves because we believe that the world faces conflict of armed force between two totally different ways of life. A man from Mars, arriving at this moment, might well ask some such question as the following: "Granted that you as a nation wish to survive and not become a servile state, still, what are the earmarks or characteristics of your way of life which you value so highly and for which you are willing to fight if need be? What are the fundamentals of your creed as compared with these new creeds of the totalitarian states?" A fair question, and one that must concern all who are engaged with the education of our youth.

What are we arming to defend?

We are arming, I take it, to prevent such a change in the political and economic situation in this country as would make us a subservient people to a foreign master state. We are arming to prevent such a revolution in our way of life as would make this land for everyone who values liberty a prison-house. But we are not arming to defend an invariant type of political system. I should be unwilling personally to declare even that we are arming to defend democracy, for the word "democracy" has suffered grievously in this last decade. Democracy can mean anything from a dictatorship of the proletariat to a preservation of the *status quo*. It can mean a belief in the divine right of 51 percent of the voters to alter in any way at any moment all laws and customs. Or it can mean the continuation in power in some locality of a privileged class.

We are not arming to defend a particular form of representative government. We may at some later time wish to modify and simplify our highly complex governmental pattern. But most of us would believe we were arming to defend certain principles embodied in our constitutional form of government. First, the civil liberties of the individual, summed up in the Bill of Rights. Second, the political machinery which enables the mass of the people to decide through elected representatives on major issues. Third, the written laws and constitutions which, together with tradition, protect the rights of the minority on the one hand, and on the other prevent sudden gusts of popular opinion from altering the structure of society.

Democracy interpreted by some of those who love to mouth this word has been at times a false shield to cover the aims of revolutionists. The Constitution, let us admit, has also been used as a false shield for others. It has been too often proclaimed as all but divine by those who seek under its protection only to hold a personal and privileged position. Between the disgruntled who would be revolutionists and the complacent privileged who would be Bourbons, a true democracy must steer a middle course.

If this be the task, how should we proceed as educators? In a recent article, Harry Elmer Barnes pleads for an educational system which he believes has the responsibility of blueprinting a new social and economic order. I shall not attempt to debate the wisdom of this proposal, which is not new with Mr. Barnes. Rather, I shall quote to show some of the dangers inherent in this point of view. Mr. Barnes writes as follows:

> This creation of an intelligent attitude toward the past is indispensable as the preparation for the second major function of education, viewed as an instrument of social progress, namely, a critical appraisal of the existing social order. . . . Until we are made completely aware of the defects of the existing social order we can have neither any incentive to work for a better social future nor any precise conception of what is actually required to bring about a better day.

Here speaks a trenchant critic. He is entitled to be heard. But one cannot help raising the question: If one indoctrinates in the youth of the country only a desire to see the defects of our existing social order, is there not a danger that dissatisfaction will become so great that a spirit of hopeless futility will prevail? There comes a point when a man can become so convinced of the weakness of a structure that he is no longer interested in making any sacrifice to preserve the foundations on which it rests. Sufficient indoctrination of "awareness of the defects of the existing social order" will certainly sap the courage of many people, sap it to a point where willingness to fight has all but disappeared. This is the danger on the one side which confronts any free democratic land. But we must recognize that the dangers on the other side are equally menacing and real. To equate the *status quo* with perfection has been the insidious disease of every civilization. To attempt to stifle criticism is the method by which a ruling class endeavors to sustain through the generations its rights and powers. Complacency will sap the courage of a nation as readily as will destructive self-criticism.

The true spirit of liberty, it seems to me, is to be found in the golden mean between destructive criticism on the one hand and complacent dogma on the other. This, it seems to me, is the first and foremost doctrine which we in our colleges and universities should seek to inculcate in our students. But the golden mean is the hardest thing in the world to maintain. It is in a sense illogical: it is a way of life. The free way of life is a hard way of life. And that fact is in itself a challenge—it is a challenge which we should every day place before our youth.

The history of this republic has been unique. And the uniqueness of our way of life rests not so much on constitutional democracy as on our social system—a system which is the embodiment of the golden mean of which I speak. I believe that fundamentally it is this unique form of society that we are really arming to defend. I believe that the ambition of every thoughtful citizen of this republic is to assist in keeping inviolate the free way of life which has developed on this continent in the last two hundred years.

I have ventured on other occasions to speak of the American ideal as that of a free and classless, or casteless, society—a society made classless through the maximum of social mobility. Let me examine for a moment the phrase "social mobility," for this is the heart of my argument. If large numbers of young people can develop their own capacities irrespective of the economic status of their parents, then social mobility is high. If, on the other hand, the future of a young man or woman is determined almost entirely by inherited privilege or the lack of it, social mobility is nonexistent. You are all familiar with the old American adage, "Three generations from shirt sleeves to shirt sleeves." This implies a high degree of social mobility, both up and down. It implies that sons and daughters must and can seek their own level, obtain their own economic rewards, engage in any occupation irrespective of what their parents might have done.

Such is the American ideal. But I gravely fear that social and economic changes during the last forty years have whittled away much of the reality on which the ideal is founded. To be sure, we are all willing still to pay lip service to such phrases as "There are no classes in America." But mere lip service does not meet the altered conditions of modern times. We must endeavor in every way possible to re-establish the validity of our ideal.

Our educational system, for example, in spite of universal schooling, is perpetuating more than we realize a hereditary class of highly educated people. I ask each one of you if you would be willing when you return to your educational institutions to compare the number of boys and girls in your colleges from families with incomes of less than $2,000 with the number of families in this income group in the region which you serve. I venture the prediction that whether your institution be tax-supported or privately endowed, you will, with few exceptions, find that you do *not* have in your student body anything like a representative cross-section of the community—that, to some degree at least, the ideal of equality of educational opportunity has not been reached. If this be so, is there not here an educational challenge to the American ideal?

There are many citizens of this nation who are less concerned than I am with the immediate danger to our integrity stated in terms of force. They worry rather lest the internal seeds of dissension, some poison indigenous to democracy, shall destroy our soul. I recognize the causes of their apprehension, but these causes are not new. May I remind you of the famous pessimistic letter of Lord Macaulay? In this letter, written in 1857, Macaulay predicted the eventual collapse of any nation which had universal suffrage. England he felt was safe, for he boasted that in England, to use his own words, "The supreme power is in the hands of a class, numerous indeed, but select, of an educated class, of a class which is, and knows itself to be deeply interested in the security of property and the maintenance of order."

On the other hand, prophesied Macaulay, when the United States comes to a period of depression and unemployment, this nation will be unable to ride the storm. Through such evil times the Whig historian wished us a good deliverance. "But," he said, "my reason and my wishes are at war; and I cannot help foreboding the worst. It is quite plain that your government will never be able to restrain a distressed and discontented majority, for with you the majority is the government, and has the rich, who are always a minority, absolutely at its mercy. . . . I seriously apprehend that you will, in some such season of adversity as I have described, do things which will prevent prosperity from returning."

Some of you may have heard this pessimistic letter repeated very often in the last half-dozen years. Some of you may feel that the crisis which Macaulay predicted is close at hand. If so, an answer given nearly seventy years ago by a future President of the United States, General James A. Garfield, may be both relevant and heartening. Personally I may say it is the only answer to Macaulay's letter that I have seen which will stand up against thoughtful analysis rather than wishful thinking. It speaks in terms of the characteristic American spirit—speaks with calm optimism of the unique nature of our institutions.

In an address in 1873 on "The Future of the Republic; its Dangers and its Hopes," Garfield referred to Macaulay's letter with these words:

I venture the declaration that this opinion of Macaulay's is vulnerable on several grounds. It leaves out the great counterbalancing force of universal education. But furthermore, it is based upon a belief from which few if any British writers have been able to emancipate themselves; namely, the belief that mankind are born into permanent classes, and that in the main they must live, work, and die in the fixed class or condition in which they are born. It is hardly possible for a man reared in an aristocracy like that of England to eliminate this conviction from his mind. . . . The English theory of national stability is, that there must be a permanent class who shall hold in their own hands so much of the wealth, the privilege, and the political power of the kingdom, that they can compel the admiration and obedience of all other classes. . . . Where such permanent classes exist, the conflict of which Macaulay speaks is inevitable.

Mark these words carefully, gentlemen, for I believe they entitle General Garfield to high credit for political foresight. To my mind, the inevitable conflict of which he speaks, a conflict which is sure to come when permanent classes and universal suffrage exist in one nation, has been in progress in Great Britain during the past few years. It seems to me that in the last decade the political forces in England have been paralyzed by a deep cleavage between the two major parties, a cleavage reflecting the struggle of which Garfield spoke.

But whether I am right or not in my interpretation of current history, let me finish Garfield's statement: "We point to the fact," said the future President,

that in this country there are no classes in the British sense of the word—no impassable barriers of caste. In our political society there run no fixed horizontal strata above which none can pass. Our society resembles rather the waves of the ocean, whose every drop may move freely among its fellows, and may rise toward the light until it flashes on the crest of the highest wave.

"Our society resembles rather the waves of the ocean, whose every drop may move freely among its fellows. . . ."

These magnificent, brave words, gentlemen, summarize for me the unique ideal of American life. As long as they express the fundamentals of our social philosophy—the vision toward which we as a people strive—we still have a firm basis on which the citizens of this country may stand united. Through the willingness of all contending groups to labor devoutly for this unique American ideal, a true national loyalty can be securely anchored, the militant faith of all can be pledged to a unifying tradition and a common cause. As long as we as a democratic free people are willing to make every needed sacrifice to preserve this cause, we can face the future with real confidence. Then, and only then, may we hope to weather the tempests of our time.

3. Unity and Diversity in Secondary Education

Address before a meeting of the American
Association of School Administrators
Boston, Massachusetts, April 7, 1952

Tonight, I should like to try to place in perspective certain features of our American system of tax-supported schools. As educators we may be well aware of the fact that our system is essentially unique in several respects, but people are inclined to take for granted certain assumptions that underlie the development of our public schools. They realize all too little what would be the consequences of drastic alterations and are, therefore, too complacent about some types of hostile criticism; they are too little willing to make the sacrifices required to maintain our schools as effective instruments of our democracy. Those involved directly with public schools themselves are at times perhaps unaware of certain challenges and reluctant to make adjustments required by these challenges. If in what I have to say this evening I appear somewhat critical of one phase of secondary education, I trust that no one here will misunderstand me. I hope that it is unnecessary for me to spend any time reaffirming my deep conviction that the expansion of our free tax-supported schools in this country has been an essential element in our national life.

According to my view, the doctrine of equality of which De Tocqueville wrote so long ago in his report on America has come to mean in the United States not parity of status for adults but equality of opportunity for children. The vast expansion of secondary education in this nation has created a new engine of democracy; it is of the utmost importance how this engine is to operate in the future. If we so desire, it can be used to restore fluidity to our social and economic life each generation and in so doing make available for the national welfare reservoirs of potential talent now untapped. At the same time, by stressing the democratic elements in our school life and the comprehensive features of our organization, we can promote the social and political ideals necessary for the harmonious functioning of an economic system based on private ownership but committed to the ideals of social justice.

We desire on the one hand to provide through our schools unity in our national life. On the other we seek the diversity that comes from freedom of action and expression by small groups of citizens. We look with disfavor on any monolithic type of educational structure; we shrink from any idea of regimentation, of uniformity as to the details of the many phases of secondary education. Unity we can achieve if our public schools remain the primary vehicle for the education of our youth, and if, as far as possible, all the youth of a community attend the same school irrespective of family fortune or cultural background. Diversity in experimentation we maintain by continued emphasis on the concept of local responsibility for our schools.

Both these ideas are to a considerable degree novel in the United States; a combination of them is to be found nowhere else in the world. Let me, therefore, remind you of the other approaches to education found in the closely related cultures of other English-speaking nations.

When I visited Australia last summer, I discovered what was to me an amazing phenomenon; a sharp dual system of education, many private independent schools and a centrally controlled state system of free education. Though we have much in common in our educational practices, this dual system serves to place in sharp contrast our American scheme. Let me make it plain I am not criticizing the educators in the Antipodes. Education is not an exportable commodity. What is a good system for one type of society may not be good for another. Nevertheless, it is interesting to see how several ways of accomplishing the same objective may be arranged.

Nowhere in the world today does the Protestant private school flourish as it does in several Australian states; this on a continent more recently settled than North America and in a society famous for its labor governments and its concern for social welfare. In two of the large Australian states there are more students sixteen to seventeen years of age enrolled in private schools than in tax-supported schools. This is no new phenomenon. Quite the contrary, the tradition of the great public schools of England (public in the British sense, not ours)—the tradition of Winchester, Eton, Harrow—was brought to Australia in the mid-nineteenth century. This tradition somewhat modified has flourished there ever since. As a consequence there is in Australia a dual system of secondary education.

What are the factors that have favored this duality in education? From my observation there are two: first, the firm belief on the part of many Australians that secondary education should not be divorced from formal religious instruction; second, the fact that there are large urban centers in each Australian state. (In spite of the size of the continent and the statistically thin population, half the inhabitants live in large cities.) The private schools are situated with few exceptions in the large metropolitan areas (Sydney, Melbourne, Adelaide); unlike the English public schools, they are not primarily boarding schools but rather day schools with a nucleus of boarders. The tuition has consequently been kept relatively low, and the range of income groups of the families patronizing them is fairly broad. In each capital city there is a group of more-or-less competing schools, each with church connections; there are Church of England schools, Methodist schools, Presbyterian schools, Catholic schools. These schools in some states are attended by students who receive state scholarships, but for the most part the schools are privately financed. The students who go on to a university (about half the graduates) must all jump the same academic hurdle. So the state to a surprising degree controls the curriculum, there is pedagogic uniformity coupled with social diversity—almost the exact reverse of the American situation.

Diversity in American secondary education is assured by our insistence on the doctrine of local control. We have no restrictions on the variety of approaches to secondary education presented by our thousands of local boards. Indeed, to an outsider I should think our diversity would look like educational chaos. But this is a characteristic of our flexible decentralized concept of democracy. The time may conceivably come when a state or the federal government may jeopardize this concept, but as far as secondary education is concerned, I do not detect any danger signals in that direction now. The NYA threat which was real in the 1930s has almost been forgotten.

I do believe, however, that there is some reason to fear lest a dual system of secondary education may in some states, at least, come to threaten the democratic unity provided by our public schools. I refer to the desire of some people to increase the scope and number of private schools. At present the proponents of such a movement are often not outspoken in their demands, but a dual system of schools with tax money flowing in some form to private schools seems to be a possibility in some people's minds. In this connection I think it is only fair to insist that the critics of our public schools should make clear their stand on two important points. To each one who attacks our public schools I would ask the simple question: "Would you like to increase the number and scope of the private schools?" If the candid answer is in the affirmative, I would then ask a second question: "Do you look forward to the day when tax money will directly or indirectly assist these schools?" If the answer is again in the affirmative, the lines have been clearly drawn and a rational debate on a vital issue can proceed.

Needless to say, I would find myself on the opposite side from this hypothetical candid critic of public education. But what I am more concerned with in the year 1952 is to make the hostile critics of the public schools in the United States show their colors. One of the most vocal of these is a Protestant clergyman who reveals himself when he writes, "The Communist is not, as a matter of fact, much of a revolutionist. The Communist would only substitute the logical secularism of Karl Marx for the pragmatic secularism of John Dewey." If this clergyman would start off all his attacks on modern education by stating that for him secularism and Communism are equal dangers, the reader would be in a better position to evaluate what he was about to read—or he might decide to skip it altogether.

There are many sincere Protestants, Jews and Catholics who believe that secondary education divorced from a denominational religious core of instruction is bad education. They erroneously assume that the tax-supported schools are not concerned with moral and spiritual values. This is essentially the point of view of the headmasters of the Australian private schools. Now, that such people have a right to organize their own schools I do not question. The United States Supreme Court settled the law on that point in the famous Oregon Case of 1926. But I do question the honesty of their tactics when they attack the public schools in an attempt to undermine confidence in secular education.

I am well aware that in several English-speaking nations public funds are used to assist church-connected schools. This is the practice in England, Scotland, and to some degree in some Australian states. Whether the state and the church or churches can develop a working arrangement that prevents a state control of the church or church control of the state is another story. My concern is with the United States. We do not have and have never had an established church. To my mind, our schools should serve all creeds. The greater the proportion of our youth who attend independent schools, the greater the threat to our democratic unity. Therefore, to use taxpayers' money to assist such a move is, for me, to suggest that American society use its own hands to destroy itself.

In some of our large Western cities, private schools are today attracting an increasing number of the sons and daughters of the well-to-do. To offset this, here in New England there seems to be a reverse tendency for fathers who attended private schools to send their children to public schools. Where the national balance lies no one can say. But I cannot help regretting that private schools have been established in the last twenty years in certain urban areas where a generation ago a public high school served *all* the youth of the town or city.

There is no use for us who are emotionally committed to public schools as schools for all to denounce or bemoan the growth of private schools. The founding of a new independent school in a locality is a challenge to those connected with public education. Granted the "snob aspect" of some of these new independent schools, nevertheless, I feel sure in many cases they would never have come into existence if the management of the local high school had been wiser. Education is a social process. This is a free country, and people will not be pushed around by educators. What is required is for those concerned to improve the high schools; public school administrators must recognize the validity of some of the criticisms now directed against them in terms of the failure of the high school to provide adequate education for the gifted. The problem is especially acute in metropolitan areas. The success of the private school in Australian cities should be a reminder of where we may be headed.

In terms of numbers involved, the dual nature of our present system may seem slight—92 percent of our secondary school pupils are in public schools. In terms of a stratification of society on economic and religious lines, however, the duality is marked, indeed. In socioeconomic terms, we are not as far from the English public school system as we sometimes like to think. Chancellor McConnell of the University of Buffalo, reporting on English education, notes the predominance of public school graduates (in the English sense) over grammar school graduates in the entrants to Oxford in 1948. A half a dozen of the best-known Eastern colleges in the United States would show a similar social phenomenon; they enroll something like half their students from private Protestant schools, which encompass only a few percent of an entire age group. But it is only fair to point out that these same colleges have been trying desperately hard in the last twenty-five years to attract a larger number of public high school graduates, particularly from various regions of the country. They aim to be national in terms of geography and representative of all income groups; that they have to some degree succeeded in moving nearer their goal is, to me, a hopeful sign.

What is the basic objection to a dual system of education? you may ask. Or put it the other way round: what are the advantages of free schools for all? To ask these questions is almost to give the answers. If one accepts the ideal of a democratic, fluid society with a minimum of class distinction, the maximum of fluidity, the maximum of understanding between different vocational groups, then the ideal secondary school is a comprehensive public high school. If one has doubts about the ability of secular schools to promote the growth of moral and spiritual values, then these doubts must be weighed against the democratic objectives I have just listed. Similarly, if a family questions the ability of a high school to prepare a gifted boy adequately for university work, the family will have to balance these misgivings against the advantages to the boy of mixing with all sorts of people when he is young.

Of this much there can be no doubt. A society which wished generation after generation to perpetuate class distinction based on hereditary status would certainly demand a dual system of schools; so, too, would a society like that in the Province of Quebec which wishes to perpetuate two different cultural groups. A dual system serves and helps to maintain group cleavages; the absence of a dual system does the reverse. This is particularly true of the secondary schools. Indeed, I would plead with those who insist on sending their children to denominational schools that they might limit their insistence on this type of education to the elementary years.

Our liberties will only be secure in the hands of the people, Jefferson declared, and in the hands of the people with a certain "degree of instruction." This belief coupled with the doctrine of equality has led to an enormous expansion of secondary school and college enrollment in the United States. With this expansion has come, by necessity, revolutionary changes in the curriculum of the schools. Unless one is prepared to maintain the thesis that there should be one type of general education for the well-to-do, another for the poor, there can be no retreat from the present position. And, let me make it clear, I advocate no retreat. Furthermore, in suggesting a greater emphasis on the identification of the scholastically gifted and their education in languages and mathematics, I have by no means repudiated the movement that has led to the liberalizing of our high school curriculum. Quite the contrary, I believe this movement should spread, for there are far too many public secondary schools today that are trying to use a program suitable for the intellectual development of a few as the basis of the general education of the many. There is too little effort made to develop a course in what has been called "common learnings" now used in some schools, but far too few.

By organizing our free schools on as comprehensive a basis as possible, we can continue to give our children an understanding of democracy by practicing it in school. Religious tolerances, mutual respect among vocational groups, belief in the rights of the individual are among the virtues that the best of our high schools now foster. An understanding of the political machinery of our federal union, of the significance of the Anglo-Saxon tradition of the common law, the distinction between decisions arrived at by "due process" and those obtained by social pressures—by duress—all this is now being achieved to some degree in the free public schools of this country.

What the great public schools of England accomplished for the future governing class of that nation in the nineteenth century the American high school is now attempting to accomplish for those who govern the United States, namely, all the people. A system of schools where the future doctor, lawyer, professor, politician, banker, industrial executive, labor leader and manual worker have gone to school together at age fifteen to seventeen is something that exists nowhere in the world outside of the United States. That such schools should be maintained and made even more democratic and comprehensive seems to me to be essential for the future of this republic. The false antithesis between education for the gifted and education for *all* American youth must be resolved. If this can be accomplished, then one demand for a further increase in private independent education will largely disappear.

The growth of free public high schools in this country would indicate to me that public opinion in the United States has been committed to a single, not a dual, system of education. The history of the rest of this century will prove whether or not the commitment is irrevocable. The verdict will depend, I believe, in no small measure on whether the comprehensive public high school can win a wide support. In short, can we have both uniformity and diversity in secondary education? My answer is that we can. The answer of this audience of school administrators, I feel sure, is that we must.

4. Social Dynamite in Our Large Cities

Keynote Address before a conference
convened by the National Committee
for Children and Youth
Washington, D. C., May 24, 1961

I appreciate the opportunity of serving as keynote speaker and chairman of this workshop Conference on Unemployed, Out-of-School Youth in Urban Areas sponsored by the National Committee for Children and Youth. It is a sobering responsibilty. I make this statement principally because I am convinced that the problem you ladies and gentlemen are here to discuss poses a serious threat to our free society. I submit that the existence in the slums of our large cities of thousands of youth ages 16-21 who are both out of school and out of work is an explosive situation. It is social dynamite.

In preparation for this Conference, a few special studies were conducted in slum areas of large cities to find out what the facts really were. In a slum section composed almost entirely of Negroes in one of our largest cities the following situation was found. A total of 59 percent of the male youth between the ages of 16 and 21 were out of school and unemployed. They were roaming the streets. Of the boys who graduated from high school 48 percent were unemployed in contrast to 63 percent of the boys who had dropped out of school. In short, two-thirds of the male dropouts did not have jobs and about half of the high school graduates did not have jobs. In such a situation, a pupil may well ask why bother to stay in school when graduation for half the boys opens onto a dead-end street?

An even worse state of affairs was found in another special study in a different city. In a slum area of 125,000 people, mostly Negro, a sampling of the youth population shows that roughly 70 percent of the boys and girls ages 16-21 are out of school and unemployed. When one stops to consider that the total population in this district is equal to that of a good-sized independent city, the magnitude of the problem is appalling and the challenge to our society is clear.

I do not have to remind this audience of the fact that the fate of freedom in the world hangs very much in balance. Our success against the spread of Communism in no small measure depends upon the successful operation of our own free society. To my mind, there is no question that a healthy body politic necessitates a sound economy and high employment. The history of Communism shows that it feeds upon discontented, frustrated, unemployed people. The present unemployment rate nationwide is roughly 7 percent for all age brackets, but unemployment among youth under 20 years of age is about 20 percent, or nearly three times greater than the nationwide rate for all workers. These young people are my chief concern, especially when they are pocketed together in large numbers within the confines of the big-city slums. What can words like "freedom," "liberty," and "equality of opportunity" mean to these young people? With what kind of zeal and dedication can we expect them to withstand the relentless pressures of Communism? How well prepared are they to face the struggle that shows no signs of abating?

A youth who has dropped out of school and never has had a full-time job is not likely to become a constructive citizen of his community. Quite the contrary. As a frustrated individual he is likely to be antisocial and rebellious. Some of this group of youth will end as juvenile delinquents. No one would claim that providing full employment for youth in the large cities would automatically banish juvenile delinquency, for we all realize that the causes of this problem are complex and there is no one solution. However, I suggest that full employment would have a highly salutary effect. Moreover, I offer the following hypothesis for professional social workers and sociologists to demolish; namely, that the correlation between desirable social attitudes (including attitudes of youth) and job opportunities are far higher than between the former and housing conditions, as measured by plumbing facilities, heating and space per family.

Unemployment is bad anywhere. Adult unemployment is grievous because it usually involves the loss of support for an entire family. In rural areas, towns and small cities, one might say that solving the unemployment of adults has the top priority; unemployment of youth may be pushed aside by some people as relatively unimportant. But in the slums of the largest cities I would say the drastic reduction of unemployment of male youth under age 21 is a greater need.

Consider for a moment the long-run consequence of persistent failure of underprivileged youth to find work. Leaving aside the human tragedies involved in each individual instance and looking at the matter solely in terms of the welfare of our free society, one sees the special position of the large-city slums. It is a matter of geography in the last analysis. Three factors are significant: first, the total size of the group of youth to whom I am referring—the larger the group, the more dangerous; second, the density of the population—the number of frustrated youth per block; third, the isolation of the inhabitants from other kinds of people and other sorts of streets and houses.

If one compares the slum areas in the largest cities with similar districts in small cities, the difference as regards those three factors is clearly evident. The youth in the big-city slums dwells in the midst of a mammoth social complex. The surrounding city extends for blocks and blocks. The business and industrial areas hem in the impoverished youth. In the case of the Negro, added to all the negative influences of a slum is the absence of any evidence that there is a pathway out. In spite of the high mobility of the family unit or perhaps because of it, a tone is set by constant talk and the prevailing attitude of the older people. And the tone is not one to encourage education or stimulate ambition. The unemployed floaters on the street are walking evidence to all the youth that nothing can be accomplished through education, that the door of the neighborhood schoolhouse indeed opens on a dead-end street.

Let me emphasize that, in my opinion, there is no reason why this should be the case. I know there are those who maintain that, on the average, Negro children are inferior to white children in academic ability. I have seen no evidence to support any such contention. In considering the relative abilities of whites and Negroes, let us examine the situation in an all-white slum in a city of considerable size. A careful study of a group of children in grade 4 of one such school showed that their average achievement level was a full year below their grade placement—a typical situation in any slum area.

What the teachers in this school have to contend with is shown by a report from the principal. Perhaps the greatest handicap to good schoolwork is the high mobility of the white population in the area. In this school mobility is very high; it is not uncommon in similar schools to have a turnover of the entire enrollment in one school year.

The principal writes:

When a residential area composed of large, old homes formerly occupied by owners and single family groups changes, economically and socially conditions of general deterioration begin. Absentee owners rent the property by single rooms or small so-called apartments of two or three rooms to large families. . . . Such conditions attract transients (who either cannot or will not qualify for supervised low income housing), the unemployed, the unskilled and unschooled, and the distressed families whose breadwinners have either just been committed to prisons or mental institutions or who have but recently been released from such. The only possession most of these families have is children. . . . In such an environment all forms of evil flourish—the peddling of dope, drunkenness, disease, accidents, truancies, physical, mental and moral handicaps, sex perversions involving children. . . .
The parents of at least one-third of the children are either in penal institutions, are on probation, or have prison records. At least 100 children are on

probation to the Juvenile Court. There has not been a day since I've been at the school that there has not been one or more children in detention at the Juvenile Court. . . .

Unless a school is able to educate its children so they may become competent and responsible citizens its work is a temporary stopgap that relieves immediate suffering only. Although the school is the only organization that has instruction as its primary responsibility, when a noble hearted teacher faces a barefoot, hungry, sick, distressed child, the result is an endless chain of efforts to relieve such a child.

We realize that little or nothing can be done for or with the parents of the children who face such serious problems in their homes. These problems directly affect the child's health, attendance, emotional and personal adjustment, his learning and his progress (or lack of it) in every respect. In all probability at least one-half of our children will be school dropouts. In our opinion the children need, desperately, for desirable development, in addition to good schools— good homes, churches and communities.

I am quoting from an official report which, in acknowledging the generally low achievement of the white children in this school, makes the interesting statment that "There is no reason to believe that these students as a group are inherently or genetically less capable than average students, but apparently because of some types of experiences in their lives they have been unable to develop their intellectual skills." The belief expressed in the first part of this sentence can hardly be based on anything firmer than an assumption as to the genetic uniformity of white children whose ancestors have for several generations lived in the United States. Such an assumption, of course, leaves out of account the possibility of a selective process occurring over the generations as some tended to move to one type of occupation and settle in one type of community. However, since I see no way of investigating the role of selective migration, I should be inclined to let the assumption stand unchallenged. *Only I would argue strongly that to date we have no evidence to indicate that the assumption should not be broadened to include both white and Negro students.* All the contrary evidence, namely, the poor work in school and low scores on tests made by Negroes, is based to a large degree on the performance of children in what are essentially slum conditions. Consequently, I start with the belief that, given a satisfactory socioeconomic background and educational opportunity, Negro children can be just as successful in academic work as any other group. You are all aware of the dramatic success that has been achieved in more than one instance in raising the aspirations and achievement levels of slum children.

The difference between the Negro slum of today and the slums of the Northern seaport cities of sixty years ago is a difference that deserves attention. The worries I have expressed about the continuation of present conditions may appear to be neutralized by contemplating the record of the past. Big cities have always had slums. In the United States it has been possible for people to raise themselves by their own bootstraps in the course of a generation. Why be alarmed about the present situation? Such a complacent projection of the past into the obscure future is fallacious for several reasons. First and foremost is the fact that in the past most of the inhabitants of slums were recently arrived white foreign immigrants. They knew that their predecessors for generations had worked their way out of poverty in the cities. They were convinced that they could do likewise. The almost complete lack of such conviction—a consequence of the tragic story of the Negro in the United States—is the outstanding characteristic of youth in the Negro slum. Secondly, a foreign immigrant came from an impoverished but stable society, for the most part a peasant society with its own ancient mores. The pride of family and often strong church connections were social cement that kept the slums from being complete social jungles in spite of the fact that the dwelling conditions were often far worse than they are today. Lastly, for most of the period of our history, labor shortages rather than labor surpluses were character- istic. Particularly, unskilled laborers were in demand. When this was not so, namely, in the depression years, organized society had to step in on a large scale to bolster up the tottering social structure. Today, auto- mation has affected the whole employment scene; there is much less demand for unskilled labor. Racial discrimination makes unemployment chronic for the Negro male North and South. In short, neither in terms of the kinds of people involved nor in terms of the economic and social setting is there much resemblance between the slum districts of 1900 and those which are the sore spots of our modern cities.

What was especially shocking to me in my visits to the large cities in the last school year was the discovery that the employment of youth is literally nobody's affair. To be sure, there are groups concerned with various aspects of the problem, but no single agency in any of the cities has the data as to the unemployment picture in that city. There is little up-to-date information about youth unemployment even city-wide and only the estimate of school people about the slum neighborhoods. Seldom are figures available to distinguish between the unemployed who are high school graduates and those who have dropped out of school before com- pleting the twelfth grade. Most important, it is not possible to say with any accuracy how the unemployed youth are distributed among various neighborhoods and among various minority groups.

The problem of unemployed youth in the large cities is in no small part a Negro problem. We do not facilitate its solution by trying to find phrases to hide this fact. And it is largely a Negro problem in the North because of the discrimination practiced quietly but extensively by em- ployers and labor unions. In an effort to overcome this unjust and na- tionally dangerous discrimination, people must not shrink from publishing statistics, unpleasant as they may be. How can we improve a situation if we are deprived of knowledge of what the situation really is? And it is my hope that in this Conference this problem of setting forth the facts will be thoroughly explored in a spirit of goodwill.

At this point I imagine many of you who are well aware of the nature of the problems I have been discussing are wondering just how I became concerned about the social problems of the big city. Therefore, I thought I might take a few moments to explain my interest and to describe briefly the situations I found which have caused my great concern.

The subject of my first report, *The American High School Today*, was the widely comprehensive high school found in independent cities that were not part of a large metropolitan complex. Aside from some short comments, I ignored suburban schools and big-city schools, both of which by my definition tend not to be widely comprehensive because they often do not include a wide variety of elective programs. In the college-oriented suburb there is not likely to be interest in vocational programs, and in the big cities the existence of separate vocational schools also means a restriction of the elective program in the general high school. However, in conjunction with my study last year of junior high school education, I decided to take a more detailed look at schools in metropolitan areas—at schools in slums and suburbs, if you will. In the large metropolitan areas of New York, Philadelphia, Detroit, Chicago, St. Louis, one has no difficulty in locating examples of both. In some cases twenty minutes' drive will enable a person to go from one to the other. A visit to the high school serving each community will open the eyes of a visitor to the complexities of American public education. Their basic problems are quite unlike, and these differences spring from the differences in the nature of the families being served. One lesson to be drawn from visiting a well-to-do suburb and a slum is all-important for understanding American public education. That lesson is that to a large degree what a school should do and can do is determined by the status and ambitions of the families within the community. I drew this conclusion after either my staff or I had visited metropolitan schools in and around many of the largest cities in the nation—New York, Los Angeles, Chicago, Detroit, Philadelphia, Baltimore, St. Louis.

In the suburban high school from which 80 percent or more of the graduates enter some sort of college the problems are the mirror image of those in the city slums, where as many as half the students drop out of school prior to graduation. The task with which the school people must struggle in the city slum is, on the one hand, how to prepare the youth for getting and keeping a job as soon as he or she leaves school and, on the other hand, to encourage those who have academic talent to aim at a profession through higher education. The task thus stated seems simple. In fact, as you all know, the difficulties are enormous. I am not nearly so concerned about the plight of the suburban parents whose offspring are at present having difficulty finding places in prestige colleges as I am about the plight of parents in the slums whose children drop out of school or graduate without prospects of employment. The latter is a much more serious social phenomenon, and too little attention has been paid to it.

Visits to a wealthy suburb and impoverished slums only a few minutes away jolt one's notions of the meaning of equality of opportunity. On the one hand, there is likely to be a spacious, modern school staffed by as many as 70 professionals for 1,000 pupils; on the other hand, one finds a crowded, often dilapidated and unattractive school staffed by 40 professionals for 1,000 pupils. Expenditure per pupil in the wealthy suburban school may be as high as $1,000; it is less than half that in the slum school. To my mind, in view of the problems one finds, conditions in the slum school necessitate more staff and more money than in the suburban school.

Leaving aside the suburban communities, I should like now to point up some of my observations in the slums of the large cities, where my staff and I made special efforts to visit schools. In each of the cities we visited, one can find neighborhoods composed of various minority groups. Many of these are areas now designated as "culturally deprived," or "culturally different," but which in my youth would have been more simply designated as "slums." The schools serving such neighborhoods have to be visited in order for one to understand the nature of the tasks which the teachers face.

The slum areas of certain big Northern cities are today largely inhabited by Negroes who have recently moved from the South hoping to improve their lot. The economic changes in the South which have forced this migration are too well known to require elaboration. The Negro is being displaced as a farm laborer, and, being unable because of discrimination to obtain other employment in the section where he was born, he becomes a migrant headed North. Between 1950 and 1960 the proportion of Negroes living in the South dropped from 60 percent to 52 percent. St. Louis is said to be the first stopping point for many who make the journey, though the school people in Chicago, Detroit, Philadelphia, Baltimore, Washington or New York indicate that their problems with the recently arrived Negroes from the South are quite as great as those which confront their colleagues in St. Louis. New York State now has the largest Negro population of any state in the Union.

The growth of Negro slums in big cities is disturbing. I wish that I could do more than direct attention. For without being an alarmist, I must say that when one considers the total situation that has been developing in the slums since World War II, one has reason to worry about the future. The building up of a mass of unemployed and frustrated Negro youth in congested areas of a city is a social phenomenon that may be compared to the piling up of inflammable material in an empty building in a city block. Potentialities for trouble—indeed, possibilities of disaster—are surely there.

Let me describe a slum that might be in any one of several of the large cities I have visited. The inhabitants are all Negroes and with few exceptions have entered the city from a state in the Deep South anywhere from the last month to the last three years. Often the composition of a grade will alter so rapidly that a teacher will find at the end of a school year that she is teaching but few pupils who started with her in the fall. In one school, I recall the principal stating that a teacher absent more than one week will have difficulty recognizing her class when she returns. The mothers move with their offspring from room to room from month to month and in so doing often go from one elementary school district to another; I am told that resident tenements look more like transient hotels.

I write "mothers" advisedly, since in one neighborhood, by no means the worst I have seen, a questionnaire sent out by the school authorities indicated that about a third of the pupils come from family units (one hesitates to use the word "home") which had no father, stepfather or male guardian. Less than one percent of the parents graduated from college; 10 percent of the parents graduated from high school; only 33 percent completed the elementary school; and the remainder did not go that far. Contrast the situation in which a third of the parents have not completed elementary school with that in a high-income suburb where as many as 90 percent of the parents have bachelor's degrees, if not graduate degrees.

These Negro slums seem to vary considerably as regards the social mores. In some there are very bad gangs with gang warfare among the boys. There are also vicious fights outside of school between girls. The condition in one such neighborhood was summed up to one of my staff by a principal of a junior high school who said even he was shocked by the answers to a questionnaire to the girls which asked what was their biggest problem. The majority replied to the effect that their biggest problem was getting from the street into their apartment without being molested in the hallway of the tenement. He went on to say that the area had a set of social customs of its own. The streets are full of unemployed men who hang around and prey on the girls. The women are the centers of the family and as a rule are extremely loyal to the children. The men, on the other hand, are floaters. Similar reports from principals and teachers can be heard by the attentive and sympathetic visitor to the Negro slums of any one of several cities.

I have so far referred only to white and Negro slums. In addition, a few words are necessary to point out that in some cities, New York in particular, there are slum areas inhabited by recent arrivals from Puerto Rico. In these sections the problems are similar to those I have described but complicated by the difference in language. Unlike the American Negro from the South, these recent arrivals bring with them a set of social mores closely associated with their own methods of communication. At the same time, they often, if not always, come with children whose schooling has been bad. Clearly, the instruction of these Puerto Rican children involves both teaching reading and teaching a foreign language. These problems are so special I shall not attempt to discuss them here. One hardly needs to point out that their existence adds one more complication to the tasks confronting the administrators and teachers in New York City schools. Add to these talks the possibilities of interracial hostility and gang warfare between Negroes and Puerto Ricans and the resentment of both toward the whites and one has a veritable witches' brew which comes to boil with unsavory vehemence in certain schools in certain areas—particularly in the junior high school years. The amazing feature of the whole situation is that pupils make any progress in schools in certain areas of the city.

One only needs to visit the type of school I am now describing to be convinced that the nature of the community largely determines what goes on in the school. For example, I have walked through school corridors in slum areas and, looking into classrooms, have seen children asleep with their heads on their hands. Is this situation the result of poor teachers without either disciplinary control or teaching ability? No, the children asleep at their desks have been up all night with no place to sleep or else subject to unbelievable family fights and horrors through the night.

Checking into one case, a principal told one of my staff that after climbing six flights of a tenement he found the boy's home—one filthy room with a bed, a light bulb and a sink. In the room lived the boy's mother and her four children. I might add that it is not unusual for teachers in these schools to take home with them children with little or no place to go at night. It is after visits to schools like these that I grow impatient with both critics and defenders of public education who ignore the realities of school situations to engage in fruitless debate about educational philosophy, purposes and the like.

As one teacher in a slum neighborhood said to me, "We do quite well with these children in the lower grades. Each of us is, for the few hours of the school day, an acceptable substitute for the mother. But when they reach about 10, 11, or 12 years of age, we lose them. At that time the 'street' takes over. In terms of schoolwork, progress ceases; indeed, many pupils begin to go backward in their studies!" What can be done to offset the demoralizing attitude of "the street" in the worst of the slums? Not much that lies within the province of the school authorities alone. Here is where the social agency people, the juvenile court people, the churches— all the various groups represented at this Conference come into the picture.

This last thought leads me to say that thus far I have spoken in negative terms for the most part, describing my own sense of shock at the slum conditions in our large cities, especially as these conditions relate to education and employment. So important are these problems that in putting together a final report for the Carnegie Corporation I decided to publish a small book that will contrast the wealthy suburban schools and the slum schools. In this small volume I shall try to create a set of anxious thoughts in the minds of conscientious citizens who while living in the suburbs may work in the cities. I wish that I had many more constructive proposals to make than I now have, and I am hoping that this Conference, composed of people thoroughly familiar with slum problems, will come up with positive, constructive ideas that will lead to solutions.

There are clearly many areas of concern. Among the more important are racial discrimination; employment practices of labor and management; federal-state laws, including insurance rates and wage scales; lack of jobs, as well as changing types of employment because of automation and the necessity for more highly skilled workers; the role of the schools in preparing youth for employment, especially average and below-average youth, and in helping them make the transition from school to work; the coordination of the efforts of the schools, the employers and labor unions, and the various community agencies that have a hand in promoting youth welfare; the role of the public sector of the economy at the local, state and federal level in providing employment if the private sector of the economy is unable to do so. All of these questions are complex and controversial but will, I sincerely hope, be thoroughly aired at the various Workshop meetings in this Conference.

In closing, I should like to express my own views on a very few of the subjects just mentioned about which I feel strongly. In the first place, there are those who would say that what goes on in the schools should not have any direct connection with the community or the employment situation. I completely reject this idea. The school, the community and the employment situation are and should be closely tied together. I am not impressed by the holding power of a school as a criterion of its quality, but neither am I impressed by the argument that a boy who fails to get along in school ought to drop out. It all depends. The situation in which a boy drops out of school only to roam the streets is quite different from the situation in which a boy drops out and finds satisfactory employment. Full-time schooling for certain youths through grade 12 may be good or bad depending upon the employment picture. What goes on in the school ought to be conditioned in large measure by the nature of the families being served, the vocational plans and aspirations of the students, and employment opportunities. *I submit that in a heavily urbanized and industrialized free society the educational experience of youths should fit their subsequent employment.* This should be so whether a boy drops out of school in grade 10, after graduation from high school, or after graduation from college or university. In any case, there should be a smooth transition from full-time schooling to a full-time job.

This is an ideal situation admittedly and one which is at present approached only in the learned professions and in a few instances the occupations for which undergraduate college courses provide the necessary training. In the case of the learned professions, those in charge of the last stage in the educational journey—the professors of law, of medicine, and those who direct the research of candidates for the Ph.D.—have usually a sense of responsibility for their students based on their own passionate interest in promoting the best interests of their profession. Graduates of some undergraduate professional courses in some institutions are also often assisted in finding employment. Sixty years ago the situation was very different. Concern with the placement of college and university graduates was a product of the depression years. The change, I believe, has been important and in the best interests of both the individual and society. For the college graduate who has received a general or liberal education without majoring in a professional or semiprofessional field, many difficulties of finding a suitable job will remain. Still, by and large, one can say at the college and university level a considerable fraction of the youth involved make a smooth transition from education to a job.

When we examine the situation at the high school level, we find quite a different state of affairs. Although in many high schools a half or more of the graduates seek employment immediately on graduation, only in a few cities does one find an effective placement service. And I make this statement without intending any reproach to either social agencies or to guidance counselors. The obligations of the school should not end when the student either drops out of school or graduates. At that point the cumulative record folder concerning a student's educational career is usually brought to an end. It should not be. To my mind, *guidance officers, especially in the large cities, ought to be given the responsibility for following the post–high school careers of youth from the time they leave school until they are 21 years of age.*

Since compulsory attendance usually ends at age 16, this means responsibility for the guidance of youth ages 16 to 21 who are out of school and either employed or unemployed. It is with the unemployed out-of-school youth that I am especially concerned—especially the boys, for whom the unemployment problem is more severe than for girls. This expansion of the school's function will cost money and will mean additional staff—at least a doubling of the guidance staff in most of the large cities; but the expense is necessary, for vocational and educational guidance must be a continuing process to help assure a smooth transition from school to the world of work. The present abrupt break between the two is unfortunate. What I have in mind suggests, of course, a much closer relationship than now exists between school, employers and labor unions, as well as social agencies and employment officers.

There is no question that the school people in the large cities face a gigantic task in their efforts to prepare youth from impoverished homes for useful lives as responsible citizens and productive workers. I have the heartiest respect for the dedicated men and women who with limited means and facilities are doing the best job they can to overcome the adverse influence of the home and street in the big-city slum. As one of my associates who had spent the best years of his life as principal of a suburban public high school put it, "I visited junior high schools in New York City in some of the worst areas. I expected to find blackboard jungles; instead I found schools with high morale, tight discipline, imaginative principals and teachers." My own visits were largely confined to similar schools in Chicago, Detroit and St. Louis, and my admiration for what is being done in those cities is equal to that of my colleague for what he saw in New York City.

Not that all problems have been solved. Far from it, as you all know. Reading is the essential tool for success in school and on the job, and although in this area much has been done, much remains to be done, particularly with respect to gaining the interest of the parents in the success of their children, reducing class size and providing for more remedial reading teachers. Decentralized administration in the big cities is surely a step in the right direction by bringing the schools closer to the people. A new look is needed at vocational programs, especially for the below-average students who are rejected by the vocational people and academic people alike. Much remains to be done for the future dropout to ease the break between school and job. It appears that the only jobs available for unskilled workers in the decade ahead will be in service occupations, a fact of considerable importance in educational planning. As you all know better than I, many of the large cities have made attempts to prepare these slow learners for work. Adult education courses, work-study programs of various sorts—these are all evidence of a continuing interest of the schools in furthering educational opportunities for out-of-school youth and ought to be expanded. Finally, I have been told many times that an important obstacle in improving the education of slum children is the fact that the teachers who may have taught in schools for a number of years with a certain kind of student body suddenly find themselves engulfed by slum children whom they do not understand and for whom they fail to recognize the need for changes in the curriculum. In many cases, a re-education of the teachers becomes necessary.

In short, there is much that schools are doing but much more that they should do. Money in many instances is the key—remedial reading teachers, smaller classes, guidance counselors cost money. I have already noted the vast disproportion between the amount spent per pupil in the wealthy suburbs and that spent in slums of the big city.

But even if the schools were to improve their services drastically, there would still remain what seems to me the crux of the situation—the presence or absence of employment opportunity. Whereas I have indicated my conviction that the problems of Negro education are no different from those of all underprivileged socioeconomic groups, the problems of Negro employment are distinctly different. The enforcement of anti-discrimination laws has proved a most difficult undertaking. I have heard it said that only those projects which are supported by public funds can really be operated on a truly nondiscriminatory basis. Therefore, it seems to me that unless local management and labor take up the challenge, it may be necessary for Congress to appropriate funds for public work programs to alleviate the problem of unemployment among youth 16 to 21 in the large cities. In view of the past discriminatory employment practices by both management and labor, action at the federal level may become a necessity. Even if there were no discrimination, it might become a necessity if the private sector of the economy is unable to provide sufficient jobs.

In conclusion, let me repeat my sense of shock as I contemplate conditions in our big cities with respect to youth in slum neighborhoods. To improve the work of the slum schools requires an improvement in the lives of the families who inhabit these slums, but without a drastic change in the employment prospects for urban Negro youth relatively little can be accomplished. I urge that our large-city problems be analyzed in far more detail than in the past and with a far greater degree of frankness. Neighborhood by neighborhood we need to know the facts, and when these facts indicate a dangerous social situation, the American people should be prepared to take drastic measures before it is too late. I wish this Conference all success as it tackles this extremely urgent and perplexing problem of unemployed, out-of-school youth in our large cities.

INDEX

Index

690 / Index

position of sexes at, 99
promotion and tenure at, 161, 176–
177, 178
during Puritan rebellion, 85
retirement tradition at, 113
structure of, 100–5
during World War II, 258

Page-Barbour Lectures, 463–64, 469–
470
Palmer, Professor, 405
Paris University of, 151
Parsons, Charles L., 347, 348
Parsons, William S., 290
Patch, Richard H., 39–40
Patterson, Richard C., Jr., 581
Patterson, Robert, 335, 341, 509
on Committee on the Present Dan-
ger, 513, 519
Pearl Harbor, 273
Pearson, Drew, 539
Pedagogical Center (Germany), 627–28
Pennock, Stanley B., 44
Pennsylvania, University of, 135
Peril and a Hope, A (Smith), 300–1
Perkins, James, 618
Perkins, Thomas Nelson, 164
on appointment of Conant to presi-
dency, 84, 88–89, 120
on Greene, 148
on loyalty oath, 449–51
on National Scholarships, 129–30
Physical Chemistry
atomic weight determinations, 27–
28, 31
in industry, 39
qualitive analysis, 15–17
Piaget, Jean, 151
Pierce, Wendell H., 649
Pilot, The, 470
Planning Board, Office of Scientific
Research and Development, 284
Plutonium, 275, 281–82, 289, 291–93
Poison gases, 49
Polyethylene, 62–63
Polymerization, 43, 61–63
Pope, Sir W., 56
Portarlington, Lady, 253
Post, Boston, 539
Post, Washington, 311
Pound, Roscoe, 109–10, 125, 143
Pratt, Joseph, 4
Price, Don K.
Government and Science, 237
The Scientific Estate, 237

Primer of American Defense (Eichelberger), 219
Princeton, University of, 30, 130–31,
134, 135
Private secondary schools, 460–72,
665–70
Problems and Plans Committee, American Council on Education, 339,
351, 352–53, 356
Public secondary schools
in Australia, 462–63, 614, 666, 668
in England, 462, 666, 668–70
in United States, 182–83, 187–93,
368, 384, 391, 462–72, 613–26,
646, 665–81
See also Roxbury Latin School
Purcell, Edward M., 125
Purnell, Adm. W. R. E., 286
Pushkin, G. M., 604–6

Qualitative analysis, 15–17
Quincy, Josiah, 651, 657
Quine, Willard Van Orman, 108

Radar, 240–41, 251, 269–70, 332
Radcliffe College, 374–83
Randall, Clarence B., 437–39, 440–41,
444
Reber, Samuel, 546, 577
Red Cross–Harvard hospital, 227, 264–
266
Reischauer, Edwin O., 125
Reserve Officer Training Corps (ROTC),
339, 341, 342, 524
Reuter, Ernst, 556, 560
Richards, Ivor A., 125
Richards, Theodore William, 53, 54–55,
74, 75
on Germany, 67
as Harvard professor, 17–18, 27–34,
36, 85
on pure and applied science, 31, 36
Richards, William T., 29, 54
Riddleberger, James, 539, 555
Robinson, Sir Robert, 99, 256, 264
Rockefeller, Nelson, 179, 471
Rockefeller Institute for Medical Re-
search, 115–16
Rocky Mountains, 198–203
Roosevelt, Eleanor, 295–97, 353
Roosevelt, Franklin Delano, 94, 117,
218, 228, 520, 638
atomic bomb and, 274, 285, 295
at Harvard Tercentenary Celebration,
153–56

Design by Sidney Feinberg
Set in Linotype Primer
Composed, printed and bound by The Haddon Craftsmen, Inc.
HARPER & ROW, PUBLISHERS, INCORPORATED